THE GREAT FOOD ALMANAC

A FEAST OF FACTS FROM

A — Z

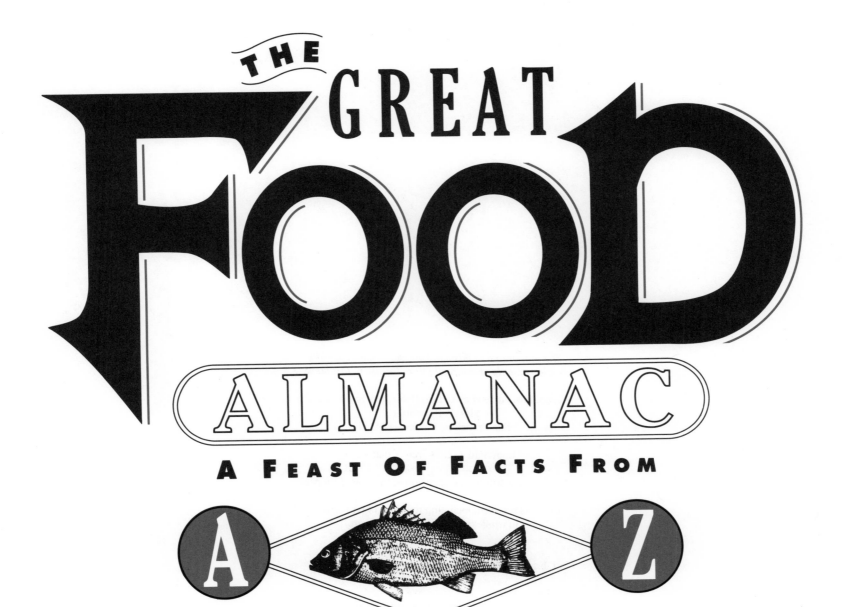

THE GREAT FOOD ALMANAC

A FEAST OF FACTS FROM A — Z

By Irena Chalmers

Designed by Shelley Heller

CollinsPublishersSanFrancisco

A Division of HarperCollinsPublishers

First published 1994 by Collins Publishers San Francisco
1160 Battery Street
San Francisco, California 94111

Library of Congress Cataloging-in-Publication Data

Chalmers, Irena.
     The great food almanac: a feast of facts from A to Z /
Irena Chalmers.
     p. cm.
     Includes index.
     ISBN 0-00-255233-7 (pbk.)
     1. Food. 2. Diet. 3. Cookery. I. Title
TX355.C38 1994
641.3'00973—dc20   94-13950 CIP

Printed in U.S.A.

9 8 7 6 5 4 3 2 1

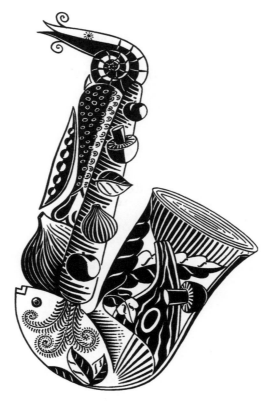

*I can't adequately thank
Joe Baum, President of The Rainbow
Room in New York City, for making
me the beneficiary of so much of his
wisdom during the many years I
have worked with him. He has been
unimaginably generous and kind, and
it is to him, and to Alan Reyburn,
Milton Glaser, Tony Zazula, Sue
Klein, Andrew Freeman, Alan Fields,
Carrie Robbins, and all my dear
"family" at The Rainbow Room
that I dedicate this book.*

It could be said of me that in this book I have only made up a bunch of other men's flowers, providing of my own only the string that ties them together.

— Montaigne

Dear Reader,

I have written and published many books about food and cooking in my career, but the book you hold in your hands today is more dear to me, I think, than any of the others, because it is the one I've been persistently dreaming about and wanting to do almost from the start.

When I took my first peek into the complex business of food, I was astounded at the size of the enterprise, by a global industry that employs every conceivable discipline and every last degree of sophistication and ingenuity to get our dinners onto our plates — from farmers and fishermen and canners and truckers, to designers of pots and pans and frozen-food containers, to the visionaries of biotechnology whose perceptions stun us almost daily as they tinker us into the world of tomorrow today.

Since that first glimpse I've been increasingly fascinated — "obsessed," some of my friends say — with the need to find out everything about everything to do with food. And I saw that a world so multifaceted and interconnected needed a very big book that could embrace all this immensity, from the frog pond to the stars. My first thought was of a book like *The Whole Earth Catalog*, which has been on my coffee table since it came out, ever pushing and prodding my imagination as I planned and made this *Almanac*.

My love of food and cooking has described the central and preoccupying journey of my life, and yet I came into the field almost by accident, and definitely at the level of the frog pond. The year was 1965, and I was living in Baltimore. As it happened, the Delmarva Chicken Festival was on at the old Lexington Market there, and the manager of the event, saying he needed "an ordinary housewife" to demonstrate prize recipes, paid me good money to fry chicken in public for four hours.

I simply loved the experience, and wondered how an ordinary housewife such as I could contrive to improve upon it. I went off to the Cordon Bleu School to take professional training, and when I returned to Baltimore I boldly opened a cooking school of my own called La Bonne Femme.

I continued the school in Greensboro, North Carolina, when I moved there, and had a little shop as well, where I offered foods that were not available anywhere else, importing croissants and breads from New York that were still warm from the bakery when I went to the airport to collect them. I also had a great selection of French wines and a wide variety of American ones.

In all this entrepreneurial time I never felt that I was as able a cook as I wanted to be, and fortunately fate intervened when Julia Child began appearing on television. I was mesmerized by her shows and watched her avidly, as a student observes a master. Since then I've always proudly claimed that Julia Child taught me to cook. The first time I was actually in the same room with her, I was too shy to speak. But I overcame my awe enough to come to know her, and later, when she cheered me for a speech I'd made, joining her hands over her head like a prizefighter, I felt lifted to the highest plateau of my professional life.

Also while in Greensboro I went into business with David Grimes at Potpourri Press to produce a series of single-subject cookbooks, resulting in more than a hundred titles. Later, in New York, I was able to publish the first cookbooks of many who are stars today in the food world, among them Rose Beranbaum, Nathalie Dupree, Jane Hibler, Martin Johner and Gary Goldberg, Barbara Kafka, Peter Kump, Carlo Middione, Richard Sax, and Phillip Stephen Schulz.

And always, my obsession kept me in hot pursuit of every interesting, telling detail I could find about the world of food. Perhaps it was my medical training that drove me to my research. In my first career I was a neurological nurse; I learned in that discipline that nothing happens for no reason, and that what occurs in the brain will almost certainly pop up elsewhere — there and there and there.

So it is with the intimate nature of food in our lives. Not long ago I clearly saw one day, in the course of my endless clipping and filing and cross-referencing of food-related news stories, that there was no part of the daily paper that I could afford to overlook. The subject saturates our entire culture, invading every section — national and international news, politics, medicine, health, business, science, fashion, and sport, not to mention the front page, the editorial page, and sometimes — as was the case with NAFTA, for example — the shrieking headlines. And just as the latest-breaking stories on food are all over the place, so is a welter of controversies about every aspect of every morsel of food we ingest or don't ingest or think that no one should be allowed to ingest. Making any sense out of the cacophony can only come from a patient attempt to put the many disparate pieces together, like a giant jigsaw puzzle. And with that approach, the guesswork has gradually gone out of the forecasting I am so often asked to do; it becomes, instead, just a matter of synthesizing the information that's coming in from a wealth of sources.

If you'd like to get a sense of the broader picture of food and think it might lie in the *Almanac* — and indeed, I think it does — please don't begin by trying to read the book from cover to cover. It would take a week to do that, and anyway, the riches won't be revealed if you approach it that way. I'd like to suggest, rather, that you open it just anywhere, by serendipity, and see what you find. I can almost guarantee that wherever you are, you'll spot some nugget of fact that will surprise and intrigue you. Then page on at will. When you read at random, a synthesis will occur as the volume of information sweeps over you and you begin to make the curious connections — between the decimation of sharks, for example, and the disappearance of crabs — that prompted me to write this book in the first place.

I used to say that I wanted the *Almanac* to save you money, make you live longer, entertain you, and inform you. I'm sure that's possible, but it's an awful lot to hope to achieve in every case. So let me put it another way by saying that I hope this book is as good for you as a good dinner.

I've always loved having dinner, making dinner for friends, people who will stay a long time with their elbows on the table, talking and laughing. And I've always said that such a wonderful evening as that happens only with good food and good friends. But now I'd like to widen my conditions just a little bit and hope that something akin to the wonderful evening can happen for you when you browse in the pages of *The Great Food Almanac*.

Of course, I intend to go right on gathering information and reporting on what's happening in the food world, and if you have any suggestions to make, or thoughts to share, I hope you'll let me know. You can call me at 212-679-2363.

Meanwhile, have a wonderful random read.

Irena Chalmers
New York, June 1994

ACKNOWLEDGMENTS

When I submitted the proposal for this book to Lena Tabori, then the president and publisher of Collins, she accepted it at once. "I only want to publish books of passion," she said, recognizing that this *Almanac* was indeed my burning passion.

My role has been to produce this book in much the same way that a producer assembles all the parts for a movie. Customarily, the book producer, or packager, delivers the work to the publisher either in the form of film or as a bound book. In this case I delivered film, and Collins then printed and distributed it — brilliantly. I would like to thank everyone at Collins Publishers for their help, especially Jenny Barry, Maura Carey Damacion, Jonathan Mills, Jenny Collins, Dayna Macy, Maria Hjelm, Ellen Georgiou, Jennifer Ward, and Cathy Quealy.

Carlotta Kerwin is the organizational genius who created order for this project from what could so easily have disintegrated into chaos. She not only refused to let me write 76 pages each on Eggs, or Lobster, or Potatoes, but astutely reduced a lot of my guff on some of the subjects dearest to my heart to a more appropriate mere page, or half page. It was Carlotta who guided me through the initial stages as we created the structure for the book and organized the flow of text and illustrations for each entry. She maintained the "road map" and the production timetable, and kept the rest of us on track by means of a highly successful combination of encouragement and death threats.

Jean Atcheson's work on this project will be admired by other editors as an example of the highest standards of her profession. Her ability to smooth a text is so remarkable that sometimes it seemed to me that she'd scarcely touched my work, when in fact she was deftly turning it into the copy I only wished I had written in my first drafts. To Jean fell the enormous responsibility of establishing and maintaining the accuracy and accessibility of the book, and it was only after many an all night siege that she was finally able to smile with satisfaction at a job superbly done.

Samara Farber walked into my office one day to ask for a job — without pay. At the end of the interview she not only had the job, and a salary, but a central role to play in the production of this book. As picture editor, she coordinated a total of nearly 1,000 illustrations from 100 illustrators. She also negotiated permissions for text reprints. She did her work so well that we piled on more: She tracked copy and kept detailed records of all meetings, remained cheerful throughout, and was invaluable in every way.

Shelley Heller, the art director/designer, was devoted to this book from the moment she saw its promise. Little did we know, then, how much detailed work it would entail. Shelley remained enthusiastic for the entire year it took to assemble the words and illustrations and translate them into designed pages. Between 6 and 7 every evening, I eagerly anticipated the arrival by fax of the day's work. No sooner had it come than I shrieked with joy and contacted her to tell her how terrific it looked. I hope our excitement will be contagious and you will glimpse some of the delight we experienced as we moved gradually from A to Z. She was ably assisted by Tim Shaner and Stephen Miller. Roy Sivertsen converted our disks into film and skillfully coaxed the illustrations into clear reproduction on the page.

Pat Baird was our esteemed nutrition consultant. Every mention of the subject in this book was passed under her professional eye for careful scrutiny. Her invaluable insights ensured that we were presenting the full picture and not erring by omission of important facts.

Richard Atcheson's bylined essays are among the brightest spots in the *Almanac*. With his skillful turn of phrase and quick blue pencil, he often intervened to make the way plain.

We were assisted, too, by Beth Hillson, who compiled the extensive lists of mail-order sources. And Lise Stern, who writes a monthly *Cookbook Review* newsletter, assembled the titles of the recommended books. Alas, we couldn't fit them all into the space allocated, but we did our best and squeezed in more than 500. Elaine Corn struggled mightily to track down an amazing collection of odd jobs in food. Bryan Lynas, Ann Hornaday, and Wayne Jebian wrote several pieces for the book, and Parris Lampropoulos and Nicholas Atcheson provided me with bulging files of research and assembled and checked the lists of information sources. Rose Grant was the greatly valued indexer.

My thanks and affection go, too, to Maggie Waldron: A stalwart supporter for many years, she helped particularly with this book. Elaine Yannuzzi and Phil Nulman gave me many marketing ideas, and my other dear friends Lou and Lisa Ekus and Merrilyn Siciak were again responsible for the publicity. They contributed some wonderfully innovative ideas, and their enthusiasm and support were invaluable.

Gabe Perle is the brilliant attorney who patiently guided the work through the contract phase and remained on hand to calm the occasionally troubled waters.

I want to thank the many authors and food experts whose words and insights appear here, as well as the artists whose work illuminates these pages. I have scrupulously tried to acknowledge everyone, and will be mightily distressed if I discover that I failed to credit every brilliant thought, word, or deed that I've appropriated. I have woven many threads from others into this tapestry, and am grateful to all who graciously allowed me to quote from their work and reproduce their art.

I am grateful, too, to all my friends and colleagues at the trade councils who provided me with masses of fascinating material and were always prompt to answer all my questions.

And I particularly want to thank Nach Waxman, founder and owner of New York's cookbook specialty store, Kitchen Arts and Letters, who bravely broke his vow never to endorse any food book and gave us all a big boost by praising ours. Thank you, Nach.

ADVERTISING

*Advertisements contain
the only truths to be relied on
in a newspaper.*

— Thomas Jefferson

HUNTING THE
HIDDEN CUSTOMER

Advertisers have several ways of enticing us to buy their products. Corporate symbols were created to establish trust in a brand name. An extension of this idea is the use of one brand to sell another — for example, using the backdrop of a famous restaurant to sell coffee or driving a Rolls-Royce to link the idea of good taste with Dijon mustard.

The association of ideas spells out a strong message. A subtler and more amusing ploy is the series of mini-adverdramas that feature a romance between two coffee drinkers. We are more likely to buy the product if the message is appealing — and this message is so appealing that it is a natural to be replicated by a dozen copycat agencies.

It costs millions to develop a new product and many companies are finding it more practical to formulate so-called line extensions of already accepted foods. Oreos, for instance,

are shrunk for the kids and for those among us who can convince themselves that three small cookies don't add up to nearly as many calories as one large one. This elephantiasis within brands has severely limited the amount of shelf space available in supermarkets, but problems beg for solutions. The answer to this one is to use one food to advertise another, so we are offered a deal: Buy two boxes of Instant Quaker Oatmeal and get the Nestlé Quik FREE! It moves a lot of product and gets us to try something we might not otherwise think of buying.

It was a creative advertising genius who persuaded us to put one food into another one. The concept of adding M&M's to cookies or Heath bars to ice cream has resulted in bonus sales for both candies. One company may also advertise another company directly on the package: The label that says their product contains Hershey's chocolate assures the customer that it will taste good.

When the advertisers run out of novel ways to get us to actually eat their food they resort to persuading us to clean our teeth or deodorize our refrigerator with it. You can, they say, catch more flies with honey than vinegar — but if you've got some vinegar in the house, you can always use it to clean the copper.

It Pays to Advertise

To judge the buying response to 22 products, researchers analyzed purchases made by a group of subscribers to a nationally distributed food magazine that carried ads for the products. Then they compared them with purchases made by a control group that had not seen the ads. The results were startling. Twenty-one of the 22 products experienced increases in sales — some by as much as 46 percent — by those who had seen the ads.

So if you think you are making an entirely independent decision about what you buy, think again. We are all actively or subliminally influenced by good or bad advertising and the number of times we are exposed to it.

What You See Isn't Always What You Get

Pity the poor bride whose husband truly believes her lasagna cannot compare with his mother's. No matter how good his wife's food is, it will always be judged inferior. The sad truth is that there is no way to fight this kind of attitude. It is rubbish, of course, because it is not the real food but the memory of it that is seen through rose-colored glasses. It is the feel of that long-ago crisply ironed white tablecloth, the intoxicating smells rolling from the kitchen, the way the sunlight fell across the room — not the lasagna (which if tasted today might be quite awful).

This is somewhat the way it is with food photographs. For advertising purposes, the law demands that food products must be shown exactly as they are sold, without any tampering; the advertiser must not deceive the public by photographing the food in a way that would be impossible to reproduce at home. But the restrictions don't apply to foods or decorations used as background.

An ad for a particular brand of ice cream, for example, *has* to use the actual variety and rely on plentiful supplies of dry ice to keep it from puddling in the intense heat of the studio lights, whereas scoops of ice cream shown in the background of a photograph featuring luscious strawberries can be created from a skillful mix of Crisco, mashed potatoes or powdered sugar, and food coloring.

Making food look beautiful for the cameras is the specialty of food stylists, who work with the photographers to produce ads for magazines, newspapers, and television, or create gorgeous-looking meals for movies. In pursuit of perfection, they may pick through countless boxes of cereals in search of exquisitely shaped flakes, cut up entire wheels of cheese to find that one ideal slice, and discard whole cases of fruits and vegetables in their rigorous selection process. Subtle touches make a difference, such as poaching "fried eggs" in warm oil so that the egg-white edges will be smooth, or adding drops of glycerine to the outside of a glass with a hypodermic needle to impart a look of dewy freshness.

Truth in advertising regulations allow for this kind of tinkering. What is not allowed is the sneaky old practice of putting marbles in the vegetable soup so that all the vegetables rise to the surface, giving the impression that the soup contains more than it actually does. But it is perfectly OK to dip sugar cubes into lemon essence to produce a yellow flame for a flambéed dish (Sterno makes a blue flame), and cigarette smoke blown gently across the food through a straw can look just like steam.

It is precisely the stylist's finicky placement of the shrimp in the salad and the photographer's skillful lighting of the mushrooms in the stew that make a professional photograph memorable. But that food is only meant to arouse the desire to eat, not to be consumed. For a dish that will live in memory for a lifetime, your own home cooking — or even your mother-in-law's — is a much better bet.

Place-Names That Sell Products

Overall, the word "America" on a label is the most popular selling buzzword, but several other places have their own magic when it comes to nostalgic associations. The number beside the name indicates the quantity of products that bore the name when New Product News compiled this list in the early 1990s.

America	62
Texas	47
Vermont	31
Southwest	26
Hawaii	25
California	23
Dakota	13
Georgia	10
Napa Valley	9
San Francisco	9
Louisiana	8
New Mexico	8
South	8
Chicago	7
Arizona	6
Florida	6

POPEYE FLIPS
HIS (SPINACH) LID

Popeye bragged, "I eats me oatmeal and I'm stronger than steel, I'm Popeye the Quaker Man . . ." but not for long. Popeye, who surrendered his spinach account to sign on with Instant Quaker Oatmeal, ran into big trouble with the peace-loving Quakers, who were appalled by his rowdy behavior. And Olive Oyl was the target of protests from women's rights advocates. They didn't like the way she looked so adoringly at Popeye, just as though she were the wife of an aspiring politician.

Do hippos that dance in tutus offend overweight viewers? Will Santa be forced to lose weight and stop smoking? Life for an advertising icon is not as easy as once it was and for Popeye to mutter under his breath, "I yam what I yam, and that's all that I yam," is no longer acceptable. Advertising characters are being modernized. Betty Crocker has evolved from a housewife into a corporate executive. Aunt Jemima now looks like a recent graduate from law school, while the Jolly Green Giant has an apprentice, Sprout, who can go where no giant has trod before. Mr. Peanut, the 1916 invention of a 13-year-old schoolboy who was paid $5 for his drawing, has slimmed down, stepped out, and danced back on center stage still decked out in top hat, monocle, and cane. But Elsie the Cow has been put out to pasture and Spuds Mackenzie has been given the boot. (He barked up the wrong tree.) Among the men, only Juan Valdez and Uncle Ben have survived the recent layoffs.

Corporate symbols today must reflect the consumers' idealized images of them in order to to retain brand loyalty in a tough competitive field.

It was so much easier to create these mythical figures in the old days, within a tightly focused market in which advertisers could deliver their message to the millions of viewers of those three omnipotent networks. Today, it's not only a question of which channel to choose out of the many that are available, but of determining the precise audience for each specific program. A hospital drama, regardless of its ratings, may attract exactly the viewers a product is seeking — or MTV may be the right medium for the message. But wherever the ad ends up, the images of those make-believe character-logos must charm the viewer into making the decision to buy, buy, and buy again — or it's back to the drawing board they go. Ho Ho Ho!

Where the Buck Stops

The Food and Drug Administration is responsible for regulations concerning food labeling, but the Federal Trade Commission and the U.S. Department of Agriculture are charged with monitoring truth in advertising.

Slogans That Have Swayed the World

Maxwell House coffee
Good to the last drop.

M&M's candy
Melts in your mouth. Not in your hands.

Wheaties breakfast cereal
Breakfast of champions.

Perdue poultry
It takes a tough man to make a tender chicken.

Lay's Potato Chips
No one can eat just one.

Coca-Cola
It's the real thing.

Pillsbury Poppin' Fresh dough
Nothin' says lovin' like somethin' from the oven.

Chiquita bananas
Quite possibly the world's perfect food.

Campbell's soup
M'm! M'm! Good!

Rice-a-Roni rice mix
The San Francisco treat.

Burger King
Have it your way.

V-8 vegetable juice
I could've had a V-8!

America's Pork Producers
The other white meat.

Kellogg's Sugar Frosted Flakes
They're grrrr-eat!

McDonald's
You deserve a break today.

Pepsi Cola
You're the Pepsi generation.

Wendy's
Where's the beef?

Alka Seltzer
I can't believe I ate the whole thing.

General Foods International coffees
Celebrate the moments of your life.

TUNING IN TO THE INFOMERCIALS

Infomercials are commercial messages that take the form of talk shows, product demonstrations, even news programming. As in home shopping broadcasts, viewers can call in to order the object of their desire (usually a relatively inexpensive self-help item). *The Wall Street Journal* reports that sales within this new industry have grown to at least $500 million a year, and we can expect to be seeing much more of this direct-response televangelism as the number of cable channels proliferates to the projected 500 by the mid-1990s.

Things have been changing very fast since the first infomercials saw the dead of night. They didn't get going until 1984, when deregulation allowed network and cable stations to sell half-hour blocks of air time for the pure and unadulterated purpose of advertising. Previously, these time slots had been devoted to horror movies in which colonies of flying bats or hatchlings from outer space made a stab at devouring the city of Los Angeles, which was always saved in the nick of time by a young researcher and the dumb but devoted daughter of the senior scientist.

Then along came Jay Kordich, the Juiceman, and the infomercial that began the mania for freshly squeezed juice. The company that produced the program saw its revenues skyrocket from $6.6 million to $100 million in two years. Most of us would happily consent to swallow even a glass of cabbage juice if it produced results like these.

If you think it is easy work to be a part of an infomercial audience, to scream with amazement, yell on cue for an hour, and be paid $40 for doing so, you would be wrong. It takes a professional actor to summon up just the right amount of energy.

The success of infomercials rests on their minimal production costs and the ability to buy air time inexpensively — at least for the moment. Thirty minutes of programming can still be had at bargain prices, whereas a 30-second commercial airing in prime time can cost $200,000 or more to make and at least $300,000 to air.

American children between the ages of four and 12 spend $2.5 billion of their own money every year on food and beverages, and influence another $80 billion in purchases.

Those Dumb Birds

As reported by Ronald Alsop in The Wall Street Journal *a little while ago, Joanne Tilove, a supervisor in the former Della Femina, Travisano & Partners ad agency, had to arrange a commercial in which chickens dressed in caps and gowns marched to the stately music of Elgar's "Pomp and Circumstance." It was a chicken commencement, Alsop reported, and the strategy was "to show that Young 'n Tender brand chickens are 'raised smarter' than ordinary birds. But the chickens in the ad hardly acted smart. They only wanted to eat and sleep, so it took three days to shoot what should have needed only a day."*

The biggest problem, according to Alsop, was that every time a cap was placed on a chicken, its head slumped to the ground. In the end, "the production crew, wearing garbage bags for sanitary protection, stood under the chickens and propped them up."

Ms. Tilove's conclusion: "Chickens are virtually untrainable. We had to go to Minneapolis just to find a director willing to do the ad."

"A FEW MINUTES WITH ANDY ROONEY"

Andy Rooney: I've been taking a survey of the words advertisers are using most often to get us to buy things we don't really want. Here's my list of the ten most common words used in advertising.

Number one: the word "new." It appears in about half of all printed and broadcast advertising. Usually, the product is not only new; it's "new and improved." If it's going to be new and improved again next year, you might want to wait.

Number two: "natural." Apparently, we like anything that says it's natural. We all know that almost everything made these days is fake, imitation, or plastic. But if the product says it's natural, we buy it.

Number three: The big newcomer to advertising in the last few years is the word "light." Apparently, we want everything light. Beer is light. They all make a light beer now. To me, light beer doesn't taste like much of anything except the bubbles. I think that light is for people who really don't like the taste of whatever it is.

The word "save" is **number four.**

Number five is "free." If we're saving so much and getting so many things free, how come we're always broke?

Number six: "rich." Rich is popular in food ads. That's funny, because the word "rich" in relation to food is the exact opposite of "light."

Number seven: "real." A lot of products want you to know they're real. I mean, would anyone bother to make fake Jell-O pudding?

Number eight: "fresh." I think they've gotten awfully *casual* about what they call fresh. Sometimes it's country fresh. They may have made it in a factory in the city eight months ago, but in the ads it's "country fresh."

Number nine: "extra." It's still popular in soap and pill ads. They have extra cleaning action.

Number ten: "discover" or "discovered" — "discovery." They're always telling us to discover something. Discovery is an accident. You can't tell anyone to go out and discover a product.

So, this is my list of the ten most used words in advertising. My job here on "60 Minutes" is to do the real, light, extra, fresh, natural comments.

Excerpted from "60 Minutes," CBS-TV, "A Few Minutes with Andy Rooney"

Coupons and Carry

Food buyers have become an increasingly diverse market for advertisers to reach. At one end of the scale are those who enthusiastically spend large sums of money to buy a cookbook devoted to the food of Vietnam or Turkey or Transylvania; at the other are the beginners who read a recipe telling them to separate five eggs, cheerfully put two whole eggs in one bowl and three in another, and then don't know what to do next.

Advertisers wrestling with such disparate market needs have found coupons an effective method of persuading customers to risk trying new foods, with the guarantee of getting money back if not satisfied (and if the store manager is in a good mood).

Product sampling in the store encourages the customer to taste and immediately decide to buy. Tasting, though, doesn't necessarily mean believing. More often it results in forgetting.

Sweepstakes, premiums, and discount certificates tucked inside packages also work with varying degrees of success but coupons are really the name of the advertising game.

In-store coupons are being used to give cents off when we buy the product again — though competing companies are also providing us with reduced prices in an effort to induce consumers to try a rival brand. Direct-mail coupons are sent to homes that have been selected by their zip code or pinpointed to specific niches. For instance, a company can narrow the market for a diet product to people who bought a size 24 dress with their credit card; or supply baby food coupons to parents who have recently subscribed to a baby magazine. But the big deal coupons are those that we find in the Sunday papers. These inserts reach a whopping 52 million households and often provide real bargains.

Restating the Truth

Exaggerated advertising claims often give misleading impressions, and sometimes public officials rise to challenge them. A recent case in point: "It is inappropriate to suggest that products such as Kentucky Fried Chicken and Dunkin' Donuts, which get up to 61 percent of their calories from fat, are healthy foods," huffed Robert Abrams, New York State's Attorney General.

Almost at once, the advertising claims were modified. KFC agreed to change the name of its new version, Lite 'n Crispy chicken, to Skinfree Crispy, and Dunkin' Donuts consented to drop its "zero cholesterol" claim after the attorney general pointed out that reducing two tiny milligrams of cholesterol didn't amount to a hill of beans considering the average doughnut gets 46 percent of its calories from fat.

AIRLINE FOOD

*The quality of food
is in inverse
proportion
to the altitude of
the dining room,
with airplanes the
extreme example.*

— Bryan Miller
Restaurant critic,
The New York Times

FREE FLIGHT
WITH YOUR MEAL, SIR?

We don't pack a hot lunch when we go for a two-hour drive, but no sooner do we soar to 30,000 feet than we start wondering, "What's for dinner?"

It's not that we are necessarily hungry, or anxious, simply because we know there are no Golden Arches in the sky. No, the problem is that, like Pavlov's dog, we have been conditioned to expect to be fed even on quite a brief journey.

Way back, when planes could fly only relatively short distances without refueling, passengers could get out,

stretch their legs, and find a sandwich in the airport. Then Marriott hit on the idea of providing box lunches . . . and within moments we were into chicken of the sky in economy class and lobster at the high end.

Today's longer flights mean that passengers want to be entertained both electronically and digestively. OK — but just imagine that, for once, you are not in the passenger seat but having to wrestle with the problem of providing 150 million meals a year. This translates to feeding 432,000 people a day, which is the equivalent of the entire population

of Oklahoma City. Visualize all these picky people packed like pickles in a metal tube hurtling through several time zones at a considerable rate of speed, and hitting occasional air pockets, pickpockets, and flirtatious and sometimes inebriated travelers who refuse to stay buckled up but insist on going to the bathroom as soon as the serving cart reaches the point of no return, so that it takes equally long to move the cart forward or backward to allow the person to pass. This is no easy task.

The thing we all tend to forget is that airlines are most definitely not restaurants; nevertheless, they are required to hand out a huge volume of food in a very limited amount of space and time — and the lettuce must be crisp and fresh, the beef must be tender, and the coffee strong. Pity the poor flight attendants, who must radiate the same qualities, appearing equally crisp and fresh, tender, and strong — and smiling, too.

Special Diet? No Problem

But no airline would be crazy enough to advertise the range of diets that are available on request. This is less a matter of hiding the service than of avoiding the logistical nightmares that develop when passengers switch flights, or even airlines. Travelers, it seems, get more overwrought about the loss of a special meal than the misplacement of their luggage.

Vegetarian and kosher are among the most frequently requested diets, but don't overlook an opportunity to sample the refugee diet that is offered by Northwest Airlines

(presumably on a first-come, first-served basis). It consists of canned fruit salad, char chiu pork, BBQ sauce, plain steamed rice, green peas, dinner roll, and cake or pudding. We have been unable to find out if you are eligible for this "special meal" as an incoming or outgoing refugee, so do

be sure to ask, just to be on the safe side.

Most meals must be ordered at least six hours in advance, especially should you wish to request a bland Hindu child's ovolacto-vegetarian plate. Simpler choices can be made from the list that follows:

Bland
Diabetic
Fruit plate
Gluten-free
Hindu
High-protein
Hypoglycemic
Infant
Kosher
Lactose-free
Low-calorie
Low-carbohydrate
Low-fat
McDonald's Happy Meals
Muslim
Ovolacto-vegetarian
Refugee
Seafood plate
Soft
Sulfite-free
Traveler's Lighter Choice
Vegan Vegetarian
Vegetarian

The Higher, the Duller

No, it isn't your imagination — airline food really *is* quite tasteless. This is not because it actually is without taste but because your taste buds are dulled by high altitude and the cabin pressure, so that food that probably would have been perfectly acceptable if it were eaten with your feet on the ground loses flavor as the plane reaches for the stars.

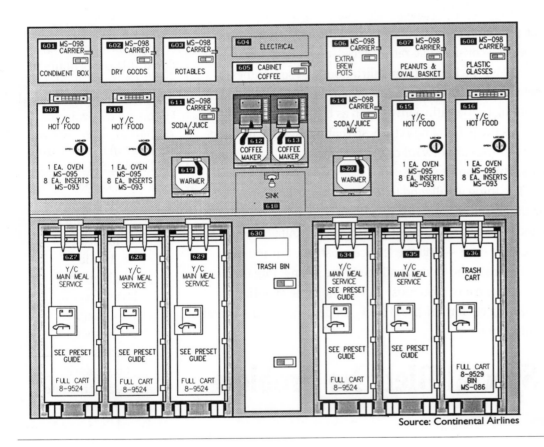

Source: Continental Airlines

Food Safety

All food for U.S. airline service has to be prepared in compliance with Food and Drug Administration safety regulations, and FDA inspectors regularly probe sample dishes with thermometers, making sure they are either hotter or colder than the danger zone (45 to 140 degrees F.) within which bacteria could multiply.

Wallop in the Skies

*I*n the old days, seasoned travelers used to pack liquor-filled hip flasks, in case a thirst emergency should arise. Today, you are offered your choice of drinks in tiny plastic bottles. It may be reassuring to know that even the amount in one of those little bottles packs a bigger wallop when airborne.

Airline wine and liquor bottles are made out of plastic rather than glass, not because glass breaks more easily but because plastic is much lighter. Northwest Airlines claims that using plastic rather than glass cuts 17½ pounds from each plane's payload, which results in fuel savings of more than $400,000 per year. Think of this when next you travel with two heavy suitcases.

To me, an airplane is a great place to diet.

— Wolfgang Puck,
Owner/chef, Spago, Los Angeles

ODD JOBS

At Caterair, one of the biggest airline catering operations in America, a single worker handles the assembling and stowing of little packaged food supplies for approximately 45 daily departures. Among the items loaded aboard: hundreds of packets of sugar, Sweet 'n Low, Equal, salt, pepper, coffee, decaf coffee, tea bags, and dry creamer.

Suffering Sickness

Traveling at 30,000 feet, your brain and inner ear, which control the sense of balance, understand that you are moving, but your eyes tell you that you are sitting perfectly still. These mixed messages induce the sympathetic nervous system to go into its fight-or-flight mode, triggering all those ghastly symptoms we know and dread.

Researchers at Pennsylvania State University have discovered that the best way to avoid air sickness is to have frequent snacks of dry crackers. Keeping your eyes closed helps, too.

Meals in the Sky

Per-passenger food costs

Domestic flights

American	$6.36
America West	$2.63
Continental	$5.81
Delta	$4.72
Northwest	$4.07
TWA	$4.86
United	$4.96
U.S. Air	$3.90

Trans-Atlantic flights

American	$31.25
Continental	$12.11
Delta	$28.67
Northwest	$20.41
TWA	$16.40
United	$18.81
U.S. Air	$26.99

Pacific flights

American	$52.92
America West	$41.07
Continental	$11.54
Delta	$27.19
Northwest	$15.10
United	$20.25

Source: Avmark, aviation management consultants, Arlington, Virginia; figures are as of June 30, 1991.

CONCORDE

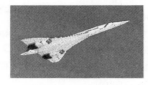

The Concorde travels so fast that passengers hear the break in the sound barrier. This is not fast food, though.

THE CONCORDE MENU

London - New York
3 h 50

DINNER

CANAPÉS
Alaskan crab, asparagus with cheese and smoked salmon

APPETIZERS
Osetra caviar and smoked sturgeon with blinis

MAIN COURSES
Grilled fillet of beef with fresh herbs garnished with leaf spinach, vegetable julienne and new parsley potatoes
or
Grilled Dover sole, lobster and king prawns with spinach, grilled vegetables and saffron rice
or
As a light alternative, we suggest cold grilled breast of Barbary duckling with cured ham

SALAD BOWL
Seasonal salad greens and herbs with grated carrot and pine kernels. Served with vinaigrette dressing

DESSERT
Passion fruit garden

CHEESE
A selection of English Stilton, Red Leicester and Comte cheese

COFFEE / TEA
Coffee, decaffeinated coffee or tea

Fine chocolates

Brave New Interactive Skies

Futurists predict that planes of the future will carry 1,000 passengers. One solution to feeding them may be not to. Let them fend for themselves, bringing a picnic from home or buying from the airport food courts, which are already offering everything from frozen yogurt to fancy feasts.

Linda Zane of Airline Food Service Industry predicts that the planes of the future will simply be equipped with more galleys.

Other forecasters hint darkly that technology that already exists may be brought to bear. When hungry, we will select a package of shelf-stable food from among the several boxes stored in the armrest of our seat and pop our choice into the built-in microwave. Beverages will come in cans. Pull a strip and the drink will be instantly heated — or chilled.

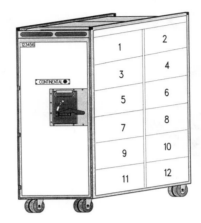

Hard Rolls, Anyone?

Why are the rolls served on airplanes almost always as hard as bricks?

Because at least half the cabin's air comes in through the plane's superheated engines, which suck all the moisture out of the air before it is cooled for use in the cabin. The result is overdry air and inedible rolls. The simple solution would be to stop serving them, but this would leave an empty spot on all those molded plastic trays.

Overheard ...

On a flight between *Pittsburgh and Albany: The plane is crowded and an elderly man is having some difficulty in choosing between the luncheon entrees: chicken Marengo, beef burritos, or fresh fruit salad. The harassed airline attendant attempts to reassure him:*

"If you don't get your first choice, sir, please don't be distressed. All our entrees taste very much the same."

MORE INFORMATION

Caterair
6550 Rock Spring Drive
Bethesda, MD 20817
301-897-7800

In-Flight Food Service Association
304 West Liberty Street
Louisville, KY 40202
502-583-3783

In Flight Services, Ogden Services Corporation
2 Penn Plaza
New York, NY 10121
212-868-5496

Sky Chefs, Inc.
524 East Lamar Boulevard
Arlington, TX 76011
807-792-2389

ALLERGIES

President Clinton has become a byword as an allergic subject, chiefly for having severe reactions not only to dust and pollen but to the Christmas greenery that decked the Arkansas governor's mansion. In the food department, he is allergic to chocolate (but loves Baby Ruth candy bars), and to milk. He drinks a lot of coffee — black.

Books

Allergy Cooking with Ease
Nicolette M. Dumke;
Starburst Publishers, 1992;
$12.95

No More Allergies
Gary Null; Villard Books,
1992; $13.00

The Gluten-Free Gourmet
Betty Hagman; Henry Holt,
1991; $12.95

The Milk-Free Kitchen
Beth Kidder; Henry Holt,
1991; $16.95

Adverse Reactions to Food
American Dietetic Association,
1984; $9.50

Allergy Overload: Are Foods and Chemicals Killing You?
Stephen Griffiths;
HarperCollins, 1992; $13.00

The Complete Guide to Food Allergy and Intolerance
Jonathan Brostroff and Linda Gamlin; Crown, 1992; $13.00

Food Intolerances

Major adult intolerances are to lactose, monosodium glutamate (MSG), strawberries, tomatoes, wine, cheese, and chocolate. Some people have trouble tolerating gluten, the protein in grains such as wheat, oats, and rye.

Food Allergies

Most adult food allergies are attributed to peanuts, shellfish, tree nuts such as walnuts and almonds, eggs, soybeans and soy products, and bisulfites.

BAD REACTIONS

A lot of people believe that they are allergic to one or another kind of food, but, in fact, genuine food allergies, which attack the body's immune system and may be life-threatening, show up in only 1 to 2 percent of the adult population. A far more common experience is a food intolerance — a disagreeable reaction that bears many of the symptoms of an allergy, among them upset stomach, vomiting, diarrhea, and itching. Food intolerances may be extremely unpleasant, but they won't kill you.

Another difference: People with a food intolerance can often consume and digest small amounts of a problem food without having a bad reaction, while those with true allergies to certain foods often have a severe reaction to even the tiniest, most microscopic quantities of it.

In the case of allergies and intolerances, seasons of the year play a significant role in the intensity of reaction to some foods. For example, someone who is allergic to cantaloupes may be more susceptible in the spring and fall, when the increase in airborne pollen can trigger a reaction. Oddly, strenuous exercise may also bring on an adverse reaction. Athletes and their trainers and doctors are always on the alert for allergic reactions that may show up when certain foods are consumed during periods of intense exercise.

Most food intolerances result from a deficiency in the enzymes that aid digestion. The most common intolerance is to the lactose in cow's milk; it occurs when the enzyme lactase, which is required to break down the lactose (a sugar), is absent from the body. Many lactose-intolerant people can consume some dairy products — hard cheeses, yogurt, sour cream — because in their manufacturing process an additive starts to break down or "predigest" lactose.

A true food allergy involves the body's immune system. Antibodies attack the offending food (usually some type of protein) by releasing chemicals that irritate the body. These symptoms frequently produce symptoms of anaphylaxis (hypersensitivity): itching, swelling of the throat and tongue, breathing difficulties, chest pain, vomiting, diarrhea, and low blood pressure. Without intervention, the body eventually goes into shock and death may occur. This reaction may happen within minutes, or within a few hours. (Symptoms of intolerance, on the other hand, may not show up for 24 hours or more.)

By means of a series of tests, a licensed allergist can determine whether someone is suffering from allergies or intolerances.

Children Have Food Allergies, Too

True food-related allergies show up more frequently in children than in adults (5 to 7 percent of children under the age of three have them). If both parents have allergies, their children stand a 70 percent chance of developing them as well. If only one parent is allergic, the risk is cut in half.

Scientists have discovered a high risk of severe allergic reaction and death in children who have both allergies and asthma. In general, a study of 355 children under the age of 15 indicates that the foods most likely to cause allergic reactions are the proteins in eggs, fish, cow's milk, legumes (specifically peanuts and soybeans), and peaches.

HOTLINES

800-822-2762
American Academy of Allergy and Immunology

703-691-3179
Food Allergy Network
8 a.m. - 7 p.m. EST

Not Allergic to Good News

Happily, by the age of three, most children outgrow the symptoms of food allergies, and after a couple of years of completely avoiding an offending food, most proven allergies will disappear in both children and adults.

Among people with proven allergies, 80 percent are allergic to only two or three foods. Those who have reached the age of 40 without developing allergies are extremely unlikely to do so.

The number-one fatal food allergy is peanut allergy; although researchers are studying an experimental injection therapy, allergists continue to stress total avoidance of anything peanutty for people suffering from this dangerous complaint.

ALLIGATORS

GATOR TAIL

ERNEST MATTHEW MICKLER

The only place you can find alligator is near the coast or the inland swamps in the South. So if you're lucky enough to get a holt to an alligator tail, there's a section about a foot long just behind the back legs that's tender and juicy. You cut it in sections at the joints just like you would a pork chop. Salt, pepper, and flour each piece of tail and then fry in hot grease until golden brown. Or you can barbecue it with Bosie's Barbecue Sauce. He had alligator tail especially in mind when he concocted it.

If you haven't eaten gator tail before you're in for a surprise. It's gonna taste a little bit like chicken, a little bit like pork, and a little bit like fish. It's so good, you'll wanna lay down and scream.

Excerpted from White Trash Cooking

See Ya Later?

The locals in Florida and Louisiana may say it tastes great, and some of us may be persuaded to try alligator tail on the strength of its supposedly heart-healthy profile: It's rich in vitamin B-12 and niacin and strong in iron. *Longevity* magazine assures us that only 18 percent of its calories come from fat, "with just 5 percent artery-clogging saturated fat."

But though all alligators may be low in cholesterol, and their meat white, they still have a long way to go in the charm department. They may be medium rare, but they're hard to bag.

So USDA agents don't inspect alligator meat. Who can blame them?

Scallopini of **Alligator**

Serves 4

Alligator receives a kind of Italian piccata treatment in this recipe. The sauce works nicely with thinly sliced boar and boneless breasts of game birds as well. Recommended wine: A Sauvignon Blanc with its citrus overtones emphasizes the citrus-tinged sauce.

1 pound alligator tail meat, thinly sliced
Salt and freshly ground black pepper to taste
1/4 cup olive oil
3 tablespoons slivered shallots
3 tablespoons white wine vinegar
1/2 cup chicken stock
2 teaspoons chopped anchovy fillet
1 1/2 tablespoons finely chopped cornichons
1 tablespoon drained capers
2 teaspoons fresh lemon juice
1 teaspoon minced garlic
3 tablespoons minced fresh parsley

Gently pound alligator slices so that they are of even thickness. Season well with salt and pepper.

In a sauté pan, heat oil and sauté alligator slices over moderately high heat, in batches if necessary. Remove to a serving platter and keep warm.

Add all remaining ingredients to pan and quickly reduce over high heat to a light sauce consistency. Taste and adjust seasoning. Pour over alligator and serve immediately.

— John Ash and Sid Goldstein
American Game Cooking

MORE INFORMATION

American Alligator Farmers Association
5145 Harvey Tew Road
Plant City, FL 33566
813-752-2836

MAIL ORDER SOURCES

Bayou-To-Go
P.O. Box 20104
New Orleans, LA 70141
800-541-6610

ALMONDS

Don't eat too many almonds; they add weight to the breasts.

— Colette,
French novelist

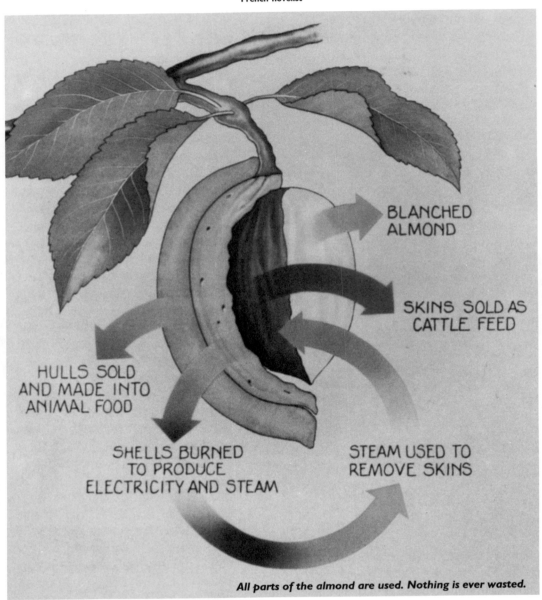

BLANCHED ALMOND

SKINS SOLD AS CATTLE FEED

HULLS SOLD AND MADE INTO ANIMAL FOOD

STEAM USED TO REMOVE SKINS

SHELLS BURNED TO PRODUCE ELECTRICITY AND STEAM

All parts of the almond are used. Nothing is ever wasted.

WHEN IS A NUT NOT A NUT?

Advertisers tell us that almonds are America's favorite nuts. In fact, the almond is not a nut but a kind of fruit called a drupe, like the cherry, the plum, and the peach. We happen to enjoy eating just the inner seed of the almond, so we discard its shell and leathery outer skin, whereas we treasure the outer parts of cherries, plums, and peaches, and throw away what we call "the pits."

As for almonds' nutritional profile: They're an excellent source of vitamin E and magnesium, a good source of fiber and phosphorus, high in fat and calories, and, like all nuts, cholesterol-free. They come in two varieties: the sweet almonds we eat and bake with, and bitter almonds, which are used to make almond extracts and flavorings (once their natural content of prussic acid has been safely removed).

Q&A

Q What is the difference between almond paste and marzipan?

A Both are made from blanched almonds, for use in baking and candy-making. Marzipan has more sugar, which makes it stiffer and lighter in color; almond paste contains more almonds, so it costs slightly more.

Diamonds in the Raw

Almond orchards occupy more farming space in California than any other crop except grapes — about 400,000 acres — and the nuts are the state's top food export, filling all of America's almond needs, and a large part of the world's as well. Fully two-thirds of the almond farmers market their nuts through Blue Diamond Growers, the gigantic cooperative whose label is familiar worldwide. Blue Diamond's sprawling headquarters in Sacramento takes up the equivalent of 33 city blocks and contains the world's largest almond factory, which can (and does) process 2 million pounds of almonds a day.

BLUE DIAMOND

Did You Know?

☞ Almonds and almond butter are accepted as meat alternates in the National School Lunch Program.

☞ According to superstition: If you eat almonds before taking a drink, you will reduce your chances of getting drunk and avoid having a hangover.

☞ Japanese teenagers like to snack on Calmond, a mixture of dried sardines and slivered almonds that is also a source of protein and calcium.

☞ According to a Chinese proverb, almonds come to people who have no teeth.

☞ California exports more than 360 million pounds of almonds annually to some 90 countries, representing about 70 percent of the world's almond supply.

MORE INFORMATION

Almond Board of California
1104 12th Street
Modesto, CA 95354
209-549-8262

Blue Diamond Growers
1802 C Street
Sacramento, CA 95814
916-442-0771

MAIL ORDER SOURCES

Luke's Almond Acres
11281 South Lac Jac
Reedley, CA 93654
209-638-3483

Nunes Farms
P.O. Box 311
Newman, CA 95360
209-862-3033

PERIODICALS

For address, see Information Sources

Almond Facts
Blue Diamond Growers
916-442-0771
Bimonthly;
free to co-op members;
$25 a year for nonmembers

ODD JOBS

An almond sorter at the Blue Diamond food processing plant needs two good eyes for tiny details. Almonds surge past sorters on a belt that moves at a rate of 1,000 pounds of nuts an hour. Workers have to scoop away flawed almonds — and know the difference between a chip and a wormhole — so that the final run will yield perfect nuts for slicing, dicing, and chopping. Their defect record: less than 1 percent.

ANCHOVIES

SALTY BUT SWEET

Lesser herringlike fish — sprats, pilchards, alewives, and the like — sometimes pass as anchovies, but they aren't. True anchovies are small fish, around three inches long, which swim in large schools where the sea is temperate. For thousands of years they have been abundant in the Mediterranean and riding the warm currents off the shores of Peru and California — though pollution and El Nino have taken their tolls.

Few people other than fishermen's families have tasted fresh anchovy; its delicate white flesh deteriorates so quickly when exposed to the air that the fish can only be preserved by being heavily salted. The ancient Romans flavored dishes with *garum*, a sauce made from unpreserved, fermented anchovies, but in modern Italy, Spain, and Greece salted anchovies are universally offered as appetizers. For the rest of the world the anchovy comes canned, with its salty fillets well oiled.

These tiny creatures are not only good to eat, they are good for us too. They contain fair amounts of iron and vitamin B-12 as well as niacin and omega-3 monounsaturated fats.

In Victorian England cooks spread anchovy paste on bread and butter at teatime. Today anchovies are most frequently seen topping pizzas and Caesar salads—and, all too often, abandoned in sad piles at the side of the plate.

MORE INFORMATION

National Fisheries Institute, Inc.
200 M Street NW, Suite 580
Washington, DC 20036
202-296-3428

ANIMAL RIGHTS

I am in favor of animal rights as well as human rights. This is the way of a whole human being.

— Abraham Lincoln

...AND JUSTICE FOR ALL

Without question, passions are aroused about the humane treatment of domesticated animals. Antagonism runs deep between advocates of animal rights and the meat and poultry producers who have the responsibility of bringing a safe and abundant food supply to market at the lowest possible cost.

Why has this become such an issue in our time? When America was still largely a farming nation, most people knew firsthand how cattle, pigs, and chickens lived — and died. Times were harder for people as well as animals, and it was understood — by the people, anyway — that an animal's sole purpose in life was to provide them with a living. Well-treated cows had healthier babies, well-fed hogs fetched higher prices, poultry that pecked about the yard certainly tasted better, but no one thought livestock had a right to a certain quality of life.

Now that both human and animal populations have increased so hugely and farming has become industrialized along with cities, we buy our meats already cut and packaged. All the dirty work has been done for us. We can barely make out the shape of the original animal, so it is hard to think about it as a living, breathing creature. Yet we feel, however briefly, concern when we think about the kind of life it may have led. In a sense, animals have become our latest — and largest — minority group, but, of course, they are really the silent majority.

THE BARBARITY OF MEAT

Nick Fiddes

If, as some authors suggest, eating meat is indeed an important statement of human power, it might seem strange that we are apparently becoming progressively more uncomfortable with reminders of its animal origins. Consumer attitudes today are in a state of flux, not least for this reason. Whereas once it was sufficient simply to display whole animals and pieces of meat, the packing of the product is now a more delicate task.

Most of us prefer not to think too directly about where our meat has come from, and unwelcome reminders can be distinctly off-putting. As one consumer put it, "I don't like it when you see . . . veins and things coming out of the meat . . . because it always reminds me of my own insides in a funny sort of a way. I suppose it's the idea of, like, blood flowing [that] makes you realize that this slab of meat was once a bit of functioning body, a bit like your own."

Meat marketing has responded accordingly, to assuage customers' sensitivity to the nature of the product. Nowadays, the consumer need never encounter animal flesh in its vulgar, undressed state. Instead it will come cooked and reshaped, in a sesame bun or an exotically flavored sauce, as a turkey roll or as chicken nuggets, in a crumb coating or a vacuum package, with not a hint of blood in sight. More and more butchers' windows sport fresh green vegetables, fragrant herbs, and perhaps a stir-fry mixture. A deliberate process of disguising the source of animal foods has gained momentum in the 20th century, reacting to our evident unease with the idea of eating dead animals.

Said one butcher, "I deplore deliveries being carried into the front of my shop on the neck of a van driver — espe-cially if they are not wrapped. . . . I can think of little more guaranteed to turn pedestrians off buying meat than the sight of pigs' heads flopping about as he struggles past them with the carcass."

The number of independent butchers' shops has declined considerably in recent years. Supermarkets have clearly derived particular competitive advantage from presenting meat in conspicuously hygienic conditions with all preparation completed out of sight. Often only the best cuts are displayed; bones, guts, and skin are nowhere to be seen. The hermetically sealed package is effectively dissoci-ated from the animal to which its contents once belonged, a service that is clearly winning customers.

The names we give to the flesh of the main meat an-imals are another device whereby we reduce the unpleasant impact of having to acknowledge their identity. We do not eat cow, we eat beef; we do not eat pig, we eat pork; we do not eat deer, we eat venison. It is as if we cannot bear to utter the name of the beast whose death we have ordained.

To some, our willingness to consume meat as well as the many other assorted products of the animal industry, but apparent unwillingness to slaughter the beasts for ourselves or even to acknowledge our complicity in that process, is a matter for moral reproof. Said one critic, "I think the meat industry is very dishonest. The people are not allowed to be aware of what's going on. To them meat is wrapped up in cellophane in supermarkets; it's very di-vorced from the animal that it's coming from. . . . People don't go down on the factory farm to see what's really going on down there. I think if a lot of people did do that or [went] to the slaughterhouse to see how the meat is produced, then a lot of them would become vegetarians."

There is some evidence to support this belief. Many first-generation vegetarians and semivegetarians directly trace their abstinence to occasions when, for one reason or another, they were brought face to face with the connection between the meat on their plate and once-living animals. The particular incident related by any individual — be it the sight of carcasses being carried into a butcher's shop, or an encounter with vegetarian polemicism, or a visit to a slaughterhouse on daily business, or merely an unusually vivid flight of imagination — is of minor importance. What matters is that many people, when confronted with this ethical perplexity, seemingly prefer to forgo meat altogether rather than to condone the treatment of animals on their path from birth to plate. And equally important, perhaps, is how new this rebellion is, or rather, how rapid its develop-ment has been in recent history.

Excerpted from *Meat: A Natural Symbol*

Brigitte Bardot was one of the first of the famous to bring animal rights issues to public attention.

Animals in the wild don't have rights. They kill most inhumanely.

— Anonymous

P. CVEY

"Rule number one, never feel sorry for the main dish."

FOOD FRIGHT

WILLIAM GEIST

The waiter has already told me more than I want to know (his name, Michael). And after reciting the specials (free-range chicken, hormone-free beef, natural-grain-fed catfish), he begins delivering a . . . *eulogy* to the entrees!

"They have all led wholesome lives," Michael says, almost solemnly, his hands folded in front of him the way they teach at funeral-director's school.

My wife — tears welling in her eyes — orders a salad.

"I'd like the . . . New York strip," I say softly. "I suppose it's too late to have a word with, you know, *the cow*?" Unfortunately, it is.

"Any photographs," I ask, "of the cow — in happier times?" Unfortunately not.

"Well," I say, "it's good to know she was drug-free. No history of alcohol or tobacco use either, I suppose?" Michael shakes his head no and begins to walk away.

"Oh! Michael, one more thing. Was she wearing a seat belt?"

I don't want to know about the cow's stress-free life-style. I don't want a medical workup. I don't want pictures of the kids. I just want to, you know, *eat* the cow, medium rare, and just as soon as the family has been notified.

I don't want to develop a close personal relationship with anything I'm about to eat. I don't go to those places where you, like, pick your own lobster — or even straw-berries, for that matter. Could be a manifestation of male intimacy-phobia syndrome. . . .

Ordering chicken is even worse. When I see free-range chicken on a menu, the first thing that comes to mind is a flock of them bounding across Montana. The second thing is "Twenty-five bucks for a free-range-chicken dinner?!" When chickens stayed home, chicken dinners were six and a quarter!

The idea is that Freeing the Chickens Now! from their cramped cages makes them healthier, happier, and better to eat. Seems like a high price to pay for recess. There are some who argue that, like us, many chickens and cows would probably be happier penned up and chowing down than wandering around wondering where their next meal is coming from. They say free-range meat is stringier, tougher, and gamy, and that gallivanting around out there makes them susceptible to all sorts of worms and parasites and infections — sort of like having a free-range girlfriend. . . .

New York menus are also sporting natural-grain-fed catfish, which one menu explained grew up in the "pure air and pure waters" of Mississippi. The menu promised that the fish had passed the exacting examinations of the Catfish Institute. So now we're getting the educational background! Another menu gives the name of the pond in West Virginia whence the trout on the menu came. Home address!

Markets and brunch menus are also carrying the new low-cholesterol miracle egg. One day I picked up a carton of low-cholesterol eggs and a carton of regulars. The eggs looked exactly alike. When I started putting them back in their cartons, I couldn't tell which was which, and ever since, I have imagined someone out there having a massive coronary because of me, and the family fingering me for manslaughter and filing a $1.5-million lawsuit.

On my behalf, a recent story on the front page of *The New York Times* raises serious questions about the ability of chickens to even *lay* such eggs. And it is asking a lot on short notice. You can imagine the chickens talking among themselves in the coop after work: "Boss calls me into his office and tells me to start layin' low-cholesterol eggs. I say, 'Jeez, boss, you're killin' us out there! You already got us doin' small, medium, large, extra large. Whadya want out of us? Pastels for Easter?' "

Dabbing her tears with a napkin after Michael's eulogy, my wife says that she is sick of all this free-range, sun-dried, stress-free, extra-virgin nonsense. "There's no such thing as being extra virgin!" she snaps, but then, she never met my high-school sweetheart. The term, of course, applies to olive oil — and, you know, looking back at my girlfriend's yearbook pictures, there is a resemblance.

Excerpted from *New York* magazine

MORE INFORMATION

Americans for Medical Progress Education Foundation
Crystal Square Three
1735 Jefferson Davis Highway,
Suite 907
Arlington, VA 22202
703-412-1111

Animal Welfare Institute
P.O. Box 3650
Washington, DC 20007
202-337-2332

Coalition for Non-Violent Food
P.O. Box 214
Planetarium Station
New York, NY 10024
212-873-3674

Farm Sanctuary
P.O. Box 150
Watkins Glen, NY 14891
607-583-2225

Humane Farming Association
1550 California Street, Suite 6
San Francisco, CA 94109
415-485-1495

Humane Society of the United States
2100 L Street NW
Washington, DC 20037
202-452-1100

People for the Ethical Treatment of Animals, Inc. (PETA)
P.O. Box 42516
Washington, DC 20015
301-770-7444

Books

The Sexual Politics of Meat: A Feminist-Vegetarian Critical Theory
Carol J. Adams; Continuum, 1990; $12.95

A Shopper's Guide to Cruelty-Free Products
Lori Cook; Bantam, 1991; $4.99

Seven Lobsters Fly the Cooler

On December 10, 1988, The New York Times reported that seven live lobsters had been purchased from a suburban Maryland restaurant and flown to a new home off the coast of Maine. It seems that the House of Chinese Gourmet in Rockville, Maryland, had been a favorite among local vegetarians until the day when its owner decided to add fresh seafood to his menu and installed a 125-gallon tank containing seven very-much-alive lobsters. "There was a big outcry," a spokeswoman for People for the Ethical Treatment of Animals told the Times. "The vegetarian clientele got very upset."

Fortunately, a crisis was avoided. The owner agreed to get rid of the tank, provided the animal rights group bought the lobsters and arranged for their freedom. Total cost of the lobster rescue was $240: $40 for the lobsters and $200 for the flight from Washington National Airport to Portland, Maine. The Coast Guard donated the cost of its services in providing an escort to a boat station where the lobsters were released in calmer, cooler waters.

Lonely lobster seeks mate for fine dining and travel. Send photo...

ANTELOPES

THE RANGE'S WILD HARVEST

Home on the range, the deer and the antelope still play, but in central Texas, at least, steps have been taken to crop a free-ranging population of some 15,000 Indian nilgai antelope — descendants of a few zoo animals introduced into the wild in the 1940s —for human consumption. The nilgai are similar to deer but leaner: the meat of the bull contains only 0.8 percent fat, and the female 5.2 percent, a far lower percentage than the more common cuts of beef. This feature alone makes antelope attractive to consumers concerned about calories and cholesterol.

Mike Hughes of the Broken Arrow Ranch in Ingram, Texas, is making serious efforts to harvest the antelope humanely without having to trap them (fear produces tainted meat). Selected animals on any of the 150 or so ranches that have nilgai herds are shot by a marksman using a silenced rifle and killed instantly. Hughes's crew dress the carcass on the spot aboard a specially designed trailer and refrigerate it. A state meat inspector accompanies them, observes the entire process, and stamps the meat approved. The mobile crew take from 15 to 20 antelope each time they make one of these excursions.

Back at the plant, the meat is hung and aged, then butchered, vacuum-packed, and aged an additional two to three weeks before being shipped to market.

Hughes reports that sales have increased by about 15 to 20 percent a year since he began operation a decade ago. Broken Arrow now produces about 12,000 pounds of antelope saddle, leg, and chuck roast annually, and supplies some 2,000 restaurants nationwide as well as many private consumers. Some of the meat bought wholesale has even shown up in supermarkets, usually classified by the USDA as venison— and it is excellent!

MAIL ORDER SOURCES ✉

Polarica
107 Quint Street
San Francisco, CA 94124
1-800-GAME-USA
fax: 415-647-6826

Broken Arrow Ranch
P.O. Box 530
Ingram, TX 78025
800-962-4263

Off the Prairie, Onto the Plate

by Richard Atcheson

I was born in Texas and raised in Oklahoma, but I never saw antelope on a plate until last year, when I was entertained to dinner at La Costa, the supremely expensive and exclusive spa resort just north of San Diego, at Oceanside. La Costa has five restaurants of ascending grandeur and we were in the grandest — a room where the walls were draped dramatically in fabric, in the Napoleonic manner. The chef suggested the filet of antelope, and as I thought the circumstance demanded something memorable, I said yes.

My filet, broiled briefly, arrived on a white porcelain plate in a shallow pool of color-coordinated brown sauce. I took knife and fork to it immediately, and enjoyed it to the last bite; it tasted exactly like very lean steak. But in such a splendid setting, in the golden glow of flickering candles and topaz chandeliers, it had to have been the thing itself — a wild idea leaping vividly to the imagination.

Fresh Black Horn Antelope
Cuts and Weights

Saddle	7.5 lb.(35-lb. pack)	Limited supply	$8.95/lb.
Hindleg	4.5 lb.(35-lb. pack)	Limited supply	$7.95/lb.
Whole	45 lb.(35-lb. pack)	Limited supply	$7.50/lb.

Source: Polarica, San Francisco, California

APHRODISIACS

Many so-called aphrodisiac recipes are basically wholesome ingredients prepared in a tasty way. The receptivity to romance probably comes from the general sense of relaxation and well-being good food induces.

— Harry E. Wedeck
A Dictionary of Aphrodisiacs

Valentine's Day Menu Suggestions

Diamond-Cut Toasts with Roses of Smoked Salmon
Mussel Soup with Golden Threads
Spears of Grass (Asparagus)
Hearts of Artichoke
Love Boat of Oysters, Clams, and Shrimp
Baby Crabmeat Dumplings

❤

Little Birds Roasted with Garlic and Rosemary
Smothered Breasts (of Chicken)
Grilled Bass Wrapped Modestly in Fig Leaves
Ring of Angel Hair Pasta
Roasted Doves with Fresh Lovage

❤

Salad of Pansies and Forget-Me-Nots

❤

Upside-Down Pair of Tarts
Coeur à la Crème • Napoleons & Josephines
Eve's Love Apples with Spun Sugar
Honey Ice Cream • Rose Petal Ice Cream
Cold Violet Soufflé

JUST SAY YES

"**P**ower is the great aphrodisiac," said Henry Kissinger (and he should know because he certainly had a lot of experience), but it has also been said that, among Arabs anyway, it is carrots that will do the trick.

These matters vary from culture to culture, but though Napoleon declared in a letter to Josephine, "Not a day passes that I have not loved you; not one night that I have not clasped you in my arms," the fact of the matter is that the only couple who were truly made for each other were Adam and Eve.

Yet since the first two pairs of bright eyes met in questioning surmise, humankind has searched for something, other than an apple, to eat or drink to produce a longed-for response on a predictable timetable.

As far as we know, no reliable solution has been found. And some of the most popular candidates of the past — tomatoes and potatoes, asparagus and even turnips — have proved to be a bust in the kiss-and-cuddle department. You could say, though, that just by feeding us over the generations, these lowly foods have kept us alive long enough for nature to run its repeated if impromptu course.

Some foods still retain a certain reputation in romantic literature. For instance, a survey of American eating habits discovered that shellfish and romance often go hand in hand.

A lobster dinner in a candle-lit restaurant is just the ticket for loving couples — but only for those with annual incomes over $30,000. Those who are not among society's upper crust settle for pizza in the parlor. But there are no figures to prove that lobster has the edge over pizza when it gets to begetting.

The modern view of oysters as aphrodisiacs boils down to mere numbers. Six oysters contain five times the government's recommended daily allowance of zinc. Men who lack this important mineral in their blood turn out to have low levels of testosterone. But if oysters are not your cup of tea, try a turkey leg. The dark meat is rich in zinc, too.

Books

Aphrodisiacs and Love Magic
Pamela Allardice; Avery Publishing, 1989; $10.95

Aphrodisiacs for Men: Effective Virilizing Foods and Herbs
Gary M. Griffin; Added Dimensions, 1991; $12.95

Cookery for Lovers: Aphrodisiacs in the Kitchen
Bettie L. Furuta; Furuta Associates, 1984; $14.95

A Dictionary of Aphrodisiacs
Harry E. Wedeck; M. Evans, 1992; $9.95

The Foods of Love
Max de Roche; Arcade Publishing, 1991; $16.95

Like Water for Chocolate
Laura Esquivel; Doubleday, 1992; $17.50

Foodie Endearments

Cookie
Dumpling
Honey
Honey-bun
Lamb chop
My little cabbage
Peaches
Pumpkin
Sugar
Sweetie
Sweetie-pie

The Foods of Love

Forget about bee pollen, mandrake root, and tiger's milk. A dip into *A Dictionary of Aphrodisiacs* reveals that even a partial list of quite common foods proposed over the centuries as aphrodisiacs is as long as — take a look!

Almonds • Anchovies • Apples • Apricot brandy • Artichokes • Asparagus
Basil • Beans • Beer • Beets • Brains • Cabbage • Caraway seeds
Carrots • Caviar • Celery • Champagne • Cheese (especially Parmesan)
Cherries • Chestnuts • Chick-peas • Chocolate • Cinnamon • Clams
Coriander • Crab apples • Crayfish • Cumin • Curry • Dates • Dill • Eels
Eggs • Endive • Fennel • Figs • Fish • Flowers • Frogs • Garlic • Ginger
Ginseng • Goat • Grapes • Halibut • Herring • Honey • Horseradish
Lavender • Lentils • Mangoes • Marjoram • Marzipan • Meat • Mint
Mushrooms • Nutmeg • Octopus • Onions • Oysters • Peaches
Pepper • Pistachios • Pomegranates • Quince jelly • Radishes • Roes, cod and herring • Rosemary • Saffron • Salmon • Salt • Snails • Tomatoes
Truffles • Vanilla • Venison • Yeast

Warning: Cucumbers, tobacco, and excessive consumption of alcohol have an anaphrodisiac effect.

APPETITE

WHAT MAKES US HUNGRY?

For thousands of years human beings have adapted to the elements. We have hunted and gathered, sowed and reaped, and toiled from dawn to dusk to get enough food to eat. And when finally we are on our own at the supermarket and can choose virtually any food in the universe, what do we want to eat more than anything?

A cookie.

One theory to account for this is that we have not surpassed our ancestors physiologically. Our brain does not know how to tell us when to stop eating junk because the subject never came up among our Cro-Magnon ancestors, who were programmed to eat anything that didn't eat them first and were equipped to store fat for times of famine.

We can't explain away our almost desperate yearning for a cookie by claiming to possess a sweet tooth. A more plausible theory is that when we are starving, inborn instinct makes us seek out high-calorie, high-fat, quick-energy foods. Imagining we are starving is a relative thing, especially when we know there is a cookie or a candy bar nearby.

Television is another phenomenon our ancestors didn't have to contend with. The excitement of seeing a pizza flashing on the screen alerts our appetite control center, which in turn sends fast and furious messages to the salivary glands to get ready for the feast. EAT? is the question. NOW is the answer. NO is not even an option. Hunger is the consequence of the sighting of food, even if we have barely rested our fork from the previous meal.

Hunger is not the same as appetite and has almost nothing to do with taste. Hunger relates to a drop in the level of blood sugar and the physical need for food. Appetite relates to the desire for food, and taste is the ability to discern between different foods. Barbara Rolls, Ph.D., a professor of biobehavioral health at Penn State University, is studying why people eat what they eat, when they do it, and how much they consume. These are matters of profound importance, because the business of controlling how much we consume eats up every bit of $30 billion every year — so we're not talking about small potatoes here. Dr. Rolls is one of many researchers who are studying hunger and appetite. Most scientists are in agreement that the neuropeptide Y urges us to eat, and its direct opposite, cholecystokinin, or CCK, tells us when we have had enough. In the laboratory, that would seem to be the beginning and the end of the matter.

It isn't, though, because it doesn't even begin to explain why we find we are hungry so soon after eating Chinese food. One hypothesis suggests that it is because the meal doesn't end properly — the shriveled orange at the bottom of the Chinese takeout bag in no way equates with the slice of cheesecake we were rather hoping for — and being deprived of what we consider a suitable ending to the meal results in a subconscious sense of loss and longing. This leads us to think we are hungry when in fact we are just being peevish.

A cookie usually solves the problem.

How the Taste Bud Translates Between Tongue and Brain

Contrary to long-held beliefs, new studies reveal taste buds to be far more than simple conduits that immediately pass on information about sweet, sour, salty, and bitter substances to the brain to tell you what you are eating and help you decide whether you want more. Rather, research has shown that cells in the taste buds communicate with each other actively, accepting, rejecting, and modifying taste stimuli through a complicated network of chemical and electrical signals before sending signals to the brain.

But that is not all. Each taste cell, it turns out, does not act independently, picking up taste messages from the environment and sending them on to the brain. Rather, as Dr. Stephen D. Roper, a neurobiologist at Colorado State University, says, the cells seem to "talk" to one another, passing taste information to and fro and modifying it in still-mysterious ways before it gets to the brain.

However, taste researchers know that the end result is a series of micro electric currents, induced by nerve-cell messenger chemicals or direct interaction of taste stimuli with taste-cell membranes, that tell the brain what the tongue has experienced less than a moment ago.

Though often inextricably linked in the consumer's mind, taste and smell are distinctly different, independent sensory systems that, in yet unknown ways, interact upon reaching the brain. Anyone whose nose has ever become stuffy because of a cold knows that what people perceive as taste sensation is based only partly on the tongue.

People differ markedly in the number and distribution of taste buds in their mouths, which may account in part for the discriminating palates of some.

— Jane E. Brody
Excerpted from
The New York Times

Onions to Ions: Pathway From Tongue to Brain

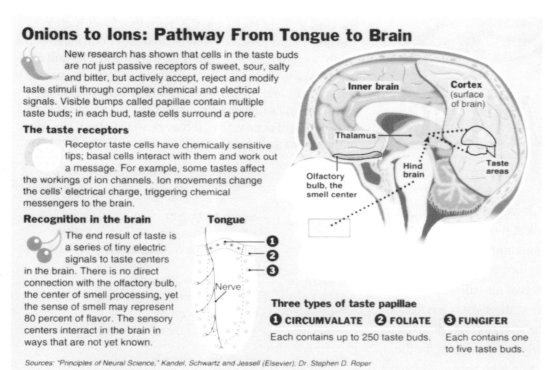

New research has shown that cells in the taste buds are not just passive receptors of sweet, sour, salty and bitter, but actively accept, reject and modify taste stimuli through complex chemical and electrical signals. Visible bumps called papillae contain multiple taste buds; in each bud, taste cells surround a pore.

The taste receptors

Receptor taste cells have chemically sensitive tips; basal cells interact with them and work out a message. For example, some tastes affect the workings of ion channels. Ion movements change the cells' electrical charge, triggering chemical messengers to the brain.

Recognition in the brain

The end result of taste is a series of tiny electric signals to taste centers in the brain. There is no direct connection with the olfactory bulb, the center of smell processing, yet the sense of smell may represent 80 percent of flavor. The sensory centers interract in the brain in ways that are not yet known.

Inner brain

Cortex (surface of brain)

Thalamus

Olfactory bulb, the smell center

Hind brain

Taste areas

Tongue
❶
❷
❸

Nerve

Three types of taste papillae
❶ CIRCUMVALATE ❷ FOLIATE ❸ FUNGIFER
Each contains up to 250 taste buds. Each contains one to five taste buds.

Sources: "Principles of Neural Science," Kandel, Schwartz and Jessell (Elsevier); Dr. Stephen D. Roper

How Sweet It Is

Our taste buds can detect sweetness in a substance even if only 1 part in 200 is sweet. We can detect saltiness in 1 part in 400. Sourness is perceived in 1 part in 130,000, bitterness can be tasted in as little as 1 part in 200,000, and odor can be discerned, though not by the taste buds, even when diluted to 1 part in a trillion (1,000,000,000). This sensitivity is partly protective: There are more bitter foods that are poisonous than sweet ones, and an off odor is a warning that the food has gone bad.

SWEET TOOTH

WHAT IS APPETITE?

Deep inside the brain, within a tiny area of the hypothalamus, is a gland that secretes neuropeptide Y. It is this chemical that stimulates appetite and controls our weight. If only we could get at it and turn it on or off like an electric light bulb, we would be able to resist temptation and fit into size 6 clothes.

Don't think for a moment that researchers are not trying to discover ways to manipulate this little gland, this naughty neurotransmitter that forces us to eat a carton of

ice cream when what we really wanted was a tofu sandwich. So far, success has been limited. Physiology and biochemistry are only two of the many factors that influence our appetite. Play loud music and we eat faster. When we sit in a brightly lit restaurant we eat more.

We eat more in the company of friends, less in the presence of strangers, and almost nothing at all when falling under the spell of a new love. At a neighborhood summer barbecue we eat more when we eat with our hands. The more formal the occasion, the fewer clothes women wear — and the less they eat.

So it seems that appetite is influenced by the company we keep, the level of our comfort, and the familiarity of the food. On the whole we prefer to eat what we have eaten before. Maybe this is a throwback to ancient imprinting that steered us away from foods that could poison us. Maybe neuropeptide Y is the conscience we have all been seeking for so long.

THE JOYS OF EATING

THOMAS WOLFE

Food! Food indeed! The great icebox was crowded with such an assortment of delicious foods as he had not seen in many years: just to look at it made the mouth begin to water, and aroused the pangs of a hunger so ravenous and insatiate that it was almost more painful than the pangs of bitter want. One was so torn with desire and greedy gluttony as he looked at the maddening plenty of that feast that his will was rendered impotent. Even as the eye glistened and the mouth began to water at the sight of a noble roast of beef, all crisp and crackly in its cold brown succulence, the attention was diverted to a plump broiled chicken, whose brown and crackly tenderness fairly seemed to beg for the sweet and savage pillage of the tooth. But now a pungent and exciting fragrance would assail the nostrils: it was the smoked pink slices of an Austrian ham — should it be brawny bully beef, now, or the juicy breast of a white tender pullet, or should it be the smoky pungency, the half-nostalgic savor of the Austrian ham? Or that noble dish of green lima beans, now already beautifully congealed in their pervading film of melted butter; or that dish of tender stewed young cucumbers; or those tomato slices, red and thick and ripe, and heavy as a chop; or that dish of cold asparagus, say; or that dish of corn; or, say, one of those musty fragrant, deep-ribbed cantaloupes, chilled to the heart, now, in all their pink-fleshed taste and ripeness; or a round thick slab cut from the red ripe heart of that great watermelon; or a bowl of those red raspberries, most luscious and most rich with sugar and a bottle of that thick rich cream which filled one whole compartment of that treasure chest of gluttony, or —

Excerpted from Of Time and The River

A Craving For Chocolate May Not Be In Your Head

Ice cream is what we crave most. Chocolate is a close second for women, less so for men. Nearly all women have cravings for specific foods but only 68 percent of men experience similar desires. There may be reasons why women yearn for pickles during pregnancy or candy bars to ward off PMS blues. A premenstrual increase in the metabolic rate consumes an estimated 150 calories a day; cravings for ice cream and other dairy products and for sweets, including chocolate and fruit, satisfy the body's need for additional calcium and calories during pregnancy. The Asian equivalent of this could be a yearning for sweet-and-sour spareribs, because the vinegar used in the recipe leaches calcium from the rib bones into the meat, where it is available for nourishing the pregnant woman and her growing fetus.

Some cravings might have a nutritional basis, while others may result from powerful emotional needs. Adam Drewnowski, director of the Human Nutrition Program at the University of Michigan, theorizes that foods high in fat and sugar stimulate the brain to produce endorphins — the "high" experienced by runners that results in a feeling of calm and well-being. It is comforting to soothe the pain of a lost job, lost love, or mournful anxiety with a candy bar — and sometimes nothing else will work — but when facing a long period of deprivation, it may be wise to heed the advice of the experts and choose from these lower-calorie alternatives.

Craving	Alternatives
Ice cream	• Low-fat yogurt • Frozen fruit bar • Iced coffee or cappuccino
Chocolate	• Diet chocolate soda • Low-fat chocolate pudding • Sugar-free candy • Just two or three tiny chocolate kisses
Potato chips	• Salt-free pretzels • Salt-free popcorn • No-fat tortilla chips with salsa • Celery sticks • Carrot sticks
Cookies	• Rice cakes thinly spread with sugar-free preserves • Fruit

Other advice involves vigorous exercise and cold showers. These may work for some; for others they simply postpone the urge. Hot soup or low-sodium chicken broth with a squirt of fresh lemon juice is the most reliable and pleasing way to distract the mind from an irrational but all too real craving.

Changing Tastes

Hardly anybody adores the taste of watery, colorless, homemade ice cream. It is the *idea* of it we like. What we really prefer is Double Chocolate Decadence ice cream or a sinfully rich Dove bar. We are addicted to commercial ice cream with all its additives and stabilizers and artificial color and flavor. We love the way it fills our mouth, mounds over the tongue, rolls about inside our cheeks, and bathes our salivary glands with sweet, smooth, fatty, creamy, crunchy richness.

It's the same way with V-8 Juice. Homemade vegetable juice just doesn't compare with the kind Campbell's makes. Skippy peanut butter is better than the stuff we make at home. And a vast number of people prefer commercial mayonnaise and canned soup to homemade.

Gradually, we are becoming accustomed to store-bought food. With little time, little enthusiasm, and fast-disappearing cooking skills, we have learned to love instant mashed potatoes, instant rice, microwaved pasta, no-beef hot dogs, and low-fat milk. We are surrendering our taste buds to scientists and economists who offer to do the cooking for us. They encourage us to substitute "quality" time for kitchen time. And in so doing we exchange genuine taste for instant gratification. The only danger — if there is a danger — is in allowing our taste buds to be manipulated by technicians who are fiendishly clever at getting us to eat more and buy more.

It is no idle boast when the advertisers say you can't eat just one… . Potato chips are specially formulated to be too big for our mouths. We have to edge them in (psychologists say this is what we like to do) and once in the mouth they have a crisp, resounding crackle that delights our sense of hearing as well as taste. "Mouth clearance" is important, too. Potato chips and popcorn are made so that they don't stick to our teeth or the roof of the mouth. The faster they can be swallowed, the faster we will reach into the bag for more and yet more.

We have reached the stage when foods can be, and are being, engineered to gratify all our senses. They taste good and they feel good in the mouth because they are loaded with sugar, salt, and fat. And because they make us feel so guilty that we swear we will reform — tomorrow — they satisfy our deepest craving of all, which is to sin and repent simultaneously.

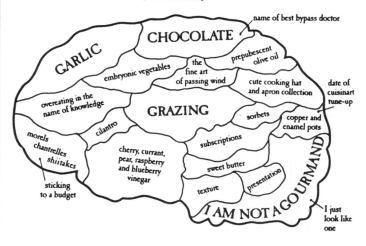

A GOURMET'S BRAIN
[RIGHT LOBE]

Outlook for the Future: Tinier Teeth?

Our little toes are getting smaller. Our appendix is slowly reducing in size. Now the word is out: Our teeth are not disappearing, but they aren't as large as they used to be. It seems that the shrinkage is not altogether gradual. For 90,000 years, teeth changed slowly, getting smaller at a rate of just 1 percent per 2,000 years. But 10,000 years ago — a mere blink of an eye in evolutionary terms — they suddenly started diminishing twice as fast.

Humans, explains anthropologist Peter Farb, differ from animals because their teeth include the cutting incisors of a rodent, the grinding molars and premolars of a herbivore, and the pointed canines of a carnivore. It is our uniquely arranged set of teeth that enables us to eat such an extremely varied diet. Most animals survive exclusively on either animal or plant food — and often on a very few items within their selected category.

In a decades-long study, anthropologist C. Loring Brace has analyzed millions of teeth and concluded that our teeth are only half the size of those of the Neanderthals. Unlike our forebears, we don't need them for tearing raw meat and chewing tough, fibrous plants. Brace attributes the down-sizing to the advent of ovens and the development of pottery. Once foods could be processed to a softer consistency, "big teeth simply became unnecessary," he says.

Futurists predict that cooking and food processing will accelerate the diminution of our teeth. But dentists won't be laying down their drills any time soon.

ORGAN MEAT DÉGUSTATION

The James Beard House in New York City was filled to capacity for the presentation of this menu in winter of 1992 by award-winning chefs Charlie Trotter of Chicago and David Bouley of New York City.

Champagne Perrier-Jouët Grand Brut

Braised Lamb's Tongue & Diver Scallops with Truffled Celery Broth & Shiso
Trimbach Riesling Alsace 1989

Warm Salad of Confit of Duck Gizzards with Fingerling Potatoes, Herb Salad & a Steamed Quail Egg
100-Year-Old Balsamic Vinegar & Chive Oil

Veal Sweetbreads in Crispy Somen Noodles with Mushroom & Pig's Feet Ragoût, Lobster Oil & Cardamom-Infused Carrot Juice
Tallot-Beaut & Fils Chorey-Côte-de-Beaune 1990

Steamed New York State Foie Gras in Sweet Pea Leaves, White Asparagus & Armagnac Sauce

Tripe & Blood Sausage Tartlet with Chino Ranch Tiny White Carrots, Mustard/Sauternes Sauce & Red Wine Essence
Château Gruaud-Larose St. Julien 1987

Organic West Virginia Quark Cheese Soufflé with Blood Oranges, Blackberries, Strawberries, Fresh Vanilla & Yogurt Sorbet
Sandeman Royal Ambrosante Rare Palo Cortado Sherry

Poached Forelle Pear in Brioche with Ennis Hazelnut Ice Cream, Mission Figs & Port Wine Sauce

Those from whom nature has withheld taste invented trousers.

— Anthelme Brillat-Savarin
Preeminent French gourmet

Books

A Natural History of the Senses
Diane Ackerman;
Vintage Books, 1991; $11.00

APPLES

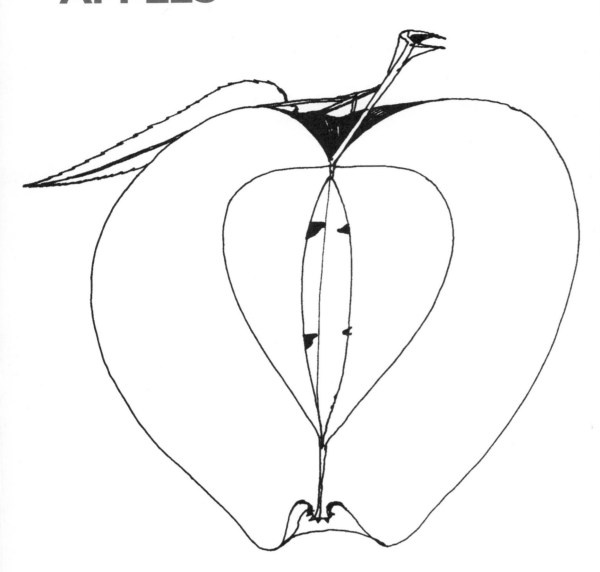

Eating Humble Pie

by Suzanne Taylor

In rural homes of the last century, pie was often served at breakfast, a good, hearty beginning to the day's work. An old friend of mine has told me that as a young boy he was sent away from his comfortable Boston home to work for a time as a lumberjack in the northern Maine woods. Breakfast was early in the lumber camp where he lived, and the men stowed away enormous quantities of food in preparation for the long day's work in the woods.

At his first breakfast, one of the numerous pies on the table was passed to our young friend, who politely declined it.

"No apple pie, boy?" one burly woodsman asked. "No, thank you, not for breakfast," he replied, passing the pie on. There was dead silence at the table and a look of utter bewilderment on the man's face. "Well, when do you eat pie, boy?" he bellowed. My friend cringed, red-faced. By the end of the week he was wolfing down pie with the best of them.

Excerpted from Cooking in a Country Kitchen

Short and Sweet

Standard apple trees grow to more than 30 feet high and picking the fruit has always been a problem requiring ladders or long poles or shaking the branches — all of which easily lead to damaged fruit. Now American orchardists are growing dwarf trees like those that have become popular in Europe.

Although the trees are less than 10 feet high they grow standard-sized apples. Picking is easy, many more trees can be planted per acre, and the trees mature in three years instead of six.

Classic Baked Apples Updated

Serves 4

Whole fruits hold their shape and keep their texture very well in the microwave. They cook best when arranged in a circle in the baking dish.

4 medium-sized apples
$1/4$ cup raisins
3 tablespoons brown sugar
$1/4$ teaspoon ground nutmeg
2 teaspoons butter, divided

Use a melon baller to remove the cores from the apples. Peel just the top halves of the apples and arrange them in a microwavable dish. Fill each of the cavities with 1 tablespoon of raisins.

Mix together the sugar and nutmeg and top the apples with equal amounts of this mixture. Finally, top each apple with $1/2$ teaspoon of butter.

Cover the apples with plastic wrap. Microwave on High (100 percent power) for 3 minutes, then turn a quarter turn and cook for 3 to 4 minutes longer until the apples are tender.

Serve warm or at room temperature with frozen yogurt, ice cream, or whipped cream.

2 APPLES A DAY GETS THE DOCTORS' OK

Apples are almost our favorite snack, and certainly the only one that is really good for us. An apple is delightfully sweet and juicy, easily portable, and fills us up in the pleasantest way with a mere 81 calories and lots of that soluble fiber we know we ought to be eating more of. We even imagine we don't need to brush our teeth again after eating an apple last thing at night. (Though dentists and nutritionists might disagree.)

Now the old saw about keeping the doctor away has been replaced by the suggestion that we should actually eat two apples a day. Among the reasons apple authorities put forward: An apple not only has no cholesterol, but pectin, one of those excellent fibers apples supply, may actually work to reduce the body's cholesterol level and help to prevent heart attacks. Pectin also slows glucose metabolism in diabetics. The apple contains potassium as well, which may reduce the chances of suffering a stroke, and the trace element boron, which is believed to increase mental vitality and also to build bones, thus helping fight off osteoporosis. Vitamins A and C are present in small amounts, sodium is almost totally absent, and every grain of dietary fiber is one more soldier in our fight to reduce the risk of cancer.

Maybe that mythical magic bullet is in our midst after all—in the shape of a round, shiny, cheerful-looking fruit we all know and love. Let's hear it for the apple. Twice.

Apple Talk

Apple Pie Order
The French description of a neatly folded cloth is *"nappe pliée en ordre."* The phrase certainly sounds like "apple-pie order." Another theory is that the phrase comes from the regularly notched "turrets" of medieval pie pastry (which was called a coffin and rather resembled one).

Apple-Pie Bed
Where this comes from is anyone's guess, and what do apple pies have to do with making up a "joke" bed in which the sheets are folded backwards halfway down so that the occupant's toes can't reach the bottom? Perhaps apple turnovers were really the source, and the hairbrushes and other torments popped in as well had their origins in the turnover's currants and spices.

Apple of His (Or Her) Eye
This phrase came into use in the early 1700s to mean a person particularly beloved.

Don't Upset the Apple Cart
The Roman playwright Plautus little knew when he coined this phrase in his play *Epiducus* in 255 B.C. that we would still be using it two millennia later.

Sniffing Apples Can Calm You Down

Yale University researchers have discovered a new route to relaxation: inhaling the scent of apples. Tests conducted with an apple spice fragrance showed a significantly calming response in the lab, so a whiff of a mug of mulled cider or the smell of a freshly baked apple may well help to allay anxiety attacks at home.

Q&A

Q Why would anyone prefer an apple with a worm in it to an apple that is perfect?

A The presence of the worm ensures the absence of pesticides.

Did You Know?

☞ The apple tree is a member of the rose family. Its blossoms are less fragrant than the rose's, but an apple is a more delicious fruit than the rose hip (though the hip is a better source of vitamin C).

☞ There are known to be fully 7,500 varieties of apples throughout the world, but only 20 are grown commercially in this country.

☞ Eight varieties of apples account for 80 percent of American apple production. The favorites, in order: Red Delicious, Golden Delicious, Granny Smith, McIntosh, Rome Beauty, Jonathan, York, and Stayman. Granny Smith recently beat McIntosh into third place.

☞ Out of 10 billion pounds of apples grown annually, 57 percent are eaten fresh and 43 percent are processed. In the processing, 53 percent are pressed as juice and cider, 29 percent are cooked as applesauce, 7 percent are dried, 6 percent frozen, and 5 percent canned. The rest are made into baby food, apple butter and jelly, and vinegar.

☞ Apples can be stored in sealed rooms filled with nitrogen and kept at a temperature of 32 to 34 degrees F. This slows the natural ripening process, enabling apples to be shipped at peak condition throughout the year.

☞ The first American orchard was planted on Beacon Hill, overlooking Boston Harbor, in the early 1600s.

Twelve Common Varieties of Apples

Variety	Color	Description and Use	Time of Year
Red Delicious	Bright red	Has 5 knobs at blossom end; mildly sweet and crunchy; major Washington State apple; America's favorite eating apple	Year-round
Golden Delicious	Speckled yellow-green	Crisp white flesh; grown almost universally; flesh retains whiteness well; good for putting in salads; bakes well, too	Year-round
McIntosh	Red and green	Juicy; tends to bruise easily; major New York State apple; excellent for applesauce	September - October
Granny Smith	Bright green	Tart, hard, very juicy; named in 1860s for Australian Maria Ana Smith, who nurtured seedlings from French crab apples thrown out in her yard; cooks and bakes well	Year-round
Rome Beauty	Dark red	Pungent, rather mealy flesh; accidental seedling from Rome, Ohio, in early 1800s; good cooker	September - July
Winesap	Dark red	Fragrant, very tasty, juicy; favorite of early 19th-century New Jersey cider makers; keeps well	October - August
Newtown Pippin	Yellow-green	Tart, crisp flesh; originated in 1700s in Long Island, New York; popular in England since Benjamin Franklin distributed samples there, now making comeback in America; excellent flavor	September - June
Gala	Yellow with red highlights	Sweet, juicy, fragrant; from New Zealand; excellent for eating and salads	August
Fuji	Yellow-green to orange	Mildly sweet, crisp flesh, generous size; Japan's most popular apple, but new to America; good for eating	October
Jonathan	Bright red	Sweet flesh, chewy skin; good for eating and baking	September - June
Stayman	Bright red	Rich flavor, aromatic, crisp; originally a sucker from a Winesap tree; good for cooking; keeps well	October
Criterion	Yellow with red blush	Sweet, juicy flesh; stays white longer than other apples; good for eating and baking	October - March

Major Apple-Growing Areas in the United States

Total crop is about 10 billion pounds, mostly from 35 of the 50 states.

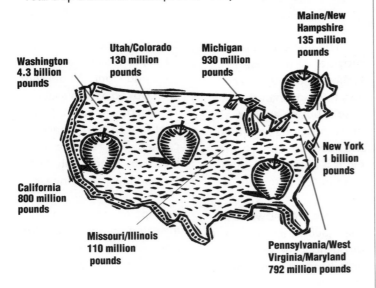

Washington 4.3 billion pounds

Utah/Colorado 130 million pounds

Michigan 930 million pounds

Maine/New Hampshire 135 million pounds

New York 1 billion pounds

California 800 million pounds

Missouri/Illinois 110 million pounds

Pennsylvania/West Virginia/Maryland 792 million pounds

ANTIQUE APPLES

Barely a century ago, hundreds of varieties of apples were grown in America — 700 kinds in New York State alone. In the days before refrigeration, apples were one of the few fruits that could last through the winter, and everyone had a favorite kind. Then the scientists got to work, breeding apples that would look good, travel well, and grow in large quantities and in almost uniform sizes. Unfortunately, this also meant that it was more practical for growers to concentrate on the few most popular varieties. The older apples almost disappeared from the market.

But apple trees are long-lived, and there has been a renaissance of interest in the russets and pippins and greenings that our ancestors valued so highly. Enthusiasts roam the countryside cutting scions from wild apples that have spread from long-vanished gardens; growers exchange seeds and cuttings from their orchards. And at farmers' markets, buyers can sample the results — apples that taste, fragrantly, crisply, deliciously, of the past. As one enthusiast put it, "One bite of a Cox's Orange Pippin, and you're hooked."

If you want to grow apples that taste like those your great-grandparents ate, your local agriculture extension service can advise you which trees will thrive in your part of the country. The sources listed here will ship trees, but only during the winter bare-root season when they are dormant. All offer free catalogs.

Southmeadow Fruit Gardens Box SM, Lakeside, MI 49116; 616-469-2865. Offers 235 varieties of trees, some dating back to the 16th century. Prices range from $17 for year-old "whips" to $25 for a mature tree.

Sonoma Antique Apple Nursery 4395 Westside Road, Healdsburg, CA 95448; 707-433-6420. More than 100 varieties of trees; mid-January - March.

Rocky Meadow Orchard Nursery 360 Rocky Meadow Road NW, New Salisbury, IN 47161; 812-347-2213. Forty-plus varieties of trees; November - April.

Applesource Route 1, Chapin, IL 62628; 217-245-7589. No trees, but ships sampler boxes of mixed antique and modern apples.

Seed Savers Exchange 3076 North Winn Road, Decorah, IA 52101; 319-382-5990. Members purchase seeds and budwoods from each other; apple scions are listed in yearbook; membership $25 per year.

America's First Environmentalist

Johnny Appleseed was born John Chapman in Leominster, Massachusetts, in 1774. Impressed with both the Swedenborgian religion and the speed with which apples grew from seed, he decided to be a missionary to the new lands along the frontier. As  the pioneers headed westward along the Ohio River, he wandered with them through what are now the states of Ohio, Indiana, and Illinois, planting little orchards, spreading his gospel, and giving away apple seeds and saplings to the settlers. His original seeds came from a cider mill in northern Pennsylvania, but he would regularly return to his orchards to care for the trees and gather fresh stock. After his death in 1847, he became a character in frontier folklore, which had him wearing a tin-pot hat and coffee-sack shirt and no shoes. But probably he was just a man who loved God, the simple life — and apples.

IN APPRECIATION OF APPLES

This menu, designed by Pamela Morgan of Flavors Catering, was served at the gala opening of "The Apple in 19th-Century American Art," an exhibition at the appropriately named Berry-Hill Galleries in New York City.

Served on trays garnished with apple blossoms and apples:

Sausage and Apple Phyllo Bundles

Fragrant Sausage and Apples mixed with Vidalia Onions and Vermont Cheddar in Flaky Phyllo Pastry

Potato and Turnip Pancakes topped with Homemade Applesauce

Miniature Sage-Apple Muffin filled with Applewood-Smoked Turkey and Apple Chutney

Apple, Leek, Gruyère, and Pancetta Tartlet

Apple Slice topped with Gorgonzola and Toasted Walnut

Warm Apple Fritters

Tiny Sweet Apple and Rhubarb Tarts dusted with Powdered Sugar

Full Open Bar with White Wine

Festive Hard-Pressed Apple Cider Punch in a Silver Punch Bowl

Ridding the World of Bad Apples

Discover magazine revealed that engineers at Michigan State University have developed an electronic apple that growers can send along with real apples on their often bumpy journey from apple tree to market shelf. Inside a three-and-a-half-inch sphere of beeswax are a tiny clock, an accelerometer, a microprocessor, and a battery. The accelerometer measures the severity of bumps; the microprocessor records those strong enough to cause a bruise; the clock notes the time they occurred. Fed into a computer, these data make it possible to locate, smooth over, or pad the bumps in the road.

A PC View of the Garden of Eden?

It's not fair. One myth after another is being exploded these days. Now we are being told that there is no basis whatever for supposing that the fruit Eve offered Adam in the garden was an apple. The account in Genesis describes the tree simply as "good for food and pleasant to the eyes, and a tree to be desired to make one wise." Archaeological evidence argues that the apple was unknown in the Middle East at the time we believe Genesis to have been written.

It is suggested that the identification with the apple happened much, much later, when Christian missionaries brought the story of Adam and Eve to Teutonic tribesmen, who worshipped an earth mother goddess. They instantly assumed that the tree of knowledge bore apples because the goddess's symbol was an apple, signifying love, knowledge, and immortality.

So now we have to question not only whether the apple that caused such problems was probably an apricot, or even a peach, but whether early converts may have believed that Eve was the most important person in the garden.

The Great Alar Debate

Was it a false alarm? In a word, yes.

As a result of a CBS "60 Minutes" report on the presumed cancer-causing dangers of spraying apples with Alar, apples were, for a while, barred from school lunches, mothers ditched innumerable jars of applesauce, and apple pie became the country's least favorite dessert. There was even a news report that a highway patrol had stopped a school bus in response to the anguished pleas of a distraught mother who had put an apple in her child's lunch box. Armed men stopped the bus, nabbed the box from the bewildered child, snatched up the apple it contained, threw it to the ground—and shot it. Dead.

In fact, Alar is not a pesticide but a growth hormone used to help the fruit ripen uniformly, and no children were hurt at all. Apple growers all over the country, however, suffered grievous losses. A group of growers in Washington State, which was particularly badly hit, sued CBS for $100 million, but lost the case.

Books

Apples
Robert Berkley; Fireside, 1991; $16.95

Apples: A Country Garden Cookbook
Christopher Idone; Collins Publishers, 1993; $19.95

The Apple Book
Rosanne Sanders; Philosophical Library, 1992; $29.95

The Apple Cookbook
Olwen Woodier; Garden Way Publishing, 1984; $9.95

APRICOTS

According to Raymond Sokolov, the apricot derives its name from the Latin word *praecox*, meaning precocious — probably because it blooms and sets fruit in early spring.

Books

Lots of Cots
Rita Gennis;
Ben Ali Books, 1989;
$6.95

RIPE APRICOTS ARE AS SCARCE AS HEN'S TEETH

Barely 5 percent of the entire population of the United States has had the chance to taste a really fresh, ripe apricot — and no one who has will ever forget it. But that honey-sweet, slightly tangy juice that runs down your chin as you bite into the glowing flesh of an apricot plucked from the tree barely survives hand-carrying to the house, let alone a thousand-mile journey in a refrigerated container. Yet the growers persist in sending the fruits to market, where their rosy cheeks tempt us with a mockery of ambrosia.

It's not entirely the farmers' fault. Almost all the U.S. crop comes from 17,000 acres in the Santa Clara Valley where Spanish missionaries introduced apricot trees long ago, and inevitably the fruit must travel long distances. Until the happy day when apricots can be transported as speedily and successfully as equally fragile raspberries and blackberries already are, we must rely on apricot preserves and the canned, crystallized, and dried fruit, all of which have delicious, distinctively different tastes.

The apricot has a long history of cultivation, starting in China some 4,000 years ago and traveling along the trade routes to the shores of the Mediterranean. In Iraq and Iran apricots are served with lamb, and a regional specialty is *kamraddin*, a kind of apricot leather. A drink is made from it to mark the end of a period of religious fasting.

Dried in the sun, glazed with sugar syrup, or fresh, apricots are eaten with relish wherever they are grown. And we have it on the reliable authority of the late, esteemed Waverley Root that, after ourselves, the chief consumers are dormice, "who dote on apricots." How sensible of them!

Take Care with Those Pits!

Apricots, in all forms, are very rich in Vitamin A and a good source of potassium. Many recent cancer sufferers have believed in the healing properties of laetrile, which is made from apricot pits, but doctors are suspicious of apricot kernels, which can be toxic when eaten in any quantity.

AQUACULTURE

THE BLUE REVOLUTION

Aquaculture — think of it as the aquatic counterpart of agriculture — is the cultivation of the sea. The term refers specifically to the intensive production of fish and shellfish in a controlled environment for human food. An ancient practice in Asia, it was begun scarcely two decades ago in America, but in virtually no time has become one of the fastest growing segments of the U.S. economy, quadrupling in both dollar value and poundage since 1980.

Today, more than 3,400 farms in 23 states raise a variety of fish and shellfish. Catfish, trout, crawfish, and salmon account for 80 percent of the total volume of all domestic aquaculture products. Other species include hybrid striped bass, tilapia, carp, crabs, clams, oysters, mussels, walleye, sturgeon, red drum, eels, abalone, lobsters, and aquatic plants. Meanwhile, it appears that virtually every species of wild fish in the sea is being fished at levels above its natural capacity to replenish supply. Thus, it's anticipated that in the near future we will be eating more farmed fish than fish from the wild.

• Offshore farming takes place in deep, navigable waters and involves the use of boats. Onshore farming is done in shallow waters where boats are not necessary.

• Both offshore and onshore farming often use a net-pen culture. Nets or hanging sacks are suspended in the water to confine groups of fish. In onshore farming, nets may be used in deep ponds to separate any one population of fish from the others — for instance, to keep smaller populations from larger ones.

• Tank culture is another form of onshore farming. Tanks, usually made of steel and reinforced cement, or fiberglass, in a variety of shapes, are used to contain populations of fish in water. The tanks answer many needs. A "raceway culture," for example, is a method used for fish such as trout that need a significant amount of circulating, temperature-controlled, and highly oxygenated water. A trout tank will be large and oblong, and a large volume of water will be pumped through it continuously.

• A pond culture is the most widely used method of fish farming. All catfish farming is pond-raised. The farming is done in man-made ponds that are drainable and often incorporate a system of dikes for harvesting.

• A tray culture involves the use of a permanent structure for mollusks to attach themselves to. Trays are set underwater in calm bays or estuaries to stimulate the growth of clams, oysters, and other shellfish. Sometimes ropes or strings are hung into the water for mussels and scallops to grow on.

• Any intervention in the growth process can be regarded as a form of sea farming. For example, oyster farmers sometimes dump old crushed shells to settle on the ocean bottom, providing a substrate on which oysters can grow. The farmers may then wait years before returning to see if there's an oyster population to harvest.

Farmed fish sent to the processors in 1992

Species	Millions of pounds
Catfish	451
Shrimp and crawfish	79
Trout	56
Salmon	19
Oysters	10 - 13
Tilapia	9
Striped bass (hybrid)	5 - 7
Mollusks (mussels/clams)	1 - 2
Scallops	unknown
Sturgeon	1 - 2
Soft-shell crabs	unknown

R U Listening?

Oysters raised on farms along the Pacific coast don't spawn, so they may be eaten all year round. But oysters in the wild do spawn, and the months in the year that have an R in them are the spawning seasons. During these times the oysters will be soft, mushy, and unpalatable. So the old saw makes sense.

Farm-Raised Fish

Catfish Named for their long, catlike whiskers, catfish are farmed mainly in man-made ponds flooding former cotton fields in Mississippi. The farming of this fish has grown dramatically since 1980; more than 450 million pounds are now produced annually. Catfish meat is white and soft and has a mild flavor. It can be used in any recipe calling for flounder, haddock, or other white-fleshed fish.

Salmon Atlantic salmon farming got its start in the late 1950s. Most domestic salmon is farmed in Maine; the state produces more than 10 million pounds a year. Other major producers of farmed salmon are Norway, Scotland, Canada, and Chile. Farm-raised salmon's fat content makes it good for grilling.

Striped Bass This fish was on the endangered species list a few years ago, but is now returning in its wild form; it has become plentiful once more as strengthened hybrids are bred in fish farms. The wild striped bass bears a continuous stripe along the back; the farm-raised fish has broken stripes.

Sturgeon Sturgeon farming is done in tanks, primarily in California. Raised in pure well water for three and half years, sturgeon may reach a weight of 30 pounds, but most are harvested at half that. It has a mellow flavor and dense texture, rather like swordfish, and tastes terrific when smoked.

Tilapia This perchlike fish is new to the American market. It hails from the Middle East and has been farm-raised in Israel for decades. Some say tilapia was the fish Christ multiplied to feed the multitudes. Its flesh when cooked has a moist, tender texture and a sweet flavor similar to that of red snapper.

Trout Advances in trout farming make it feasible to produce as many as 2,500 tiny trout fingerlings in a space about the size of a small bedroom. This news prompted Claudia H. Deutsch of *The New York Times* to observe that the new technology "would make fish farming as viable in abandoned inner-city warehouses as it is in Idaho's open fields."

Tastes Good?

Some American chefs are sniffy about farmed fish. They don't challenge its nutritional value. Farm-raised fish have essentially the same protein, cholesterol, and vitamin content as their wild counterparts, with the only deviance lying in the fat department. Farmed finfish tend to have more total fat than their wild cousins. But it's not enough to fuss about. Even the Atlantic salmon, weighing in with 11 grams of fat per 3.5 raw ounces, is within the margins of heart-healthy guidelines for occasional eating. In fact, much of the salmon's fat comes from the so-called good omega-3 fatty acids that are linked to a lower risk of heart disease. Indeed, farmed salmon and trout tend to have higher omega-3 contents than the salmon and trout of the wild.

Notwithstanding which, some discerning palates find the farmed fish boring: too flaccid from lazing about, it's said, and too bland compared with the wild variety. "Texture is the biggest difference," says Wayne Ludvigsen, chef at Ray's Boathouse in Seattle. "There's very little muscle in farm-raised fish." But most Americans have little conscious appetite for muscular fish, and bland seems to be just what they want in their fish dishes.

Like poultry, fish tastes like what it eats. Thus it is that the channel catfish, once a strongly flavored delicacy of the Mississippi Delta, has become the fifth most popular fish in America. It was made into something other than what it used to be; it was carefully bred and fed to the very zenith of blandness. In fact, the Catfish Institute describes their channel cats today as "chickens that don't cluck."

Pinking Salmon

Salmon reared in pens have white flesh because they're not exposed to the natural foods that color the flesh of wild salmon salmon-pink. So fish farmers are now adding a synthetic pigment to the domesticated salmon's diet, to put their product back in the pink.

Quick Catfish Gumbo

Serves 8

1 cup chopped celery
1 cup chopped onion
1 cup chopped green pepper
2 cloves garlic, minced
3 tablespoons cooking oil
4 cups beef broth
16-ounce can whole tomatoes, cut up
1 bay leaf
1 teaspoon salt
$^1/_2$ teaspoon dried thyme
$^1/_2$ teaspoon ground red pepper
$^1/_2$ teaspoon dried oregano
2 pounds catfish fillets, cut into bite-sized pieces
10-ounce package frozen sliced okra
4 cups cooked rice

In a large kettle or Dutch oven cook the celery, onion, green pepper, and garlic in hot oil until tender. Stir in the beef broth, tomatoes, bay leaf, salt, thyme, red pepper, and oregano. Bring to a boil; reduce heat. Cover and simmer for 15 minutes. Add the catfish and okra to the kettle. Return to boiling. Cover, reduce heat, and simmer for 15 minutes or until the fish flakes easily. Remove from the heat and discard the bay leaf. Serve in bowls over hot cooked rice.

MORE INFORMATION

Aquaculture and Food Engineering Laboratories
University of Wisconsin
1605 Linden Drive
Madison, WI 53706
608-263-2003

California Aquaculture Association
Box 1004
Niland, CA 92257
619-359-FISH

National Aquaculture Council
National Fisheries Institute
1525 Wilson Boulevard, Suite 500
Arlington, VA 22209
703-524-8881

World Aquaculture Society
Louisiana State University
143 J. M. Parker Coliseum
Baton Rouge, LA 70803
504-388-3137

Catfish Farmers of America
1110 Highway 82E, Suite 202
Indianola, MS 38751
601-887-2699

Catfish Institute
P.O. Box 247
Belzoni, MS 39038

PERIODICALS

For addresses, see also Information Sources

Aquaculture Magazine
Achill River Corporation
Box 2329
Asheville, NC 28802
704-254-7334
Bimonthly; $17 per year

Aquatic Farming Newsletter
California Aquaculture Association
619-359-FISH
Quarterly; free

World Aquaculture
World Aquaculture Society
504-388-3137
Quarterly; $90 per year

Constant Care + Smart Feeding = Happy Fish

Farm-raised fish may suffer a certain crimping of the spirit. After all, they'll never know the briny deep, plunging and soaring; they'll never swim with the wild ones — in fact, they couldn't survive if they tried because they don't know how to hunt for their food. But they do enjoy a pretty cushy kind of womb-to-tomb health plan back on the farm that would be the envy of a wild fish living rough, if fish had the wit to be envious.

For fish on farms, nothing is left to chance. They live in water that is stabilized throughout their life cycles, and they are served up specialized feeds by brainy and watchful marine biologists. Mostly their feeds consist of flours, soybeans, and fish oil, though a major potato processor in Idaho is currently raising tilapia on feed made from potato scraps. The usual diet — in the form of dry pellets prepared by commercial mills that are routinely examined by the Food and Drug Administration — must be high in protein (30 to 40 percent, depending on the stage of growth) and contain a balance of essential vitamins and minerals. A balanced diet of the floating pellets is mechanically scattered on the fish pond's surface once or twice daily.

Of course, there is the danger of disease, which dense populations of penned fish can communicate faster than fish in the wild. Fish farmers use drugs, usually mixed in the feed, to treat diseases and discourage parasites. They use chemicals as disinfectants and to kill bacteria. They employ herbicides to maintain just the right balance of aquatic vegetation in and on the edges of the pond.

Long before the fish go in the water, farmers must make sure that the pond's soil is free of pesticides and not contaminated. The water quality has to be constantly checked for optimum growth requirements — proper temperature, the right amount of oxygen, the appropriate water chemistry. In order to operate, farmers have to obtain the appropriate EPA water permits and meet state and local requirements about the water they use and how and where they discharge it. Only drugs approved by the FDA may be used.

Thus coddled, the farm fish of America are a far cry from the angst of the briny deep. They comprise a new school, a contented kettle of seafood such as we have never seen on our plates before and are only too glad to welcome into our kitchens.

MEAN STREAMS

During the past half century, fish biologists released billions of hatchery-reared fish into streams, rivers, and lakes, giving little thought to the ecological and genetic consequences. Today, it has become clear that this practice may pose a serious threat to the long-term survival of wild fish.

When hatchery-raised trout and salmon are released into waters where wild species already live, the result can be the depletion of both kinds of fish. When wild trout feed, for example, they spread their fins to signal interlopers away. Hatchery trout don't know the signals and get into fierce and lethal fights with the wild fish.

Farmed salmon, which travel from the hatchery to the sea by truck, lack the knowledge of home rivers which wild salmon imprint at birth. Farmed salmon will enter a river at random and by reproducing in the "wrong" river, they handicap their progeny. This next generation of salmon will imprint where they hatch, but once out to sea may lack the inherited ability to find their way back.

Hatchery fish lack both the fear and caution of wild fish, and are easily caught. When they breed with wild fish the resulting generations end up with the least desirable characteristics of both. They lose their self-preservation instincts along with their ability to judge currents, and fail to feed efficiently. The result is a shorter life span that often ends before spawning.

It is now recognized that wild streams need to be managed carefully and that hatchery fish are a hostile element that must not be released into the waters. Meanwhile, researchers are experimenting with releasing fish into the streams at the infant fingerling stage in the hope that they will be able to grow up wild. At a recent conference of scientists from North Atlantic countries with salmon interests, several proposals were introduced. One was the designation of aquaculture-free zones in the vicinity of threatened wild stocks. Another was the sterilization of farmed stocks at the hatcheries. It was also urged that gene banks should be established to retain the genetic diversity of wild fish for the future.

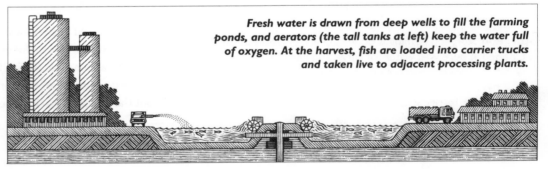

Fresh water is drawn from deep wells to fill the farming ponds, and aerators (the tall tanks at left) keep the water full of oxygen. At the harvest, fish are loaded into carrier trucks and taken live to adjacent processing plants.

Fish and Feed

Because feed is such a big part of the cost of raising fish, studies are continuously being made to find ways of increasing what farmers call the conversion of feed. Today a pound of fish meal converts into a pound of fish — a ratio of 1 to 1. In contrast, a broiler chicken converts feed at the rate of approximately 2 to 1 pound of chicken. Beef cattle are the least efficient feeders, requiring 15 pounds of feed to produce just 1 pound of meat.

Cheap fish meal is to modern aquaculture what cheap chemical fertilizer is to a land-based corn or soybean farm: the stuff that enables the crop to grow, fast and free of disease. What's more, some fish farmers have been able to reduce their labor costs by using robots to feed their underwater "flock."

All this is good news for consumers, as reduced costs at the production end will ensure a steady supply of fresh, affordable fish.

FISHPOPS

Forecasters glimpse the day when processed fish will be sold from vending machines. You'll put in your money and out will pop fish "dogs" on a stick, with a dripless sauce inside — ready to eat in seconds.

Some call this progress.

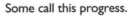

ARTICHOKES

MEMORIES ARE MADE OF
ARTICHOKES

It takes the average person 20 minutes to eat an artichoke, but some average people get through a whole lifetime without ever tasting one — and, I'm sad to say, never knowing what they are missing.

There are several best ways to eat artichokes: steamed with a just-made hollandaise is about as satisfying as life can get, unless you prefer them at room temperature, as I often do, with a fresh rémoulade sauce, which is nothing more than a tarted-up oil and vinegar dressing.

The baby artichokes that appear in the market for barely two days a year are lovely braised with plenty of young garlic, a fruity olive oil, and a light touch of lemon juice to bring the flavors into focus. I could eat 50, given half a chance.

Of the hundreds, possibly thousands of artichokes I have eaten, one stands out above the rest. I ate it for lunch on a sunny Friday afternoon in a long, narrow restaurant in New York's Greenwich Village. My friend said it was a Mafia place and I am sure he was right. It was impeccably clean, with crisp, heavily starched white tablecloths, chunky china, and the unmistakable smell of roast veal coming from the kitchen in the back.

Only a few tables were taken but everyone sat with his back to the wall. No one spoke but us — and we talked a lot because we ordered a bottle of red wine, and artichokes stuffed with sweet sausage and breadcrumbs flavored with fresh rosemary and thyme. They were hot from the oven and served with a rich, red tomato sauce that, once I knew I was in such a dangerous place, made me think, just for a moment, it could be blood (but it wasn't). The memory of that artichoke still haunts me in the night.

I never found the place again, though I've looked for it for more than a dozen years.

I don't think I imagined it.

Did You Know?

☞ The globe artichoke belongs to the thistle family. The "choke" in the center is actually an immature flower, enclosed in leaf scales (the parts we nibble at).

☞ Jerusalem artichokes are the tuberous roots of a member of the sunflower family and are sometimes called sunchokes. They are a source of insulin.

In 1947, Marilyn Monroe was crowned the first Queen of the Artichokes.

Tips

Preparing: Pull off lower petals of artichoke. Cut stem to one inch or less. Cut off top quarter of artichoke; if desired, snip tips of remaining petals.

Cooking: To tell if an artichoke is cooked, pull out a leaf after it has been simmering for 50 minutes. If the leaf comes away easily, the artichoke is ready to eat. Drain it upside down to remove the excess water.

To cook a large (8-ounce) artichoke in the microwave, put it in a small, microwave-safe bowl and add an inch of water. Cover with wet paper towels and cook it on High (100 percent power) for 4 minutes.

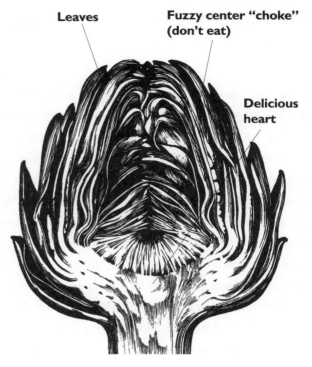

Leaves — Fuzzy center "choke" (don't eat) — Delicious heart

How to Eat an Artichoke

There are few things more intimidating than being presented with a whole lobster in its shell or a whole artichoke, and not knowing what on earth to do with them. Escape from the table is rarely an option.

There are other alternatives. One possibility is to embark on an animated monologue on any subject of interest to you (though not necessarily to others at the table). This will allow enough time to watch what the other guests are doing and enable you to copy them without letting on that you are way out of your depth.

Another camouflage tactic is to sit quietly and toy with the beverage in your glass while observing the rules of the game.

Basically, though, the way to deal with an artichoke is to start with the outer layer and pull off one leaf. It will slip off

easily. The bottom of the leaf is dipped into the sauce and pulled gently through the front teeth to extract the tiny edible portion, then discarded at the side of the plate. The process is repeated — and repeated. (British people are born with special genes that enable them to eat artichokes and talk at the same time; acquiring this skill ungenetically takes years of practice.)

As you get to the center, the edible parts of the leaves become more and more succulent until you reach the "choke," which you pry up and place gently at the side of the plate. What is left is the artichoke heart. Ideally, this should be eaten with your eyes closed to ensure the utmost concentration.

An angelic chorus would add just the right touch of class to the occasion.

These things are just plain annoying. After all the trouble you go to, you get about as much actual "food" out of eating an artichoke as you would from licking 30 or 40 postage stamps. Have the shrimp cocktail instead.

— Miss Piggy

Too Much Is Sometimes More Than Enough

Author John del Valle recalls an episode that involved the enlisted personnel of A Battery, U.S. Army Coast Artillery, during World War II. A well-meaning mess sergeant had spent a considerable portion of the battery's mess fund to purchase artichokes as an intended special treat for the 300 rookie artillerymen. As del Valle tells it, "The young soldiers, mostly West Virginia farm boys, stared with suspicion at the unfamiliar objects awaiting them on the steam table like so many limp green grenades. They had been expecting steak. 'What are them (bleep) things?' they demanded — all but one, Frank Banker, who being a Californian, knew his artichokes. While the other 299 soldiers banged their tableware, griped loudly, and even threw artichokes on the floor and stomped on them, Banker ate until he could eat no more — about seven, he remembers.

"Meanwhile, the mess sergeant, mindful that he could lose his stripes if so much good food was to be wasted, offered PFC Banker the privileges of the mess hall at any hour if he could just eat the remaining artichokes.

"Banker cheerfully did what he could, three meals a day for three days, and personally accounted for 53 artichokes before throwing in the sponge."

He emerged from the war a full colonel with ribbons on his chest, del Valle remembers.

Q&A

Q Why do some drinks taste sweet when one has just eaten an artichoke?

A This is because artichokes contain two compounds, chlorogenic acid and cynarin, that inhibit the taste buds' sweetness receptors. Drinking water or milk or even wine clears away the reaction and the receptors return to normal — bringing with them the illusion that the liquid tastes sweet.

Not everyone experiences this so-called Artichoke Effect, which seems to be genetic, but people who take wines seriously strike artichokes from the menu when vintage wines are being served.

Welcome to the Original Foggy Bottom!

Castroville, California, some 110 miles south of San Francisco and 16 miles north of Monterey, claims to be the artichoke center of the world. Actually, Italy, Spain, France, and Greece (in that order) produce many more tons of the vegetable. But their climates are not ideal, it seems — too sunny.

Artichokes prefer fog. And certainly no artichokes taste better than those grown around Castroville, where the fogs creep in nightly from the Pacific Ocean to cool acre upon acre of the silvery green, low-lying plants. Stands selling every size of artichokes by the crate line every roadside, but the main attraction is a restaurant shaped like a gigantic artichoke where artichokes are cooked in as many ways as there are leaves on the vegetable.

ASPARAGUS

Pray, how does your asparagus perform?

— John Adams in a letter to his wife, Abigail

HOW DOES YOUR ASPARAGUS GROW?

Under the right circumstances, asparagus plants grow very well — and grow, and grow some more. Beds may require two or three years of cultivation before they begin to yield a crop, but if the plants are well tended, they will produce abundantly for 20 years or more. During optimum growing conditions, the plants require two harvestings every day — one in the morning and another in the evening. Spears grow rapidly and exuberantly, often increasing by as much as 10 inches in a day.

It is said that spears continue to grow even after they are picked, and indeed, many farmers pack them in crates that are large enough to allow for an increase in size during shipping. In fact, the spears are not actively growing so much as swelling in size as they absorb moisture from the air. So, if you are very early to market and the asparagus you buy is very fresh, you stand a good chance of watching your own spears extending on your own kitchen counter — over cocktails, say, before the water boils.

White Treasures

White asparagus, particularly favored by Europeans, is grown beneath mounds of earth that are watched closely for the first hints of cracking — an indication that the stalks are about to push through the dirt. At this crucial point, harvesters rush to the asparagus fields in the pre-dawn to snip the subterranean beauties from their dark gardens before a tip can inch through the earth toward the sun. Once the sun touches those tender tips, they turn light purple and the stalks lose their grade-A status.

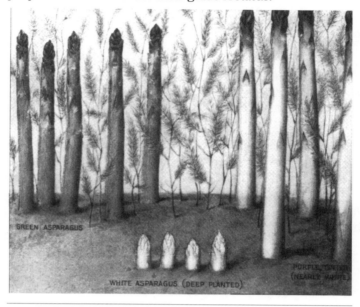

GREEN ASPARAGUS
WHITE ASPARAGUS (DEEP PLANTED)
PURPLE-TINTED (NEARLY WHITE)

Walking on the Wild Side

It is more than 30 years since Euell Gibbons's best-selling Stalking the Wild Asparagus *opened our eyes to the foods that could be found growing wild. Doors opened wide, and seekers streamed into the countryside to harvest a bounty ranging from asparagus to yucca blossoms, by way of fiddlehead ferns and thimbleberries.*

Asparagus grows wild wherever it can find a footing, in the lee of ancient hedges along undisturbed country roads. Mark where the ferns grow in summer and come back with a knife in the spring.

Cooking and Eating
Asparagus

Conventional wisdom aside, it is not necessary to buy an expensive asparagus steamer in order to cook asparagus beautifully. It can be simmered, uncovered, in a saucepan or skillet and will be ready to eat in 8 to 12 minutes, depending on its thickness. The only way to know if it is tender is to taste it and drain it when it is a shade on the underdone side. The heat that it retains will finish it off nicely.

Some people like to tie the spears in bundles before putting them in the pan, because when they are cooked, all the spears will point in the same direction, like a chorus line. If you are feeling particularly elegant, it is graceful to serve scrupulously well-drained asparagus within the folds of a starched white napkin. And if you were Martha Stewart, you might well tie a bow of lavender ribbon around it, causing everyone to exclaim how terribly clever you are.

Serve the asparagus with warm, melted butter, regardless of what "they" say. Anything that tastes this good can't possibly be bad for you.

ATHLETES' FOOD

ATHLETES CAN TEACH US HOW TO EAT — AND WHAT TO DRINK

Is it really useful for ordinary people to pay attention to how athletes fuel their bodies? You could argue that the new, widespread interest in sports nutrition is just another food fad. But might there be wisdom here even for those of us who live more or less sedentary lives, and are unlikely to get any closer to a hockey stick or a volleyball net than the couch we sit on when we watch a high-powered game on TV?

The answer is yes, because athletes are also ordinary people who just happen to live their lives a lot more vigorously than the rest of us do.

What is to fuel our active lives? The average American man consumes 2,150 calories a

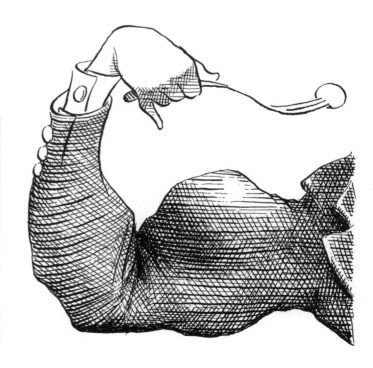

day, and a woman 1,600; in each case, the diet consists of 47 percent carbohydrates, 36 percent fat, and 17 percent protein. Most serious athletes would go far lower in fat (perhaps down to 20 percent or less) and in protein (which is our least efficient energy source) and would boost carbohydrates. Their influence on the frequent consumption of water is also now an article of faith among many people who work all day at desks.

Ordinary people may also be at risk for dehydration — even though the day's normal activities won't even raise a sweat. The word is out from researchers that it's a good idea to drink water frequently during the day because the body requires it to process high-protein foods such as meat, milk, and cheese. The kidneys need the water to wash out nitro-

gen, a by-product of protein digestion.

Other factors, too, contribute to dehydration: the diuretic effects of drinks that contain caffeine, or alcohol; the fact that we tend to spend long periods of time in sealed, air-conditioned rooms or offices; and our increasing use of air travel. In fact, nutritionists recommend drinking at least a cup of water for every hour spent in the air — and we might be well advised to remember that ratio when our feet are on the ground, as well.

Gatorade

Sports drinks are intended to boost energy and to replace salts and other minerals that are lost when we exercise. Gatorade, the first such drink to come on the scene, was introduced in 1967 after researchers at the University of Florida concocted it for their football team, the Gators. Quaker Oats bought the brand in 1983 and now offers it in five flavors: lemon-lime, orange, fruit punch, lemonade, and citrus cooler. But the tastes are not the point; when consumed, the drink's basic ingredients — water, sugar (for energy), salt (for fluid balance), and potassium (for nerve transmission) — are rapidly absorbed, and the body's fluid and mineral balance is restored. Among sports drinks, also known as isotonics, Gatorade is far in the lead, with 85 percent of an $800-million-a-year market.

Books

Eat to Win: The Sports Nutrition Bible
Robert Haas, M.D.; Signet Books, 1985; $5.99

Nancy Clark's Sports Guidebook
Nancy Clark, M.S., R.D.; Leisure Press, 1990; $14.95

Eating for Endurance
Edward Coleman (revised edition by Ellen Coleman); Bull Publishing, 1992; $12.95

Training Foods

The charts show the number of servings that are recommended for athletes at different times in their training season. The suggested number of servings, as defined in the Nutrition section, is always a minimum — the actual number is an individual decision based on age, sex, body size, weight, and activity levels.

Basic Diet	Modified Training Diet	Training Diet	Carbohydrate-Loading Diet
1600 calories • For athletes during the off-season	**2200 calories** • For endurance athletes on the first 3 days of carbohydrate loading • For athletes in training who want to lose weight • For high school athletes throughout the training season	**2800 calories** • For athletes throughout the training season (See a Registered Dietitian)	**3000 calories** • For endurance athletes 3 days before competition (Not useful for all athletes; experiment prior to actual event. An experienced sports nutritionist should be consulted before using this technique)
Types of Food	Recommended Daily Servings	Recommended Daily Servings	Recommended Daily Servings	Recommended Daily Servings
Milk, cheese, yogurt, cottage cheese, ice cream **Nutrients supplied:** protein, riboflavin, vitamin B-12, calcium, and magnesium	For teenagers, adults under 24, and women who are pregnant or breast-feeding: 4 or more servings. For adults over 24: 2 or more servings	For teenagers and adults under 24: 4 or more servings For adults over 24: 2 or more servings	3 or more servings	4 or more servings
Meat, fish, poultry, eggs, dried beans and peas, nuts **Nutrients supplied:** protein, vitamin B-12, iron, zinc	2 or more servings (total 5 ounces)	2 or more servings (total 6 ounces)	3 servings (7 ounces approximately)	3 or more servings
Fresh, frozen, canned, dried, and juiced fruits. **Nutrients supplied:** vitamins A, C, potassium	2 or more servings	3 or more servings	4 or more servings	6 or more servings
Fresh, frozen, canned, dried, and juiced vegetables **Nutrients supplied:** iron, magnesium, folate	3 or more servings	4 or more servings	5 or more servings	8 or more servings
Cereals, breads, rolls, pasta, muffins, pancakes, grits **Nutrients supplied:** thiamine, niacin, folacin	6 or more servings	9 or more servings	11 or more servings	18 or more servings

Adapted from "Food Power," National Dairy Council, and The Food Guide Pyramid, HG 252

AVOCADO

'AVE A CADO, MY DEAR?

The avocado is not a vegetable, but a fruit — that of a tree belonging to the laurel family, There are three main types: small, thin-skinned Mexican avocados; large, bumpy-skinned Guatemalan varieties, some of which can weigh up to three pounds; and West Indian avocados, which can be equally big, but have slightly more watery flesh and leathery skins. Each country uses them differently. Nicaraguans like their avocados cooked; in Ecuador and Colombia sliced avocado is added to soups; in Chile you will find avocado topping hot dogs; in Brazil avocado can be mixed into ice cream.

Avocados got their name from the Spaniards' efforts to pronounce the Aztec word for the fruit, which was known as *ahuacatl*, "testicle," because of its shape. The Spanish equivalent became *aguacate*. A popular Aztec delicacy was agave worm, served with a special hot sauce made from avocado mixed with chili pepper and tomato, and the Spaniards called this fiery sauce *aguacamole*, leading, of course, to the guacamole we know today.

The worms supplied protein, but the avocado, too, was rich in nutrients. An average-sized avocado contains 17 vitamins and minerals — a cup of pureed avocado has 1,378 milligrams of potassium as against 890 milligrams in a cup of mashed banana — and very little sodium. But it also supplies 324 calories, 88 percent of which are "contributed" as fat, even though most of it is monounsaturated. This is a fact that the average Aztec could make good use of, but most modern people might want to think twice about.

Guacamole

Makes 2 cups

2 medium-sized ripe avocados	**2 tablespoons lemon**
4 scallions, thinly sliced	**or lime juice**
1 teaspoon salt	**A few drops Tabasco sauce**

Peel and pit the avocados and cut them into small pieces. Either put the pieces in a food processor, add the scallions, salt, lemon juice, and Tabasco, and process until the mixture is almost smooth; or mash all the ingredients with the back of a fork to a slightly coarser texture. Serve with tortilla chips.

To prevent the guacamole from darkening, put the avocado pit in the bowl and cover the surface of the guacamole closely with plastic wrap.

TIPS

Buying

Although there are three kinds of avocado, they basically have two different skin types: there are avocados with thin, shiny green skins, and avocados that have leathery, pebbly-looking dark skins. The smooth-skinned ones stay green even when ripe; the rough-skinned Hass avocados turn from green to purple to black, so their ripeness can be judged to some extent by their color. Avocados do not start to ripen until they are off the tree, so it is important to check each one for ripeness.

Hold the fruit in the palm of your hand. If it yields to even slight pressure, it is ripe and ready to eat. Hass avocados can wait another 24 hours to reach optimum condition.

Storing

To avoid the possibility of bruising from the journey to market or from over-rough handling by other shoppers, buy the fruits while they are still hard and store them at room temperature for a few days until they pass the ripeness test. To accelerate the process, put them in a brown paper sack with an apple or a tomato and leave them in a warm place. The warmth and the natural ethylene gas emitted by the fruit help the avocados ripen nicely in a day or two.

How to Prepare an Avocado

1. Cut the fruit in half lengthwise around the pit. Use a stainless steel knife; carbon steel will make the flesh discolor.
2. Rotate the two halves to separate them. The pit will stay in one half. If you are not using the whole fruit, set aside the half with the pit.
3. Gently remove the pit with a spoon.
4. To peel the avocado, turn it flesh side down and peel the skin off with a knife or your fingers.
5. Sprinkle the cut flesh with lemon or lime juice or white vinegar to prevent it from darkening.

Books

The Avocado Lovers' Cookbook
Joyce Carlisle; Celestial Arts, 1985; $9.95

The Major Varieties of California Avocados

Hass: California's leading variety, available year-round; pear-sized with rough pebbly skin that turns from green to purplish black when ripe; creamy texture and great taste
Bacon: available fall through spring; medium-sized, with shiny green skin; good texture for guacamole and sauces
Zutano: available fall through winter; similar to Hass in size, but with smooth yellow-green skin; light in taste and texture
Gwen: available late winter through late summer; slightly larger than Hass, but similar in appearance, taste, and texture, though the skin remains green when ripe
Pinkerton: available winter through spring; similar to Hass in taste and texture, but larger, with a small seed and medium-thick slightly pebbled green skin
Fuerte: available winter through spring; similar to Hass in taste and texture, but with smooth, slightly mottled thin green skin
Reed: available in summer and early fall; large, round, with slightly pebbled green skin; smooth texture and nutty flavor

(Hurricane Andrew devastated Florida's chief avocado-growing areas, and the state is no longer shipping avocados in quantity.)

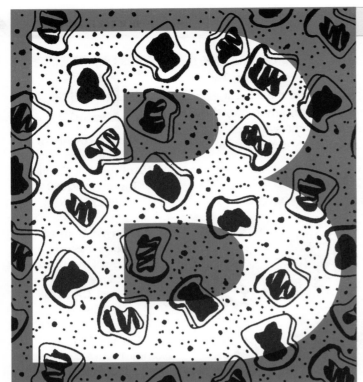

BABIES' FOOD ❖ BAGELS ❖ BANANAS ❖ BARBECUE ❖ BASS ❖ BATS ❖ BEANS ❖ BEEF ❖ BEETS ❖ BETA CAROTENE ❖ BIOTECHNOLOGY ❖ BISTROS ❖ BLUEBERRIES ❖ BREAD ❖ BREAKFAST ❖ BROCCOLI ❖ BRUSSELS SPROUTS ❖ BUTTER

BABIES' FOOD

**The brain gets bigger right after birth.
By the age of two, it's close to adult size.
Man's future depends on what
his food is as an infant.**
— William Conor, M.D.
Oregon Health Sciences Center

WARFARE AT THE SUPERMARKET

ANNA QUINDLEN

On the subject of feeding my first child, I was what you might call a real pain. For the first six months of his life he got nothing but breast milk, accompanied by the occasional rhapsody about nourishing him from my own body. When I put him on solids, I carried a little food mill everywhere: It became traditional at family gatherings to see me hunched over a plate of steamed carrots, grinding them and mixing them with yogurt.

I knew those days were gone forever when I found myself recently splitting a bag of Cheez Doodles with my kids. (You know everything about Cheez Doodles by the way Cheez is spelled. I mean, would you buy a sauce for asparagus called Holl-N-Daze?) It was not companionable; none of us were talking, just scarfing down those little curlicues like attack dogs at feeding time. Finally my first child, he of the breast milk and pureed carrots, looked up and grinned, a salty orange grin. "Mommy, I like this stuff," he said.

The father of the children remembers a time when I was a careful shopper and a devoted cook. He forgets that at the time my Tupperware was not being used as bathtub toys, my vegetable steamer basket had not become a pond for the plastic dinosaurs, and nobody was using the garlic press as a gun. (It was also a time when I sublimated my true nature and pretended that I thought Ring Dings were revolting, which is a lie.)

I once had a theory that if you fed children nothing but nutritious foods, with no additives, preservatives, or sugar, they would learn to prefer those foods. I should have recognized the reality at the first birthday party, when tradition triumphed over nutrition and I made chocolate cake for the guest of honor. He put one fistful in his mouth and gave me a look I would not see again until I brought a baby home from the hospital and told him the baby was going to stay. The cake look, roughly translated, said, "You've been holding out on me." He set about catching up. The barber gave him lollipops, the dry cleaner a Tootsie Roll. At the circus he had cotton candy, which is the part of the balance of nature designed to offset the wheat germ.

The other night for dinner he was having vegetable lasagna and garlic bread, picking out the zucchini, the spinach, even the parsley — "all the green stuff" — and eating only the parts of the bread that had butter.

"Know what my favorite food is, Mom?" he said. "Sugar."

Excerpted from The New York Times

Books

Baby, Let's Eat
Rena Coyle; Workman, 1987; $8.95

Breasts, Bottles, and Babies: A History of Infant Feeding
Valerie Fildes; Columbia University Press, 1989; $18.00

Child of Mine: Feeding with Love and Good Sense
Ellyn Satter; Bull Publishing, 1991; $14.95

Feed Me: I'm Yours
Vicki Lansky; Meadowbrook Press, 1990; $8.00

Feeding Your Baby: From Conception to Age Two
Louise Lambert-Lagace; Surrey Books, 1991; $10.95

Mommy Made and Daddy Too! Home Cooking for a Healthy Baby and Toddler
Martha Kimmel; Bantam, 1990; $13.95

The Nursing Mother's Companion
Kathleen Huggins, R.N., M.S.; Harvard Common Press, 1990; $11.95

BREAST IS BEST

Babies, like all young mammals, do best with milk from their own species. Babies on a formula diet are at greater risk for illness and hospitalization. Diarrheal infections, respiratory illnesses, and ear infections are more frequently seen among those babies. Formula-fed infants also have higher incidences of colic, constipation, and allergic disorders. Bottle feeding with formula more commonly leads to overfeeding and obesity, which may well persist into adulthood. For all these reasons, the American Academy of Pediatrics recommends that infants be offered only breast milk for the first four to six months after birth, and that breast-feeding continue throughout the first year."

So says Kathleen Huggins in *The Nursing Mother's Companion* and there is ample evidence to back up the pediatricians' recommendations. A 1992 article in the British medical journal *The Lancet* reported findings that breast-fed babies developed IQs more than eight points higher than those of babies who were fed formula, even after adjusting for differences in mothers' education and social class. And in Goteborg, Sweden, Professor Sven Decker claims that mother's milk contains natural tranquilizers that help the baby sleep through the night.

Although it seems the most natural thing in the world, successful breast-feeding is surprisingly hard to accomplish. For many mothers, even those convinced of the advantages, nursing is not an option because they have to leave the baby and get back to work. Breast-feeding in public is still frowned upon by some, and more complications result if the baby's father is not wholly supportive.

And now it appears that some useful resources in helping women adjust to life with a new baby aren't as solid as they seemed. Nursing mothers used to be encouraged to drink beer or a little wine to increase their milk flow, but a recent study in the *New England Journal of Medicine* found that drinking even one beer had the effect of reducing rather than enlarging milk supply. It also changed the taste and smell of the mothers' milk and their babies not only drank considerably less than usual, but had restless nights after consuming the alcohol-tainted milk.

Exercising, too, raises the levels of lactic acid in breast milk and makes it taste sour. And if breast milk has been expressed in advance to avoid these problems, warming it in the microwave can zap away the infection-fighting properties that make it superior to formula.

In the end, the age-old advice still holds: Don't worry, be informed, and do the best you can. When babies are loved, they will thrive, no matter how they are fed.

There are three reasons for breast-feeding: the milk is always at the right temperature; it comes in attractive containers; and the cat can't get it.

— Scottish midwife

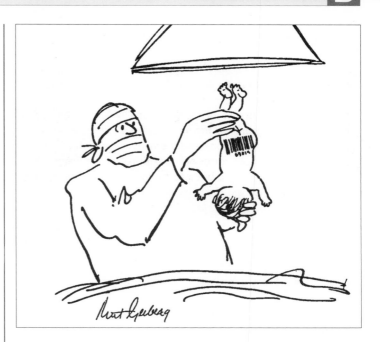

Babies Need Feeding, Not Dieting

Babies grow at an astonishing rate, tripling their birth weight and adding 10 to 11 inches to their height by their first birthday. To fuel this growth, they need the most nutritious food nature can provide.

Well-meaning parents who are concerned that their babies may become overweight sometimes water down the infants' formulas and cut back on fat by serving unbuttered vegetables, low-fat or skim milk, and lean meat. The end result is that the diet may not contain sufficient calories for nourishment.

Tufts School of Nutrition studies show that a diet that includes skim milk, lean meat, and eggs without the yolks may be wise for parents and older children who are trying to follow a heart-healthy regimen. For infants under the age of two, however, limiting foods that contain fat and cholesterol could spell real trouble. Skimming off the fat, and thereby the calories, from a baby's diet can actually stunt his growth; limiting an infant's dietary cholesterol could deprive her of the cholesterol she needs to form body cells, including those of the nervous system.

The American Academy of Pediatrics Committee on Nutrition recommends that 30 to 40 percent of a baby's calories should come from fat. It is essential to the baby's diet, providing a concentrated source of energy as well as vitamins A, D, E, and K, and linoleic acid.

"If you think of her as Isaac Newton you won't mind the droppings on the floor."

For Babies, Bland Is Better

The current concern about eating healthy foods has hit the baby-food market, too. Here, Gerber is still the giant in the field, with a market share that is larger than AT&T's share of long distance. Heinz, "the value brand," strong in the South, has the bottom end of the market, while in the Northeast and the West, Beech-Nut gives Gerber a run for the money.

Gone are the days when baby food was salted so Mom would think it tasty enough for her baby, heavily sugared to appeal to baby's natural sweet tooth, or filled with starch to swell the profit margins. These days, baby foods proudly proclaim their lack of salt, sugar, filler, and preservatives.

How fortunate it is that babies really *prefer* foods without much taste. Funny, that it took us so long to find this out. But considering how dismal the stuff tastes to us as adults, perhaps fate is kind to spare us the memory of relishing strained squash with tapioca and banging our spoons for more.

Infant Feeding at a Glance

This chart is simply a guide; each baby will have his or her own sequence which should always be discussed with the child's pediatrician or a dietitian.

Age	Birth to 6 months	6 months	7 to 9 months	9 to 12 months	12 to 18 months	
Suggested Food Sequence	• Breast milk and/or iron-fortified formula satisfies all nutritional requirements • Solid foods not nutritionally needed but infant may want	Starter foods: • Bananas • Rice cereal • Pears • Applesauce	• Avocados • Peaches • Carrots • Squash • Mashed potatoes • Barley cereal • Teething biscuits • Pear and apple juice	• Lamb, veal, poultry • Bagel • Rice cakes • Egg yolk • Cheese • Yogurt • Tofu • Noodles • Beans • Peas • Yams • Oatmeal	• Whole milk • Cottage cheese • Ice cream • Whole eggs • Beef • Peanut butter • Fish: salmon, tuna • Broccoli • Spinach • Cauliflower • Melon • Mango • Kiwi	• Papaya • Apricots • Grapefruit • Grape halves • Strawberries • Tomatoes • Pasta • Graham crackers • Wheat cereal • Honey • Pancakes • Muffins
Presenting Foods	• Breast and/or bottle	• Strained, pureed • Fingertip full • Spoonful	• Introduce cup • Finger foods begin • Puree and mash • Holds bottle	• Lumpier consistency • Finger foods mastered • Bite-sized cooked vegetables • Melt-in-mouth foods • Holds sippy cup	• Participates in family meals • Chopped and mashed family foods • Begins self-feeding with utensils	

Source: *Baby Talk* magazine

Pick, Pick, Pick

Research from *American Baby* magazine verifies that parents who try to force their infants to eat the "right" foods wind up with the pickiest eaters. When small children are forced to eat when they are not hungry, the biological mechanism that lets them know they have had enough to eat becomes permanently damaged. A new school of nutritionists thinks that this may eventually become a cause of lifelong battles with overeating and obesity.

The problem is compounded by the fact that, on average, today's working mothers return to their jobs when their babies are no more than six weeks old, so it is all the more important that their replacements offer plenty of nurturing care. "Babies cared for by adults who do not hold or touch them, except while feeding them, can wrongly teach baby that eating relieves not just hunger but also anger, depression, anxiety, and loneliness," says Martha Kimmel in *Mommy Made and Daddy Too!* "Food should be a great pleasure, but it shouldn't answer emotional needs."

Children, even young ones, are very smart. Caregivers or parents who worry openly about what they eat and when they eat provide them with a powerful weapon for manipulation. Psychologists suggest beating them at their own game. If a child refuses all vegetables, offer alternatives, such as fruits that contain many of the same nutrients. Don't dwell on the success or failure of a single meal; consider each as part of a long chain of experience with eating.

Vegetarian Kids

Babies fed an exclusively vegetarian diet mature more slowly than their meat-eating counterparts, according to a study conducted by the Nutrition Division of the Centers for Disease Control. The 404 children in the study lived in a religious cooperative in Tennessee and ranged in age from four months to ten years. All were following a vegan diet, which avoids all animal foods, including milk and dairy products such as cheese. Each child's statistics were compared with the standard U.S. growth reference for their age, and although all the younger children were slightly smaller than their contemporaries in the reference, the Tennessee ten-year-olds had almost caught up, both in height and weight. Growing more slowly means that a child takes longer to mature, and this could yield long-term health benefits.

The only real danger in a meatless and dairyless diet is the possible lack of a nutritionally balanced selection of foods, but professional nutrition counseling can ensure that children's total nutritional needs are properly taken care of with a vegan diet.

LISA HANEY

Totally Pure

Two new organic baby-food companies, Earth's Best, from Vermont, and Simply Pure, from Maine, use only water-processed fruits and vegetables grown on land that has been pesticide-free for at least three years.

HOTLINES

800-523-9393
Beech-Nut Nutrition
9:00 a.m. - 7:00 p.m. CST

800-443-7237
**Gerber Consumer
Information Services**

800-525-3243
La Leche League
9:00 a.m.– 3:00 p.m. CST

PERIODICALS

For addresses, see also Information Sources

American Baby Magazine
P.O. Box 53093
Boulder, CO 80322-3093
303-447-9330
Monthly; $19.88 per year

New Beginnings
La Leche League International
708-455-7730
Bimonthly; free for members;
$18 per year for nonmembers

BAGELS

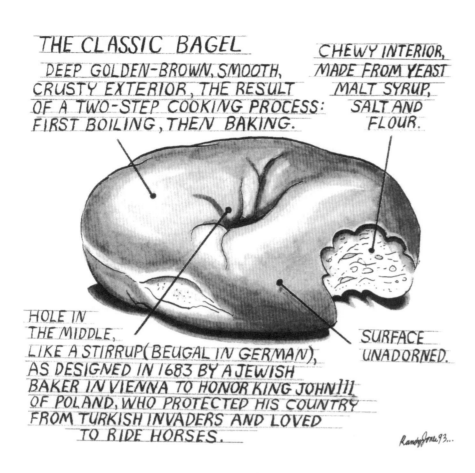

THE CLASSIC BAGEL
DEEP GOLDEN-BROWN, SMOOTH, CRUSTY EXTERIOR, THE RESULT OF A TWO-STEP COOKING PROCESS: FIRST BOILING, THEN BAKING.

CHEWY INTERIOR, MADE FROM YEAST MALT SYRUP, SALT AND FLOUR.

HOLE IN THE MIDDLE, LIKE A STIRRUP (BEUGAL IN GERMAN), AS DESIGNED IN 1683 BY A JEWISH BAKER IN VIENNA TO HONOR KING JOHN III OF POLAND, WHO PROTECTED HIS COUNTRY FROM TURKISH INVADERS AND LOVED TO RIDE HORSES.

SURFACE UNADORNED.

Randy Jones 93...

BEGETTING THE BAGEL

CRAIG CLAIBORNE

One of the most interesting breads known to man is the bagel. Curiously, in America, bagels have their greatest appeal in the Northeast and they are generally considered "Jewish food." I am told, however, that many years ago they were eaten in many European countries by the populace at large. In *The Joys of Yiddish*, Leo Rosten notes that "the first printed mention of bagels . . . is to be found in the Community Regulations of Kracow, Poland, for the year 1610 — which stated that bagels would be given as a gift to any woman in childbirth." He adds that the word is derived from the German word *beugel*, meaning "a round loaf of bread." There are those who dispute this and claim that it derives from the middle High German word *bugel* . . . a twisted or curved bracelet or ring.

To prepare a bagel, you make a dough with flour, yeast, water, and oil or other fat. You knead the dough and let it rise until it is double in bulk. After shaping the bagels into a circle, drop them into a basin of boiling water and let them "cook" 2 or 3 minutes to a side, turning once. Drained, they are generally brushed with egg and baked until golden brown.

It therefore seemed logical to me that any properly made bagel could be referred to as a water bagel. But I was chastised by a New Yorker.

"Though it is true," she wrote, "that 'any properly made bagel' is boiled before being baked, the term water bagel refers not to this process but to the content of the dough. Any bagel eater or baker will tell you that there is a world of difference between the classic water bagel and the modern (infamous to purists) egg bagel. I wouldn't want to sound unduly harsh as regards the egg bagel — which is actually very good, albeit a little rich — but the true and traditional bagel, the water bagel, is absolutely eggless, both inside and out."

Reprinted from *Craig Claiborne's Food Encyclopedia*

A Bewilderment of Bagel Varieties

Somewhat Traditional	Far Out
Bialy	Apple and cinnamon
Egg	Blueberry swirl
Garlic	Cheddar cheese
Onion	Chocolate chip
Plain	Cranberry-orange nut
Poppy-seed	Fruits and nuts
Pumpernickel	Ham
Pumpernickel and raisin	Ham and cheese
Salt	Herbed
Sesame-seed	Honey
Sourdough	Jalapeño
Whole-wheat	Oat-bran
	Pesto
	Spinach
	Sun-dried tomato
	Walnut
	… and Everything

The Bagel Takes Flight

Bagels are hot. *American Demographics* reports that gay women buy more honey-wheat bagels than the rest of the population. No one knows why. Nor do we know why businessmen in suits buy plain bagels during the week and come in for funky varieties on the weekend, when they are wearing blue jeans. We understand why athletes buy salt bagels and teething babies are comforted by chewing on a plain bagel, but why professors prefer poppy-seed bagels is anyone's guess — unless it's their alliterative attraction. And how do the demographic researchers know the line of work or sexual preference of those who buy bagels, anyway? Is there a register at the counter? Or are the retailers just guessing?

What they're not guessing about is the runaway success of the bagel all over the United States. Americans are now consuming more than 5 million bagels a year, although many who bake them and eat them have never tasted the solid, chewy real thing. An authentic food quickly gets obscured whenever a new food fad erupts. The first thing that happens, as it has in turn with croissants, cookies, muffins, and now bagels, is that they double in size so that stores can charge more for them. Then dozens of flavors proliferate. The virtuoso who dreamed up larding the originally kosher bagel with ham and cheese surely takes the grand prize in the incongruity department.

Without question, part of the reason bagels have been so successful is because they are filling, inexpensive, and widely available. But people also mistakenly believe that they are pure because they are kosher, and that they won't make you fat. Myth number one is blown away with the discovery that Bruegger's Bagels, headquartered in Burlington, Vermont, of all unlikely places, already has a chain of 65 bagel stores and anticipates having 1,000 by the end of the decade with sales of a cool $1 billion — a lot of nonkosher dough by any reckoning. As for myth number two, a plain bagel contains 200 calories before you add even the tiniest smear of butter or cream cheese, let alone any of the other goodies. Nevertheless, people continue to fantasize that the hole in the middle makes the bagel into a doughnut with the sin removed.

The real proof that bagels are here to stay: The Swiss army knife has added a new blade alongside the gadget that gets stones out of horses' hooves, and its express purpose is splitting bagels.

Make Mine A ...

In *The Bagel Bible*, authors Marilyn and Tom Bagel (yes, that really *is* their name) list the bagel preferences of some famous people:

Larry King: salt bagel with lox and cream cheese

Ed McMahon: onion bagel with peanut butter or cream cheese and lox

Geraldo Rivera: poppy-seed bagel with cream cheese and olives

Willard Scott: sesame-seed bagel with cream cheese

A bagel creation that would have my parents turning over in their graves is the oat-bran bagel with blueberries and strawberries. It's a bagel nightmare, an ill-conceived bagel form if there ever was one.

— Ed Levine
New York Eats

Books

New York Eats
Ed Levine; St. Martin's Press, 1992; $16.95

The Bagel Bible
Marilyn and Tom Bagel; Globe Pequot, 1992; $9.95

MAIL ORDER SOURCES

H&H Bagels
2239 Broadway
at West 80th Street
New York, NY 10024
212-595-8000

BANANAS

Voice

I'm Chi -qui-ta Ba-na - na and I've

Ai Ai-ai-aye

by Richard Atcheson

When I was a kid, one of my favorite people on radio was Chiquita Banana. Chiquita hit the airwaves in 1945 — when I was 11 — as the star of a commercial designed to boost banana sales, and she went straight to my heart with her memorable ditty with a samba beat: "I'm Chiquita Banana and I've come to say/ That bananas have to ripen in a certain way."

Of course, I never saw Chiquita. I knew she wasn't a real person. But I was smart enough to realize that she was based on a favorite movie star of mine, Carmen Miranda, so I endowed her in my imagination with Carmen's fantastic frou-frou, platform heels, and banana-bearing turban.

The part of the lyric that I liked best was about how to use bananas. "You can put them in a salad," she would sing, "You can put them in a pie-aye./ Any way you want to eat them / It's impossible to beat them." And then came the cautionary close: "But you must never put bananas / In the refrig-er-ator. No-no-no-no!"

A word like "pie-aye" could really break me up in those days. It still can. Olé.

Bananas Are Growing Smaller

The trend in bananas is toward the new, smaller ones. The familiar nine-inch-long Cavendish has been shrunk to the seven-inch Chiquita Junior, which is actually about one-third the size, and most people, young and old, seem to prefer the smaller ones.

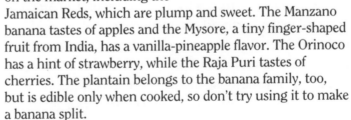

New varieties are coming on the market, including the Jamaican Reds, which are plump and sweet. The Manzano banana tastes of apples and the Mysore, a tiny finger-shaped fruit from India, has a vanilla-pineapple flavor. The Orinoco has a hint of strawberry, while the Raja Puri tastes of cherries. The plantain belongs to the banana family, too, but is edible only when cooked, so don't try using it to make a banana split.

TIPS

Buying

All bananas are picked while they are still green. If they ripen on the stem they lose their taste and texture. After they are picked, the sugar content increases from 2 percent to 20 percent. The yellower the skin, the sweeter the fruit will be. Brown spots on the skin indicate the amount of sugar in the banana.

Storing

If you want to delay ripening, store bananas in the vegetable crisper of the refrigerator. The skin will turn brown but the banana inside will remain firm at this temperature.

To speed ripening, put the bananas in a paper bag. They will produce ethylene gas, which hastens the ripening process. If you add an apple to the bag, the bananas will ripen even faster.

Did You Know?

☞ A banana of average size contains 95 calories.

☞ Bananas are the least expensive and most popular fruit in the market.

☞ Every year Americans eat, per capita, more than 25 pounds of bananas.

☞ Bananas come in some 400 varieties, all belonging to the same family as lilies and orchids.

☞ Bananas are a $5 billion business in the United States. We import 15 billion bananas a day into this country.

☞ Bananas grow in almost all tropical countries, but are exported chiefly by Colombia, Ecuador, Panama, Costa Rica, Honduras, and Guatemala, nations long known as the Banana Republics. Oddly enough, bananas are also grown in Iceland, in soil heated by geysers.

A BANANA A DAY

Eating bananas can chase away the blues. Why? Because they contain serotonin and norepinephrine, which are believed to alleviate mental depression.

And according to a University of California study the risk of stroke can be reduced by as much as 40 percent simply by eating one banana a day. The medication patients take to control high blood pressure depletes the body's store of potassium, and a single banana every day restores the correct balance.

Nutritionally, bananas are high in vitamin B-6, low in sodium, and a good source of fiber; they also come in their own convenient, biodegradable containers.

Banana Bread
Makes 1 loaf

½ cup softened butter or
   margarine
1 cup sugar
2 eggs
1⅓ cups mashed ripe banana
   (3 to 4 medium-sized bananas)
1 tablespoon milk
1 teaspoon vanilla extract
2 cups unsifted all-purpose flour
1 teaspoon baking soda
¼ teaspoon salt
½ cup chopped walnuts

Preheat the oven to 350 degrees F. Butter and flour a 9-by-5-by-3-inch loaf pan.

In a large bowl, cream the butter and sugar together until light and fluffy. Add the eggs and fold in the mashed bananas, milk, and vanilla. Mix the flour, salt, and baking soda in a separate bowl, then fold them into the banana mixture. Fold in the walnuts. Transfer to the prepared loaf pan and bake for 1 hour and 10 minutes until a cake tester comes out clean.

Remove from the oven and cool in the pan for about 10 minutes. Then turn out onto a wire cooling rack to cool completely before slicing.

Not Just Something to Slip On

A banana peel can substitute as a polishing rag for leather shoes; its slippery qualities clean and condition the shiny surface nicely.

BARBECUE

HOME ON THE RANGE
(ON TOP OF OLD SMOKY)

Cooking is among the most competitive of indoor and outdoor sports. Otherwise quite normal people, who would never think of bragging about the speed with which they can pull out a tooth or paint a house, puff themselves up embarrassingly when they talk about their skill with the grill. I think they actually *prefer* it when their neighbor burns the steak or undercooks the chicken. It makes them feel smug and superior.

Actually, there isn't a whole lot to making a terrific barbecue. All you need is the right equipment, the right fuel, the right weather forecast, the right ingredients, a good nose to let you know when the meat is ready to eat, and a loving companion who will fetch

and carry all the stuff you forgot.

All these things, of course, have existed since the beginning of time, especially the charcoal, which was in use at the time of the Neanderthals — with whom many contemporary outdoor cooks have much in common. Primitive peoples found that relighting already charred wood produced a fire that burned more hotly and with less smoke than freshly cut branches.

Nothing much else happened in the outdoor cooking business until about 1920, when Henry Ford, flushed with the success of the Model T, made another contribution that would profoundly change the American way of life.

A believer in thrift, Ford had purchased a sawmill in Iron

Did You Know?

☞ Americans spend more than $400 million a year on charcoal briquettes.

☞ The word "barbecue" may stem from the French *barbe à queue*, meaning "from whiskers to tail." The expression indicates that the whole animal has been cooked. (And every part is eaten except the piggy's squeak.)

☞ Some 83 percent of U.S. households own a barbecue grill; 62 percent own a charcoal grill, and 54 percent own a gas grill.

☞ Hamburgers are America's favorite food. Chicken claims the second spot, steak is third, and hot dogs fourth. Fish is fast swimming into the mainstream.

Mountain, Michigan, to make wooden parts for his automobiles. As he watched the growing mountain of wood scraps, the frugal Ford fretted about the wasted leftover wood. But not for long. He hit on the idea of burning it to form charcoal, which was then ground into a powder. With the aid of a starch binder, the mix was compressed into the familiar pillow-shaped briquettes in a manufacturing plant designed by Ford's pal Thomas Edison. Cooks pounced on the briquettes. At last they were able to have a reliable source of heat to light their "camp fires" and a steady supply of good Grade A, government-inspected red meat to feed to their families.

The home barbecue grill soared in popularity after the Second World War, when GIs used their benefits to buy the low-cost homes, with backyards, that sprang up like mushrooms on the edges of towns, beyond walking distance to the store. The need to drive to market spawned the demand for bigger stores where Mom could shop once a week for food in economy-sized packages, buy meats in quantity, and find a large freezer to take home and put everything in. Naturally enough, Dad took on the role of cave man, tending the grill.

Men have traditionally viewed red meat as having more charisma than vegetables. They like to swagger about the yard with a beer and a spear. The gene that tells all men they are warriors and therefore must bring home the bacon renews itself with each generation. Hurrah!

MANLY CHORES

William Geist

I'm a man. Men cook outside. Women make the three-bean salad. That's the way it is and always has been, since the first settlers of Levittown. That outdoor grilling is a manly pursuit has long been beyond question. If this wasn't firmly understood, you'd never get grown men to put on those aprons with pictures of dancing wienies and things on the front, and messages like "Come N' Get It." Some men wear little chef's hats, too, accessorized with big padded barbecue gloves. They wear them willingly without a whimper. Try putting that stuff on the family dog.

Excerpted from The New York Times Magazine

cent ashy gray in daylight, glowing red at night — this usually takes from 30 to 40 minutes after it is lit. The rule of thumb is that it always takes longer than you expected.

When using dry aromatic woods, such as mesquite, hickory, alder, fruitwoods, or grapevine cuttings, or when using herb packages, soak them in cold water for 30 minutes before putting them on the hot charcoal. This stops them from burning away before their flavor reaches the food.

To light the briquettes, stack them into a pyramid to allow the air to circulate. Use lighter fluid, an electric coil starter, or compressed lighter cubes. You can also use a cylindrical chimney starter by lighting crumpled newspaper in its base and piling the briquettes on top of the paper.

Instant-lighting briquettes are presoaked with lighter fluid. Spread them in a single layer under the cooking grid and light the edges with a match. They light faster than regular briquettes, so don't add lighter fluid.

It is easier to clean the grill while it's still hot. And it is wise to clean it thoroughly from time to time, even though this is definitely the down side of the whole business.

Choosing the Right Barbecue Equipment

Kettles and Covered Cookers

These deep, round-bottomed grills are the most popular and versatile barbecues on the market.

Water Smokers

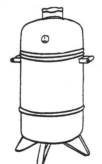

A water smoker is a tall, cylindrical, covered cooker

with a fire pan for the coals, a water pan, one or two grids, and a dome-shaped cover. The food cooks very slowly in a dense cloud of smoke and steam, and becomes wonderfully moist and tender.

Portables or Tabletops

These range from simple hibachis to small versions of covered cookers. They are great for campsite or beach cookouts, tailgate parties, and picnics.

Braziers

These are shallow grills with optional hoods, good for quick grilling.

Gas Grills

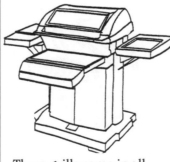

These grills come in all shapes, sizes, and price ranges. They can be used as open braziers for grilling, or as covered kettles for roasting.

Fire Away!

To provide charcoal for the fire, pour briquettes into the base of the grill widely enough to extend in a single layer approximately two inches beyond the surface area that the food will cover.

To judge the temperature of the burning charcoal, hold the palm of your hand over the fire at the height where the food will be cooked. If you can keep it there and recite only "One Mississippi, two Mississippi," the temperature is high. At three seconds it will be medium-high; at four seconds, medium; and at five seconds, low. The temperature can be adjusted by raising or lowering the cooking grid, and by spreading out the charcoal.

The charcoal is ready for cooking when it's 80 per-

Barbecue Industry Association
710 East Ogden Avenue, Suite 113
Naperville, IL 60563
708-369-2404

800-446-1071
Weber-Stephens Products Company
7:00 a.m. - 6:00 p.m. CST

Barbecue Tips

PREPARING

Minimize sticky-food buildup by spritzing the grid surface before grilling with nonstick cooking spray, or wiping it with vegetable oil. Marinate low-fat foods such as chicken, turkey, fish, and vegetables for a few minutes before cooking to prevent them from sticking to the grill.

For health reasons, never return cooked meat or poultry to the plate it was sitting on when it was raw. If the uncooked juices were contaminated, they will be absorbed into the cooked meat.

GRILLING

Beef and Hamburgers
Select tender cuts such as sirloin, T-bone, fillet, or rib steaks.

Marinate flank steaks before cooking to tenderize them. Trim the excess fat and cut small nicks in any fat around the edges of thin steaks to prevent them from curling. Turn steaks with flat-bladed tongs or a spatula to prevent the juices from escaping.

To see if the meat is ready to turn, make a small cut near the bone. Bright droplets of blood will appear if it is still rare. Turn it once only. The blood will rise to the surface when the second side is cooked. Press it with your thumb. The harder the meat and the greater the resistance, the more "done" it will be.

Assuming that the coals are ready, a 1-inch steak is rare when cooked 5 to 6 minutes on each side. In 10 to 12 minutes on each side it will be well done.

For rare hamburgers, grill 3 to 4 minutes on each side; medium takes 5 to 6 minutes, and well done will require 7 to 10 minutes.

Use a meat thermometer to ensure that hamburgers have an internal temperature of 155 degrees F., for safety.

Add salt *after* cooking, not *during* cooking. Salting during cooking will bring the juices to the surface. You want the juices to stay evenly distributed to flavor the meat.

Lamb
Lamb chops, ribs, and other cuts are cooked in the same way as beef. A whole butterflied leg of lamb, prepared by the butcher without a bone, will lie more or less flat on the grill, providing a feast of varying "doneness" as the peaks and valleys cook in a range from pink to perfection. It is rare and ready when it reaches an internal temperature of 160 to 170 degrees F.

Pork
Spare ribs can be cut into individual pieces, or a whole rib may be impaled on a wooden skewer — threaded through the meaty parts — enabling the cook to turn the whole thing at one time. Brush frequently with sauce.

Poultry
Cook poultry over medium to low heat and turn it frequently until the juices are no longer tinged with pink. There are few things less palatable than undercooked chicken, turkey, or duck. Use a meat thermometer to be sure the internal temperature at the thickest part reaches 190 degrees F.

Fish
The best way to cook fish is in an oiled hinged basket, so that it can be turned easily. Don't prod it with a fork, or the juices will escape, and don't overcook it or it will be dry and tasteless. When the flesh is opaque, not pink or translucent, it is done. The experts tell us the best way to time the cooking is to measure the fish at its widest part. If it is 1 inch thick, cook it for 10 minutes; add time if it is thicker.

To tell if fish is ready to eat, slide a spatula beneath it and lift it up an inch or two. If the fish feels heavy, leave it a little longer. If it is fully cooked, it will tend to flake away.

Vegetables
Soft and juicy vegetables are easily cooked in an oiled hinged basket, so they can be turned easily. This method is good for tomatoes, eggplant, zucchini, and mushrooms.

To cook fresh corn, pull back the husks, remove the silk, put the husks back in place, and tie them with butcher twine. Soak the corn in ice water for 15 minutes. Squeeze out the water and grill the corn over medium heat, turning two or three times.

To cook potatoes, coat them in barbecue sauce and roast them wrapped in foil for 45 minutes to an hour.

Parboil carrots, sweet potatoes, and other root vegetables before finishing them on the grill so that they will cook relatively quickly.

Seven Little Details That Make All the Difference

Your barbecue guests' pleasure will be greatly enhanced if

1. They are not required to wait more than an hour to eat

2. The food is not totally burned at the edges and raw in the middle

3. The temperature of the air outdoors doesn't fall below 75 or rise above 85 degrees F.

4. There are tolerably few mosquitoes

5. There are relatively few children whose bedtimes have long since passed

6. There are places for all the guests to sit and sufficient light for them to see what they are eating

7. There is enough to drink and enough ice to put in the drinks

Health Hazards

Fears that outdoor barbecues may be hazardous to your health stem from studies that link meats grilled over charcoal with cancer in laboratory animals. Grilling produces heterocyclic aromatic amines (HAAs) during prolonged high-heat cooking. These "mutagens" may damage DNA and result in genetic mutations down the road.

The National Cancer Institute is concerned about any meat — beef, pork, lamb, or chicken — that is cooked at temperatures above 212 degrees F. (Most barbecues cook at 350 degrees or even higher.) An equal concern is that foods should be no more than four to five inches from the heat source.

It should, however, be noted that there are carcinogens in everything we eat, from peanut butter to raw mushrooms, that nitrites occur naturally in some vegetables, and that at least seven people are struck by lightning every year.

Books

Barbecuing and Sausage-Making Secrets
Charlie and Ruthie Knote; Pig-Out Publications, 1993; $14.95

Grill It Right!
Better Homes & Gardens editors; Meredith Press, 1993; $19.95

The Art of Grilling
Kelly McCune; Harper Perennial, 1990; $17.00

The Backyard Barbecue and Grill Book
Carolyn Wells; Pig-Out Publications, 1992; $12.95

The Grilling Encyclopedia; An A-to-Z Compendium of How to Grill Almost Anything
A. Cort Sinnes; Atlantic Monthly Press, 1992; $24.95

The Joy of Grilling
Joe Famularo; Barron's, 1988; $22.95/$12.95
Morrow, 1990; $24.95

BASS

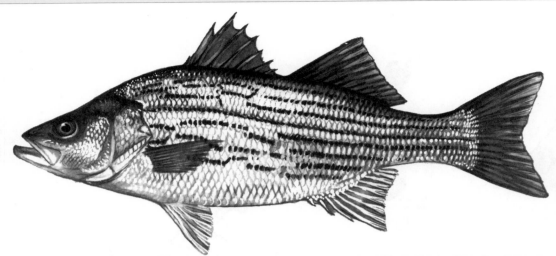

The "striper" is the most highly esteemed of American bass.

— Alan Davidson
European food connoisseur

HYBRID BASS GET BACK IN THE SWIM

At the beginning of the 1600s, the Chesapeake Bay teemed with hundreds of varieties of fish. The diary of an early colonist reported a staggering catch of 100 tons of striped bass on a single tide. In those days, some fish weighed up to 70 pounds, but by the 20th century the stripers were considerably smaller, and frighteningly fewer.

In fact, by the early 1980s, they nearly disappeared altogether. The bass were reported to be contaminated with PCBs and the polluted Chesapeake fishing grounds were closed. Intense conservation efforts were needed to protect striped bass from becoming an endangered species.

Rescue came from an unexpected source. Stripers, like salmon, live in the sea but return to freshwater rivers to spawn. In the 1940s, construction of a South Carolina dam had interrupted bass on their migratory route, trapping them upriver — where they remained and bred successfully, thriving in a totally freshwater environment. White bass, a related freshwater species, interbred with the striper population — and natural hybridization was the result.

Realizing that this new cross had possibilities both for game fishing and for farming for food, the hatcheries took over and within decades rivers, lakes, and reservoirs in every state but Alaska were being restocked with farmed hybrid bass fingerlings. Bass anglers (28 million American fishermen admit to a passion for bass) were delighted, and by the late 1980s, the hybrid bass were also being farmed in steadily increasing quantities. The anticipated supply this year is close to 5 million pounds.

Nutritionally, bass flesh is an excellent source of vitamin B-12 and also contributes vitamin B-6 and iron. In addition, it provides heart-healthy omega-3 fatty acids, and is low in fat and cholesterol.

Today, most of the bass eaten in America are hybrids. They are sold at around a year old, weighing about 1½ to 2 pounds, just the right size to yield two 6-ounce fillets — an ideal portion — of sweet, firm, white flesh. To assure buyers that these are indeed hybrid striped bass, the processors usually leave the skins on.

Did You Know?

☞ Striped bass are also known familiarly as greenheads, squidhounds, and, in the region of the Chesapeake Bay, as rockfish.

☞ Cooks prefer small striped bass to large because their flesh is more tender and succulent.

☞ You can tell the difference between wild and hybrid striped bass by the stripe along the back; in a wild fish it runs straight and unbroken, in the farmed fish it is fragmented and irregular.

The Rise of Hybrid Striped Bass

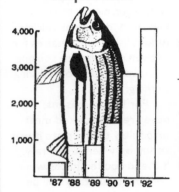

Source: Striped Bass Growers Association

U.S. harvests of farm-raised striped bass in thousands of pounds.

BATS

BATS HAVE A ROLE IN THE FOOD CHAIN, TOO

When Merlin Tuttle, the founder and director of Bat Conservation International, appeared on Charlie Rose's late-night interview show on PBS, viewers learned both how misunderstood and how essential bats are.

There are 1,000 kinds of bats, the only mammals that can fly. Bats perform almost entirely beneficial and largely unseen functions, such as protecting crops from insects, dispersing seeds, and pollinating key food plants. Seventy percent of the world's most important economic tropical fruits — among them, avocados, mangoes, dates, figs, and breadfruit — depend upon bats for pollination or dispersal.

Rose: There are 40-some species in the United States,  right? And these incredibly valuable insect-eating bats can eat up to 3,000 insects a night?

Tuttle: There are single bat colonies that actually eat up to 250 *tons* of insects in a night — and one bat can catch 500 to 1,000 insects in an hour.

Rose: Wow! I remember reading about people wanting to install bat houses around their property to give them an insect-free environment….

Tuttle: A study done in Indiana shows that for the number of bats you could house in one small bat house, one small part of the insects they could eat in the course of a summer would result in preventing 18 million rootworms from attacking crops.

Rose: Are there any successful efforts by farmers to use bats to control insects?

Tuttle: Tony Cox, an organic farmer in Oregon, has put up all kinds of bird houses in his orchards to control insects that fly by day, and bat houses to control insects that fly by night. He's reduced pesticide spraying from 13 times a season to just one or two. And between the birds and the bats he's getting a marvelous job done.

MORE INFORMATION

Bat Conservation International
P.O. Box 162603
Austin, TX 78716-2603
512-327-9721

BEANS

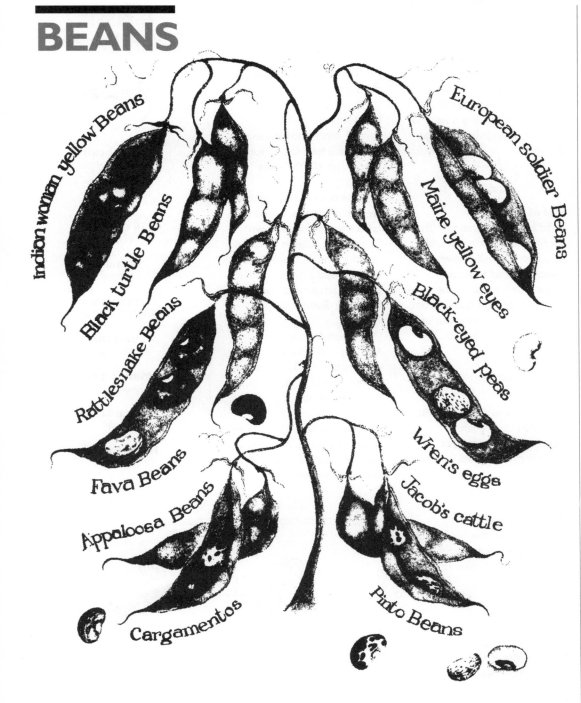

Legumes are truly a culinary treasure.

— **Jimmy Schmidt**
Owner/chef, The Rattlesnake Club, Detroit

BEANS HAVE SOME MAGIC, AFTER ALL

Several studies have found that beans help fight cancer because they carry high concentrations of enzymes that counteract the development of cancer-causing compounds in the intestine. Anne Kennedy, a researcher at the Harvard School of Public Health, reports that laboratory animals fed a diet of beans did not develop colon or breast cancer. More information about this study is available from the American Cancer Society (800-ACS-2345).

Beans are also thought to be beneficial in lowering blood cholesterol and the American Diabetic Association recommends a diet high in beans and other legumes because they help stabilize blood glucose.

LEANING TOWARD LENTILS

Jon Carroll

Current thinking is that the lentil is one of nature's most perfect foods. I remember when milk was one of nature's most perfect foods, but that was a long time ago. Now it is the lentil, the kidney bean, the unmilled husks of ragged cereals; these are the perfect foods.

The lentils do not look perfect in their bag. They look like remnants of a large machine-tooling project. A bag of lentils is tactilely pleasing, however. It feels as though it would be fun to throw.

Perhaps if we promoted lentil-hurling as a sport, we wouldn't have to eat them. That would be just fine with me. A little lentils goes a long way. No lentils at all go even farther.

Here's what I want to know: Why are the least appealing foods inevitably the healthiest? Why don't humans crave foodstuffs that interact optimally with their digestive systems and brain chemicals? Is there no gain without pain?

That would suggest that the universe is a stern, puritanical place after all, as rigid as a Cotton Mather and twice as nasty. Pleasure kills, from one end of the galaxy to the other. Become one with the cosmos: Suffer.

What if God really is the Jehovah of the Old Testament? Bum-mer.

But for instance: In many parts of the world they eat lots o' lentils. They have lots o' lentils, and not much else. Some of these lentil-eaters come to this country. Do they stick with the comforting, soothing lentils of childhood?

Nope. They eat ice cream and Snickers bars and french fries and pizza. Doesn't matter what they were raised on: Offered the entire cornucopia of international foodstuffs, most people will opt for salt, sugar, and grease. The body craves what seeks to injure it.

Naturally, the government is on the side of the lentil. The Agriculture Department has thrown out the old Food Wheel and replaced it with an "Eating Right Pyramid." Why you'd want to eat a right pyramid I'll never know.

In the Eating Right Pyramid, lentils are at the big end. Fats and oils are at the pointy end. Ice cream is near the point; rutabagas are near the broad part. This is indeed the government we have come to know and love.

But notice: I carefully wrote that last paragraph so that you'd see what the government was driving at, conceptually speaking. In a more normal formation, we'd say that ice cream was toward the top and lentils were toward the bottom. Ice cream above lentils; the world as it should be.

I can only conclude that the Agriculture Department was suffering from heavy graphic ambivalence. It was trying to say the right thing, but its choice of metaphors gave the game away. Generations of schoolchildren will see candy at the pinnacle of the Food Pyramid and say: Knew it all along.

Excerpted from "Lentilmania: Food Chain of Fools," *San Francisco Chronicle*

The Government's Response

Because leguminous lentils are a vegetable, they do not supply all the essential amino acids (building blocks of protein) in the ideal amounts necessary to make them a complete protein. To make their protein complete, just add grains, nuts, seeds or a small amount of meat, fish, poultry, eggs, or dairy products. (Not a word about ice cream.)

HILLS AND HILLS OF BEANS

One of the world's most productive areas for growing dry peas, lentils, and chick-peas is the hilly region of the Pacific Northwest known as the Palouse, where the states of Idaho, Oregon, and Washington come together. The volcanic soil of the Palouse is fertile, the sun gentle, and the spring moisture generous, hence its name, which means "green lawn" in French. As a result, the area produces about 500 million pounds of dry peas and lentils annually, 75 percent of which are exported to 90 countries around the globe.

In addition to putting cash into the farmers' pockets, the nitrogen-fixing legumes also return a bounty to the land, when they are plowed into it in the form of "green manure." Planted in rotation with wheat and barley, they replenish the soil between plantings and need almost no fertilizer.

Bean Talk

Spilling the Beans
This phrase originated with the gypsies, whose fortune-tellers used to predict the future from the way a handful of beans was spilled on a flat surface.

Full of Beans
Used to mean bursting with energy, this phrase probably refers to the well-known gaseous sequel to eating beans; more prosaic inter-preters suggest it comes from beans' habit of popping out of their skins when boiled.

Just Beans
Another phrase equated with emissions from beans — meaning that the subject, whatever it is, is best ignored.

Bean Counter
A reference to the time when gold used to be balanced on a scale with beans used as a counterweight.

I Don't Have a Bean in My Pocket
This used to mean that a person was penniless because beans have always been one of the few foods available to poor folk. Beans still retail for barely 80 cents a pound, but they have become the chic, as well as cheap, alternative to meat.

☞ There are more than 70 different varieties of legumes.

☞ Beans are an important part of every known cuisine. They have been eaten for more than 10,000 years.

☞ The original bean eaters were the Pilgrims in Boston (also known as Beantown). Their strict religion forbade cooking on the Sabbath. So they devised a bean pot that baked overnight and was ready to eat for Sunday supper.

☞ Robert Burton's *The Anatomy of Melancholy*, published in 1621, proposed 64 remedies for gas produced by eating beans.

☞ The average American eats about 15 pounds of beans a year, and consumption is increasing steadily.

Bean Positive
Beans are cholesterol-free and high in vitamins, minerals, and soluble fiber. A cup of cooked kidney beans supplies 219 calories, 16 grams of protein, and 0.9 grams of fat.

Classic Bean Dishes

Baked beans
(Boston)

Cassoulet
(France)

Chili con carne
(Texas)

Feijoada
(Brazil)

Hoppin' John
(Southern United States)

Hummus
(Middle East)

Minestrone
(Italy)

Pasta e fagioli
(Italy)

Refried beans
(Mexico)

Three-bean salad
(United States)

Holy Cow

Fee, fie, foh, fum. When Jack traded the family cow for the handful of beans that grew into the Beanstalk, he ended up with the Goose that Laid the Golden Egg.

The moral: He who eats low on the Food Pyramid eventually ends up on top of the heap.

10 BEANS & THEIR FLATULENCE LEVELS

Here is a list of beans in order of their flatulence production, from most to least. The compiler of the list, Dr. Louis B. Rockland of the USDA's Western Regional Research Laboratory in Berkeley, California, cautions that "the state of the art is not very advanced," so these preliminary findings might prove to be a lot of hot air.

Soybeans
Pea beans
Black beans
Pinto beans
California small white beans
Great Northern beans
Lima beans (baby)
Garbanzos (chick-peas)
Lima beans (large)
Black-eyed peas

Although not technically beans, garbanzos and black-eyed peas were included in the tests because they are also gas producers and are often categorized as beans. The researchers (who did not reveal their methodology for tabulating their measurements) did offer the advice that cooking soybeans with an equal portion of rice eliminates two-thirds of their flatulence production, as well as increasing their content of usable protein.

Further investigation yields the following wisdom from Corby Kummer, writing in *The Atlantic Monthly*: "Why beans cause gas is fairly straightforward, yet even people who devote a great deal of time to researching how beans are metabolized seem a bit self-conscious discussing it. (Scientists I talked to often began by reciting the rhyme beginning 'Beans, beans, the musical fruit' or by chuckling over the memory of the campfire scene in *Blazing Saddles*.)

"As beans dry, they store complex sugars called oligosaccharides. Normal digestive enzymes are unable to break down these chains of sugar, so they pass whole into the lower intestine, where friendly bacteria, to which we play host, eat the sugars and ferment them. This process is similar to the fermenting of other sugars, and a natural by-product is gas."

BEANO
to the rescue

Fear of flatulence can be alleviated by adding about five drops of Beano to cooked beans, broccoli, and whole-grain cereals. Beano is a natural food enzyme that helps digestion and averts the socially unacceptable consequences of eating gas-producing foods.

I have no truck with lettuce, cabbage, and similar chlorophyll. Any dietitian will tell you that a running foot of apple strudel contains four times the vitamins of a bushel of beans.

— S. J. Perelman
American humorist

Legumes

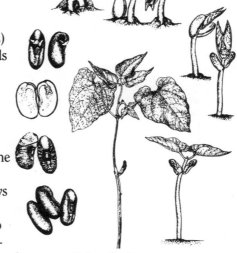

Legumes (also known as pulses) are the mature seeds that grow inside pods. We call these seeds peas, beans, and lentils. We also call some of these peas beans, and some of the beans peas, but lentils are always called lentils. The garbanzo bean (also known as the chickpea) is both a bean and a pea, so it is called a legume. There will not be a quiz on this.

Senate Bean Soup

Serves 6

1 ¹/₂ cups Great Northern beans
2 quarts water
1 meaty ham bone or smoked ham hock (about 1 pound)
1 medium-sized potato, peeled and diced
1 onion, chopped
3 cloves garlic, finely chopped
¹/₂ cup chopped celery
Salt and pepper
Chopped parsley for garnish

Soak the beans if necessary, and drain them. Cover with cold water. Bring to a boil and boil, uncovered, for 2 minutes. Skim off any foam that rises to the surface. Cover and let stand for 1 hour.

Drain the beans and put them in a large pot. Add 2 quarts of water and the ham bone. Cover and simmer for 2 hours. Add the potato, onion, garlic, and celery and simmer for 1 hour. Remove the ham bone and cut up the meat. Set aside.

Remove 1 cup of the beans and some of the liquid and puree in a blender. Return the pureed beans and the ham meat to the soup. Season with salt and pepper. Heat until piping hot and serve, garnished with chopped parsley.

Soaking Beans

Not all dry legumes require a period of soaking, but a great many do. Directions are always given on the package; the important thing is to discard the soaking water and cook the beans in fresh water.

Overnight Soak

Put the beans in a bowl and cover with cold water to a depth of 2 inches above the beans. Cover and set aside to soak for at least 12 hours or overnight. Drain the beans and proceed with the recipe.

Fast Soak

Put the beans in a saucepan, cover with cold water to a depth of 2 inches above the beans, and bring to a boil. Boil for 2 minutes. Remove from the heat, cover, and let stand for 1 hour. Drain the beans and proceed with the recipe.

Microwave Soak

Mix 2 cups of beans with 2 cups water in a microwave-safe bowl. Cover and microwave on High (100 percent power) for 15 minutes. Let stand for 5 minutes. Add 2 more cups cold water. Cover and let stand for 1 hour. Drain the beans and proceed with the recipe.

Pressure Cooker Soak

Put the beans in a bowl, cover with at least 2 inches of cold water, and set aside to soak for at least 4 hours. Following the manufacturer's instructions, cook in a pressure cooker for 30 minutes.

MORE INFORMATION

American Dry Bean Board
115 Railway Plaza
Scottsbluff, NE 69361
308-632-1258

American Soybean Association
540 Maryville Center Drive
St. Louis, MO 63141
314-576-1770

California Dried Bean Advisory Board
531-D North Alta Avenue
Dinuba, CA 93618
209-591-4866

Idaho Bean Commission
P.O. Box 9433
Boise, ID 83707
208-334-3520

Michigan Bean Commission
1031 South U.S. 27
St. Johns, MI 48879
517-224-1361

National Dry Bean Council
1200 19th Street NW, Suite 300
Washington, DC 20036
202-857-1169

MAIL ORDER SOURCES

Kennebec Bean Company
P.O. Box 219
North Vassalboro, ME 04962
207-873-3473

Nilsdotter
P.O. Box 220
Orono, ME 04473
207-866-4110

Books

The Bean Cookbook
Judith Choate; Simon & Schuster, 1992; $20.00

Boutique Bean Pot
Kathleen Mayes and Sandra Gottfried; Woodbridge, 1992; $14.00

The Brilliant Bean
Sally and Martin Stone; Bantam, 1988; $14.00

The Versatile Grain and the Elegant Bean
Sheryl London and Mel London; Simon & Schuster, 1992; $27.50

BEEF

MAKING THE GRADE

All meat is graded by the U.S. Department of Agriculture (USDA) based on three factors: conformation (the proportion of meat to bone), finish (the proportion of fat to lean meat), and overall quality. There are eight grades: prime, choice, select, standard, commercial, utility, cutter, and canner.

Most prime meat is sold to the nation's finest restaurants. Choice, select, and standard grades, identified with the familiar purple vegetable-dye stamp, are available in butcher shops and supermarkets. The lesser grades wind up in hot dogs and in cooked and canned meat products, such as chili.

In the prime grade, the most tender meat is baby beef, from cattle 7 to 10 months old. The best-flavored beef comes from females 18 to 24 months old that have borne one or more calves.

Books

Beyond Beef:
The Rise and Fall of
the Cattle Culture
Jeremy Rifkin; Dutton, 1992;
$21.00

James McNair's Beef
Cookbook
James McNair; Chronicle
Books, 1989; $11.95

Light Ways with Beef,
Lamb, and Pork
Sunset Editors; Sunset, 1991;
$8.95

Williams-Sonoma Kitchen
Library: Beef
Joyce Goldstein; Time-Life
Books, 1993; $14.95

Woman's Day Beef,
Veal, and Lamb
Woman's Day Editors;
Meredith Books, 1991; $12.95

HOTLINES

800-535-4555
USDA Meat and Poultry
Hotline
10:00 a.m. - 4:00 p.m. EST

IT'S NO BULL

For a very long time Americans put beef on a pedestal along with the flag and the Constitution — a meal without beef on the table was no more than a snack. However, the country's favorite meat has been under attack in recent years as potentially dangerous to health, and its critics are reaching a large audience.

Reports of beef's potential dangers have changed habits of a lifetime. We still like our steaks and roasts but we've found our way to a wider, more diverse array of foods in which meat still figures but is no longer prime. There's been a real change in attitude and emphasis. Where we once ate meat and potatoes, we now eat potatoes and meat.

Cutting out beef.

Beef is the most dangerous food in herbicide contamination and represents about 11 percent of the total cancer risk to consumers from all foods on the market today. Each year hundreds of thousands of Americans die from heart attacks, cancers, and strokes caused in part by their addiction to grain-fed beef.

— Jeremy Rifkin,
Activist

Is Beef Getting a Raw Deal?

Meat is the most tested and inspected food we buy at the supermarket. The USDA devotes eight times as many resources to the inspection of meat and poultry as the Food and Drug Administration expends for the rest of the entire food supply. In round numbers, it costs the federal government more than $1 million a day to employ the 7,000 meat and poultry inspectors of the USDA, who are physically present in every packing plant during every minute of operation. By comparison, FDA-inspected food plants may receive a visit from an inspector less than once a year.

The beef industry acknowledges that meat (and other foods) will never be completely free of bacteria; indeed, scientists agree that it would not be beneficial to our health to strive for a completely sterile food supply. Quite apart from the enormous increase in cost that would be involved, sterile food would lower our resistance to infection and would be detrimental to our immune system. Notwithstanding some claims of chemical pollution of cattle, there is no evidence that conventionally raised beef is any less safe than "organically" produced beef. Extensive testing has proved that the drug and chemical residues in beef are virtually nil.

Mustard's no good without roast beef.

— Chico Marx
Monkey Business

Forecast

You may not have heard about the Great Cattle Reef Project. In brief, it's a scheme in which cattle are being taught to breathe underwater as a first step in teaching them how to swim. The idea is that if cows were more like fish, we'd eat a lot more of them. What's more, all that high-fat milk that nobody wants anymore would be turned into fatty fish oil, which everybody's crazy about. And thus it is that beef will go with the flow.

(Just kidding.)

Safety Q&A

Q Why don't we ban the use of all hormones in beef production?

A Mainly, it's a question of cost. Without hormones, the price of beef would go up by 20 to 30 cents a pound. When steers and heifers are implanted with growth hormones, they gain weight significantly faster and convert a larger quantity of body mass to beef more efficiently than untreated animals. This results in a reduction in the cost of raising cattle by $50 to $80 per steer. Hormones have been used in cattle ranching for more than 30 years; 90 percent of cattle raised in the United States receive a "growth promotant" at some time during their development. The implant, about the size of a pencil eraser, is placed beneath the skin on the back side of the animal's ear.

Q But isn't it dangerous to introduce hormones like estrogen into the food chain?

A No. Consider that the estrogen level in a 3-ounce serving of beef — think of it as about the size of a pack of playing cards — is about 1.85 nanograms. A nanogram is one *billionth* of a gram, which is analogous to one blade of grass in a football field. The level of estrogen in a nonimplanted steer is 1.3 grams. By comparison, a nonpregnant woman produces 480,000 nanograms of estrogen a day, while a pregnant woman produces 20 million! So you can see that the overall hormonal effect of eating a steak is statistically inconsequential.

MAIL ORDER SOURCES

Brae Beef
P.O. Box 1561
Greenwich, CT 06830
203-869-0106

Great Plains Meats Company
836 Mobile Court
Naperville, IL 60540
708-983-8827

Omaha Steaks International
P.O. Box 3300

Omaha, NE 68103
800-228-9055

Whippoorwill Farms
P.O. Box 717
Lakeville, CT 06039
203-435-9657

PERIODICALS
For address, see Information Sources

The Beef Brief
National Cattlemen's Association
303-694-0305
Weekly; free

Moo-Off
in the Big Apple

*I*n a bizarre product promotion, the folks at Fleischmann decided to celebrate their Move Over Butter spread by staging a sounds-like-moo-cow competition. Would-be contestants were urged to call a special telephone number and moo their hearts out. Finalists among these bovine balladeers were brought to Carnegie Hall in New York City for a glittering moo-off. The winning mooer received a free trip to — where else? — Maui. But in the course of the competition many callers dialed the letter O instead of the zero in the special phone number, and mooed incorrectly into the answering machine of a man in Atlanta . . . who wasn't exactly jumping over the moon.

The "Bad Fat" Thing

Our ancestors recognized that beef was a powerful source of fuel. It is a *nutrient-dense* food. The protein in beef is nutritionally complete and it is the major source of five of the B-complex vitamins and essential minerals, including iron and zinc. On a cattle drive, no cowboy would have been without at least some beef jerky in his saddlebags, and home on the range more than likely meant a big, juicy steak every night. Men who were in the saddle from dawn to after dark under grueling conditions needed all the refueling they could get; for today's largely inactive American life-style smaller portions a few times a week are more appropriate.

But beef also contains saturated fat. An article in the *New England Journal of Medicine* reports on a study of 89,000 women that showed a diet high in saturated fat as increasing the risk of colon cancer — and implicating the saturated fat in beef and other red meats. Few nutritionists advocate banning beef altogether, but they do urge moderation. However, there is a growing trend to cut down on the consumption of fat from all sources, especially meats, and the meat producers have got the message. Cattle, too, are on a diet that produces a steak much less marbled than that of old — maybe almost as lean, in fact, as the meat from the steers that trudged the Chisholm Trail.

MORE INFORMATION

American National Cattlewomen
P.O. Box 3881
Englewood, CO 80155
303-694-0313

National Cattlemen's Association
5420 South Quebec Street
Englewood, CO 80111
303-694-0305

National Live Stock & Meat Board
Beef Industry Council
444 North Michigan Avenue
Chicago, IL 60611
312-467-5520

The Beef Board
P.O. Box 3316
Englewood, CO 80155
303-220-9890

BEETS

The beet is the most intense of vegetables. The radish, admittedly, is more feverish, but the fire of the radish is a cold fire, the fire of discontent, not of passion. Tomatoes are lusty enough, yet there runs through tomatoes an undercurrent of frivolity. Beets are deadly serious.

— Tom Robbins
A Cook's Book of Quotations

THE BEET IS NOT REALLY A DEAD HORSE

It is not surprising that Harvard College, an institution with a pronounced affection for the color crimson, should have invented Harvard beets — although their color is closer to magenta than crimson. But I wouldn't say the dish is popular outside alumni circles. A much better bet is cold borscht with a nice hot potato nestled in the bowl and a dollop of sour cream to muddle into the soup. Pickled beets are a puzzle, though. You see them on every salad bar, but you never see anyone actually *eating* them.

Eastern Europeans seem to have got the hang of cooking beets and profess to like them, but that's probably because they are cheap. At some of the poshest European spas, however, too-well-nourished patrons are given regular doses of fresh beet juice, which holds out the promise of weight reduction. Out in the country they grow a big orange-colored beet known as the mangel-wurzel, which tastes just as horrible as it sounds. The natives eat it, but only if there is no alternative.

There may be more to beets, though, than meets the eye or gets under the fingernails. An article in an old, old *Harper's Bazaar* says they are good for tightening up that sagging skin and those bulbous bags under the eyes. The explanation has to do with the beets' content of manganese, a trace mineral said to produce collagen, which tightens

everything up nicely, enabling *Bazaar* readers to slip into the kind of slinky gown Cinderella might have dreamed of.

For a while the National Cancer Institute took an interest in the theory that betaine, an alkaloid contained in beets, has a useful role as an anticarcinogen, but the beet's lack of charisma was rather a turnoff. Besides, it does turn urine red, a condition known as beeturia, which can be startling, but is perfectly harmless.

In fact, beets are high in folate, which is said to help prevent fatigue and depression, and are a nice source of fiber. Beet lovers suggest cooking them in the microwave, where 15 minutes on High will zap a pound of unpeeled medium-sized beets and ¼ cup of water into a splendid side dish while you are busy elsewhere.

In fact, there has been a flurry of enthusiasm for beets among the more forward-thinking American chefs, who hit upon the idea of cooking up beet-tinged risotto, beet-flavored couscous, beet soup with tofu dumplings, even lobster with beet sauce.

Florence Fabricant, the indefatigable restaurant critic, had a red-letter day when she stumbled on one of the oddest of beet bonanzas: beet sorbet served in a hollowed-out cooked beet. "The presentation was stunning," she commented, "and the sorbet mildly sweet, mellow, and intriguing." She went on to suggest that a splash of vodka on top would have provided just the right sharpening touch.

To my mind, a splash of vodka can be counted on to sharpen the wits in many a dismal situation, and I fervently hope Craig Claiborne and Pierre Franey had plenty of it on hand when they baked their pie with pureed beets, a little corn syrup, eggs, raisins, and nuts. Nuts indeed!

BETA CAROTENE

WHAT IS THIS THING CALLED BETA CAROTENE?

Do you remember the old wives' tale about eating carrots so you could see in the dark? Lately researchers have come to think that those old wives knew something after all. Carrots contain beta carotene, the nutrient that gives them (and pumpkin and sweet potatoes, among other fruits and vegetables) their orange color, and scientists have recently recognized that it's beta carotene that prevents the lens of the eye from becoming cloudy, a condition that can lead to cataracts. Researchers at the Tufts University Center on Aging have found that people with cataracts are five times more likely than others to have low levels of carotenoids (a family of some 500 nutrients to which beta carotene belongs).

Moreover, it's now believed that beta carotene plays a crucial role in slowing progressive heart disease, which is the leading cause of death in the United States today, responsible for more than half a million deaths every year. In 1990, evidence was presented at the annual meeting of the American Heart Association indicating that men who took 50-

milligram supplements of beta carotene every other day halved their risk of developing heart attacks or stroke, and of dying from cardiovascular disease. The test, involving 333 men, was part of a larger study of 22,000 male doctors, dentists, and other medical practitioners. (The study was restricted to men because, statistically, they appear more likely to suffer these calamities than women are. This is because historically they have been studied more and are likely to receive better care when complaining of certain ailments. However, a women's study is now under way.)

Beta carotene is now also thought to ward off melanoma, a deadly form of skin cancer, and it is known to prevent the debilitation of epithelial tissues that can result in cancer of the mouth, esophagus, lung, stomach, gastrointestinal tract, breast, and bladder. One thing is common to all those who suffer these diseases: They don't eat enough fruits and vegetables. This was proved in a study, endorsed by the National Cancer Institute, which found that women who eat at least five servings a day of beta carotene-rich fruits and vegetables improve their chances of avoiding breast and other cancers.

When we eat foods that are rich in beta carotene, the body converts part of this natural pigment into vitamin A. But beta carotene is not the same thing as vitamin A, although they are related. The body can quickly rid itself of excess beta carotene; too much vitamin A, on the other hand, can be toxic.

A real understanding of beta carotene's importance in the diet requires a little knowledge of carotenoids, antioxidants, and free radicals.

How Much Is Enough?

Dr. Paul Lechance of Rutgers University says we should be eating about four times as much beta carotene as we currently do. Just adding two rich sources of beta carotene to our daily diet is enough to keep us healthy, he says. This translates into one large carrot or one medium-sized sweet potato per day. Not many of us manage even this much; the Food Intake Survey of the U.S. Department of Agriculture shows that the average American diet contains only about a quarter to a third of this amount.

Though there is no specific recommended daily requirement for beta carotene, it seems you cannot harm yourself by eating as many beta carotene-rich foods as you want, because the body is able to get rid of any excess. But when you take large amounts of beta carotene in the form of supplements, it can interrupt the body's natural absorption of vitamins.

Nevertheless, the pharmaceutical companies are gearing up for a major new demand on supplies, and Hoffman LaRoche, the leading supplier of beta carotene, estimates that its plant in Freeport, Texas, will produce 350 metric tons a year. This looks like a mighty heap of beta carotene. Maybe this company knows something that we have only begun to glimpse.

Q&A

Q What are carotenoids?

A Carotenoids are nutrients found in certain foods. Beta carotene is among some 500 of these compounds. Carotenoids have strong antioxidant properties and are effective against a wide range of diseases. They play a role in safeguarding the health of the immune system and in fighting off damage caused by free radicals.

Q What is an antioxidant?

A There is a chemical reaction in nature known as oxidation. Oxidation is what makes a bike rust when it's left out in the rain. A somewhat similar effect takes place in the cells of the body, and antioxidants, such as beta carotene, vitamins C and E, and the mineral selenium, slow the rate of this destructive process.

Antioxidants prevent the bad kind of cholesterol (LDL) from combining with oxygen. When LDL is not oxidized, the particles are less likely to settle on artery walls and cause blockages that lead to stroke or heart disease.

To visualize how this works, imagine a crowd of passengers getting off a train and being funneled toward a narrow gate. The wider the gate, the faster the passengers can flow through. The narrower it is, the more their flow will be impeded. In the same way, the narrower the artery, the slower will be the rate of the blood flow and the greater the chance that a blood clot will form.

Q What are free radicals?

A These are chemically unstable, naturally occurring oxygen molecules that can damage inner and outer cell walls and are thought to be an important factor in the development of cancer.

The body normally creates a certain number of free radicals as a result of specific metabolic processes. Their production is greatly increased among smokers and people who consume high fat diets, or are exposed to chemical carcinogens, X rays, and too much sunlight. Cholesterol, for example, does the most damage to the arteries when it is oxidized or damaged by free radicals.

If beta carotene can prevent the oxidation of cholesterol, it may minimize this damage. In fact, you could think of beta carotene as a hit squad of computer PacMen, scurrying around the screen devouring the free radical villains.

MORE INFORMATION

American Cancer Society
1599 Clifton Road NE
Atlanta, GA 30329
800-ACS-2345

American Heart Association
7272 Greenville Avenue
Dallas, TX 75231-4599
214-706-1220

National Center for Nutrition and Dietetics
American Dietetic Association
216 West Jackson Boulevard
Chicago, IL 60606-6995
312-899-0040

What to Eat

Beta carotene can be found in orange and yellow fruits and vegetables, and in dark-green ones whose orange color is masked by chlorophyll. The richest sources are:

Apricots
Broccoli
Cantaloupe
Carrots
Chard
Collard greens
Grapefruit
Kale
Mangoes
Melons
Papayas
Peaches
Pears
Spinach
Sweet potatoes
Winter squash

BIOTECHNOLOGY

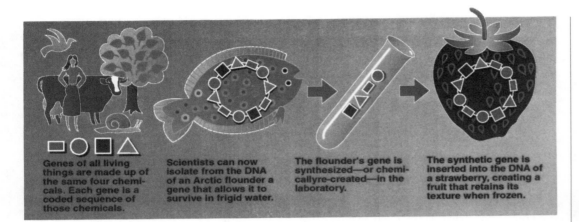

Genes of all living things are made up of the same four chemicals. Each gene is a coded sequence of those chemicals.

Scientists can now isolate from the DNA of an Arctic flounder a gene that allows it to survive in frigid water.

The flounder's gene is synthesized—or chemically-created—in the laboratory.

The synthetic gene is inserted into the DNA of a strawberry, creating a fruit that retains its texture when frozen.

BIOTECHNOLOGY:
A SPLICE OF LIFE

The word *biotechnology* has two parts: *bio*, meaning the life processes of biology, and *technology*, which is a scientific method of achieving a practical purpose.

Biotechnology has literally exploded into our awareness since its beginnings in 1954, when Cambridge University scientists Francis Crick and James B. Watson unraveled the double helix of the DNA molecule. These pioneers opened a new chapter in agriculture for an ancient line of farmers who from the beginnings of tilled soil have struggled to increase the quality and yield of their crops and to nurture the most desirable characteristics of their domesticated animals.

One of the most astonishing facts about biotechnology and gene splicing is that *all genes*, whether they come from animals, plants, or humans, are made up of the same four chemicals, designated with the letters A, G, C, and T for the compounds they represent. These are arranged in combinations ranging from a few to hundreds of thousands, but a gene is always a gene, just as a red rose, or a white or yellow rose, is a rose.

Genes (and water) are present in all living things. There is no such thing as a frog gene, a tomato gene, or a camel gene. There are genes in humans and animals that also exist in plants. For example, a gene that occurs in rice is also present in the human brain. But this wouldn't prevent vegetarians from eating rice, would it? Or would it, if they knew?

Biotechnology works, not by breeding but by splicing. A copy of a gene that has a desired specific attribute is spliced into the DNA of a plant or animal cell, adding the attribute of the gene into that new cell, where it is then replicated in the normal process of cell division. So we don't

really have pieces of animals turning up in vegetables, as some people fear. The nutrients in the plant, whatever their genetic source, are absorbed by the human digestive system, after which the gut breaks down and eliminates the residue.

The purpose of isolating and introducing a *specific* gene with *specific* characteristics into another living organism is to improve a species in a *specific* way, rather than by the haphazard methods used since the beginnings of agriculture. Biotechnology's goal is to use *specific* genes directly.

So far, the process has worked best in simple organisms, such as bacteria. There are "good" kinds of bacteria just as there is a "good" kind of cholesterol. These good bacteria are the kind that gobble up oil spills. Now if only someone would invent bacteria that would gobble up leftovers, that really would be something!

Education is important, but trust will be a decisive factor in consumers' ultimate acceptance of food biotechnology.

— Marion Nestle, Ph.D.
Chairman of the Department of Nutrition, New York University

A MATTER OF
HISTORICAL INEVITABILITY

Biotechnology is going to change the way we live as radically as the Industrial Revolution did. The changes will be eventual and inexorable. By altering the way food is grown, produced, and distributed, biotechnology will improve its taste and enhance its nutritional qualities. Prognosticators foresee plants that are resistant to damage from frost, drought, and hail, and crops that can grow with little water or in salty seawater. New varieties of seeds are being created that will have an advanced tolerance to disease and higher resistance to insects. This will lessen the farmer's dependence on fertilizers and pesticides, which in turn means that fewer chemicals will seep through the soil to contaminate the underground water that flows into our streams, rivers, and lakes — a flow that threatens the ecological balance of nature.

The new agriculture is environmentally friendly, even in hostile climates. Everywhere there will be a reduction of the need for the petrochemicals that are the basis of many fertilizers. Moreover, emerging technologies will enable Third World countries to grow food on what is now infertile soil and to feed many hungry populations, thus altering political landscapes all over the world.

Lack of understanding makes people fear change. About 300 years ago, people were afraid that tomatoes were poisonous. Potatoes, coffee, and, in more recent times, sugar substitutes have been denounced in turn. When microwave ovens were introduced, there were warnings that if you even passed one you risked becoming sterile or losing your hair.

In the short term, the controversy will probably be decided not on the issues but according to which groups of scientists have the best spokesmen. There will be continuing pleas to hold back progress. But, in the end, common sense and good science — backed by millions of dollars in research funds — will prevail.

I think biotechnology is terribly exciting and interesting. Of course, it needs thorough investigation and testing, but if you're never going to venture anything, you're never going to find out anything. If there's a way to improve the taste and quality of our food, we should be very much for it.

— Julia Child

The Loyal Opposition

The biggest food fight since the filming of *Animal House* is heating up over biotechnology. The whole idea of transgenetic transfer shocks certain people profoundly. There are theologians who worry about contamination with taboo foods and regard any "tampering" between species as a desecration. Other people simply find the transfer of genes from one species into another to be morally and ethically repugnant. (Yet no one has ever objected to the use of activated yeast in bread-making.)

It's true that pigs implanted with growth hormone grow 18 percent faster on 15 percent less food — and produce leaner pork; it's also a fact that the animals die sooner than untreated animals. Critics like to point out that after scientists managed to produce chickens without feathers, the chickens became so neurotic about their nudity that they failed to breed and refused to lay any eggs.

The overriding consumer argument against biotechnology involves a question of informed consent. If the food tastes better, costs less, and is more nutritious, people will try it. But many worry about loss of control. We don't want to eat food that has been "improved" without our knowledge. We like to think that food is a subject we know something about, and that no government agency can take away our choices.

Blue Genes

In May of 1992 the Food and Drug Administration issued policy guidelines for evaluating the safety of foods developed through biotechnology. They are the same as those already in use for the evaluation of other foods; thus, decisions will be based on the food itself, not on the processes used to manufacture it.

Companies are encouraged to consult with the FDA on issues related to nutrient content, the presence of possible allergens, naturally occurring toxicants, impact on the environment, and any other issues that could relate to the food's safety.

According to premarketing regulations from the FDA, marketers of a new food brought to the agency for review will be required to give satisfactory answers to the following questions:

1. Has the concentration of naturally occurring toxicant in the plant increased?

2. Has an element to which some people are allergic (such, for example, as peanuts) not commonly found in the plant been introduced?

3. Have the levels of important nutrients changed?

4. Have accepted, established scientific practices been followed?

5. What are the environmental effects?

All foods developed by means of new techniques will be subjected to extensive chemical analysis and animal feeding studies; when a procedure has been used that significantly changes the composition of a food, labeling will be required. The FDA can remove a food from the market if there is a "reasonable" possibility that a substance added by human intervention might be unsafe. But the best safeguard remains the grower or processor, for no company would force itself out of business and into the law courts by knowingly contaminating the food supply.

Marvels of the New Age

Let's say it's the year 2020, and biotechnology has come completely into its own. As you wander the supermarket you find:

• **Apricots that taste delicious more than ten feet from the tree.**

• **Avocados with the seeds in the skin instead of in the center.**

• **Beans without strings.**

• **Perfectly shaped corncobs that are sweeter, juicier, and totally bug-resistant.**

• **Crossbred seedless fruits of every sort. Some you won't recognize.**

• **Melons with edible rinds.**

• **Lettuce that won't wilt.**

• **Sweet peppers in rainbow colors.**

• **Potatoes without a mark on their skins, and that absorb less oil when fried.**

• **Chili peppers, tree-ripened and harvested by machine.**

• **Tomatoes with fewer** seeds and less water, just off the vine and fully flavored.

• **Cheeses, fully mature, that were made barely a week ago.**

• **Oils with a lower ratio of saturated to unsaturated fat than you ever thought possible.**

• **Vanilla in synthetic form.**

• **Nutritious breads made from wheat that is impervious to bacteria and fungi.**

• **Low-caffeine coffee beans.**

• **An aisle devoted to a variety of foods specially designed to avert heart disease, cancer, osteoporosis, and other diseases.**

• **In the pharmacy, medicines derived directly from livestock that have been bred specifically for that purpose.**

ALICE IN BIOTECHLAND

CHARLES MEMMINGER, JR.

I knew that huge steps had been made in genetic engineering, but I assumed it was being used to fight hunger and disease. I hadn't realized it was also being used to develop designer foods for those lucky enough to be able to afford it.

But there they were — Little Cows, smaller than chicken drumsticks, Little Sheep, and wonderful Little Pan-Fried Pigs, so tender they almost melted in your mouth. And nothing could compare to the Sweet-and-Sour Chicken, each the size of a brussels sprout….

Just when I thought I had tried all of the little food there was, I chanced upon a Japanese restaurant and sat down at the sushi bar. There they were, lying on a bed of ice! Northwest Salmon the size of sardines; Pacific Swordfish the size of anchovies. (I learned that the sword makes a handy toothpick.)

They cooked the midget fish in rice wine or served them raw. Dungeness Crabs, baked crispy as popcorn, were served by the bowlful as an appetizer. But the biggest surprise was the Humpback Whale dinner for four. Scientists had long since managed to save the whale from extinction, but I never would have guessed that genetic entrepreneurs would develop whales the size of sockeye salmon. The whale dish became a guilty pleasure of mine.

After some months I succeeded in sampling all of the establishments in town that served little food. I went into a sort of depression. Could this be the end? Was there no other little food to try?

Then, as I was wandering around the city, I ended up in a dark basement bar. The waitress asked if I wanted something for dinner. "Bring me anything," I said. What difference did it make? A few minutes later she returned with a sizzling platter and put it on the table.

"This might cheer you up," she said.

The smell of roasted meat was like none other I had experienced. My fork easily cut through the tender 10-ounce fillet. It had more flavor than chicken but it was not as heavy as beef. It was wonderful. But what was it? I asked.

"Mouse," the waitress replied.

"But this is the size of a New York steak!" I said.

"We only serve USDA prime mouse shank, the best cut from genetically enlarged animals."

"Enlarged? You mean they have managed to make mice the size of cows?"

"Mice, gerbils, shrews … you name it," she said. "The little critters that used to hide under the barns now can hardly fit inside them. The scientists found out that rodent meat is much more tender than beef, and it tastes terrific with a dry white wine. Our specialty is barbecued hamster ribs, served every Friday. But I warn you, bring a hungry friend; they are huge. A half a hamster can feed two."

… I went back Friday, and the ribs were incredible. And I have just heard of a place across town that serves a marvelous 20-ounce chipmunk sirloin. For Thanksgiving I think I will have several friends over to share a plump, 25-pound hummingbird, roasted over hot coals on a rotisserie…. Ah, science.

Excerpted from "Last Word," *Omni* magazine

CAFE BIO-TECH

This mock menu was originally circulated at a press conference held by the Pure Food Campaign, opponents of gene-altered foods. Although the menu notes that all of the cross-species genetic transfers listed have already been developed and field-tested, it does not reveal which property of each food was positively affected by the introduction of a foreign gene.

A Dinner of Transgenic Foods

APPETIZER

Spiced potatoes with wax moth genes

Juice of tomatoes with flounder gene

ENTREE

Blackened catfish with trout gene

Pork chops with human genes

Scalloped potatoes with chicken gene

Cornbread with firefly gene

DESSERT

Rice pudding with pea gene

BEVERAGES

Milk with genetically engineered bovine growth hormone (BGH)

Reprinted from the *National Culinary Review*

Did You Know?

☞ Japanese scientists combined a common agricultural virus with an amino-acid derivative that reduces high blood pressure and applied it to the leaves of a cherry tomato plant. The plant became "infected" with the virus and began producing the hypertension drug in tomatoes.

☞ A plant geneticist has cultured juice vesicles — the part of the orange that yields juice — and has grown them into juice without an orange and without a tree.

☞ Berries and tomatoes have been grown without plants in nutrient-packed mediums.

**Biotechnology Industry
Organization**
1625 K Street NW
Washington, DC 20006-1604
202-857-0244

**Biotechnology and
Sustainable Agriculture**
Union of Concerned Scientists
1616 P Street NW
Washington, DC 20036
202-332-0900

**Center for Nutrition
and Dietetics**
American Dietetic Association
216 West Jackson Boulevard
Chicago, IL 60606-6995
800-366-1655

**Center for Science in
the Public Interest**
1875 Connecticut Avenue
NW, Suite 300
Washington, DC 20009
202-332-9110

**Foundation for
Economic Trends**
1130 17th Street NW
Washington, DC 20036
202-466-2823

**Institute of Food
Technologists**
221 North LaSalle Street
Chicago, IL 60601
312-782-8424

**Institute of Biosciences
and Technology**
Texas A & M University
2121 Holcomb
Houston, TX 77030
713-677-7700

**International Food
Biotechnology Council**
1126 16th Street NW
Washington, DC 20036
202-659-0789

**International Food
Information Council**
1100 Connecticut Avenue
NW, Suite 430
Washington, DC 20036

Office of Biotechnology
Food and Drug Administration
200 C Street SW
Washington, DC 20204
202-205-4144

**Public Voice for Food
and Health Policy**
1001 Connecticut Avenue NW
Washington, DC 20036
202-659-5930

**Journal of Food
Biochemistry**
2 Corporate Drive
P.O. Box 374
Trumbull, CT 06611
203-261-8587
Bimonthly;
$137 per year

Meow!

BISTROS

> *Bistro cooking is good,
> traditional food,
> earnestly made and
> honestly displayed.
> It is earthy, provincial,
> or bourgeois; as befits
> that kind of food,
> it is served in
> ample portions.*
>
> — David Liederman
> New York restaurateur

THE BLOOM IS ON THE BISTRO

Bistros belong to France. We think of them as neighborhood restaurants behind white lace curtains that serve *big food*: pork and beef and all their moving parts — *têtes*, tails, tripe and trotters, liver and kidneys, along with leeks, blood sausage, mustard and sauerkraut, garlic soup, *escargots*, *entrecôte* and *pommes frites, lapins, gratins, pâtés* and *mousse au chocolat*. The handwritten menu, run off in smudged purple ink, is always a promise of good food and lots of it. And on each table stands an open bottle of the local red wine, ready to pour into heavy glass tumblers. There are rarely more than a dozen tables. Large white plates are used. And there's a ruddy-cheeked *patronne* who leans over the table at the end of the meal and totes up *l'addition* on the white paper tablecover. When she returns her pencil to its place beneath her ample bosom, she confidently expects to see you again tomorrow, and says so.

In fact, to the French this is not a bistro, but a restaurant. Although trendy contemporary eating places are sometimes called bistros, the genuine French bistro is a sleazy corner joint that serves cheap wine and beer to locals for whom the food matters little — hence there is very little to eat in them.

The American bistro serves up a totally different experience. You find yourself surrounded by young people on the fast track, who are dining on grilled duck breast with pomegranate juice, pizza with goat cheese, and smoked salmon and lobster ravioli with grapefruit sections. You may think you're in the wrong place but, for America, it's the right place. It's just that all ideas don't cross the Atlantic with absolute authenticity.

Jacquot, Be Quick!

The word *bistro* comes from the Russian *bistrot*, meaning "quick," and derives from the time when Paris was occupied by members of the Allied forces (chiefly British, German, and Russian) that had defeated Napoleon at Waterloo in 1815. The Russian soldiers would pound their fists on the zinc counters of Parisian cafes, demanding fast service by shouting, *"Bistrot! Bistrot!"*

Books

**America Eats Out: An
Illustrated History of
Restaurants, Taverns,
Coffee Shops, Speak-
easies, and Other
Establishments**
John Mariani; Morrow, 1992;
$25.00

Bistro Cooking
Patricia Wells; Workman,
1989; $12.95

Paris Bistro Cooking
Linda Dannenberg; Clarkson
Potter, 1991; $30.00

BLUEBERRIES

Star Berries

Native American tribes valued the wild blueberry especially highly because at the blossom end of each berry the calyx forms a perfect five-pointed star. Their legends tell of a time when children were dying of hunger during a famine and the Great Spirit sent "star berries" to feed them.

Blueberry Benefits

Blueberries are a luscious source of vitamin C: one cup supplies almost one-third of the recommended daily allowance for an adult, tossing in some fiber for good measure and very little sodium. Half a cup of berries has only 41 calories — unless you surrender to temptation and add a scoop of ice cream.

Blueberries have entered the new domain of so-called pharmafoods — foods that are therapeutically beneficial. Dr. Nathan Sharon, a biochemist at the Weizmann Institute of Science and Tel Aviv University in Israel, has found that both blueberries and cranberries have bacteria-fighting capabilities that are particularly useful in combatting urinary-tract infections. Could it be that future doctors may prescribe a glass of blueberry juice instead of an antibiotic?

Q&A

Q Is there a difference between wild blueberries and the cultivated kind?

A The wild berries are smaller and sweeter than cultivated berries, but are rarely available fresh outside the Northeast. The berries grow in clusters on low bushes, about 6 to 18 inches high, and are harvested by hand, using metal rakes.

The cultivated "high-bush" berries grow to heights of 12 feet or more; their berries are bigger and pulpier than the wild kind, but somewhat less flavorful. After an initial hand picking, they are harvested by machines that shake each bush gently so that only the ripe berries fall into the catching frame.

BERRY BIG BUSINESS

Blueberries are as much a part of the American heritage as country quilts and parades on the Fourth of July. They were growing here when the first human beings set foot on this continent. The Native Americans ate them fresh, stewed, and dried long before the colonists arrived and baked them into grunts, slumps, cobblers, buckles, and crisps, as well as puddings, pies, and tarts. And then modern folk started stirring them into yogurt, baking them into cheesecake and muffins, adding them to everything from pancakes to bagels and blintzes, even composing them into flavored vinegars.

The industry is a lot larger than most of us think, second only to strawberries among all berry crops. The annual commercial crop of blueberries in North America averages well over 200 million pounds —and this doesn't include all those pailfuls picked by little fingers for Mom's blueberry pie. Ninety-five percent of the world's commercially produced blueberries are grown here and demand is building for them overseas as well. American and Canadian growers export blueberries to Europe, Great Britain, Australia, and Japan, and in turn we import blueberries from New Zealand's summer crop to meet our winter-season craving for those fresh, blue-bloomed berries.

Blueberries as big as the end of your thumb,
Real sky-blue, and heavy, and ready to drum
In the cavernous pail of the first one to come!
And all ripe together, not some of them green
And some of them ripe! You ought to have seen!

— Robert Frost
Blueberries

Blueberry Muffins
Makes 18 muffins

2 cups flour
2 teaspoons baking powder
1 teaspoon powdered cinnamon
¹/₄ teaspoon salt
2 eggs
1 cup milk
³/₄ cup sugar
¹/₂ cup vegetable oil
1 cup fresh or frozen and thawed blueberries

Preheat oven to 400 degrees F.

Combine the flour, baking powder, cinnamon, and salt; mix well. Break the eggs into a bowl, beat them lightly, and stir in the milk, sugar, and oil. Quickly stir the egg mixture into the dry ingredients, then carefully stir in the blueberries. Spoon into greased muffin cups. Bake for 15 to 17 minutes.

TIPS

Storing: Freeze blueberries in a single layer on a tray, then transfer them into freezer containers. Frozen berries can be stored for up to two years.

Cooking: Always add the blueberries at the last minute and stir them gently so that the skins do not break, or they will "bleed" into the other ingredients as they cook.

BREAD

BAKERS
BY THE DOZEN

A dozen years ago bakers were a rare breed. It was almost impossible to find a decent loaf of bread anywhere and squishy soft white bread blanketed the land. It was a miracle of sorts when Alice Waters and her merry band of cooks opened a restaurant in a small house in Berkeley, California, and named it Chez Panisse. Steve Sullivan was the pioneer baker and he introduced a hungry world to the heady smells and tastes of fresh baked, thick-crusted breads that have become the inspiration for several other star bakers, Eli Zabar and Nancy Silverton among them. They are fueling their ovens with imagination and expertise.

Potato bread and sourdough, whole-grain bread and brioche, pepper bread and bread flecked with sun-dried tomatoes, olives, herbs, and seeds — all these are appearing in boutique bakeries and in bountiful baskets handed around to guests in restaurants. Some chefs are even baking their own signature breads and breadsticks as long as your arm and skinny as the waiter's ponytail. Irresistibly, they tease the appetite while diners sip a glass of cool white wine and contemplate the menu. Grainy yellow cornbread muffins, fresh from the oven, are on the tables, too. So are feather-light, lily-white biscuits, sweet muffins with carrots and cranberries, or raisins and walnuts, and hot scones flecked with melting morsels of white and dark chocolate. Soft focaccia, brittle baguettes, crackling croissants, and hearty seven-grain breads taste so good that they barely need butter.

But butter almost always makes them all taste even better — save for those times when we are offered a saucerful of virgin-green pure olive oil for bread dunking until we have had our fill and hardly have room left to eat an actual *meal*.

Bread has become the icing on the cake.

Best Breads

The types of bread listed here are in the order of preference recommended by *The Tufts University Guide to Total Nutrition.*

100 percent whole-wheat
Whole-grain
Multigrain
**Rye (but check
the sodium content)**
Oat
Cracked wheat
Stone-ground
Whole-wheat bagels
Whole-wheat pita
**Whole-grain English
muffins**
Corn tortillas

---

*Where
there's smoke,
there's toast.*
— Anonymous

James Beard's
French-Style Bread

1½ *packages active dry yeast*
1 *tablespoon granulated sugar*
2 *cups warm water (100 to 115
degrees F., approximately)*
1 *tablespoon salt*
5 to 6 *cups all-purpose or
hard-wheat flour*
3 *tablespoons yellow cornmeal*
1 *tablespoon egg white, mixed
with 1 tablespoon cold water*

Combine the yeast with the sugar and warm water in a large bowl and allow to proof. Mix the salt with the flour and add to the yeast mixture, a cup at a time, until you have a stiff dough. Remove to a lightly floured board and knead until no longer sticky, about 10 minutes, adding flour as necessary. Place in a buttered bowl and turn to coat the surface with butter. Cover and let rise in a warm place until doubled in bulk, 1½ to 2 hours.

Punch down the dough. Turn out on a floured board and shape into 2 long, French bread-style loaves. Place on a baking sheet that has been sprinkled with the cornmeal but not buttered. Slash the tops of the loaves diagonally in two or three places, and brush with the egg wash. Place in a cold oven, set the temperature at 400 degrees F., and bake 35 minutes, or until well browned and hollow sounding when the tops are rapped.

Reprinted from Beard on Bread

DOWN WITH CATCH-ALL
LOAVES

JAMES BEARD

One doubtful fashion in bread-making today, however, is the tendency to acquire as many different flours and meals as can be found and incorporate them all into a single loaf, without thought for texture, for crumb, or for the other attributes by which a fine loaf is judged. The aim seems to be merely to fill the bread with vitamins and *health*, and the coarser it is, the healthier, some people think. To my mind, not only is this folly, but the result is also often quite indigestible. I love a fine bread with cornmeal, a rye bread, a whole-wheat meal bread, and breads made with wheat germ and a judicious mixture of flours, as well as various white breads, and any one of them is as healthful as one could want. What's more — they are so much more delicious than the catch-all loaves.

Excerpted from Beard on Bread

Q&A

Q Why is a speech proposing someone's health called a toast?

A Because in 17th-century England it was customary to float a piece of spiced toasted bread in a bowl or carafe of wine to improve its flavor before it was drunk. When people raised their glasses in the traditional custom of drinking to wish someone good health, it would have been rude, as well as unwise, not to finish every drop, and so the toast was consumed along with the wine. The custom came to be called "toasting," but the toast was jettisoned. The drinking was the point anyway.

PRIMAL KNEADS

Ken Haedrich

The kind of baking I do is neither of the New Age whole-grain school, nor would you call it traditional. It is somewhere between the two: relaxed, eclectic and earthy, but not heavy; you might say it is baking that speaks the various tongues of a generation that grew up on Betty Crocker, turned hippie, then saw the dawning of a New American Cuisine. The whole-grain baking movement of the 1960s introduced us to a panoply of little-known grains and flours and brought a new health awareness. But it was destined to fade: For most of us it was too heavy, too uncompromising, and it took itself too seriously.

… For a novice, getting the knack of kneading is the primary problem, not surprisingly, given the limitation of language to describe the process…. [Kneading is] an art — like the potter's — that's learned to a great extent by touch. For instance, I can tell you to knead a dough until it feels elastic, but until you feel that elasticity for yourself, the instructions have no real meaning. Different doughs have their little behavioral quirks; some require a gentler hand, others like a little rough-housing.

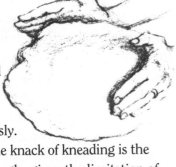

The standard line is to "push, fold, and turn," and that will get you started. But if you've ever watched an experienced baker knead dough, you know that these words no more describe the beauty of kneading than "tap, tap, tap" describes the way Fred Astaire moves on the dance floor.

The challenge, then, is to translate that "push, fold, turn" into something fluid, something that feels like more of a dance. That takes some experimenting with your hands and the way you manipulate the dough. Don't be timid. Using little half runs, push the dough this way and that until you achieve a rhythm that feels right.

A good way to find your rhythm is to play music while you knead. I used to think that kneading had to be some sort of meditative exercise done in absolute silence in a contemplative state of mind. Ten minutes of contemplative kneading can seem like an eternity, however.

Eventually, I discovered I was more of a rock-and-roll kneader. Maybe you're a classical kneader or a country-western kneader or a rap kneader. With George Harrison up loud, I could knead all day.

Making yeast breads does take more than music, however. It requires some level of commitment because expertise does not come overnight and there are sure to be frustrations along the way. Stick with it, though, because there's wisdom to be found in the process. Baking is more than mere mechanics, mixing this and that and putting it in the oven; it demands your involvement and your ability to read the messages that the dough and loaves provide. Expect a little stumbling, but by all means, bake bread.

Excerpted from Ken Haedrich's Country Baking

The Benefits of Brown

Some people think enriched white bread is every bit as nutritious as whole-wheat bread. They are wrong, of course. Essentially, white bread is made from white flour, which has had the bran and the wheat germ — the fiber — removed from it in the milling process. (Fiber touches almost immediately upon good health and "regularity," subjects that we are choosing not to address, at least not here.)

The only way to be sure of getting fiber-rich bread is to read the label carefully. Very carefully — because some bakers have started adding oat- or wheat-bran fiber to fortify their so-called white bread. And bread that looks brown may not necessarily be especially good for you. Sometimes caramelized sugar is added to the dough to bring color to bread that is of borderline merit in terms of nutritional content.

Multigrain bread, and whole-wheat and rye breads are all good places to find fiber. But check the label before you buy.

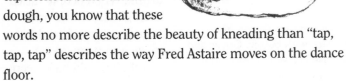
Croissants Wouldn't Have Worked, Either

*M*arie Antoinette did not say "Let them eat cake." What she actually said was "Qu'ils mangent de la brioche," meaning a soft, slightly sweet bread, which would, in fact, have been quite a sensible food for people starving as the Parisians were. But, of course, no brioche was available, and she lost her head anyway.

The Nutritional Content of Breads

Bread	Calories	Protein	Fat	Comments
Whole-wheat, 1-ounce slice	70	3 grams	1 gram	Must be made from 100 percent whole-wheat flour. Good source of vitamins, minerals, and fiber. May contain sugar, honey, and molasses, which add calories. Bread labeled "wheat bread," "cracked wheat," or "sprouted wheat" usually contains white flour.
White, enriched, 1-ounce slice	75	3 grams	1 gram	Made from white flour, which lacks the bran and germ of the wheat grain. Most of the lost nutrients are not replaced, even in "enriched" flour, which has only niacin, thiamines, riboflavin, and iron added. Fiber is reduced. Avoid bleached flour.
Rye, 1-ounce slice	70	3 grams	Trace	Most rye breads contain mostly white flour. Look for rye flour, especially whole-rye flour, as a primary ingredient.
Pumpernickel, 1-ounce slice	70	3 grams	Trace	Most American loaves are made from white and rye flour colored with caramel, so they have no advantage over white or rye bread.
Italian/French, 1-ounce slice	80	3 grams	Trace	Loaves made at local bakeries are usually free of preservatives and may contain little or no sugar or fat. Look for whole-grain varieties.
Bagel, plain, 2½ ounces	200	7 grams	2 grams	Usually made of high-protein flour and little or no fat, making it dense. Egg bagels contain added fat and cholesterol.
Pita, 2 ounces	165	6 grams	1 gram	Often made just of flour, salt, and water. May have sweeteners and additives.
Croissant, 2 ounces	235	5 grams	12 grams	Contains butter and sugar. High in saturated fat, cholesterol, and calories.
English muffin, 2½ ounces	140	5 grams	1 gram	Has no nutritional advantage over white bread.

Source: *The Wellness Encyclopedia*

BREAKFAST

To eat well in England you should have breakfast three times a day.

— W. Somerset Maugham
English novelist

THE CRACK OF DAWN

Eggs, once the cornerstone of the new day for most of us, just don't cut the mustard anymore for the righteous. And all their talk these days about being healthy all the time gets to me. It's harder and harder now to enjoy the "fry-ups" of my youth, which were my main reason, once, for getting out of bed. Two fried eggs, two slices of meaty bacon, three small sausages floating on their backs in a small pond of grease, two big, black mushroom caps oozing black liquid into melted butter, half a grilled tomato — all served lukewarm — that's what I once adored. It all came on a big plate painted around the edges with entwining flowers. Soggy cold toast upended on a silver toast rack. Serious, chunky, dark-brown marmalade and hot, strong tea in the pot under the tea cozy. That was the breakfast for righteous folk in those days. Backbone of the British Empire.

Alas, the food patrol has lowered the truncheon and almost everywhere now (except at truck stops on the nation's better highways) traditional breakfasts have nearly vanished. Even when we get a chance to have one we don't much fancy it. A carton of yogurt and a scoop of berries, some herb tea and the check, please — that's what squares us with our conscience now as boredom overwhelms.

But there are many kinds of anarchy within easy reach. Chocolate cake, I find, is a splendid alternative to bran flakes, first thing in the morning. So is a bowl of cold spaghetti with a scattering of Parmesan cheese — slips down nicely and can be carried around while you dress.

And who says that breakfast foods are only for breakfast? College students, I'm told, stock up on three different kinds of cereals for three different meals a day, breakfast, lunch, and dinner. Why not? They're cheap and nutritious, and sometimes the mind has to be given over to great thoughts and spared the mundane question of what to eat and when to eat it.

So if you find yourself in a rut, try a spot of rice pudding for breakfast, or a toasted cheese sandwich, or a spoonful of chili on a Saltine cracker, or a BLT. As Julia Child once said, "You are alone in your kitchen. No one can see you." Anyway, what you eat is nobody's business. In fact, just one fried egg would taste really good right now.

A Typical English Breakfast

Egg and Chips

Two Eggs and Chips

Egg, Bacon and Chips

Two Eggs, Bacon and Chips

Sausage and Chips

Two Sausages and Chips

Bacon, Sausage and Chips

Egg, Sausage and Chips

Two Eggs, Two Sausages and Chips

Egg, Bacon, Sausage and Chips

Two Eggs, Bacon, Sausage and Chips

Egg, Bacon, Two Sausages and Chips

Two Eggs, Bacon, Two Sausages and Chips

Egg, Bacon, Sausage, Beef-burger and Chips

— George Lang
Lang's Compendium of Culinary Nonsense & Trivia

Top-of-the-Morning Breakfasts

Upscale
Freshly squeezed orange juice
Tofu omelette with dried cherries and three chilies
Sourdough rolls
Butter
Herb tea
Cafe latte

Midscale
Juice from a carton
Eggs Benedict
English muffins
Margarine
Regular tea
Brewed coffee

Lowbrow
Root beer
Two fried eggs, sausage, and hash browns
Toasted white bread
Margarine
Iced tea
Coca-Cola

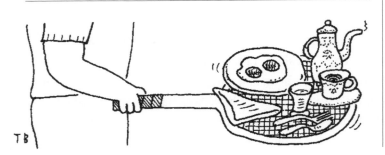

Less Keeps Adding Up to More and More

In the old days, Mom used to tell us we should eat breakfast like a king, lunch like a prince, and dinner like a pauper. Those kings that remain enthroned may well be eating beggarly breakfasts on principle, but mothers still *know* they know best, and a regular breakfast is something they insist on.

Some reinforcement:

• Experts at Baylor College of Medicine in Houston back up Mom; they say that *skipping breakfast hinders a child's late-morning problem-solving ability*, a consequence of tumbling blood-sugar levels.

• Professional athletes eat hearty breakfasts at their training tables. They want the energy to perform as close to their peak as they can.

• A study at Canada's St. John's University concluded that *having a sensible breakfast may reduce the risk of heart attack*. (It's always when the study is in favor of something that the word *may* is introduced into the findings. But what nutritionists mean by *sensible* may not coincide with what old folks mean by *healthy*. It's an argument reminiscent of the drinker who points out that there are more old drunks than old doctors.)

• Doctors of any age are pretty convinced that we should all have *something* to eat in the morning. *People who regularly deny themselves food for 14 hours are more likely to develop gallstones*, they say.

• A three-month study conducted by nutritionists at Vanderbilt University revealed that *women dieters who eat three meals a day lose more weight than those who skip breakfast*. All the women participating consumed 1,200 calories a day during the study, with 25 to 30 percent derived from fat. Those who skipped breakfast lost about 13 pounds each; those who *ate* breakfast lost 17 to 19 pounds!

Did You Know?

☞ Breakfast is the most frequently skipped meal in America. Fifty-eight percent of the population don't eat breakfast every day.

☞ Dry cereals are the favorite breakfast food for most Americans: 10 pounds per person every year.

☞ Some 20 percent of adults eat breakfast out at least once a week, but (figure this out) 90 percent of breakfasts are eaten in the home.

☞ Twelve percent of the total quantity of colas sold are consumed with — or instead of — breakfast.

☞ Breakfast coffee accounts for half of all the coffee that's consumed in America on any given day. How much is regular and how much is decaf? It's fifty-fifty. (With or without half-and-half.)

My wife and I tried to breakfast together, but we had to stop or our marriage would have been wrecked.

— Winston Churchill
British statesman

Books

The Bed & Breakfast Book
Martha W. Murphy;
Stemmer House, 1991; $30.00

The Breakfast Book
Marion Cunningham;
Knopf, 1987; $19.95

Favorite Recipes from Country Inns and Bed & Breakfasts
Meredith Books, 1991; $19.95

Grant Corner Inn Breakfast and Brunch Cookbook
Louise Stewart; Grant Corner Inn, 1986; $12.95

Morning Food
Margaret S. Fox and John Bear;
Ten Speed Press, 1990; $19.95

Micro-Granola

Makes 3 cups

2 cups quick-cooking oatmeal
¹/₂ cup chopped walnuts or
    pecans
¹/₃ cup wheat germ
¹/₄ cup flaked coconut
¹/₄ cup brown sugar
¹/₄ cup vegetable oil
¹/₄ cup honey
1 teaspoon vanilla extract
¹/₂ cup raisins or chopped dried
    apricots

In a large, microwave-safe baking dish, combine the oatmeal, nuts, wheat germ, and coconut. In a small bowl stir together the brown sugar, vegetable oil, honey, and vanilla. Combine the raisins with the oatmeal-coconut mixture in the baking dish, pour the liquid mixture over the top, and toss thoroughly. Microwave on High (100 percent power) for 5 to 6 minutes, stirring twice.

Cool completely, stirring occasionally to break up any lumps. Store in an airtight container.

BRUNCH AT THE CAFE BEAUJOLAIS

This is the menu that greets visitors to this small cafe in Mendocino, on the Northern California coast, which features the lovingly prepared, intrinsically organic creations of husband and wife chef/owners Margaret Fox and Christopher Kump.

Freshly squeezed orange or grapefruit juice

Ricotta and chestnut blintzes
with maple cream, two chicken-apple sausages and
gingered dried winter fruit compote

Tangy buttermilk waffle
with toasted hazelnuts & wild rice, smoked chicken-
apple sausage and half a grapefruit

Homemade cashew granola
with bananas & dried currants and yogurt

Mexican tofu scramble
(with sautéed potatoes, roast garlic, fresh vegetables,
guacamole & black bean chili), served with Brickery
toast and freshly squeezed juice

Omelettes
served with a choice of Brickery toast, Noah's onion
bagel, buttermilk coffeecake or muffins

* Spicy black beans, salsa, guacamole,
cheddar cheese, sour cream

* Smoked chicken-apple sausage, sautéed leeks &
mushrooms, Jarlsberg cheese & sour cream

* Bacon, green onions, grilled potatoes, toasted
walnuts, jack cheese and sour cream

McEats Hits the Road

When McDonald's introduced the Egg McMuffin to a hungry work force, the chain started a trend that has galloped into many other fast-food outlets. Taco Bell, for example, is scooping up the low-price breakfast market by offering assorted burritos priced from 39 cents to 79 cents. Even with a drink, these first meals of the day do little to lighten the wallet; however, they promise to make a significant deposit to the hips.

Breakfast pizzas are now appearing on the market, as are dozens of other foods that can be held in one hand while the purchaser holds a newspaper or a steering wheel in the other. Croissant sandwiches, bagels layered with ham and cheese, stuffed pitas, pancake-wrapped sausage dogs on a stick, hefty breakfast cookies, and breakfast sandwiches, as well as the more traditional Danish, muffins, and cinnamon buns, are consumed now by the ton as Americans make their way to work. Lite they may claim to be, but heavier is what we become when we succumb.

Perhaps it's time to reexamine our breakfast choices and try to lighten up by doing a little advance planning. A banana is as easy to hold in one hand as a muffin. A desk drawer can be stocked with cereals that are prepackaged with bowl, spoon, and shelf-stable milk, and shelf-stable orange juice keeps "fresh" without refrigeration for four months.

Alternatively, have a cup of hot soup for breakfast. It tastes just as good as or even better than bacon and egg on a roll and will get the day going with a minimum intake of fat.

BROCCOLI

"By the way, broccoli is biodegradable, in case you want to throw it out."

IS BROCCOLI THAT MAGIC BULLET?

There it was, in March 1992, on the front page of *The New York Times*: "Broccoli harbors what could be the most powerful anticancer compound ever discovered." The immediate result was a doubling in the retail price and what was popularly referred to as a broccoli feeding frenzy. Americans (other than former President George Bush) are now eating eight times as much broccoli as they were just 20 years ago.

What prompted the *Times* story was the news that researchers at Johns Hopkins and Mount Sinai Medical Center had isolated sulforophane, a chemical found in broccoli that is thought to detoxify carcinogens. Other studies had already proved that cruciferous vegetables (those with cross-shaped flower petals) — a group that includes broccoli, kale, brussels sprouts, cabbage, carrots, and scallions — may play a significant role in reducing the risk of developing certain forms of cancer.

Although no one believes that broccoli can be relied on exclusively to prevent disease, it does appear that eating broccoli along with a variety of other vegetables and fruits can have a markedly positive effect on the health.

Broccoli has one of the highest concentrations of calcium of any vegetable. It is rich in vitamins A and C and supplies several of the B vitamins, as well as potassium and iron. It is also a good source of dietary fiber. Beats out cheeseburgers, anyway, hands down.

Offspring of a Vegetable Marriage

Broccoflower is a hybrid vegetable that combines the best characteristics of broccoli and cauliflower. It is lighter in color and milder and sweeter tasting than either broccoli or cauliflower, and therefore appeals to small children. A serving of about a cupful of broccoflower has more than the recommended daily allowance of vitamin C, but somewhat less beta carotene than its two popular parents.

Books

Broccoli and Company
Audra Hendrickson and Jack Hendrickson; Storey Communications, 1989; $9.95

Broccoli by Brody
Lora Brody; Morrow, 1993; $6.95

The Big Broccoli Book
Georgia Downard; Random House, 1992; $10.00

TIPS

Cooking: If steaming broccoli, lift the lid two or three times to allow the gases to escape. This will also keep the color bright green.

How Broccoli Grows

Broccoli springs from a taproot and secondary roots that anchor the plant firmly in the ground and take up moisture and nutrients from the soil. The outer petioles or stalks support the major leaves, which utilize the sun's heat and light, carbon dioxide and moisture from the air to produce growth. Encircled by the leaves is the flower head on the main stalk, which is really there to produce seeds, but whose florets are the most desirable parts to eat.

If This Is Heaven, What the Hell!

At a recent cooking contest sponsored by the White Castle chain, the prize was awarded to a recipe for a Celestial Hamburger (presumably a White Castle) topped with broccoli, Velveeta cheese, and Ritz crackers.

There was no word on submissions by the losers.

Did You Know?

☞ Broccoli was developed some 2,500 years ago on the island of Cyprus.

☞ Broccoli was frequently served at banquets in ancient Rome, sautéed in oil and seasoned with onion, cumin, and coriander.

☞ The word *broccoli* comes from the Italian *brocco*, which means "arm branch." It was popularized in the United States by Italian immigrants.

☞ The first crop of broccoli commercially raised in America was grown in Brooklyn, New York.

☞ Ninety percent of the fresh broccoli sold in America is grown in the Salinas Valley in California.

BRUSSELS SPROUTS

BUT WHY BRUSSELS?

There are several things to be said about brussels sprouts. Frenchmen say *"Mon petit chou,"* which means "little cabbage," as a term of endearment. Some say Britain is a nation possessing only three vegetables and two of them are brussels sprouts. Botanists tell us the real name is *Brassica oleracea gemmifera*. Californian farmers inform us that three-quarters of our supply comes from Santa Cruz County and the Monterey Bay area. Marketers advertise the peak of the season as being mid-August through April. Nutritionists point out that sprouts are low in calories and virtually fat-free. Low in sodium, high in fiber, and rich in vitamins A and C, potassium, and iron, they also contain folic acid, found in dark-green leafy vegetables, which may protect against cervical cancer and some birth defects.

And *I* can tell you that once, at dusk, hurtling through Belgium on a train, I saw miniature forests of brussels sprouts: knobby, four-foot-tall stalks sticking awkwardly out of the ground like old men's legs with clenched green fists clinging to them. Years and years later, stores in the United States began selling brussels sprouts on the stem, and this is by far the best way to buy them because they are at their freshest when they are still being breast-fed, so to speak.

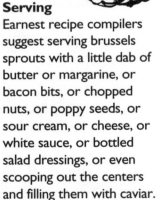

TIPS

Serving
Earnest recipe compilers suggest serving brussels sprouts with a little dab of butter or margarine, or bacon bits, or chopped nuts, or poppy seeds, or sour cream, or cheese, or white sauce, or bottled salad dressings, or even scooping out the centers and filling them with caviar. *Caviar!*

None of these ideas has any merit whatsoever except adding just a little pat of butter.

The best way of serving them, to my mind, is to cook them in a lot of salted water until they are barely tender, drain them, and add a handful of hot chestnuts.

BUTTER

RICH MAN, POOR MAN, BUTTER MAN...

There is something mystical about the way butter forms in golden globules simply from agitating pure white cream for a given amount of time in the dark confines of a churn. Butter-making is in a sense an act of creation, and in declining its rich rewards, whatever our reasons, we fail to complete a ritual that has been in place around the world since prehistoric times.

The origin of butter is thought to have been when early herdsmen carried milk sloshing about in a bag made from an animal's stomach, and found its contents divided into fat (butter) and milk solids and whey (buttermilk).

In medieval Europe, butter was plentiful, so it was viewed as fit only for poor folk to eat. But by the 19th century, butter had become accepted in aristocratic kitchens largely because of the development of French classic cuisine, which was founded on the use of butter.

According to food historian Margaret Visser, when this century began, upper-class families were eating three times as much butter as the rest of the population. "It was one of the ways in which they demonstrated their superiority," she writes in her intriguing book *Much Depends on Dinner*. But increasingly, "people in wealthy countries feel it behooves them to reduce their intake of visible fat. Now, eating little fat although plenty of it is available, and managing — through an aristocratic combination of expense, pride, and self-control — not to *be* fat, has attained the kind of ineffable prestige which once accrued to soft hands and clean linen. Yet the *idea* of butter and words like 'buttery,' 'deep-buttered,' and 'butter-ball' retain their enticing power in the North American language."

NO GREAT SHAKES

Butter substitutes are "all natural" sprinkle-on alternatives. Because they contain fewer calories and no fat or cholesterol they are recommended for weight-loss and cholesterol-controlled diets. The "natural" ingredients include maltodextrin (a carbohydrate derived from corn), salt, rice starch, lecithin (an emulsifying agent derived from soybeans), and annatto and turmeric (colors).

Natural these ingredients may be, but real butter is closer to nature and a wise man knows that when a food contains no sugar, no cholesterol, and no calories, it also has no taste. So those of us who yearn for the real thing might settle for eating a little less butter rather than abandoning it entirely. Compromise does not always mean surrender.

Eat butter first, and eat it last, and live till a hundred years be past.

— *Old Dutch proverb*

Fat Chance

The law stipulates that both butter and margarine must contain at least 80 percent fat — but not all fats are alike. Butterfat, the kind found in butter, milk, cream, cheese, and the richest, best-tasting kind of ice cream, is derived from animal products. It is saturated fat and contains cholesterol, whereas the plant-derived oils used to make margarine are cholesterol-free.

There are about the same number of calories in butter as in margarine, but butter lovers tend to eat more butter than margarine eaters.

And don't think you are cutting down on calories by eating whipped butter. It is true that a tablespoon of whipped butter contains less fat. But if you actually *weighed* whipped and regular butter, ounce for ounce, they have the same number of calories because the air only adds volume, not weight.

So if you think you are being virtuous by spreading your muffin with twice as much whipped as regular butter, think again. You may be deceiving yourself, but your hips will betray you.

Did You Know?

☞ Butter is made from the milk of cows, sheep, goats, donkeys, horses, water buffaloes, camels, and yaks.

☞ French butters have a higher butterfat content than most American butters, which are required only to have 80 percent butterfat (the remainder is water — 18.5 percent — and milk solids).

☞ In Europe, cultures are added to butters to give them flavor. American-made Plugrá butter, developed by Hotel Bar Foods, closely resembles French butter in taste and texture.

Butter Sauces

Beurre noisette (hazelnut butter) is heated until just lightly browned. It has a delicious flavor, used with green beans or added to cakes.

Beurre noir (black butter) is cooked until dark brown, then deglazed with a little vinegar. It is a sauce for bland foods such as brains or eggs.

Beurre blanc (white butter) is a sauce primarily for fish. It contains dry white wine, vinegar, shallots and heavy cream, with tiny pieces of cold butter whisked in, one at a time, over high heat.

Maître d'hôtel butter is not cooked; softened butter is mixed with parsley, lemon juice and seasonings and served with fish or meat.

MORE INFORMATION

American Butter Institute
1250 H Street NW
Washington, DC 20005
202-296-4250

United Dairy Industry Association
O'Hare International Center
10255 West Higgins Road,
Suite 900
Rosemont, IL 60018-5616
708-803-2000

HOTLINES

800-782-9606
Land O'Lakes Holiday Bakeline
November 1 - December 24,
8:00 a.m. - 6:00 p.m., CST

DEATH TAKES A HOLLANDAISE

CABBAGE

I wonder if the cabbage knows
He is less lovely than the Rose;
Or does he squat in smug content,
A source of noble nourishment;
Or if he pities for her sins
The Rose who has no vitamins;
Or if one thing his green heart knows —
That self-same fire that warms the Rose?
— Anonymous

THE VIRTUOUS CABBAGE

Judith Valente

Shed a tear for the lowly cabbage. Even as vegetables go, it is particularly friendless. The Department of Agriculture collects data on everything from asparagus to zucchini — but it stopped bothering with cabbage back in 1982. "There was just no lobby for the cabbage," a department statistician says.

The American Cancer Society says that because cabbage is loaded with fiber it helps prevent certain cancers, particularly of the esophagus, stomach, and colon. It is also high in vitamin C, low in sodium and calories — good things all. Crushed fresh cabbage leaves, applied as a poultice, are said to reduce the swelling of varicose veins. So why doesn't cabbage get its day in the sun?

Across the nation, farmers have been tearing up their cabbage patches. Cabbage, you see, is cheap, not chic. It grows just about anywhere, even in cold climates. And there's too much of it already. . . .

Cabbage's few but staunch defenders say it is getting a bum rap. "Cabbage always was a staple of peasant cooking," says Barbara Wheaton, a culinary historian at Radcliffe College, in Cambridge, Massachusetts. Sauerkraut, the commonest cooked cabbage, became "Liberty Cabbage" during World War II when things German became *verboten* in the United States and Britain. When citrus was scarce during the war, the British government touted cabbage as a source of vitamin C. Maybe that's why many people in England shun cabbage still. Too common, too many bad memories.

Also, it stinks. Cabbage contains sulfurous compounds that, when heated, give off vapors that remind some people of rotten eggs and ammonia. Boiling cabbage to death, as many cooks do, especially when making corned beef and cabbage, *really* gives people the vapors. . . .

In other ways, cabbage tries so hard to please. It costs as little as 19 cents a pound; it isn't as prone to wilt as lettuce; it can withstand a 15-degree frost. Cooks can prepare it sweet, tart, bland, or creamed. . . .

But the smell is always a big hurdle. "Blaagh," groaned fifth graders (more or less in unison) at Bowman Elementary School in Lexington, Massachusetts, when they heard that chef Marian Morash was planning to prepare for them cabbage with curry and butter.

Ms. Morash is host of the "The Victory Garden" cooking show, and after she had sautéed her first batch for the kids, they "didn't want to stop eating it," she says.

So score one for a head of cabbage in the hands of a good cook.

Excerpted from The Wall Street Journal

From Khan to Cook, Kraut Wins Out

It is said that when Genghis Khan plundered China, he took a shine to a certain dish of cabbage pickled in wine, popular there since the building of the Great Wall, centuries earlier. His Mongol hordes brought back the recipe, and transported it across Europe, where the Germans, in particular, became very fond of it, substituting a process of fermenting the cabbage with salt instead of wine and giving it the name of *sauerkraut*, which means "sour cabbage" in German.

In 1772, Captain James Cook, hearing that sauerkraut had great health-giving properties, ordered 25,000 pounds of it for his second great voyage to explore the Pacific.

The magic in the kraut, which we now know to be vitamin C, lasted for the length of his years-long voyage. In more than 1,000 days, he lost only one of his 118 men to scurvy, and the ogre of all seafaring men was banished forever.

MORE INFORMATION

National Kraut Packers Association
c/o Myers Communicounsel, Inc.
510 Thornall Street, Suite 380
Edison, NJ 08837
908-494-1111

Books

Cabbage: Cures to Cuisine
Judith Hiatt; Naturegraph, 1989; $6.95

CAFETERIAS

HELPING YOURSELF

The cafeteria was born in San Francisco in the Gold Rush of 1849. The town was jammed with strangers and saloon-keepers wooed them with free lunch — an array of edibles placed on the bar. The idea of helping yourself to a meal was so sensational that canny entrepreneurs soon jumped in: They offered good fare, provided trays so the suckers could really load up, and made them pay at the end of a line for what they had formerly got for free.

Cafeterias soon popped up everywhere. By the 1940s, there was always at least one big cafeteria downtown in every American city, contiguous to the department stores and movie palaces. It had two serving lines, hot food, cool Art Deco trappings, and *everybody* went there. But fashions change. By the 1960s, corporations were providing company cafeterias for employees, who immediately lost any taste for eating in cafeterias on their own time.

As downtowns bit the dust, so did cafeterias. The only traces we find now are in company cafeterias, where the employer defrays some or all of the costs of employee meals. Most of them feature plain fare, paper plates, and formica-topped tables; in staff dining rooms, however, which are sometimes known as messes (the allusion is military, not derogatory), there are tablecloths, service — and sometimes splendor, too.

MESSING ABOUT IN THE ULTIMATE COMPANY CAFETERIA

People who have worked at the White House talk about the mess in a nostalgic way. Aides go there to gossip, or to size each other up. They take their cousins and grandmothers there to show off. It is a constant, tangible perk — a place to relax in and to feel special in. Peggy Noonan, in her memoir of the Reagan White House, makes it sound like an old prep-school dining hall. She says she never enjoyed eating there alone. "Young men would look up, look down, and continue to chew," she wrote, noting that "when they gestured, the light caught their Presidential cufflinks."

The main mess dining room (there are two others) feels like a stateroom on a prosperous ship. There are no windows, and the walls are paneled in polished dark wood. To get there from the press office, you go down a narrow flight of stairs and through the West Wing, past pictures of Presidents and deep-blue submarines. Near the entrance are a silver bowl filled with M&M's and, above that, a battered mess gong from the U.S.S. *Constitution*. The cramped, nautical feel is deliberate, for the Navy manages the establishment, and has done so since Harry Truman opened the staff dining room in the White House, in 1951.

The menu has changed over the years, with gastronomic fashion. You can order a taco salad at the White House, or tomato bouillon, or spicy rice and chicken, only 450 calories a plate. Regulars say the food is decent, but when it isn't no one complains, because everyone is so happy to be there. There are crackers at every table, and elaborate orange flower arrangements at some. There is a salad bar, which, like any other salad bar, is stocked with creamy packaged dressings, wet sunflower seeds, and crusty lettuce tongs. The french fries look abnormally long as they go by, and all sandwiches come with a luminous green pickle. . .

Menus come printed on white paper board, corded with a blue sash. You can have one for a souvenir if you like. The stewards also used to dispense packs of Presidential cigarettes, but the Bushes weren't smokers and abolished that practice. Now you can take away handfuls of M&M's instead.

Excerpted from The New Yorker

CALCIUM

WHAT IS CALCIUM?

Calcium is an essential mineral that the body needs in order to build and maintain its skeleton, to enable its muscles to contract, its blood to clot, its heartbeat to be regular, and its membranes to stay healthy.

Since kindergarten we have been told that calcium builds strong teeth and bones. It's true. More than 90 percent of bone density develops by the age of 18, though the process continues until the mid-30s. Whenever the body needs more calcium, it drains it from bone as needed. Calcium cannot be manufactured on its own, so the only source of this vital nutrient is through what we eat and drink.

Nutritionists urge a calcium-rich diet in early life to form a strong, healthy bone structure and promote growth; if we continue to make healthy food choices, we can maintain this good bone structure permanently.

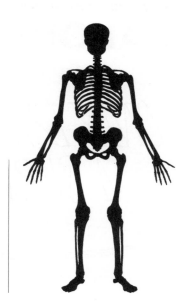

Foods High in Calcium

Foods	Percentage of RDA (child/adult)
Nonfat yogurt (unflavored), 8 ounces	35/52
Low-fat yogurt (fruit-flavored), 8 ounces	29/43
Skim milk, 8 ounces	25/38
Low-fat milk (1 percent), 8 ounces	25/38
Low-fat milk (2 percent), 8 ounces	25/37
Whole milk, 8 ounces	24/36
Tofu (raw, firm), 1/2 cup	22/32
Cheddar cheese, 1 ounce	17/26
Canned salmon (with bones), 3 ounces	17/25
Broccoli (fresh, cooked), 1/2 cup chopped	7/11
Orange, medium-sized	5/7

Note: Low-fat and nondairy products have more calcium per ounce than their whole-milk counterparts.

Source: USDA

Recommended Dietary Allowances for Calcium Consumption

(1 serving is equivalent to 1 cup skim milk, or 302 milligrams)

Children up to age 11
800 milligrams a day
(or 2 - 3 servings)

Pregnant and nursing women
1,200 milligrams a day
(or 3 - 4 servings)

Teens and young adults 11 - 24
1,200 milligrams a day
(or 3 - 4 servings)

Adults 25 and older
800 milligrams a day
(or 3 servings)

Source: Food and Nutrition Board of the National Academy of Sciences

Grow For It

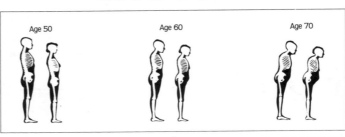

Age 50   Age 60   Age 70

Osteoporosis is the debilitating bone-thinning disease (its literal meaning is "porous bone") that produces an abnormal loss of bone density. It affects an estimated 25 million Americans. Most of them are older women, partly because women have smaller skeletal frames than men, hence less stored calcium, but also because changes in hormone levels during and after menopause leach calcium from women's bones, leaving them fragile and easily fractured. Interestingly, women also tend to eat fewer dairy and other calcium-rich foods than men.

Foods such as leafy green vegetables, the edible bones in canned salmon and sardines, and milk in all its forms are considered more effective sources of calcium than supplements, although a recent study in New Zealand reported that bone loss was reduced by as much as 43 percent in older women who took daily supplements of 1,000 milligrams of calcium.

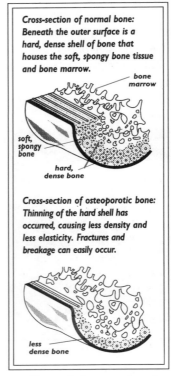

Cross-section of normal bone: Beneath the outer surface is a hard, dense shell of bone that houses the soft, spongy bone tissue and bone marrow.

bone marrow

soft, spongy bone

hard, dense bone

Cross-section of osteoporotic bone: Thinning of the hard shell has occurred, causing less density and less elasticity. Fractures and breakage can easily occur.

less dense bone

Nevertheless, eminent nutritionists fear that postmenopausal women whose childhood diet was deficient in calcium may receive little benefit from increasing their calcium intake either in their diet or in supplements. Osteoporosis does not occur solely as a result of calcium deficiency, but stems from many factors including a hereditary disposition to the problem.

MORE INFORMATION

Calcium Information Center, Clinical Nutrition Research Unit
Division of Nephrology, Hypertension, and Clinical Pharmacology, Oregon Health Sciences University
3314 SW Veterans Hospital Road PP262
Portland, OR 97201
800-321-2681

National Center for Nutrition and Dietetics
American Dietetic Association
216 West Jackson Boulevard, Suite 800
Chicago, IL 60606-6995
312-899-4853

National Dairy Council
O'Hare International Center
10255 West Higgins Road, Suite 900
Rosemont, IL 60018-4233
708-803-2000

HOTLINES

800-321-2681
Calcium Information Center

800-366-1655
American Dietetic Association's Nutrition Hotline
9 a.m. - 4 p.m., CST

CALORIES

ONLY 12 CALORIES A SERVING!

A SERVING

WHAT IS A CALORIE?

When referring to food, a **calorie** is the measure of energy made available when a food is eaten. The word comes from the Latin *calor,* meaning "heat," and the calorie we view with such misgivings in the context of food is exactly the same unit as the calorie we learned about in physics — the amount of energy needed to raise the temperature of one gram of water by one degree Celsius. Food scientists measure the amount of heat given off by different foods when they burn, and the measurements are expressed in terms of **food calories,** or simply calories.

Low-Calorie Foods

(Foods with from 0 to fewer than 20 calories per ½-cup serving)

Water
Club soda
Coffee
Tea
Freshly harvested
Jerusalem artichoke
Sour pickle
Sauerkraut juice
Dill pickle
Cooked zucchini
Raw Boston lettuce
Cooked New Zealand
spinach
Cooked cabbage
Cooked celery
Cooked summer squash
Cider vinegar
Raw Belgian endive
Raw cucumber
Raw rhubarb
Raw celery
Radish

High-Calorie Foods

Food	Portion	Calories	Fat (grams)
Avocado	1 avocado (medium)	324	31
Blue cheese salad dressing (regular)	2 tablespoons	154	16
Cheeseburger	Large double-meat patty with condiments and vegetables on bun	706	38
Cheesecake (prepared from recipe)	2-ounce slice	202	15
Chuck roast (braised and trimmed)	4 ounces	443	35
Duck (dry-roasted)	½ medium-sized bird	1,287	108
Eggnog (packaged, nonalcoholic)	1 cup	342	19
Frankfurter (beef)	1 5-inch-long frank (8 per 1-pound package)	184	17
French fries	Large order	355	19
Fried clams (breaded)	¾ cup	451	26
Ice cream (French vanilla, 16 percent fat)	½ cup	178	12
Italian sausage (pork)	1 link (dry-cooked)	216	17
Macadamia nuts (roasted, salted)	10 – 12 whole	205	22
Mayonnaise (regular)	1 tablespoon	100	11
Pancakes with butter and syrup	3 6-inch cakes, 1 ounce butter, 2 tablespoons syrup	519	14
Peanut butter	1 tablespoon	95	8
Pepperoni pizza	2 slices of 12-inch pizza	270	11
Ricotta cheese (whole milk)	½ cup	216	16
Salmon fillet (dry-cooked)	4 ounces	247	13
Red table wine (dry)	3.5-ounce glass	74	0

Both charts source: USDA Handbook 8

NOT ALL CALORIES ARE ALIKE

JEANNE JONES

Recently I was the keynote speaker for the opening of the Peninsula Spa, a state-of-the-art urban fitness club at the top of the Peninsula Hotel in New York City. For the occasion the hotel's executive chef created a wondrously delicious and stunningly beautiful brunch entree: a tall, cone-shaped tower of vanilla yogurt mousse resting on a crunchy granola cake in the middle of a swirling sea of colorful fruit purees.

The first question asked by one of the guests was, "How many calories are in that granola cake?" My answer was, "Who cares?"

The important thing to know about any meal is not how many calories or how much fat is in any one item but the total calories and how many of them come from fat.

Calories come from only four sources: the three food groups and alcohol. The number of calories in one gram varies considerably depending on its source:

1. **Carbohydrates** (both simple and complex): 4 calories per gram
2. **Proteins** (both animal and plant): 4 calories per gram
3. **Fats** (saturated, polyunsaturated, and monounsaturated): 9 calories per gram
4. **Alcohol** (wine, beer, distilled spirits): 7 calories per gram.

As you can see, fats have more than twice as many calories per gram as either carbohydrates or protein; therefore, fats have the greatest calorie density.

Many people have the wrong idea about how to lose weight. They think the way to lower calorie intake is to cut down on carbohydrate foods such as breads, cereals, potatoes, and pastas and eat more protein foods such as poultry, meat, eggs, and cheese. [But] a large percentage of animal protein is fat, not protein. Since fat has more than twice as many calories as protein, these people are actually adding calories instead of cutting them. Picture yourself sitting at a table with an 8-ounce steak, an 8-ounce baked potato, and 8 ounces of steamed broccoli on a plate in front of you. If you chopped them all up and put them in measuring cups, you would have one cup of steak, two cups of potato, and three cups of broccoli.

Even though in terms of volume the steak is the smallest-sized portion on the plate, it has four times as many calories as the baked potato and 12 times as many calories as the steamed broccoli! You can certainly see that if you are trying to cut calories, the first thing to do is cut the steak in half, not the potato and certainly not the broccoli. It's not the protein in the steak that makes it so high in calories, it's the fat hiding in the red muscle, or the *calorie density*. . . .

Fortunately, you can leave the fat off a baked potato, but you can't get the fat out of a well-marbled steak. . . . [If you *do* add] butter or margarine, sour cream, and chopped bacon to a plain 8-ounce baked potato, you can increase the calories from 240 to over 1,000.

Excerpted from Eating Smart, ABCs of the New Food Literacy

MORE INFORMATION

Calorie Control Council
5775 Peachtree-Dunwoody
Road, Suite 500-G
Atlanta, GA 30342
404-252-3663

**National Center for
Nutrition and Dietetics**
American Dietetic Association
216 West Jackson Boulevard,
Suite 800
Chicago, IL 60606-6995
312-899-4853

The Sugar Association
1101 15th Street NW,
Suite 600
Washington, DC 20005
202-785-1122

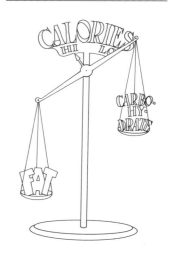

CAMELS

DESERT MILKING MACHINES?

While his fellow researchers "sift through the feces of desert crustaceans, grow tomatoes on sand dunes, and use the migratory patterns of quails to theorize about Moses' path to Mount Sinai," as *The Wall Street Journal* put it, Dr. Reuven Yagil of Israel's Ben Gurion University is cultivating — camels. Camel milk, he says, could be a valuable source of the water and protein so desperately needed by drought-stricken populations. Cattle die under such conditions, but camels can go for long periods without water and are able to get nourishment from just about any growing thing. Their milk is complete, nutritionally speaking, and in steady supply, and the less water available, the more water turns up in the milk, which is something close to a miracle when you think about it.

Poor farmers in arid areas have traditionally raised cattle rather than camels because they don't cost as much and breed faster. Using fertility drugs, Dr. Yagil has been able to increase his camels' breeding rate, and he is convinced that camel herding could, and should, replace cattle herding in impoverished desert economies.

The point is that camels' milk is already the beverage of choice for thousands of nomadic people and a well-fed camel can produce 10 gallons of it a day — as much as an American Holstein cow, and infinitely more than African cattle. What's more, camels produce meat and don't deplete the soil like cattle do. It's true that they are said to be intensely disagreeable, and smelly, to boot. But if Dr. Yagil's proposals are successful, camels could nourish a lot of impoverished people — and end up smelling mighty like a rose.

CANCER AND DIET

FRUITS & VEGETABLES PREVENT CANCER

JEAN CARPER

Ever since scientists started probing a cancer – diet connection in the 1970s, the antidote to cancer has been coming up "fruits and vegetables," consistently and relentlessly. It is a striking read-my-lips kind of message. In the words of Dr. Peter Greenwald, director of the Division of Cancer Prevention and Control at the National Cancer Institute: "The more fruits and vegetables people eat, the less likely they are to get cancer, from colon and stomach cancer to breast and even lung cancer. For many cancers, persons with high fruit and vegetable intake have about *half the risk of people with low intake*."

The fact is substantiated by massive evidence. A recent review of 170 studies from 17 nations by Gladys Block, Ph.D., of the University of California at Berkeley, came up with the same exciting message: People everywhere who eat the most fruits and vegetables, compared with those who eat the least, slash their expectations of cancer by about 50 percent. This includes cancers of the lung, colon, breast, cervix, esophagus, oral cavity, stomach, bladder, pancreas, and ovary. Nor are we talking about huge amounts of fruits and vegetables. Some research shows that eating fruit twice a day, instead of less than three times a week, cut the risk of lung cancer 75 percent, even in smokers. It is almost mind-boggling, says one researcher, that ordinary fruits and vegetables could be so effective against such a potent carcinogen as cigarette smoke.

The evidence is so overwhelming that Dr. Block views fruits and vegetables as a powerful preventive drug that could substantially wipe out the scourge of cancer, just as cleaning up the water supply eliminated past epidemics, such as cholera.

Excerpted from Food — Your Miracle Medicine

MORE INFORMATION

American Cancer Society
1599 Clifton Road NE
Atlanta, GA 30329
800-ACS-2345

National Cancer Institute
Cancer Information Service
Building 31, Room 10A24
9000 Rockville Pike
Bethesda, MD 20892
800-4-CANCER

Books

Cancer: Special Diet Cookbook
Clare Shaw and Maureen Hunter; Thorson's, 1991; $8.95

Food—Your Miracle Medicine
Jean Carper; HarperCollins, 1993; $25.00

Nutrition for the Chemotherapy Patient
Janet Ramstack; Bull Publishing, 1990; $18.95

High Stakes

The National Cancer Institute believes that one-third of all cancers are linked to diet; British researchers put the figure as high as 60 percent. Since one out of five Americans dies of cancer, Jean Carper suggests that "altered food choices might help prevent some 385,000 to 700,000 new cancer cases."

CANDY

A LITTLE SOMETHING SWEET

The great thing about candy is that it has no redeeming social characteristics. Its only purpose is to please— to taste so sweet and so good that we simply have to go back for more. When we bite into a favorite confection, there's no speculation whatever about whether this food is good for us, whether we are going to become slimmer, more beautiful, more virtuous; at first taste, these questions are out the window. Lick it, suck it, crunch it, chew it — candy delivers instant gratification.

Children love candy unreservedly; adults love it too, but often guiltily. Some struggle mightily to resist, but often the child within wins the moral wrestling match. And thus it is that holiday sales of candy now top $1 billion — an estimated $5.00 for every man, woman, and child in America.

A century ago, much of our candy was made in the home, by such processes as boiled-sugar syrups and candied fruits, that hadn't changed appreciably in centuries. A passion for something sweet goes all the way back through the history of human development: The earliest candy fanciers were Stone Age peoples, who raided beehives for their honey. And we know that by 1566 B.C., the ancient Egyptians were making gobs of honey and nuts to satisfy their sweet tooth.

Honey was long the main source of sweetness in much of the world, but our word "candy" comes from the Arabic *qand*, which means "sugar." Sugar came out of India, where it was first made from sugar-cane sap around 3000 B.C. In these early times Indians had the genius to develop nougat from boiled sugar and marzipan from nut pastes. By 700 A.D., traders were taking sugar cane west into the Arab countries, along with the techniques for refining it to make sugar. Not long after that, cane shoots and the knowledge of what to do with them crossed the Mediterranean, and in fairly short order, candy-making began on the shores of Italy and France.

In the Middle Ages, bonbons (literally, "goodgoods") were on the tables of only the very rich; by the 15th century they were more common, and the astrologer and prognosticator Nostradamus was so taken by the art of candy-making that he wrote a book about it. But it was not until the late Renaissance that sugar became accessible to just about everybody. Columbus took sugar cane to the West Indies, where it became a major crop to meet the growing demands of Europe. Amazingly, penny candy came into being in England as early as the 17th century, and the first corner candy store popped up in America just as soon as there was a corner to put it on.

This sweet story has left out any mention of chocolate, by far the most popular form of candy in the world. Its taste and rewards are so special that it is featured in a section of its own.

From Mutton Pies to Chocolate Bars

The Kit Kat bar probably gets its name from the Kit-Cat Club, which was an exclusive group of Whig politicians and writers formed around 1700. Its members met regularly over dinners at the house of a pastrycook named Christopher Cat, who was famous for his savory mutton pies, which were known, in a play on his name, as Kit-Kats. They were very sustaining — and so are Kit Kat bars.

Ruthie, Toot, Toot

The Baby Ruth candy bar was not named for the famous Yankee slugger, Babe Ruth. It was named to honor the daughter of President Grover Cleveland, who had been born in the White House and was the nation's darling. In fact, when the Babe tried to bring out a candy bar of his own, the makers of Baby Ruth went to court and got an injunction preventing him from using his own name in competition with them.

One day in 1896, as Leo Hirschfield rolled some chocolates for his daughter Tootsie in his candy store in New York, it occurred to him to call them Tootsie Rolls and offer them for sale to the children in the neighborhood. The rest is history. On any average day, 17 million Tootsie Rolls now roll off the factory line.

Did You Know?

☞ On an average day, 2,160,000 Hershey's Kisses are produced.

☞ Life Savers were the first candies in America to be wrapped in tinfoil to preserve their flavor and freshness. The label on the wrapper bore the slogan: "For that stormy breath."

☞ The first lollipop was a commercial candy on a stick, made at the turn of the century. It was named after the finest racehorse of that day: Lolly Pop.

☞ The Dutch have the biggest sweet tooth in the world. They consume 64.2 pounds of candy per person a year (compared with the American average of 20.7 pounds a year).

MORE INFORMATION

National Association of Chewing Gum Manufacturers
2 Greentree Center
Marlton, NJ 08053
609-985-2878

National Confectioners Association
7900 Westpark Drive
Suite A-320
McLean, VA 22102
703-790-5750

Retail Confectioners International
1807 Glenview Road
Suite 204
Glenview, IL 60025
708-724-6120

*"A most advanced communication system
Jenkins ... Pictograms, Ideograms and Candygrams!"*

Rush to Virtue

Although Americans are eating an average of 21 pounds of candy per person every year, a jump from 17 pounds per head a decade ago, the folks who run the candy-maker giants — Hershey, M&M/Mars, and Nestlé — don't sleep easy in their beds. Because their products are rich in calories and fat, they are worried to death about sinister implications for their tremendous business profits in the relentless American diet craze. And the fact that sugar-free gums and candies recently captured a whole 1 percent sliver of the confectionery market sent shivers down their collective spine.

In reaction, M&M/Mars has already introduced the Milky Way II bar, featuring 25 percent fewer calories and less fat than the original. One of the new bar's ingredients is caprenin, a fat introduced by Procter & Gamble that combines the taste and thickness of ordinary fat with half the calories. The other biggies are sure to follow soon with slimmer products of their own.

Hershey has a low-calorie bar in development, and Nestlé USA Inc. has been test-marketing Aero, a candy bar that's divided into 12 bite-sized portions and is targeted at women. The marketing idea is that men chomp and women nibble; the company hopes that women will like the idea of consuming an Aero bit by bit. There's no reduction in calories, though; a 1.4 ounce bar contains 210. Meanwhile, D. L. Clark Company is developing a bar called Clark Light, which they claim will have even fewer calories than Milky Way II.

But it's the small companies that are leading the way in the healthy-candy department. Sorbee International Ltd. has leaping sales reports with sugar-frees. Source Consumer Products Inc. has a chewing gum that is citrus-flavored and loaded with vitamin C . Estee Corporation, which originally targeted diabetics, has found a substantial commercial market for a range of its sugar-free products, including hard candies and gummy bears. On the fringe, Legume Inc. has introduced rice cakes made with whole- grain rice covered in tofu chocolate.

Candyland knows that even sugarplums are going to be called into the court of public opinion pretty soon, for a critical scrutiny of their nutritional content and social virtue — if any.

Understanding Rubbish

According to William Rathje, author of Rubbish!, *"After Halloween one finds lots of candy wrappers and almost no candy in garbage, while after Valentine's Day one finds that the candy itself (along with the wrappers, which still enclose it) often gets thrown away."*

Perhaps on Halloween what's important is the candy; on Valentine's Day, what's important is the gesture.

Books

Truffles, Candies, and Confections
Carole Bloom; Crossing Press, 1992; $22.95

Oh Fudge!
Lee E. Benning; Henry Holt, 1990; $19.95/$12.95

PERIODICALS

For addresses, see Information Sources

Candy Bar Gazebo
6 Edge Street
Ipswich, MA 01938
508-356-4191
Quarterly; $15 per year

Kettle Talk Monthly
Retail Confectioners International
708-724-6120
Monthly; free to members

The Sweet Journal
National Confectioners Association
703-790-5750
Every other month; free to members

A View of the Top Commercial Candies

Brand / Annual U.S. sales	Portion	Calories	Grams of fat
1. **Snickers**, made by M&M Mars, invented in 1930: $61.3 million.	2.07 ounces	280	13
2. **Reese's** peanut butter cups, made by Hershey Foods Corporation, invented in 1923: $41.3 million.	1.6 ounces	250	15
3. **Kit Kat**, made by Hershey Foods Corporation since 1973, under license from Rowntree's in England, where it was invented in 1933: $36.2 million.	1.5 ounces	230	5
4. **M&M's** plain, made by M&M/Mars, invented in 1940: $31.7 million.	1.69 ounces	230	10
5. **Butterfinger**, made by Nestlé, invented in 1923: $31.6 million.	3.8 ounces	250	10
6. **M&M's** peanut, made by M&M/Mars, invented in 1940: $29.6 million.	1.74 ounces	250	13
7. **Nestlé's Crunch**, made by Nestlé, invented in 1938: $26.0 million.	1.55 ounces	230	12
8. **Hershey's** milk chocolate bar, made by Hershey Foods Corporation, invented in 1900: $24.4 million.	1.45 ounces	230	14
9. **Hershey's** milk chocolate bar with almonds, made by Hershey Foods Corporation, invented in 1907: $24.0 million.	1.45 ounces	230	14
10. **3 Musketeers**, made by M&M/Mars, invented in 1932: $19.9 million.	2.13 ounces	260	8

CANNED FOOD

INTO THE CAN

JEAN ATCHESON

It seems quite simple, really: Food will keep almost indefinitely if you can kill off the microorganisms that would otherwise thrive in it and make it go bad.

Cooks knew centuries ago that you could preserve fruits in jars or bottles in honey, as the Romans did, or in sugar syrup, by heating them in a water bath, then corking them tightly. But it was only housewives who "put up" fruit in this way; the bottles were small and easily broken, the seals were not always airtight, and there were no precise instructions about how hot the water should be or how long the heating should last.

The father of modern commercial canning was a French confectioner named Nicholas Appert, who spent most of the 1790s experimenting with preserving meats, vegetables, and fruits under controlled, hygienic conditions. In 1803, he sent samples of his foods to the French navy for trials at sea and received glowing praise. The government awarded him 12,000 francs to publish a full account of his work, which appeared in 1810. Almost immediately, it was translated and published in Germany, England, Sweden, and America, and manufacturing operations similar to Appert's canning factory outside Paris were set up all over Europe.

At first, everyone used glass bottles and one English firm, seeking testimonials, was complimented by the President of the Royal Society on the high quality of its "embalmed provisions." Soon, however, tin-plated iron cans were used instead for everything but fruit, because they were more practical for stowing provisions aboard ship.

In 1824, a British naval expedition in search of a Northwest Passage around Canada had to abandon one of its vessels that became icebound, along with a considerable quantity of canned foods. Some four years later, a second expedition, running dangerously short of food, was able to survive by using the cached supplies, which, luckily, had not deteriorated. Its leader brought back one unopened can, which became a major attraction at the Great Exhibition of 1851, 22 years later.

The can subsequently reposed at London's Science Museum until, in 1938, a brave crew of taste explorers opened it and found the contents "quite like recently cooked veal" after 114 years. They put the empty can back on the shelf, where it remains to this day.

New Lifts for Old Standbys

Add a few touches of your own to pick up canned foods' flavor:

To canned black bean soup, add a tablespoon or two of sherry and top with finely chopped onions and chopped hard-cooked egg.

To canned clam chowder, add freshly chopped cilantro and crisp crumbled bacon.

To canned tuna, add mayonnaise, capers, and a touch of fresh lemon juice.

To canned yellow corn, add chopped yellow pepper and chopped mango, and serve in a leaf of red lettuce.

To canned chick-peas, add freshly chopped scallions and diced tomatoes.

To canned rice pudding, stir in plump raisins and a tablespoon of apricot preserves.

To canned pears, add pureed frozen raspberries and serve in a wineglass.

Cannery Rows Upon Rows

More than 1,500 kinds of foods are canned for the American market. Billions of cans are sold every year and the variety is stupendous: Over 40 kinds of beans, 75 kinds of juice, 130 vegetable products, and 100 soups.

For produce, for example, the process begins when the freshly harvested vegetables arrive at the cannery. After being washed and trimmed, the food is blanched to preserve its flavor and texture and to neutralize enzymes that cause spoilage, then packed in steel cans, vacuum sealed, and cooked. When the cans have cooled, they are labeled, cased, and sent on their way. Many foods are

packed without preservatives, and most will keep their quality for two years or more, if stored in a cool, dry place.

CARBOHYDRATES

IN THE MOOD

Are carbohydrates a pick-me-up or a calm-you-down? One mother of two believes sugar makes her kids hyperactive, so she bans not only candy bars, but fruit juice from their daily diet. An office manager, tired and under deadline pressure, munches chocolate to achieve that quick burst of energy he needs to complete the project. Yet that man's mother would swear that a hot sweet drink before bedtime guarantees a good night's rest, and *her* father was renowned for nodding off at birthday parties almost as soon as he had finished his last mouthful of cake.

According to Susan Chollar, writing in *Psychology Today*, recent studies have shown that carbohydrates don't cause hyperactive behavior, nor do they keep you alert. In fact, they have a calming effect, which can be quite pronounced, even unsettling, if the amount of carbohydrate is not balanced by some protein. Even cream cheese on a bagel can be enough to block the sedative effect of an unbalanced-carbohydrate meal.

Though people often attribute this feeling of fatigue to hypoglycemia, the sharp drop in blood sugar that can follow carbohydrate consumption, it is more likely that they are being affected by an increase in the brain's levels of serotonin, the chemical messenger that controls sleepiness and motor activity.

Other researchers, however, who have studied groups of people who report feeling uplifted and alert after eating carbohydrate-rich foods, hypothesize that they may be suffering from a biochemical deficiency and are unwittingly craving carbohydrates in order to raise their serotonin levels.

Even patients suffering from Seasonal Affective Disorder, who become tired and depressed during the winter months, tend to overeat because it makes them feel better. Experiments with exposure to bright light suggest that low levels of sunlight may induce a seasonal serotonin deficiency, which the patients are attempting to alleviate by bingeing on carbohydrate-rich foods.

Reading Between the Lines

Health professionals tell us that, ideally, 55 to 60 percent of the calories in our daily diet should be coming from complex carbohydrates and fiber (the remainder should be made up of no more than 30 percent fat, and the balance can come from protein).

This involves a drastic reordering of our priorities. "Instead of having a chicken dinner, we should be thinking of having chicken *with* our dinner," says syndicated columnist Jeanne Jones. To work with energy to spare, we should be eating a plate filled with

rice and a small amount of chicken, not chicken with a small amount of rice. There is a side benefit to this diet: It's less costly. Serving carbohydrates is the most economical way of eating well.

When you think about it, this is the way poor people have always eaten. In America, too, this was how we used to eat. Then, early in this century, powerful advertisers began enticing us to eat more and more meat and dairy products, which are where the money is, so we started eating fewer grains and lowly legumes, which are where the advertising

money is not. Over the last 100 years we have drastically reduced our consumption of complex carbohydrates, and have radically increased our health problems in consequence.

Athletes realized more quickly than the rest of the population the advantages of eating a high-carbohydrate diet Their goal is to get 60 to 70 percent of their daily calories from complex carbohydrates in order to have the energy and endurance they need for their big event, whatever it may be. There is more about "carbo loading" in the section on Athletes' Food.

Q&A

Q What is the difference between complex carbohydrates and simple carbohydrates?

A **Complex carbohydrates** are long strands of simple sugars. Also called polysaccharides, they are starches and fiber that are found in many of the foods we have been avoiding because we thought they were fattening: potatoes, bread, and pasta; peas, beans, and lentils; corn, wheat, oats, and rye; and vegetables, some fruits, nuts, and seeds. A single starch molecule may contain from 300 to more than 1,000 sugar units. The giant molecules are packed side by side in a plant root or seed, to provide energy for the plant to grow. All starches are plant material; all fiber comes from plants, too.

Simple carbohydrates are simple sugars, whose bonds are easily broken, or digested. All sugars are described in words ending in *ose. Lactose*, for instance, is the sugar found in milk; *sucrose* is just plain sugar; *dextrose, glucose, and maltose* are other types of sugars you see listed on the labels of syrups, honey, preserves, candies, and soft drinks. *Fructose* is the natural sugar found in fresh and dried fruit.

Did You Know?

☞ Manna, the food that sustained the children of Israel during their journey through the wilderness, was and is a complex carbohydrate.

☞ Complex carbohydrates are the only food category that is not in some way linked to dread diseases.

MORE INFORMATION

American Dietetic Association
216 West Jackson Boulevard
Suite 800
Chicago, IL 60606
312-899-0040

Books

Eating Smart
Jeanne Jones; Macmillan, 1992; $17.00

CARROTS

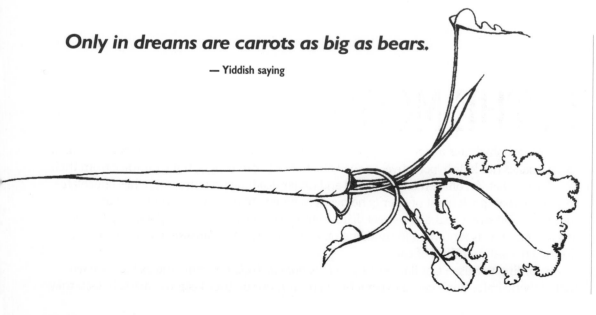

Only in dreams are carrots as big as bears.
— Yiddish saying

WHAT'S UP, DOC?

A lot. Eating just one carrot a day is like signing a daily health insurance policy. You may be surprised to know that cooked carrots are even better for you than raw ones. This is because the cellulose-stiffened cell walls are partially dissolved, making the nutrients more readily available. Three and a half ounces of cooked carrots contain a form of calcium that is easily absorbed by the body, as well as a whopping 15,000 units of vitamin A.

Like teenagers, the younger and slimmer they are, the sweeter the carrots will be — but chop off the fuzzy fronds on top before storing them in a plastic bag in the refrigerator. The leaves rob the carrots of moisture.

Old Wives' Tale

The link between carrots and male fertility was known long before the arrival of Bugs Bunny and his friends that breed — well, like rabbits. Carrots are also said to relieve menstrual pain and to blow away premenstrual irritability.

Supercarrot

A four-year-long collaboration between a geneticist and a horticulturist has resulted in the development of Beta III, a carrot that looks like a generously sized regular carrot, but contains five times the amount of beta carotene. This is converted in the body to vitamin A, which will make the carrot a potentially invaluable food in countries where the diet is lacking in vitamin A, causing serious and widespread vision problems. Fortunately, vitamin A deficiency is not prevalent in the United States, but the supercarrot may also be helpful in inhibiting the development of cancer.

Carrots
with Oranges

Serves 4

1 pound young carrots, scrubbed
3/4 cup orange juice
1 1/2 teaspoons sugar
1/2 teaspoon salt
1/2 teaspoon powdered ginger
1 tablespoon butter
2 oranges, peeled and cut into segments

Simmer the carrots in the orange juice mixed with the seasonings and butter for about 10 minutes. Add the orange wedges and heat through.

Books

The Carrot Cookbook
Audra Hendrickson and Jack Hendrickson; Storey Communications, 1987; $9.95

MORE INFORMATION

California Fresh Carrot Advisory Board
531-D North Alta Avenue
Dinuba, CA 92705
209-591-0434

Produce Marketing Association
P.O. Box 6036
Newark, DE 19714-6036
302-738-7100

"All your organic carrots and nobody gets hurt … "

CATFISH

If I go down for anything in history, I would like to be known as the person who convinced the American people that catfish is one of the finest eating fishes in the world.

— Willard Scott
'The Today Show'

WHY THE CATFISH ARE COMING TO THE TOP

It used to be that the whiskery catfish — bottom-feeding, sometimes muddy to the taste — was entirely ignored outside the South. But today it's the fifth most popular seafood in America — ahead of salmon, scallops, sole, clams, and crab — and the basis for a $500 million industry.

How did catfish come up from the bottom and break into the big time? The feat was accomplished mostly by Mississippi farmers, who built dikes around their former cotton fields, created ponds, and started raising "channel cats" in huge numbers — some 178,000 metric tons per year.

The channel catfish is the fastest-growing and the best-tasting of all catfish, with a deeply forked tail and spotted sides. There are also blue catfish and white catfish, but they are bottom feeders, unlike the channel cats, which frequently rise to the surface. This has been a great advantage in farming, because they can be fed special "puffed" pellets made of soybean, wheat, corn, and fish meal, which float on the surface, attracting the fish upward and effectively banishing the possibility of any muddy taste. The water in the farm ponds, too, is aerated and constantly monitored for temperature and oxygen level.

With the successful production of tasty cats came a product image makeover led by the Catfish Institute. A designer even proposed changing its name to "Tiffany fish," but the Institute preferred the plain old "channel cat." And, in less than a decade, its canny efforts shifted the catfish image out of the bayous and right out into the mainstream.

Did You Know?

☞ There are 100,000 taste buds on the surface of a catfish tongue.

☞ Americans eat nearly eight-tenths of a pound of catfish per capita per annum.

MORE INFORMATION

Catfish Institute
P.O. Box 247
Belzoni, MS 39038
601-247-4913

Catfish Farmers of America
1100 Highway 82 East
Suite 202
Indianola, MS 38751
601-887-2699

Books

Classic Catfish
Evelyn and Tony Roughton; The Antique Mall, 1993; $14.95

CAULIFLOWER

*Cauliflower is nothing
but a cabbage
with a college education.*

— Mark Twain
Pudd'nhead Wilson

NOTHING BORING HERE

The head of the cauliflower, which is known as "curds," looks like a single large flower, but it is actually a closely packed collection of stems, which, to confuse matters further, are referred to as florets.

Thinking that we might be getting bored with plain white cauliflower, farmers have been producing new varieties that are a delicate shade of purple. They say there is no difference in texture between the plain white (snowball) and the colored version (pearl); some folks think the tinted cauliflower is a little less crisp.

Broccoflower, the newest member of the family, is a cross between broccoli and cauliflower. Its appealing green color is echoed by its sweet, unpeppery taste. Just one cup of broccoflower contains 124 percent of the recommended daily allowance of vitamin C.

Despite its more humdrum image, cauliflower is also a good source of vitamin C; it contains vitamin B-6 and potassium, too, as well, of course, as fiber.

Interestingly, though most U.S. cauliflower is grown in California, almost all the rest of our supply comes from Arizona.

MAIL ORDER SOURCES

Diamond Organics
P.O. Box 2159
Freedom, CA 95019
800-922-2396

Lone Pine Farm
P.O. Box 38
Inglefield, IN 47618
812-867-3149

Books

Broccoli and Company
Audra Hendrickson and
Jack Hendrickson; Storey
Communications, 1989;
$9.95

TIPS

Serving

• Toss blanched, chilled cauliflower florets with sun-dried tomatoes, toasted pine nuts, fresh basil, and a roasted garlic and balsamic vinaigrette dressing.

• Toss blanched cauliflower and broccoli florets with cherry tomatoes, radishes, and diced yellow peppers. Serve with a creamy tarragon dressing.

• Puree cauliflower with a Dijon cream sauce and serve with grilled ham steaks or pork chops and applesauce.

• To make a great soup, simmer cauliflower with Spanish onions and russet potatoes in chicken broth. Puree, add cream, and a touch of horseradish and fresh dill.

ALERT

Cauliflower contains vitamin K, which has blood-clotting properties and may reduce the effectiveness of anticoagulant drugs. Like other cruciferous vegetables, cauliflower contains chemicals known as goitrogens that may cause problems with people who are taking medication for a thyroid condition.

CAVIAR

*Caviar is to dining what a
sable coat is to a girl
in evening dress.*

— Ludwig Bemelmans

SOMETHING FISHY HERE

As a young man I had a cozy picture about caviar production. In my mind's eye I saw the broad mouth of a river, which I comfortably called the Malossol; in it a lot of big Russkies were singing boat songs and wading and carefully lifting immense sturgeons out of the water while relieving them gently of their eggs with a soft, sluicy swish and then putting them back again, like milked cows let out to pasture."

So said Ludwig Bemelmans. How elegant the process was in his mind; how civilized. Not a bit like what's been going since the collapse of the Soviet Union. Now everyone is fighting about how many sturgeon can be caught without endangering the species and killing the sturgeon that "lays" the little black eggs. The Kazakhs are yelling at the Turkmen, and the Azeris are at loggerheads with the Russians. What with Kalmyk and Dagestan joining the fray, it's not surprising that the underwater crooks are out there raking in the roe and the dough. It would be nice to say that, in consequence, the prices are tumbling down. But it wouldn't be true. Prices have fallen a little, but as of May 1994 Petrossian was selling its Beluga for about $475 for 250 grams (8¾ ounces) while Macy's claimed to have one of the lowest retail prices around: "only $295" for 14 ounces.

America's Best

At the turn of the century the United States produced more than 600 tons of caviar a year, largely from the Atlantic sturgeon that swam up East Coast rivers to spawn. It was exported all over the world, but could hardly be given away here. In fact, it was offered as a free come-on in bars, like pretzels. Southern fishermen used to throw it away or use it for catfish bait. Then the caviar industry collapsed — the result of overfishing.

Thanks to conservation measures and the fact that the American appetite for caviar has broadened to include roe from other species such as the paddlefish, we are now getting home-grown caviar ranging from fairly awful to really very good quality from both coasts, the Great Lakes, and the Mississippi River in Arkansas. Fresh American sturgeon caviar costs about $6.00 an ounce. Laban DeFriese of Continental Caviar in Chattanooga, Tennessee, is the country's largest caviar producer, but there are also small companies such as Walter's Caviar, which supply knowledgeable buyers (Ted Turner and Jane Fonda took some Walter's Caviar on their honeymoon) at around $160 per pound.

The problem is that the female has to perish for the

Types of Caviar

Beluga, the most highly prized and highly priced caviar with the largest eggs, comes from the beluga sturgeon of the Caspian Sea.

Osetra and **Sevruga** both come from smaller sturgeon than the beluga. The eggs are smaller, too, and are preferred by some caviar connoisseurs.

Malossol may come from either the beluga, osetra, or sevruga sturgeon. The word itself, translated from the Russian, means "lightly salted" and usually designates a shipper's highest grade of caviar. By Russian law, it must contain no more than 5 percent salt.

Salmon (red) caviar of superb quality is processed in Alaska, mostly by Japanese workers. The bulk of the supply is shipped to Japan, where it is held in high esteem.

Whitefish (golden) caviar, mostly from the Great Lakes, was much in vogue until people discovered that it has very little taste.

Lumpfish caviar is a good description of these hard little eggs whose black dye weeps like mascara after a good cry.

processor to garner her eggs. Humanitarian Californians tried removing the roe sac by cesarean section, but when the fish are stressed they secrete adrenalin, which softens the eggs and makes them flaccid. Still, research is continuing on how not to kill the source of so much pleasure — and treasure.

How Caviar Is Made

Caviar is made by extracting the roe sac from the fish. The eggs are separated, washed, drained, salted, and shaken in fine sieves to dry them. They are then packed in specially made tins and stored at or slightly below freezing temperature.

There is more simplicity in the man who eats caviar on impulse than in the man who eats Grape-Nuts on principle.

— G. K. Chesterton
English novelist

CELERY

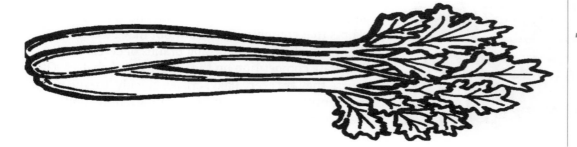

Stirring It Up

The celery stick garnish originated at Chicago's Ambassador East Hotel in the 1960s. A celebrity (unnamed) received the Bloody Mary he had ordered but not the customary swizzle stick. He grabbed a stalk of celery from the relish tray and used it to stir his drink. Thus is history made.

Ancient Cure —
Modern Explanation

No question, celery has its merits. Sears, Roebuck & Co. advertised a celery tonic in its 1897 catalog, claiming it was good for the nerves; a forerunner of valium, apparently. And long before celery was made into a patent medicine, the Romans and Greeks said it cured a hangover. They also thought that it chased away ancient-civilization blues and purified the blood at the same time. Their reasoning may have been that because the wild celery tasted so bitter, it *had* to be good for you.

We still feel in our bones that good medicine ought to taste bad, but cultivated celery has achieved the feat of tasting agreeable without sacrificing its mysterious powers. And now scientists have established a solid basis for the health claims made for it.

Anecdotal evidence suggested that eating two stalks of celery a day lowered blood pressure. Further investigation revealed that 81 percent of people on a high-potassium diet that included celery could control their blood pressure while taking only *half* the usual medication. Celery is high in potassium, but also high in sodium — there are 35 milligrams in a stalk. Sodium tends to be bad for hypertension, but, surprisingly, one factor doesn't cancel out the other. There are about 30 chemicals in celery, one of which is a substance called 3-n-butyl phthalide. Laboratory studies have shown that this significantly reduces the blood pressure by relaxing the muscle tissue in artery walls, thus making a wider channel for the blood to flow through.

It seems the Greeks found the solution to a problem without fully understanding either the problem or its solution.

Kalamazoo —
And Celery, Too

The celery we all now know, Pascal celery, was first cultivated in Kalamazoo, Michigan, in 1874. To popularize the new vegetable, crisp stalks were offered free to passengers traveling through the area by train.

Pascal celery is now the second most important salad crop in the nation, available year-round, from **California, Florida, Texas,** and **Michigan.**

MORE INFORMATION

American Celery Council
P.O. Box 140067
Orlando, FL 32814
407-894-2911

**California Celery
Research Advisory Board**
531-D North Alta Avenue
Dinuba, CA 93618
209-591-0434

Did You Know?

☞ About 2 billion pounds of celery are grown annually in the United States. The average per-capita consumption is almost 8 pounds a year.

☞ ½ cup of raw sliced or diced celery contains only 9 calories.

☞ Celery's crunch comes from teeth biting through the plant's air-filled cells, rather like puncturing small balloons.

☞ Would-be medieval magicians used to put celery seeds in their shoes, hoping this would help them fly. It didn't.

CEREALS

*I tell kids they should
throw away the cereal
and eat the box.
At least they'd
get some fiber.*

— Richard Holstein, D.D.S.

CEREAL KILLERS?

What's in your cereal box this week? How about plastic guns, ghosts, Ninja turtles, dinosaurs, cavemen, Batmen, and Barbies? Along with the artificial colors, artificial flavors, salt, sugar, marshmallows, dried fruit, and added vitamins and minerals, of course. When, really, the most important thing we ask of a cereal is that it won't go soggy as soon as the milk is added.

After that, we hope it will taste decent, and way down the scale of importance is that it should actually be good for us. Nevertheless, breakfast cereal can be the ideal way to get enough fiber into our diet and if there is a health bonus in getting the day off on the right foot, we ought to be thinking about what we put in our mouths.

The FDA has cracked down hard on food companies that make misleading advertising claims and forced them to withdraw or modify their messages or face formidable punishment. Compliance is mandatory, albeit grudging, but consumers, too, need to be alert to claims that comply with the law but may be ever so slightly misleading. Some 200 brands of cereal are in desperate competition on the supermarket shelves. Of course they try every flaky, crispy, crackly, toasty, puffy, fruity, nutty way they can to get our attention and coax the disposable dollar from our pockets. So it's up to us to keep it there — until we've read the fine print.

The Content of 20 Brand-Name Cereals as Defined by Their Manufacturers

Brand	Portion	Calories	Sugar (grams)	Fiber (grams)	Sodium (milligrams)
Bran Flakes (Kellogg)	²/₃ cup	90	5	5	220
Cap'n Crunch (Quaker)	³/₄ cup	110	12	N/A	220
Cheerios (General Mills)	1¹/₄ cups	110	1	2	290
Corn Flakes (Kellogg)	1 cup	100	2	1	290
Cracklin' Oat Bran (Kellogg)	¹/₂ cup	110	7	4	140
Frosted Flakes (Kellogg)	²/₃ cup	110	12	0	190
Grape-Nuts (Post)	¹/₄ cup	110	3	3	170
Honey-Nut Cheerios (General Mills)	³/₄ cup	110	10	1¹/₂	250
Life (Quaker)	²/₃ cup	100	3	3	230
Nutri-Grain Wheat (Kellogg)	²/₃ cup	100	6	2	150
Nutri-Grain Almond Raisins (Kellogg)	²/₃ cup	90	2	3	170
100% Whole Grain Wheat Chex (Ralston)	²/₃ cup	140	7	3	220
Puffed Wheat (Quaker)	1 cup	50	0	1	0
Raisin Bran (Kellogg)	³/₄ cup	120	13	5	220
Raisin Bran (Post)	²/₃ cup	120	14	6	200
Rice Chex (Ralston)	1¹/₈ cups	110	2	N/A	240
Rice Krispies (Kellogg)	1 cup	110	3	0	290
Shredded Wheat (Nabisco)	1 biscuit	80	0	3	0
Special K (Kellogg)	1 cup	110	3	1	290
Trix (General Mills)	1 cup	110	12	N/A	140

Note: None of the cereals contained more than 2 grams of fat.

FIBER
IN THE BELLY

COLIN MCENROE

I am not in the habit of shedding tears for gigantic, bloated American corporations, but I do feel a stab of pity nowadays for the makers of some breakfast cereals. They have a right to feel confused. They knew us as little kids, when our idea of a great cereal was one step short of an IV drip of dextrose — something that ricocheted off the pancreas and up into the brain, allowing us to experience, for brief seconds, the heightened state of consciousness shared by mass murderers and game-show hosts. Back in those days, the cereal makers felt they were practicing restraint by not tossing Hershey's Kisses right in there with the corn puffs.

And now we are 26, 36, or 46. Our idea of a great breakfast cereal is something that scours the intestinal tract with the ferocity of a wolverine, allowing us to experience, for many long hours, the heightened state of consciousness of a dairy goat. Today, the cereal makers feel they are practicing restraint by not tossing bits of gravel in with the pine husks.

Don't get me wrong. I think the world of fiber; I eat bushels of it. But fiber, like anything else, can suffer from the attention of extremists. There are people out there who are not content with a mere bowel movement. They want to pass a textile. They are fiber wonks.

. . . I used to favor a certain cereal that contained whole-grain rolled oats, wheat, brown sugar, raisins, almonds, coconut, and honey. I know it wasn't up there with the cereals that contain, say, cattails and steel wool, but it tasted good, and I figured it was at least better than those breakfasts where you cut a little hole in the bread so the yolk of the fried egg can peek through at you.

But then a fiber wonk caught me eating it one day and told me it contained rather a lot of . . . fat. . . .

So I don't eat that stuff anymore. I found something else that contains no significant fat and tastes good and consists of flakes that magically resist getting soggy in milk. I know in my heart it is a little on the wimpy end of the continuum, and, sure enough, when *Consumer Reports* recently [November 1992] rated all the cereals, it was in the middle.

I was sort of reassured to discover that they still sell Sugar Smacks, although it is no longer possible to be so bold-facedly honest. They are now called, simply, Smacks. I refuse to let my children eat any of that stuff, but it's out there. Somebody's eating it. We can only hope that, before it's too late, those poor innocents are located, converted into fiber wonks, and force-fed malted-barley stalks until the last shred of chocolate marshmallow mutant turtles are torn loose from their colons.

Excerpted from Men's Health

Did You Know?

☞ Consumers spend nearly $8 billion on breakfast cereals and consume nearly 3 billion pounds of cereals annually.

☞ More and more cereals are being eaten at dinnertime — the 68 million pounds consumed in 1991 was an increase of 2,000 percent over the year before.

Dr. Kellogg's Dream

In his later years, John Harvey Kellogg told how he came to invent the first ready-cooked flaked cereal food in 1894:

"I prescribed zwieback for an old lady, and she broke her false teeth on it. She demanded that I pay ten dollars for her . . . teeth. I began to think that we ought to have a ready-cooked food which would not break people's teeth.

"One night about three o'clock I was awakened by a phone call from a patient, and as I went back to bed I remembered that I had been having a most important dream. Before I went to sleep again I gathered up the threads of my dream, and found I had been dreaming of a way to make flaked foods.

"The next morning I boiled some wheat, and while it was soft, I ran it through a machine Mrs. Kellogg had for rolling dough out thin. This made the wheat into thin films, and I scraped it off with a cake knife, and baked it in the oven.

"That was the first of the modern breakfast foods. Later, I invented nearly 60 other foods to meet purely dietetic needs."

As quoted in A Food Lover's Companion

Making Sense of the Cereal Aisle

• Ignore the package phrase "all natural." It has no legal or nutritional meaning.

• Choose a product made from unrefined or whole grain. It will contain trace minerals like magnesium, manganese, chromium, and copper that are not added when a cereal is fortified. Look for the words "whole wheat," "whole wheat kernels," or "whole grain barley." Wheat flour is not the same. On oat cereals, look for "whole oat flour" or "rolled oats."

• Cereals that are even a moderate source of fiber, containing two to four grams, provide the fiber information on the label.

• Avoid cereals with a lot of sugar. Watch for the term "sucrose" on the label. Three to five grams of sucrose are acceptable, about one teaspoon per serving. Cereals that use honey in place of sugar are no better.

• If the cereal contains dried fruit, the label may make a separate category for "naturally occurring sugar." This added sugar, which comes from fruit, is acceptable because the fruit contains important nutrients.

• Some cereals, especially granolas, can contain significant amounts of fat. But most cereals have no fat, though a few have one gram. None have cholesterol.

Do not choose a cereal on the basis of whether it contains all of the Recommended Daily Allowance of vitamins and minerals. If a child is eating well-balanced meals the rest of the day, there is no need to get all the vitamins and minerals at one sitting. And for those who really need additional vitamins, a pill is cheaper.

— Marian Burros
Excerpted from The New York Times

CHEESES

Milk's leap to immortality.

— Clifton Fadiman
Cheese lover

JUST FOR STARTERS:
A REVIEW OF MODERN CHEESE-MAKING

Imagine a teaspoon containing 5 trillion living organisms. That's how power-packed modern cheese-starter cultures are. Early cheese-makers just hoped for the best, relying on the milk-souring lactic acid bacteria that occur naturally in milk. Now specialist companies grow pure cultures of bacteria in the whey that separates from the curds in the process of cheese production. The selected bacteria, such as *Lactococcus* and *Lactobacillus*, ferment lactose, a type of sugar that occurs in milk, forming lactic acid. The acid helps stop undesirable microbes from growing in the cheese, by preserving the milk solids; later, it is involved in the important process of "curing" the cheese to give it flavor.

Pure starter cultures and clean, pasteurized milk are the starting point in cheese-making. Without cleanliness, harmful bacteria such as *Listeria* can contaminate cultures and cause food poisoning. But deliberately introduced molds also have a role. Without *Penicillium* mold, we'd have no Camembert nor Roquefort cheeses, and no penicillin-based antibiotics, either.

After cheese-makers introduce bacteria to the

milk, they add an enzyme called chymosin to the mix; this will aid in clumping the milk protein into curds as the milk is gradually heated, leaving behind the watery whey. Until recently, the sole source of chymosin was the rennet extracted from calves' stomachs, a by-product of veal production; several companies are now producing it from genetically modified bacteria.

In the completion of cheese-making, the cheese-maker mills the curds, then salts and molds them, and, finally, stores the young cheese to let it mature and ripen — a process that may take many months. During the curing process proteins and fats slowly break down into their flavorful component parts — amino acids, sulfur compounds, and fatty acids — which give each cheese its specific taste and character.

Low-Fat Cheese: Not Much There

Sales of reduced-fat cheeses are gaining all the time — at last report they had increased 60 percent in just over a year — but what people are doing with them remains something of a mystery. One thing we definitely know is that you cannot bring these cheeses anywhere near heat without reducing them to the flavor and consistency of rubber. Thus it's unlikely that anyone is doing much cooking with them: It *can* be done, but only with the utmost care. Cheese sauces are out of the question; low-fat cheeses can be added to casseroles only when grated and then at the very last moment. Fat-free cheeses make their only plausible appearance in salads and sandwiches, or in cheesecakes and other refrigerated desserts.

The Classics — A Sampler

Soft and Semisoft Cheeses

Bel Paese: Italian, from cow's milk; it has a mild, buttery taste.

Bleu de Bresse: French, from cow's milk or goat's milk; soft and creamy with blue veins, it's milder than most other blues.

Boursault: French, from cow's milk, cream-enriched; very smooth and mild.

Brie: French, may be pasteurized or raw, from cow's milk whole or raw; creamy, buttery.

Bûcheron: French, from raw goat's milk; soft and creamy with a tang.

Camembert: French, from raw or pasteurized cow's milk; creamy and somewhat tangy.

Feta: Greek, from sheep's, goat's, or cow's milk; crumbly, tangy, salty.

Gorgonzola: Italian, from cow's or goat's milk; a semisoft pungent blue.

Havarti: Danish, from cow's milk, cream-enriched; buttery, often contains caraway seeds.

Liederkranz: American, from cow's milk; smooth, highly flavored and strongly aromatic.

Limburger: Belgian, from cow's milk, with a very strong taste and aroma.

Monterey Jack: American, from cow's milk; semisoft and mild.

Montrachet: French, from raw goat's milk; creamy and mild.

Mozzarella: Italian, from whole or skimmed cow's milk; tender, spongy, mild.

Muenster: German, from cow's milk; mild and pungent.

Port-Salut: French, from cow's milk; smooth and buttery.

Roquefort: French, from raw sheep's milk; semisoft and blue-veined, with a sharp flavor.

Hard Cheeses

Appenzeller: Swiss, from raw cow's milk; firm, with a fruity taste.

Caerphilly: Welsh, from raw cow's milk; firm, flaky, slightly salty.

Cheddar: English, from cow's milk; firm, mild when new, sharp when aged.

Cheshire: English, from cow's milk; firm, like Cheddar if white or orange, piquant if blue-veined.

Edam: Dutch, from cow's milk; known for its red wax casing; mild when young, sharper later.

Emmentaler: Swiss, from partially skimmed raw or pasteurized cow's milk; mild with a nutty flavor.

Fontina: Italian, from cow's or sheep's milk; nutty, with a strong aroma.

Gouda: Dutch, from cow's milk; mild, nutty when young; tangy after long curing.

Gruyère: Swiss, from cow's milk; firm, with widely dispersed holes and a nutty flavor.

Jarlsberg: Norwegian, from cow's milk; firm, buttery, with a slight tang.

Parmesan: Italian, from partly skimmed cow's milk; only those stamped Parmigiano Reggiano are authentic; hard and dry, with a sharp flavor.

Provolone: Italian, from cow's milk and usually smoked; firm, mild when new, piquant when aged.

Stilton: English, from cow's milk; a crumbly blue.

MORE INFORMATION

American Cheese Society
34 Downing Street
New York, NY 10014
212-727-7939

Cheese Importers Association of America
460 Park Avenue
New York, NY 10022
212-753-7500

International Dairy, Deli, Bakery Association
313 Price Place, Suite 202
P.O. Box 5528
Madison, WI 53705-0528
608-238-7908

National Cheese Institute
1250 H Street NW, Suite 900
Washington, DC 20005
202-296-1909

Wisconsin Cheese Makers Association
P.O. Box 2133
Madison, WI 53701
608-255-2027

Books

A Gourmet's Guide to Cheese
Carol Timperley and Cecilia Norman; HP Books, 1990; $9.95

Chèvre! The Goat Cheese Cookbook
Laura Chenel; Addison Wesley, 1990; $9.57

The Cheese Primer
Steve Jenkins; Workman, 1993; $15.95

The Simon & Schuster Pocket Guide to Cheese
Sandy Carr; Simon & Schuster, 1992; $13.00

Les Brousses

Le Roquefort

Le Brie

Le Hollande

Classic Cheese Fondue

Serves 6

1 clove garlic, halved
2 cups dry white wine
1 pound Gruyère cheese, grated
1 pound top-quality Swiss cheese (such as Emmentaler), grated
Freshly ground black pepper
2 tablespoons cornstarch dissolved in 2 tablespoons kirsch
French bread cut into 1-inch cubes, for dipping

Rub the garlic all over the inside of an enameled cast-iron fondue pot. Add the wine. Place the pot over moderate heat until the wine begins to simmer. Add the cheeses, a little at a time, stirring slowly in a figure-eight pattern. When the cheese has melted, season with pepper to taste.

Stir the dissolved cornstarch into the cheese mixture. Continue stirring until the mixture has thickened, about 2 to 3 minutes. Place the fondue over a small burner at the table and invite everyone to pull up a chair. Spear the bread on fondue forks and dip it into the cheese, which will gradually cook more and more and become crustier on the bottom.

Note: If you do not have a fondue pot and the correct long thin forks for dipping into the cheese, you can use a deep heavy saucepan and conventional forks instead. Though a little of the charisma will be lost, the fondue will taste just as good. Serve the fondue with small boiled new potatoes, cornichons, and radishes.

Velveeta Visions

by Richard Atcheson

My friend the food snob was over the other day and went into the kitchen for a cold drink.

"You have Velveeta in your refrigerator!" he cried, as if he had found some live alligators in there.

"Of course I do," I replied, *"but it doesn't have to be in the refrigerator. It's the perfect emergency food. It has the shelf life of stick-on floor tiles."*

"But you eat that stuff?" he asked.

"With pleasure," I replied. *"I love the taste. I've loved it since I was a kid. And if I make a sandwich for a train ride from New York to Boston, my Velveeta is as fresh at New Haven as it was in Penn Station. Velveeta is forever."*

"You never take train rides to Boston," he said.

"I might," I replied. *"Meanwhile, if a tsunami should engulf Manhattan and I'm marooned in my apartment . . ."*

". . . and the floor tiles pop up . . ."

"Velveeta is for any occasion," I replied, with a certain smug satisfaction.

What Cottage Was That, Exactly?

Cottage cheese was not, in its beginnings, the fashionable diet food it is today. It got its name because until well into the 20th century it was a true cottage industry, a food made in home kitchens all over Europe and America. Housewives would skim the milk for butter-making and put the pan of excess milk aside at the back of the stove. When the milk curdled and whey formed, they would pour the curds into a cloth bag and let the whey drain off. The residue became an important source of protein for the entire family.

Today's cottage cheese differs in few respects from what was made in those humble cottages, though the dimensions of the process have burgeoned. Giant processing plants handle tons of milk in a day, using 100 pounds (46½ quarts) of pasteurized skim milk to produce 15 pounds of cottage cheese.

The process starts with coagulation, which is aided by lactic-acid-producing bacteria or food-grade acids, with or without the addition of rennet. When the curds form they are cut and agitated slowly in a vat. After about two hours the whey is drained off, and the curd is washed to remove any residue of whey. In the last stage, a mixture of cream and milk is added to create a creamy consistency. Then the product is packaged and sent to stores and restaurants.

As often as not a dollop of it will find its way to a dieter's plate, where it will be garnished by a sprig of parsley, a slice of orange, a couple of carrot curls, and other mouthwatering elements. What once was a crucial family staple has become in our time the last resort of weight-watchers.

Le Camembert

Le Munster

Cheese Dreams

Cream cheese seems like the kind of cheese weight-watchers ought only to dream about while they nibble at their cottage cheese. Made in a similar process, cream cheese differs in the amount of cream and milk that is added to the curds — usually enough to yield a total milk-fat content of about 12 percent. Its smooth creamy taste goes wonderfully well with strongly flavored foods or crispy crackers and it blends beautifully into dips. Cream cheese also comes preflavored, making a great marriage with chives, scallions, pimientos, olives, pineapple, and nuts.

But an ounce of regular cream cheese has only half a gram more fat than an ounce of Cheddar, and the whipped or low-fat styles such as Neufchatel have considerably less, so a cream cheese dream needn't be a dieter's nightmare. Indeed, spread thinly on a plain bagel, it could even be an acceptable lunch. Definitions of *thinly*, of course, vary.

Caerphilly Fights Cavities

Most cheeses — especially the hard ones, such as Cheddar, Gouda and, yes, Caerphilly — literally help prevent cavities by counteracting the harmful effects of acids on the teeth. You should also know that the fat content of cheese includes fatty acids that have an anti-bacterial effect that actually prevents tooth decay. So the next time your dentist tries to intimidate you with a giant toothbrush, simply fend him off with a wheel of Fontina or, for convenience, a pocket-sized package of Edam.

Baa-aah!

Goat cheese — *Chèvre* for those who know how to pronounce it in French — is a hit in chic circles. At its finest it comes direct from the Loire Valley of France, using methods that date back more than 400 years. For the genuine article, look for a cindering in the black ash of birches mixed with pulverized sea salt, a texture as insinuating as satin, and a voluptuous melange of flavors that astonishes the most sophisticated palate. Excellent American versions also now exist; domestic goat-cheese sales now total about 2 million pounds a year, double what they were in 1989, but that's still just a tiny share of the total American cheese market.

Cheese from goat's milk was not an easy sale in the United States. It's expensive — goats don't give as much milk as cows do, and the process requires a lot of handling. And it's weird. In too much of the American collective mind, a goat is an ill-tempered horned animal that eats trash. In fact, goats are just as friendly and intelligent as dogs are, and they would rather graze on bushes and shrubs than tin cans anytime. It has taken producers a lot of time and effort to overcome sales resistance. But the business is looking up, and it's estimated that there are currently more than 150 small domestic goat-cheese makers in America. Says Dave Thompson, editor and publisher of the *Dairy Goat Journal*: "I get a dozen or two calls and letters a week from people who would like to make a living at it."

CHERRIES

I gave my love a cherry
That has no stone,
I gave my love a chicken
That has no bone,
I gave my love a baby
That's no cryin'.
How can there be a cherry
That has no stone?
How can there be a chicken
That has no bone?
How can there be a baby
That's no cryin'?
A cherry when it's buddin',
It has no stone.
A chicken in the eggshell
It has no bone.
A baby when it's sleepin'
Is no cryin'.

— Old Appalachian song

CHERRY RIPE

There are two kinds of cherries, the sweet varieties we like to eat by the handful, such as the dark Bing and Lambert, and the tart, sour cherries, chiefly Montmorency and Morello, that are canned, frozen, juiced, and made into jams, jellies, and pastry and pie fillings. Both are good sources of vitamin C and fiber.

Sweet cherries

Almost anyone can grow a cherry tree in their backyard (though the birds usually steal most of the fruit), but the western states of Washington, Oregon, California, Idaho, and Utah — produce most of the sweet cherries we see so briefly in our markets from June until the middle of August. Cherries are among the few crops that are truly seasonal.

Cherries are a delicate fruit. They demand specific growing conditions that are superbly met in the fertile, well-watered valleys of the Pacific Northwest, where warm days and cool nights combine with expert modern technology to produce the finest quality sweet cherries in the world.

Cherry growers do not fit the stereotype of "big business" farmers and ranchers. Most orchards are quite small and are tended by doctors, teachers, and business people who also grow other "tree fruits" such as apples, peaches, pears, apricots, plums, and nectarines. Almost no one grows sweet cherries as their sole crop. Fickle weather patterns — an early spring frost as the blossoms emerge, a cold snap at pollination time, rain during the harvest — can snatch away their livelihood in minutes. No one can count on a good crop every year.

Tart cherries

Michigan is the leading producer of tart cherries, and 75 percent of the nation's crop comes from the five-county area around Traverse City. The region yields up to 80 million pounds of fruit annually. The orchards are planted in the sandy soil along stretches of Lake Michigan where the weather is tempered by the huge body of inland water. The cherries ripen fast and the season is even shorter than for the sweet cherries of the Northwest. Michigan's harvesting begins and ends in July.

Did You Know?

☞ There are more than 1,000 varieties of cherries in the United States, but fewer than 10 are produced commercially.

☞ New York's Broadway takes a jog westward at its intersection with East 10th Street because a cherry tree once stood there.

☞ The flowering cherry trees around the Tidal Basin in Washington, D.C., were a gift from the Mayor of Tokyo in 1910.

☞ Only 20 countries in the world have the correct growing conditions for producing commercial crops of cherries.

☞ The world's leading cherry producers are the former Soviet Union, the United States, Germany, Italy, and France.

Cherries Jubilee
Serves 4

1-pound can dark sweet cherries
1 tablespoon sugar
1 tablespoon arrowroot or cornstarch
1/2 teaspoon almond extract
Grated rind of 1 orange
Grated rind of 1 lemon
1/4 cup Grand Marnier
1 tablespoon brandy
Vanilla ice cream

Drain the cherries, reserving the juice. Set them aside in a bowl.

Pour the reserved juice into a saucepan and stir in the sugar and arrowroot. Stir over low heat until the liquid is clear and slightly thickened. Add the almond extract, grated rinds, and cherries and heat until hot.

In a separate pan, heat the Grand Marnier and brandy until slightly warmed. Bring the hot cherries with their sauce to the table. Light the Grand Marnier and brandy with a match and pour the flames slowly over the hot cherries. Serve with vanilla ice cream.

Mr. Maraschino

You know, those bright red cherries that crown the piles of whipped cream atop old-fashioned sundaes and banana splits, or lurk in the russet depths of a Manhattan cocktail. Their name comes from the Italian word for a pungent liqueur distilled in Croatia and Italy from the marasca, a bitter Dalmatian wild cherry, in which cultivated cherries used to be steeped until appropriately fortified. Commercial maraschino cherries retain the name, but the original fiery glow has been replaced by food flavors and coloring. Glacé cherries also are maraschinos, boiled in their sugar syrup until it has the consistency of molasses and the cherries are about 75 percent sugar.

Old Wives' Tale
Cherries, they say, help to relieve the pain of gout and arthritis. Perhaps the old wives are remembering the days when they were young wives, with lips like cherries —sweet, plump, luscious, and irresistible. Cherries, they tell us, are an aphrodisiac. No wonder, if they can obscure the pains that attack aged limbs.

MORE INFORMATION

Cherry Central Cooperative
P.O. Box 988
Traverse City, MI 49685-0988
616-946-1860

Cherry Marketing Institute, Inc.
2220 University Park Drive
Suite 200
Okemos, MI 48864
517-347-0010

Northwest Cherry Growers
1005 Tieton Drive
Yakima, WA 98902
509-453-4837

National Cherry Foundation
190 Queen Anne Avenue N.
Seattle, WA 98109
206-285-5522

New York Cherry Growers Association, Inc.
P.O. Box 350
Fishers, NY 14453
716-924-2171

MAIL ORDER SOURCES

American Spoon Foods
P.O. Box 566
Petoskey, MI 49770
800-222-5886

Chukar Cherry Company
306 Wine Country Road
P.O. Box 510
Prosser, WA 99350-0510
800-624-9544

C. J. Olson Cherries
Route 1, Box 140
El Camino
Sunnyvale, CA 94087
408-736-3726

Country Ovens
229 East Main Street
P.O. Box 195
Forestville, WI 54213
414-856-6767

L'Esprit de Campagne
P.O. Box 3130
Winchester, VA 22604
703-955-1014

Van Dyke Ranch
7665 Crews Road
Gilroy, CA 95020
408-842-5423

Sweet Cherry Varieties

Kind	Description and use	Availability
Bing	Large, firm, juicy, sweet, almost black when fully ripe; the West's leading commercial sweet cherry. One of the best shipping and fresh market varieties; also used in commercial canning.	Mid-June to mid-August
Lambert	Dark red, heart-shaped, slightly smaller than the Bing, firm texture and rich flavor. Second to Bing as the West's leading commercial variety.	Late June to mid-August
Van	Much like the Bing, red to dark red, with sweet, juicy flavor. Profitable commercially.	Mid-June to mid-August
Rainier	Large, golden yellow, thin-skinned, with superbly delicate flavor; the cream of the crop — juicy, plump, sweet, but in short supply because of its fragility.	Last week in June to first week in August
Black Republican	Medium-sized, very dark red, turning to black when fully ripe; distinctive taste.	Mid-June to mid-August
Royal Ann	Also known as Napoleon, light yellow skin with pink blush; large, firm, flavorful with colorless juice.	Mid-June to mid-August
Stella	Good-sized, moderately firm, heart-shaped, with flavor comparable to Lambert; resistant to splitting from rain.	Mid-June to mid-August

Picking Cherries

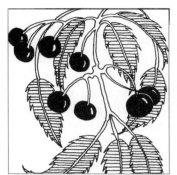

Cherries bruise easily and must be gathered with great care by workers — you guessed it — on cherry pickers, reaching up to detach the fruit gently from the 15-foot-high branches. In the old days, Michigan's tart cherry growers relied on hundreds of migrant workers who moved north every year to hand-pick cherries. They were equipped with a harness and pails, which freed their hands to gather the fruit. Picking with both hands, a skillful worker could harvest more than 400 pounds of cherries a day from trees with abundant crops, though 200 pounds was more usual.

Today, because of the high cost and irregular supply of hand laborers, tart cherries are harvested with a mechanical shaker, which looks rather like an upside-down umbrella. The shaker, attached to the trunk, vibrates the tree gently, causing the ripe cherries to fall into the canvas catcher. With the machine's aid, a single worker can harvest 25 to 30 trees in an hour.

In the Northwest, all cherries are still picked by hand, but the most prized and most fragile Rainier is often picked directly into packing containers in the field and shipped immediately to market. Rainier cherries comprise less than 5 percent of the total cherry crop, partly because they are so labor-intensive to gather. It takes as much effort to handle five acres of the yellow, rosy-cheeked Rainiers as to pick 50 acres of dark sweet cherries.

The cherries in each Rainier tree ripen at different rates, with those at the top usually maturing last. The workers are trained to touch only the stems, and each cherry is literally hand-selected for ripeness. One worker may take two weeks to pick 24 trees, and return to the same tree as many as eight times.

The last 20 years have seen the introduction of mechanical sizers, stem cutters, even automatic packers that fill the boxes. As soon as they are collected the cherries are sluiced with icy-cold water to prevent rapid deterioration. The boxes of fruit are loaded quickly into refrigerated trucks and are on their way to market within 24 hours. So if you want to eat sweet cherries at the peak of perfection, buy them from a busy store that is resupplied frequently.

A cherry pitter cuts the cherry more neatly than a knife does. It also prevents stained fingers.

Spit It Out There!

The International Pit Spit Competition, in Eau Claire, Michigan, is held just before the annual Cherry Festival in nearby Traverse City. In 1988, hometown boy Rick Kraus made it into *The Guinness Book of Records* for a second time with a super spit of 72 feet, 7½ inches — that's 13½ inches farther than a pitcher *throws* a baseball to the plate.

Books

Cherry Time!
Judith Bosley; Grand Books, 1989; $8.50

CHESTNUTS

THAT OLD CHESTNUT

Chestnuts are one of the few foods that can be used, literally, from soup to nuts. Versatile, nutritious (low in fat, low in calories, high in fiber), they add flavor to savory entrees, make luscious sweet desserts, and can be dried and made into flour. The Chinese roast them in hot sand; the French steam them slowly in cast-iron kettles; and in Austria, as in America, the fragrance of hot, slightly charred chestnuts rises from charcoal braziers in the wintry streets. The nut's only drawback is the time it takes to get the eatable part out of its shiny brown shell and tightly adhering inner husk. Though there are almost as many methods of doing this as there are ways of serving chestnuts, most cooks secretly depend on canned or vacuum-packed nuts, where others have done the peeling ahead of time.

Alas, there are almost no native chestnut trees left in the eastern United States, where the giant trees once used to dominate the forests, providing quantities of superb hardwood and tasty, nutritious nuts. They were wiped out in the billions in the first half of this century by an accidentally introduced blight to which they had no resistance. Scientists recently developed a way of inoculating young chestnut sprouts with a genetically engineered, less virulent form of the blight that would enable the trees to resist its ravages, but they have as yet to win permission to experiment in the open forest.

Almost all the chestnuts we eat nowadays are imported from Europe, chiefly from Italy, where the chestnut is almost the national nut. The name itself comes from the Latin *Castanea*, and the Roman legions spread chestnuts across Europe, planting the nuts during their campaigns.

Cream of Chestnut Soup
with Prosciutto and Sage

Serves 6

2 tablespoons unsalted butter
6 ounces thickly sliced
   prosciutto, coarsely chopped
   (about 1 cup)
2 medium-sized onions,
   coarsely chopped
9 cups homemade chicken
   stock or canned low-sodium
   broth
2 large boiling potatoes,
   peeled and cut into 2-inch
   pieces (about 12 ounces)
1 16-ounce jar vacuum-packed
   whole chestnuts
1 teaspoon dried sage
1/4 teaspoon salt
1/4 teaspoon white pepper
1/2 cup heavy cream
Fresh sage or celery leaves, for
   garnish

In a large saucepan, melt the butter over low heat. Add the prosciutto, onions, and celery. Cover and cook, stirring occasionally, until the onion is softened, about 10 minutes. Add the chicken stock, potatoes, chestnuts, sage, salt, and pepper and bring to a simmer. Cook, covered, until the potatoes are tender, 20 to 30 minutes.

Using a slotted spoon, transfer the soup solids to a food processor fitted with the metal blade and puree until smooth. Stir the solids back into the saucepan. (The soup can be prepared to this point up to 1 day ahead, cooled to room temperature, covered, and refrigerated.)

When ready to serve, add the cream and reheat gently over low heat. Ladle into soup bowls and garnish each serving with a sage leaf.

Peeling Chestnuts

Using a sharp paring knife or a special chestnut knife, cut a shallow X through the flat side of the chestnut, just through the tough peel to reveal the flesh. Bake the chestnuts in a preheated 375-degrees F. oven until they are split open and beginning to brown underneath the peel, 20 to 30 minutes. Remove the peel and inner skin while the chestnuts are still warm. (It helps to use a damp tea towel.) If the chestnuts cool and become difficult to peel, return them to the oven for a few minutes to rewarm.

Other Chestnuts

The chestnut, *Castanea sativus*, is a different tree altogether from the horse chestnut, *Aesculus hippocastanum*, which has pink or white candle-shaped flowers in spring and big green fruits in fall, which split open to reveal shiny round brown nuts which are *not* edible. And the Chinese water chestnut is not a nut at all, but a vegetable tuber.

CHICKEN

Chicken for the cook is what canvas is for the painter.

— Anthelme Brillat-Savarin
French gourmet extraordinaire

CHEAP, CHEEP

Chicken is just about the world's most popular protein, eaten by people of all ages, in every country, and in every culture. We eat it before it is born and after it is dead. We roast it, poach it, fry it, and never seem to get enough of it. Indeed, we praise more mysterious meats by saying they taste "just like chicken." The only problem is that chicken is losing its taste.

Today's chickens are almost man-made — mini-machines with no spare parts, designed to produce meat and eggs as quickly, cheaply, safely, and efficiently as possible. And in many ways the chicken breeders have succeeded. The birds our grandparents raised took infinitely longer to mature. Even in 1960 it took 10 weeks and 10 pounds of feed to produce a 4-pound broiler. By 1990 a bird the same size could be produced in 6 weeks with only 8 pounds of feed. Some scientists have even suggested that chickens might be able to reach this weight in as few as 25 days, although, as *Science of Food and Agriculture* points out, "the amount of time and feed required to raise a chicken to market size can be reduced only so far; the question is, how far?" Some breeders think we have already gone far enough, and are slowing down chickens' growth for fear the birds may literally be outgrowing the capacity of their vital organs.

Already the average hen's egg production has increased from 120 a year in the 1920s to 255 in the 1990s. Fewer days off are scheduled in the hens' future, though no one is as yet admitting the possibility of getting them to lay an egg every day.

A Classical Clavicle

The custom of two people each making a wish, then tugging at a dried chicken "wishbone" or clavicle until it breaks in two halves, indicating that the wish made by the person with the larger half will come true, dates back almost 2,500 years. The ancient Etruscans used to keep chickens in their temples that would provide answers to questions by pecking at grains of corn placed on a circle marked with alphabetical letters; a priest interpreted the results. When one of these sacred birds died, its collarbone was dried and believers would stroke it and make a wish — but not break the bone.

That part of the ritual came a century or two later, when the custom passed to the Romans, and there was a shortage of sacred bones — hence people started tugging at the bone to get the half with the "head."

The Romans brought the custom to Britain, where the wishbone was called the "merrythought," because people usually wished for good things to happen when they pulled at it. And it is suggested that this was also the origin of the phrase "to get a lucky break," applied to the person who got the bigger piece.

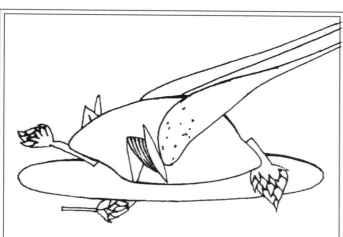

White Meat Or Dark?

As explained by Harold McGee, meat is muscle, and muscle that is active stores a lot of oxygen from the blood. This makes it darker than meat from muscles that are less frequently exercised. Chickens walk around quite a lot, so their leg meat is dark, but they very rarely fly, so their breast meat is quite pale, and turns white when cooked. Dark meat is higher in calories and fat than white meat.

Safety in Numbers?

There may actually be more likelihood of finding bacteria in chickens that are allowed to wander about freely than in those confined in large breeding operations that must pass the 43 quality checks mandated by USDA regulations. (Perdue, in fact, likes to boast that its birds undergo an *additional* 24 checks.) Range-fed chickens may have acquired superior flavor and texture from their country lives, but it is important to buy them from a good butcher who knows that his sources enforce strict safety standards.

A Chicken What's What

Free-range chickens are allowed to forage for food outdoors; by USDA rules, the door to their coop must be open so that they can roam outside at will. Understandably, chickens that range freely taste much better than mass-produced birds because they have the opportunity to eat a variety of natural foods; some people would also say it's because they lead happier lives. They are usually sold whole.

Organic chickens are understood to have been raised on land that has not been treated with chemical fertilizers or pesticides for at least three years, and fed entirely on chemical-free grains, although the precise USDA definition of "organic" has not yet been established. They are likely also to be free-range birds, usually available whole.

Mass-produced chickens are raised commercially, in quantities that almost defeat the imagination, in crowded but carefully supervised conditions that bring them to market at exact sizes and weights. They are available whole, quartered, and cut up into parts, often sold in multiple packs.

Kosher birds have been killed according to Jewish dietary laws under the supervision of a rabbi.

Broiler-fryers are chickens about seven weeks old, usually weighing from 2½ to 4½ pounds.

Roasting chickens usually are meaty hens eight or nine weeks old, weighing from 5 to 8 pounds, with enough fat to brown well as they roast.

Stewing hens or fowls usually weigh from 4 to 8 pounds, and are more than a year old, having spent most of their lives as laying hens. They tend to be tough, so they need long, slow cooking, but are full of flavor.

Capons are castrated roosters, about 10 weeks old, weighing from 8 to 10 pounds. They have generous amounts of tender, white breast meat and are ideal for stuffing and roasting.

Poussins are baby chickens, about a month old, weighing about a pound. They are tiny and toothsome, without much flavor, best for grilling and roasting.

Cornish hens are also babies, five to six weeks old; they weigh about 2 pounds, and taste best roasted or grilled. They have been crossbred away from the original separate breed of Rock Cornish Game Hen, but still have White Rock and Cornish bloodlines and a slightly gamy flavor.

Did You Know?

☞ Chickens have been raised domestically for at least four thousand years.

☞ When inflation is figured in, chicken costs less today than it did 30 years ago. Overproduction keeps the price low.

☞ Between them, America's five top chicken producers raise more than 200 million pounds of ready-to-cook poultry annually. In order of production, they are Tyson Foods, Inc. (Holly Farms), with 80 million pounds; ConAgra, Inc., with 38 million; Gold Kist, Inc., with 35 million; Perdue Farms, Inc., with 26 million; and Pilgrim's Pride Corporation, with 22 million pounds.

☞ Americans' consumption of chicken has increased 280 percent since 1900.

☞ Fifty-two percent of all poultry entrees ordered in restaurants are for fried chicken.

Books

Faye Levy's International Chicken Cookbook
Faye Levy; Warner Books, 1992; $29.95

Look & Cook: Chicken Classics
Anne Willan; Dorling Kindersley, 1992; $19.45

Perdue Chicken Cookbook
Mitzi Perdue; Pocket Books, 1991; $18.95

The Whole Chicken Cookbook
Jim Fobel; Ballantine, 1992; $12.00

365 Ways to Cook Chicken
Cheryl Sedaker; Harper & Row, 1986; $16.95

"And don't let me catch you hanging out with those free-range chickens!"

Bathing Your Chickens Before They're Packed

The USDA's Food Safety and Inspection Service has moved with uncharacteristic speed in approving TSP (trisodium phosphate) as a means of reducing salmonella contamination in freshly killed raw chickens. This chemical, manufactured by Rhône-Poulenc under the trade name AvGard, has proved effective in commercial tests, reducing the salmonella contamination rate from 25 percent in untreated birds to one-half of 1 percent in birds dipped in a bath containing TSP.

At an estimated cost of 1 cent per dipped chicken, the TSP bath looks promising — especially when compared with the alternative, irradiation, which can cost up to 12 cents per bird.

Frank Perdue gets the straight peep from the chicken assembly line, and it's good news — for him anyway.

TIPS

Storing
Keep frozen chicken breasts on hand to give weight to a quick pasta meal. They are easy to defrost in the microwave. Take care to barely thaw the breasts; if they are allowed to cook in the microwave, the fast change of temperature will toughen the meat. To ensure the breasts will stay tender, cut them into strips while they are still lightly frozen.

Preparing:
When preparing chicken breasts, remove the white tendon that runs the length of the breast; this helps prevent the meat from becoming tough.

• Truss all chicken and other poultry before roasting so that the wings and thighs will not be overcooked.

• When preparing a chicken for a salad or sandwiches, poach it in chicken broth; it will be moist and flavorful.

Cooking
Dark meat takes longer to cook than white meat, so when frying chicken parts, put the legs into the pan first and add the breasts later.

• To tell whether a roasted bird is completely cooked, pierce the thigh with a fork. If the juices run clear, it is done; if they are slightly pink, return the bird to the oven for 5 or 10 minutes longer.

• When chicken is cooked in a casserole, the leg meat shrinks, exposing the bone. To make a more attractive presentation, trim away the bone ends and wing tips with poultry shears.

I did not become a vegetarian for my health, I did it for the health of the chickens.

— Isaac Bashevis Singer, Jewish-American novelist

We Don't Wing It With Chickens

Today's doctors use magnetic resonance imaging (MRI) to detect and diagnose human ills. This state-of-the-art technique has been modified to allow poultry breeders and scientists to measure muscle and fat development in chickens from the moment they hatch. The use of MRI enables them to select for breeding those birds with a greater-than-usual proportion of lean muscle to fat tissue.

MORE INFORMATION

National Broiler Council
Madison Building, No. 614
1155 15th Street NW
Washington, DC 20005
202-296-2622

HOTLINES

800-535-4555
USDA Meat and Poultry Hotline

Nutritional Content of Dry-Roasted Chicken Parts

Part	Portion	Calories	Fat (in grams)	Cholesterol (in milligrams)	Sodium (in milligrams)	Protein (in grams)	Iron (in milligrams)
Breast	½ breast (86 grams) with skin	193	8	83	69	29	1
	½ breast without skin	142	3	73	63	27	1
Wings	2 wings (68 grams) with skin	198	13	58	56	18	1
	2 wings without skin	86	3	36	38	13	0
Drumstick	1 drumstick (52 grams) with skin	112	6	48	47	14	1
	1 drumstick without skin	76	2	41	42	12	1
Thigh	1 thigh (62 grams) with skin	153	10	58	52	16	1
	1 thigh without skin	109	6	49	46	13	1

Source: USDA Handbook 8

CHICKEN SOUP

SAY IT WITH SOUP

It's odd how you can have the same thing time and again and it's almost as if it doesn't register until that one rarefied moment when all other memories of that particular food are banished. This one time, it is in such sharp focus, engraved forever, and even becoming more intense as you savor it on the palate of the mind.

This is how it was for me with chicken soup with matzoh balls. I was suffering intensely at the time, with the gusting depth of pain you can only experience when you have finally accepted the awfulness that "he" won't ever call again. But my then-truest love, albeit in the surrogate form of a delivery boy, sent me a plastic, wide-necked bowl of . . . yes, that's what it was . . . and I sat in bed and smiled my way to the last drop. And I knew I was loved.

Why It Works in Scientific Terms:
Chicken Soup Inhibits Neutrophil Chemotaxis

In the 12th century, Maimonides wrote "soup made from an old chicken is of benefit against chronic fevers . . . and also aids the cough . . ." (20th treatise). While our grandmothers also advocated this traditional remedy, social and cultural changes have both called such practices into question and resulted in a loss of such traditional wisdom. We postulated that an anti-inflammatory action of chicken soup (CS) might explain its general salutary effects. As an initial test of this hypothesis, we tested the ability of CS to inhibit neutrophil (PMN) chemotaxis (CTX).

CS was prepared by a standard traditional method (C. Fleischer, grandmother of BOR, personal communication). Nineteen aliquots of the soup were sampled at various stages of preparation. Fraction 18 (completed soup without matzoh balls, prepared separately) was tested for its ability to block human PMN CTX in the blind-well assay system. Inhibitory effect of CS was observed whether the soup was added to the neutrophils or below the chemotaxis membrane. The inhibitory effect of CS on neutrophil chemotaxis was dose-responsive with significant activity detected at dilutions up to 1:200. Analysis of the various samples indicated the CS acquired inhibitory activity after the addition of the first set of vegetables: onions, sweet potatoes, carrots, turnips, and parsnips. Cytotoxicity was not observed, 93 - 98% of PMNs excluded trypan blue after incubation in suspension with CS.

This study suggests that chicken soup contains biologically active substances capable of inhibiting neutrophil migration. This may account in part for its traditional use as a remedy. It is likely that many other traditional remedies also have biological activity, and the worldwide loss of this information as a consequence of social and cultural changes is to be regretted.

— Barbara O. Rennard and associates University of Nebraska Medical Center

Chicken Soup
with Matzoh Balls
Serves 6 to 8

Broth:
- 1 3 1/2-pound chicken
- 3 quarts (12 cups) water
- 1 unpeeled onion, halved
- 2 stalks celery, coarsely chopped
- 1 carrot, coarsely chopped
- 2 bay leaves

Matzoh Balls:
- 2 eggs
- 1 1/2 tablespoons chicken fat
- 2/3 cup matzoh meal
- 1/8 teaspoon salt
- 1 tablespoon chopped parsley (optional)
- 2 tablespoons chicken broth or water

Remove the giblets from the chicken. Put the chicken and the giblets, except for the liver, in a large pan and add the water. Add the onion, celery, carrot, and bay leaves. Bring to a boil, then lower the heat, and simmer for 2 1/2 to 3 hours, skimming off the foam and fat that rise to the surface. Chill for 4 hours until a semisoft layer of fat has formed. Reserve 1 1/2 tablespoons of the fat for the matzoh balls; discard the rest.

Reheat the broth and strain it through a colander into a large saucepan. Discard the chicken bones and skin, the vegetables, and bay leaves. Reserve the cooked chicken meat for another use.

To make the matzoh balls: In a small bowl, combine the eggs and chicken fat and stir until well blended. Stir in the matzoh meal, salt, and parsley, if using. Add the 2 tablespoons broth and stir until just combined. Chill the mixture for at least 30 minutes.

In a large saucepan, bring about 6 cups of water to a boil. Bring the saucepan of chicken broth to a gentle simmer over low heat. Form the chilled matzoh mixture into 12 balls by rolling between the palms of the hands. Drop the balls into the boiling water, 4 at a time, and cook for about 2 minutes, or until they rise to the surface. Remove the balls with a slotted spoon and add them to the hot chicken broth. Cook the remaining matzoh balls in the same way. Serve at once.

Why We Believe It Works

Chicken soup with or without matzoh balls will always be comforting, especially when it's cold outdoors or someone is feeling cold and rotten (it is not recommended for anyone feeling sick to the stomach, however). The reason it helps is primarily because it is hot, and the heat spreads quickly through the body, opening the pores, as they used to say. Of course, the soup is also nutritious, and the floating, starchy matzoh balls are easy to eat and digest. But, in fact, any hot liquid would probably do the trick, too — especially when administered by someone who really cares.

CHILDREN'S FOOD

*I like children,
if they're properly
cooked.*

— W. C. Fields
American comedian

MORE OF THE RIGHT STUFF, PLEASE

Pediatrics reports that, given a choice, one-third of a group of elementary schoolchildren selected low-fat meals. We may be raising the first generation of Americans who are eating-literate, but the down side is that we are certainly raising the first generation of children anywhere who are cooking-illiterate. Average American kids neither see, touch, nor smell their food until they unwrap it hot from the microwave oven. They may be learning about good nutrition, but few of them know where their food comes from or how it is produced.

Should we be alarmed? Probably not. It isn't that children don't care about food, but that they care differently from adults. When many a parent calls the children to come to dinner, they run not to the kitchen or dining room but to the garage, assuming they are going to a fast-food restaurant — but they *do* run!

Even at home, most children do not eat the way their parents and grandparents used to. Fully 65 percent of all American mothers are now working, so very young children learn self-reliance early on. More than a third of mothers of 5- to 8-year-olds and nearly half of mothers of 9- to 12-year-olds let their children use the microwave on their own, and at least 63 percent of American children under 13 are now preparing at least one meal a week for themselves. Just about the same number also participate actively in selecting what the family eats.

Interestingly, whether or not mom is employed makes little difference to children's diet. Researchers have uncovered the fact that children of full-time or part-time working mothers eat just as well, or as badly, as the children of full-time homemakers.

The Food Pyramid recommends that young children should eat 6 or more servings from the bread group, 3 or more from the vegetable group, 2 or more from the fruit group, 3 to 4 from the milk group, and 2 to 3 servings from the meat group. Parental intentions to fulfill these require-

ments may be firm but are seldom resolute when confronted with a child who at a very early age has learned implicitly and explicitly how to say no. The experts tell us that most children have to be offered an unfamiliar food at least eight times before they will venture to taste it, that they learn to hate food they are forced to eat, and crave foods that are used as rewards.

Always offer smaller portions than children are likely to eat, and let them ask for more. And if bribe you must, stick to offering a chicken wing *only* if all the ice cream has been finished and the plate licked clean.

Remembrances of Things Past

In a letter to a playmate in Ohio, an expatriate child mourned the food inadequacies of a faraway country:

"There's no chocolate syrup, peanut butter, Spaghetti-Os, Hawaiian punch, Good Humor bars, hot dogs, potato chips, grape juice, bubble gum, Fluffer Nutter, Pop-Tarts, fish fingers, tuna melts, bologna sandwiches, popcorn, Slurpees, M&M's — there's nothing to eat in France."

Did You Know?

☞ A child between the ages of 4 and 6 needs as much calcium as a 25-year-old woman, and more vitamin D. Excessive consumption of soft drinks may inhibit absorption of the calcium children receive from milk and other sources.

☞ Only nine states mandate that nutrition be taught in schools.

☞ Nine out of ten children eat with their family three to five times a week. Fifty-four percent eat with their family every day.

☞ Seven million children provide snacks for themselves and their siblings after school.

Children and Cholesterol

Concerned physicians agree that eating habits formed in childhood play a critically important role in preventing heart disease. Louisiana's Bogalusa Heart Study of 10,000 children has found that children with high blood cholesterol exhibit signs of developing atherosclerosis, the process that leads to heart attacks later in life. We know from surveys that one-third of all American children 2 to 18 years old have blood cholesterol levels of 176 milligrams, or more, per deciliter, and are consequently at increased risk for developing heart disease as adults. Both the American Heart Association and the National Academy of Sciences advocate a heart-healthy diet for children over the age of 2, with no more than 30 percent fat, and no more than a third of that from saturated fats. (Fat is vital, however, for younger children's brain growth and their overall development.)

Andrew's Turkey

One of 21 recipes prepared "for your dining pleasure" by students in Mrs. Alicia Sarles's kindergarten class at Transfiguration School in Tarrytown, New York.

TURKEY
by Andrew
———

10 lbs. turkey
3 cans gravy
Nothing inside the turkey
No salt and pepper

PUT
the turkey in a big
glass thing. Put
the gravy on it and put it
in the oven for
12 hours. Let it warm
off and eat it.

Books

Fanny at Chez Panisse
Alice Waters; HarperCollins, 1992; $23.00

Healthy Yummies for Young Tummies
Ann L. Shrader; Rutledge Hill Press, 1993; $14.95

Jenifer Lang Cooks for Kids
Jenifer Lang; Harmony Books (Crown), 1991; $22.50

Meals Without Squeals: A Childcare Nutrition Guide and Cookbook
Christine Berman and Jackie Fromer; Bull Publishing, 1991; $14.95

The Book of Children's Food
Lorna Rhodes; HP Books, 1992; $10.95

Obesity Is a Growing Problem

American children and their parents have become obsessed with weight, and there are good reasons for them to be alarmed. Dr. Robert Mendelson, a spokesman for the American Academy of Pediatrics, believes that "the single most important health issue for pediatricians in this country today is overweight children."

In the last two decades there has been a 54 percent increase in obesity among children aged 6 to 11, and a 39 percent increase in the 12-to-17 age range. At least one out of every four children of school age is significantly overweight, and consequently at risk for a number of health problems that are likely to persist into adulthood. Not the least is the loss of self-respect, which can cause psychological difficulties every bit as debilitating as physical illness.

The problems begin early in life. Obese infants under the age of six months are twice as likely to become obese adults as are babies whose weight is normal. The risk rises as they grow older; from six months to age 7, the likelihood increases by seven times, and the longer the obesity persists, the higher the probability that the overweight teenager will become an obese adult.

The worst possible thing to do for overweight children is to put them on a diet. The best approach, say the experts, is for the whole family to support each other in *gradually* changing their life-style. Doing it cold turkey doesn't work; nor does serving an overweight child food different from everyone else's. The key is dividing the responsibility: parents are responsible for what, when, and where children eat; the children decide how much or even whether they do so. Interestingly, weight problems often arise in households where there are problems in setting limits, researchers have found.

The ultimate success comes from setting realistic goals — and in letting children know they are loved and admired for sticking to them. A bowl of Jell-O with berries and apple slices may not seem as appealing at first as a quart of super-premium ice cream cradled in a darkened room, but steady loss of weight has a powerful allure, too.

On the subject of spinach: divide into little piles. Rearrange again into new piles. After five or six maneuvers, sit back and say you are full.

— Delia Ephron
How to Eat Like a Child

The Food World According to Children

1. Children's Concern About Fat and Cholesterol

Children	73 percent
Adults	56 percent

2. Children's Influence Over Meal Decisions

Breakfast	65 percent
Lunch	46 percent
Dinner	8 percent
Snacks	74 percent

3. Children's Preparation of Their Own Meals

Breakfast	80 percent
Lunch	73 percent
Dinner	38 percent
Snacks	83 percent

4. Children's Record on Skipping Meals

Breakfast	57 percent
Lunch	41 percent
Dinner	17 percent

Source: International Food Information Council

MORE INFORMATION

American Academy of Pediatrics
Dept. C, Division of Publications
141 Northwest Point Boulevard
Elk Grove Village, IL 60009-0927

American Dietetic Association
216 West Jackson Boulevard, Suite 800
Chicago, IL 60606-6995
312-899-0040

American Health Foundation
Public Relations Department
1 Dana Road
Valhalla, NY 10595
914-592-2600

Kids Against Junk Food
1875 Connecticut Avenue NW, Suite 300
Washington, DC 20009
202-332-9110

Shapedown
Balboa Publishing
11 Library Place
San Anselmo, CA 94960
415-453-8886

CHILIES

AI CARAMBA!

RICHARD ATCHESON

There's hot and there's hot. This is a fact about chilies that people grow up with south of the border. Two chilies may look alike in every respect. Bite into one and it'll be mild, amusing. Bite into the other and it'll take your head off and put you through an out-of-body experience. Latins know this from an early age, so they grow up with a natural, healthy respect — not only for chilies but for all things.

Up north, we don't know from chilies *or* respect, and I think this is what makes us gringos. We have to learn respect the hard way.

My turn came about a decade ago in a Mexican restaurant on La Cienega Boulevard in Los Angeles. While waiting for my combination plate and Diet Coke, I noticed a clear glass jar by the napkin dispenser that seemed to contain a lot of pale green jalapeños. I thought, "How nice. Mild-mannered jalapeños such as I sometimes buy at the supermarket. I'll just have one." So I popped one into my mouth and chomped down.

As my teeth met I had a spiritual experience. Every cell in my body flipped over, tucked in, and said "Yaaah!" Tears gushed from my eyes, sweat exploded all over me tip to toe, I couldn't speak. The water I sluiced down my throat set my lips and mouth aflame and burned its way down tracheal lacunae that I had never before known were there. For a long time I sweated vigorously, gasped, wept — I think I was with the angels.

Food brought me back. No combination of cheese enchilada, chicken taco, rice and beans had ever tasted so … vivid. My Diet Coke swam into my mouth and was such a balm to my attentive taste buds that I had another. At the end of the meal my shirt was plastered to my body, and hot tears still seeped down my cheeks.

The lesson to gringos is clear. Playing fast and loose with chilies is never a good idea. You have no way of knowing, even on a bright day in L.A., when one of those pale green peppers is primed to blow you into the middle of next week. That calls for respect.

BUT IT HURTS SO GOOD

Do we really want to put into our mouths a substance that's used to repel grizzly bears and muggers? Well, yes, we really do. We want that chile in our chili, the whole five-alarm fire. We want the gustatory blowtorch effect of capsaicin, the chemical agent in chilies that delivers the heat. It's why we're willing to wear rubber gloves when we slice and prepare chilies as a food ingredient, and God forbid you forgetfully touch your eye with the finger of one of those gloves, lest the fire alarm travel straight to your brain and put you out of action for the first part of the picnic.

Can't touch but can eat? How is this possible? Well, for one thing, our palates tend to translate the heat as burningly tasty. For another, there's the adrenaline rush that comes with this territory; we get so excited about eating hot chili that the excitement whets the appetite. Then our endorphins kick in; some say we get the equivalent of a runner's high. Also, first tastes stun, almost anesthetize us, so that second and third bites will be a lot less dramatic than the first. It literally thwarts the sensation of pain.

This last fact moves us away from the dinner table and into the pain wards of hospitals, where capsaicin, in creams applied topically, has been recognized as capable of relieving the agony of shingles, arthritis, and other painful conditions. The cure may initially seem worse than the complaint — capsaicin salves may stun before they help — but they do eventually inhibit pain sensation.

Folklore was there before us, of course. Chilies have been recognized for hundreds of years as a cure for everything from indigestion to impotence — good for the heart, good for long life. They are commonly used in South America to kill parasites. And if you have a head cold — well, it's not an illusion when eating chili that the fiery pepper is clearing out your  sinuses. It's going through them like a hot wind off the desert.

Hotter than a firecracker, chilies are. And don't try to feed them to a dog or any animal; the sensible creatures flee. Only masochistic man will eat this stuff. But in pleasure and in pain, chilies are good for what ails us.

TIPS

Preparing

If fresh chilies are soaked in cold water for 1 hour, they will be slightly less fiery. Remove the ribs and seeds before using.

• Rinse canned chilies in cold water before using them.

• Rinse dried chilies in cold water, remove the ribs and seeds, then cut the chilies into small pieces. Let these soak and soften for at least 30 minutes before using them.

A Chart of Chilies

There are over 100 varieties of chilies, and many of them have more than one name. Here are the most popular ones (in order of heat). Bell peppers are not hot; look for them later in the book.

Kind	Description and use	Flavor
Anaheim chilies	Fresh, they are long, narrow, green; ripened and dried, they are brick-red. Good for stuffing, sauces, stews.	Sweet, fruity flavor, mild to moderately hot
New Mexico chilies	Related to Anaheims, with similar uses. Available fresh most of year; freeze well.	Hotter than Anaheims, with clearer, more cutting flavor
Poblanos	Large, fleshy, good for roasting, stuffing (as in *chiles rellenos*); never eaten raw.	Earthy flavor
Anchos	Dried poblanos, essential in *mole* (the dark sauce of chilies, chocolate, nuts, and spices).	Aromatic, sweet flavor
Jalapeños	Most widely eaten, most versatile. Add kick to salsas, stew, breads, sauces, dips; can be roasted, stuffed or eaten raw.	Hot
Chipotles	Dried, smoked jalapeños; used mainly in soups, salsas, sauces.	Smoky-sweet, with a hint of chocolate flavor
Yellow wax or Hungarian chilies	Named for their waxy look; related to sweet banana peppers, but much hotter; brought from Hungary in 1932. Good for yellow *mole* sauces.	Slightly sweet, with a "waxy" taste; quite hot
Serranos	Used fresh in salsas, pickles, roasted, or in sauces.	Hotter, more flavorful than jalapeños, hottest chile regularly available in United States
Pequins	Tiny, ¼-by-¾ inch, domesticated from wild *tepin* chilies; used for salsas, soups, sauces, and vinegars.	Intense, but transitory heat
Thai chilies	Thin, 1½-inch-long, many-seeded red and green peppers; provide the heat in most Southeast Asian dishes.	Fiery, lingering heat
Habañeros	Lantern-shaped, about 2 inches long, dark green to orange, to red when fully ripe. Used fresh with tropical fruit, or in salsas, chutneys, and seafood marinades.	Incredibly hot, 30 to 50 times the fire of jalapeños; said to taste of apricots (if any taste buds still function). Beware!

Based on material from Mark Miller, author of *The Great Chile Book*

Old Wives' Tale

In cold weather, sprinkle a little cayenne pepper in your socks to keep your feet warm. Many skiers do this, but you don't have to wear ski boots to use this trick.

Books

Hot Spots
David DeWitt; Prima Publishing, 1992; $14.95

Peppers: A Story of Hot Pursuits
Amal Naj; Knopf, 1992; $23.00

The Great Chile Book
Mark Miller; Ten Speed Press, 1991; $14.95

The Tabasco Cookbook
McIlhenny Company with Barbara Hunter; Clarkson Potter, 1993; $14.00

MAIL ORDER SOURCES ✉

Los Chileros de Nuevo Mexico
P.O. Box 6215
Santa Fe, NM 87502
505-471-6967

Mo Hotta-Mo Betta
Tim and Wendy Eidson
P.O. Box 4136
San Luis Obispo, CA 93403
800-462-3220

Tabasco Country Store
McIlhenny Company
Avery Island, LA 70153-5002
800-634-9599

CHOCOLATE

Cole Porter got a kick from fudge.
He had nine pounds of it shipped to him every month
from Arnold's Candies in Peru, Indiana —
his hometown.

PASSIONATE CHOCOLATE

The Aztec emperor Montezuma was so crazy about hot chocolate that he drank 50 golden goblets of it every day. It wasn't the hot chocolate that we know today. His was thick as honey, dyed red, and flavored with chili peppers. And when he was done, he threw the goblets away, the way we throw away paper cups. They weren't important to him, but the chocolate was. He believed it strengthened his purpose when he went to visit his wives.

Hernando Cortez, upon conquering the emperor and his people, sampled Montezuma's drink, but couldn't stomach it. His interest was in the golden goblets. How-

ever, he did take some cacao beans back to see if they could find a market in Spain, and before long the Spaniards had found a way to make the beans into an agreeable drink by substituting sugar and spices for the chili peppers. The new beverage quickly caught on in Spain and cacao plantations became a new source of wealth in its overseas colonies. For nearly a century, the making of chocolate was a guarded secret; once it was revealed, chocolate quickly became the fashionable drink all over Europe, renowned for its health-giving powers. The first chocolate house opened in London in 1657, advertising "this excellent West India drink."

The notion that you could *eat* chocolate was unknown until the 19th century, when someone at J. S. Fry and Sons, a British chocolate maker, found out how to make smooth, velvety fondant chocolate. Then, in the 1870s, Swiss manufacturers got into the act and added milk — and created the first milk chocolate, the product that has since become America's most beloved.

Chocolate may not actually be an aphrodisiac, but it does have some very pleasant qualities. It contains both theobromine, a mild relative of caffeine, and magnesium, a component of some tranquilizers, so it could be said to perk you up and calm you down simultaneously. It also contains stearic acid, a saturated fat that, unlike other saturated fats, may actually lower cholesterol — fractionally.

Few would claim that these constituents make chocolate into a health food, but unquestionably it is beneficial for the soul. And probably never more so than when a boy buys a heart-shaped box of chocolates and takes it to his sweetheart.

Marcel Desaulniers'
Bittersweet Chocolate Sauce
Yields 3 cups

Marcel says one of his favorite desserts is four scoops of his White Chocolate Ice Cream positioned in a cluster on a pool of this sauce.

2 cups heavy cream
³/₄ cup granulated sugar
2 tablespoons unsalted butter
¹/₄ teaspoon salt
4 ounces unsweetened chocolate, broken into ¹/₂-ounce pieces
¹/₂ teaspoon pure vanilla extract

Heat the heavy cream, sugar, butter, and salt in a 2¹/₂-quart saucepan over medium - high heat, stirring to dissolve the sugar. Bring to a boil. Place the unsweetened chocolate in a stainless steel bowl. Pour the boiling cream mixture over the chocolate and allow to stand for 5 minutes. Whisk vigorously until smooth.

Cool the Bittersweet Chocolate Sauce in an ice-water bath to a temperature of 40 to 45 degrees F., about 15 minutes. When cold, stir in the vanilla. Transfer to a plastic container. Securely cover and refrigerate until ready to use. The Bittersweet Chocolate Sauce may be kept refrigerated up to 5 days.

Reprinted from
Death by Chocolate: The Last Word on a Consuming Passion

It flatters you for a while, it warms you for an instant; then all of a sudden, it kindles a mortal fever in you.

— Marie, Marquise de Sévigné
17th-century French letter-writer

Dessert in the Desert

Temperature has a lot to do with our perception of chocolate. It must break neatly into squares at room temperature, yet melt sublimely in the mouth at just a shade below body heat.

Three 4-ounce chocolate bars have formed part of the U.S. Army's D-rations since World War II. Fortunately, by the time of the Gulf War, researchers had discovered how to prevent chocolate from melting at 105 degrees F. This "miracle" is brought about by distributing minute quantities of water throughout the chocolate bar; they prevent the fats from blending together as they warm up.

Books

Cocolat: Extraordinary Chocolate Desserts
Alice Medrich; Warner Books, 1990; $35.00

Death by Chocolate: The Last Word on a Consuming Passion
Marcel Desaulniers; Kenan (Rizzoli), 1992; $25.00

Faye Levy's Sensational Chocolate
Faye Levy; HP Books, 1992; $14.95

Look & Cook: Chocolate Desserts
Anne Willan; Dorling Kindersley, 1992; $19.45

Maida Heatter's Book of Great Chocolate Desserts
Maida Heatter; Knopf, 1980; $15.00

The Chocolate Book
Sara Perry; Chronicle Books, 1992; $8.95

Jean Harlow savoring chocolates in **Dinner at Eight**

A Chocolate Glossary

Cocoa butter is the vegetable fat content of the cacao bean. The cocoa nibs (the edible part of the bean) are roasted, then ground by a process that liquifies them into chocolate liquor, and the fat is extracted when the liquor is subjected to high pressure.

Bitter chocolate is unsweetened chocolate liquor (nonalcoholic) that has been cooled and molded into blocks. Also called baking, or cooking, chocolate, it contains roughly 53 percent cocoa butter, the same amount present in the cocoa nibs before they are ground.

Semisweet (bittersweet) chocolate is chocolate liquor to which sweeteners and cocoa butter have been added. Also known as "dark" chocolate, it must contain, by government regulation, at least 35 percent chocolate liquor. Its fat content averages 27 percent.

Sweet chocolate contains more sugar than semisweet chocolate and at least 15 percent chocolate liquor. It is most often used in decorating and in making streusel toppings. Its fat content is similar to that of semisweet chocolate.

Milk chocolate is made by adding cocoa butter, milk, sugar, and flavorings to chocolate liquor. The most popular form of eating chocolate in the United States, milk chocolate also lends itself to decorations and candy coatings. All American-made milk chocolate contains at least 10 percent chocolate liquor and 12 percent whole milk.

Cocoa powder is the brown powder remaining after most of the cocoa butter has been extracted from chocolate liquor. Standard for use in baking is medium-fat or American-process cocoa, which contains between 10 and 22 percent cocoa butter. "Dutched" or European-style cocoa, which has been treated with a mild alkali such as baking soda, has a slightly stronger flavor and darker color; it is also used in baking.

White chocolate contains cocoa butter but no cocoa solids. Its content is not currently standardized in the United States.

Filling Chocolates

Filled chocolates are made in one of two ways. In one method, machines create hollow-molded chocolate shells in distinctive shapes, which are filled with soft or liquid centers, sealed with chocolate, then released and inverted onto a tray. In the other process, known as enrobing, lines of assorted centers, from jellies to caramels to nuts, pass through a machine that showers them with a gentle waterfall of liquid chocolate that solidifies around each one.

Although enrobing, the usual American method, would seem particularly apposite for Godiva chocolates, which bear the name of the lady who rode through Coventry without a stitch on, in fact all Godiva chocolates are still made by the more expensive shell-molding process which was standard in Brussels in 1926, when the chocolatier Joseph Draps introduced them. When Godiva came to America in 1966 — in chocolate form, that is — the original recipes and designs came too.

TIPS

Storing
Chocolate can be refrigerated or frozen without loss of taste. It loses its shine, but for cooking purposes this does not matter.

Cooking
The easiest way to melt chocolate is to put it on a plate over a pan of simmering water. Cover the plate with a saucer. Or melt it in the microwave, following the specific instructions for the model you are using. Be sure to remove the dish with the chocolate *just before* it all seems to have softened; then, as it is stirred, the rest will melt too.

Never let chocolate become too hot or the cocoa butter will be released and it will become hard and grainy. Sometimes tragedy can be averted by beating in a drop or two of salad oil with a wire whisk.

Annual World Chocolate Consumption

Country	Pounds per capita
Switzerland	19
Norway	17
United Kingdom	17
Belgium/Luxembourg	15
Netherlands	15
Germany	15
Austria	15
Ireland	13
Denmark	12
Sweden	12
United States	10
France	9
Yugoslavia	6
Japan	3
Italy	3

Source: Chocolate Manufacturers Association

CHOLESTEROL

Don't become too excited about all those products hyped as having "zero cholesterol." Only foods derived from animals have any cholesterol to begin with.

WHAT IS CHOLESTEROL?

Cholesterol is a steroid alcohol that is vital to human existence. Despite all the negative messages about cholesterol, it is needed to make sex hormones and bile salts, forms an important part of nerve insulators, and is essential to the production of vitamin D. Cholesterol is made chiefly in the liver. About 85 percent is made by the body; the rest comes from the diet.

The body creates all the cholesterol it needs in an internal synthesis. However, we take on additional cholesterol when we eat meat and dairy products, which means that unless we are strict vegetarians, we all ingest more cholesterol than we need. Saturated fat, which is also found in animal products, raises the blood cholesterol levels. Elevated blood cholesterol is one of the main risk factors for coronary heart disease. Fat and cholesterol in the blood leave deposits of plaque on the arterial walls, eventually narrowing them so that the blood cannot reach the heart.

However, increases in dietary cholesterol do not automatically increase blood cholesterol levels in all people. Excessive weight, age, family history, and diets high in saturated fat are all factors associated with increasing levels of blood cholesterol.

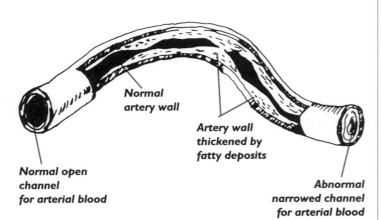

Normal artery wall

Artery wall thickened by fatty deposits

Normal open channel for arterial blood

Abnormal narrowed channel for arterial blood

Q&A

Q What are LDL and HDL?

A LDL and HDL are two types of *lipoproteins* — packages of cholesterol, fat, and protein that the body makes to carry fat and cholesterol through the blood.

LDL stands for "low-density lipoprotein." It is LDLs that carry most of the cholesterol in the blood. If the level of LDL cholesterol is elevated, cholesterol and fat can build up in the arteries, contributing to atherosclerosis — the accumulation of deposits of plaque inside the artery walls. This is why LDL cholesterol is often called "bad cholesterol."

An HDL, the acronym for "high-density lipoprotein," contains only a small amount of cholesterol. HDLs are thought to pick up cholesterol from body tissues and carry it back to the liver. Thus HDLs help to remove cholesterol from the blood, preventing cholesterol buildup in the walls of arteries. HDL cholesterol is often called "good

IT'S IN THE BLOOD

SCOTT MOWBRAY

The righteous are among us, and they have low blood cholesterol. Several times lately I've heard people — *men*, I should say — boast publicly and with smooth satisfaction about their cholesterol levels, as if this were some sort of crowning achievement like winning a Rhodes scholarship or defeating a five-year-old at Nintendo Game Boy. It was not that these people once had high cholesterol, saw the writing on the arterial wall, adopted a Dean Ornish-style diet and dropped their count by 75 points. No, I didn't hear any recovery stories. The lipid-crowing was all about inheritance, which is like bragging about shoe size or bushy eyebrows. But listen closely and you hear a claim to virtue, as if clear arteries breed a clear conscience. What we may have is the beginning of a new royal bloodline whose privileges include protection from ticker trouble and a dispensation to eat foods that people with high blood cholesterol feel sinful even *thinking* about.

Cholesterol boasting is part of an irrepressible nutrition numerology, in which human health is reduced to a few magic numbers that are supposed to predict how long each heart will beat upon this Earth....

We all face the problem of dealing with numbers in an age of rapidly expanding nutrition knowledge. Numbers are useful — fat content on food labels or in *Eating Well* recipes, vitamin values in everyday foods — but health is not math, and it is easy to get lost in the numerical woods. It is easy to lose sight of what it means to eat (and live) well and not self-consciously. Which is not to say that those of us who do not have the new royal blood in our veins wish anything ill upon those who do. It's just that these are probably the same people who, in Florida in the year 2022, will be boasting about their bowel transit times. And do we really want to be around to listen to that?

— *Excerpted from Eating Well*

cholesterol." The soluble fibers found in beans, oats, fruits, and vegetables — and regular exercise — may increase HDL.

Books

Food Values: Fats and Cholesterol
Patty Bryan; HarperCollins, 1992; $6.00

10 Easy Steps to a Healthier Heart: Vest Pocket Cholesterol Counter
Susan Kagen Podell, M.S., R.D.; Doubleday, 1991; $2.50

Low-Cholesterol Cuisine
Anne Lindsay; Quill (Morrow), 1992; $17.45

Understanding and Managing Cholesterol
Kevin P. Byrne; Human Kinetics, 1991; $40.00

PERIODICALS

Cholesterol Blood Pressure Update
Citizens for Public Action on Blood Pressure and Cholesterol
7200 Wisconsin Avenue
Bethesda, MD 20814
301-907-7790
Quarterly; $9.00

CITRUS FRUITS

Citrus fruits come in all sizes and make everyone fit.

CITRUS IS GOOD FOR YOU

Citrus fruits are low in calories and very high in vitamin C. They also are good sources of potassium, have no, or almost no sodium, and provide fiber and other nutrients. The high vitamin C content of citrus fruits means that they are regarded as helpful in fighting certain viruses. Vitamin C improves cellular immunity, bolstering the cells that repel invading organisms; it also enhances the absorption of iron. Eating citrus or other foods rich in vitamin C at the same meal as foods that contain iron greatly helps the body's iron utilization.

There is evidence that citrus fruits, which are high in pectin, are valuable in lowering blood cholesterol and reducing arterial plaque. And epidemiological research indicates that these fruits help in the treatment of several forms of cancer, notably pancreatic cancer, and may also assist in retarding the formation of cataracts.

Florida oranges are so juicy that you have to eat them in the bathtub.
— Californian saying

You have to drive a truck over a California orange to get any juice at all.
— Floridian rebuttal

There is a lot more juice in a grapefruit than meets the eye.
— Anonymous

Citrus Equivalents

1 medium-sized orange
10 - 12 sections
1/3 - 1/2 cup juice
4 teaspoons grated peel

1 medium-sized grapefruit
10 - 12 sections
2/3 cup juice
3 - 4 tablespoons grated peel

1 large lemon
3 - 4 tablespoons juice
2 - 3 teaspoons grated peel

1 large lime
2 - 3 tablespoons juice
1 - 3 teaspoons grated peel

So far I've always kept my diet secret but now I might as well tell everyone what it is. Lots of grapefruit throughout the day and plenty of virile young men at night.

— Angie Dickinson
Film actress

Residues Pay Major Dues

The residue from making orange juice is worth millions of dollars. Elements from the discarded pulp, seeds, and peel go into food products such as cake mixes, candies, and soft drinks, but also into paints and perfumes. More than 100 million pounds of peel oil is sold annually for cooking (it's unsaturated), and peel oil is also the base for a synthetic spearmint oil that Coca-Cola buys in quantity for flavoring purposes. Even the dried orange-sac residue, mixed with water into a thick coating, is used by firefighters to aid in dousing forest fires.

☞ Ponce De Leon did not discover the first orange grove in Florida while searching for the Fountain of Youth. He may have brought orange seeds or small trees with him from Europe, a common practice among New World explorers. Oranges have been cultivated in Europe since the first century A.D. when they were imported from Asia by Roman traders.

☞ It is said that the acid in lemon juice will even dissolve a pearl.

☞ The name *tangerine* is thought to come from Tangier, Morocco, the port from which mandarins were originally shipped to Britain in the 1840s.

☞ The blossom end of the orange is said to be the sweetest part.

☞ Oranges don't ripen after they are picked, but lemons do.

☞ No citrus fruits are reproduced commercially from seed; all are grown by grafting selected "slips" onto young rootstocks.

Books

Citrus: A Cookbook
Ford Rogers; Fireside, 1992; $18.00

Lemons: A Country Garden Cookbook
Christopher Idone; Collins Publishers, 1993; $19.95

The Citrus Cookbook
Josephine Bacon; Harvard Common Press, 1983; $8.95

ALERT

People who are taking felodipine, a drug used to treat high blood pressure, should be aware that drinking grapefruit juice seems to have the effect of producing much greater absorption of the drug than is customary.

Kinds of Citrus Fruits

Thanks to the climatic differences between the citrus-producing states, oranges and grapefruit are in season, one way or another, year-round. Lemons and limes, too, are available either freshly picked or from cold storage around the year. The tangerines, tangelos, tangors, and other specialty fruits have limited seasons — which makes us appreciate them the more.

Fruit	Description and Availability
Oranges	
Valencia	Medium-large, usually seedless, with yellow-orange, sometimes green-tinged thin skin; famous for its finely flavored juice; Florida, March - August; California and Arizona, February - November; Texas provides winter fruit, too
Navel	Large, seedless, with bright orange, pebbly, thick skin; peels and sections easily; California and Arizona, November - May; Florida, November - February; Texas provides winter fruit, too
Hamlin	Medium, usually seedless, with deep yellow-orange, smooth, thin skin; good juice; Florida, October - December
Blood	Medium, few seeds, with orange-red, pebbly skin; dark red flesh, fragrant, dark, tangy juice; Italy and California, December - spring, at peak in January
Grapefruit (a cross between a pummelo and sweet orange)	
Ruby red	Medium-large, flattened at ends, few seeds, with smooth, yellow skin with pinkish areas; flesh is pink or red, very juicy and sweet; between California, Arizona, Texas, and Florida, available year-round
Pink	Like Ruby, but with paler skin and flesh; as above
White seedless	Medium-large, usually seedless, with smooth yellow skin; white to honey-colored flesh, plenty of tart-sweet juice; as above
Mandarins/Tangerines	
Dancy	The fruit we all think of as a Christmas tangerine; medium, rather seedy, with vivid orange, shiny skin that almost zips off; sweet, low acid juice; California raises 12 varieties of mandarins between November and May; Florida raises three main varieties, November - February, and calls them tangerines
Clementine	Small, seedless, with bright orange, shiny skin that peels easily; very fragrant juice, flavorful flesh; small quantity from California, most from Spain and North Africa, November - January
Kinnow	Medium, some seeds, with light orange, smooth skin that peels easily; mild, sweet flavor; plentiful from California, January - May
Tangors (a cross between mandarin and sweet orange)	
Murcott	Also known as honey tangerine. Medium, seedy, with smooth gold skin that peels easily; very juicy, high in vitamin A; Florida, February
Temple	Called royal mandarin in California. Medium-large, some seeds, with deep orange, sometimes pebbly skin that peels easily; plenty of sweet, snappy-tasting juice; Florida, mid-January - mid-March; California, January - April
Tangelos (a cross between mandarin and grapefruit)	
Minneola	Medium-large, almost seedless, knobby at stem end, with medium-thin, slightly pebbly skin that peels easily; flavorful juice; Florida, January; California, December - April
Orlando	Like Minneola, but smaller and rounder with no knob; flesh has grapefruitlike tang; Florida, November - January; California, December - April
Lemons	
Lisbon and Eureka	Lisbon has a pointy knob opposite the stem end, Eureka a short neck; otherwise similar, with virtually no seeds, yellow, shiny skin, and extremely acidic juice; lemons from Florida are a Lisbon variety known as Bearss
Meyer	A cross between lemon and mandarin. Large, with golden, thin sweet skin and sweet, aromatic juice; not commercially grown but available through specialty stores
Bergamot	A rare fruit, grown largely for its aromatic leaves and skin, which are used in making perfumes and Earl Grey tea; large, yellow, lightly acidic fruits have deliciously fragrant juice
Limes	
Persian	Despite the name, probably originally from Tahiti; now Persian limes come from Florida, and a variety known as Bearss from California; both are marketed unripe, dark green, with extremely acidic juice
Key	All key limes come from southern Florida. Smaller, rounder, and paler than other limes sold commercially; distinctive, slightly sweet flavor (all limes grow yellower as they ripen, and if left on the tree, can become quite sweet)
Specialty fruits	
Pummelo	Also known as Chinese grapefruit. Very large, with thick, smooth yellow skin; white to deep pink flesh in large, sweet, juicy segments; very popular in China, not yet a U.S. commercial crop
Ugli fruit	A cross between mandarin and grapefruit, originally from Jamaica. Aptly named, looks like a coarse-skinned, discolored large grapefruit; flesh is soft, tangy, incredibly juicy
Kumquat	Available at holiday season, often sold with its decorative leaves and stalks attached. Tiny, some seeds, with bright orange, thin, pungent skin; little flesh or juice, but superb flavor, especially for adding to preserves

CLAMS

Down to the Sea with a Pail and Shovel

by Susy Davidson

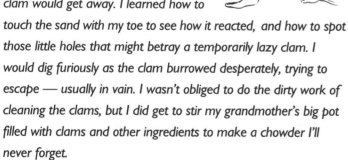

My grandparents had a house on the Oregon coast. It was a lovely old adventure of rising at the crack of dawn to go clamming with my grandfather. We would set out with our boots, pails, and shovels and I would promise to dig so fast that not one clam would get away. I learned how to touch the sand with my toe to see how it reacted, and how to spot those little holes that might betray a temporarily lazy clam. I would dig furiously as the clam burrowed desperately, trying to escape — usually in vain. I wasn't obliged to do the dirty work of cleaning the clams, but I did get to stir my grandmother's big pot filled with clams and other ingredients to make a chowder I'll never forget.

Illegal Immigrants

Some West Coast steamer clams are not natives. When the barges that brought logs from the Pacific Northwest to the East Coast at the turn of the century loaded on sand ballast for their return journey, Atlantic soft-shell clams were scooped up in the sand and off-loaded along the beaches of Puget Sound and British Columbia, where they multiplied unobserved for decades. Unfortunately, lack of regulation has led to very short-lived fisheries. More than 400,000 pounds of soft-shell clams were dug from Puget Sound in 1985; within five years, the harvest was barely 1,500 pounds.

EAST COAST CLAMS

All clams are mollusks that live in the sediments of bays, estuaries, or the ocean floor. There are three major types: soft-shell, hard-shell, and surf.

Soft-shell clams with their protruding siphons are dug from shorelines from Maine to the Chesapeake. Known as steamers, manninoses, or squirts, they have brittle shells that break easily. It is safe to eat them even if the shell is broken if you are confident they are fresh. Steamers are served steamed, and eaten dipped first in hot clam broth and then in melted butter; in New England they are sometimes fried.

Hard-shell clams are found inshore in estuaries and shallow bays. They have strong, oval shells and are identified by size:

• **Littlenecks**, named after the bay on Long Island which used to be the center of the half-shell trade, are the smallest and most expensive, with an average size of about 2 ½ inches. They are sweet and succulent and best eaten raw.

• **Cherrystones**, named after a creek in Virginia, are slightly larger, about 3 inches across. They are eaten raw on the half shell, but used mostly for baked dishes or chowder.

• **Topneck clams** are larger but usually marketed as cherrystones.

• **Chowder clams** are larger, and tougher; as the name implies, they are used in dishes such as chowders that require chopped or minced clams.

• **Ocean quahogs** are big, deep-water clams with mahogany brown shells.

Surf clams make up the bulk of the commercial catch. They are found along the inner Continental Shelf and most are shipped from New Jersey. They have large, smooth tan or white shells and fairly tough meat, used for prepared packaged chowders, clam sauces, and the fried clam strips sold at roadside stands and under the orange roofs of Howard Johnson.

WEST COAST CLAMS

Pismo clams get their name from Pismo Beach in central California; they are the prized Pacific clams with a sweet, briny taste and are eaten raw, fried, or chopped for use in clam sauces and other dishes.

Butter clams have a flavor like Pismo clams and a heavy shell similar to that of the Atlantic hard-shell clam. They are found around Puget Sound, but are not harvested commercially.

Littlenecks and **Manila clams** are cultivated, mostly in the Puget Sound area. Manila clams originated not in the Philippines but in Japan, and were introduced accidentally along with oyster seed in the 1930s. Dark-shelled and similar to littlenecks in size, they are eaten raw or steamed, and have become the West Coast's major commercial clam.

Geoducks (pronounced gooey-ducks) are funny-looking giant clams found mostly in Washington and British Columbia, which can weigh up to 6 to 8 pounds, with siphons that protrude as much as 3 feet. The flesh is supposed to taste like abalone, but sweeter, and like abalone, it is harvested by divers, sliced into cutlets, pounded to soften it, then fried as steaks or eaten raw. The body meat is also canned or smoked or chopped for use in cooked clam dishes, and even the siphon or neck is eaten by those with strong stomachs.

COD

Cod is my favorite fish.

— Anne Rosenzweig
Owner/chef, Arcadia,
New York

THE SACRED COD

New England fishermen first brought cod into Gloucester, Massachusetts, in 1623 and the fish was so commercially valuable that its image appeared on seals, stamps, coins, letterheads — and, of course, it gave its name to the Cape that resembles its silhouette.

Today, cod is fished in both the North Atlantic and the North Pacific. Both species have flesh that is easily digestible, has a mild, delicate flavor, is naturally low in calories and fat and has 1.5 grams of the valuable omega-3 fatty acids.

But overfishing has taken its toll. Recently, cod prices have more than doubled, and cod has been replaced by cheaper fish in lower-priced restaurants. In America's white-tablecloth establishments, however, cod is emerging in new and grander guises, because it is still less costly than most other "name" fish — and it still has those snowy-white, moist, tasty flakes that first made it so popular centuries ago.

Did You Know?

☞ Almost 10 percent of the world's total fish catch is cod.

☞ Americans eat close to 400 million pounds of cod a year — about a pound and a half per person.

☞ Scrod is a small cod, weighing less than three pounds.

☞ Norwegian scientists attract young cod to feeding sites by playing recordings of tuba music underwater.

Just Call Me...

Bacalao — in Spain and Latin America

Cabillaud — in France and Quebec, Canada

Dorsz — in Poland

Kabeljau — in Germany

Merluzzo bianco — in Italy

Porskur — in Iceland

Torsk — in Denmark, Norway, and Sweden

Treska — in Russia

Turska — in Finland

ALERT

People who are taking multivitamin supplements should not take cod-liver oil, because it might raise levels of vitamin D and vitamin A above safe limits.

COD-LIVER OIL:
TASTES TERRIBLE, WORKS WONDERS

PENNY WARD MOSER

How could something that smells like low tide in July still be a health food staple? And who first got the idea to catch a cod, pluck out its liver, and drink up?

Well, probably the Vikings. [But] the first clinical use was in 1782, when London physician Thomas Percival reported that the oil helped relieve the symptoms of chronic rheumatism, or "old pains."

By 1885, Philadelphia physician Roberts Bartholow's *Materia Medica and Therapeutics* was listing an amazing range of ailments touched by the oil's "special therapeutic virtue." Taken orally or rubbed on the skin, the manual said, cod liver oil could aid digestion, stimulate appetite, increase the red blood cell count, help reconstruct damaged tissue, ease the pain of psoriasis, prevent colds, remedy problems of the nervous system, and forestall hardening of the arteries.

All along, the oil had but one drawback. As Bartholow put it, "Cod-liver oil is extremely repugnant to many patients."

...Doctors proposed ingenious ways to get it down. Bartholow recommended "washing the mouth out with raw whisky" before and after swallowing the oil. Or you could just mix it *in* the whisky and knock it all back. Or carefully bury the oil under the foam of a good beer. Another doctor suggested powdered ox pancreas mixed with cod-liver oil, with a cognac chaser. And one textbook suggested that patients could trick their tongues by "chewing a smoked herring" before and after a dose.

I was burping up something redolent of linseed oil and aged sardines. So I switched to tasteless cod-liver oil gel capsules and was fine.

Excerpted from *Health* magazine

COFFEE

Good coffee should be black like the devil, hot like hell, and sweet like a kiss.

— Old Hungarian saying

That Old Black Magic

Nobody knows who actually discovered coffee, but it originated in ancient Kaffa, in Abyssinia (now Ethiopia). There are many legends about it in the Arab world, where it made its popular debut and where it is loved as passionately as it is here. One story from the ninth century A.D. tells of a goatherd named Kaldi, tending his flock near Kaffa, who noticed that his animals were unusually frisky after they ate the berries of a certain leafy tree. So he chewed a few of those berries himself and had, presumably, the world's first caffeine rush.

Who Grows What

Colombia — a medium-bodied, mellow coffee; the top grade is Supremo.

Costa Rica — a rich, full-bodied coffee.

Ethiopia — a rich, tangy, heavy-bodied coffee.

Guatemala — a rich, full-flavored coffee.

Hawaiian Kona — a mild, smooth, often expensive coffee.

Jamaica — a smooth, full-bodied coffee, sometimes hard to find.

Java — a smooth, aromatic coffee.

Kenya — a sharp, winy-tasting coffee; AA is the highest grade.

Mexico — a mellow, aromatic coffee, usually from Oaxaca.

Puerto Rico — a mild, heavy-bodied coffee.

Sulawesi — a full-bodied, aromatic coffee.

Sumatra — a smooth, aromatic coffee similar to Java, but heavier.

Yemen — a light, sharp coffee, often known as Mocha.

No Thanks!

Sumatran coffee-plantation workers track a discerning marsupial who eats only the best beans. What he excretes becomes Kopi Luwak, the world's most expensive coffee blend ($130 per pound).

Types of Grinds

Coarse — large particles; for use in percolators, urns, plunger pots, and cold-water extraction brewers.

Medium — less coarse, but still sizable; for uses cited above.

Drip — finer than Medium; for use in electric-drip coffee makers.

Fine — finely ground, for use in cone-shaped filters and drip pots.

Espresso — very finely ground, for use in espresso machines.

Turkish — so finely ground as to be pulverized and flourlike, for use in the traditional Turkish brewer.

Coffee has two virtues: It is wet and warm.
— Old Dutch saying

THE CLASSICAL COFFEEHOUSE REVIVAL

JOSEPH MAZO

America lacks the decadence required for a truly great coffeehouse," says Brian McNally, "but we're acquiring it, I think."

What McNally calls "decadence" is really nothing more than a proper respect for leisure, a trait shared by most mature, properly civilized societies and honored by them with the institution of the coffeehouse. A cafe is not a filling station for fueling the human engine with a quick caffeine (although Italian espresso bars can serve that very purpose); it is a way station where travelers may dawdle for 10 minutes or three hours as their dispositions and appointment calendars demand. Good coffee, dispensed in several styles, is certainly a requirement, but coffee and its accoutrements are not the reason for visiting a cafe; they are the excuse.

Excerpted from Food Arts

Where Coffee Comes From

Mainly two varieties of coffee beans come into the United States: the **arabica**, grown at high altitudes, the best, low-yielding, and expensive bean, for fine coffees; and the **robusta**, which is cheaper, high-yielding, and destined for supermarket blends, instants, and decafs. Robustas have 30 to 40 percent more caffeine.

It all starts when a coffee tree bears what are called its cherries. Once picked, cherries are dried in the sun or soaked in water to expose the coffee seeds, called green beans — it takes about 2,000 to make five pounds of coffee.

Green beans stay fresh for years. Once they are roasted, however, they lose their freshness rapidly.

Books

A Cup of Coffee: From Plantation to Pot, A Coffee Lover's Guide to the Perfect Brew
Norman Kolpas; Grove Press, 1993; $19.95

Cooking with Coffee
Carol Foster; Fireside, 1992; $8.95

Making Your Own Gourmet Coffee Drinks
Mathew Tekulsky; Crown, 1993; $12.00

Perfect Cup: A Coffee Lover's Guide to Buying, Brewing, and Tasting
Timothy J. Castle; Addison Wesley, 1991; $10.53

The Complete Coffee Book
Sara Perry, Edward Gowans, and Judith Anne Rose; Chronicle Books, 1991; $19.95/$12.95

MORE INFORMATION

National Coffee Association of U.S.A.
110 Wall Street
New York, NY 10005
212-344-5596

Specialty Coffee Association of America
1 World Trade Center, No. 800
Long Beach, CA 90831
310-983-8090

MAIL ORDER SOURCES

Coffee Connection
6 Drydock Avenue
Boston, MA 02210
800-284-JAVA

Community Kitchens Coffee
The Art of Food Plaza
Ridgely, MD 21685
800-535-9901

Oregon Coffee Roaster, Inc.
P.O. Box 223
North Plains, OR 97133
800-526-9940

Starbucks Coffee Company
2203 Airport Way South
P.O. Box 34510
Seattle, WA 98124-1510
800-445-3428

JAVA JIVE

A cup of coffee contains 80 to 100 milligrams of caffeine, more or less, depending on the strength of the brew. (A cup of tea usually has less because less tea is used per cup.) Is the caffeine in one cup going to keep you awake, make you think more clearly? Yes, depending on your sensitivity to caffeine; someone else might need two or three cups to do the trick.

How does caffeine do this? The prevailing theory is that it stops the effects of adenosine, a chemical the body makes to control neural activity. Caffeine may block the adenosine receptor sites in cells. Thus we're able to plow away when we're tired — but we don't necessarily do better work. Caffeine increases intellectual speed but not brain power.

It also speeds up some people's metabolism and may burn calories faster. It's diuretic and dehydrating, has a laxative effect, and can cause heartburn. Caffeine can even counteract the effects of Valium and other tranquilizers. But if you're drunk, strong black coffee won't sober you up, despite its fabulous reputation for doing so.

The Big D in Decaf

You probably haven't lost any sleep lately worrying about how they take the caffeine out of the coffee beans. Did you even know it was the beans they take it from? Maybe you thought it was a strictly liquid transaction in a vat somewhere. Wrong.

Several decaffeination methods are currently in use.

• **The direct-contact method**, in which the beans are treated with methylene chloride to extract the caffeine, has long been regarded as best for preserving flavor. But in 1989, the FDA banned the use of methylene chloride in hair sprays because studies showed that it caused cancer in animals. Soon thereafter, General Foods

"Sorry, darling — I thought it was decaffeinated."

converted its decaffeination process from methylene chloride to carbon dioxide.

• **The soaking method** extracts caffeine by first soaking the beans in water, then drawing the water off and treating it with ethyl acetate, a compound found in fruit. The chemical binds with the caffeine and the water goes back to the beans.

• **The water process method** soaks the beans in hot water to remove the caffeine. But supposedly many flavor components come out in the wash, and the caffeine is burned off and lost for any other use.

COLAS

COFFEE, TEA, OR COKE?

Morning consumption of Coke now accounts for 12 percent of total soft-drink sales, up from 9 percent a decade ago, and the Coca-Cola Company is encouraging the trend with banners at points of sale that herald "Coke in the Morning." Breakfast cola is more a habit in the South than elsewhere — they even cook with Coke in that part of the world. But in any situation where a beverage has to be portable, as when driving to work or riding the bus, a cold drink in the hand is more manageable than a hot one. Meanwhile, average daily coffee consumption has been declining for some time — from 3.12 cups per person in 1962 to about half that recently. However, breakfast Coke won't be an easy sell, owing to what an industry spokesman has called "the yuck factor." As in, "Coke for breakfast? Yuck!"

The Cola Kings

Coca-Cola came first, in 1886. Pepsi-Cola arrived two years later and has been running hard for more than a century, trying to catch Coke and pass it by in American popularity. Meanwhile, Coke is ever maneuvering to keep Pepsi in its dust. The cola business has always been a horse race, with the two leaders jockeying for position, but Coke still holds the lead with 41 percent of the market. Pepsi is right behind with 31 percent.

Americans drink about 13 billion gallons of soft drinks every year — about a gallon a week for every man, woman, and child in the country. Traditionally, soft-drink preferences are unshakably strong: As Pepsi knows better than most, it's very hard to get people to switch. But the market has been changing in recent years. Cola's share of grocery-store soft-drink sales has been slipping as the public searches restlessly for something new, and noncolas — New-Age beverages, drinks you can see through — are rising in popularity. Bottled waters, flavored seltzers, juice drinks, and "natural" sodas appeal to the new appetite for variety — not enough to threaten the primacy of the cola leaders, but sufficient to spark the Coca-Cola Company and PepsiCo Inc. into vigorous competition. Pepsi is pushing Mountain Dew, Crystal Pepsi, and Ocean Spray juice drinks. Coke has Nestea iced tea, Sprite, and Fresca, and the recently introduced Nordic Mist sparkling waters, which are sweetened and flavored with black cherry, raspberry, peach, pineapple, or a medley of kiwi, pineapple, and guava. Pepsi's answer? A sparkling water called H20h, [set up like water but with Oh] which comes unflavored or in berry and lemon-lime flavors. And both giants now provide sports drinks for an expanding market of runners, joggers, and rock climbers — Pepsi has All Sport Thirst Quencher, Coke has PowerAde.

PepsiCola beverage ad. Robert Day. 1947. Pepsi-Cola Co.

"That's what I call smart merchandising."

Meanwhile, any domestic slippage in the cola market is made up for in international sales. Years ago Pepsi got a toehold in Russia; Coke has China, and opened a new plant in Uzbekistan in March 1994. Both companies do well in the teetotal Arab world, and are eyeing the Pacific countries, where the cola consumption is currently about that of the United States in 1939. "When I think of Indonesia — a country on the equator with 180 million people, a median age of 18, and a Muslim ban on alcohol — I feel I know what heaven looks like," confessed a Coca-Cola officer.

Smaller, independent soft-drink competitors may make further slight inroads on the giants' 70 percent share of the American soft-drink market. But with whole continents left to conquer, the cola companies are still looking up.

Music Has Power...

Pepsi-Cola was the first company to use a musical jingle in its national advertising — in the depths of the Depression, "Pepsi-Cola Hits the Spot" offered twice as much cola as other companies: 12 ounces for a nickel.

What's in a Soft Drink?

Water, the main ingredient, makes up 90 percent of regular soft drinks, 99 percent of diet drinks. Bottlers filter it to remove any impurities and standardize the taste.

Flavors create distinctive tastes. Bottlers use artificial flavors in combination with herbs and spices, natural extracts, oils, and fruit extracts.

Carbon dioxide gas is forced into soft drinks under pressure just before containers are sealed. The carbonation ensures the fizz. (In early soft-drink making, carbon dioxide was made from sodium salts. Thus people used to refer to soft drinks as "soda water.")

Colors are added, sometimes chemically, to draw the eye. Caramel is a natural color ingredient that's often used in soft drinks.

Caffeine in small amounts — much less than is found in an equal quantity of coffee or tea — is added to regular soft drinks to enhance flavor.

Sodium present in soft drinks comes from the water supply and from other ingredients.

Potassium, like sodium, is an essential nutrient found in drinking water.

Preservatives commonly used in many foods are also used in soft drinks.

Acidulants, such as phosphoric acid and citric acid, provide a tart taste and also serve as preservatives.

Sweeteners for regular soft drinks are usually sucrose (the granulated sugar we know well, made from sugar cane or beets), high fructose corn syrup, or mixtures of the two. The amount ranges from 7 to 14 percent.

In diet drinks, saccharin is the only noncaloric sweetener approved for soft drinks. Aspartame, approved for soft drinks in 1983, is a "nutritive" sweetener, meaning that it provides calories. However, it's so flavor-intensive that only about 15 milligrams of it per ounce is used when it's on its own, even less when combined with saccharin.

Further alternative sweeteners are waiting in the wings for FDA approval. One is acesulfame K, brand name "Sunette," which has already been approved for certain food uses. Others include sucralose, a derivative of sucrose that is 600 times sweeter, and alitame, a compound similar to aspartame that is 2,000 times sweeter than sucrose.

Source: National Soft Drink Association

Coke or Pepsi?
Depends on the Party

The Coca-Cola Company can produce photos of every President since Truman with a Coke in hand, but according to industry lore, Coke does best in Democratic administrations, while PepsiCo comes to the fore under the Republicans. Both companies claim cordial connections with politicians of all stripes, of course, but Coke's alliance with the Democrats probably began when FDR asked James Farley, his Postmaster General and a former Coca-Cola executive, to help get Cokes to the troops in World War II.

PepsiCo sprang forward in 1959, during the Eisenhower administration. Pulling strings behind the scenes, a PepsiCo executive arranged for Pepsi to be the only soft drink represented at the American National Exhibition in Moscow. When Soviet Premier Nikita Khrushchev drank one while U.S. Vice President Richard Nixon drank another, they created one of the most famous images of the Cold War era.

During the Nixon presidency, Pepsi became the first foreign consumer product to be sold in the Soviet Union. Jimmy Carter was a Coke man. George Bush was a Pepsi man. President Clinton has been photographed drinking Sprite, a Coke product, but his true allegiances remain unclear. White House spokesmen will say only that he has a cordial relationship with all diet drinks.

COMPANIES

You either eat or you are eaten.
— Didier Rabattu
Financial analyst with S. G. Warburg, Paris

IS BIG BEAUTIFUL?

For a long time, consumers have been locked in an intricate dance with the large food-producing companies. When we decide to buy a can of soup or chicken broth, we are likely to choose Campbell's because this company literally "owns" this food category just as Fleischmann owns the market for yeast. Skippy's name is almost synonymous with peanut butter, and when we think of macaroni and cheese we think of Kraft. Almost all processed foods such as breakfast cereals, colas, cookies, and ice cream are produced by a relatively few corporate entities. A mere handful of giant companies supply us with such basic ingredients as salt, sugar, tea, coffee, cocoa, preserves, rice, and flour. Even meats, poultry, fruits, and vegetables often carry the brand names of just a few major producers.

A big company seeks to defeat its competition. And a company that's able to make products with its own machinery, package those products, deliver them in its own trucks and ships, and command space at the retail level, is a company that can control its own costs and — except in the face of bad weather, recession, and revolution — can be said to have some mastery over its prices and profits.

With big money, big companies can bulldoze their way through the market. They can afford to undercut the competition and withstand losses until smaller companies go broke, leaving the field clear for the big companies to establish new, higher price points.

However, while a company may own the lion's share of the soup market, the mayonnaise market, or the cookie

The Big Time Together, the more than 40 separate U.S. industries that specialize in making	various food products comprise the second largest manufacturing industry in this country — surpassed	only by the transportation-equipment industry, which makes cars, buses, trains, and planes.

market, it cannot indefinitely contain the rising costs of labor and raw materials. And sooner or later there comes a price at which customers balk, a price they will not pay. A door of opportunity then opens for new competitors, and an array of cheaper house brands floods the supermarkets. Competition rises again.

But it is hard for local growers and small start-up companies to get a foothold in the nation's supermarkets. They are shut out because they cannot fulfill the rigid entrance requirements demanded by the powerful chains. In turn, the growing trend toward monopoly severely limits customers' choices. We may enjoy a new product, but when we return to the store it is nowhere to be found. It was tossed off the shelf because it did not sell briskly enough to satisfy the accountants.

No question that the system works well for the sellers. Customers rarely protest to the store manager when cans or boxes remain the same size, but their contents shrink. Until recently, people simply shrugged off a small price increase and just dug deeper into their pockets for a favorite and familiar product. They felt unable to beat the system, however concerned they were about the amount of additives, or the quantity of salt or sugar or unwelcome residues in specific foods.

But things are changing rapidly. Changing demographics have propelled American food production in new directions. Once consumers were glamorized by everything big — hypermarkets the size of 40 football fields, giant packages of food that would feed a family of eight in Tibet for a week, vegetables bigger than footstools. Today, one in four Americans lives alone. There are few large families. Half of married households are working couples who have little time to shop, and less inclination. What we want now is small: boutique and convenience stores, individually wrapped single slices of cheesecake, one-bite bananas and artichokes; prepared meals, ready to eat.

The 40-to-60 age group will grow by 20 million in the coming decade; the fact that older people tend to dislike spicy foods will show itself in the supermarket. Middle-aged consumers are increasingly concerned with good health, spurring demands for organic, pesticide-free produce and fewer additives in processed foods; low-cholesterol and low-fat food sales have climbed to $33 billion a year. Shifting ethnic balances encourage bilingual packaging and products designed to reach expanding populations.

Now consumers are demanding healthier foods at lower prices, and companies are responding by providing full disclosure of their ingredients. Health claims are being scrutinized intensely, not only by the government but by an ever more aware public. For ultimately, it is the informed consumer who decides what to buy and at what price — and even the largest companies listen attentively to the chorus at the cash register.

More of this, less of that. Less red, more white. More green, more fiber. Down home. Upscale. No drip. Fast. Fresh. Microwavable. Now.

Philip Morris Takes Over

Philip Morris, the second largest food company in the world after Nestlé, has the stated goal of becoming the most successful consumer packaged-food company in the world. Already we could live entirely on the products it owns and never be hungry again. With consolidated revenues of $60.9 billion, the company is America's biggest taxpayer and has a work force of 173,000, 50 percent of them employed outside the United States.

The company operates around the globe from Australia to Venezuela — in fact, it probably takes less time to name those countries where it *doesn't* have a presence — and its list of acquisitions and joint ventures is staggering. The company markets more than 3,000 different products in the United States. Here is a partial list of the more familiar brands:

Baked Goods
Boboli
Entenmann's
Freihofer's
Oroweat

Beverages

COFFEE
Maxwell House
Sanka
Brim
Yuban
General Foods International Coffees
Cappio
Maxim

BEER
Miller (6 varieties)
Löwenbräu
Milwaukee's Best
Meister Bräu
Molson (2 varieties)
Foster's
Leinenkugel's
John Courage
Sharp's nonalcohol brew

SOFT DRINKS
Country Time
Crystal Light
Kool-Aid
Tang
Capri Sun

TEA
Maxwell House
Crystal Light

Dairy Products
Breakstone's
Breyers yogurt
Foremost
Knudsen
Light n' Lively
Sealtest

Frozen Food

DESSERTS
Cool Whip

DINNERS/ENTREES/SIDE DISHES/BAGELS/PIZZAS
The Budget Gourmet
Lender's bagels
Jack's pizzas
Tombstone pizzas

Grocery

CEREALS
Nabisco
Frosted Wheat Squares
Fruit Wheats
Shredded Wheat
Shredded Wheat 'n Bran
Spoon Size Shredded Wheat
Team Flakes
Post
Alpha-Bits
Banana Nut Crunch
Bran'nola
Fruit & Fibre
Golden Crisp
Grape-Nuts
Great Grains
Honey Bunches of Oats
Honeycomb
Natural Bran Flakes
Oat Flakes
Pebbles
Raisin Bran

CONDIMENTS & SAUCES
Bull's-Eye
Kraft
Miracle Whip
Sauceworks

CONFECTIONS
Côte d'Or
Callard & Bowser
Kraft
La Vosgienne
Toblerone

DRY DESSERTS
D-Zerta
Jell-O
Minute tapioca

DRY GROCERY
Baker's

Calumet baking powder
Log Cabin & Country Kitchen syrups
Minute rices
Shake 'N Bake & Oven Fry coatings
Stove Top
Sure-Jell & Certo

FRUIT SPREADS/TOPPINGS
Dream Whip
Kraft

SALAD DRESSINGS
Good Seasons mixes
Kraft
Seven Seas

TABLE SPREADS
Chiffon
Miracle
Parkay
Touch of Butter

SIDE DISHES
Kraft dry dinners
Velveeta shells & cheese

Refrigerated Foods

PICKLES & SAUERKRAUT
Claussen

CREAM CHEESE
Philadelphia Brand
Temp-Tee

FRESH PASTA & SAUCES
DiGiorno
Digiorno Lighter Varieties

FRESH & PROCESSED MEATS
Oscar Mayer
Louis Rich

Cheese

GRATED
Kraft

LOAF
Old English
Velveeta

NATURAL
Casino
Cracker Barrel
Harvest Moon
Knudsen
Kraft Deluxe
Kraft Healthy Favorites
Select-A-Size

OTHER CHEESES
Athenos
Churny
Elkhorn
Kraft
Mohawk Valley
Polly-O
Rondelé

SLICES
Kraft
Light n' Lively
Velveeta

SNACKS
Kraft Cheez Whiz
Handi-Snacks
Zap-A-Pack Cheez Whiz

World Wrestling Championship

In the view of an international marketer, the politics of nations is virtually irrelevant. For him the world divides itself chiefly into three major economic entities — the European Community, the Asian block, and the alliance of the

United States, Canada, and Mexico. And what most interests that businessman is the speediest possible dissolution of tariffs and quotas within and among the member states of those entities, so that manufacturing may be dispersed to points where it costs the least, production may be speeded up and goods made to flow more freely to eager markets in every likely part of the world — and money may be made.

This is nothing new. The Kellogg Company, for one, has had expansionist visions since its formation. The company was selling cereal to Canada in 1914, barely eight years after it came into being as the Battle Creek Toasted Corn Flake Company. By 1938 it was in Australia and England, and today Kellogg produces more than 40 different cereals in 17 countries and distributes them to 150 countries. It is currently building plants in Guangzhou, China, and in Riga, Latvia.

Meanwhile, General Mills and Nestlé have forged Cereal Partners Worldwide, an alliance designed to advance the sales of Cheerios, Wheaties, Total, and newer cereal treats in reluctant markets. A possible result of vigorous marketing: The Japanese, who once ate rice and fish for breakfast, are laying aside their chopsticks and taking up spoons, the better to devour cereals with flavors to their liking: seaweed, carrot, coconut, and papaya.

The great international food conglomerates — Nestlé and Philip Morris, to name the top two — play hardball on the global scene. In 1991, for example, Nestlé sold 10 million tons of products worldwide, from all the dehydrated yam flakes available in the Ivory Coast to 70 percent of the instant coffee bought in Japan. Meanwhile, Philip Morris, slightly behind and growing by acquisition, doubled its European presence through its purchase of Jacobs Suchard AG. Said one European trader: "Philip Morris has teeth."

Other American leaders in the field include ConAgra, Archer Daniels Midland Company, Cargill, Inc., PepsiCo, Inc., the Anheuser-Busch Companies, Inc., and the Coca-Cola Company, and the fact is that they and their international competitors *all* have teeth. Indeed, they could be likened to a pack of giant squid with dentures of Krupp steel and tentacles reaching around the globe.

The maneuvering of these companies bears watching. They are caught in a marketing contest to determine which one will ultimately most universally embrace the face of the earth. It is a struggle from which none may withdraw but in which many smaller players will be consumed.

Developing a Yen

The lushest market still largely untapped by Western industries and consequently most alluring to international food businesses is the Pacific Rim. The densely populated countries gathered under that parasol term include Japan, South Korea, China, Taiwan, Hong Kong, the Philippines, Thailand, Malaysia, Singapore, Indonesia, and Australia — in all, some 1.7 billion potential consumers. They are expected to constitute a larger market for American goods than the European Community does now, and to provide a customer base almost as wealthy as that of the United States itself.

As their economies expand, the countries of the Pacific Rim are about to ride a wave of unprecedented prosperity. Western businesses are on the scene, buying in, buying out, cementing alliances. As opportunities for further acquisition float in the wake of Asia's new wealth, creating new jobs and generating ever stronger economies, forecasters envision a river of cash flowing massively back from the shores of the Far East into the waiting wide pockets of the West.

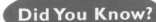
The Top Ten Companies

(ranked by food revenues)

1.
Nestlé

2.
Philip Morris

3.
Unilever

4.
Conagra

5.
Ferruzzi Finanziaria

6.
Grand Metropolitan

7.
BSN

8.
Sara Lee

9.
Barlow Rand

10.
IBP

Source: *Fortune* magazine

CONVENIENCE STORES

CONVENIENCE MAY COME
CLOSER SOON

The words "convenience store" evoke those late-night hunger pangs when the refrigerator is empty that force you out the door to someplace, anyplace, that can assuage them. Defining convenience better than any dictionary, these businesses offer late hours, good locations, easy-to-heat food, and a handy microwave. Many, especially those linked to gas stations, accept credit cards.

Their owners call them C-Stores. They're small, they're open, you can run in and out in a hurry, and you find them everywhere you look. They have names like Jim Dandy, Li'l'Champ, Wawa, Majik Market, U-Tote-Em, convenience stores are at your service all over the country 24 hours a day, more than 80,000 of them.

Lately, owners have been expanding the range of services offered at their locations. Video rentals, photocopiers, and fax machines keep the customers coming, and fresh-baked goods, prepared foods, and other perishables are moving onto shelves that once held chiefly long-life presealed snacks.

Many city dwellers have the good fortune to live near an all-night grocery or Korean deli, the C-store's urban cousins. Salad bars and prepared pastas service immediate food cravings while staples such as cheese, milk, cereals, and vegetables ensure that convenience and a balanced diet are not incompatible.

Oil companies, particularly Chevron and Arco, have been moving into the C-store niche, and mini-markets are now common fixtures at gas stations around the country. These stores offer a wide range of prepared foods, including hot dogs, hamburgers, pizza, egg rolls, nachos, burritos, and fried chicken, often with prices lower than those at fast-food chains. In fact, some industry experts believe that foods sold hot and/or microwavable at such stores for consumption at home may be the wave of the future.

In a truly effortless and convenient future, the food will drive to *us*. Bob Messenger, the publisher of *Food Business* magazine, has predicted that convenience stores *on wheels* will be one of the biggest trends of the current decade. Until that happens, we'll just continue to run to the corner and the lazy among us will keep the home delivery folk in business.

National Association of Convenience Stores
1605 King Street
Alexandria, VA 22314-2792
703-684-3600

You Pay a Little More

Here's some 1994 comparison pricing on standard items available both in a convenience store and a the supermarket in the suburban New York area. It took our shopper under 7 minutes to buy these items in a convenience store. At the supermarket it took twice the time: 15 minutes.

Food	C-store	Supermarket
13-ounce can, Maxwell House coffee	$2.99	$2.29
10¾-ounce can, Campbell's Chicken Noodle Soup	0.89	0.59
5½-ounce package Kraft Macaroni and Cheese	0.99	0.67
32-ounce carton Tropicana orange juice	1.89	1.29
1 gallon 2 percent milk	2.45	2.37
1 dozen large eggs	1.29	1.29
2-liter bottle Pepsi	2.13	1.19
5½-ounce can 9 Lives cat food	0.55	0.30
12-ounce can SPAM	2.69	1.69
4-ounce jar Beech-Nut strained baby food	0.55	0.43

COOKBOOKS

Half the cookbooks tell you how to cook the food and the other half tell you how to avoid eating it.

— Andy Rooney
"60 Minutes" curmudgeon

COOKBOOKS PROLIFERATE
BUT PICKINGS ARE SLIM

Now we no longer need cook in order to eat. We can buy all our food totally or partially prepared at a take-out store or the supermarket; we can eat as cheaply at a fast-food restaurant. Cooking has really become a hobby, yet some 330 cookbooks are published each year, and the figure shows little sign of dwindling.

There is an outdated belief that all cookbooks sell thousands of copies and guarantee a lifetime income for the author. Alas, the life of an average cookbook is somewhere between that of milk and yogurt. Very few authors earn their living by writing cookbooks. We hear of staggeringly large advance payments of upwards of $600,000 being made to one or two "celebrity" authors, but most cookbook writers are lucky to receive as much as $20,000. Large as this may seem, initially, by the time you have planned a recipe, made a shopping list, gathered the ingredients from the store, loaded them into the car, taken them out of the car, put them in the refrigerator, taken them out of the refrigerator, cooked the food, washed the dishes, typed the recipe carefully, and then repeated the process three or four times until the recipe is absolutely right and can be re-created by someone who has rarely cooked before — mighty little is left.

Cookbook authors have a responsibility that is not imposed on writers of fiction. A person who doesn't like a novel simply puts it down and picks up something else. If a recipe doesn't work, the reader has wasted not only money but time, which becomes an ever scarcer, and hence more valuable commodity. There is also the suspicion, often justified, that the fault lay with the teacher, not the trusting pupil.

Many people have the quaint idea that they could easily write a cookbook if only they had the time. But there is a craft to it, as well as an art. If you really want a cookbook, as many authors have discovered, it is far less effort to go out and buy one than to make one yourself.

Cheaper, too!

Old, Rare, and Beloved

For people who love cookbooks, the old ones are often the best — and the hardest to find or to replace when lent out and lost by some undeserving person who does not understand their true, inestimable value.

Those in the know treasure such people as Jan Longone, of the Wine and Food Library, whose collection, amassed over two decades, includes rare books from as far back as the 1500s, as well as America's earliest cookbooks, and originals, facsimiles, and reprints of classic books on wine, food, and cooking equipment; or Nach Waxman, of Kitchen Arts and Letters, who keeps some 7,000 new and older cookbooks on hand in his store in New York City.

Some of the cookbook dealers and stores listed here specialize in certain areas; nearly all are prepared to help customers locate titles that are out of print or hard to find; some will search for specific books; several have catalogs and do business by mail, with visits arranged by appointment. And most stock new books as well. After all, those, too, will turn out to be treasures.

The First American Cookbook

A Facsimile of "American Cookery," 1796 by Amelia Simmons

So You Want to Write a Cookbook?
A multiple-choice quiz.

1. Writing a cookbook is:
   a. Easy and fun
   b. All-consuming
   c. A labor of love
   d. A cross between Mardi Gras and a root canal

2. The most important prerequisite is:
   a. Practical and theoretical food knowledge
   b. A unique contribution or viewpoint
   c. Organizational skills
   d. A staff of thousands
   e. A life of leisure

3. The single most critical phase is:
   a. Signing the publishing contract
   b. Selecting the recipes
   c. Testing the recipes
   d. Cutting 75 percent of the recipes

4. The project's most exacting cost to you will be:
   a. Time and money
   b. Energy
   c. Putting aspects of your business on hold
   d. Dealing with everything you put on hold

5. The biggest reward from writing a cookbook is:
   a. Professional
   b. Personal
   c. Monetary
   d. A sense of accomplishment

Answers to questions 1 through 5: All of the above with the possible exception of 5c.

Reprinted from *Restaurants & Institutions*

COOKBOOK STORES

Books for Cooks
301 South Light Street
Baltimore, MD 21202
410-547-9066

Cookbook Cottage
1279 Bardstown Road
Louisville, KY 40204
502-458-5227

Marian L. Gore, Antiquarian Bookseller
P.O. Box 433
San Gabriel, CA 91778
818-287-2946

Hoppin' John's
30 Pinckney Street
Charleston, SC 29401
803-577-6404

Household Words
P.O. Box 7231
Berkeley, CA 94707
415-524-8859

Kitchen Arts and Letters
1435 Lexington Avenue
New York, NY 10128
212-876-5550

Powell's Books for Cooks
3739 Southeast Hawthorne Boulevard
Portland, OR 97214
800-354-5957

The Cookbook Store
850 Young Street
Toronto, Ontario M4W 2HI
Canada
416-920-2665

The Cook's Book Shop
3854 Fifth Avenue
San Diego, CA 92103
619-296-3636

The Cook's Library
8373 West Third Street
Los Angeles, CA 90048
213-655-3141

The Wine and Food Library
1207 West Madison
Ann Arbor, MI 48103
313-663-4894

Record Breaker

In the Kitchen with Rosie, Rosie Daley's Oprah-diet cookbook, was published in spring 1994 and instantly became the biggest, fastest seller of all time, with 4.1 million copies in print as of June 1994.

A Table of Many Contents

Imagine how difficult the Campbell Soup Company would find it to advertise 350 versions of tomato soup. This approximates the dilemma faced by the cookbook publisher, who tries, in theory at least, to make each new cookbook stand out and be noticed. The average customer in a bookstore spends less than three seconds looking at a book's jacket before taking it from the shelf or passing it by. Every year close to 55,000 new general interest books are published and must jostle for shelf space with the 700,000 titles already in print. No wonder few books or authors ever achieve star status. There simply isn't enough room in a store for the many competing titles.

Several factors influence a decision to buy a cookbook. We tend to trust brand names, and this is true in cookbooks too. *Better Homes & Gardens New Cookbook* is the equivalent of a brand name. It was first published in 1930 and since then has sold more than 26 million copies. The 10th revised edition was issued in 1989, supported with an advertising budget of $750,000. With that amount of muscle behind it, it was certain that customers would be aware of it. *Better Homes & Gardens New Cookbook* sells an average of half a million copies every year.

Joy of Cooking, the great American classic, made its first appearance in 1931 with a printing of 3,000 copies. It has since sold more than 11 million copies; an average of 150,000 copies are still bought every year.

The first edition of *Betty Crocker's Cookbook* appeared in 1921, a response from Pillsbury, the Minneapolis miller of Gold Medal Flour, to many letters from home bakers asking for recipes. Betty Crocker has changed her image many times over the years and continues to be as popular a mythical figure as ever. Other cookbook institutions are *The Family Circle Cookbook*, *The New York Times Cookbook*, written by Craig Claiborne, and *The Doubleday Cookbook*, authored by Jean Anderson and Elaine Hanna. All have found cherished places in kitchens throughout the country. The books may be battered and dog-eared, splotched with gravy, but they are never thrown away. We depend on them to remind us of everything we need to know, from how to make a bowl of Jell-O to how to roast a perfect chicken. These, together with compilations of recipes from our favorite magazines — *Gourmet*, *Bon Appétit*, *Cook's Illustrated*, *Food & Wine*, and *Eating Well* — constitute a significant slice of the cookbook pie.

On the upper crust of that pie is Julia Child, of whom it has been said that she need never eat another meal because she is nourished by the affection of a nation. Television brought her and her books into our lives. Martha Stewart, Jeff Smith a.k.a. the Frugal Gourmet, Jacques Pépin, Sharon Tyler Herbst, and dozens of others now fill the screen with their ebullient personalities, and we respond by buying their books.

Every now and again one book captures our imagination like no other. Sheila Lukins' and Julee Rosso's *Silver Palate* books from Workman — with sales hovering around the 5 million mark — were in perfect sync with the good times of the 1980s.

Scholarly works by such brilliant minds as Harold McGee, Elizabeth Schneider, and Shirley Corriher find their own niches. So do books devoted to good, healthy food, fast preparation, ethnic cooking, special interests, and single subjects. Fad books like *The Firehouse Cookbook* blaze for a moment. Celebrity books like *Cooking with Regis and Kathie Lee* find thousands of fans ready to stand in line for them when they are well thought out, as this one was.

Picture books become more exquisite every year. Collins's Beautiful series — *America the Beautiful*, *Italy the Beautiful*, *Mexico the Beautiful* — takes the concept to dazzling heights. Smaller books with unique vision dazzle, too. These include Leslie Forbes's *A Taste of Provence*, published by Little, Brown; the James McNair series of single-subject cookbooks, published by Chronicle Books; the lovely *Potager*, by Georgeanne Brennan, also from Chronicle; and *Food Tales*, with photographs by Laurie Rubin, published by Viking Studio Books.

For those who love to read about food, the works of M. F. K. Fisher are prized. Another of the very best is *Blue Trout and Black Truffles*, by Joseph Wechsberg, who was writing in the mid-1940s and into the 1950s. His work is newly available from Academy Chicago Publishers. *Between the Meals*, by A. J. Liebling, first published in 1959, was recently brought out again by North Point Press and is a wonderful read. And there is the all-time favorite, *Lang's Compendium of Culinary Nonsense and Trivia*, by George Lang, published by Clarkson Potter. Also important to mention are Ed Behr's *Good Taste* and John Thorne's *Simple Cooking*, both published by Viking. Behr and Thorne also write fascinating food newsletters.

And this is just a tiny sampling. Remember, a new cookbook is coming out of the oven almost every day!

How to Choose a Cookbook

• Look at the author's credentials.

• Look up a recipe you are familiar with and see how it compares with the one you like to use.

• Are the recipes easy to read and understand?

• Can you find the ingredients?

• Can you afford the ingredients?

• Judge your time and be honest about your abilities. Will you be able to make any of these recipes?

• If you can't make the specific dishes, will the book give you some good ideas anyway?

Recipes aren't everything. Some books are just for having — or adding to a collection — or for making you interested in eating all over again.

Of making many books there is no end: And much study is a weariness of the flesh.

— *Ecclesiastes 12:12*

HEAVY, HEAVY

Close to 20 percent of cookbooks are given as gifts, so be careful when choosing one for others. A friend may be delighted to receive a book on cookies but less pleased to unwrap a diet book with its implied criticism!

THE BEST OF THE BEST

Top prize in the food world is winning the annual award for best cookbook of the year. Annual awards have been in place since 1966, when R. T. French, the mustard manufacturers, set up the Tastemaker Awards, the first national competition that specifically honored cookbooks. R. T. French sponsored the awards for many years, then Seagram's took over the Tastemaker sponsorship; since 1990 two sets of awards have been presented, one by the International Association of Culinary Professionals (IACP) and the other by the James Beard Foundation. Each event, one named for Julia Child, the other for James Beard, honors those books that panels of judges have recommended as outstanding in a series of categories, and one of these winners is also selected as the best book of the year.

Scanning the list offers a fast overview of the changes that have taken place in American cooking over nearly 30 years, and who was primarily responsible for them.

1966 **The Thousand-Recipe Chinese Cookbook**
Gloria Bley Miller (Grosset & Dunlap)

1967 **America Cooks**
Anne Seranne (Putnam)

1968 **The New York Times Large Type Cookbook**
Jean Hewitt (Golden Press)

1969 **A Kitchen Primer (Best Basic Book Award)**
Craig Claiborne (Knopf)

1970 **Splendid Fare (Best Basic Book Award)**
Albert Stockli (Knopf)

1971 **The New York Times International Cookbook**
Craig Claiborne (Harper)

1972 **James Beard's American Cookery**
James Beard (Little, Brown)

1973 **The Seasonal Kitchen**
Perla Myers (Holt)

1974 **Simple French Food**
Richard Olney (Atheneum)

1975 **The Doubleday Cookbook**
Jean Anderson and Elaine Hanna (Doubleday)

1976 **Michel Guerard's Cuisine Minceur**
Michel Guerard (Morrow)

1977 **James Beard's Theory and Practice of Good Cooking**
James Beard (Knopf)

1978 **Julia Child & Company**
Julia Child (Knopf)

1979 **La Méthode**
Jacques Pépin (Times Books)

1980 **Craig Claiborne's Gourmet Diet**
Craig Claiborne with Pierre Franey (Times Books)

1981 **The New James Beard**
James Beard (Knopf)

1982 **The Book of Bread**
Judith and Evan Jones (Knopf)

1983 **Country Weekends**
Lee Bailey (Clarkson Potter)

1984 **Giuliano Bugialli's Foods of Italy**
Giuliano Bugialli (Stewart, Tabori & Chang)

1985 **Glorious American Food**
Christopher Idone (Random House)

1986 **Roger Vergé's Entertaining in the French Style**
Roger Vergé (Stewart, Tabori & Chang)

1987 **The Art of Indian Vegetarian Cooking**
Yamuna Devi (Dutton)

1988 **The Cake Bible**
Rose Levy Beranbaum (Morrow)

1989 **The Foods of Vietnam**
Nicole Routhier (Stewart, Tabori & Chang)

1990 **Cocolat: Extraordinary Chocolate Desserts**
Alice Medrich (Warner Books) — James Beard

The Savory Way
Deborah Madison (Bantam) — IACP

1991 **Sauces: Classical and Contemporary Sauce Making**
James Peterson (Van Nostrand) — James Beard

Bread in Half the Time
Linda West Eckhardt and Diana Collingwood Butts (Crown) — IACP

1992 **The Splendid Table**
Lynne Kasper (Morrow) — James Beard & IACP

1993 **A Taste of the Far East**
Madhur Jaffrey (Carol Southern Books) — James Beard

The Georgian Feast
Darra Goldstein (HarperCollins) — IACP

Books

A Guide to Collecting Cookbooks
Colonel Bob Allen; Collector Books, 1990; $14.95

Cookbooks Worth Collecting
Mary Barile; Wallace-Homestead, 1993; $17.95

Food from the Heart: Creating a Heritage Cookbook
Mary Barile; Heritage Publications, 1992; $12.95

Food Writing Guidelines
Food Writers and Editors Committee; International Association of Culinary Professionals, 1993; $10.00

Price Guide to Cookbooks and Recipe Collections
Linda Dickinson; Collector Books, 1993; $9.95

Recipes into Type: A Handbook for Cookbook Writers and Editors
Joan Whitman and Dolores Simon; HarperCollins, 1993; $25.00

MORE INFORMATION

International Association of Culinary Professionals
304 West Liberty Street, Suite 201
Louisville, KY 40202
502-581-9786

James Beard Foundation
167 West 12th Street
New York, NY 10011
212-675-4984

PERIODICALS

CookBook
P.O. Box 88
Steuben, ME 04680
6 times a year;
$18 per year

The Art of Eating
Box 242
Peacham, VT 05862
Quarterly;
$25 per year

The Cookbook Review
60 Kinnaird Street
Cambridge, MA 02139
617-868-8857
6 times a year;
$24 per year

COOKING FOR A CAUSE

The community cookbook — that tried and true collective enterprise that women have turned to, historically, to raise money for causes — now accounts for 20 percent of all cookbooks published in the United States. The cost of launching such projects may run as high as $25,000, plus uncounted hours of volunteer labor, or it can be as low as a few thousand dollars (for a simpler, one-time-only product). Generally speaking, with an average run of 5,000 to 10,000 copies, these books will bring a return of three times the original investment.

The first formal community cookbooks came into being after the Civil War as a means of raising money for war widows and orphans. Many have become classics, reissued constantly over the years. *The Picayune's Creole Cookbook*, for example, was first published in 1901, and reprinted in every decade afterward until 1989, when Random House published a trade edition to capitalize on the new vogue in Cajun cooking.

The Wimmer Companies of Memphis, Tennessee, is one of the largest printer/publishers in the field. "We view books differently from commercial publishers," says Sheryn Jones, vice president for sales. "We've developed a definition: Community cookbooks preserve American regional traditions and change the quality of life. No more little mimeographed products — the groups take great pride in creating a quality book."

To assist them, Wimmer's Education Division offers two-day Community Cookbook Seminars twice a year, covering development, manufacturing, marketing, and distribution, and many groups come back again and again.

Other publishers, such as Cookbook Publishers, Inc., of Olathe, Kansas, and Favorite Recipes Press, of Memphis, Tennessee, are geared to serve small organizations seeking a less costly approach. These firms publish books with few frills and in short runs.

Since 1990, the McIlhenny Company has sponsored the annual Tabasco Community Cookbook Awards, with prizes going to three national and six regional winners. Cookbooks that have sold more than 100,000 copies are named to the Walter S. McIlhenny Hall of Fame — so far there are 31 members, led by *River Road Recipes*, from the Junior League of Baton Rouge, Louisiana, which has sold in excess of 1.2 million. The company also publishes a brief guide to crafting a community cookbook, which is available free of charge from *Compiling Culinary History*, c/o Hunter MacKenzie, 41 Madison Avenue, New York, NY 10010.

The latest wrinkle: The community cookbook community is no longer all-female. The Beavers Club, a prominent men's organization in Lafayette, Louisiana, has its first cookbook in production at Wimmer — and the men are doing the work, no wives allowed. "Women might be too literal, too detailed," says Wimmer's Sheryn Jones. "We want to keep the flavor and personality of the way men tell the stories and write their recipes."

Schlesinger's Culinary Collection

The Arthur and Elizabeth Schlesinger Library on the History of Women in America was founded more than 50 years ago at Radcliffe College in Cambridge, Massachusetts. Originally a collection of works on women's rights, it has become the foremost women's history library in the world. Its culinary collection is one of the most complete in the nation and contains invaluable research tools for those in the developing field of food history.

The collection was born in 1961 when the library received a legacy of historic cookbooks. In the mid-1970s Samuel and Narcissa Chamberlain donated their sizable collection of French regional cookbooks and other culinary materials; another boost came when Eleanor Lowenstein, renowned rare book dealer in New York, bequeathed her correspondence to the library.

"We feel this is a time when people are growing in awareness of the possibilities presented by the serious study of food for furthering our understanding of history and culture," says Barbara Haber, the Schlesinger Library's curator. Under her guidance, and that of Barbara Wheaton, honorary curator of the culinary collection, the library has grown into a true learning center, with outreach programs geared to reach as wide a population as possible. Both the Women's Culinary Guild and the Culinary Historians of Boston came into being through close ties with the library; a new group, Radcliffe Culinary Friends, offers a monthly First Mondays program on topics such as how to publish a cookbook or what's hot in food, intended primarily for food professionals but open also to anyone interested.

The collection is fully indexed on HOLLIS (Harvard Online Library Information System), and although the books do not circulate, there are open stacks and pleasant work areas that invite leisurely browsing. Appropriately, the research area is named for Julia Child.

COOKIES

I am still convinced that a good, simple, homemade cookie is preferable to all the store-bought cookies one can find.

— James Beard

COOKIE CAVALCADE

Cookies of one kind or another have been rolling down through history since the third century B.C., when a baker in Rome came up with a wafer of dough that became all the rage. He didn't sweeten his wafer, though; the sugar didn't get into the dough for literally ages.

The Roman wafer was called a *bis coctum*, which is Latin for "twice baked," and if you hear in the name the root of our word *biscuit*, you're on the right track. It was flat, firm, and very dry, so that it kept its crispness for a long time. This was handy in a time when most foods couldn't be preserved. The Romans were always hitting the road in those days, extending their empire in all directions, and at the end of a long day's march, a traveling Roman could always look forward to a beaker of wine and the sharp snap of a nice, crunchy *bis coctum*.

Something similar showed up in the Middle Ages called, in Middle English, a *cracken*, precursor of the modern cracker. It was named for the sound produced when you bit into one. Like the *bis coctum*, it was made of plain dough; its main virtue was that it kept for a long time.

Sugar came into the mix in Holland with the invention of a little cake called a *koekje* — Dutch for "little cake." The *koekje* promptly jumped the English Channel and became, of course, the cookie. The idea traveled to America with the early colonists and cookies became as popular as pie in American homes, but they didn't become a commercial item until the emergence of the Graham Cracker, a "digestive biscuit" born in New England in the 1830s.

Fig Newtons made their appearance in 1895 and were well received; because of the jam inside, they were considered an ingenious novelty. Animal Crackers, introduced by Nabisco in 1902 and beloved by children, were such a huge hit that the company saw a vast potential market looming, and determined to create "new varieties of the highest class biscuit." They launched several, but the smash hit, the one that soon had America cheering and went on to conquer the world, was "two beautifully embossed, chocolate-flavored wafers with a rich cream filling" — the Oreo.

The only true rival the Oreo has ever had in the hearts of Americans is the chocolate chip cookie, which is said to have originated in 1930 at the Toll House Inn near Whitman, Massachusetts. Ruth Wakefield, proprietor of the inn, tried adding bits of chocolate to her basic butter cookies and was so pleased with the result that she sent the idea to the Nestlé Company. The company printed her recipe on the wrapper of their large semisweet chocolate bar, calling it the Toll House cookie. Everybody started making chocolate chip cookies like crazy, and Ruth Wakefield won a lifetime supply of Nestlé's chocolate.

Hillary Rodham Clinton's Cookie Recipe

Makes 7½ dozen cookies

- 1½ cups unsifted all-purpose flour
- 1 teaspoon salt
- 1 teaspoon baking soda
- 1 cup solid vegetable shortening
- 1 cup firmly packed light brown sugar
- ½ cup granulated sugar
- 1 teaspoon vanilla extract
- 2 eggs
- 2 cups old-fashioned rolled oats
- 1 12-ounce package semisweet chocolate chips

Preheat the oven to 350 degrees F. Grease baking sheets. Combine the flour, salt, and baking soda on waxed paper.

In a large bowl, beat together the shortening, sugars, and vanilla until creamy. Add the eggs, beating until light and fluffy. Gradually beat in the flour mixture and rolled oats. Stir in the chocolate chips.

Drop the batter by well-rounded measuring teaspoonfuls onto the greased baking sheets. Bake in the preheated oven for 8 to 10 minutes or until golden. Cool the cookies on the sheets on a wire rack for 2 minutes. Remove to the rack to cool completely.

Fig Names We Never Knew(ton)

The city of Newton, Massachusetts, gave its namesake cookie a 100th birthday party in 1991. The Fig Newton, third best-selling cookie in America, was actually created in Cambridgeport, Massachusetts, but the makers never considered calling their cookie the "Fig Cambridgeport." They wanted to name it for some nearby town, and thought seriously about calling it the "Fig Shrewsbury" before Newton got the nod.

Books

Maida Heatter's Book of Great Cookies
Maida Heatter; Knopf, 1977; $10.00

Rose's Christmas Cookies
Rose Levy Beranbaum; Morrow, 1990; $22.50

Sweet Miniatures
Flo Braker; Morrow, 1991; $24.50

The International Cookie Cookbook
Nancy Baggett; Stewart, Tabori & Chang, 1988; $30.00

The Joy of Cookies
Sharon Tyler Herbst; Barron's, 1987; $15.95

MAIL ORDER SOURCES

M. A. O'Halloran
A Family Baking Company
472 Tehama Street
San Francisco, CA 94103
415-777-2578

Mrs. Peabody's Cookies
715 North University
Ann Arbor, MI 48104
313-761-2447

Santa Fe Select
410 Old Santa Fe Trail
Santa Fe, NM 87501
800-243-0353

TRUTH IN NIBBLING

In the midst of the nation's no-fat, low-fat binge, consumers are making a lot of silly choices. Just because a package of cookies has words on it that sound healthy — oat, nut, bran — buyers assume they're going to get skinny eating what's inside. But just take a for instance: The country's most popular cookie, the Oreo, has 50 calories and 2 grams of fat. The Pepperidge Farm Wholesome Choice Apple Oatmeal Tart cookie has exactly as much fat and 20 more calories. About the same goes for Health Valley's Fruit and Nut Oat Bran cookies (55 calories and 2

grams of fat). Nabisco's Fat-Free Fig Newtons are different, though; they have no fat, but they have 10 *more* calories than the regular Fig Newton.

If you can resist the seductive language that is dragging you down the aisle to happy oat heaven, try turning to some old favorites that really *are* low in fat: graham crackers, Animal Crackers, vanilla wafers, gingersnaps. But remember: There's more to a cookie than meets the eye. Read the numbers, not the names, to make your choice.

CORN

Sex is good, but not as good as fresh sweet corn.

— Garrison Keillor
Ultimate Prairie Home Companion

Classic Corn Dishes

Corn fritters — Fried cornmeal batter cakes, sometimes with fruit stirred in

Corn pone — Oval-shaped cornbread made without eggs, baked or fried

Corn sticks — Cornbread baked in a special cast-iron pan with indentations that look like ears of corn

Cracklin' bread — Cornbread with fried pork cracklings stirred into the batter

Dodgers — Baked, bite-sized cornmeal pancakes

Hominy — Dried, ground

white corn grits, boiled and served as a side dish

Hush puppy — A deep-fried cornmeal dumpling made with eggs

Indian pudding — A custard made with cornmeal, eggs, and milk, flavored with molasses and spices

Johnnycake — A flat cake made from cornmeal and water or milk, cooked on a griddle or cast-iron skillet

Spoonbread — A bread that is more like a pudding, made from cornmeal and baked in a lidded casserole

THE LORE OF CORN

ANNE RAVER

When the dogwoods have leafed out and the leaves of the shadblow are the size of a squirrel's ear, it's time to plant the corn. It's best to get it in the ground before the moon is full — which was last Saturday, so I'm a little late.

"The leaves are signs that the soil is warm enough to plant, and the gravitational pull of the moon helps the growing of the corn," said Nanepashemet, whose Wampanoag ancestors fished and hunted and farmed along the coast of Massachusetts a thousand years ago.

"Tradition states that the crow brought the first corn and bean from the Creator's cornfield in the Southwest, where the Creator lived," he said. "He brought the corn in one ear and the bean in the other."

I had called Nanepashemet, who is the director of the Wampanoag Indian Program at Plimoth Plantation in Massachusetts, to find out how to plant the ancient varieties I had gotten from Seeds of Change, an organic heirloom-seed company in Santa Fe, New Mexico.

I have Black Aztec, which was grown in southern Mexico 2,500 years ago, and Rainbow Inca, a multicolored sweet corn with origins in Peru. When fresh, Black Aztec is white and sweet, but as it dries, it turns purplish black, and its hard kernels can be ground into purple cornmeal. Rainbow Inca is red, yellow, and bluish black, and a single ear can have 750 seeds.

Biologists think that corn evolved from a wild grain called teosinte that still grows in the Mexican highlands. Popcorn as old as 6,000 years (like what I had at the movies last week) has been found in caves outside Mexico City. But it took thousands of years before that for teosinte to turn from a grassy plant into the first husked kernels of corn that somebody probably threw into a fire one day and watched pop.

Corn cultivation in the Northeast probably began about

1,000 years ago, Nanepashemet said. "They received corn by trading seed with people farther south, and they also learned the techniques that had developed thousands of years before in South America."

Years ago, when I gardened on a hill overlooking a tidal estuary in Massachusetts, I planted my corn the way the Wampanoags did, putting a few seeds in a loose, sandy mound about three feet across with a herring buried beneath, because the soil was a bit poor.

When the corn was about a hand's breadth high, I hilled soil about the young stalks and kept them weeded. When they were up about seven inches, I planted scarlet runner beans right at the base of the stalks. Then I planted acorn squash at the edge of the mounds — which were six feet apart center to center — and let the vines ramble along the ground. The squash plants kept the soil moist and the weeds down.

The first corn growers in Mexico planted beans next to the corn, without knowing that the legumes were working to help the nitrogen in the soil fertilize the very plants that gave them support. They just copied the combinations they saw growing wild in the highlands.

"It's just how the plants grow in nature," said Alan Kapuler, a microbiologist who searches for heirloom seeds and grows them for his research company, Peace Seeds, in Corvallis, Oregon. "Mexico is the origin of corn, as well as some of the squashes and beans, and you find them growing wild together."

And eaten together, these "three sisters of life," as many native peoples called them, provide the 20 amino acids necessary for complete protein, Mr. Kapuler said. Of course, no one had a chemistry lab 6,000 years ago — people just ate what was there.

Excerpted from The New York Times

Types of Corn

Dent corn — This is the hard yellow field corn that is America's second most important crop, grows throughout the Midwest, and is exported worldwide. It feeds livestock, makes cornflakes, cornmeal, sweets, starches, and ethanol fuel. **White dent corn** flour is used in Mexican cooking.

Sweet corn — This is eaten fresh, as corn on the cob, canned, or frozen. New varieties and rediscovered old varieties are constantly appearing that retain sweetness and moisture longer or have intriguing colorations. **Baby sweet corn** is just sweet corn picked while still immature.

Flint corn — This is not grown commercially in the United States, but several brightly colored varieties are popular in South America.

Flour corn — One of the oldest types of corn, flour corns were an early American staple. They are well adapted to dry conditions but require too much care to be mass-produced. With increased interest in Southwestern cuisine, several varieties have become very popular, especially **blue corn**, traditionally revered by the Hopis and Zunis because of its color. It is now used to make flours and popcorn.

Popcorn — Most dried corns will pop when heated, but Americans' fondness for popcorn has led to the development of specialized varieties with maximum puff and minimum hard parts left unpopped.

A CORNY MEAL

Celebrating publication of Betty Fussell's *The Story of Corn*, chef Brendan Walsh of the North Street Grill in Great Neck, New York, served an All Corn Dinner at the James Beard House in New York City. This was the menu:

Johnnycakes with American Golden Caviar
Soft Blue Tacos with Spiced Rock Shrimp
Fried Oysters with Charred Tomato Salsa
Mumm Cuvée Napa Blanc de Noirs

Maine Lobster Croustade
with Green Corn Cream
Red Chili Crêpes
with Cuitlacoche
Tamales
Roast Striped Bass
with Succotash and Corn Salad
Chicken and Sage Sausage
with Hominy Grits and Spoonbread

A Summer Fruit Atole

Fresh Corn Rolls
Cornbread
Corn Sticks
Blue and Yellow Corn Chips
Popcorn
Fried Hominy

Books

James McNair's Corn Cookbook
James McNair; Chronicle Books, 1990; $19.95/$11.95

Lee Bailey's Corn
Lee Bailey; Clarkson Potter, 1993; $14.00

The Story of Corn
Betty Fussell; Knopf, 1992; $30.00

MORE INFORMATION

Corn Refiners Association, Inc.
1701 Pennsylvania Avenue NW, Suite 950
Washington, DC 20006
202-331-1634

Florida Sweet Corn Exchange
P.O. Box 140155
Orlando, FL 32814-0155
407-894-1351

National Corn Growers Association
1000 Executive Parkway
St. Louis, MO 63141
314-275-9915

COTTAGE INDUSTRIES

STARTING UP POTS OF GOLD

Many of America's giant conglomerates started life as tiny companies, built around ideas that took form on the kitchen table or in a basement workshop or garage. People are still starting small every day, but the general impression is that it was easier to grow in the old days than it is now.

As a rule, small companies today have an uphill battle if they try to expand in an economy that benefits the strongest players. A start-up company seldom has adequate resources to keep going during bad times or when faced with unanticipated problems — unless there is an understanding "banker" to come to the rescue. However, neither a person nor a company can afford to stand still in a highly competitive world. If a little company is content to supply its products only to friends and neighbors, it soon loses its momentum. It becomes a small service "hobby" rather than a growing enterprise. On the other hand, if the product is good, customers clamor for it, almost forcing the entrepreneur to grow.

Celestial Seasonings is a good example of how an idea became a real zinger. Its founder, Mo Siegel, was a barefoot hippie flower child who turned out to be a marketing genius. He built a herbal tea company with sales in the multimillions. As he began to draw sales away from other tea producers and distributors, the Establishment took a closer look at him. Eventually, Kraft, one of the largest food companies in the country, began a courtship that resulted in a prenuptial agreement without the nuptials. Kraft bought Celestial Seasonings, and the bells on Mo's cash registers rang many a merry peal, enabling him, not long afterward, to leave and found another business, producing environmentally friendly cleaning products and trash bags. Latest chapter in the saga has seen his return as CEO of Celestial Seasonings and the development of a new line of iced teas, which are being distributed by Perrier USA.

This is a true success story, the kind Harvard Business School likes to use as a model. However, another kind of story is more common. An entrepreneur has an idea for a product — it could be a hot fudge sauce, a recipe for salsa, new fruit preserves or bagel bits or vegetable chips. The maker distributes samples to friends, relatives, coworkers, and they love the stuff. "Give us more," they say.

At first the entrepreneur regards this crispy, crunchy, spicy, sweet, hot, cool new product as just a way to make a little extra money. He or she persuades the local specialty store to stock it. It flies off the shelf and the store orders more. The maker glimpses a pot of gold at the end of a very short rainbow and rushes off to exhibit the wonder wares at the nearest Fancy Foods show. But few buyers are interested in the product. Hardly any one even looks at it. No orders are written. Gloom, doom, and depression descend, but not for long.

The entrepreneur decides that while the product is terrific, the packaging is at fault. He hires a designer, using up a lot of the earlier profit for the development of a fancy label for a fancy package. Suddenly, Dean and DeLuca wants 124 cases — immediately. Overextended and undercapitalized, the entrepreneur hires more people to fill the jars. More money goes out to buy shipping boxes and invoice forms, and a billing department is needed to keep up with the volume. Sales increase, but so do the costs. The profit margin shrinks while — who would have thought it? — respectable stores with big names delay 90 days or 120 days or even longer in paying their bills.

The entrepreneur turns to advertising to increase volume. It does, but it also drains more dollars from the enterprise. Meanwhile, the entrepreneur can't raise prices because there's a limit to how much the public will pay for a jar of preserves, no matter how good they are.

As all this frantic activity is going on, the entrepreneur has to learn how to handle the snags of running a business that operates on a paper-thin margin. He's distracted trying to deal with problems he's never faced before and he makes mistakes, all of them costly. And he's sorely missed on the production line; without his hand stirring the pot, the quality of the product is likely to slip.

This is not to say that small business is always in crisis. It isn't. Hundreds, indeed thousands of cottage industries are alive and well, providing hundreds of thousands of jobs and generating ideas for the foods we will be enjoying in the future. But experience shows that fast growth isn't always the best thing for a fledgling company.

The Name of the Game

Obviously, many cottage industries have decided that there's nothing like a name. Here are some of them:

Before the Frost

Big Belly Cajun Jelly

Blue Planet Trading Company

Boomer's Oogies

Chocolate Lace

Claire's Angels

Colts Bolts

Drake's Ducks

Floribbean

Larder of Lady Bustle

My Mother's Knish

Nervous Nellie's Jams and Jellies

Nuts D'Vine

Olive Schmear

Pork Schop of Vermont

Prosperity Farms

Severance Foods
(founded with someone's severance pay)

Southern Comforts

Southern Presence

What's Poppin'

Whistling Wings

Word of Mouth Food

MORE INFORMATION

National Association for the Specialty Food Trade, Inc.
8 West 40th Street, 4th floor
New York, NY 10018-3901
212-921-1690

Books

Specialty Food Resource Handbook: A Comprehensive Guide to Resource Information for Food Entrepreneurs
Beth Hillson; Connecticut Specialty Food and Beverage Association, 1992; $12.95

CRABS

J. DATOR

BUNGEE CRAB

There are three species of creatures who when they seem coming are going, when they seem going they come: diplomats, women, and crabs.

— John Hay
19th-century American diplomat

Spawned, Then Spurned

by Sandra Soehngen and Melanie Young

Female blue crabs mate only once. Only during this brief period when the female or "Sook" sheds her shell can she be mated to the "Jimmy" or male crab. The mating session can last up to 48 hours. Afterward, the male cradles his female partner until she regenerates a hard shell. Once the female's shell hardens, she proceeds to attack and eat her male partner unless he makes a quick getaway. Talk about "till death us do part!"

INSIDE A CHESAPEAKE
CRAB HOUSE

WILLIAM WARNER

Most Atlantic blue crabs are caught hard and processed for meat. Although soft-shell crabs are rapidly gaining a new nationwide popularity, the meat of hard crabs — fresh, pasteurized, or canned — remains the heart of the industry. First stop for most of the market-bound catch, therefore, is a place where crabmeat is extracted by hand. In the Chesapeake an establishment performing this function is known as a picking plant or more often simply a "crab house," as opposed to a "crab shanty," which is the shacklike structure used by soft-crab pound operators to watch over their shedding floats.

Although Chesapeake crab houses exhibit great variety, all have two essential elements. The first is a device to cook the crabs whole, since the flesh of the blue crab, like that of nearly all other crustaceans, cannot be removed from the shell until it is firmed up by thorough cooking. Large steaming vats or "cookers" are used for this purpose. Their design has not changed much since the beginning of this century. Some are boxlike chambers into which crates holding almost a ton of crabs fit very snugly. Others are large kettles, the size and shape of which make you think of savages and the parboiling of missionaries, capable of receiving three circular steel baskets each holding about 350 pounds of crabs. Both types function in the same manner. Handlers push the crates into the chambers on dollies or let the baskets down into the kettles from overhead rail systems. The steam does the rest, or, more exactly, pressurized steam at 250 degrees Fahrenheit for about 12 minutes. Since so

many of the cookers are old, accidents are not uncommon. Crab house proprietors will tell you about them with great relish. Omar Evans, a waterman who at the age of 71 runs the only picking plant on Smith Island, vividly remembers the time the door of his ancient Nilsen and White chamber-type cooker let go at the hinges. "Oh, my heavens, did she blow!" Evans says. "I wa'nt very popular around here, I tell you that. Crabs was scattered all over town. Found one stuck by his spike in the mast of a buy boat half a mile yonder."

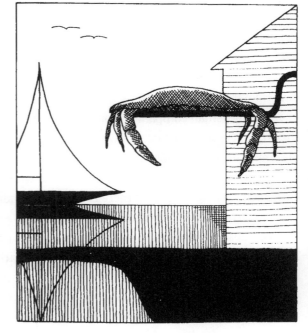

Barring such problems the crabs emerge from the cooker very much dead and with their top shells and claws almost lobster-red. (The shell of the sternum and abdomen remains obstinately white.) Their muscle tissue is now both free of live bacteria and very firm. They are thus ready for the other crab house essential, or the "picking room," where they will be split, quartered, and dissected for every last gram of meat.

A man enters a picking room at his peril. As many as 30 or 40 ladies will be seated around stainless-steel-topped tables, talking loudly and carrying on. Open the screen door and all activity halts. Within seconds the ladies resume their work, but silence, curious stares, and a slower production pace remain, much to the annoyance of the manager. You go up to the head lady, traditionally seated nearest the hinged receiving window through which the crabs are shoveled, and try to think of something to say. Her hands fly so fast that it is impossible to see what she is doing. The skill commands immediate respect. You ask her how long it takes to learn.

"Some never do," she replies tartly, looking at the slower apprentices.

Excerpted from *Beautiful Swimmers*

The Most Common Crabs

Type	Habitat	Description and Use
Alaskan king crab	Alaska, North Pacific	Large spiny legs are a very popular delicacy; so is backfin meat, used for canning. Can weigh up to 25 pounds and produce at least 6 pounds of meat, sold brine-frozen.
Snow crab	Alaska to Northern California	Long, spidery legs, often substituted for king crab; claws and legs are most popular. Can yield up to 2½ pounds of meat; sold frozen.
Dungeness crab	Alaska to Northern California	Brownish-red top shell turns bright red when cooked; deep, heavy body averages 2 to 4¼ pounds. So popular that catch has had to be limited to males more than 6½ inches; meat nearly always sold cooked fresh or frozen; also available whole, live or cooked.
Jonah crab	Off Maine and Canada	Large, elliptical reddish-yellow shell, about 6 inches; usually caught along with lobsters from deep water. Production being increased with special pots. Sold fresh, whole, or as cooked meat and claws.
Stone crab	Southeast coast, Florida into the Gulf	Only heavy, black-tipped claws are eaten. Fishermen take the smaller claw from each crab, which is then put back to regenerate another, a process that lasts 18 months. Claws have to be cracked with a stone or mallet, hence the name; are cooked and sold chilled or frozen.
Blue crab	Cape Cod through Florida into the Gulf	Mottled dark blue-brown oval shell, up to 8 inches. Swims sideways; very abundant; males are larger, usually sold whole. Meat is available picked in three grades: lump or backfin (from body); flake or body (smaller pieces); and claw meat. Often pasteurized and sold in cans.
Soft-shell crab (Blue crab in molt)	Cape Cod through Florida into the Gulf	Blue crabs caught just as they have shed their hard shells, which is how they grow bigger. The molting stage lasts very briefly, the shell starts to toughen within hours, and if the crab can escape the fishermen the new hard shell forms in a day. Soft-shell crabs vary from 5½ to 3½ inches and are totally edible. They are usually kept in water for 8 hours, then shipped and sold live; they have already hardened slightly and are often fried crisply to disguise it. Available fresh from May through mid-October; frozen year-round.

Did You Know?

☞ A female blue crab may carry up to 2 million eggs.

☞ There are 4,500 species of crabs in the world. Some are less than an inch long, others measure 12 feet, claw to claw.

☞ Crabs are the second most popular crustacean consumed in the United States. After shrimp, that is.

☞ The largest American crab catch is of snow crabs — some 357 million pounds annually, worth more than $200 million. By comparison, just over 28 million pounds of king crabs, the most expensive, sell for $82.8 million.

Some Crab Expressions

A crab or **a crabby person** — Someone who is constantly cross.

To catch a crab — To fail to raise the oar clear of the water when rowing, or to miss a stroke altogether.

A crab apple — A small, very sour wild apple, often grown as an ornamental because of its blossom and decorative fruit. "Crab" may, in fact, refer to the bright red skin rather than the tart taste.

Crabwise — A sideways movement, like a crab scuttling across the sand.

To crab the wind — To move an airplane into a crosswind, which produces an apparent sideways motion.

Books

The Chesapeake Bay Crab Cookbook
John Shields; Addison Wesley, 1992; $10.95

The Complete Crab and Lobster Book
Christopher R. Reaske; Lyons & Burford, 1989; $16.95/$9.95

The Crab Cookbook
Whitey Schmidt; Marian Hartnett Press, 1990; $12.95

CRANBERRIES

THE CONTENT OF CRANBERRIES

Cranberries are almost 90 percent water, and the remaining 10 percent is carbohydrates and fiber. Their major nutrient is vitamin C — early New England sailing ships used to put to sea carrying barrels of berries to supplement the sailors' diet of salt pork and crackers.

More recently, researchers have found a special factor in cranberries that seems to act as a urinary antiseptic, by preventing bacteria from coating the surface of cells in the bladder and urinary tract. This could well explain the widespread belief in cranberry juice as a folk remedy for urinary infections.

Did You Know?

☞ Cranberries are one of only three major fruits native to North America (Concord grapes and blueberries are the others). Of more than 100 varieties of cranberries, four are grown commercially: Early Blacks, Howes, Searles, and McFarlins.

☞ The Ocean Spray cooperative is the world's largest producer of cranberry products; close to 80 percent of U.S. cranberry growers belong to it.

☞ Cranberry farms range in size from 4 or 5 to 1,200 acres.

☞ More than a third of the $200 million-plus annual cranberry harvest is made into juices.

☞ Massachusetts, Rhode Island, New Jersey, Wisconsin, Oregon, and Washington are the major cranberry-producing states.

TIPS

Cooking
When making a whole-berry cranberry sauce, it is a good idea to add the sugar *after* the cranberries have been cooked, letting it dissolve in the juice. Adding sugar earlier tends to toughen the skins.

Old Wives' Tale

Long before modern science confirmed cranberries' role in preventing scurvy and treating urinary infections, Indian women believed the berries possessed the power to heal. They brewed hot cranberry poultices — just the thing to pull out the poison from arrow wounds.

Books

Cranberries
William Jaspersohn; Houghton Mifflin, 1991; $14.95

Cranberries from A to Z
Ann Kurz; Cranberry Originals Press, 1989; $13.95

The Cranberry Connection
Beatrice Ross Buszek; Nimbus, 1977; $11.95

PERIODICALS

Cranberry Institute Newsletter
Cranberry Institute
P.O. Box 535
East Wareham, MA 02538
508-295-4895
Quarterly; free to members

Crane Berries

The Pilgrims called them *crane berries*. Some people say this was because the flowers crane their necks at the end of their stalks; others say the name came from the cranes' fondness for the pungent red berries.

CRAWFISH

A Crawfish Legend

by Bernard Clayton

The little creature is a descendant of the Maine lobster. After the Cajuns were exiled from Nova Scotia, the lobsters yearned for the Cajuns so much that they set off across the country to find them. The journey over mountains was so long and treacherous that the creatures began to shrink in size. By the time they found the Cajuns in Louisiana, all that was left of the crustaceans' former greatness was their tremendous flavor, which they managed to store in their succulent tails. Upon their arrival, a great festival was held, and all the great Cajun crawfish dishes — étouffée (stew), jambalaya, gumbo, bisque, boulettes (meatballs), pies, and fried and boiled crawfish — were created.

Excerpted from Bernard Clayton's Cooking Across America

TIPS

Buying
Try to find live crawfish if you can because they taste better; frozen crawfish, however, are much less trouble to deal with.

Cooking
Wash the crawfish in two or three changes of cold water, then slide them gently into a large pot of boiling salted water. Let the water return to a slow simmer, cover the pot, and cook for about 3 minutes, depending on their size. Err on the side of undercooking, so that they don't toughen.

Drain the crawfish and remove the shells from the tails, saving the orange-colored livers to enrich sauces.

HOW TO EAT CRAWFISH

EMERIL LAGASSE

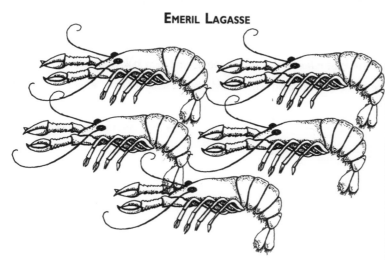

Hot boiled crawfish are served in restaurants and homes all over New Orleans. You can always spot first-time crawfish eaters because they haven't a clue as to how to eat these freshwater crustaceans that look like mini-lobsters. Here's how to eat boiled crawfish like a native.

1. Twist the tail off the body and immediately suck the juices out of the body shell. (It's what we mean by "sucking the heads.")

2. Hold the tail by the bottom and peel off the top ring of the shell.

3. Place the meat between your teeth, pinch the bottom of the tail with your thumb and forefinger, and pull out the meat with your teeth.

Excerpted from *Emeril's New New Orleans Cooking*

Jude Theriot's
Crawfish Skillet

Serves 8

¹/₄ cup peanut oil
¹/₂ cup (1 stick) unsalted butter
1 pound fresh crawfish tails
1 tablespoon minced celery
1 tablespoon minced carrot
1 bunch green onions, tops and bottoms, chopped
2 medium-sized bell peppers, sliced into strips
8 large mushrooms, sliced
2 firm red tomatoes, sliced into wedges
2¹/₂ cups cooked white rice
1¹/₄ teaspoons salt
¹/₂ teaspoon each Tabasco sauce and black pepper
¹/₄ teaspoon each dried sweet basil and filé powder
1 tablespoon white wine
¹/₄ cup sliced toasted almonds
¹/₂ cup minced fresh parsley

Have ready a very heavy 10- to 12-inch skillet with high sides — since it must hold the entire dish at various stages.

Heat the peanut oil in the skillet over medium-high heat, until it begins to smoke. Add the butter and move it around so that it melts quickly. Add the crawfish, celery, and carrot, and sauté for 3 minutes.

Add the green onions and mix well. Add the peppers, mix well, and sauté for 30 seconds. Add the mushrooms and tomatoes. Stir briefly just to coat the mushrooms. Remove the skillet from the heat.

Add the cooked rice, salt, Tabasco, black pepper, sweet basil, filé powder, and wine and mix until all of the rice is coated with the pan liquid. Add the almonds and parsley and mix very well.

Serve at once!

Reprinted from *Bernard Clayton's Cooking Across America*

What to Drink with Crawfish

Paul, high priest of the Cajuns, thirteenth child of the family Prudhomme that did a lot of begetting near the bayou close to Opelousas, who has done more than anyone to spread the word about Cajun cooking, would probably recommend a Cajun Martini. His own brew, composed of gin and chili peppers, is hot enough to blow off the top of your head. It is served straight up — in a jam jar, filled to the brim. Did some faint-hearted person murmur, "Iced tea?" *This* potion has been known to raise the dead.

Did You Know?

☞ Deep-fried crawfish tails are known as Cajun popcorn.

☞ It takes seven pounds of crawfish to produce one pound of edible meat.

☞ Louisiana produces more than 90 percent of the U.S. crawfish catch.

☞ There are more than 300 species of crawfish; most popular are Red Swamp and White River varieties. Only a handful of species grow to a size that makes them worth the trouble of shelling — 3½ inches, approximately the length of an index finger.

☞ The crawfish industry is anticipating annual production of some 500,000 pounds as consumer demand increases.

Pearls of the Bayou

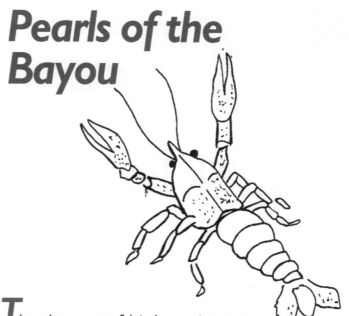

The red swamp crawfish is the most important species in the Atchafalaya Basin, accounting for about 80 percent of the 40 million pounds of crawfish harvested annually with baited traps from the warm-water crawfish ponds. (A related species, the signal or California crayfish, lives in the cold waters off Northern California and Oregon. About 1 million pounds are taken annually, primarily for sale to the European market under the name of crayfish.)

Down on the bayou, where 90 percent of red swamp crawfish are consumed, nobody cares what they call the crawfish, provided they're good and tasty. Soft-shell crawfish, taken during the molting process, are the latest craze — one with an unexpected dividend. When crawfish molt, the calcium in the shell migrates to two glands in the head, leaving the shell soft enough to shed. These stones have to be removed before the crawfish are served. The size of split peas, they are known as "Cajun pearls," and the bayou folk make jewelry from them.

MORE INFORMATION

Crawfish Research and Promotion Board
P.O. Box 3334
Baton Rouge, LA 70821-3334
504-922-1280

MAIL ORDER SOURCES

Baton Rouge Crawfish Company
9121 Amber Drive
Baton Rouge, LA 70809
504-756-4807

Deanie's Seafood
1713 Lake Avenue
Metairie, LA 70005
504-834-1225

J. Bernard Seafood
P.O. Box 623
Cottonport, LA 71327
800-869-5616

Pacific Crayfish Company
12924 Athens Way
Los Angeles, CA 90061
310-538-5155

Books

Around the Southern Table
Sarah Belk; Simon & Schuster, 1991; $24.95

Bernard Clayton's Cooking Across America
Bernard Clayton; Simon & Schuster, 1993; $25.00

Emeril's New New Orleans Cooking
Emeril Lagasse and Jessie Tirsch; Morrow, 1993; $23.00

La Cuisine Cajun
Jude Theriot; Pelican, 1986; $12.95

Southern Food: At Home, on the Road, in History
John Egerton; Knopf, 1987; $22.95

Coming Up Roses — Crawdads and Mudbugs

Louisiana has arrived at a highly satisfactory system of crop rotation. In the hot summer months while the farmers are growing rice, the crawfish bury themselves in the soft mud to escape the heat. In the fall the rice fields are flooded.

The crawfish come out of the mud to spawn.

The farmers gather rice and crawfish, praise the Lord, and eat gumbo.

Naming Crawfish

by Calvin Trillin

There are crawfish (or crayfish, or crawdads) all over the country, but outside of Louisiana they are all but ignored — lumps of clay lacking a sculptor. People outside of Louisiana, in fact, often scoff when they hear of people eating crawfish — the way an old farmer in Pennsylvania might scoff at the New York antique dealer who paid $14.00 for a quilt that must be at least a hundred years old and doesn't even look very warm. A New York crawfish craver who couldn't make it to the Atchafalaya Basin would have to settle for Paris, where crawfish are called écrevisses, except by people from Louisiana, who always call them inferior.

Excerpted from American Fried

CUCUMBERS

A cucumber should be well sliced, and dressed with pepper and vinegar, and then thrown out, as good for nothing.

— Dr. Samuel Johnson
18th-century encyclopedist

BLAND BUT NEVER BORING

The cucumber is one of the oldest cultivated vegetables — it's been growing around human dwellings since at least 7750 B.C., traveling originally from India and Burma to Europe. In Roman times, the Emperor Tiberius grew cucumbers in carts, and had his slaves wheel them around to catch the sun. He ate them saturated in wine. Eventually, cucumbers were cultivated all over Europe. And when the first explorers came to the New World, cucumbers came with them.

The popularity of the cucumber over time might seem curious, in light of the fact that it doesn't taste like anything in particular. Nor does it have any food value to speak of — it contains virtually no fat, fiber, or sodium, and absolutely no cholesterol. You could eat 10 big ones without gaining a pound. It has literally nothing to give us. So why are we so crazy about this gourd?

Perhaps it's because the cucumber is so cool. It literally maintains its insides at a temperature several degrees cooler than the surrounding atmosphere. This chilly demeanor gives it an aristocratic air of detachment that makes other vegetables look cloddish in comparison.

Though the English cultivated the cucumber to an enormous size, they've always liked its innate restraint. Slivers of cucumber peel in festive "cups" were supposed to distract the unwary from the fact that they were drinking gin.

Americans like it in salads, mainly for its crispness — guaranteed if it comes straight from the ice-cold refrigerator. We like especially the English kind, now grown hydroponically here and known as "burpless" — after all, burping isn't cool.

TIPS

Preparing
When using cucumber in salads, cut it lengthwise and scoop out the seeds. Then cut it crosswise. Without the seeds, the cucumber won't weep onto the plate.

A cucumber that has begun to soften can be made crisp again by slicing it and sprinkling it with salt. Leave to stand for an hour, drain off the water that forms, and pat the slices dry on paper towels.

Cooking
Cucumber makes a terrific hot vegetable. Cut it into small pieces and simmer in salted water for about 5 minutes, until translucent. Throw a handful of freshly shelled peas into the pot and they will cook in the same time.

Serving
Mix cucumber slices with sour cream and fresh dill and serve as a side-dish salad.

Did You Know?

☞ The cucumber is a member of the gourd family.

☞ As a crop, cucumbers rank 12th in cash value among all vegetables grown in the United States.

☞ The cucumber can hold up to 30 times its weight in water.

☞ Each person in the United States eats more than four pounds of cucumbers a year.

☞ In 1930s slang, a cucumber meant a dollar bill.

ALERT

People who are allergic to pollen or to aspirin should avoid cucumbers, peeled or not, as they contain ingredients that can make the mouth itch unpleasantly.

To Wax, Perchance to Eat

Cucumbers are waxed to prevent them from shrinking during the (considerable) lapsed time from being picked to being eaten. Eating the waxed skin will do you no harm — the wax is edible — although waxed cucumber skin may not be among the foods you crave. If you discard the skin, waxed or unwaxed, wait to do so until you are ready to eat what lies beneath or you will remove the cucumber's small amount of vitamin C.

DATES

*It's never too late
To succumb to a date
that's plump
as a camel's hump
And far sweeter
than an old potate(r).*

DATES
OF THE DESERT

The United States produces 35 million pounds of dates every year, almost entirely from date palms in the Coachella Valley of southern California, in the vicinity of Palm Springs and Indio. These monumental palms, which can live and bear fruit for a hundred years and may grow to an equal number of feet, are a natural wonder and a great enhancement to the beauty of the desert.

There is evidence that date palms were growing along the Nile in the fifth century B.C. The date palm is identified as the "Tree of Life" in Genesis, and there are 60 references to it in the Old Testament.

Nomadic tribes took the date palm into the Sahara about 2,000 years ago. The Moors brought it to North Africa and Spain. And Spanish missionaries brought it to the coast of California. It didn't fare well there because the climate was too moist. But early in this century, USDA researchers tried planting the date palm in the desert at Mecca, California, and it flourished, bearing so quickly and so generously — a healthy palm will produce up to 300 pounds of dates in a season — that by 1915 an industry was launched.

Inside Dates

The fruit of the date palm is actually a berry with a ridged seed. Our word for it comes from *dactylus*, the Latin word for finger. The fruit, about three inches long and oblong, was thought to resemble one.

An average date has only 24 calories, but it's rich in folic·acid and fiber. Dates contain neither sodium nor fat.

There are two types of dates: soft and semisoft. The soft types have soft flesh, high moisture content, and relatively low sugar content. They are harvested by hand. Semi-soft dates are firmer, have a fairly low moisture content, and are high in sugar. They can be picked by machine.

There are about 30 varieties of dates, most bearing Arabic names. The Deglet Noor, "date of light," a semisoft type, accounts for 85 percent of California's production. It is medium-large, oblong, and amber-colored. The Zahidi, "nobility," is smaller, egg-shaped, and golden. Soft varieties include the Khadrawy, "green," the Halawy, "sweet," and the big, flavorful Medjool, which means "unknown."

Soft dates should always be stored in the refrigerator. Semisoft types can be kept, tightly wrapped, at room temperature, but will keep longer if refrigerated. In airtight containers, dates will stay moist in the refrigerator for as long as eight months.

ODD JOBS

The date palm's male and female flowers grow on separate trees, and the female flower emits no scent to attract insects. So *palmeros*, the elite workers of the date industry, climb up the 60-foot-high male trees to collect pollen. Each male produces enough pollen for 49 female trees. The palmeros then climb to the tops of the female trees, carefully blow the pollen onto the pods, and slip a paper bag over each to generate heat and ensure that the pollen isn't blown away.

Once the trees bear fruit, up the workers go again to tie each fruit stalk to a lower leaf to provide support and wrap paper parasols around the bunches to protect them.

Books

Date Recipes
R. I. Heetland; Golden West, 1986; $6.95

DELIS

DELICATE EATING

In Germany, *delikatessen* means particular food — literally, an abundance of delicacies — a wonderful array of good things to eat; rice pudding and cheesecake, to be sure, but notably cooked meats, done to perfection. With the change of a single letter, the word and reality of delicatessen translated to America with the waves of German-Jewish immigrants in the late 19th century. The kosher deli, a wildly popular attraction that's now considered an American institution, can be found in most cities and towns around the country. But New York remains its true home — the seat of all its traditions, the place where it started.

Though most delis maintain a casual air — just a comfortable, informal place to have a *nosh* (Yiddish for a bite to eat) — there's nothing casual about the service. The men at the counter may well have spent their entire working lives learning to slice meats exquisitely. At Zabar's, one of the legendary New York counter delis (no table service, just heart-stopping food encounters at the counter), the average salary for a lox slicer with ten years' experience is $60,000 a year.

In a proper New York deli restaurant, pickles must be on the table when you sit down, and the portions have to be gargantuan, the sandwiches piled so high — six inches, minimum — that you couldn't possibly get your mouth entirely over the top of one. Another tradition is that the waiters have to be surly; many New Yorkers believe that if a waiter is nice to them, they're in the wrong place. However, it's not grumpiness that motivates the waiters so much as a delicacy of feeling about the foods they serve.

The story goes that a greenhorn once went to a deli and ordered a lean pastrami sandwich. "Pastrami isn't lean," the waiter replied, deeply offended by such ignorance. "If you don't like fat, don't order pastrami." Whereupon he walked off and never came back. It was evidently too painful for him to conceive of serving anybody so dumb.

Many New Yorkers would stand in line — and do — in hopes of getting a waiter like that. It's part of the price of authenticity.

The Carnegie Deli, near Carnegie Hall, was made nationally famous by Woody Allen in his movie *Broadway Danny Rose*, but it has been a New York institution since 1933. The Carnegie is widely regarded as having the best pastrami in the city, and no more so than by its owner. After the restaurant was robbed not long ago, he said to reporters, "Stupid fools! They took the money and left the pastrami."

The Carnegie offers only the best, and serves about 750,000 customers a year. The management estimates that some 80 percent of patrons are non-New Yorkers; menus are available in several foreign languages, including Japanese.

Pastrami sandwiches here contain a full pound of meat. But people who are *really* hungry can ask for combination sandwiches up to two pounds, such as "Carnegie Haul," "Nova on Sunday," "Tongues for the Memories," "The Mouth that Roared," and "The Egg and Oy."

Top-selling sandwiches are:

"**Club Dear**" — a triple-decker of roast turkey, grilled bacon, lettuce, tomato, and mayonnaise.

"**Broadway Danny Rose**" — heaps of corned beef and pastrami.

"**Brisketball**" — brisket of beef and white meat of turkey, with onion, lettuce, and tomato.

Cutting the Mustard with
Deli Meats

The way they're slicing it these days, Americans are eating about 70 slices of bologna per person per year — in all, that's nearly 800 million pounds annually. Most of it — 88 percent — is traditional beef and pork, or beef, but chicken is coming along at 8 percent, and turkey at 4 percent. Turkey's the lowest in fat, with a third of the 30 percent fat content allowed in the traditional kinds.

Americans eat more than 5 billion pounds of various deli meats a year, and there are something like 200 varieties to choose from. Traditional kinds are as popular than ever, turkey's low fat notwithstanding.

According to a survey conducted by the National Livestock and Meat Board, 99 percent of all Americans eat deli sandwiches, and 31 percent eat them two or three times a week. The most enthusiastic eaters are those between 18 and 34: With them, it's deli meat more than five times a week.

What do people cry for at the deli counter? Among those surveyed, ham sandwiches came in first with 30 percent. BLTs were next with 28 percent. Corned beef followed at 10 percent, pastrami at 8 percent, salami and bologna at 5 percent, and liverwurst at 4 percent.

Super-Dels

What might be called the "new" deli has been showing up in supermarkets all over the country since 1988, with great success so far and ever more accelerated sales foreseen by industry observers. Supermarket owners like having them — their deli profit margins average 43 percent and account for more than 14 percent of store profits.

DIETING

TO LIVE AND DIET

WENDY WASSERSTEIN

A few years ago at an obesity support group, I met a nice, rather substantial man who told me that women refused to sit next to him on buses. Later he wrote me a note saying that he had lost weight and that he hoped I was well and happy. I still think about that man occasionally. I think about how he could move to London, Paris, Los Angeles — someplace where no one would know his past — and start again. Except . . .

Except it's always there. If tomorrow, through the miracle of liposuction, I weighed 90 pounds, I still would never dream of wearing the Sonia Rykiel dress, the one in the Madison Avenue window that is the width of a fabric bolt. That dress is for the other faction. I could never go to Le Cirque, eat a fig, play with dessert, and complain that I ate too much. Only thin people do that. And I could never feel completely at home among the girls in leather pants and spike heels or strapless cocktail dresses. We parted company at age eight. No matter what happens, we are different. I've been a player for the other side. I can't abandon the home team. When the girls in the strapless cocktail dresses say they are enormous, I smile or change the subject. Size is relative.

When I embark on any new romantic or career venture, there is for me always the same bottom line. Namely, I will assume that, no matter what happens, no matter how deeply I fall in love or how successful the project, if anything goes wrong it is because I prefer buttered rolls to bran flakes for breakfast. Or: I don't have fear of intimacy; my date has fear of flesh. OK, maybe I'm exaggerating a little. But the paranoia, the impulse to blame everything on excess tonnage, is undeniably real.

More than anything it's my hope, my fantasy, that someday this horribleness will all go away. Yes, triglycerides are bad, and lack of muscle tone on someone so young is horrendous. But so is such a superficial standard for rating human quality. We treat melons with more dignity. At least we wait to make a judgment until we know what's inside.

Excerpted from Bachelor Girls

A Piece of American Pie

The average American eats about 3,500 calories a day, about the same as in 1910. But the average American weighs more now; he doesn't live on a farm anymore, and has been exercising less since the invention of the horseless carriage.

A Concatenation of Diets

The "I Love New York" Diet

The Scarsdale Diet

The Beverly Hills Diet

The Airline Stewardesses Diet

The Fit for Life Diet

The Eat to Win Diet

The Bloomingdale's E.A.T. Healthydiet

The Grapefruit Diet

The Water Diet

The Drinking Man's Diet

The Rice Diet

The Nutritech Diet

The White Diet

The Never Say Diet Diet

The Slim-Fast Diet

The Cider Vinegar Diet

The California Diet

The Cambridge Diet

The Acutrim Diet

The Tone Tabs Diet

The AYDS Diet

The Hollywood Pineapple Diet

The Runner's Diet

The Long Weekend Diet

The Bahamian Diet

The Steak and Salad Diet

The Bran Diet

The Nutrisystems Diet

The L.A. Diet

The Popcorn Diet

The Permanence Program

Q&A

Q Are you an apple or a pear?

A (Answer without looking in the mirror.)

Q Which is better for your health?

A A pear. Pear-shaped people store excess fat below the belt, around the hips and thighs, and are relatively slim in the upper body. Apple-shaped people accumulate fat around the chest and abdomen, some of them near the internal organs, others just beneath the skin. Researchers have found that apple-shaped people are at greater risk for such problems as high blood pressure, heart disease, stroke, and diabetes.

But not all apples are equal. Those with fat just under the skin — the kind that can be pinched into a thick fold between the fingers — are not at great risk. But a firm, protruding belly can signal midbody fat carried deep in the abdomen, which is more dangerous. And in such cases, say obesity specialists, even a small weight loss can bring major health benefits.

"How long does getting thin take?" Pooh asked anxiously.

— A. A. Milne
Winnie the Pooh

THE RIGHT SHAPE

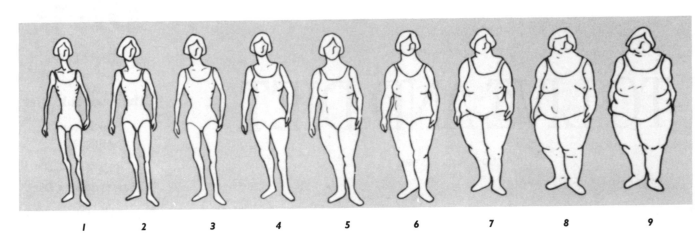

How do you see yourself? Most women see themselves as slimmer than number 4, believe men would be most attracted to number 3, but would like to be even thinner than that.

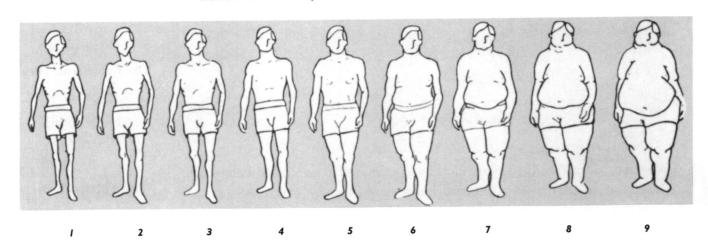

Most men actually think that they look like their ideal, which is number 4, and that women find that weight attractive — although women say they like men leaner.

In late 1993, *People* magazine did a cover story on supermodel Kate Moss. "SKIN & BONES" was the cover line, which went on to note in smaller type that Moss "is the ultrathin symbol of the underfed waif look."

At 5 feet 7 inches and 100 pounds, Moss is a smidge less anorexic-looking than Twiggy, the original waif of the 1960s; Twiggy was 5 feet 6 and weighed in at 92 pounds. Like her paper-thin predecessor, Moss is being rushed to fame, showing up in all the most prestigious ads and lauded by all the fashion mags. It took a writer for the New York *Daily News* to say what many privately thought, that "she should be tied down and intravenously fed."

Indeed, all these fashionable looks are about food and who dares to have some. The painful dichotomy: Studies show that the *average* female fashion model — the national ideal against which women compare themselves — is 5 feet 9 ½ inches tall and weighs 123 pounds. But, according to the National Council for Health Statistics, the average American woman is 5 feet 4 inches tall and weighs 144 pounds. And gaining.

Are women dieting frantically to shed the embarrassing difference? They used to. There is already some evidence that teenage girls are starving themselves to look like Kate Moss. But, in general, dieting took a nosedive between 1986 and 1991, when the number of American dieters dropped from 65 million to 48 million. Significantly, this is the period when television host Oprah Winfrey made a national spectacle of the futility of dieting by losing 67 pounds while her audience cheered, and putting it all back on again within a year.

Commercial weight-loss centers are still doing a good business, generating about $2 billion in annual revenue, but today's public is well aware that crash diets don't keep weight off. These days the weight-loss centers emphasize the need to develop healthy eating habits, and stress the value of small weight losses. People are realizing that human beings never lose weight once and for all, and that a weight loss of 5 percent in a year is not only a significant victory but enough to reduce by 50 percent the risk of having high blood pressure. This kind of wisdom, which reaches mature dieters, has little impact on fad-dieting adolescent girls. Nevertheless, as the overall American dieting frenzy tapers off, and more women focus on doing what they can with what they have, we might well find ourselves on the leading edge of another sea change in body fashion.

The fashion in body shape is as mercurial as the fashion in clothes, and just as dictatorial. Like the tides, it flows for a few generations in billows of curves, then ebbs into angles and skinny elbows. And what fashion decrees, we struggle to be.

A century ago, billows were the thing. Perfection for women was to be "pleasingly plump." So pleasing was it that, in 1878, Dr. T. C. Duncan published a dieting handbook entitled *How to Be Plump, Or Talks on Physiological Feeding.* Basically, Duncan advised his readers to belly up to the table and eat their fill "so that we observe the golden mean — florid plumpness, which is the picture of health the world over."

How did we travel from those amplitudinous attitudes to the asperity of today? In part, it's a result of the information network now in place worldwide, constantly informing us how badly off everybody is in the parched and barren parts of the globe. Bad news elsewhere tweaks the conscience of the affluent, who are ashamed of being able to eat all they want, so eating less becomes a fashion.

Equally influential are those stop-press bulletins incriminating yet another popular food product in a miasma of possibly dangerous side effects. This, too, is a function of affluence. Where food is hard to find, very little time is spent analyzing its potential hazards.

Finally, there is the growing awareness that the traditional simple foods of peasants are far and away the most healthful for us. A strict diet of rice and beans, for example, is guaranteed to keep us looking like . . . well, peasants, which is exactly the current fashion ideal.

But the problem for most of us is that we want more tastes and textures than rice and beans can provide. We crave variety. Also, because we're social creatures, we like to eat our meals in the company of other people, and when animals see other animals eating, they want to eat *more.*

And then there's stress. Laboratory experiments show that stress can increase food consumption to abnormal levels. This could explain why the poor people in rich countries are often fat, while the reverse is true for the rich people in poor countries: Consciously or unconsciously, anxious people tend to overeat. And if they live in economic hard times, as we do, worry adds another stress factor.

So it's really not surprising that it's only teenage girls who can manage not to eat a bite.

Winning Weights

Use this formula for a rough estimate of the desirable weight for your height. This is only a guide; everyone's body is different.

Women: 100 pounds for the first 5 feet, then add 5 pounds for each additional inch.

Men: 106 pounds for the first 5 feet, then add 6 pounds for each additional inch.

Both: Add 10 percent for a large body frame; subtract 10 percent for a small body frame.

Source: American Diabetes Association/American Dietetic Association

Why Diets Don't Work

You can't really put anything over on your body. If you skip breakfast, the body responds by slowing down the metabolic rate in order to make the stored fat last as long as possible. A result is that you start thinking about food more often, and maybe get depressed.

Similarly, dieting doesn't work because the shortage of food sends a false famine-alert to the brain, which, with great efficiency, directs the body to store fat for use in the emerging crisis. The more a person diets, the more efficient the fat-storage system becomes and the more the odds are stacked against you.

The truth is that if you want to lose weight, the worst thing you can do is to stop eating. You're a lot more likely to lose weight and keep it off if you eat pleasurably — a balanced diet with healthy and nourishing lean foods, and some occasional goodies so that you won't feel deprived.

Nutritionists now talk about a "set point" — the right weight for *you.* The theory rests on the belief that if you fall below your genetically predisposed weight, your body keeps wrestling to get back to where it wants to be — a weight that some may consider heavy, others comfortable.

"We cannot struggle with destiny," these researchers say. Adopted children end up looking like their biological parents, not their adopted ones. When several sets of twins were overfed 1,000 calories a day, each pair gained weight identically, but no two pairs alike — different metabolic rates, different biochemistry, and different inheritance made different results in every case. "One of the biggest mistakes people make when going on a diet is not having realistic expectations," says Jodi-An Zahra, the director of a weight-loss program created by the National Dairy Council. "Everyone has a basic body frame and if you're 5 feet 2 inches tall and pear-shaped, you're not going to be 5 feet 10 with an hourglass figure when you finish."

It's not women's fault that diets don't work. It's not perversity or lack of willpower. God did this — in Her great wisdom.

— Wayne Callaway, M.D.
George Washington University

Diets are for those who are thick and tired of it.

— Anonymous

MEN AND DIETS

A great unfairness in nature — that men lose weight more quickly and easily than women — is often observed and has been confirmed by endocrinologist Donald Smith of the Mt. Sinai Medical Center in New York. When men and women are put on exactly the same diet, the men lose twice as many pounds in a week as the women do.

It's because the sexes don't burn calories in the same way. Metabolism increases according to the muscle mass you have, Smith says, and men have testosterone, which builds muscle. So that a man of average build burns more calories sitting still (1,900 a day) than any woman of average build (1,430). A body must burn 3,500 stored calories of fat for each pound of weight loss. So put a man and a woman on the same diet and the man starts dipping into his stored supplies of fat a lot sooner.

Not that many couples are going to engage in this experiment. Most men tend to be satisfied with the body type they end up with, even if they're not literal Giants; little boys dream of growing up to be as big as their football heroes. Little girls will be dieting by the age of 13.

"A man's weight is not affected by his wife's education level," says Stanley Garn of the Center for Human Growth at the University of Michigan at Ann Arbor. But, he points out, a woman's weight *is* affected by her husband's social status. Women who marry men on a lower rung of the economic ladder tend to gain weight, while those who marry above themselves slim down.

However, all of the above could soon be old sociology. Men are increasingly being bombarded on TV and in magazines with models of the ideal male, and the more the condition of the body becomes a metaphor for ability, energy, and competence, the more men start to feel that they have to measure up. When Bill Clinton started to gain weight during the presidential campaign, the press treated it like a character flaw; the next we knew, the candidate was jogging fiercely every day.

For the men of America, the pressure is on as never before to prove just how much metabolism can do.

Pass Me That Tiny Fork

It's a good ten years since Psychology Today *told about a potential victory in America's unending battle against weight gain. A Detroit advertising man named Monroe D. Molner had invented something called the Mini-Bite System, which used undersized utensils to encourage slower eating. The theory was that the brain takes 15 to 20 minutes to sense how much food has entered the stomach — by which time compulsive eaters have finished everything on the plate. On Molner's plan you were to cut up your food into crouton-sized portions with the special Mini-Bite Dietware, timing yourself with the Mini-Bite Dietwatch, and set your tiny fork down between each bite "until all motion of mouth, lips, and tongue has ceased!"*

But in the very next column was a rebuttal from a British psychologist, insisting that "unlearned postingestional effects are unlikely to contribute refined wisdom to the choice of what amount to eat." As translated by the magazine's thoughtful editors, this means "there is no little meter in the gut that measures our intake and flips a mental circuit breaker at the right moment." In fact, if we could eat sufficiently slowly we might never ever feel we had eaten enough.

Which explains why we have heard no more of the Mini-Bite System — the motion of mouth, lips, and tongue has never ceased.

But Gaining Weight Is Not a Disease

According to the Centers for Disease Control, the average person gains seven pounds between the ages of 25 and 34. The CDC also suggests that after the age of 55, Americans start losing weight (some Americans, maybe).

Books

American Heart Association Low-Fat, Low-Cholesterol Cookbook
Scott Grundy and Mary Winston; Random House, 1992; $13.00

Eat More, Weigh Less
Dean Ornish; HarperCollins, 1993; $22.50

Food for Life: How the New Four Food Groups Can Save Your Life
Neil Barnard, M.D.; Harmony Books, 1993; $23.00

Lose to Win
Stephen T. Sinatra; Lincoln-Bradley, 1992; $19.95

Low Fat and Loving It
Ruth Spear; Warner Books, 1991; $19.95

Never Satisfied: A Cultural History of Diets, Fantasies, and Fat
Hillel Schwartz; Free Press, 1987; $19.95

The Choose to Lose Diet
Ron Goor, M.D., Nancy Goor, and Katherine Boyd, R.D.; Houghton Mifflin, 1990; $10.95

The New Pritikin Program
Robert Pritikin; Simon & Schuster, 1990; $5.99

The 10 Percent Solution for a Healthy Life
Raymond Kurzweil; Crown, 1993; $20.00

MORE INFORMATION

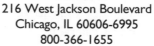

National Center for Nutrition and Diet
The American Dietetic Association
216 West Jackson Boulevard
Chicago, IL 60606-6995
800-366-1655

HOTLINES

800-366-1655
American Dietetic Association
8 a.m. - 4 p.m., CST

ALCOHOL
SOMETIMES HANGS OVER THE BELT

If you're wondering where those love handles came from, you might consider the possibility that more weight is accumulating from the booze than from the burgers. *The American Journal of Clinical Nutrition* reports that meals consumed with alcohol tend to contain 350 to 500 more calories than those consumed without wine or preprandial cocktails. What's more, diners spend nearly three times longer at the table when they're drinking. Putting bottled water on the table does not miraculously turn it into wine, but it does aid digestion and *may* cut down on the wine consumption.

A 12-ounce can of beer contains 150 calories. A 4-ounce glass of wine contains 80 calories. And a 1 ¼-ounce tot of gin, rum, vodka, or whiskey contains 80 calories, too.

Weight A Minute

1917 — *Diet & Health*, published by Lulu Hunt Peters, teaches "calories" and recommends a low-fat, high-carbohydrate diet.

1939 — Diet pills (amphetamines) generate sales of $30 million.

1961 — Jean Nidetch, a New York housewife, launches a dieting discussion group. Seventeen years later she sells her Weight Watchers empire for $100 million.

1970 — Seventy percent of American families are buying low-calorie foods.

1982 — The National Football League endorses Diet Coke for Real Men.

1990 — Oprah Winfrey loses 67 pounds on Optifast liquid diet.

1991 — Oprah Winfrey gains 67 pounds and declares: "No more diets."

1993 — Moderation becomes the new buzzword.

1994 — Most diet books are reclassified as fiction.

Fat of the Land

Lots of Americans worry about their weight, but an estimated quarter of the population is actually obese — defined as 25 percent or more above their so-called ideal weight. Most have tried over and over again to reduce, but to little or no avail. And many of them live lives of great unhappiness, mocked and rebuked by strangers, turned down for jobs, and regarded as such a source of embarrassment in their families that often their own children ask them not to attend school events.

Fat people are told that they could be thin if they wanted to. "There's that implicit assumption," says Dr. Albert Stunkard, an obesity researcher at the University of Pennsylvania, "that you really could lose weight if you settled down and stopped being such a fat slob."

But the assumption is false. According to a panel of experts recently convened by the National Institutes of Health, "there is increasing physiological, biochemical, and genetic evidence that overweight is not a simple disorder of willpower, as is sometimes implied, but is a complex disorder of energy metabolism."

Yet even some doctors disparage fat people, and refuse to treat them. Lynn Meletiche, a 48-year-old nurse who is chairwoman of the health committee for the National Association to Advance Fat Acceptance (NAAFA), often counsels members who have been ill-treated by doctors. Abuse can come in every avenue of life. Studies have shown that, in overwhelming numbers, formerly fat people would rather have a leg amputated than be fat again.

People have many peculiar prejudices against fat people, says William Fabrey, NAAFA's founder. "People are real wary that if a fat person sits next to them, the person will be smelly," he says. "There's also a feeling that a fat person is violating territorial limits. They're larger than their allotted space."

Researchers who study the psychology of body image have suggested that people of normal weight fear the fat person because obesity is emblematic of what they fear most in themselves — loss of control, a reversion to infantile desires, failure, self-loathing, sloth, passivity, gluttony.

Will society ever confront such inner fears? The news of scientific findings that obesity has a genetic or physiological basis beyond individual control should help. But until it does, the longing of fat people to be accepted will have to remain just a longing.

Changing Habits Forever

So you've absolutely decided to change your life, lose weight sensibly and keep it off, and affirm good eating habits for the rest of your life. Sounds good. So what are you going to eat from now on? Had you considered rat chow? Well, it makes an ideal diet for rats, so why not for you? Their feed consists of brown, crunchy, nutritionally balanced pellets, and on this food and nothing else, rats maintain a

healthy weight. So could you, munching away at the same mix every day.

But there's no need to be grim about it. The notion of dieting simply disappears when you follow the Food Guide Pyramid, which is explained in the section on Nutrition. The pyramid emphasizes foods from the five major food groups and naturally lowers fat intake to less than 30 percent of calories. Best of all, there are no forbidden foods here. You choose a number of servings that are appropriate for your age, sex and activity levels and make lower fat choices whenever possible. Wise

selections should enable you to eat well — *and* lose weight if you wish to — and to feel good for the rest of your life.

It is exercise that plays the predominant role in weight control. Studies that compared groups of women who changed nothing at all about the way they ate found that the group that took regular walks consistently lost weight — and these women were simply walking, not doing aerobics or following a planned program. Exercise, in whatever form you take it, relieves a lot of tension, which is why you feel less tired afterward than before. It also increases the level of good cholesterol (HDL), ups the ratio of muscle to fat, and helps you sleep. And you really do look better and feel better — particularly when you're zipping the zipper and it goes right up.

DINERS

LUNCH WAGONS WITH A CURFEW

SYLVIA CARTER

The idea that diners originally were railroad dining cars is a widely cherished legend. But it's not true. The diner business got its start with Walter Scott's first horse-drawn lunch wagon in 1872 in Providence, Rhode Island. Scott sat inside on a wooden box, sheltered from the elements. Customers ordered through window openings on both the street side and the sidewalk side. Mostly, Scott sold nickel items: ham sandwiches, boiled eggs with buttered bread, and pie, but for the *crème de la crème* there was sliced chicken, 30 cents.

From this beginning, the diner evolved to include counters and space for customers to stand inside.

At first, night lunch wagons plied their wares near locations where people worked all night. They were licensed to stay out no later than 10 a.m., so operators had to find spots where they could get off the street by curfew. Eventually, the owners made a big to-do about throwing away their keys and staying open 24 hours. When they stopped roving about, proprietors covered the wheels, hooked up to utility lines, and offered more varied menus.

Among the big diner manufacturers were T. H. Buckley and his White House Cafes, introduced in 1890; Jerry O'Mahony, who started to build rugged lunch cars in Bayonne, New Jersey, in 1913, and Patrick Joseph (Pop) Tierney, who is credited with first bringing the toilet inside. Whatever the make, diners had to be narrow to be transported to their sites. And for a time, the railway image *was* a popular style.

Diner Speak

"A radio, a 51, a stretch, and squeeze it." This sort of talk, in diner lingo, means a tuna sandwich on toast, hot chocolate, a Coke, and make it fast. The evolution of "radio" as the equivalent of tuna on toast comes from the phrase "whiskey down," which means rye toast, from rye whiskey and the downward motion a diner cook makes when toasting bread on top of the grill; "tuna on down," spoken by a true New Yorker, sounds like "tuner on down" — shortened to "radio."

Some others: "Full house" — a grilled cheese, bacon, and tomato sandwich. "Adam and Eve on a raft" — two poached eggs on toast. "Cowboy with spurs" — a western omelet with fries. "Takes a flower" — with onion. "Hold the grass" — no lettuce. "Cremate a blue, bikini cut" — well-done, toasted blueberry muffin cut in three or four pieces instead of the normal half. "Seaboard" — to go.

Excerpted from New York Newsday

Greek Meat Loaf with Tomato Sauce

Serves 4

2 tablespoons plus 1 teaspoon
    olive oil
3 cloves garlic, chopped
2 11-ounce cans plum
    tomatoes, drained, seeded,
    and coarsely chopped
¼ cup red wine vinegar
1 tablespoon honey
Salt and freshly ground pepper
2 pounds very lean ground
    beef
1 medium-sized onion, finely
    chopped
1 egg
½ cup fresh whole-wheat
    bread crumbs
    (about 1 slice bread)
½ cup chopped parsley
1 tablespoon chopped fresh
    oregano or 1 teaspoon dried

Heat the teaspoon of oil in a medium-sized saucepan over moderate heat. Add 1 clove of garlic and cook for 1 minute. Add the tomatoes and cook for about 5 minutes. Add the vinegar and honey and simmer for 20 to 25 minutes until thickened. Season to taste with salt and pepper.

Meanwhile, preheat the oven to 350 degrees F. Lightly combine the remaining ingredients, adding 1 teaspoon salt and ½ teaspoon pepper, being careful not to mash the meat. Pack the mixture into a loaf pan. Bake for 30 minutes. Spread the meat loaf with a little more than half of the tomato mixture and bake for another 30 minutes.

Bring the remaining tomato mixture back to a simmer. Slice the meat loaf and serve the tomato sauce on the side.

Old Diner, New Diners

Old diners are as Yankee Doodle as a ball game on a summer afternoon. Go up the steps, push open the door, pass the racks of newspapers and the bulletin board advertising the church bazaar and the lost dog. Bump into the bubble-gum machine with the telephone book on top. Twirl on a counter stool at a spotless counter; stare at a glass cabinet containing three tiers of pies. Or slide sideways into a booth, settle into the vinyl, take in the unobstructed view of the parking lot.

Old diners never change. Neither does the music on the jukebox. Drop in a coin and Frank Sinatra croons your old sweet song as you hold hands across the formica tabletop. Next Elvis murmurs, "Love me tender, love me true," and we're transported to another time, when we

were too young to wonder why the bottle of ketchup here is always full, when the one at home is usually empty.

The thick plastic water glasses come with the plastic-covered menu listing the blue plate special — usually meat loaf, with a pool of brown gravy filling a crater in the mashed potatoes, and a sorry heap of canned carrots. Old diners don't hold much with fresh ingredients. Even the pies — apple, peach, blueberry — await a mound of whipped cream from an aerosol can. We pretend dismay, although this was exactly what we had hoped for.

Gladys, in pink pastel with bright yellow hair, refills our heavy white china coffee cup. She calls everybody "hon." Her feet have aged. That's what happens when you serve a breakfast of eggs sunny side up, sausages, bacon, and hash browns 24 hours a day with toasted Wonder bread. The short-order cook has his back to the customers but carries on a lively nonstop conversation. Nobody is a stranger here. And when you get the check on a slip of green paper and take it to the cashier, she will wish you a good day and you know she means it.

New diners serve white wine, imported water, and cappuccino. They have crisp white cloths and fresh flowers on the tables. The furnishings are funky, the colors vibrant, and neon lights crash in brilliant zigzags. Background music throbs and rocks. The kitchen is open and the action is intrinsic to the ambiance. Slim waitpersons wearing cheerful smiles and sneakers, snowy white aprons tied flatly around their waists, are interchangeable in age, education, and income level with the young guests. Will it be sauteed duck breast with a sauce of pomegranate and blood oranges, or risotto with four wild mushrooms? The crowd is having a glorious time, sharing in the abundance of the good earth, shouting applause and encouragement for the chefs, spurring them on to fresh creations.

In the new diners, the chefs are like jazz musicians, playing set after set, variation after variation, until we are presented with one of those awesome achievements — five different kinds of smoked salmon reclining in four different rippling rivers of sauces, topped by three different kinds of caviar, and counterpointed by a lone crawfish pirouetting on a single sublime pea.

That new diner crowd doesn't know what it's missing.

Books

American Diner Then and Now
Richard J. S. Gutman; HarperCollins, 1993; $20.00

Fog City Diner Cookbook
Cindy Pawlcyn; Ten Speed Press, 1993; $24.95

DISHES, EDIBLE

SAY ADIEU TO DISHPAN HANDS

Appropriately enough, the idea of getting rid of china began in China. It was there that two scientists (some call them crackpots) formulated the first edible plate. No, no — "edible" does not mean we are meant to eat them. These plates are designed to be consumed by birds and dogs, which leads us to wonder why bark was not the material of choice rather than oatmeal, which was what the scientists ultimately settled on. It takes a nice glaze, they say — and Chinese artisans are expert with glaze.

No sooner did the startling news of the fabrication leak out than other nations started leaping into this fresh field. First were the Australians, who built on the oatmeal concept and added potato peelings to make the the dishes more sturdy. Then Belgium's leading newspaper, *Le Soir*, reported the shocking news that its citizens discard 3.5 million containers immediately after eating their contents: french fries. (Belgians are crazy about french fries and eat them topped with a dollop of mayonnaise.) Belgian burghers set to work at once, using the potato as their inspiration. They bonded potato starch with cornstarch to produce biodegradable bags for their hot spuds.

In no time at all, our own domestic statisticians began denouncing waste. They figured out that Americans discard 1.1 million tons of disposable plates and cups every year—enouugh to serve a picnic to everyone in the world six times over. This revelation led two enterprising entrepreneurs at Iowa State University in Ames, Iowa, to produce their own version of an edible plate, appropriately fortified with corn and soybean starches and protein. The plates cost 12 cents a pound — not a bad price when you consider they can be recycled into animal feed.

Recycling is what edible plates are all about. Make a plate out of corn, feed it to the dairy cows, and what you get back is a glass of milk — no, not in a glass, but in an edible corn mug, maybe, which in turn is fed to the meatmaking cows, and at some time in the future the recycled mug reappears as a slice of steak.

All this low-tech technology is wonderfully good for the environment. We save water because we don't have to wash the dishes, and while edible dishes may be hard to swallow for the dishwasher manufacturers and the detergent makers, they could mean good eats in the future for the squirrels, rabbits, and other wild dears.

Rumor has it that work has already begun on edible spoons and forks. So the future looks very bright for the consumable crockery industry, and we eagerly await the time when being called to dinner means that we truly will be able to eat the whole thing.

DRIED FOOD

GETTING THE WATER OUT

Human beings have been drying foods to preserve them since the Stone Age. The Persians dried figs, dates, apricots, melons, and peas, and the Greeks got the knack from them. In ancient Babylonia, the Sumerians dried fish and grapes. By the Middle Ages, drying was the major means of food preservation, after salting, in all of Europe. Native Americans were drying corn, squash, pumpkin, and meat long before explorers reached these shores. The Chinese dried eggs, and the Japanese dried fish and rice.

Taking the moisture out of foods inhibits the growth of mold, bacteria, and other microorganisms that normally break down animal and vegetable matter; thus dried foods can be kept almost indefinitely. And because dehydrated food has about ⅟₁₅th the bulk of the original product, storage and transportation are lesser problems than with whole foods (something that campers and hikers know well and appreciate).

Drying Techniques

Hot-air drying, which was invented in France in 1795, was the first commercial method developed for drying foods. Modern techniques vary with the kinds of foods to be dried: Natural air drying is usually used for fruits and beans, and artificial air drying is used to process flour and certain vegetables, to dry apples, and turn plums into prunes and grapes into raisins.

Natural air drying involves setting foods in the sun for varying periods, then stacking them in trays in the shade until they are uniformly dry both inside and out — a process that can take several days. **Artificial air drying** places food in a dehydrator where currents of very hot air (often more than 400 degrees F.) circulate around it, speedily evaporating most of its moisture. For both methods, kits for use at home are available for those who like to do it themselves.

Vacuum drying is a process similar to artificial air drying that takes place in a closed vacuum at relatively low temperatures. This makes it especially suitable for drying heat-sensitive foods such as tomatoes and bananas, and for turning fruit and vegetable purees into powders that reconstitute easily in water.

Spray drying is frequently used for dairy products, such as whole milk, skim milk, buttermilk, and eggs, and has the advantage of retaining their nutrients. In their liquid state these foods are atomized into a mist that, when brought into contact with hot air, almost instantly loses its moisture content and becomes a fine powder.

Freeze drying is used to preserve a variety of foods, such as meat, eggs, mushrooms, berries, and coffee. The product is first quick-frozen, then put into a vacuum under very low pressure and carefully heated so that the ice crystals vaporize without ever becoming liquid. The process takes some hours, but the food ends up almost exactly the same size as it was originally, but weighing about two-thirds less. It can also be rehydrated in minutes and, if necessary, cooked very quickly. Meat, especially, can be freeze dried when already frozen, which bypasses intermediate thawing and produces, on rehydration, a product very much like fresh meat.

"Sound" drying may be the newest method of food dehydration. Food science researchers at Purdue University discovered that by "blasting" low-frequency sound waves past food at high speed they could suck the moisture out at a rate four to ten times faster than is possible with current techniques. And because quicker drying means less exposure to heat, which degrades the quality of food, the result promises to improve both taste and nutrition.

Books

How to Dry Foods
Deanne DeLong; HP Books, 1992; $14.95

Mary Bell's Complete Dehydrator Cookbook
Mary Bell; Morrow, 1994; $15.00

Preparing for Air Drying

Fruit to be air dried is always picked when ripe, so that it contains the maximum amount of sugar, and is cut, peeled, or pitted appropriately *before* being dried. Plums are dipped into a hot alkaline solution which produces tiny cracks in the skin that allow the moisture in the fruit to escape more quickly. In commercial processing, peaches, apricots, and pears are exposed to sulfur fumes or dipped in sulfite solutions, to preserve their natural colors and help keep them soft.

MORE INFORMATION

California Dried Fruit Export Association
P.O. Box 270-A
Santa Clara, CA 95052
408-727-9302

DRUGS IN FOOD

You said there would be more milk but this is udderly ridiculous!

DRUGS IN ANIMALS: NO BIG DEAL?

Ours is the safest food in the world, thanks to diligent inspection and monitoring by the Food and Drug Administration, the agency that is responsible for ensuring the safety and effectiveness of veterinary drugs.

Before a drug is approved for use in animals, its manufacturer must demonstrate that it is both safe and effective, and prove that it leaves no residue to pose a threat to human health. After FDA approval is given, meats, poultry, and milk are still subject to rigorous surveillance, and inspectors monitor the food at every step from farm to market.

It is initially alarming to learn that close to 750 drug products from about 100 basic drugs are approved for use by farmers. Most are designed to prevent outbreaks of disease and to make the animals grow faster on less feed. Dr. Gerald Guest, director of FDA's Center for Veterinary Medicine, has acknowledged that about 30 percent of chickens, 80 percent of veal calves and pigs, and 60 percent of beef cattle are routinely given medicated feed. However, he reassures us that residues above the legal limits are found in only 0.5 percent of poultry sampled and barely 1 percent of livestock.

The percentage of meat with drug levels in excess of FDA limits has been declining steadily in recent years. Because the FDA takes only random samples, though, some of the meat that wouldn't be acceptable if sampled may end up being sold. It is a relief to know that this tiny percentage still does not contain drug residues high enough to pose a health threat.

Levels for drug residues are established by the FDA as low as possible; in some cases only a zero tolerance is acceptable. The risk of harm from drug residues is considered to be one in 1 million — a statistically insignificant figure that means, not that one in every million people will possibly be harmed, but that the risk is increased by one in 1 million over the *normal* risk in the course of a lifetime. Nevertheless, we continue to fret.

There is legitimate concern about the presence of antibiotics in livestock because these may be passed along to us in our food, reducing their effectiveness when we are prescribed them for some illness in the future. Also, bacteria can become resistant to antibiotics that are administered over long periods, so health officials are always on the lookout for high-resistance strains. Their presence means that larger doses of a drug or even different drugs may be required to eliminate them. Alternative drugs have recently become available but have not been put to widespread use because health experts see no immediate cause for concern.

A five-year study begun in 1988 by the National Academy of Sciences found that pesticide residues in food may have a stronger effect on children than on adults, and recommended that levels be multiplied by ten in considering their effects on children. This finding may cause the FDA to rethink what it considers acceptable levels of some substances.

In our hearts, we would like all our food to come from Sunnybrook Farm, where the farmer's wife throws handfuls of organic corn to the chickens from a basket resting on her hip. But this isn't the way things work in industrialized societies where more people live in cities than in the country. Our romantic visions should not blind us to the truth: Drugs are necessary for maintaining animal and human health and the risks appear to be far outweighed by the reward of a plentiful supply of safe and inexpensive food.

Q&A

Q Why has the European Community (EC) prohibited the import of beef containing hormones?

A Anabolic hormones or steroids are given to beef cattle to increase their growth and muscle. In 1989, the EC banned the use of such hormones or the import of any beef from animals where the hormones are allowed, which affected the United States and many other countries.

EC's decision was not based on human safety concerns, but on economics and consumer preferences. Europe itself had a large surplus of beef, and European consumers indicated a preference for non-hormone-raised meat.

Reprinted from Food Insight

Supermarket Come-ons

Lately, some supermarkets have been advertising meat from drug-free animals. Since the FDA monitoring programs effectively protect the public, there is no real health advantage in buying these meats, though we may want to indulge ourselves by thinking that they taste better.

DUCK

THE DUCK STOPS HERE

Consider the role of the duck through good economic cycles and bad. In colonial times, having roast duck on the table was a sign that all was right with the world. The duck would be served with an orange sauce or surrounded with cherries and garlands of greenery, with a plentiful bowl of wild rice nearby.

This was the way things were for a couple of centuries. Then the decadent 1980s arrived and the old canard was replaced by rare duck breast, its transparently thin, bloodily red slices arranged in a fan shape, accompanied by pumpkin ravioli and zucchini blossoms. Truly, it was a time of excess.

This artifice was quickly followed by heady nights of $100-a-plate smoked South Central Indiana duck breasts served with Northwest Quadrant Oregon berries. (We *had* to know where *everything* came from.) Then there was a brief moment when all the smart restaurants were simultaneously serving duck carpaccio with a whisper of lemon grass set off by an accompaniment of grilled duck sausage as large as an index finger. Each reincarnation of duck resulted in smaller quantities of duck at ever escalating prices. Then the stock market plummeted.

Members of the President's Council of Economic Advisers took to the Sunday morning airwaves, pontificating about the budget with such inner-directed observations as "If it looks like a duck, walks like a duck, and quacks like a duck, it probably *is* a duck." Astonishingly, once one person had made this budgetary revelation, dozens of others quickly fell in line and in no time at all the remark began appearing on the evening and morning news programs and hovering on every serious reporter's lip.

The duck was designated as a future economic indicator and the phrase "to duck" became a tenet of government.

Along with all this, roast duck has reappeared in its purest form, which is very good news because it makes for a fine and tasty dinner.

TIPS

Preparing
Defrost a frozen duck by leaving it in its original wrapper and setting it on a plate in the refrigerator. It will take 24 hours to thaw. To speed the process, immerse it, still in its wrapper, in a bowl of hot water and keep substituting fresh hot water as the previous batch cools. The thawing time will be reduced to 2 to 3 hours.

• Some experts say you can defrost a duck in the microwave oven. Others vigorously disagree. A frozen duck is one thing; what emerges from the microwave can be a dead duck.

Cooking
A lot of duck fat is stored just beneath the skin. Before roasting a bird, prick the skin all over with the point of a sharp knife and set the duck on a rack to allow the fat to drain off into the roasting pan beneath.

• To produce a fabulously crisp, almost black skin, brush it with equal parts of melted butter and honey.

• Preheat the oven to 350 degrees F. and roast a 5-pound bird for 90 minutes, uncovered. Drain off the fat that collects in the roasting pan.

Serving
The easiest way to cut a duck into portions is to use poultry shears.

Sitting Ducks

The breed most favored for domestication in North America is the Peking, also known as Pekin, duck. Always referred to as "duckling" (to make it seem younger and more tender, perhaps?), it is usually table-ready when it weighs about five pounds, which is only enough for four people. A big-boned bird, it is relatively short on meat, but so rich that a small amount goes quite a long way.

Domesticated ducks are fed a high-protein diet and almost all are treated with antibiotics as they are relatively delicate and need careful nurturing. Fortunately for us, there is no fear of residues of the drugs remaining in the meat. Of greater concern is the amount of fat. Duck is considerably fattier, and therefore much tastier, than any other kind of poultry, except goose — which has even more fat than duck.

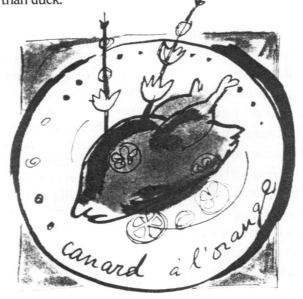

canard à l'orange

Books

Beard on Birds
James Beard; Warner Books, 1989; $10.95

Working a Duck
Melicia Phillips and Sean O. McElroy; Doubleday, 1992; $20.00

MAIL ORDER SOURCES

D'Artagnan
399-419 St. Paul Avenue
Jersey City, NJ 07306
800-327-8246

Durham Nightbird Game & Poultry Company
358A Shaw Road
South San Francisco, CA 94080
800-255-7457

The Game Exchange
107 Quint Street
San Francisco, CA 94124
415-282-7878

Wild Game, Inc.
2315 West Huron Street
Chicago, IL 60612
312-278-1661

EELS ◆ EGGPLANT ◆ EGGS ◆ ELECTRONIC
SHOPPING ◆ ETHNIC FOOD ◆ EXTRUDED FOOD

EEK!
IT'S EELS!

Eels are very big abroad — absolutely adored in the Netherlands, for example, where freshly caught pan-fried or smoked eels, offered by street vendors, sell better than hotcakes and are eaten in the hand. But the eel business is very small in America. Indeed, a recent survey of "odd" foods showed that few American adults had ever tasted one. Snakes did worse in this survey — they were slithering along the rock bottom of the list — but it isn't saying much for eels that the only creature they could top was the lowest of the low.

Yet eels have their charms, lacking only an industry board or council to trumpet their cause. Gourmands attest to their deliciousness when cooked. Alive, they are sensitive, moody creatures with a romantic life story. All eels, in Europe and America, spend seven years of their lives in fresh water, then start downstream, and meet their mates at the mouths of their rivers. Then the females travel thousands of miles to the becalmed, salty, weed-covered waters of the Sargasso Sea, between Bermuda and Puerto Rico — in an area said to be the site of lost Atlantis, certainly in the vicinity of the Bermuda Triangle — where they release huge quantities of eggs, and die. The tiny hatchlings make the long, long journey back to waters they have never known; for the European ones, floating with the Gulf Stream, it can take three years.

No one has been able to simulate the lure of the Sargasso Sea, and commercial cultivation in the United States is minimal because of the lack of demand, but there is *some* eel farming in Florida. One entrepreneur there says he produces some 50,000 pounds of aquacultured eels a year, almost entirely for export. And although there are no formal figures on the American crop, the National Marine Fisheries Service estimates that in 1990 about 4.3 million pounds of eels, mostly the wild kind, were exported abroad.

Where eel admirers are very glad to get them.

EELS

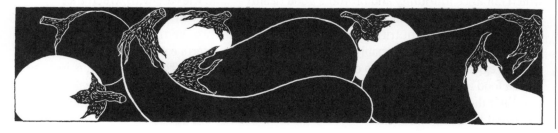

> **I think the eels prefer to be eaten by someone who loves them.**
>
> — Samuel Applebaum
> Israeli aquaculturist

*If you were a female eel
How do you think you would feel
If a male eel came wooing
And all you were doing
Was wriggling
And squiggling
And giggling . . .
Why, any potential suitor
Might have to declare himself neuter,
And then where would you be?
Not bound for the Sargasso Sea.*

ODD JOBS

Small game hunters enjoy "pole-poking" for monkey-faced prickleback eels. They use a long pole to fish in the dark crevices where the slithery darlings hide. They don't use bait, just a hook attached with a wire to a long pole. When caught, the eels express little surprise or resistance.

EGGPLANT

A MOST ADAPTABLE VEGETABLE

It was Thomas Jefferson who first brought eggplants to the United States, and they have since become one of our 22 principal vegetable crops. Curiously, the eggplant is the least popular of these here — although it is held in high regard in the Near East, the Middle East, the Far East, and all through Europe and South America, where it goes by a variety of names.

The eggplant is said to be indigenous to India, where it has been grown for at least 4,000 years. In early days ordinary folk were afraid to eat it because, like its relatives the tomato and the potato, it belongs to the nightshade family, some of whose members are poisonous. Maybe it is because of this that even today some people sprinkle slices of eggplant with salt before cooking it, "to draw out the bitter juices." Some myths hang on for ages.

Once the fear of eggplants was more or less overcome, another set of rumors sprang up, suggesting that those who ate eggplant would go mad and naming it *mala insana*, which is easy to translate.

It is harder to know why one of Turkey's most famous dishes, which is made with eggplant, got the name of *Imam bayildi*, which means "the fainting Imam." Did the Imam faint with delight or with horror when he found out how much precious olive oil had gone into the preparation of this delicacy?

Eggplant does drink up a huge quantity of oil. Its porous flesh is chockablock with air cells, and when it is heated, the air flies out like a genie from the cell and the oil rushes in to take its place. This is why some cooks press eggplant with a heavy weight before cooking it: Getting rid of the air enables it to be cooked with less oil.

Eggplants have a little bit of several nutrients but not a significant amount of anything, and they are almost endlessly adaptable. Many interesting dishes result from matchings of eggplant with garlic, onions, tomatoes, and green and red peppers. Ratatouille is among the very best of them. It is a versatile summer dish that is good served hot or cold, with roast lamb, with egg dishes, or even on its own, to be scooped up with triangles of toasted pita bread.

Ratatouille
Serves 6

1 medium or 4 small eggplants
4 tablespoons olive oil
2 large onions, thinly sliced
3 cloves garlic, finely chopped
1 green bell pepper, seeded and cut into strips
1 red bell pepper, seeded and cut into strips
2 thin zucchini, sliced
3 medium-sized fully ripe tomatoes, cut into wedges and seeded
¼ teaspoon salt
¼ cup chopped fresh basil leaves
1 bay leaf
2 tablespoons finely chopped fresh parsley

Cut the eggplant into ¼-inch slices and then into cubes. Heat the oil in a large skillet; cook the eggplant cubes in the oil for 6 or 7 minutes until lightly browned all over. Add the onions, garlic, and peppers and cook for 3 minutes more. Add the zucchini and the remaining ingredients. Cover the skillet and cook over low heat for 15 minutes. Remove the lid and continue cooking until most of the liquid has evaporated, about 10 minutes more. Stir occasionally just to make sure that the vegetables are not sticking to the bottom and burning. Serve hot, at room temperature, or cold.

Au Bergine

In her *International Vegetable Cookbook*, author Faye Levy tells us that *aubergine* is the French word for eggplant. Its derivation is a Sanskrit word that later was adopted in Arabic and Persian. Interestingly, this was also the geographical route the aubergine took on its predestined journey towards Bloomingdale's (where it has now been taken up as the ultimate fashion statement, but in silk).

Books

The Eggplant Cookbook
Norma S. Upson; Pacific Search, 1979; $5.95

EGGS

Love and eggs are best when they are fresh.

— Russian proverb

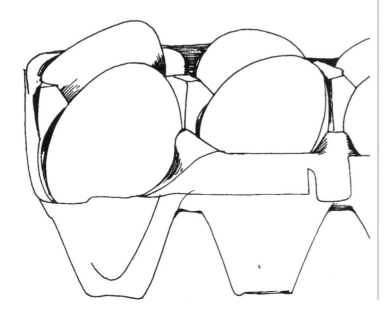

THE "PERFECT" FOOD

We used to think that a rounded, pristinely perfect egg was just as good for us as it was beautiful. Now so many Americans have listened to the warnings about eggs' high cholesterol content that consumption has literally been cut in half since the 1970s. An egg no longer even seems like a whole unit; in our minds we separate white from yolk as carefully as any chef, but in terms of good and bad.

Nutritionally speaking, a large egg's white has only 17 calories and 3.5 grams of high-quality protein, with no fat and no cholesterol, whereas a large egg's yolk has 59 calories, 2.8 grams of protein, more than 5 grams of fat, two-thirds of it unsaturated, and a cholesterol count that was recently downgraded from 274 to 213 milligrams — though this is still more than two-thirds the daily limit that is recommended nowadays. However, egg yolks also contain good amounts of B vitamins and vitamin A, as well as riboflavin and iron, all of which enhance immunity and promote good health — and the ease with which these nutrients can be assimilated is what made eggs popular in the first place.

Dr. Lynn Carew, a nutritional scientist at the University of Vermont, sees nothing wrong with people who have reasonably low levels of blood cholesterol eating four eggs a week, or even an egg a day, "though two eggs a day might be too much." The egg, in fact, is just as good a food as it ever was — for those who understand how its strengths and weaknesses fit into their dietary needs. The most important message, it seems, is to cook eggs thoroughly and to eat them with restraint.

MOTHER HEN

Margaret Visser

Light rouses the cock to crow, and it is light which passes through the hen's eye, activates the pituitary gland at the base of her skull to secrete certain hormones in her body, and starts her ovary working to lay eggs. Every baby hen hatches with five or six thousand microscopic egg-germs already awaiting completion in her body. She is ready to begin creating and laying from this vast store when she is about six months old.

The hen's ovary is a very large organ, because although she is a big bird, her eggs are enormous in relation to her body size — they are so big that she can carry only one egg to completion in her body at a time. Hens, like all female vertebrates, begin with paired ovaries; but in her case the right ovary withers away so that only one egg needs to be given space. Only a tiny fraction of the egg-germs she carries will eventually end up as eggs; what it is that makes these privileged few do so is unknown. Quite naturally, scientists would dearly like to understand and then draw profit from knowledge of the mechanism.

The female hormone estrogen is partly responsible for the hen's behavior, both in making her submissive to the cock at coition, and in causing her to seek and prepare a nest in which to lay her eggs. It apparently even causes her to emit a pre-laying call. Nest-preparation is so biologically necessary as part of the laying process that caged battery hens will often cry out and struggle to obey this part of nature's demand.

Excerpted from Much Depends on Dinner

An egg is always an adventure; the next one may be different.

— Oscar Wilde

Let Me Count The Ways

Theoretically, our per capita consumption of eggs is 232.8 eggs a year. The 1990 census found the population of the United States to be 248,709,873. Therefore, as a nation we eat 232.8 × 248,709,873 = 5,789,966,400 eggs per year, which, divided by 365, amounts to 158,629,210 eggs a day. Expressed in personal terms — i.e., divided by 248,709,873 — this number becomes less than two-thirds of an egg per day per person per year.

As for the hens, each of the 230 million laying hens in the United States produces just about 300 eggs a year. This amounts to 5,757.8 million dozen eggs a year, for a total of 69,093.6 million eggs altogether. Now, if we divide this number by that of the population in 1990, it should prove that every American eats 232.8 eggs every year — but in fact the number is closer to 250 eggs per person, because everyone knows that hens don't know how to use a calculator.

Grading Eggs

Eggs are graded by a system that ensures they are of good quality. Sample eggs are selected randomly, then broken out onto a level surface, where they can be carefully examined. The grader measures the height of the thick albumen, or white, with a micrometer, then correlates this with the egg's weight to give a measurement known as a Haugh unit. A high Haugh value means high egg quality. The condition of the yolk is noted as well.

Eggs are then graded as AA, A, or B; there is no difference in their nutritive value.

The Grade AA egg stands tall, with a firm yolk and a small area of white, almost all of which is thick.

The Grade A egg is smaller, with a round yolk and a fairly sizable white, more of which is thick than thin.

The Grade B egg spreads out more, with a flattened yolk and as much, or more, thin white as thick white.

Brown vs. White

There is no difference between brown-shelled and white-shelled eggs as far as content is concerned. The shell color is determined by the breed of the hen. Those that lay brown eggs (originally strains of Rhode Island Reds) are slightly bigger than the White Leghorn hens that lay white eggs. This means that they eat more food, which is why brown eggs cost slightly more. (Those who fancy brown eggs say that the shells are stronger and the eggs taste better, which make it worth paying the higher price. White egg lovers just smile, and save.)

Did You Know?

☞ The cost of a 2-ounce egg is 11 cents. The cost of a 1-egg portion of an egg substitute ranges between 24 and 36 cents.

☞ Two blind men must surely claim the prize for total concentration. In the course of a 7¼-hour shift in a hotel restaurant, they shelled 1,050 hard-cooked eggs.

☞ The records for eating eggs are, in this order: 14 hard-cooked eggs in 58 seconds, 32 soft-boiled eggs in 78 seconds — and an astonishingly slippery 13 raw eggs in 2.2 seconds.

☞ The farthest anyone has thrown a fresh egg without breaking it is 317 feet, 10 inches, according to *The Guinness Book of Records.*

☞ One large egg white weighs 1 ounce.

☞ Use of the term *egghead* to mean an intellectual seems to date from the early 1950s; it probably derives from "highbrow" — having a forehead shaped, like Shakespeare's or presidential hopeful Adlai Stevenson's, very much like an egg.

Books

Book of Crêpes and Omelets
Mary Norwak; Price Stern Sloan, 1988; $9.95

Eggs: Basics and Beyond
American Egg Board, 1989; $2.50

Omelettes: Eggs at Their Best
Laurence Sombke; St. Martin's Press, 1992; $7.95

The Egg Cookbook
Marion Maxwell; HarperCollins, 1993; $7.00

The Omelette Book
Narcissa G. Chamberlain; Godine, 1990; $17.95

Safe Eggs Or Sorry

The Egg Nutrition Center reports that, overall, *Salmonella enteritidis* outbreaks are steadily decreasing. In 1991, for example, there were 66 outbreaks, half of them in the New England and mid-Atlantic states, but only 13 were positively identified as caused by eggs. Despite the public's fears, even eggs from a flock known to be positive for salmonella are very rarely contaminated — researchers have had to test more than 10,000 eggs from an infected flock before finding one carrying the bacteria.

It should be noted, however, that an outbreak can affect thousands of people, and the egg industry has been somewhat reluctant to admit the problem and tends to downplay the danger, estimating the chances of an egg being contaminated as one in 14,000 in the areas where most recent outbreaks were located, and even lower elsewhere.

Most cases of salmonella poisoning result from cross-contamination and poor sanitation practices, which are more likely to occur in restaurants and commercial operations where eggs are pooled together, enabling a single bad egg to spoil a whole batch. In large feeding institutions, too, eggs are often not chilled quickly enough, and salmonella bacteria thrive at room temperature, multiplying tenfold in an hour.

The studies indicate that the possibility of acquiring a food-borne illness from raw eggs is small, but, should this rare chance occur, the risk of developing serious illness is increased during pregnancy, and among the frail elderly, the very young, and people with impaired immune systems.

To play it safe:

• Don't wash eggs. Most eggs sold commercially have already been washed and sprayed with a protective oil that prevents bacteria from penetrating the porous shell.

• Never leave eggs or foods containing eggs at room temperature for more than 2 hours, including preparation and serving times, because bacteria thrive in temperatures between 40 and 140 degrees F. Refrigerate all such foods as soon as possible.

• Cook eggs until both the yolk and the white are firm, not runny. Soft-scrambled, soft-cooked, or sunny-side-up eggs present some risk.

• Avoid dishes containing raw eggs, such as Caesar salad, and homemade products such as mayonnaise, ice cream, and egg nog. (Commercial products, on the other hand, are safe because they are made with pasteurized eggs.)

TIPS

Preparing
One of the easiest ways to separate an egg is to break it into your (clean) hand and let the white drip between your fingers.

• Beat egg whites only when you are ready to use them. If beaten whites are not used immediately, the air beaten into them escapes and they become watery.

Storing
Store extra unbroken egg yolks in the refrigerator for a couple of days in a small container, covered with cold water. Store leftover raw egg whites in a tightly covered jar; they will keep for up to four days in the refrigerator.

• Raw whole eggs, yolks, and whites can be frozen; beat the whole eggs lightly first to combine yolks and whites.

Cooking
Simmering, not boiling, prevents so-called boiled eggs from cracking. Start cooking the eggs in cold water. When it reaches boiling point, reduce the heat to a simmer and count 3 minutes for soft-boiled eggs, 12 minutes for hard-cooked eggs. After 12 minutes, put the saucepan in the sink under cold running water. Peel the eggs as soon as they are cool enough to handle. The shells will slip off easily, along with the inner membrane.

• Eggs poached ahead of time can be kept warm in a bowl of hot, not boiling water. They do not continue to cook, so the yolks will remain soft.

Serving
To prevent stuffed hard-cooked eggs from sliding on a serving dish, anchor them in place with a tiny dab of the stuffing.

Egg Without End

If you encounter slices of hard-cooked egg on an airplane, perhaps, or in a hospital or school cafeteria, each slice was most probably cut, not from a single egg, but from a very, very long egg roll, created by food processors to make sure the yolk is dead center in every slice.

To accomplish this, they produce an elongated roll of cooked yolks and then encase it in an elongated ring of cooked whites.

Which means that, paradoxical as it may seem, your slice is actually a single slice of a great many eggs.

The Old Man and the Eggs

Not long ago, researchers discovered an 88-year-old man in a Colorado retirement home who had eaten 25 soft-boiled eggs a day for well over 15 years as part of an otherwise sensible diet. In all this time he had maintained good health and a normal cholesterol level.

Gerontologist Fred Kern, Jr., of the University of Colorado School of Medicine in Denver, said that his patient had "extremely efficient compensatory mechanisms." His intestines were absorbing only 18 percent of the cholesterol he ingested, compared with a normal 50 to 60 percent; also, his liver manufactured double the normal levels of bile acids that break down cholesterol.

After eating something like 131,400 eggs in getting on for two decades, the old guy complained only of loneliness since his wife's death — and before too long, he had joined her.

Eggs are very much like small boys. If you overheat them or overbeat them, they will turn on you, and no amount of future love will right the wrong.

— Anonymous

MORE INFORMATION

American Egg Board
1460 Renaissance Drive,
Suite 301
Park Ridge, IL 60068
708-296-7043

United Egg Association
1 Massachusetts Avenue,
Suite 800
Washington, DC 20001
202-842-2345

United Egg Producers
1301 Hightower Trail,
Suite 200
Atlanta, GA 30350
404-587-5871

PERIODICALS
For addresses, see Information Sources

American Egg Board Newsletter
708-296-7043
Monthly; free

United Egg Producers Newsletter
404-587-5871
Biweekly; free

Shrunken Eggs

Food scientists have developed a dehydrating technology that enables them to shrink eggs into tiny pellets. They place the eggs — which are 70 to 80 percent water — in a vacuum that evaporates the water, leaving behind a thick yellow substance. This is frozen with liquid nitrogen, then dried to remove the last of the water. The pea-sized egg that remains can be rehydrated and used like an ordinary egg for cooking or baking.

Other technologies such as hyperpasteurization and irradiation will probably be used to minimize the possibility of salmonella-infected eggs ever entering the market. And nutritionists may soon be able to recommend "super eggs" containing fatty acids, produced by adding a mixture of fish, cod liver oil, and canola oil to standard chicken feed, as a novel means of fighting coronary disease. Australian researchers assert that such eggs can enhance brain development in babies.

ODD JOBS

When chicks hatch at Hy-Line International near Des Moines, Iowa, it takes a crew of chicken sexers to separate the females from the males (which are useless in the fresh-laid-egg business). Each sexer looks at about 1,000 chicks an hour, 80,000 a day, picking them up in the hand to examine their sex organs under a 300-watt light. Accuracy is estimated to be 99 percent. Females are retained for laying, along with 1 in 10 of the males, which are kept for breeding. For the rest, it's the end of a very short road.

Egg Substitutes Nestle In

If you taste an omelette made with a liquid egg substitute, you may not realize you are eating eggs without yolks. Egg substitutes look like eggs and have close to the same texture but contain less cholesterol and fewer calories. They cost a little more, but can successfully replace eggs in baking and for some cooking procedures.

Substitutes have varying salt contents so it is prudent to read the label carefully and test more than one manufacturer's product before deciding which brand suits you best. The refrigerated rather than the frozen form is handy when you are in a hurry; defrosting can take an hour or more.

HOTLINES

800-535-4555
USDA Meat and Poultry Hotline
in Washington, DC:
202-447-3333

If you boil an egg while singing all five verses and chorus of the hymn, "Onward Christian Soldiers," it will be cooked perfectly when you come to Amen.
—Letter to the Editor
London's *Daily Telegraph*

ELECTRONIC SHOPPING

NOT QUITE READY FOR PRIME TIME

It's ahead of its time" is what most people say about electronic shopping. It's certainly how Prodigy, the interactive network, described its reasons for abandoning the electronic shopping system it used to offer. One of Prodigy's problems was that many of us don't really know what we want until we see the food in the supermarket.

"Shopping is a visual and tactile experience," a Prodigy spokesperson explained. "People may know they like the medium-sized green and yellow box of squiggly pasta, but they may not know the brand name nor the size in ounces." So, if they don't know whether it is a 10-ounce or a 12-ounce box, they don't know whether the pasta is agnolotti, bucatini, or capelletti, and they can't recall the name of the manufacturer, the electronic system fails them — and they have to send out for pizza. Customers simply don't want to take the time to look through a book-length order form in order to pull together a shopping list.

Marketing in person is time-consuming, but the idea of checking off items on a list and placing the order seems even more burdensome. And once the order form has been used, how will the check marks be erased? Other problems flood to mind. Where will the delivery truck leave the ice cream? Will apartment houses be prepared to supply refrigerated storage space? Whose responsibility will it be if the groceries are stolen? And who will prove that they *were* stolen, not eaten?

Supermarkets operate with huge inventories and minuscule profit margins; electronic shopping would add large costs in equipment and personnel, and customers are unused and unwilling to pay premium prices for such service.

The basic problem is that human beings don't like being programmed. Shopping, especially shopping for food, is a time when even the most scrupulous list-makers may turn into an aisle, find something they cannot resist, and toss the preplanned meal into oblivion. When was the last time *you* went to the store to buy three items and got through the checkout without having picked up at least three more?

Time will not catch up with electronic shopping until we can think of the computer not as a piece of office equipment masquerading as a house guest but as a family member totally at home in the kitchen.

Futurist Wizardry

Merchandising experts predict that when the age of electronic shopping dawns, consumers will be supplied with a stylus pen similar to the ones Federal Express already uses. Swipe the bar code and a record will be made of the exact package size required. Tap a personalized bulletin board and a shopping list will be sent direct to the store. Funds will be simultaneously deducted from your checking account (provided all your assets are not frozen). Delivery will be made in temperature-controlled packages that have coded locks.

ETHNIC FOOD

Everything old is new again.

— Peter Allen
Australian songwriter

CHERISHING
THE PAST

Food memories are gloriously evocative. In our mind's eye, we conjure up time-enhanced remembrances of our immigrant grandmothers' kitchens and their wealth of tastes and smells. It has been said that politics consists of the remembered foods of our childhood. Whether we yearn for clam chowder or *chlodnik* or egg drop soup, moussaka or manicotti, we almost all were awakened to the joys of eating at a shared family table.

For those who cook the traditional dishes of our individual ethnic heritages there is enduring pleasure and comfort in preparing the food that is familiar to us. We go on loving the same music no matter how often we hear it and we are comforted by the same simple foods no matter how often we eat them. Indeed, the repetition is part of the joy of remembrance and renewal.

The hallowing of tradition appears most clearly in our food heritage. Every time we prepare and share the food of our immigrant culture we forge strong links both with our ancestral past and with future generations. For some, this may be a long-simmered stew; for others it is a peanut butter and jelly sandwich. For one family a once-a-year feast has to include *tsouriki,* the traditional Greek Easter bread; others will feast on *lebkuchen, rugalach,* or plum pudding, made from recipes originally written down long ago and far away.

Almost everything around us has changed since our grandparents' day, but the soups, the roasts, the cookies, and the dishes associated with national and religious holidays have remained the same — in reality as in memory.

Setting America's Table

The variety and quality of food in America today is unmatched anywhere, yet when the first colonists arrived in Jamestown, Virginia, in 1607, it did not at first appear that there was anything to eat in the new land. There were no domesticated animals, so there was no beef, no pork, and no chicken. Consequently, there was neither milk, butter, cheese, nor eggs, and no animal fat or oil for cooking. The only pots and utensils were those the settlers brought with them. No kind of cuisine was possible — there wasn't even a kitchen.

On other continents regional dishes were developed based on the ingredients that were available; their origins have been lost in time but their essential characteristics have remained. Noodles have been made in China for thousands of years and porridges of one kind or another have existed throughout Europe for as long as humans have gathered grains. Similarly, foods based on corn have formed the foundation of Mexican cooking.

But Americans have been continuously on the move from one region to another in a restless search for a better life. The raw ingredients were carried from one settlement to the next and in consequence little effort was ever made to develop a range of recipes based on uniquely regional foods. Once transportation improved and large food processing plants opened up, there was less and less reason to depend on local produce. In this century many of the foods we eat daily will have traveled hundreds, even thousands, of miles before they arrive in the local store. Pineapples from Hawaii are flown to Nevada; New England's live lobsters are steamed in Oklahoma; Florida oranges are squeezed in Maine.

A few regional differences do exist — the food of New Orleans is an outstanding example — but most local specialties have evolved as adaptations of dishes brought by newly arriving immigrants. Each influx of new arrivals in turn has had an impact on the foodstuffs we buy and how we prepare them. The large Cuban population is influencing the food in and around Miami. Recent waves of immigration from the Pacific Rim countries

have resulted in literally hundreds of ethnic restaurants on the West and East coasts. The fast-growing Hispanic population has created a demand for niche supermarkets.

Yet these newcomers have not wholly dispelled the patterns and values established by the early settlers, who viewed fancy food as sinful. It is understandable, too, that people who were once hungry and poor would emphasize the particular blessing of having plenty to eat. Even today a feast usually denotes quantity rather than variety or quality. The offer of "all you can eat" is more attractive to more people than an invitation to a fine, formal dinner.

If there is a single ethnic characteristic of American food, it has to be the value we place on sweetness. Our forefathers' first foods in the new land were intensely sweetened with honey and we have never lost our sweet tooth since. Breakfast pancakes, waffles, and french toast are considered inedible without sweet syrup; sweet rolls, coffee cakes, Danish pastries, muffins, and doughnuts are still the favorite morning foods. We consume cookies, candies, sweet snacks, and sweet sodas throughout the day, and many an evening meal is not complete without thickly frosted cake, ice cream, or pudding.

Some things are changing, though. We go on eating foods that taste sweet, but the sugar today is often artificial. We still like our food fast, but the ultimate in kitchen convenience is the take-out food store. We like "ethnic" foods, but are more likely to eat them at a restaurant. And though there was once a time when we thought foreign food was superior to our own, we are coming to believe that the best food of all may be grown in our own gardens.

THE HEART OF FRANCE

A typical Frenchman thinks the world is made up of the French — and those who are less fortunate.

Indeed, it is impossible to think of food without putting France into a separate, exalted place. Listen to a group of French carpenters or plumbers sharing lunch on the job, a meal made up of bread, cheese, perhaps a little sausage, and a measure of wine. Eavesdrop on a group of housewives waiting their turn in the butcher's shop, or three or four businessmen assembled in a fine restaurant. They will be sharing memories of their Breton grandmother's *matelote* of eel with wine, cream, eggs, shallots, even prunes. "Did you ever eat a matelote with prunes?" one will ask, and another will launch into a tale of a cassoulet from Toulouse, full of beans and sausage, duck, pork, and lamb, taking six hours to cook and three more to eat. Another will recall, with his tongue passing over his lips, a certain earthenware pot that was always filled with a Burgundian beef stew — a stew perfected by time and hallowed by generations, a noble stew with *lardons* of salt pork, dark woodland mushrooms, tiny white onions, a crust of bread to soak up the gravy, and a liter or two of wine, all served on Sundays that seemed never to end.

Food and wine are important topics of conversation in France and everyone knows that good cooking begins with the selection of the freshest and finest of ingredients in the open-air markets that are still the nation's pride. Jostling throngs fill the village squares and narrow streets, buying, bargaining, and carrying home their evening meal in string bags and wicker baskets. And the displays of food are seductive enough to jolt the most disinterested of palates into a lathering of salivation.

Cascades of tomatoes explode in brilliant redness. Purple-black, round-bellied eggplants are displayed alongside skinny asparagus. Crackling brown-skinned onions appear in a family grouping with their heroic garlic cousins, fat leeks, delicate scallions, and baby shallots. Blushing apricots herald the promise of summer, and the profusion of strawberries, cherries, melons, peaches, and pears sends the mind reeling in a hundred different directions of choice.

White and yellow cheeses, some touched with blue, some with green, are brought to the cheese stall from nearby dairies. Soft cheeses ooze their richness onto cold marble and hard cheeses are piled one upon another. There are pyramids of cheeses made from the milk of mountain goats. Some can be spooned from a bowl like flowing cream; others are as dry in the mouth as the crumbling of chalk.

Then there are the boxes of trout, *rouget, dorade,* flat-chested sole, and dozens of their fellow travelers, snatched from dawn waters with still a gleam of surprise in their eye and moisture glistening on their skins. Mussels and sea urchins are scooped with small shovels into the darkness of paper bags. Eels lazily coil and uncoil themselves in shallow troughs. There are shrimps and *langoustes* in full armor and oysters on the half shell.

Recently expired ducks hang upside down from hooks while still-living chickens cackle in coops, unaware of their impending doom. Guinea hens and woodcock, some still wearing their feathered socks, are trussed and ready for the oven. There is baby lamb from the salt marshes and red beef from lush pastures. And over all this abundance wafts the seductive fragrance of bread, fresh from the oven.

This piece was inspired by a visit, long ago, to the market in Beaune with Richard Olney.

Q&A

Q What makes a foreign food acceptable in the United States?

A It must possess at least four of the following attributes:

1. Not drip or fall apart if eaten with one hand while driving.

2. Have energetic, amusing, or convincing advertising — preferably, all three.

3. Be easy to make or reheat without difficulty or danger of harming either cook or consumer — in effect, be foolproof but still taste good.

4. Be adaptable for serving in fast food outlets, in a form, e.g., chicken nuggets, that children can try with ease and without pressure (and hence be likely to make it their favorite food).

5. Be inexpensive, yet offer value for money — i.e., look like more than can be eaten in a couple of mouthfuls.

6. Be balanced between bland and spicy so that people of all ages can feel adventurous when eating it, with at least one component that is crispy or crunchy.

7. Be guilt-free — i.e., capable of being described as healthy food without stretching truth beyond belief.

All Wrapped Up

Almost every nation encloses small amounts of its main-meal foods — meat, chicken, fish, or cheese — in outer wrappings in order to make them go further, but the choice of wrapping seems to be a regional distinction.

In Western countries, it is primarily bread, top and bottom. American hamburgers and hot dogs are always served within a soft, squishy "roll," and sandwiches of all kinds extend a small amount of filling into a filling meal. (The exception is the genuine kosher deli sandwich where the rye bread is merely the vehicle enabling the colossal filling to be hefted to the mouth.)

In Israel and the Middle East, the bread of choice is pita, stuffed with ground chick-peas and called falafel, or in Greece, crammed with slices of roast lamb, onions, and peppers, and known as a gyro. In Mexico the big enchilada is meant for enclosing a roll-up of meat, chicken, or cheese.

Elsewhere, other foods are wrapped in packages some of which are intended to be consumed as well, while others were simply the most convenient containers at hand: lettuce leaves, cabbage leaves, grape leaves, banana leaves, palm fronds, corn husks, envelopes of baked mud. Tasty fragments nestle neatly in noodles or in pastry — phyllo pastry, plain pastry, puff pastry — or in paper: rice paper, parchment paper, even newspaper.

A bewildering variety of meats, fish, cheese, vegetables, nuts, and fruits turn up inside blintzes, buns, burritos, cannelloni, chimichangas, Cornish pasties, crêpes, dumplings, egg rolls, empanadas, fajitas, knishes, kreplach, quesadillas, ravioli, spring rolls, strudels, tortellini, turnovers, and won tons. Minute amounts of expensive protein are rolled in inexpensive rice and even cheaper seaweed.

And an entire fortune can be contained inside a cookie.

CHOP-CHOP

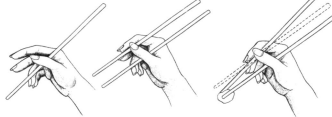

In China, it is considered barbaric to present a piece of meat that at all resembles the animal from which it came, and it is thought very impolite to expect a guest to do the work of cutting food into bite-sized pieces. This task belongs to the cook, and the food must leave the kitchen ready to be consumed without the slightest delay.

Such a philosophy of eating naturally led to the invention of chopsticks. The Chinese word for them, *kwai-tsze,* means "quick little fellows," hence *chop,* which in pidgin English means "quick." Chinese chopsticks have square tips and are made in different lengths — 10 inches, usually, for eating and up to 20 inches when used for cooking.

The Japanese also use chopsticks, which they call *hashi,* or "bridge," because they serve as the bridge that carries food from the bowl into the mouth; their chopsticks have pointed ends.

How
People Eat

Everybody has to eat, but the methods that people all over the world use to get food from plate to mouth vary. Figures from the Japanese Restaurant Association divide the world's population into four categories:

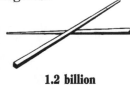

1.2 billion
eat with chopsticks

1.5 billion
eat with fork, knife,
and spoon

350 million
eat with knife and hands

250 million
eat with hands only

Source: *Restaurants and Institutions*

THE AFRICAN LEGACY

JOHN **E**GERTON

From Africa with the people in bondage came new foods; okra, black-eyed peas (also called cowpeas), collard greens, yams, benne seed (the mystical and luck-bringing sesame), and watermelons. From Central and South America, meanwhile — sometimes by circuitous routes through Europe and Africa and Asia — came hot and sweet peppers, peanuts, tomatoes, lima beans, chocolate, white potatoes, and sweet potatoes, the latter a look-alike nonrelative of the yam. . . . Up from Florida came oranges and peaches, natives of China brought to the New World by the Spanish.

With eggs from the chickens, milk and butter from the cows, honey from native and imported bees ("white man's flies," the Indians called them), native black walnuts and pecans, and syrup extracted by the Indians from the sap of maple trees, colonial cooks enriched and expanded the diet. The food of Virginia gradually took on a distinctive character as English and Indian and African cooks all contributed from their diverse experiences. To the rather dull and plain cookery of 16th-century England they added American foodstuffs, Indian harvesting and cooking knowledge, African tastes and seasonings, and such Spanish, French, Dutch, and German touches as managed to penetrate the English circle of colonial power. Within 50 years of the founding of Jamestown, a distinctly American cookery was beginning to emerge. . . .

It is difficult to reconcile the glory of the feast with the ignominy of slavery. To praise the food, and then to say that such dining excellence would not have been possible without slave labor, seems almost to amount to an endorsement of slavery itself. But there is another consideration: To throw out the superlative dishes of the colonial and antebellum periods because of their association with slavery would be to ignore the creative genius of generations of black cooks, and thus to discredit one of the truly outstanding achievements in American social history.

In the most desolate and hopeless of circumstances, blacks caught in the grip of slavery often exhibited uncommon wisdom, beauty, strength, and creativity. The kitchen was one of the few places where their imagination and skill could have free rein and free expression, and there they often excelled. From the elegant breads and meats and sweets of plantation cookery to the inventive genius of Creole cuisine, from beaten biscuits to bouillabaisse, their legacy of culinary excellence is all the more impressive, considering the extremely adverse conditions under which it was compiled.

Excerpted from Southern Food

ETHNIC SOUPS

Every country has its own traditional, beautiful soup, because soups have always been the mainstay of the large families people used to have, providing nourishment in quantity and inexpensively. Here are just three distinctive soups, reprinted from my book *Good Old Food: A Taste of the Past*. They are easy to make and delicious to eat.

French Onion Soup

Serves 6

6 tablespoons butter
8 medium-sized onions, sliced (about 8 cups)
8 cups beef broth
¼ cup Madeira (optional)
Salt and freshly ground black pepper
Long loaf French bread, sliced into 24 ½-inch-thick rounds
1½ cups grated Gruyère cheese

In a large saucepan over medium-low heat, melt the butter, add the onions, and stir to coat them with the butter. Reduce the heat to low and cook gently until the onions are soft, about 30 minutes, stirring occasionally. Raise the heat to high and cook the onions for about 5 minutes, stirring continuously, to brown them. Add the broth and the Madeira, if you are using it, and season to taste with salt and pepper. Cover the pan and simmer very slowly for 30 minutes. (The longer the soup cooks, the greater the depth of flavor, but keep checking to make sure the broth is not disappearing.)

Meanwhile, lightly toast the bread slices.

Heat the broiler until very hot. Pour the soup into a large ovenproof tureen or individual bowls. Float the toasted bread slices on the surface and top with the grated cheese. Broil just until the cheese has melted and is lightly browned.

Dutch Green Pea Soup

Serves 6

2 tablespoons butter
½ cup coarsely chopped onion
1 small clove garlic, finely chopped
1¾ cups quick-cooking split green peas
6 cups water
2-pound cooked ham shank, bone in
2 tablespoons finely chopped parsley
1 bay leaf
½ teaspoon sugar
Salt and freshly ground black pepper
1½ cups chicken broth

In a stock pot over moderate heat, melt the butter, add the onion and garlic, and cook for about 5 minutes, stirring occasionally, until softened and translucent. Add the split peas and cook, stirring, for another 5 minutes.

Pour the water into the pot. Add the ham shank, herbs, sugar, salt and pepper to taste, and the chicken broth. Raise the heat and bring to a boil. Reduce the heat to low, cover the pot, and simmer for 2 hours.

Remove the ham shank, cut the meat from the bone, and discard the bone. Chop the meat into small pieces and reserve. Remove and discard the bay leaf.

Pour the soup into a blender or food processor and process until smooth. (This will have to be done in several batches).

Return the soup to the pot, add the reserved ham meat, and heat through before serving.

Jewish Shchav

Serves 4

1 quart vegetable broth
1 small bunch watercress, washed and coarsely chopped
½ pound sorrel, washed and coarsely chopped
½ cup chopped celery
2 tablespoons lemon juice
1 tablespoon freshly grated lemon rind
4 teaspoons sugar
Salt and white pepper
1 cup sour cream

Put the broth, watercress, sorrel and celery in a large pan and bring to a boil. Lower the heat and simmer for 40 to 45 minutes until the watercress and sorrel leaves have just about dissolved in the liquid.

Add the lemon juice, lemon rind, and sugar. Season to taste with salt and pepper. Stir the soup well and simmer for about 5 minutes to give the flavors time to blend.

Pour the soup into a glass or porcelain bowl, cover with plastic wrap, and chill for at least 4 hours, or until cold.

Serve with sour cream and love.

Did You Know?

☞ At last count, New York City had exactly 3,033 ethnic restaurants.

☞ The 1990 census reported nearly 20 million people living in the United States who had been born abroad. The actual number is considerably higher both because of illegal immigration and because of undercounting in many areas with large first-generation populations.

☞ Ethnic dishes now comprise 30 percent of the choices offered on restaurant menus.

Favorite Foods

A poll conducted by *Healthy Choice* showed that America's most popular ethnic cuisines are Italian (55 percent), Mexican (39 percent), and Chinese (38 percent). Next up, in order: French, Spanish, German, Japanese, Greek, Latin American. Rankings in the third group: Indian, Caribbean, Eastern European, Middle Eastern, Korean, Thai, Vietnamese, Scandinavian, Russian, and the foods of the 54 countries that comprise the African continent.

EATING ABROAD RIGHT HERE AT HOME

The most popular ethnic restaurants may produce food of dubious authenticity, but their patrons can experience a mini-vacation nonetheless — the waiters speak with an accent, though not always an ethnically correct one, and the wall posters depict never-never lands (outside the normal range of frequent flier miles) where the Taj Mahal is always bathed in moonlight, the toreador is always preening in front of the bull, and the Tower of Pisa always leans.

These unintimidating eating establishments have a common touch, appealing particularly to students who prefer their booze by the jug and to those who appreciate cheap eats accompanied by deafening noise and ketchup bottles on the table. Such places are not concerned with nuance, subtlety, or even authenticity.

Thus, Spanish cooking is reduced to paella, castanets, and sangria, served by waiters wearing wide-brimmed embroidered black hats, tight toreador pants, and designer sneakers. Millions of Americans innocently equate Italy with pizza, parmesan, and pepper on the pasta, in places where Mom may or may not be thrilled to be addressed as "signorina."

More adventurous diners may be rewarded with the fresh tastes and textures created in Japanese, Thai, and Vietnamese restaurants where immigrant "chefs" stir up dishes from exotic ingredients that for most of their patrons would involve making a 3,000-mile round trip shopping expedition. Their cooking techniques are all the more impressive because they seem so difficult to master, especially by those whose skills are limited to pressing buttons on the microwave. Most diners here are simply grateful to be served a decent meal at a decent price in a place where they don't have to wear a tie and a high chair is provided for the toddlers.

Many well-intentioned ethnic restaurants quickly realize that few will risk ordering tripe, trotters, rabbit, or jellyfish. So, instead, they offer us what they think we want.

What we really want is not to have to think too much about the food. It is far more important to relax and have a good time. Only if it genuinely interests us will we delve a little deeper and find the treasures that teem beneath the surface in ethnic restaurants. Only subversives and radical crazies have time these days to spend six hours cooking dinner or are prepared to shell out $100 per head to eat the genuine food that requires skilled hands and years of training to prepare.

In the meantime, I'll have whatever she ordered.

> *When it comes to foreign food, the less authentic the better.*
>
> — Gerald Nachman
> *San Francisco Chronicle*

EXTRUDED FOOD

NEW AGE FOOD
TURNS ON THE SCREWS

If you have ever wondered how they make those pasta letters for alphabet soup, you may be relieved to learn that it's all done by machine. Similar machines form the Os in Cheerios, the Xs in Friskies, the curls of Fritos, and the shapes of dozens of other breakfast cereals, pet foods, and snacks. They're called extruders.

To visualize how extrusion works, imagine a metal tunnel in which a spiraling screw or twin screws are continuously turning. At one end is a large funnel or hopper into which all the ingredients are dumped. In an entirely automated process they are mixed mechanically, kneaded, and continuously pushed forward by the side-by-side screws that are synchronized to clean the mixture off each other as they move it along. The mixture is cooked, meanwhile, partly by the pressure generated inside the extruder and partly by outside heating devices. At the far end, it is forced through dies similar to those on cake-decorating tubes, and then chopped into pieces.

Different-sized dies determine the shape just as the size of a toothpaste tube opening forms the width of the ribbon of toothpaste squeezed through it. For example, the die that generates the O shape of each Cheerio has a "nail prong" in its center. As the mixture is pressed through the die it squeezes around the nail, leaving a central hole. Pasta shapes are formed using dies similar to those available for home pasta machines. By combining the streams from two extruders, a specific product can be given a center of one substance and a coating of another. As the endless ribbons of formulated food emerge, whirling blades cut them into flakes, shapes, curls, and curlicues of the exact size required.

Almost all extruded foods are processed from oats, wheat, corn, rice, or a blend of these grains, and the different characteristics of each one have to be considered when the cycle is being programmed, especially if two different grains are to be bonded together. In addition, any sudden changes in heat or pressure can affect a grain's flavor or the degree to which its starch will gelatinize.

Extrusion is a triumph of physics and technology married to food chemistry. The cooks in their tall hats and checkered trousers have left the kitchen and in their place have come the food scientists and engineers. And surely they sense fulfillment as they see the mountains of puffs, doodles, crisps, and kibbles that fill our shopping carts.

FAMILY MEAL ◆ FARMING ◆ FAST FOOD ◆ FAT ◆

FIBER ◆ FIGS ◆ FLAVORINGS ◆ FLOUNDER ◆ FLOUR

◆ FLOWERS, EDIBLE ◆ FOIE GRAS ◆ FOOD ADDITIVES

◆ FOOD AND MEDICINE ◆ FOOD SAFETY ◆

FROGS ◆ FROZEN FOODS ◆ FRUIT ◆ FRUITCAKE

◆ FUNERAL FOOD

FAMILY MEAL

After a good dinner, one can forgive anybody, even one's relatives.

— Oscar Wilde

THE ENDANGERED KITCHEN TABLE

ROB KASPER

An American institution is under attack. It is the kitchen table. Everybody knows that most of the world's great ideas — the theory of light, the theory of making potato salad without mayonnaise, the theory of who will win the pennant — take shape around the kitchen table.

Yet, whenever I visit a modern kitchen and look around for a place to sit and chew the fat, I don't find a table. What I find is a breakfast bar or a kitchen "island" surrounded by stools. While it is possible to position yourself on such perches, they don't encourage serious sitting.

Instead, they seem to be designed for "quick bites," wherein people hurry in, wolf down some fiber-filled muffins, and then sprint out into the fast lane. Perched at a breakfast bar, there is little inclination to smell the coffee, to count the raisins in the raisin bran, to talk.

In contrast, a kitchen table, with its easy-to-plop-in chairs and vast flat surface, invites you to spread out and linger. And lingering is the essence of kitchen life. Without it, a kitchen is nothing more than a work station. . . .

Lots of things remain on our kitchen table. The goldfish bowl, magazines, notes from teachers, and stacks and stacks of newspapers. It is our ready reference center, a place to find the answer to questions ranging from "Are the Simpsons on tonight?" to "Why are these people protesting in the Philippines?"

. . . But the main attraction a kitchen table holds for me is that it is a good place to hear things. As a parent, you sit at the table and, as the kids talk to each other, you sometimes hear the real version beyond the "school-was-OK" line of what went on in the classroom.

And, as a kid, you can learn about the unsanitized you'll-never-guess-what-happened-today accounts of adult behavior — especially if the kid sitting at the table keeps quiet and pretends he isn't listening. . . .

It's hard to imagine such stories getting started at a breakfast bar.

Excerpted from *The Baltimore Sun*

My dear, I love you ardently
Adore your charm, the way you look,
I'm captivated by your voice,
I've read with pride your latest book,
And yet I will not marry you
Until, sweetheart, you've learned to cook.

— Martyno
Ultimatum

Books

Dinner in Minutes
Linda Gassenheimer;
Chapters, 1993; $19.95

Good Old Food
Irena Chalmers; Barron's,
1988; $19.95

Home Cooking in Minutes
Thelma Snyder and Marcia
Cone-Esaki; Simon & Schuster,
1992; $25.00

The Family Circle Cookbook
Editors and David Ricketts;
Simon & Schuster, 1992;
$23.00

The Working Family's Cookbook
Irena Chalmers; Barron's,
1993; $24.95/$12.95

Half the Truth

Once when we were hungry we went home to eat. Now when we are hungry we go out to eat. Already many families eat together only when they eat out. A survey conducted by *Better Homes & Gardens* magazine and the Food Marketing Institute suggests that seven out of ten families eat dinner together three or more times a week, and that more than half the families eat together every night. *Newsweek* writer Laura Shapiro reported the survey but took pains to point out that "as with most surveys, families were phoned at dinnertime, so those not eating at home were excluded." Hmm.

Norman Rockwell, Where Are You?

The good news is that we are returning to the cooking of our grandmothers.

The bad news is that our grandmother could not cook.

The up side is that in her day there was plenty of food. The down side is that most of it tasted terrible.

The reality is that Mom is not sitting in a rocker on the back porch shelling peas. Father no longer knows best, nor does he stand at the head of the table wielding a carving knife. Almost all the food we take home is boneless, so there is nothing left to carve.

The entire hierarchy of the traditional family table has gradually changed. For the first time in our history, the "average" American is now female; the number of families headed by a single woman increases each year, and the majority of families have no parent at home full time. Those of all ages who have become accustomed to receiving an answer from a computer in two seconds are disinclined to spend two hours preparing the evening meal. Furthermore, the independent children of working parents demand, and often receive, the right to eat what and where they please. Arguments are exhausting.

Forecasters anticipate that by the end of the decade more than 90 percent of all food purchases will be fully prepared and ready to eat within 10 minutes. We are fast approaching the millennium.

All of this bothers us terribly. Though we know it is true, we would like to believe that this state of affairs is only temporary. We have found it far easier to stop cutting our own hair, stop cleaning our own clothes, and stop being responsible for growing our own food than to confront the reality: We are spending less time cooking and less time gathered around the family table.

FARMING

THE CHALLENGE OF THE 21ST CENTURY

ORVILLE FREEMAN

In the next two to four generations, world agriculture will be called on to produce as much food as has been produced in the entire 12,000-year history of agriculture.

The estimated population growth for the next quarter century is so enormous that warning bells should be sounding in every quadrant of the globe. Feeding this population may well be the greatest challenge we have ever faced — one that will test the world's productive and technological capabilities to their very limits.

Even conservative projections call for a population increase of over one billion people — bringing the world's population to 6.2 billion by the year 2000. These same projections predict a population of nearly 11 billion by the year 2050. This increase will take place in a world where already over 75 percent of the population can barely feed themselves, almost 500 million people are severely malnourished, and 15 million children worldwide die each year from starvation and related illnesses — that is over 41,000 every day. In this regard, I think that many people, particularly those in the relatively well-fed industrialized world, simply cannot relate to the concept of subsistence, where securing enough food to sustain life is the focal point of each day's activities.

In the United States, for all but a relatively small segment of the population, the task of securing food means no more than a trip to the nearby supermarket, where we choose from more than 11,000 items to meet our needs. In fact, one of our major food-related concerns is how to eat less!

In order of priority, then, the first challenge we must address is how to bring the goals of feeding the world's population and protecting the world's environment into harmony. They need not and must not be mutually exclusive. To maximize our productive capabilities and minimize the effect this production has on the environment, the vital connective tissue is technology. We must foster and harness the technological means through which both goals can be served — applying science to meet the objectives of both humanity and our environment. But there is a very serious danger that the voice of the world's hungry will not be heard if the environmental and food-related agenda is written to meet only the needs of well-intentioned but well-fed interests.

Excerpted from
"Meeting the Food Needs of the Coming Decade," *The Futurist*

The earth does not belong to man; Man belongs to the earth. This we know. Whatever befalls the earth befalls the sons of the earth. Man did not weave the web of life, he is merely a strand in it. Whatever he does to the web, he does to himself.

— Chief Seattle
19th-century Native American

Farmers Are Fewer, But Yields Are Way Up

In 1850, most Americans lived and worked on farms, and the average farmer produced enough food for four people. Today, one farmer produces the food for 80 people, a 20-fold increase in 140 years.

In 1925, farms averaged 143 acres. In 1940, the average had reached 168 acres. By the early 1990s, this had swelled to nearly 470 acres. Crop yields per acre have climbed steadily by around 2 percent a year. Some 80 percent of annual output is produced by 15 to 20 percent of farms. Thus, costs to the consumer are still falling. Today, we spend only about 15 percent of our disposable income on food.

Sustainable Agriculture: Buzzwords Or Serious Stuff?

What is sustainable agriculture? How does it differ from mainstream farming? Simply put, it's growing food as naturally as possible, working with nature. "It has four essential components," according to Terry Gips, an agricultural economist and founder of the International Alliance for Sustainable Agriculture, writing in *Buzzworm: The Environmental Journal.*

"First, it must be ecologically sound. It must not destroy the environment or our health, while conserving energy and using renewable resources.

"Second, it must be economically viable, assuring farmers a fair return, and at the same time, accounting for all the hidden costs and subsidies in the system.

"Third, it must be socially just, assuring full participation for all people, from their access to land and resources to their ability to make decisions about their own destinies.

"Fourth, it must be humane, which means to embody our highest values. Most often we think about our treatment of animals, but it applies just as well to our treatment of human beings.

"Sustainable agriculture is concerned with respect for all life as well as preservation of rural communities and culture."

What sustainable agriculture tries to do :

• Increase plant nutrients and tackle pests by understanding how and why they function

• Reduce the input of potentially lethal substances onto the farm

• Utilize plants or animals selected for vigor or disease-resistance

• Be aware of what can or cannot be grown, matching crops to soils and climate

• Take care of the soil, water supply, energy use, and living organisms, including animals and the farmers themselves, with a view to efficiency and profit

WHO DOES WHAT?
Three federal agencies are responsible for agriculture.

United States Department of Agriculture (USDA)
The Food Safety and Inspection Service conducts random tests for drug residues at the time animals and poultry are slaughtered. The Animal and Plant Health Inspection Service regulates and approves all drugs, vaccines, and biological products that are used to detect or enhance an animal's immunity to infection.

The Food and Drug Administration (FDA)
The Center for Veterinary Medicine oversees the development of animal drugs and feed additives and monitors animal health products to ensure they are safe and effective. The Center for Food Safety and Applied Nutrition monitors drug residues in milk through its own Milk Safety Branch.

The Environmental Protection Agency (EPA)
The Office of Pesticide Programs is responsible for approving chemicals used topically on livestock to control pests.

HOTLINES

800-FARM-AID
(327-6243)
Farm Aid

800-676-3608
Food Watch Information Center, Agriculture Council of America

Books

Farming in Nature's Image: An Ecological Approach to Agriculture
Judith D. Soule and Jon K. Piper;
Island Press, 1992; $19.95.

The Land That Feeds Us
John Fraser Hart;
W. W. Norton, 1991; $25.00

FOOD FOR THE FORAGING

There are wild plants growing in the American Southwest that predate the coming of Columbus by hundreds, perhaps thousands of years. Certainly we know that native people began turning many of them into crops in prehistory, and that many continue to do so to the present day. Among these plants are the chili pepper, tepary beans, cotton, squashes, and the tequila plant.

It has been estimated that as many as two-thirds of North America's native crop varieties have been wiped out over time. This came about through the clearing of land for cultivation, and because of the introduction of new, more dominant crop plants. Moreover, the federal government has not until recently taken any steps to preserve those native crops that remain.

Now, a nonprofit organization in Arizona called Native Seeds/SEARCH (NS/S) has joined forces with the U.S. Department of Agriculture in a conservation plan for wild native crops. The project aims to study the dietary values of these crops and to exploit them as food for native people of Arizona, who on a diet of typical American high-fat foods put on weight all year round and show a strong tendency to diabetes after the age of 35. Nutritional tests have shown that when they switch back to their traditional foods — tepary beans, pods from mesquite trees, acorns, and corn — they lose weight, their general health improves dramatically, and their blood sugar levels drop significantly.

Long before Columbus, native American people were feeding themselves well. In their back gardens are hundreds of edible native plants that are often far more nutritious than the common crops eaten in America. The NS/S project workers hope that their efforts will bring traditional crops once again to the support of the people.

WHAT AMERICA PRODUCES

The chief U.S. agricultural commodities are ranked below by "value of production," which is based on the average price at which the farmer sells a crop, or, for livestock, their estimated mean value per head. The figures are derived from the government's *Agricultural Statistics 1992.*

Cattle and calves: $30.6 billion

Milk: $18.3 billion

Corn: $18 billion

Hogs: $11.1 billion

Soybeans: $11 billion

Broilers (chickens): $8.4 billion

Wheat: $5.8 billion

Eggs: $3.9 billion

Turkeys: $2.3 billion

Potatoes: $2.1 billion

Apples: $1.8 billion

Tomatoes: $1.8 billion

Grapes: $1.7 billion

Oranges: $1.7 billion

Sorghum: $1.3 billion

Rice: $1 billion

Lettuce: $810 million

Mushrooms: $648 million

Strawberries: $634 million

Onions: $581 million

Almonds: $540 million

Beans, dry: $524 million

Sweet corn: $493 million

Peaches: $393 million

Grapefruit: $383 million

Sheep and lambs: $341 million

Pecans: $310 million

Carrots: $309 million

Lemons: $295 million

Plums and prunes: $283 million

Walnuts: $280 million

Pears: $274 million

Broccoli: $242 million

Cranberries: $207 million

Celery: $206 million

Cauliflower: $188 million

Avocados: $179 million

Asparagus: $150 million

Sweet potatoes: $142 million

Cherries, sweet: $138 million

Beans, snap: $137 million

Cucumbers: $131 million

Peas, green: $128 million

Pineapples: $108 million

Pistachios: $96 million

Nectarines: $86 million

Tangerines: $78 million

Honeydew melons: $69 million

Olives: $37 million

Apricots: $37 million

Macadamia nuts: $35 million

Kiwifruit: $24 million

Dates: $21 million

Hazelnuts (filberts): $18.5 million

Papayas: $16 million

Figs: $13.5 million

Bananas: $4.5 million

Did You Know?

☞ It would take about 110 million tons (dry weight) of animal manure to give us a third of the nutrients now supplied by synthetic fertilizers.

☞ With a gross farm income totaling nearly $20 billion annually, California tops the 50 states in American food production. Closest competitors are Texas with nearly $15 billion, and Iowa with over $12 billion.

☞ American farmers use, on average, about 2 million gallons of water each year on every acre of crops. Typically, 360 gallons of water are consumed in raising one pound of beef.

☞ A year's supply of meat for the average American family takes the equivalent of 50 gallons of fuel to produce.

☞ The United States ships 6 to 7 million tons of food aid to foreign countries every year.

Seventy years ago, farmers were seduced into going for mechanization and, later, the use of chemicals, because these practices gave good returns. No one could have foreseen the damage that this approach to growing food would wreak.

— Bryan Lynas
Science writer and farmer

Slicing Up the Buck

What a dollar spent on food actually pays for. About one-third goes for food marketing labor costs. The breakdown includes food eaten both at and away from home. Other costs include property taxes and insurance, accounting and professional services, promotion, bad debts, and many miscellaneous items.

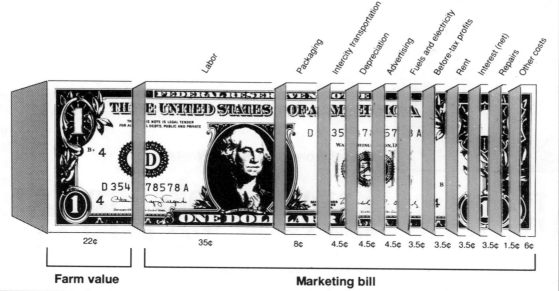

	Farm value	Labor	Packaging	Intercity transportation	Depreciation	Advertising	Fuels and electricity	Before-tax profits	Rent	Interest (net)	Repairs	Other costs
	22¢	35¢	8¢	4.5¢	4.5¢	4.5¢	3.5¢	3.5¢	3.5¢	3.5¢	1.5¢	6¢
	Farm value	Marketing bill										

MORE INFORMATION

Agriculture Council of America
927 15th Street NW,
Suite 800
Washington, DC 20005
202-682-9200

American Farm Bureau Federation
225 Touhy Avenue
Park Ridge, IL 60068
312-399-5700

Council for Agricultural Science and Technology
4420 West Lincoln Way
Ames, IA 50014-3447
515-292-2125

Farm Aid
334 Broadway, Suite 5
Cambridge, MA 02139
617-354-2292

U.S. Department of Agriculture Information Center
14th Street & Independence Avenue SW
Washington, DC 20250
202-720-2791
The USDA publishes a free booklet: *How to Get Information from the USDA.*

U.S. Department of Agriculture
National Agricultural Library
Alternative Farming Systems, Room 111
Beltsville, MD 20705
301-504-6559

FARM SUBSIDIES

Almost all over the world governments hand out subsidies to their farmers, either to help them grow more crops less expensively so that prices can be lowered in the marketplace, or to reward them for *not* farming portions of their land in order to avoid glutting the market and piling up overlarge reserves of foods and grains.

These practices, always controversial, tend to become politicoeconomic footballs, tossed into play by one party against another or one country (most recently, the United States) against others (the European Community). As

always, there are valid arguments on both sides.

In America, the idea of giving agricultural subsidies originated in the Depression, with the Agricultural Adjustment Act of 1933, which was set up to establish a program of soil conservation, storage of surplus farm goods, and control of agricultural production. Its purpose was to reduce crop surpluses and thereby raise farmers' incomes. But in 1936 the Supreme Court declared the act unconstitutional, and it was replaced by the Soil Conservation and Domestic Allotment Act, which

authorized payments to farmers who raised soil-building crops rather than staple grains. In 1938 this was replaced by the Agricultural Adjustment Administration Act, which established a system of price supports by agreeing to purchase crops at specified minimum prices and to store surplus production. During World War II and the Korean War, the surpluses were almost eliminated, but the problem of excess productivity reappeared almost immediately afterward.

Despite the Soil Bank and Rural Development programs of the 1950s, agricultural surpluses grew

massively, and the government mounted a major new effort on two fronts — to use them up by instituting new domestic food programs, such as Food Stamps, and to divert more acreage from production by paying farmers to keep their land idle. Both have been successful from the government's point of view, although both farmers and taxpayers may see it differently. And now that drought, famine, and civil wars are gripping one country after another, the world's supplies of food are dwindling — and we may once again hear a call for increased production.

What the Farmer Gets

Generally speaking, the farmer gets a 27 percent share of the retail price of his products. But various types of foodstuffs are handled differently from one another, and what with the cost of marketing, transportation, advertising, processing, packaging, and so on, his actual cut can be a movable feast. Here are some spot comparisons, based on information from the American Farm Bureau Federation:

Foodstuff	You pay	The farmer gets
1 pound of choice beef	$2.88	$1.60
1 pound of lemons	$1.23	$0.38
1 pound of green beans	$1.02	$0.11
1 pound of sugar	$0.40	$0.15
1 pound bag of potato chips	$1.96	$0.31
12-ounce box of oatmeal	$2.48	$0.14

The best fertilizer is the footprint of the farmer.

— Anonymous

BIG FARMS, BIG BUSINESS

American farming today is a Brobdingnagian under-taking — cultivation of the land on an enormous scale to feed a demanding and multitudinous population, all done by a relative handful of people, a mere 2.5 percent of the work force, or 2.8 million people, to be exact. The crop and grazing land they work comes to an astounding total of 983 million acres nationwide, and the only way to maintain it is by using machinery on a large scale, plus pesticides and synthetic fertilizers. Farmers find themselves locked in a cycle of inputs and outputs. To increase outputs (produce = profit), inputs must increase (these include bought-in fertilizers, pesticides, seeds, machines, and fuel). To keep up, most farmers have to borrow, and while the average debt-to-asset ratio is 15 percent, 40 percent is normal for many of them.

The technical knowledge now required by anyone running a large farm is greater than that required of a businessman with an equal investment, and the capital required is beyond the reach of most people. In making his decisions, the farmer has to draw on information from the biological, physical, and social sciences. Nor is ownership of the land and resources the only way to farm anymore. Farmers rent land, which enables them to increase the scale of their operations. Those who don't want to tie up their money in machinery can contract out the harvesting of their crops. Vegetables, fruits, and nuts may be picked under contract by shipper-packers whose crews move from farm to farm. The rental of machinery is commonplace; in

the northeastern United States, some dairy farmers even rent the cows.

The result is that American farmers feed America and other countries, too. About 44 percent of all the world-exported production of rice, wheat, corn, and soybeans comes from the United States. And American supermarkets are chockablock with choice foods of all descriptions at prices lower than in most other countries.

Report from the Ground Roots:

Farmers Make Profits But Crops Miss Rotation

Recently, the National Academy of Sciences surveyed the farm scene and discovered that government policies encourage the highest per-acre yield possible for a given crop. Under the current commodity program, it is too costly for farmers to use eligible corn acreage to rotate crops even though this is beneficial to the soil. Thus, most farmers plant the same crop in the same place each year. This method of farming established by politicians rather than farmers results in crops that are highly susceptible to insect damage,

and that fact in turn leads to the necessity of using large quantities of pesticides and contributes to the erosion of 1.6 billion tons of soil from 417 million acres each year.

Because rotation with nitrogen-fixing crops such as alfalfa is not economically feasible, the nutrient-starved land needs huge quantities of fertilizer to enable it to sustain the single crop. The fertilizer may boost the yield, but that which is not absorbed by plants is carried via eroded soil into streams, rivers, lakes, and ground-water where it endangers drinking water, encourages the growth of algae and other microorganisms, and alters the balance of nature.

Current farm policy also encourages the farmers to plant marginal farmland with crops that are far from ideally suited to the growing area. These

require disproportionately higher uses of chemicals and fungicides.

Unfortunately, there is no "single" or "right" answer to any of these problems. What is clear, though, is that we are going to have to come to grips with the notion that a battle rages between the militant naturalists (con-temporary shepherds and shepherdesses) and the might of industry. The truth may be that both camps are wrong — and right.

Agriculture cannot be an industrial process any more than music can be. It must be understood differently from stamping this metal into that shape. ... The major workers— the soil microorgan-isms, the fungi, the mineral particles, the sun, the air, the water — are all part of a system, and it is not just the employment of any one of them but the coordination of the whole which achieves success.

— Eliot Coleman
Environmental writer

The Beef Cattle Chain

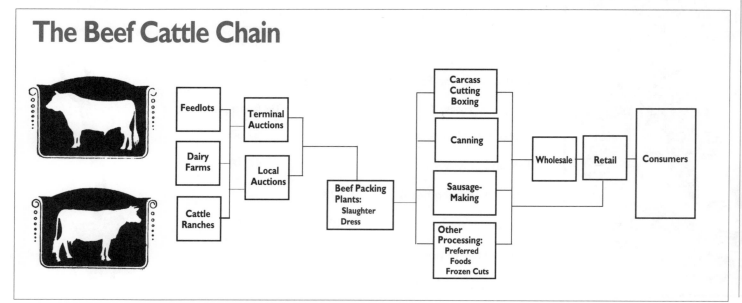

Feedlots → Terminal Auctions → Carcass Cutting Boxing / Canning / Sausage-Making / Other Processing: Preferred Foods Frozen Cuts → Wholesale → Retail → Consumers

Dairy Farms → Local Auctions → Beef Packing Plants: Slaughter Dress

Cattle Ranches

ANIMAL HUSBANDRY NEEDS A CARING TOUCH

BRYAN LYNAS

Animal husbandry in America today is geared to decades of "nutritional wisdom" that recommend a high-protein diet. But as the Worldwatch Institute puts it: "Abundance in the world's butcher shops has its costs — many of which are currently billed to the earth. Current methods of rearing animals around the world take a large toll on nature."

Almost half the energy used in agriculture in the United States goes into livestock rearing, and in California — now the major dairy state — one third of all irrigation water goes into animal production. On the great plains, beef feedlots depend on grain and fodder grown by irrigation at 13 trillion gallons of water each year. The federal government sells water from irrigation projects at a fraction of its real cost, which makes it possible for farmers to grow feed and fodder crops for livestock. Without the effective subsidy, estimated by Congress to be close to $1 billion, their efforts would more than likely be uneconomic.

The main problem is that current farming operations tend to be specialized. One farm may concentrate wholly on animals, producing tons of "waste" (i.e., fertilizer in the wrong place) which can't be economically used. Another farm grows corn or wheat, and buys in artificial fertilizers because there's no animal manure to spread on the fields. And so on down the line.

However, there is good news on the horizon. There are many people today who advocate a revolution in the way we produce food. Protests about pollution of soil, air, and water; about inhumane treatment of animals; about pesticide residues; about animal hormone and antibiotic treatments; about flavorless produce, are hitting the target. Sustainable agriculture is the coming vogue, based on a return to mixed, diversified farming in which animals play a vital role. This may sound like two steps backwards to an Amish life-style but it won't be; no farmer will be able to work his farm without machines and an increasingly high-tech approach.

Humans originally domesticated cattle to be beasts of burden. For millennia, draft animals have tilled fields but also have yielded food, fuel, fertilizer, and clothing. Cattle, goats, and sheep are adapted to live on tough grasses and it is this ability to survive on inedible fodder that has made them so useful to humans. These grazing animals provided us with food from land where soils were poor or rains too sparse for arable crops. Hogs and poultry like to forage for their food, but they also turn over the soil and convert some farm wastes and food scraps into meat and eggs. So animals became integrated into mixed farming, with their manures returned to the land as high-quality fertilizer.

The aim today is to reintegrate animals with crops for the benefit of all. This method invariably involves giving the animals more space to roam, an obvious and natural requirement. One result is less disease — and less need for antibiotics.

Studies by Cornell University researchers show that America can save enormously on natural resources, slashing energy inputs by 60 percent, by going for a sustainable livestock industry without feed grains. But there is a price to pay: It would yield only half the animal protein we get right now.

The bottom line is this: We don't have to stop eating meat, dairy products, and eggs; we just have to eat less of each. And studies tell us that the more moderate our consumption of animal products, the better our health will be.

PERIODICALS

For addresses, see also Information Sources

Food Review
ERS-NASS
341 Victory Drive
Herndon, VA 22070
800-999-6779
3 times a year; $17 per year

Food Watch Update
Agriculture Council of America
202-682-9200
Bimonthly; free

Science of Food and Agriculture
Council for Agricultural Science and Technology
515-292-2125
Biannual; $10 for 4 issues

Successful Farming Magazine
Meredith Corporation
1716 Locust Street
Des Moines, IA 50336
800-374-3276
12 times a year;
$14 per year

THE FARM OF THE FUTURE

Ten to 50 years in the future, a traditional farm is converted into a fully integrated system for producing energy, chemicals, plastics, and other products, in addition to food.

The traditional farmhouse (A) and barn (B) have a high-tech twist, receiving power from a photovoltaic array (C) and advanced windmill machines (D). Beside the barn is a grain storage and transfer system (E), and in front is a greenhouse (F). Livestock (G) provide manure that is transferred to a biogas plant. In the foreground, a truck (H) sprays fertilizer made from a by-product of the waste-management system. Beyond the farm is a plantation of trees (I) genetically created to grow to harvestable maturity in six to eight years.

Three sections of crops at the bottom left of the drawing (J) represent feedstocks such as switchgrass, sorghum, and corn that are grown for both food and fuel production. The central diagonal of the drawing illustrates several crop-to-product conversion facilities, including an ethanol fuels production plant (K), which transforms feedstocks into the alcohol-based fuel. One by-product is a dry material made into pellets for feed. To the right (L) is a facility for converting logs into biocrude, a petroleumlike material.

Another facility (M) converts biocrude into plastics, and another (N) uses wood chips, recycled paper, and sawdust to make paper. The biogas facility (O) converts cow manure into biogas, which is then converted into electricity and sent to the city via power lines.

The fountains at the upper left of the drawing (P) are sewage-treatment facilities, which draw out gas for electricity. To the right is the high-efficiency bioelectric plant (Q), which takes almost anything and burns it, producing steam-generated electricity. These facilities are also attached to the power grid (R) leading to the city on the horizon. All vehicles depicted operate on hybrid fuels and are highly efficient, running as much as 100 miles per gallon.

Reprinted from
The Futurist

Farming in a High-Tech World

Just a Thin Coat

Anti-Stress 2000 is a spray-on plastic coating for plants that, according to its makers, will help to protect crops from frost, heat, and other climate quirks. It's nontoxic, it stretches, and after a couple of months it biodegrades. Early tests showed that it protected lemon trees from frost.

It Must Have Been Moonglow

Plowing by moonlight could drastically cut the need for herbicide. A team from Oregon State University found that night plowing stops light-induced activation of buried, broad-leaf weed seeds. Night-plowed plots grew only half as many weeds as those plowed by day.

Stress-Busters

Plants manufacture their own form of aspirin — a powerful defense-system hormone that switches on immunity-enhancing genes. It turns out that we can help many plants in their battle against disease by using aspirin sprays. But that's not all. Methionine, an amino acid, and vitamin B-2 kill certain fungi and bacteria that cause plant diseases. The antioxidant vitamins C and E have similar effects, helping stressed plants back to vigor by stimulating them to help themselves.

Color Codes

The U.S. Department of Agriculture, not noted for its whimsy, reports that the color of mulch has an effect on the growth of plants. When red mulch was used on tomato beds, the result was a 20 percent increase in the yield. Potatoes prefer red mulch to white. Mulches in designer colors are being studied for the increased production of green, red, yellow, orange, and black peppers.

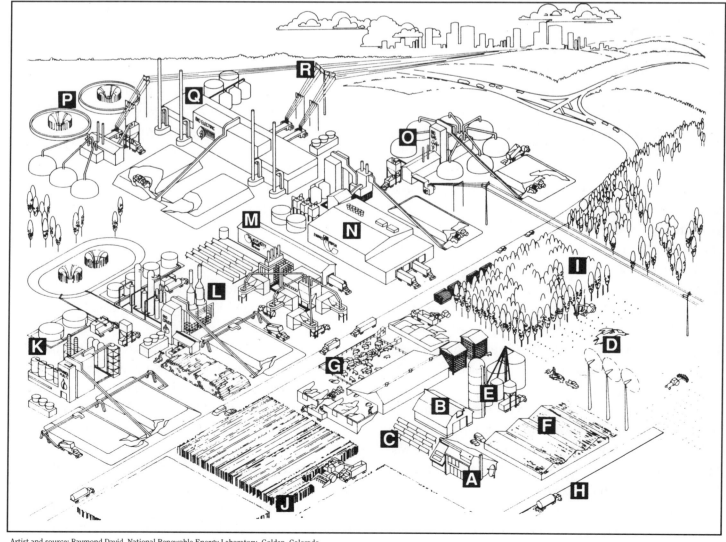

Artist and source: Raymond David, National Renewable Energy Laboratory, Golden, Colorado

THERE'S NO PLACE LIKE A FARM

JANEEN ALETTA SARLIN

Tractors Run on Software

Thomas Colvin, an agricultural engineer at the National Soil Tilth Laboratory in Ames, Iowa, has linked government satellites and tractor-mounted computers to tell farmers where to apply fertilizer or pesticides and how much to use. First you create a computer database, including detailed information about soil and crop conditions for each acre of a given field. Then you equip a base station and your tractor with radio receivers able to pick up signals from 21 satellites orbiting the earth as part of the Department of Defense's global positioning system. A tractor-mounted computer uses these signals to plot the exact position of the tractor as it moves across the field. Colvin's system correlates information from the database with the tractor's position and calculates adjustments in the amount of chemicals to be applied.

Colvin has named his system JANUS: Joint Agricultural Navigation Using Satellites, and says that owners of big farms in the Midwest have talked to him about trying it in their fields, at a cost of about $50,000 each.

Excerpted from
Harrowsmith Country Life

Farm life is about the balance between nature's way and human needs. Farmers provide food — both directly to the people and for the animals that nourish people, who in turn nurture the land — that supports the food chain. Farm life is seasonal: frantic summer fieldwork; the satisfying fall harvest; winter — when we "rest," repair the machinery, fix things around the house; and then spring and the blossoming of new life. This cyclical phenomenon directs, undermines, and surprises, breathing life and death with an even hand. In the barnyard, the strong and the hearty live, but the weak and the sickly pass on. The old dog dies, but each year of her life she whelped a litter of puppies.

Farmers talk freely about these everyday occurrences. They are friendly, curious, and interested. Because the drive down an unpaved gravel road in the country is slower than on smooth, paved state highways, the farmer can observe the progress of a crop, determine the immediate condition of the farmyard and the buildings, check out the progress in the garden, and notice that a new calf is nursing. If you on your drive observe a farmer (or his wife) plowing, cultivating, picking corn, combining soybeans, or cutting hay, wave to him. He will wave back, often wondering to himself, "Who is that fellow (or that lady)? That's a different car for these parts. I wonder where he (or she) is going." His concern is genuine, though guarded at times in front of strangers.

The farmer conducts his business face-to-face; he would no more think of calling you on the phone for an appointment than he would give his prize bull away. Instead, he will hop in his pickup and drive over to see you about the business at hand. Food naturally is incorporated into all visits — a cup of coffee and a fresh doughnut at the neighbors, the extra chair pulled up to the dinner table for someone who "just happened to be in the area." Even a quick trip to town to get a part fixed ends with an ice cream cone and a "Fine weather we're having . . ." at Hansen's drugstore. Then there are the daily meals, organized gatherings, impromptu socials, and grand traditional holiday family dinners.

Most babies in the 19th century and the early part of the 20th century were birthed in the same beds where their mothers and grandmothers were born. Not only Grams and Granddad, but Mom and Dad as well were born on the "home place" where their families farmed. Although my brother and sisters and I were born in a hospital, we thrived, learned, loved, and laughed on our farm.

"Our Farm" is a 160-acre piece of land in southern Minnesota. It is located in the section of this great country that borders the northern edge of the Iowa Corn Belt. As the crow flies over the fertile rolling hills heading north, he'll see strips of rich black dirt and green alfalfa or clover. There next to that patterned field is a cluster of buildings, surrounded by trees, with a vegetable garden and flower patch and the dog — the home place.

Life on our farm was romantic, humorous, and full of adventure. We shared sadness and happiness with our friends, family, and neighbors, and everyone worked very hard.

Excerpted from *Food from an American Farm*

FAST FOOD

*There are only two things
our customers have,
time and money —
and they don't like
spending either of them,
so we better
sell them their
hamburgers quickly.*

— James McLamore
Founder of Burger King

The Top Ten Chains

Chain	Systemwide Sales (in billions of dollars)
McDonald's	13.99
Burger King	6.50
Pizza Hut	4.78
Hardee's	4.15
Taco Bell	3.64
Wendy's	3.61
KFC	3.60
Marriott Management Services	2.50
Little Caesar's Pizza	2.31
Domino's Pizza	2.20

Source: *Nation's Restaurant News*

☎ HOTLINES

For consumer inquiries

800-2-ADVISE
Arby's

800-YES-1800
Burger King

708-575-FOOD
McDonald's

800-262-1744
Pizza Hut

800-735-8226
Taco Bell

800-443-7266
Wendy's

Two-all-beef-patties-special-sauce-lettuce-cheese-pickles-onions on-a-sesame-seed-bun

Invocations like this fill the air at the eating establish ments that have become the sanctums of our inner cities and the beacons for travelers on America's network of long, long roads. They offer clean, air-conditioned, brightly lit, plant-filled environments, with soft music, spotless bathrooms, and somebody else to do the cooking.

People of all ages, all income groups, and diverse ethnic backgrounds congregate here, seeking the instant gratification of being waited on and served a filling meal at an affordable price within 60 seconds, more or less. Countless babies' first taste of solid food is a french fry, and by the time their two front teeth appear, ketchup is flowing through their veins.

The restaurants that initially limited their role to the service of fast, cheap, easy-to-eat food have recognized their essential niche in the community and learned to change with the times. They are lengthening their long arm to reach the older population by expanding their seating areas, providing table service, and offering grown-up beverages — and luring families with young children to their brightly colored play spaces as well as with the promise of gifts along with dinner.

Street-smart fast-fooderies recognized long ago that working mothers are not seeking methods of making cooking easier; they are looking for an economical, guilt-free way of avoiding cooking altogether.

A BURGER KING FRY WORK STATION

ESTER REITER

The fries arrive in the store in plastic bags, frozen and precut. About two hours before serving, a worker removes them from the bag and places them in a fry rack. There are explicit directions for every step in this process, including how to empty the frozen fries from the bags and place them in the wire baskets. Workers must line up three (or four) baskets in a row and shake the bag six (or eight) times, working their way across the baskets and then back again to create an even distribution.

A worker wheels the rack filled with fry baskets over to the fryer, which contains two vats of oil in which four fry baskets can cook simultaneously. The crewperson on fry station places the fry basket on a lift arm above the hot oil and presses a computer button that causes the arm to lower the basket into the shortening. When the fries are ready, a buzzer sounds and the lift arm automatically raises the basket of fries out of the shortening. A worker then empties the fry basket into the fry bagging station and bags the fries with a special scoop designed to control the portion of each bag of fries. Each move in the bagging process — how to pick up the scoop, how to hold the bags, how to scoop up the fries — is described in careful detail in the manual.

Each move in the preparation of fries is timed: 7 seconds are allotted to placing the fry basket in the fry pot, 13 seconds to dumping the fries into the bagging station and returning the basket to the holding rack, 5 seconds to filling the first bag in the bagging cycle, and 3 seconds to packing each subsequent one.

Fry portioning is watched particularly carefully: Despite the special scoop used, the bags can still be filled too much for management's taste. Indeed, most people like being generous because the counter people get complaints if they offer skimpy portions.

Excerpted from *Making Fast Food: From the Frying Pan into the Fryer*

MAKING INFORMED CHOICES

PAT BAIRD, R.D.

American fast-food restaurants keep customers coming back because they are quick and convenient, and the foods are familiar and consistent, no matter where in the world you eat them. But it may take awareness and planning to achieve a really nutritious meal.

Foods served in these restaurants tend to be low in fiber, high in sodium, and loaded with calories from fat, particularly saturated fat. In all fairness, we should remember that when most of these chains started, that's how most Americans ate — we were a meat-and-potatoes population. In the intervening years, evidence has emerged about the relationship of diet and health. In response to the nutrition concerns of consumers, and their demands for more nutrition information, many of the chains have developed nutrition analyses of their food and beverage items. Most companies now provide this information in brochures at the counter.

Try to make choices at fast-food restaurants the same way you make choices at any other time during the day. Always consider the principles that form the backbone of the Food Guide Pyramid: Variety, Balance, and Moderation. Choose foods from each of the Pyramid's layers, or food groups. Remember that no one food supplies all of the protein, vitamins, and minerals you need for good health.

You can incorporate *variety* with food selections you make throughout the day. Vary choices wherever you go. In a fast-food restaurant have a soft drink one time and low-fat milk the next. Order fries on one visit, a salad on the next.

Balance what you're ordering with what you have had, or are going to have, in the rest of the day. You can have just about whatever you want — even if you make the higher fat choices — when you balance out the day's other meals. For instance, if you've decided that nothing can replace your favorite deluxe burger with the works, then simply fit it into your eating agenda for the day. To accommodate the burger and fries, choose a lower-fat breakfast — a bagel, fat-free yogurt, or cereal with skim milk; and for dinner have some poached fish with lots of vegetables, or perhaps rice or pasta and a light sauce, with some fresh fruit for dessert.

Moderation lies in planning your menu selections, and choosing average portion sizes. At right are some notes about the major fast-food chains and suggested selections from their menus.

Make-the-Right-Choice Sample Menus

McDonald's has been providing nutrition information to consumers since 1973. There are cards with specifics on food exchanges and calories, fat, cholesterol, and sodium in every restaurant. The company has also added highly nutritious menu items.

In 1986, McDonald's introduced fresh salads. Only 100 percent vegetable oil is used for frying, all the shakes and frozen yogurts served are 99 percent fat-free, and all milk is 1 percent low-fat. Whole-grain cereals are on the breakfast menu, as well as fat-free and cholesterol-free blueberry and apple-bran muffins. Fat in the Big Mac sauce has been reduced; so has the fat content of the tartar sauce used in the Filet-O-Fish sandwiches. Margarine has replaced butter in all McDonald's restaurants, fat and calories have been reduced in some salad dressings, and shredded carrots have replaced shredded cheese on salads. In 1991, the company introduced the McLean Deluxe, which is 91 percent fat-free and contains just 10 grams of fat.

Breakfast
- Wheaties or Cheerios Whole-Grain Cereal
- 1 percent Low-Fat Milk, 8 ounces
- Orange Juice, 6 ounces
  270 calories, 3 grams fat, 10 milligrams cholesterol, 340 milligrams sodium

Substitute McDonald's Fat-Free Apple-Bran Muffin for the cereal, and the count becomes 370 calories, 2 grams fat, 10 milligrams cholesterol, 330 milligrams sodium

- Scrambled Eggs
- English Muffin
- Orange/Grapefruit Juice, 6 ounces
  390 calories, 14 grams fat, 425 milligrams cholesterol, 560 milligrams sodium

Lunch or Dinner
- Chunky Chicken Salad, Lite Vinaigrette Dressing, 1 packet
- Iced Tea, medium
  198 calories, 6 grams fat, 78 milligrams cholesterol, 470 milligrams sodium

- McLean Deluxe
- Side Salad, Lite Vinaigrette Dressing, 1/2 packet
- Diet Coke, small
  375 calories, 12 grams fat, 93 milligrams cholesterol, 845 milligrams sodium

- Chicken Fajita
- Vanilla Low-Fat Frozen Yogurt Cone
- Diet Coke, medium
  297 calories, 9 grams fat, 38 milligrams cholesterol, 415 milligrams sodium

Some meals at Burger King may be low-calorie and low-fat, but quite high in sodium. For example, the BK Broiler Chicken Sandwich provides 280 calories, 10 grams fat, and 770 milligrams sodium. The Chunky Chicken Salad is a better choice, providing 142 calories, 4 grams fat, and 443 milligrams sodium. If sodium is a concern, request that salt be omitted from the preparation.

Lunch or Dinner
- BK Broiler Sandwich
- Side Salad with Light Italian Dressing
- Diet Coke, medium
  335 calories, 11 grams fat, 50 milligrams cholesterol, 1480 milligrams sodium

- Chunky Chicken Salad with Light Italian Dressing
- French Fries, medium (salted)
- Orange Juice, 6.5 ounces
  626 calories, 25 grams fat, 49 milligrams cholesterol, 1393 milligrams sodium

Jack in the Box has a new brochure that provides complete nutritional information for menu items. Also included are suggested meal combinations and some "good health tips" on such subjects as learning more about your body, maintaining a healthy weight, eating regular meals, etc. The brochure also gives a graphic of the Food Guide Pyramid and the number of servings suggested in each food group.

Breakfast
- Breakfast Jack
- Orange Juice, 6.5 ounces
  490 calories, 13 grams fat, 203 milligrams cholesterol, 871 milligrams sodium

- Sourdough Breakfast Sandwich
- Orange Juice, 6.5 ounces
  564 calories, 20 grams fat, 236 milligrams cholesterol, 1120 milligrams sodium

Lunch or Dinner
- Hamburger
- Side Salad with Low-Calorie Italian Dressing
- Diet Coke, small
  344 calories, 16 grams fat, 26 milligrams cholesterol, 1485 milligrams sodium (Not for those watching sodium)

- Chef Salad
- Diet Coke, small
  325 calories, 18 grams fat, 142 milligrams cholesterol, 900 milligrams sodium

- Chicken Fajita Pita
- Diet Coke, small
  293 calories, 8 grams fat, 34 milligrams cholesterol, 738 milligrams sodium

Wendy's was the first company in the fast-food industry to introduce baked potatoes and salad bars nationwide. The chain offers many lower-fat food choices, including the Grilled Chicken Sandwich, the Chili, and Wendy's Garden Spot Salad Bar. Two tablespoons of Wendy's Reduced-Calorie Italian Dressing provide only 50 calories and 4 grams of fat, but 340 milligrams of sodium. If sodium is a concern, try pairing 1 tablespoon of Salad Oil (120 calories, 14 grams fat, 0 milligrams sodium) and 1 tablespoon Wine Vinegar (2 calories, less than 1 gram fat, and only a trace of sodium). Beware of Wendy's Superbars, where the prepared salads are loaded with mayonnaise and oily dressings.

Lunch or Dinner
- Grilled Chicken Sandwich
- Side Salad with Reduced-Calorie Dressing
- Diet Coke, small
    500 calories, 14 grams fat, 60 milligrams cholesterol, 1210 milligrams sodium

- Small Chili, 9 ounces
- Side Salad with Reduced-Calorie Dressing
- Iced Tea, small
    250 calories, 9 grams fat, 40 milligrams cholesterol, 870 milligrams sodium

- Fresh Salad To Go
- Deluxe Garden Salad with Reduced-Calorie Dressing
- Baked Potato
- Diet Coke, small

461 calories, 9 grams fat, 0 grams cholesterol, 750 milligrams sodium

Hardee's

Hardee's offers a selection of healthful options for breakfast and lunch or dinner that are lower in fat and also lower in calories. Three Pancakes are an option at breakfast; healthier options at lunch and dinner include the Regular Roast Beef Sandwich, Grilled Chicken Breast Sandwich, and the Garden Salad.

Breakfast
- Three Pancakes
- 1 percent Low-Fat Milk
- Orange Juice
    530 calories, 4 grams fat, 25 milligrams cholesterol, 1025 milligrams sodium

Lunch or Dinner
- Grilled Chicken Breast Sandwich
- Side Salad with Fat-Free Dressing
- Diet Coke, medium
    331 calories, 9 grams fat, 60 milligrams cholesterol, 905 milligrams sodium

- Hamburger
- Garden Salad with Fat-Free French Dressing
- Diet Coke, medium
    445 calories, 22 grams fat, 64 milligrams cholesterol, 760 milligrams sodium

Founding Fathers

RAY KROC

Ray Kroc was over 50, and selling milk-shake mixers for a living when, one day in 1954, he walked into a busy little hamburger restaurant in San Bernardino, California. The next day he returned and persuaded the proprietors, the McDonald brothers, to let him franchise their ideas.

DAVID R. THOMAS

Dave Thomas had made a million dollars in fast food, turning around losing Kentucky Fried Chicken restaurants, before he struck out on his own, in Columbus, Ohio, in 1969, with the first Wendy's (named for his daughter).

Big MacCurrencies

Since 1986, *The Economist* **has been using a so-called Big Mac index as a rough-and-ready means of determining whether currencies are at their correct exchange rate — "as a tool to make exchange-rate theory more digestible." The most recent chart sets the price of a Stateside Big Mac, including sales tax, as $2.28, and lists the costs of local Big Macs in 24 of the 66 countries where they are now available, translated into U.S. dollars. The magazine goes on to derive values such as purchasing power parity and over- and undervaluation from these comparisons; here we list simply the comparative costs of what** *The Economist* **calls "the perfect universal commodity."**

THE HAMBURGER STANDARD		
Country	**Prices in local currency**	**Prices in dollars**
United States	$2.28	2.28
Argentina	Peso3.60	3.60
Australia	A$2.45	1.76
Belgium	BFr109	3.36
Brazil	Cr77,000	2.80
Britain	£1.79	2.79
Canada	C$2.76	2.19
China	Yuan8.50	1.50
Denmark	DKr25.75	4.25
France	FFr18.50	3.46
Germany	DM4.60	2.91
Holland	Fl5.45	3.07
Hong Kong	HK$9.00	1.16
Hungary	Forint157	1.78
Ireland	I£1.48	2.29
Italy	Lire4,500	2.95
Japan	Yen391	3.45
Malaysia	Ringgit3.35	1.30
Mexico	Peso7.09	2.29
Russia	Ruble780	1.14
South Korea	Won2,300	2.89
Spain	Ptas325	2.85
Sweden	SKr25.50	3.43
Switzerland	SwFr5.80	3.94
Thailand	Baht48	1.91

Source: *The Economist*, based on exchange rates of April 13, 1993

Did You Know?

☞ Burger King's ideal fry yield: 410 portions of fries for each 100 pounds of precut potatoes used.

☞ Every day Americans eat 14 million hamburgers.

☞ The National Restaurant Association projects that fast-food restaurant sales will hit $86 billion in 1994, outperforming full-service restaurants for the first time ever.

☞ The largest McDonald's in the world has 700 seats and 29 cash registers. It is in Beijing.

☞ Those sprinklings of sesame seeds on McDonald's buns amount in one year to 2,500 tons.

☞ Forty-seven percent of the U.S. food dollar is spent away from home.

1993 Consumer Choices

Every year *Restaurants & Institutions* magazine conducts a poll to determine America's favorite chain restaurants. Here are the 1993 winners:

Burgers
Wendy's

Cafeterias/Buffets
Old Country Buffet

Dinner Houses
The Olive Garden

Family Dining
Cracker Barrel

Mexican
Chi-Chi's

Pizza
Pizza Hut

Sandwiches
Rax Restaurants

Seafood
Red Lobster

Steak Houses
Golden Corral

Sweets
Baskin-Robbins

FAT

FAT-FREE DOESN'T EQUAL
NO PRICE TO PAY

Fat has become the most feared word in the language. Cutting back is difficult, abstinence damn near impossible, and banning fat merely enhances its appeal.

Fat is what makes food taste sublime. It's that elusive, smooth slide across the tongue that makes you close your eyes and moan, Mmm.

Fat is what makes a steak taste tender and juicy. It causes croissants to crackle and keeps cookies crisp, crackers brittle, and ice cream smooth. Fat is the element in food that carries its flavor; without it, the taste is flat, dry, and unsatisfying. Take away the fat and we feel deprived. We *are* deprived.

We may not see the fat in our food, but we detect its absence when it is replaced by technology in the form of gums, starches, and laboratory-formulated substitutes.

The FDA has begun to approve synthetic fat substitutes for commercial use. Already on the market is the Nutra-Sweet Company's product Simplesse, a low-calorie, zero-cholesterol, all-natural fat substitute composed of whipped protein obtained from milk and egg whites. Simplesse can replace the fat in cold foods such as ice cream, salad dressings, cheese spreads, and yogurt, but it cannot be used in cooking. Meanwhile, Procter & Gamble is gambling that its Olestra will become a $10 billion industry practically overnight, but is still poised on tippy toe awaiting the kiss of acceptance. According to its manufacturers, Olestra will remove all the disagreeable nutritional consequences of eating *real* fat by tricking our taste buds into believing they are onto something equally good.

Olestra, which is a compound of sugar and fatty acids, is designed, when used with other oils, to reduce the fat content in fried foods. This amounts to nothing less than a giant step in culinary evolution and a welcome one at that. Olestra, they say, will taste like fat, but slide unnoticed past the body's detection mechanisms, leaving not a trace of its presence and without depositing an extra ounce of weight. It is what is called, politely, digestively inert — although, when pressed, some of the testers admitted, quietly, that they had had a little bit of diarrhea. Olestra's manufacturers say they have fixed this problem.

These and no doubt other yet-to-be-devised fat substitutes are sure to provide a major boost to the snack food industry, which has been suffering (slightly) from our concerns about health.

For the first time in history we are making a conscious attempt to make our food less nutritious so that we can look better in a bathing suit.

Meanwhile, we may have to settle for food that is labeled "fat-free," meaning that it contains less than half a gram of fat in a serving — a very small serving. It is time to revise the old dictum that man cannot live on bread alone. Bread alone is what's on our plate now. It's not buttered on both sides; it's not even buttered on one side. The saints are marching thin.

Chewing the Fat

Bulging files of conclusive evidence have led the American Heart Association, the U.S. Department of Agriculture, the National Cancer Institute, and the National Institutes of Health as well as other government agencies to recommend that Americans reduce their intake of calories derived from fat from the current level of 37 percent to 30 percent. A reduction of 7 percent is considered do-able, although other leading researchers, including Dr. Dean Ornish, insist that our dietary fat intake should be considerably lower. They are probably right, but for many people such radical changes seem too difficult to achieve. As always, success depends on individual motivation.

BEFORE

AFTER

The reason fat people are happy is that the nerves are well protected.

— Luciano Pavarotti
Tenore robusto

FACING THE FATS

Saturated fats are almost all derived from animal origins and are found in meat, poultry, and butter. They are solid at room temperature. These are the ones to avoid because they tend to raise blood cholesterol levels. Tropical oils, such as coconut oil, are plant oils, but they are high in saturated fats; however, these do not become solid at room temperature.

Polyunsaturated fats come from plants and include safflower, soybean, sunflower, corn, and cottonseed oils. They are liquid at room temperature and do not raise blood cholesterol levels. They should be used in moderation.

Monounsaturated fats include canola, peanut, and olive oils. They help reduce levels of LDL (the bad) cholesterol, so these, along with polyunsaturated oils, are the ones to choose and use, again in moderation.

Hydrogenated fats are those that begin as liquid fats but are solidified by adding hydrogen, which causes them to harden. As a result of this procedure, the fats act like undesirable saturated fats, and like them, should be eaten sparingly. Crisco, margarine, and some commercial peanut butters fall within this category. Read labels to find the amount of saturated fat in hydrogenated products.

Big Fatties

Food	Amount	Total fat (in grams)	Calories
Salad or cooking oil	2 tablespoons	28	250
Whipping cream	½ cup	44	410
Ice cream bar	Haägen-Dazs	23	320
Peanut butter	2 tablespoons	16	190
Avocado	½ medium-sized	15	153
Doughnut	1 plain	11	190
Mayonnaise	1 tablespoon	11	100
Butter and margarine	1 tablespoon	11	100
French fries	20 (about 3 ounces)	13	274
Fritos	1 ounce	10	155
Potato chips	10	7	105
Bacon	2 slices	6	73
Almonds	1 ounce	15	167
Cheesecake	¹⁄₁₂ of cake	13	278
Croissant	4½ x 4 x 2¾ inches	12	235
Apple pie	⅙ of pie	18	405
Tuna, chunk, packed in oil	4 ounces	21	285

Fat Has Virtues, Too

As nutritionists know, fat is a vital nutrient. Like carbohydrates and protein, dietary fat is an important source of energy for the body. In fact, fat is the most concentrated source of energy in the diet, providing 9 calories per gram as compared with 4 calories per gram from either carbohydrates or protein.

Dietary fat supplies essential fatty acids, such as linoleic acid, which is especially important for young children's proper growth. Fat also is required for maintenance of healthy skin, regulation of cholesterol metabolism, and as a precursor of prostaglandins, the hormonelike substances that regulate some body processes. An excess of fat in the diet, however, is increasingly being recognized as a risk factor influencing the development of several chronic diseases.

> *No diet will remove all the fat from your body because the brain is entirely fat. Without a brain you might look good, but all you could do is run for public office.*
>
> — Covert Bailey
> Noted fitness expert

MORE INFORMATION

National Center for Nutrition and Diet
American Dietetic Association
216 West Jackson Boulevard
Chicago, IL 60606-6995
800-366-1655

HOTLINES

800-366-1655
American Dietetic Association
8 a.m. - 8 p.m., CST

Fear of Fat

According to the *Nutrition Action Health Letter*, in 1984, 8 percent of shoppers said that they were more concerned about fat than anything else to do with their food; in 1992, the number of concerned shoppers had risen to 48 percent.

FIBER

"Is it a high fiber cracker?"

WHAT IS FIBER?

Our grandmothers called it "roughage" and in all well-regulated households it has long been known that roughage is good for you — the secret of regularity, in fact.

Fiber has no nutritional value whatsoever. It doesn't even break down during its long journey through the digestive system. Think of it instead as a personal scouring pad for internal use only.

Fiber is not a specific thing, like a piece of old rope, but a complex of components, all of which are found in plants. Almost all fiber-containing foods have a combination of both soluble and insoluble fibers. This is fortunate because we should be eating both kinds in order to have a sunny disposition and a happy outlook on life. Show me a grinch and I'll show you a person who hasn't eaten his fiber today.

Soluble fibers come from fruits, vegetables, dried beans and peas, barley, and some cereals such as oats. Soluble fiber seems to affect the absorption of substances into the bloodstream and reduce cholesterol levels, so it can play a beneficial role in alleviating diabetes and heart disease.

Insoluble fibers are found in whole-grain foods including brans, whole-wheat and other cereals, and the skins and peels of vegetables and fruits. Apart from its valuable role as roughage, insoluble fiber is very good at making us feel we have had quite enough to eat, enabling us to push ourselves away from the table. It may also aid in preventing colon cancer.

Bread is one of the most readily available sources of fiber, but be careful about the kind of bread and its ingredients. *Unbleached flour* has no meaning in terms of fiber content; *enriched flour* may or may not contain fiber, depending on whether the fiber (or bran) removed in the milling was put back along with the vitamins and minerals added to enrich the flour. *Multigrain breads* also may not necessarily contain fiber, despite their reassuring title. To be sure what you are getting, read the label carefully.

A commercially prepared bread labeled "high in fiber" may contain only just enough bran to enable the label to be legally used. If the first ingredient listed is anything other than whole-grain flour, the bread is not the kind you want. But if one slice of a bread is listed as containing two or three grams of fiber, grab it at once and spread it with mashed beans. It will keep you on the go.

Q&A

Q How much fiber is enough?

A Don't worry, you are most unlikely to be getting more than enough. "They" say we should be eating a lot more fiber than we are: at least 20 to 30 grams a day. Most of us consume less than 11 grams.

Books

Fabulous Fiber Cookery
Elaine Groen and Jane Rubey; Bristol Publishing, 1988; $8.95

The Moosewood Cookbook
Mollie Katzen; Ten Speed Press, 1992; $19.95/$16.95

FIGS

LET'S GIVE A FIG

The fig, a member of the mulberry family, has been cultivated since Adam and Eve set the fashion for fig leaves, a movement toward modesty encouraged by some of our lawmakers to this day. California's fig growers describe their product as nature's most nearly perfect fruit. Figs have more dietary fiber than prunes, bran flakes, broccoli, or popcorn, and just five little figs pack 60 percent more potassium than one banana. Ounce for ounce, figs are also higher in calcium than cow's milk, though a lot less convenient. To get approximately the amount of calcium contained in a pint and a half of milk, you would have to consume a pound and a quarter of dried figs, which could be a digestive nightmare.

Whether green, brown, or purple, fresh or dried, figs have something in them for everyone.

Shape is a good part of the fig's delight.

— Jane Grigson
British food writer

MORE INFORMATION

California Fig Advisory Board/California Fig Institute
P.O. Box 709
Fresno, CA 93712
209-445-5626

Valley Fig Growers
P.O. Box 1987
Fresno, CA 93718
209-237-3893

FLAVORINGS

~ EATING WELL ~

petit.roulet

FLAVOR ME CINNAMON

As the demand for low-fat and reduced-calorie foods and beverages surges ever onward, large companies that specialize in creating flavorings are expanding their operations. Adding tastes that are lost in processing to reduce the fat content that once gave foods their special flavors is just a small part of the flavor-makers' capabilities. All foods that are to be frozen must be given heightened flavor because freezing will mute their tastes. The act of microwaving convenience foods such as TV dinners and pasta side dishes will destroy their flavor compounds, and flavors must be added to replace those that are lost.

According to Jeffrey Kluger, writing in *Discover* magazine, "In the United States alone there are more than 75 different companies working full-time to churn out artificial flavors. Each of these labs serves hundreds of brand-name food manufacturers, who buy the labs' inventions and put them into nearly everything we eat, from TV dinners to tacos to Tootsie Rolls."

Flavor-makers create roasted, baked, fried, or brothy chicken flavors for hundreds of uses ranging from pan-dripped beef flavors for burgers, tallow flavor for potato chips and fries, or deep, dark woodland flavor for mushrooms. They create distinctive tastes for cheese, yogurt, and other dairy products. The scientists provide the tastes for deli and other meats, as well as fruit extracts for everything from ice cream to herbal teas. They can make drab rice cakes taste like buttered popcorn without increasing their calorie or fat content; they can fabricate a flavor, real or imaginary, for dozens of snack foods, candies, and coffees.

In fact, if a food has a distinctive taste, the chances are good that it has received a boost from the laboratory. The interesting thing is that, given a choice, we often prefer what we have come to accept as the "real" taste of artificial or synthetic flavors to the *real* taste.

But make mine a Ben & Jerry's Rocky Road, please.

The Mighty IFF

International Flavors & Fragrances is the world's leader in creating and producing the intense tastes found in many of the new clear beverages that are so vibrant they could almost change the color of contact lenses. And as IFF's own literature makes plain, the palette of titillating tastes for fresh culinary products is being constantly expanded:

"Our marketing groups continually track flavor preferences worldwide for all beverage categories. Mango or apple. Durian or orange.

"We've collaborated with customers on flavors for every type of processing — retorted, aseptic, frozen, refrigerated, or fresh — in whatever packaging form you choose. . . .

"With our network of flavor laboratories, staffed by local experts and serving 107 countries, we are strategically positioned to create and provide flavors that appeal to the tastes of adults and children, region by region. . . .

"Think of flavors to enhance corn or masa. Think of onion or other savory flavors to fortify the impact of many snacks. Think of chicken, prawn, beef, pepperoni, mushroom, scallion, garlic, sesame, and other flavors for topical or internal use. If it makes snacks taste good, IFF's got it." Got it.

As described by Ursula Sohn, spokeswoman, Quest International: "Flavors are extremely complicated things. A flavorist may sit down with, say, a mango flavor and notice a sweetness, a tang, a tartness, a whole range of things. Then he'll go to a shelf and say, 'Well, citric acid has one of these flavor components, another type of acid has another component,' and on and on. After a long time and dozens of ingredients, he'll assemble the entire mango. It's really remarkable when it all comes together into a complete flavor."

A Flavor Sampler

Tastemaker is a group that develops "brilliant, extraordinary flavors, custom-created for each new product by the world's most talented flavorists." The range of flavors spans natural, artificial, or natural *and* artificial flavors, extracts, seasoning blends, oils, and essences; they are available in liquid, dry, and paste forms. Among the 290 tastes ranging from Almond, Roasted, to Yogurt:

Asparagus	**Oat**
Beef (10 flavors, from Crusty to Rare Juicy)	**Oriental, Fry Peanut**
Butter, Sautéed	**Passionfruit**
Cantaloupe	**Pepperoni**
Charbroil	**Plum Pudding**
Cheese (11 flavors, from Alfredo to White Cheddar)	**Pork (6 flavors, from Fatty to Low Sodium)**
Cherry-Apricot	**Quince**
Chrysanthemum	**Ranch**
Crab Apple	**Replacers (5 flavors, from Beef Extract to Salt)**
Fried Flavor	**Rhubarb**
Ginseng	**Sarsaparilla**
Guacamole	**Sour Cream & Onion**
Lychee	**Thai Peanut**
Mixed Grain	**Tutti Frutti**
Mixed Vegetables	**Watermelon**
Mushroom	**Yeast Types**
Nacho	

FLOUNDER

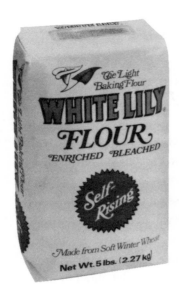

FISHERMEN RARELY FLOUNDER WHEN SELLING SOLE

Flounder and *sole* are used interchangeably in American fish markets, but they are names for biologically different species. True soles have thicker bodies and are more oblong in shape than flounders, but the early settlers, who ate sole as often as they could get it in Europe, were thrilled to discover solelike fish off the Canadian and American coasts and called many of these flounders soles.

The Seafood Leader, an industry publication, informs us that bottom-dwelling flounder and sole are near the top of the list of fish preferred worldwide. "About 540 species of Pleuronectiformes are recognized in 117 genera and six families, but fewer than 20 are commercially viable," it continues. "They range in size from the pan-sized rex sole to the 500-pound Pacific and Atlantic halibut."

Pleuronectiformes are better known to most of us as flatfish, so called for obvious reasons. As well as flounder and sole, the order includes brill, dab, sanddab, fluke, plaice, turbot, halibut, and a fish called whiff. All are asymmetrical, with both eyes on one side of their head, and are the only vertebrates that are arranged in this way. Though peculiar to us, it makes perfect sense for a bottom-dwelling fish to have both eyes available for looking upward, but why some species look right and others left is less clear. When the fish is young the eyes are not in their final position, but they gradually move around in all but a few species, such as starry flounder, which has eyes on either side of the top of its head.

Usually, the eyed side is dark and the blind side white. So if you want to catch a flounder unawares, approach it on the blind side. (In fact, most flatfish live at depths where seeing is almost impossible, and are harvested by trawlers.)

Did You Know?

☞ English sole is not found in England. It's a small Pacific flounder.

☞ Dover sole *is* found in England, but not in America. All genuine Dover soles sold in U.S. restaurants are imported, usually by air, from European waters.

☞ Lemon sole is the American name for a winter flounder weighing more than three pounds. Flounders lighter than three pounds are known as blackbacks.

FLOUR

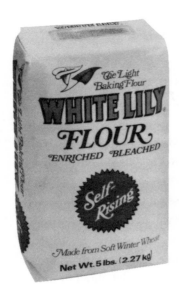

Any Southerner worth his piecrust knows that White Lily is the only flour worth stocking in the larder.

— **Richard David Story**
New York magazine

FLOUR POWER

SHARON TYLER HERBST

Most supermarkets carry *steel-ground flour,* meaning it's crushed with huge, high-speed steel rollers or hammers. The heat that is generated with these high-velocity machines strips away the wheat germ and destroys valuable vitamins and enzymes.

The more naturally nutritious *stone-ground flour* is produced by grinding the grain between two slowly moving stones. This process crushes the grain without generating excess heat and separating the germ. Stone-ground flours must usually be purchased in health-food stores, though some large supermarkets also carry them.

A flour can range in texture from coarse to extremely soft and powdery, depending on the degree of sifting it receives at the mill. Wheat is the most common source of the multitude of flours used in cooking. It contains *gluten,* a protein which forms an elastic network that helps contain the gases that make mixtures (such as doughs and batters) rise as they bake.

All-purpose flour is made from a blend of high-gluten hard wheat and low-gluten soft wheat. It's a fine-textured flour milled from the inner part of the wheat kernel and contains neither the *germ* (the sprouting part) nor the *bran* (the outer coating). U.S. law requires that all flours not containing wheat germ must have niacin, riboflavin, thiamine, and iron added. (Individual millers sometimes also add vitamins A and D.) These flours are labeled "enriched." All-purpose flour comes in two basic forms — *bleached* and *unbleached* — that can be used interchangeably. Flour can be bleached either naturally, as it ages, or chemically. Most flour on the market today is presifted, requiring only that it be stirred, then spooned into a measuring cup and leveled off.

Bread flour is a specially formulated, high-gluten blend of 99.9 percent hard-wheat flour, a small amount of malted barley flour (to improve yeast activity), and vitamin C or potassium bromate (to increase the gluten's elasticity and the dough's gas retention). Bread flour, available bleached and unbleached, is ideally suited for yeast breads.

The fuller-flavored **whole-wheat flour** contains the wheat germ, which means that it also has a higher fiber, nutritional, and fat content. Because of the latter, it should be stored in the refrigerator to prevent rancidity.

Cake or pastry flour is a fine-textured, soft-wheat flour with a high starch content. It makes particularly tender cakes and pastries.

Self-rising flour is an all-purpose flour to which baking powder and salt have been added. . . .

Instant flour is a granular flour especially formulated to dissolve quickly in hot or cold liquids. It's used mainly as a thickener in sauces, gravies, and other cooked mixtures.

Gluten flour is high-protein, hard-wheat flour treated to remove most of the starch (which leaves a high gluten content). It's used mainly as an additive to doughs made with low-gluten flour (such as rye flour) and to make low-calorie "gluten" breads.

All flour should be stored in an airtight container. All-purpose and bread flour can be stored up to six months at room temperature (about 70 degrees F.). Temperatures higher than that invite bugs and mold. Flours containing part of the grain's germ (such as whole wheat) turn rancid quickly because of the oil in the germ. Refrigerate or freeze these flours tightly wrapped and use as soon as possible. Other grains — such as barley, buckwheat, corn, oats, rice, rye, and triticale — are also milled into flours.

Excerpted from *Food Lover's Companion: Comprehensive Definitions of Over 3,000 Food, Wine, and Culinary Terms*

MAIL ORDER SOURCES

FOR BREAD FLOUR
Arrowhead Mills
P.O. Box 866
Hereford, TX 79045
800-749-0730

FOR SOFT WHITE BISCUIT FLOUR
The White Lily Foods Company
P.O. Box 871
Knoxville, TN 37901
615-546-5511

FOR ORGANIC BREAD FLOURS AND GRAINS
Walnut Acres
Box 8
Penns Creek, PA 17862
800-433-3998

MORE INFORMATION

The Wheat Foods Council
5500 South Quebec, Suite 111
Englewood, CO 80111
303-694-5828

Books

The King Arthur Flour 200th Anniversary Cookbook
Brinna Sands; Countryman Press, 1991; $21.00

The Classic Wheat for Man Cookbook: 300 Ways with Stone-

Did You Know?

☞ Potatoes were once considered worthless because they could not successfully be made into flour.

☞ A new white whole-wheat flour is now available. It is said to combine the nutritiousnes of regular whole-wheat flour with all-purpose flour's milder flavor and ease of use.

Ground Wheat
Vernice G. Rosenval; Woodbridge Press, 1975; $5.95

FLOWERS, EDIBLE

Please Don't Eat The Daisies.
—Jean Kerr
Comic author/playrwright

LUNCHING ON FLOWERS

ZACK HANLE

The colonial gentlewoman cherished her centuries-old heritage of recipes: flower waters for flavoring cakes, dried herblike blossoms for enhancing teas and punches, fresh posies for dressing up special salads, and fragrant leaves and blossoms that would add exotic tastes to jellies, jams, and conserves.

Much of this great American heritage came from England, where Shakespeare's audiences delighted in such delicacies as stewed primroses (popularly called oxlips), gillyflower cordials (made from pinks or carnations, as we know them), and violet and rose waters. In fact, the joys and delights of flower cookery date back to the beginnings of human history, reaching a high peak of artistry in medieval and Elizabethan times.

Today, the use of flowers in the kitchen is an almost lost art that is once again being revived. Carnations and chrysanthemums, nasturtiums and marigolds, violets and roses no longer grace our tables purely as decorations, but as delectable foods from the flower garden. Don't forget to urge your guests to "please *do* eat the flowers" — and often the green leaves, too.

Excerpted from *Cooking with Flowers*

Pause
Before You Pick

If you find the idea of eating flowers charming, wait just a moment. Not all flowers are edible, and poisonous blossoms can be as dangerous as any other poisons. Make it a rule never to eat a flower you haven't checked out with a botanical authority. Equally, don't float an unknown blossom on a summer drink or decorate a cake with its petals until you are sure it is one of the many flowers that are both good to eat and good for you.

Experts advise against eating flowers purchased at a florist's, which may have been sprayed with pesticides, or picked from a roadside, where they may have been exposed to lead from exhausts. When picking edible wildflowers, such as daylilies, yucca blossoms, white elderflowers, and wild roses, be sure of the community's regulations and laws, or you may find yourself unexpectedly in hot water.

The Floral Big Ten

Cathy Wilkinson Barash, an expert on edible flowers, recommends the ten most easily grown, most commonly known, and most flavorful edible flowers:

Chives

Calendulas

Daylilies

Marigolds

Mint

Nasturtiums

Pansies

Roses

Sage

Squash blossoms

Mum Soup

Serves 4 to 6

2 10¾-ounce cans chicken broth
8-ounce can water chestnuts, thinly sliced
2 scallions, green parts only, sliced in small rounds
Peel of 1 fresh lemon, slivered
2 slices cold boiled ham, cut in julienne strips
1 medium-sized chrysanthemum flower, washed and drained
Soy sauce
6 sprigs parsley

In a medium-sized saucepan, heat the broth to boiling point and add the water chestnuts, scallions, lemon peel, and ham. Pull off the chrysanthemum petals and drop them into the soup. Bring it to a boil again, add a dash of soy sauce, and pour into bowls. Garnish with sprigs of parsley.

Reprinted from Cooking with Flowers

Books

Cooking with Flowers
Zack Hanle; Chalmers, 1982; $3.50

Edible Flowers: From Garden to Palate
Cathy Wilkinson Barash; Fulcrum, 1993; $29.95

Flowers in the Kitchen
Susan Belsinger; Interweave, 1991; $14.95

The Forgotten Art of Flower Cookery
Leona W. Smith; Pelican, 1985; $15.95

A Potpourri of Pansies
Emelie Tolley and Dania Petek; Crown, 1993; $15.00

MAIL ORDER SOURCES

Diamond Organics
P.O. Box 2159
Freedom, CA 95019
800-922-2396

Paradise Farms
P.O. Box 436
Summerland, CA 93067
805-684-9468

FOIE GRAS

*Christmas is coming,
The goose is getting fat,
Please put a penny in
the old man's hat.*

— Old English begging rhyme

What Was That Again?

Several years ago, the French chef Jean Troisgros created his signature dish: fresh foie gras and haricots verts (skinny string beans) with a warm vinaigrette dressing. An American columnist raved about it and printed the recipe but in a slightly altered form that she thought her readers would prefer: sliced bologna, frozen string beans, and Thousand Island dressing.

Some things just don't translate.

THE BIG FOIE GRAS FLAP

Foie gras has always been regarded as one of the richest of all foods and, like caviar and champagne, a delicacy for the wealthy. Suddenly, quite recently, foie gras was on the front pages in quite a new light.

"Can Foie Gras Aid the Heart? A French Scientist Says Yes," was *The New York Times*'s headline above Molly O'Neill's report from Auch in France:

"Here in the land of the Three Musketeers, the Gascony region of southwest France, goose and duck fat are slathered on bread instead of butter, the people snack on fried duck skin and eat twice as much foie gras as other Frenchmen, and 50 times as much as Americans," she wrote. A ten-year epidemiological study had just concluded that Gascons eat a diet higher in saturated fat than any other group of people in the industrialized world. Yet "the foie gras eaters of the Gers and Lot Departments in southwest France have the lowest rate of death from cardiovascular disease in the country," according to the study's director.

A World Health Organization monitoring study of habits and mortality rates in Toulouse and a surrounding area that included much of Gascony confirmed this remarkable finding. "Out of 100,000 middle-aged Frenchmen, approximately 145 die of heart attacks annually, but in

Toulouse the number is about 80. In the United States, 315 of every 100,000 middle-aged men die of heart attacks each year," O'Neill reported.

One would imagine that at this remarkable news church bells would have rung carillons and there would have been dancing in the streets. Not on your life. A wail of dissenting voices immediately claimed that we were looking only at part of the picture. Presumably, this anti-pleasure lobby would have been far happier had the study shown the poor peasants dropping in droves as fit punishment for feasting on foie gras.

In their search for an explanation of what has come to be called the French Paradox, learned men suggested that goose and duck fat is more like olive oil (which is definitely preferred over saturated fat) than butter (which has in recent times come to be considered "bad"). Others proposed that the Frenchmen's longevity had less to do with diet than with regularity — early to bed, early to rise, and similarly uplifting guidelines for leading a good life.

And there the matter might have rested, had not "60 Minutes" soon afterward broadcast a segment offering "proof" that it is better for your health to drink a glass of red wine every day than not to do so. Which led the alarmists to become very agitated all over again about the virtues of regularity and the importance of bodily exercise other than the bending of elbows.

Does this suggest that if we want to be healthy we should eat a little foie gras, when we can afford it, and jog from bar to bar, where we can sip a drop of red wine? Or, that what we put into our minds is more important than what we put into our mouths?

Feathers Fly at Foie Gras Farm

Though almost everyone associates foie gras with France, it is also produced and eaten in Austria, Bulgaria, Czechoslovakia, Hungary, Israel, Luxembourg, and even in the United States.

About a decade ago, a group of Israeli-trained farmers got together in order to raise ducks and produce foie gras; they formed a company called Commonwealth Enterprises that was thriving in the Catskill Mountains of New York — until PETA, People for the Ethical Treatment of Animals, tried to close it down, along with another foie gras farm in the Sonoma Valley of California.

The PETA people want to stop restaurants from serving foie gras and their customers from eating it. They claim that it is horribly inhumane to force a funnel down the throat of a duck or goose and force it to eat more corn mush than it needs or wants. The farmers claim that what they are doing is perfectly ethical and that ethical people treat animals ethically.

Clearly this is a case of one man's meat being another man's poison, even though in this case the meat is poultry.

THE FAT OF OUR FATHERS

ANDRÉ DAGUIN AND ANNE DE RAVEL

The technique of producing foie gras may indeed go back as far as the ancient Egyptians. Relief paintings on tombs dating from the fourth and fifth Egyptian dynasties (2600 B.C.) depict farmers holding geese by the neck and feeding them packed balls of grain, presumably to fatten them quickly. This method, called *gavage*, is fundamentally unchanged today. The rich diet causes the livers to swell up to four to five times their normal size.

Some have speculated that foie gras, like so many important inventions and recipes, was discovered by accident. As the theory goes, a farmer in Egypt had a flock of geese, and for some reason, one bird developed a nearly insatiable appetite; when killed for its meat, the farmer discovered that the oversized goose had an enormous liver that was exceptionally delicate and delicious.

Ancient Roman poems and literature are replete with tales of sumptuous banquets that featured the fattened livers of geese. According to at least one source, it is a Roman who deserves credit for advancing the technique of producing foie gras. Consul Quintus Caecilius Metullus Pius Scipio, the father-in-law of Pompey, a Roman general and statesman (106 - 48 B.C.), fed his geese a diet of figs to give the livers and the meat extra sweetness. A by-product was an enlarged liver with an ineffably delicate flavor. A half century later another Roman, Marcus Gaius Apicius, applied the technique to ducks and pigs.

Following the Roman occupation of Gascony, the local people continued to produce foie gras. By the 15th century they had established a thriving cottage industry, first with geese, later with ducks. It was not until 1747, however, that the first published recipe turned up for *pâté de foie gras* in a book called *Le Cuisinier Gascon*, published in Amsterdam. It called for slicing fresh foie gras, seasoning it with truffles, and baking it in pastry.

The endless gastronomic skirmish over which is better, foie gras from ducks or geese, continues to this day. Some contend that the liver of a fattened goose is finer in texture, firmer, and tastier. But the duck partisans counter with the same ammunition. Who is right? Of course, it comes down to personal tastes.

Excerpted from Foie Gras, Magret, and Other Good Food from Gascony

Anything to Declare?

In the course of one of Alfred Hitchcock's many transatlantic journeys a customs officer who did not recognize him asked what his occupation was. Hitchcock said he was a producer.

"Oh?" said the official. "What do you produce?"

"Gooseflesh," said the famous producer of thrillers.

FOOD ADDITIVES

Better Living Through Chemistry
— Slogan of the 1939 World's Fair

What's in a Twinkie?

Though a 1.5-ounce Twinkie cake has been reputed to have the longest shelf life of any American food (some estimates have put it at 12 years), the company is prepared to guarantee freshness only up to 14 days, after which a Twinkie is no longer at its best. The following additives assist it in staying moist and creamy:

Modified food starch — Processed cornstarch, added to improve solubility and texture in the cake; it imparts moistness.

Whey — The watery component of milk, dried to a powder; it is a source of dairy protein.

Mono- and diglycerides — Vegetable (soybean)-based emulsifers; they keep the water and fats in the creamy filling from separating.

Lecithin — Another vegetable-derived emulsifying agent, which has the same function.

Calcium caseinate — Protein derived from milk; it adds body and dairy flavor to the creamy filling.

Sodium stearyl lactylate — A dough conditioner that promotes improved mixing tolerance, grain, texture, and tenderness; it extends the life of the cake.

Cellulose gum — A gum derived from plants and used in icings to prevent the crystallization of sugars.

Polysorbate 60 — A preservative; it inhibits the growth of molds and wild yeasts associated with spoilage.

2-3 (3-PHENYLPROPYL) TETRAHYDROFURAN AND OTHER GOOD THINGS TO EAT

What *is* food today and how much of it is actually unadulterated? Why are we concerned about chemicals in our food? Should we be concerned?

"Better Living Through Chemistry" was the brave slogan of the 1939 World's Fair, and for quite a while we thought it true. We changed our tune when we found out that we are now eating close to 400 million pounds of additives every year. This figure, large as it is, should not cause undue alarm. The chemicals used to process foods are unlikely to do us harm when eaten in "normal" quantities. Saccharin, for instance, was once considered potentially dangerous, but its adverse effects would have appeared only after ingestion in absurdly abnormal quantities. Therefore, it has remained on the market.

Additives are used in foods for all kinds of reasons: to extend a food's shelf life, to improve its nutritive value, to make its preparation easier, and, yes, to make it taste better. Without additives, food would spoil more rapidly, potatoes would sprout, bugs would erupt in the flour, mayonnaise and puddings would separate — and loud would be the wails across the land if all the cookies were soft.

As any good cook knows, too, when food is subjected to heat, it loses color. Food processors regularly add artificial colors and flavors to foods to make them look more attractive. Theoretically, we consumers are not too worried about the safe use of additives because most of us believe they are being carefully monitored by the government and by big business — though it is unfortunate that most consumers do not put a lot of faith in either of these institutions.

The really important concerns about additives, however, lie less with the various chemical elements that are added in the course of processing our foods, and which are dutifully listed on the food labels, than with the residues of the antibiotics and hormones that are fed to animals and poultry. These issues are discussed elsewhere in the book in the section on drugs in food and under specific foods.

We should take some comfort from the fact that ours is a litigious society, and any company that flirts with danger by risking unsafe practices is unlikely to survive scrutiny — so there is a strong incentive of self-interest to keep everything honest. In safeguarding the consumer, farmers and food processors ensure their own longevity.

Incidentally, *A Consumer's Dictionary of Food Additives* defines 2-3 (3-Phenylpropyl) Tetrahydrofuran as a synthetic fruit, honey, and maple flavoring agent for beverages, ice cream, ices, candy, gelatin, puddings, and chewing gum. It has no known toxicity.

Public debate about the proliferation of additives in our food is more likely to be constructive if we all recognize two basic facts: that our food has never been perfectly safe or free from additives, and that consumers share the responsibility for whatever risk there may be in eating today.

— Harold McGee
On Food and Cooking

Books

A Consumer's Dictionary of Food Additives
Ruth Winter;
Crown, 1989; $10.95

On Food and Cooking
Harold McGee;
Collier Books, 1988; $21.00

ADDITIVES IN THE BALANCE

At a forum on diet and behavior presented by the National Center for Nutrition and Diet, Susan Borra, R.D., then director of consumer affairs for the Food Marketing Institute, summed up the benefits and risks of food additives:

The Good News

Additives make our food safer, and from a microbiological point of view, that is extremely important. The addition of additives to food is essential in order to provide safe food and also to minimize the number of microbiological infection-related deaths. In addition to providing us with safe, nutritious foods, additives also make possible a wider range of food choices and more convenience.

Finally, food additives ensure lower-priced foods, an appealing fact for the public. The United States has the best, safest food supply of any country in the world. In fact, Americans spend a lower percentage of their income on food than do citizens of any other country in the world.

The Bad News

Some people have become sick, and there have been allegations regarding asthmatic responses to additives. On the other hand, thousands of people die every year from microbiological infections and intoxications. In fact, there are probably as many deaths caused by such infections as there are automobile-related deaths.

There are some drawbacks to the use of food additives. For example, we risk the production of more "fun foods" with lower nutrition density. There also are sensitivities to food additives. A number of people are hypersensitive to certain compounds, such as bisulfites and soy derivatives.

Finally, there are toxicological risks when we deal with thousands of compounds — it is the nature of the game. Compounds may have been previously sanctioned or generally recognized as safe by experts who were only able to work with the data available at the time.

"Henry likes nothing more than to curl up with a good label."

Q&A

Q What's the difference between a natural and an artificial additive?

A Natural additives are derived from natural sources, such as soybeans and corn, which provide lecithin, or beets, which are powdered and used as food coloring. Artificial additives are man-made, such as ascorbic acid or monosodium glutamate, and can often be produced with more purity and consistent quality, and also more economically, than their natural counterparts. But both are composed of the same chemicals and meet exactly the same standards.

Did You Know?

☞ Up to 16 chemicals can be added to help breads keep "fresh" and retain the moist and yielding qualities customers expect. So-called balloon bread even contains a small quantity of plaster of paris.

☞ Butter has been colored yellow since the 1300s.

☞ Annatto, the vegetable dye that makes margarine yellow and turns cornflakes the color of corn, comes from the seed of a tropical tree.

☞ Dr. Harvey W. Wiley, who investigated food additives in the early 1900s, organized a "poison squad" of brave young men who were prepared to eat measured amounts of chemical preservatives such as boric acid, formaldehyde, and salicylic acid to find out how toxic they were.

☞ The demand for food additives is expected to increase nearly 9 percent per year.

Additives We Add to Our Lives

What they do	What they are	Some examples	Foods in which they are found
Impart or maintain a desired consistency or texture	Emulsifiers	Lecithin, polysorbate, di- and monoglycerides	Baked goods, cake mixes, salad dressings, ice cream, processed cheese, puddings
	Stabilizers	Gum arabic, agar-agar	
	Thickeners	Pectin, xanthan gum, guar gum	
	Anticaking agents	Calcium phosphate	Table salt
Improve or maintain a food's nutritive value	Vitamins	Vitamins A and D, niacin, thiamine	Flour, bread, breakfast cereals, pasta, margarine, milk, iodized salt
	Minerals	Iron, zinc oxide	
Maintain "freshness" by preventing spoilage and deterioration	Antioxidants	Benzoic acid, butylated hydroxyanisole	Margarine, oils, potato chips
	Preservatives	Sodium and calcium propionate, acetic acid, sodium nitrite, ascorbic acid, sodium and potassium salts	Bread, crackers, cake mixes, meats, cheese, syrup, pie fillings
Control acidity and alkalinity and aid in leavening	Acids, alkalis	Tartrates, ammonium carbonate, yeast, citric acid, malic acid	Cakes, cookies, quick breads, colas and soft drinks, candies
	Buffers and neutralizers	Calcium carbonate, sodium aluminum phosphate	
Enhance flavor	Natural flavors	Salt, malic acid	Soft drinks, confections, ice cream, cheeses, jams, chewing gum
	Synthetic/artificial flavors	Monosodium glutamate, aspartame	
Impart a desired coloring	Natural colors: pigments from natural sources	Turmeric, caramel, beet powder	Baked goods, colas
	Synthetic colors	Seven approved for use in food: FD&C Blue Nos. 1 & 2, FD&C Green No. 3, FD&C Red Nos. 3 & 40, FD&C Yellow Nos. 5 & 6	Confections, baked goods, jam, butter, cheeses

REGULATING THE ADDITIVES

T hough additives have been used for centuries, we have never regulated both food and color additives as strictly as we now do. The original law on the books is the Federal Food, Drug, and Cosmetic (FD&C) Act of 1938, which empowers the Food and Drug Administration (FDA) with authority over food and food ingredients and defines requirements for truthful labeling of ingredients.

In 1958, the Food Additives Amendment to the Act was passed; it requires that the FDA approve the use of an additive before it can be included in a food. The manufacturer must prove that the additive is safe in all the ways in which it will be used.

Two groups of substances were exempted from this amendment. The first, known as "prior-sanctioned substances," included such additives as sodium nitrite and potassium nitrite, which were already in use for preserving luncheon meats. The second was substances "generally recognized as safe," or GRAS, which had a long history of being acceptable. These included salt, sugar, spices, vitamins, and many other substances.

Amendments governing color additives were added in 1960, requiring dyes used in food, drugs, cosmetics, and certain medical devices to be approved by the FDA before being marketed. Every one of the provisionally listed 200 colors already in use had to pass further testing and only 90 of these survived to be declared safe. The remainder have been withdrawn.

Both laws prohibit the approval of an additive if it is found to cause cancer in animals or in people. The FDA cannot prevent excessive fortification of a food with nutrients, however, unless its toxicity is proven.

What Is a Food Additive? Legally, the term refers to "any substance the intended use of which results or may reasonably be expected to result — directly or indirectly — in its becoming a component or otherwise affecting the characteristics of any food."

A direct additive is a substance added to a food for a specific purpose — in effect, as an ingredient. Most of these are identified on the food's label. An indirect food additive can become part of the food in trace amounts as a result of the way it is packaged, stored, or handled. All materials that come in contact with food must be certified by the FDA as safe before they can be used in packaging.

Steps in Getting the FDA's Approval The manufacturer of a new food or color additive first has to petition the FDA for its approval. About 100 new petitions are submitted annually, most for indirect additives such as packaging materials.

Each petition must provide convincing evidence in the form of animal studies showing the effects of large doses over long periods, or studies of the effects in humans, as proof that the proposed additive performs as it is supposed to.

The FDA considers the composition and properties of the substance, the amount likely to be consumed, its probable long-term effects, and various safety factors. Because absolute safety can never be proven, the FDA has to determine whether the additive is safe under the proposed conditions of use, based on the best scientific knowledge available.

If approval is given, the FDA issues regulations governing types of foods in which the additive can be used, in what amounts, and how it must be identified on food labels. Additives for meat and poultry must also receive authorization from the U.S. Department of Agriculture. And even then the process is not over. Federal officials continue to monitor the new product to check on the extent of its consumption and whether any new research presents challenges to its safety.

The FDA also operates an Adverse Reaction Monitoring System (ARMS) that acts as an ongoing safety check of all additives. It investigates any complaints and through its vast database can help officials decide whether reported adverse reactions constitute a genuine food health hazard.

As long as consumers demand convenience and processed foods, additives will be a part of those foods.
—Rita Storey, R.D.
ConAgra Foodservice Companies

Without food additives, we'd live like the caveman.
— Richard Ronk
FDA's Center for Food Safety and Applied Nutrition

All I ask of food is that it doesn't harm me.
— Michael Palin
World-traveling "Monty Python" alumnus

Come Back, Big Red!

Were you aware that for a terrible 11 years, between 1976 and 1987, there were NO red M&M's in those M&M's bags, neither in plain nor in peanut? The lack of redness originally followed hard upon the FDA ban on the supposedly cancer-causing Red Dye No. 2 — although M&M's have always been reddened by Red Dyes Nos. 3 and 40, which are on the approved list. Protesting red M&M's lovers around the country wrote in to complain; a student at the University of Tennessee even founded a Society for the Restoration and Preservation of Red M&M's ("there wasn't that much to do at college," he explained); and eventually, the M&M organization brought back the red ones. Tentatively, at first, in 1985, under the guise of a "Holidays" Christmas package, when everyone knows you can't have green without red. Finally, the bags started coming out in the proportions favored by M&M focus groups: 30 percent brown, 20 percent each red and yellow, and 10 percent each orange, green, and tan for plain; and 30 percent brown, 20 percent each red, yellow, and green, and 10 percent orange for peanut.

Interestingly, the ban was lifted just about the time of glasnost and the crumbling of the anti-Red scare. Was this a coincidence? M&M keeps mum.

What Does GRAS Mean?

Not what you might expect. GRAS stands for Generally Recognized As Safe, the term the FDA established in 1958 to define those additives already in use, many of which had historically been used to color or flavor or retard spoilage in foods. Not everything on the GRAS list stays that way; subsequent developments have brought to light all kinds of anomalies due to the inadequate testing of additives.

For example, cyclamates were originally on the GRAS list, but once research in the 1960s showed them to cause cancer in lab animals, they were promptly removed. President Nixon subsequently ordered a total review of the GRAS list, which has been continuing ever since.

Currently, some 1,750 additives are designated as GRAS, but should the ongoing evaluation turn up any new evidence to suggest that a formerly accepted GRAS substance may be unsafe, federal authorities will prohibit its use or initiate a review.

I Go for — Indigotine

No, Indigotine, Erythrosine, and Tartrazine are not the names of the Three Graces — they are FD&C's colorants Blue No. 2, Red No. 3, and Yellow No. 5, and you may be more familiar with them than you think. Traces of royal blue indigotine turn up in ice cream, confections, and the cherries in fruit cocktails and salads. Erythrosine makes cherries' somewhat pallid cheeks glow red. And no packaged custard or eggnog would look good without a judicious dash of lemon-yellow tartrazine.

These and the other color additives the FDA has certified for use in food are available as dyes or lakes. Dyes are water-soluble and come in powdered, granular, or liquid forms. Despite their name, lakes are the water-insoluble form of dyes, used to color items that lack moisture, such as coated tablets, cake mixes, and chewing gum.

The color of food has played a major role in cooking since the earliest times. The Romans added saffron to dishes to brighten them as well as to improve their taste, and 19th-century milk puddings would be dyed an all-too-rich pink with cochineal — which the cooks would have disdained had they known it was squeezed from beetle scales.

Expertly used, modern food colorings can offset color loss caused by exposure to light, air, or temperature extremes. Since they have no taste, they do not alter the foods whose appeal they heighten — though we have all noted the effect when an overgenerous dose has turned the birthday-cake frosting into a fright. With color, as with all questions of taste, it's a case of less is more.

Risks Versus Benefits

When it comes to potentially harmful food additives, we often take the risk while the food processors take the benefits. For example, nitrites combine with natural stomach chemicals to cause nitrosamines, powerful cancer-causing agents, but nitrites also prevent botulism, a potentially fatal illness caused by contaminated food. Food processors [point out] that one part per billion is equal to one inch in 16,000 miles. But how much exposure to a carcinogen does it take to damage a gene or to cause cancer? No one knows for certain. The FDA estimates that exposure to diethylstilbestrol as low as one part per trillion may be associated with the risk of one cancer per million consumer lifetimes. That's pretty low, except if you are the consumer.

— Ruth Winter
The Consumer's Dictionary of Food Additives

Fortification:
The New Bulwark Against Disease

Foods were first fortified just before World War II to correct nutritional deficiencies that caused serious illnesses. Vitamin D was added to milk to stop rickets. Treating salt with iodine prevented goiter from developing. Cereal products and bread fortified with niacin could fight pellagra.

The efforts were so successful that most deficiency diseases have ceased to exist in the United States, and people have come to expect — indeed, to rely on — the addition of various nutrients to our foods. The American Medical Association has recommended expanding the number of nutrients and proposed suggested guidelines for fortification with vitamins and minerals which the National Academy of Sciences and the Institute of Food Technologists cordially endorsed. It all seems sensible enough — but the food manufacturers have taken it to extremes.

Do we really need to have more calcium in our orange juice than in our milk, or turn to Kellogg's Bran Flakes to receive 100 percent of our daily requirement of iron? There is a risk here that we may try to subsist on certain foods alone, and abandon the principles of eating a balanced diet. Milk and orange juice are not comparable, for example; milk contains other important nutrients as well as calcium, which we need just as much. There are more than 40 essential nutrients to be found in foods, and no one product, however well fortified, can or should provide them.

FOOD AND MEDICINE

**Let your food be your medicine,
and your medicine be your food.**

— Hippocrates
Greek father of medicine

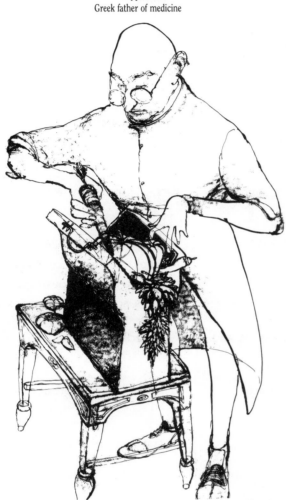

EAT GREEN TO FEEL IN THE PINK

The issue of food and its relationship to medicine has assumed greater importance as the nation wrestles with mounting medical costs. Epidemiological experts now estimate that up to 70 percent of modern diseases have a dietary link.

We have no trouble believing that if we swallow arsenic we will surely die, but we have a much harder time convincing ourselves that a healthy diet improves the quality of our life. Dr. Ernst L. Wynder, founder and president of the American Health Foundation, talking with Frances Lear in *Lear's*, explained this reluctance:

"We had a conference several years back on the subject of the illusion of immortality, asking why people are not more aware of their responsibility for their long-term health. And the answer, after a day and a half of erudite discussion, was that we find death unacceptable. Because we find it unacceptable, we deny death for as long as possible. So prevention of disease is rarely a pressing issue, and public support [for eating wisely] is difficult to obtain."

Maybe another reason for our lack of interest in controlling our urge to splurge is because the subject of nutrition is very often still held in low esteem by the medical profession. Few medical schools acknowledge its importance and even fewer consider the subject worthy of inclusion in the curriculum. Traditionally, nutrition has been regarded, derisively, as "woman's work," but attitudes changed once it was observed that men eat more meat than women. Women eat more fruits and vegetables than men. And women, on average, outlive men!

The serious study of food and medicine is still in its infancy but the tools are being refined for searching out microscopic elements in food. For example, it has been discovered that when garlic is steamed, one of its components that is known to fight microbes is destroyed, but a new anti-inflammatory property is acquired. Scientist sleuths at the University of Georgia found that centenarians' intake of nutrients is much like that of other older Americans save that most 100-year-olds eat six servings of green and yellow vegetables a week, while most 60- to 80-year-olds eat only four servings. The oldest oldsters are also more likely to eat breakfast. Meanwhile, USDA researchers have found that cinnamon stimulates insulin production and that the omega-3 fatty acids found in some fish may prevent cancer, alleviate the pain of migraine, ease the aches of rheumatoid arthritis, prevent blood clots, lower the blood pressure, and promote the healing of psoriasis. And there is absolutely incontrovertible proof of the benefits of vegetables and fruits in preventing illness.

The absurdity of some of the fad messages about food has had the unfortunate effect of making many people discount all the solid advice. However, there is overwhelming evidence to prove that eating well is an essential element in our well-being. Indeed, we soon may be eating even better. As described earlier in this book, the biotechnologists are already at work in the "kitchen," hand-in-hand with the cooks, nutritionists, and insurance agents — to bring us, perhaps, a food containing a built-in contraceptive, a drink to sip during a heavy negotiation, or a snack to cure baldness. Surely the day is not far off when the doctor will prescribe a bowl of chicken soup with garlic, ginger, and ginseng, and tell us to leave a message on his fax in the morning!

The crucial relationship between food and health should not come as a surprise. After all, our ancestors depended entirely on diet to shorten or prolong life. Folklore and old wives' tales are coming full circle and the gainers are those who can keep an open mind.

Not Lizzie, But Elsie?

Lizzie Borden's lawyers argued almost a hundred years ago that the ax murder of her parents was the result of premenstrual tension. If only she had been on a calcium-rich diet, or had eaten a foie gras sandwich, she might have blown away the PMS blues and saved everyone a lot of grief.

An old-fashioned vegetable soup, without any enhancement, is a more powerful anticarcinogen than any known medicine.

— James Duke, M.D.
USDA medicinal phytochemicals expert

Mind Food

Some foods are good not only for physical ailments but for psychological ones, too. In addition to the well-recognized role of chocolate in making us happy, *The Harvard Health Letter* claims that vitamin B-12 is helpful for treating some kinds of dementia and just the scents of strawberries, jasmine, and bananas have been found to have a tranquilizing effect.

Maybe advertisers will replace those perfume ads in magazines with inserts of paper impregnated with the aroma of freshly baked pizza or sizzling bacon.

Food By Design: Nutraceuticals

The idea that everyday foods could prevent major disease may create the next specialty: nutraceuticals — the practice of prescribing certain foods that have druglike attributes. If it's true, for instance, that resveratrol, a naturally occurring substance found in red grapes and red wine, lowers levels of harmful cholesterol, we may be about to take a completely new look at what we eat and drink.

Certain foods contain substances, such as phytochemicals, that could prevent certain types of cancer, blood clots, and osteoporosis. Though the National Cancer Institute is still cautious about such possibilities, it has funded some $20 million to the Designer Foods Program to develop methods of measuring these substances and studying their impact in the prevention of disease.

Citrus fruits, for instance, contain flavonoids — antioxidants that enhance the body's detoxification system and protect cell membranes. Saponins and triterpenoids, also found in citrus fruits, have inhibited the growth of breast cancer in rodents; they could have a biochemical action similar to that of a drug currently given to women with breast cancer.

Through selective breeding, scientists may be able to achieve high concentrations of vitamin A or defined amounts of antioxidants in certain foods.

A Food Pharmacy

A potpourri of naturally occurring substances that may fight disease

Active Food Component	Possible Disease-Fighting Properties	Found in the Following Foods
Allylic sulfides	Inhibits cholesterol synthesis and protects against carcinogens.	Aged garlic extract
Alpha-linolenic acid	Reduces inflammation and stimulates the immune system.	Flaxseed, soy products, purslane, walnuts
Carotenoids	Antioxidants that protect against cancer and may help reduce accumulation of arterial plaque.	Parsley, carrots, winter squash, sweet potatoes, yams, cantaloupe, apricots, spinach, kale, turnip greens, citrus fruits
Catechins	Studies have linked catechins to low rates of gastrointestinal cancer; they may aid the immune system and lower cholesterol.	Green tea, berries
Coumarins	Prevents blood clotting and may have anticancer activity.	Parsley, carrots, citrus fruits
Flavonoids	Block receptor sites for certain hormones involved in cancer promotion.	Parsley, carrots, citrus fruits, broccoli, cabbage, cucumbers, squash, yams, tomatoes, eggplant, peppers, soy products, berries
Gamma-glutamyl allylic cysteines	May have a role in lowering blood pressure, and elevating immune system activities.	Aged garlic extract
Indoles	Induce protective enzymes that deactivate estrogen.	Cabbage, brussels sprouts, kale
Isothiniocyanates	Powerful inducers of protective enzymes.	Mustard, horseradish, radishes
Limonoids	Powerful inducers of protective enzymes.	Citrus fruits
Lycopene	Powerful antioxidant that helps the body resist cancer and its progression.	Tomatoes, red grapefruits
Monoterpenes	Cancer-fighting antioxidants that inhibit cholesterol production and aid protective enzyme activity.	Parsley, carrots, broccoli, cabbage, cucumbers, squash, yams, tomatoes, eggplant, peppers, mint, basil, citrus fruits
Phenolic acids	May help the body resist cancer by inhibiting nitrosamine formation and affecting enzyme activity.	Parsley, carrots, broccoli, cabbage, tomatoes, eggplant, peppers, citrus fruits, whole grains, berries
Phthalides	Stimulate the production of beneficial enzymes that detoxify carcinogens.	Parsley, carrots, celery
Plant sterols	Block estrogen promotion of breast cancer activity, help block the absorption of cholesterol.	Broccoli, cabbage, cucumbers, squash, yams, tomatoes, eggplant, peppers, soy products, whole grains
Polyacetylenes	Protect against certain carcinogens found in tobacco smoke and help regulate prostaglandin production.	Parsley, carrots, celery
Triterpenoids	Prevents dental decay and acts as an anti-ulcer agent. Binds to estrogen and inhibits cancer by suppressing unwanted enzyme activity.	Citrus fruits, licorice-root extract, soy products

Source: *Eating Well*

Food and Medicine Do Not Always Mix

Because reactions can vary, always speak to your doctor about any *specific* medication being prescribed. Some antibiotics, for instance, should be taken on an empty stomach; others should be taken with food to minimize stomach irritation. Taking drugs with milk can often reduce their absorption by the body. Eating iodine-rich foods such as soybeans, seafood, turnips, and salt can reduce the effects of some thyroid medications. The efficacy of iron supplements is lowered by food, milk, and wine; taking them with vitamin C, however, enhances their absorption. Foods rich in tyramine or tryptophan — fava beans, certain wines, cheeses, beer, yogurt, or other fermented products — can create a dangerous rise in blood pressure or high fever, possibly even with fatal results, when they are ingested along with certain antidepressant drugs. Even some over-the-counter preparations such as aspirin or Motrin can cause stomach irritation or increase the risk of vitamin C deficiency.

Books

Cold Spaghetti at Midnight: Feel-Good Foods to Heal Your Body and Soothe Your Soul
Maggie Waldron; Morrow, 1992; $16.00

Eat Smart, Think Smart
Robert Haas; HarperCollins, 1994; $22.00

Food: Your Miracle Medicine
Jean Carper; HarperCollins, 1993; $25.00

Healing Foods
Judith Ben Hurley and Patricia Hausman; Rodale Press, 1989; $25.95

Superfoods: 300 Recipes for Foods That Heal Body and Mind
Dolores Riccio; Warner Books, 1992; $26.45

The Food Pharmacy Guide to Good Eating
Jean Carper; Bantam, 1992; $13.50

No disease that can be treated by diet should be treated with any other means.

— Maimonides
Jewish father of medicine

The Lord hath created medicines out of the earth.

— Ecclesiastes 38:4

MORE INFORMATION

American Medical Association
515 North State Street
Chicago, IL 60610
312-464-4818

International Food Information Council
1100 Connecticut Avenue NW, Suite 430
Washington, DC 20036
202-296-6540

Drug development is necessary and I'm not against it, but the fastest way to make real public health changes is to reach the food supply. And the idea that everyday foods could prevent major diseases — you couldn't come up with a hotter topic to change the whole damn world.

— Herb Pierson, M.D.
Designer foods pioneer, National Cancer Institute

FOOD SAFETY

FEAR OF FOOD

Why are we so worried about food safety today? The number of outbreaks of food-borne illness has been gradually declining for a decade, but more efficient methods of reporting mean that an outbreak of any magnitude almost instantly becomes headline news. And, despite improved scientific knowledge, misunderstandings about the causes of food poisoning still abound.

Many people continue to believe that farm animals are the primary source of contamination, but the Centers for Disease Control and Prevention in Atlanta report that 77 percent of problems stem from improper food handling in restaurants and other institutions that prepare large quantities of food that must be held until it can be eaten. Another 20 percent of illnesses are the result of improper storage and cooking at home. This leaves only 3 percent of outbreaks that can be traced to infection at farms and unclean processing plants. Yet the vast majority of inspectors still focus their attention on the farm, not on the plate.

Today, there are 9 million foodservice employees who prepare foods for salad bars, cafeterias, and restaurants, as well as for institutions such as schools, hospitals, and airlines. Many of these jobs are paid at minimum wage, and are performed by workers with a poor command of English and standards of hygiene that could stand improvement. The more people handle a food on its way to our plates, the more likely it is to be exposed to contamination. And the more frequently we eat away from home, the greater becomes the risk.

The history of government regulation of food safety is one of government watchdogs chasing the horse after it's out of the barn.
— David A. Kessler, M.D.
Commissioner, Food and Drug Administration

Causes of Food Poisoning

(in order of frequency)

Salmonella — Found in improperly cooked or thawed meats, poultry, eggs; unpasteurized cheese and milk; chocolate made from contaminated cocoa beans.

Listeria — Found in undercooked meat and poultry; soft cheese, pâté, unpasteurized milk.

Campylobacter — Found in undercooked poultry; unpasteurized milk.

Escherichia coli (E. coli) — Found in improperly handled, undercooked beef, especially ground beef; unpasteurized milk.

Clostridium botulinum — Found in foods that have been improperly canned, with insufficient heat for processing; secretes botulin, the toxin that causes botulism.

Staphylococcus aureus — Carried by food preparer from infected wounds or coughing and sneezing.

Trichina — Found in undercooked pork or wild game; a parasitic worm that causes trichinosis.

Adapted from *Eating Well*

Risky Business

*O*nly in America is death considered to be an option.

The National Safety Council reported 40,300 deaths from automobile accidents in 1992; the Centers for Disease Control and Prevention reported 9,300 deaths as a result of food poisoning. The risk of becoming ill from contaminated food is 1 in 100,000. The risk of being involved in a car accident is 1 in 65, yet this isn't going to stop most people from getting into a car. Apparently, 95 percent of all drivers sincerely believe they are better than average behind the wheel; we are less sure of our invincibility when it comes to food.

To put things further into perspective: It is somewhat irrational for a skydiver to take the risk of jumping from a plane, and then refuse to eat an egg because it may be hazardous to his health.

THE ROLE OF GOVERNMENT

Responsibility for food safety is shared between the USDA and the FDA. The Food Safety and Inspection Service (FSIS) of the USDA is responsible for ensuring that all U.S. meat and poultry products are safe, wholesome, and accurately labeled. By law, every carcass and bird must be inspected for cleanliness, wholesomeness, and absence of disease, and FSIS's 7,400 inspectors visually check 126 million head of cattle, hogs, and sheep and 6.9 billion turkeys and chickens a year at 6,000 processing plants.

But visual inspection alone does not guarantee safety. The prevailing laws date from 1907, and the agency, led by Secretary of Agriculture Mike Espy, is urging that they be changed and expanded to take better advantage of modern technology. USIS scientists can analyze samples down to parts per trillion, for instance, but samples are usually taken only after an outbreak of disease, not as a routine measure.

The reformers point out that with the steady expansion of the food industry and our increasing demand for convenience and takeout foods, greater and more consistent safety checks are needed at every stage in the distribution system. The FDA, for example, has been inspecting annually only operations that are judged high risk, checking other facilities once every three years. But the agency is putting in place a new, systematic approach to food safety that Health and Human Services Secretary Donna Shalala called a "sea change." "We will be reviewing whether the safety system is in place rather than taking a snapshot," she said.

THE ROLE OF INDUSTRY

For a long time the food industry refused to admit that there were potential problems with certain dyes, chemicals, and additives, and tended to play down stories about the presence or transmission of food-borne diseases. More recently, its members have been funding studies designed to improve food safety.

The problem is that the public distrusts industry-funded research. If the egg producers, for instance, pay the salaries of independent scientists and the results are positive, the researchers were "in the pocket" of those who supplied the big bucks. If the conclusions are negative, the media publicizes them as "bad" news and we conveniently forget who paid whom to do what.

Naturally, the food industry is concerned to provide safe food — it can't afford to do otherwise.

THE ROLE OF THE ADVOCATES

Consumer advocates play an important watchdog role in protecting the public interest, but they don't always have all the facts straight, and they frequently have private agendas. When their advocacy conflicts with the views of other authorities, the public has to make its own judgments and arrive at its own conclusions.

Few of us are willing to take the time to examine scientific data; for obvious reasons, government and industry are not always the most credible sources of information. And it is all too easy to accept the opinion of some well-coached Big Name over specifics provided by a professional who knows the field and tells us more than we really want to know. Still, if we decide to join a cause, or even express an opinion, we should look beyond the headlines before speaking out or acting up.

Food Imports

The USDA regulates imports of meat and poultry; all other foods are subject to examination by the FDA. They must meet the same standards as domestic foods — be pure, wholesome, safe to eat, and produced under sanitary conditions. Eighty-six percent of the 1.5 million shipments a year are food products. Every entry is screened but not all are inspected. Each record is reviewed, then the food is either released for distribution, held for physical examination, or sent for sampling and analysis.

Inspectors check for signs of dirt, spoilage, contamination, or mislabeling. Perishables are also inspected for insects, or illegal pesticide residues; samples collected are examined within 24 to 35 hours.

TIPS

Buying

❏ Buy eggs from a case that is 45 degrees F. or colder. Check the temperature with the manager if you don't see a thermometer.

❏ Check the hamburger package date and always buy on the day it was ground (it spoils within two or three days of grinding). Ask for an extra plastic bag to wrap meat and poultry, because although these are already wrapped, raw meat juices can leak out and could contaminate other foods.

❏ Distrust fish that looks limp. If it has defrosted and thawed more than once, it may be unsafe to eat. Smell is a good indication of freshness. Find out when fish is shipped to the store and buy when a shipment has just come in.

❏ Locally grown produce is often safer than fruits and vegetables that have traveled from afar. Avoid produce that has been waxed, because if pesticides have been used the wax can seal them in and the produce will need extra washing.

❏ At the salad bar, trust your eyes. If the food doesn't look fresh, don't risk it.

❏ Never rationalize buying any food because it is convenient. The intestines prove more persuasive than the brain.

Storing

❏ Take expiration dates seriously. They can have an impact on your own longevity.

❏ Check the cupboard shelves at regular intervals and throw out stale dry products and any canned goods that arouse suspicion.

❏ In hot weather, carry perishable food home in a cooler containing ice. Don't leave any perishables unrefrigerated for more than 2 hours.

❏ An opened jar of mayonnaise will keep in the refrigerator for up to a year if you don't allow it to sit at room temperature for extended periods. Similarly, opened jars of jelly or marmalade will keep for several weeks if refrigerated.

❏ If soft or liquid foods in the refrigerator show any signs of mold, discard them. You can save some hard or firm foods, such as cheese, salami, bell peppers, or potatoes that show tiny mold spots by cutting out the spots carefully without touching the knife to the mold.

❏ When in doubt about a food, throw it out. Don't taste it first!

Home Rules

Cook all foods to at least 160 degrees F.

Keep the refrigerator at 40 degrees F. or below.

Keep freezers at 0 degrees F. or lower.

Scare, Scare!

It's time to set some facts in order about a few of the stories that made recent news headlines:

• The Pepsi syringe scare, which turned out to be a hoax, cost the company about $15 million in sales.

• The quantity of benzene actually detected in Perrier water was the equivalent of taking a single step after walking the breadth of the country from Los Angeles to New York and back again *30 times*. The company's loss from the scare ran into several million dollars.

• Saccharin is harmful to your health . . . but only if you were to drink the equivalent of 8,000 soft drinks a day!

• A 1989 scare, which started with an anonymous telephone call, warned that grapes en route from Chile were laced with cyanide. Two million crates of Chilean grapes were impounded at airports and docks, but only two poisoned grapes were ever found. Chilean losses were in excess of $600 million. Domestic grape producers were also severely harmed by the fact that most Americans stopped eating any kind of grapes for weeks.

• A scare about cantaloupe melons was traced not to the fruit but to the ice in which it was shipped, which had been made from contaminated water from a Mexican river. American melons also experienced plummeting sales.

MORE INFORMATION

Americans for Safe Food
Center for Science in the Public Interest
1875 Connecticut Avenue NW, Suite 300
Washington, DC 20009-5728
202-332-9110

PERIODICALS

For addresses, see also Information Sources

Food Protection Report
Charles Felix Associates
P.O. Box 1581
Leesburg, VA 22075
703-777-7448
Monthly; $135 per year

Nutrition Action Healthletter
Americans for Safe Food
202-992-9110
10 times a year; $24 per year

FROGS

Frogs were here when the dinosaurs were here, and they survived the age of mammals. They are tough survivors. If they're checking out now, I think it is significant.

— David Wake
Director of the Museum of Vertebrate Zoology, University of California, Berkeley

FROGS TAKE A LEAP
BACKWARDS

Frogs seem to be disappearing all over the world these days, and scientists are becoming increasingly alarmed. They are less concerned about frogs' legs vanishing from restaurant menus than about the reasons for the swift and sudden decrease in frog and other amphibian populations. Some believe they are victims of habitat destruction, climate change, and acid snow, others blame contamination from pesticides and herbicides, which may be causing irreparable damage to frogs and other animals, too, during vulnerable stages in their life cycles.

But whatever the cause, or combination of causes, the results are alarming. Declines in frog populations have been reported from every continent and on a global scale. When biologists, zoologists, herpetologists, and ecologists from 63 countries met at a conference a few years ago and compared notes, they discovered that out of some 4,000 known species of amphibians in the world only a few dozen were thriving. Since then, the Declining Amphibian Populations Task Force has been formed to study the extent and causes of the decline, with more than 1,000 researchers at work in 40 countries.

Miners used to carry caged canaries with them because the birds' sudden silence and speedy death would betray the lethal presence of carbon monoxide at the coal face. Similarly, the silences where once there were frogs may be an early warning signal to us. Frogs, like all amphibians, are at home on land and in the water. With porous skins and neither fur nor feathers, they may be sensitive to pollution problems not yet recognized — dangers to which we should be paying close attention.

JUMPING OFF THE BANDWAGON

ELIZABETH SCHNEIDER

DATELINE: BIG CYPRESS SWAMP, FLORIDA

Midnight, a canal near Alligator Alley in the preserve adjacent to Everglades National Park in southern Florida. The chairman of the Tribal Council of the Seminoles, James E. Billie, perched high above the hull at the controls of the airboat, touched a switch and a beam of light sprang from the band encircling his wide brow. He pointed a visitor into a seat in the prow. An airplane engine and propeller contained in concentric steel circles eight feet in diameter formed an imposing backdrop.

"Hang on and don't let go," he warned. In seconds the boat was skimming across the tar-black channel at 45 miles an hour, past literally hundreds of gold-gleaming alligator eyes. Negotiating narrow sloughs, accelerating over sawgrass hummocks, gliding through shallow water, stopping on a dime: Mr. Billie's reputation as an ace pilot of both watercraft and aircraft was not exaggerated. Nor was his skill as a frog catcher.

Zooming alongside each tiny prey, discernible only by the emeralds of its eyes, Mr. Billie plucked it from the canal with a flick of the wrist, unerringly pinioning it with a long four-pronged pole, a gig, the frogger's traditional tool.

"No one can really make a living catching frogs any more," Mr. Billie said. "This is still the only way to get them, one at a time in the middle of the night. It takes too much time and energy and isn't well paid."

The primary domestic source of edible frogs is the Everglades, but most of the legs consumed in America are imported.

Beginning in the 1940s, real-estate developers, citrus growers, cattle ranchers, and produce farmers encouraged the diking and draining of most of Florida's frog country, according to Foster Crippen, owner of the Frogleg Ranch, the major Florida supplier of frogs' legs. "Compared to cattlemen — sales, profits, net worth — froggers are nothin'," he said. "That's the truth. And compared to real estate, we're double nothin'." . . .

In the 1930s there were 23 frog farms in southern Florida. "And I guess we'll be the last, since we're the only one left," said Mr. Crippen. . . .

Those who are fond of frogs' legs, it seems, must prepare for a dry spell.

Excerpted from "Frogs' Legs, Hunt to Table," in *The New York Times*

Low-Tech Insect Control

Bangladesh used to supply most of the frogs' legs consumed in the United States until the Bangladeshi government discovered that a reduced population of frogs resulted in a vastly increased population of flies. It was costing more to import insecticides to control the flies than could be earned by exporting the frogs that ate the flies at no cost at all. So the government prohibited the export of frogs. No word, as yet, on the effect this has had on the flies.

It's not easy being green.

— Kermit the Frog

FROZEN FOODS

THE BIG CHILL

When it comes to frozen food, we believe what we selectively choose to believe. For instance, we have a hard time accepting the fact that frozen vegetables really are considerably fresher than fresh ones. Produce to be frozen is picked and packed within six hours of being harvested so, unless we grow our own, or buy from a farmers' market, the vegetable bought frozen in a box will be more economical, more convenient, more nutritious, and considerably less wasteful than the equivalent purchased from the supermarket produce section. For example, vegetables like carrots and broccoli have the same amount of vitamin A, whether fresh or frozen. And, interestingly, after three days in the supermarket and three days at home in the refrigerator, fresh green beans retain 40 percent *less* vitamin C than frozen ones; vitamin C is locked in by freezing.

But, somehow, we prefer the vision of ourselves buying fresh peas and beans, squeezing the fruit knowledgeably, and picking out the bunch of carrots with the prettiest topknot. No one feels close to nature rattling a box of frozen string beans.

Once frozen foods were the only means of eating certain foods year-round but, in fact, with every advance in the technology of keeping fresh vegetables and fruits in tiptop condition, sales of frozen equivalents have been falling off. Meanwhile, supermarket house brands of frozen staples like peas and potatoes have cut into the profits of giants like Birds Eye and Green Giant. The most popular frozen items these days are ice cream — which has amply earned its own section further on in the book — and high-end combinations such as fresh pastas with and without vegetables and stir-fries with interesting sauces.

Many supermarket customers demand "fresh" fish too, though it should be obvious that fish flash-frozen at sea, literally within a couple of hours of being caught, is likely to be in far better condition than the sad specimens languishing on crushed ice for days on end. The question to ask here is no longer "Is it fresh?" but "Has it been carefully frozen?"

One morning, as I went to the freezer door, I asked my wife, "What should I take out for dinner?" Without a moment's hesitation, she replied, "Me."

— Anonymous

Did You Know?

☞ Clarence Birdseye perfected the process of freezing vegetables in 1929.

☞ The first frozen vegetables to be sold were June peas and spinach.

☞ More than 1,500 frozen foods are now available to consumers.

MORE INFORMATION

American Frozen Food Institute (AFFI)
1764 Old Meadow Lane
McLean, VA 22102
703-821-0770

Frozen Vegetable Council
c/o Creamer Dickson Basford
1633 Broadway
New York, NY 10019
212-887-8010

National Frozen Food Asssociation (NFFA)
4755 Linglestown Road
P.O. Box 6069
Harrisburg, PA 17112
717-657-8601

Books

Dinner's in the Freezer
Jill Bond; Bonding Place, 1993; $18.00

Fresh from the Freezer
Michael Roberts; Morrow, 1990; $19.45

FRUIT

With Americans exposed to less than 250 of the 20,000 to 80,000 edible plants available in the world, the potential for our growth is phenomenal.

— Frieda Caplan
Founder and CEO of Frieda's, Inc.

WHAT IS A FRUIT?

A botanist would define a plant's fruit as the fleshy or dry ripened ovary that contains one or more seeds — a broad-brush definition that includes plants we wouldn't dream of eating, such as poppies. In narrower terms, a fruit is the fleshy, edible part of a perennial plant that is associated with the development of its flower — and that tastes good to the human palate because of its balance between astringency, acid content, and carbohydrate, mostly in the form of sugars.

Gimme Five!

A t last, fruits are being recognized as a vitally important part of our diet, contributing nutrients, fiber, and an intriguing variety of tastes and textures. The magic number is at least five servings daily — of either fruits or vegetables, though most of us seem to prefer eating fruit. Some fruits play such major roles in our lives that they have sections of their own: apples, apricots, bananas, blueberries, cherries, citrus fruits, cranberries, dates, figs, grapes, kiwifruits, melons, peaches, pears, pineapples, plums, prunes, raspberries, and strawberries.

Many more recently introduced fruits are constantly expanding our palates, thanks to the efforts of entrepreneur importers such as Frieda Caplan and the increasing number of U.S. specialist growers. A few are described here; all are worth adding to any fruit lover's shopping basket.

MORE INFORMATION

Fresh Fruit Produce Council
1601 East Olympic Boulevard
Los Angeles, CA 90021
213-629-4171

Frieda's, Inc.
P.O. Box 58488
Los Angeles, CA 90058
800-421-9477

Rare Fruit Council International
P.O. Box 561914
Miami, FL 33256
305-378-4457

United Fruit and Vegetable Association
727 North Washington Street
Alexandria, VA 22314
703-836-3410

Did You Know?

☞ Americans' favorite fruits in descending order are bananas, apples, seedless grapes, and oranges. Fruit accounts for approximately 39 percent of retail produce sales.

☞ The average store carries some 225 fruits and vegetables in its produce department.

☞ Americans are currently eating four pounds *less* fruit annually than in 1985.

☞ Ranked by the fruit's content of vitamins A and C, folate, potassium, iron, thiamine, niacin, riboflavin, calcium, and fiber, papaya places first, followed by cantaloupe, strawberry, orange, tangerine, kiwi, mango, apricot, persimmon, and watermelon.

I can't understand how they are able to locate a single fertile fruit fly over the city of Los Angeles but they can't track down 100,000 drug dealers.

— Johnny Carson

Some Less Common Fruits

Fruit	Description and Use
Carambola (Starfruit)	A waxy yellow five-sided fruit which, sliced horizontally, forms a star. Sweet to sour, depending on ripeness. Can be eaten out of hand, sliced as a garnish, or made into preserves and relishes.
Cherimoya	A heart-shaped fruit with gray-green skin indented all over. The black seeds are inedible; the flesh, soft and creamy white, combines the flavors of banana, papaya, and pineapple. Can be eaten out of hand, added in chunks to salads, or made into a custardy pie.
Guava	Guavas are round, green or yellow-skinned, and have white to deep pink flesh with many small seeds in the center. Some taste like pineapple, others like strawberries. Can be eaten out of hand, juiced, or made into jams and jellies.
Kiwano (Horned Melon)	A small oval fruit with a spiky orange skin; emerald green crunchy flesh has lots of seeds and a mild, melonlike flavor. The pulp can be scooped out and chopped in salads or pureed (with seeds strained off) for adding to fruit sauces and drinks. The shells make colorful dessert containers.
Lychee	Lychees are strawberry-sized, with rosy-brown, thin, rough shells that strip away to reveal whitish, opaque flesh surrounding a big brown inedible seed. Taste is similar to a peeled muscat grape with a hint of roses. Best eaten out of hand, or added to fruit desserts, but can be frozen in the shell or in light syrup; offered dried or canned in Chinese restaurants.
Mango	A large round or oval fruit, with smooth skin varying from green to yellow and red; colors increase and fruit softens as it ripens. Bright orange flesh has rich flavor and spicy aroma, but clings to the large hairy seed; it can be sliced into fruit desserts or blended into drinks or sauces.
Papaya	This pear-shaped fruit should be golden skinned when ripe. Soft orange-pink flesh around a central cluster of black seeds is sweet but bland. It can be sliced lengthwise and sprinkled with tart juice or served with seafood or chicken salads, with the seeds ground up and added to the salad dressing.
Passion Fruit	A round, small fruit with deep purple skin that is shriveled when ripe; within is a fragrant greenish-yellow pulp studded with tiny, crunchy black seeds. Flavor is both sweet and sour, lemony and tropical. The pulp can be added to fruit drinks or spooned over fruit desserts; it freezes well.
Persimmon	An oval fruit with shiny orange skin and orange-pink soft flesh, it is edible only when soft and yielding to the touch like an overripe tomato. Good chilled, eaten out of hand or with a spoon, or cooked into puddings or cakes.
Pomegranate	The size of a large apple, with a tough yellow to bright red rind. Each of the mass of seeds has a gelatinous coating with a sweet, pungent flavor and bright red juice. The seeds can be eaten out of hand or sprinkled on salads, and the juice can be squeezed to be made into fruit drinks or frozen for later use.
Prickly Pear (Cactus Pear)	The small, oval fruits of the Nopal cactus, with thick green, orange, or red skins. Fresh is soft and sweet with a watermelon flavor and edible seeds. Skinned, the fruit is served in quarters, or diced and added to desserts and sauces.
Quince	A ripe quince looks like a knobbly pear with a fuzzy yellow, fragrant skin, but is never eaten raw. When cooked, the whitish, granular flesh turns pink and has a distinctive flavor. May be baked, poached in syrup, or made into fruit sauces and preserves.
Sapote	Several fruits are called sapotes; the black and white sapotes are akin to the persimmon, the mamey sapote is not. The black sapote has bright green skin and chocolate-colored flesh that must be completely soft and slightly blackened to be edible. The custardy flesh is sweet and bland, and may be pepped up with liquor, sugar, and cream. The white sapote has very thin green to yellow skin, and pale sweet creamy flesh that hints of peaches, citrus, or vanilla. Like a persimmon, it is eaten out of hand, or can be frozen. The mamey sapote is like a brown-skinned avocado, with a large nut and honey-sweet, dense orange flesh that is spooned from the shell and added to fruit shakes, or eaten out of hand.
Tamarillo	Sometimes called a tree tomato, this egg-shaped fruit has smooth red-gold skin and flesh like a dense tomato. It has the tart-sweet flavor of an unripe plum. It can double as a vegetable, and is mostly used cooked as a base for chutneys or sauces, or raw in salsas or salads.
Tamarind	A fruit with brown, hard-shelled pods that look dried but actually contain glossy "beans" surrounded by sticky pulp with a strong sour-sweet taste. Soaked, the pulpy beans yield a puree used for seasoning sauces, chutneys, and nectars; some people like to nibble them raw.

Books

A Feast of Fruits
Elizabeth Riely; Macmillan,
1993; $25.00

Cooking with Fruit
Rolce Redard Payne and
Dorrit Speyer Senior; Crown,
1992; $22.00

Fruit
Amy Nathan; Chronicle
Books, 1988; $29.95/$16.95

**Fruit: A Connoisseur's
Guide and Cookbook**
Alan Davidson; Simon &
Schuster, 1991; $30.00

**Sweet Onions and Sour
Cherries**
Jeannette Ferrary and Louise
Fiszer; Simon & Schuster,
1992; $25.00

**Uncommon Fruits and
Vegetables**
Elizabeth Schneider; Harper &
Row, 1990; $20.00

FRUITCAKE

FRUITCAKE IS FOREVER

RUSSELL BAKER

Thirty-four years ago, I inherited the family fruitcake. Fruitcake is the only food durable enough to become a family heirloom. It had been in my grandmother's possession since 1880, and she passed it to a niece in 1933.

Surprisingly, the niece, who had always seemed to detest me, left it to me in her will. There was the usual family backbiting when the will was read. Relatives grumbled that I had no right to the family fruitcake. Some whispered that I had "got to" the dying woman when she was *in extremis* and guided her hand while she altered her will.

Nothing could be more absurd, since my dislike of fruitcake is notorious throughout the family. This distaste dates from a Christmas dinner when, at the age of 15, I dropped a small piece of fruitcake and shattered every bone in my right foot.

I would have renounced my inheritance except for the sentiment of the thing, for the family fruitcake was the symbol of our family's roots. When my grandmother inherited it, it was already 86 years old, having been baked by her great-grandfather in 1794 as a Christmas gift for President George Washington.

Washington, with his high-flown view of ethical standards for government workers, sent it back with thanks, explaining that he though it unseemly for Presidents to accept gifts weighing more than 80 pounds, even though they were only eight inches in diameter. This, at any rate, is the family story, and you can take it for what it's worth, which probably isn't much.

There is no doubt, though, about the fruitcake's great age. Sawing into it six Christmases ago I came across a fragment of a 1794 newspaper with an account of the lynching of a real-estate speculator in New York City.

Thinking the thing was a valuable antique, I rented bank storage space and hired Brink's guards every Christmas to bring it out, carry it to the table, and return it to the vault after dinner. The whole family, of course, now felt entitled to come for Christmas dinner.

People who have never eaten fruitcake may think that after 34 years of being gnawed at by assemblages of 25 to 30 diners my inheritance would have vanished. People who have eaten fruitcake will realize that it was still almost as intact as on the day George Washington first saw it. While an eon, as someone has observed, may be two people and a ham, a fruitcake is forever.

It was an antique dealer who revealed this truth to me. The children had reached college age, the age of parental bankruptcy, and I decided to put the family fruitcake on the antique market.

"Over 200 years old?" The dealer sneered. "I've got one at home that's over 300," he said. "If you come across a fruitcake that Julius Caesar brought back from Gaul, look me up; I'll give you $10 for it."

Excerpted from The New York Times

A geological homemade cake

—Charles Dickens
Martin Chuzzlewit

Books

An Edible Christmas
Irena Chalmers; Morrow, 1992; $23.00

Favorite Fruitcakes
Moira Hodgson; HarperCollins, 1993; $12.50

Ruth and Skitch Henderson's Christmas in the Country
Ruth and Skitch Henderson with Judith Blahnik; Viking Studio Books, 1993; $30.00

FUNERAL FOOD

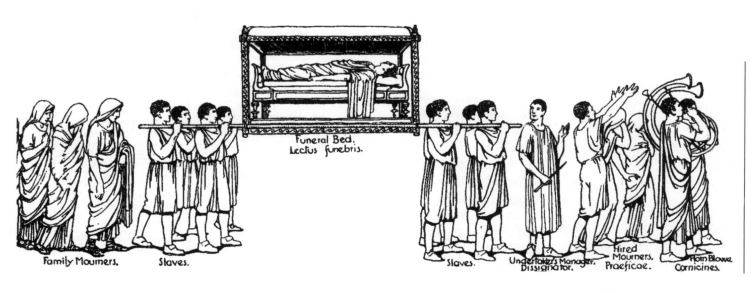

Family Mourners. Slaves. Funeral Bed. Lectus funebris. Slaves. Undertaker's Manager. Dissignator. Hired Mourners. Praeficae. Horn Blower. Cornicines.

The bringing of funeral food may be our last unexamined rite. There's no use taking it to pieces, because all it means is friendship, a token that your friends are there for you.

— Anonymous

THE FUNERAL FEAST

RICHARD ATCHESON

In the early 1930s, when I was growing up in Houston, Texas, the matriarchs and patriarchs of my family were virtually lined up to meet their Maker. So before I was five years old I had been to a lot of funerals, had been lifted into the coffin to kiss the rigid cheek of many a great-aunt, and knew all there was to know about the social aspects of mourning.

People died at home in those days, and I observed that after the undertaker had removed the remains to a black Pierce-Arrow hearse and glided silently away, it was only a matter of minutes before the neighbors were at the door with tearful condolences and covered dishes.

Because I was just a boy, the covered dishes interested me particularly. I wondered, first, what was in them, and second, how soon I would get to sample them. I knew that, owing to the solemn nature of the occasion, there would be no early stampede to the table.

First would come the great ingathering of the clan to my grandmother's house, for she was the functioning head of the family. Everybody would be in a state, no matter how tenuous their connection to the deceased. All the in-laws were there, and the cousins who showed up only for funerals, who never spoke to anyone but expected to be seated in the front pew.

Throughout the day, neighbors and friends would keep turning up on the porch with heaping platters veiled in tea towels, and these would be received with grateful thanks ("Oh, I declare, you shouldn't have," etc.) and removed to the dining room. As there was never any coordination of edibles, my grandmother would sometimes wonder aloud if we would be eating 18 versions of macaroni and cheese for days.

By about six the great throng would be peckish, and poised to surge into the dining room. At a nod from my grandmother, some uncle would part the oaken doors and in we would sweep to discover the accumulated dishes uncovered: a buffet laid out over every inch of the dining room table, cold meats, casseroles, and salads, and along the length of the mirrored sideboard fresh-baked cakes and pies. And everything, I thought from thoroughly sampling the fare, just delicious. It was all homemade, of course; nobody ate store-bought dishes or baked goods then.

To drink, there was iced tea and buttermilk, supplied from my grandmother's kitchen, and coffee. Period. My grandmother was a teetotaler and wouldn't have whiskey in the house. But mourners who were looking for more emphatic refreshment could speak to my Uncle Harry, who always saw to it that there was bourbon in the barn. So that as the evening wore on, some people who slipped in and out

of the house forgot the gravity of the occasion and made more merry than their older relations thought fitting.

My grandmother remained oblivious to these displays of high spirits, though she couldn't have been ignorant of what prompted them. If fights broke out, which they sometimes did — resentments that had been simmering for decades were likely to burst into a rolling boil at such times — my grandmother would make one of the combatants go upstairs and lie down.

This family rout would go on more or less nonstop for three days or more, picking up to high volume right after the funeral, then slowly tapering off as relatives gradually overcame their reluctance to take their leave. And right along, neighbors and friends kept coming over with the funeral food, supplying the family's needs for sustenance and relieving the household of the obligation to provide. And though I was just a little boy, I saw the generosity and practical sense in it, and knew my grandmother did just the same when death came to the families of her friends.

I rarely go to funerals now but when I do, I still look around to see what the neighbors brought. I think how I used to stand in my grandmother's front yard and wave to my last departing cousin. And then of going in to eat another dish of macaroni and cheese.

There is nothing like a morning funeral for sharpening the appetite for lunch.

— Arthur Marshall
Witty Englishman

Brunches for the Bereaved

The restaurant trade magazines recently noted a flurry of midday action in northern New Jersey, where there are a lot of cemeteries. Restaurateurs are offering so many "mercy lunches" that the local paper now runs a Funeral Brunches ad department on the obituary page.

In North Arlington, for example, Eagan's, which is barely a block from Holy Cross Cemetery, caters a $9.95 special to mourners, who may choose between full roast beef or fish dinners. In Kearny, the Lisbon Gardens also has a good thing going with death, and draws more than 100 funeral groups a year.

Price per head in Kearny is $7.95 and groups run around 60 people each.

"Once you have a few you get a lot of repeats," one restaurateur told a *Restaurant Business* reporter. "They'll remember the lunch they had when they buried Aunt Mary."

My grandfather had a wonderful funeral.... It was held in a big hall with accordion players. On the buffet table there was a replica of the deceased in potato salad.

— Woody Allen
Witty American

Dark Suggestions for a Funeral Buffet

Black china on black tablecloth, black balloons

Black caviar on pumpernickel croutons

Black olives

Black sausage

Black bean soup

Squid-ink pasta garnished with black truffles

Eggplant on black bread

Prunes

Blackberries

Black coffee

Black Sambuca (served in silver goblets)

Elvis's Finale

The very last food that Elvis ate was four scoops of Sealtest ice cream and six Chips Ahoy! cookies.

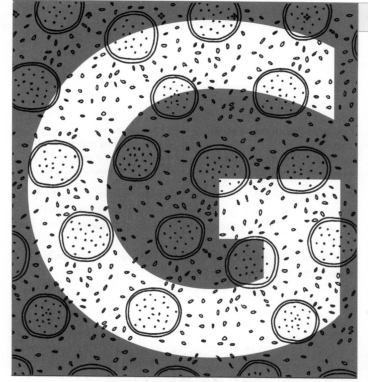

GAME ❖ GARBAGE ❖ GARLIC ❖ GINSENG ❖ GOATS

❖ GOOSE ❖ GRAINS ❖ GRAPES ❖ GREEN MARKETS

GAME

If you want intrinsic flavors with loads of character and meat that tastes good without a lot of dressing up, you should be eating game.

— George Faison
Co-owner, D'Artagnan game distributors

NO GROUSING
ABOUT GAME, PLEASE

If you would like to serve game for dinner today, you don't need a gun. You don't have to be counted among the 16 million registered hunters in the United States. You don't even need to know how to shoot. All you need is a credit card and access to a telephone: Some of the best quality game comes by mail. These days, too, supermarkets as well as specialty meat stores are starting to feature game birds and venison cuts that will lend a touch of adventure to a city dinner party or a homey Big Game Hash.

What a curious turnabout this is. We are entranced with the idea of wild animals and free-range chickens, but in reality almost everything we eat is farm-raised — including game, fish, and even "wild" mushrooms. And in another odd anomaly it has become more dangerous to live in the city than in the forest where once wild animals roamed.

Just 50 years ago there were estimated to be some 50 million pheasants in South Dakota; now loss of habitat has taken a heavy toll, as it has on wild populations almost everywhere. There are still plenty of birds around but most of the pheasants — the most popular game bird — and squabs and quails, as well, are hatched on farms and raised on chicken feed. So it's no surprise that they end up tasting a lot like chicken, too.

Big game such as venison is raised on a grand scale by professionals such as Mike Hughes, who are the modern successors of yesterday's Big Game Hunters. Hughes, whose name is synonymous with quality and responsibility, nurtures deer, antelope, and other game animals on a vast ranch in Ingram, Texas, known as the Texas Wild Game Cooperative. His animals come about as close as you can get nowadays to "wild" ones.

Rabbits, of course, hardly count as wild game, but pop up in smaller-scale operations, along with doves and bigger game such as bison and elk. Exotic species such as alligator, emu, llama, ostrich, and rattlesnake are rarer, but can be found. So can guinea pigs, which are a South American delicacy. If you stumble across them on a U.S. restaurant menu, they will be called *cavies*, which doesn't sound appealing. Better stick with the toasted cheese sandwich.

Or try Gordon's Restaurant in Aspen, Colorado, where grilled quail is served on a bed of red cabbage with goat cheese and thyme butter, or with spinach tossed with chilies and moistened with a touch of chili-orange vinaigrette. And Patrick O'Connell's Inn at Little Washington, in Virginia, sautés peppercorn-coated medallions of venison with lingonberry salsa and wild mushrooms. The whole thing is served in a potato nest. Well, not the *whole* venison, my dear, just a small portion of it.

Saucing Game

Robust is the word that comes to mind when pondering game. Birds and beasts from the wild cry out for big, bold tastes when they arrive in the kitchen: ruby, fruity wines for the sauces, flavored vinegars to focus flavors, braised chestnuts, brussels sprouts, red cabbage, turnips, intensely flavored dried fruits and tart-sour fresh fruits like gooseberries and lingonberries that squinch the face and pucker the tongue.

Books

Game
John Ash and Sid Goldstein; Aris Books, 1991; $25.00

Going Wild: A Guide to Field Dressing, Butchering, Sausage-Making & Cooking Wild Game & Fish
Urban Gaida and Martin Marchello; Watab Marketing, 1994; $16.95

New Game Cuisine
Janet Hazen; Chronicle Books, 1990; $29.95/$16.95

MORE INFORMATION

North American Gamebird Association
P.O. Box 2105
Cayce, SC 29171
803-796-8163

MAIL ORDER SOURCES

D'Artagnan
399-419 St. Paul Avenue
Jersey City, NJ 07306
800-327-8246

Durham Nightbird Game & Poultry Company
358-A Shaw Road
South San Francisco, CA 94080
800-225-7457

Broken Arrow Ranch
P.O. Box 530
Ingram, TX 78025
800-962-4263

TIPS

Preparing

GAME BIRDS, including dove, grouse, partridge, pheasant, pigeon, quail, squab, wild duck, and woodcock, should be trussed with butcher twine or their little legs will dry out before the breast is done. They are often roasted covered with bacon slices.

PARTRIDGE AND PHEASANT: Allow half a bird per person. Roast them or cook them in a casserole, adding a few shavings of white truffle to the sauce, or cook them in a casserole with sliced apples and raisins or with green olives (and mashed potatoes with lashings of butter).

SQUAB: In the game bird context, a squab is a young pigeon. Allow one bird per person and roast or braise the squabs in a casserole with citrus fruit and a spoonful of sweet preserves such as red-currant jelly or apple jelly. They are nice served with white or red cabbage.

WOODCOCK, GROUSE, AND SNIPE: These small birds can be roasted or baked into a pie with small white onions, cubed ham — and, traditionally, calves' kidneys, though this may be a tradition you prefer to ignore.

WILD DUCK OR GOOSE: A wild duck will serve only two people but some domesticated "wild" ducks have put on enough weight to serve four. As a general guide allow one pound per person. Wild duck and wild goose are best stuffed with breadcrumbs, rosemary, and walnuts, roasted or braised in a casserole with port wine, and served with wild woodland (meaning not white button) mushroom sauce.

RABBIT is a much neglected game meat. Don't roast it, because the meat is tough, but it will be wonderfully tender and tasty when cooked in a casserole and served with a creamy mustard sauce and an accompaniment of white beans or lentils.

Love That Bunny

Subjects being studied at Los Angeles's Institute for Sexual Longevity reported that their sex lives markedly improved after eating rabbit two or three times a week.

VENISON'S choice cuts are the loin and the saddle. It can be cut into steaks, roasted, or cooked like any other large animal meat, but benefits from a long slow bath in a red wine marinade.

Serving

Traditional accompaniments for game birds are freshly made croutons (3-inch rounds of firm-textured bread sautéed in equal parts of butter and vegetable oil until brown and crisp), wild rice, braised celery or root vegetables, and red cabbage or sauerkraut. Duck and goose, being all dark meat, marry well with orange, chestnuts, wild rice, and watercress.

Janie Hibler's Big Game Hash

Serves 3 to 4

1 pound venison round steak, finely ground	1/2 teaspoon salt
1/2 cup finely chopped onion	3 tablespoons safflower oil
1 cup grated raw potato	Freshly ground pepper
	Pinch of cayenne pepper

Combine all the ingredients and shape into patties. Heat the oil in a skillet until moderately hot and fry the patties about 8 to 10 minutes, until they are thoroughly cooked and nicely browned on both sides.

Serve plain or with a simple sauce of prepared horseradish mixed with sour cream.

Reprinted from *Fair Game*

"I'm so glad you didn't shoot that deer, I much prefer wine and cheese."

GARBAGE

Today's most coveted object inevitably becomes tomorrow's garbage.

— *Anonymous*

TALK ABOUT TRASH

In the course of heading up the University of Arizona's Garbage Project, anthropologist William Rathje has discovered that the foods that are thrown away reveal a great deal about the throwers. For instance, the more repetitious a family's diet is, the less food they throw away. They buy the same limited number of foods and learn precisely how much of each item they will eat within a short time. More fresh food is apparently thrown away than portion-controlled packaged meals. This is partly because the portions are small but also because they are usually reheated quickly in the microwave and produce less waste than the preparation of fresh fruit and vegetables. All those peels and pits *could* go to the compost heap, but most of us secretly pop them into the trash bin, along with the faded flowers.

Rathje's group also discovered clues to a family's ethnic background by examining their garbage. Apart from the obvious identification of specialty foods, they found that in Hispanic households the most popular baby food is squash. (Squash has been a staple in the diet in Mexico and Central America for 9,000 years.) In Western European households the most popular baby food is peas.

Another discovery was that consumers do not always tell the truth about what they eat. They may claim to be eating healthily but their garbage may reveal discarded wrappings that tell another story altogether. And garbage that contains discarded empty containers from "status" brand-name foods is more likely to have come from a middle-income family than from one that is more affluent.

China Isn't All It's Cracked Up To Be

*I*t is easy to dismiss styrofoam cups as villains and extol the virtues of china, but this is only part of the story. Every time the china is put into the dishwasher it uses up precious water resources; in addition, energy is required to heat the water, and the detergent may leave polluting residues. Even the box containing the detergent adds to the trash.

A study conducted in Holland points out: "A cup and saucer need to be used 1,800 times before they have less impact on the air during their lifetime than a polystyrene mug. However, if the china cup is refilled, it need only be used 114 times before it beats polystyrene on energy use and only 86 times before it imposes less damage to the air. Paper cups are more harmful than polystyrene on every count except their impact on water resources."

MORE INFORMATION

Council on Plastics and Packaging in the Environment
1001 Connecticut Avenue
NW, Suite 401
Washington, DC 20036
202-331-0099

Center for Waste Reduction Technologies
345 East 47th Street
New York, NY 10017
212-705-7407

Paper Versus Plastic

Plastic weighs less than paper and takes up one-seventh the space of paper in landfills. Yet many people firmly and wrongly believe that they are being environmentally correct in choosing paper bags at the supermarket. The fact is that plastic bags require less energy to produce than paper does, and, like paper, can be reused and recycled into new products after original use.

Furthermore, modern landfills are designed to prevent discarded materials from breaking down and releasing toxic substances into the groundwater; the biodegradability of waste is of less concern than the volume of space taken up by trash. The best personal solution for reducing the mountains of trash in the modern world is to take your own string bag to the store.

What Do We Throw Away?

Paper and paperboard	35.7 percent
Yard wastes	20.1 percent
Food wastes	8.9 percent
Metals	8.9 percent
Glass	8.4 percent
Plastics	7.3 percent
Wood	4.1 percent
Rubber, leather	2.8 percent
Textiles	2.0 percent
Miscellaneous organic wastes	1.8 percent

Source: Franklin Associates, Prairie Village, Kansas

Did You Know?

☞ The average American makes about 3½ pounds of garbage a day.

☞ Some communities spend as much on garbage disposal as on educating their children.

☞ A paper cup that is used for 10 minutes takes 500 years to biodegrade — so they say, but how can they be sure?

☞ On an average day 93 million aluminum cans are produced. More than half are recycled.

☞ We throw away 60 million pounds of food a day.

Books

Recipes from an Ecological Kitchen
Lorna Sass; Morrow, 1992; $25.00

Rubbish! The Archaeology of Garbage: What Our Garbage Tells Us About Ourselves
William Rathje and Cullen Murphy; HarperCollins, 1992; $23.00

GARLIC

**Shallots are for babies;
Onions are for men;
Garlic is for heroes.**

— *A folk saying*

THE BREATH QUESTION

Eating garlic is bound to lead to garlic breath, a wrathful draft against which no sure remedy has ever been found. Unless everybody is eating garlic, the person eating garlic will stand out in the crowd by simply standing there and breathing. Suggestions abound: Try sipping a cup of coffee or a glass of milk; eat honey or yogurt; chew on some parsley. In French society, a glass of red wine is regarded as a good idea when garlic mouth is rampant; in French society, a glass of red wine is regarded as a good idea in any event.

BULB DOCTOR

Garlic, sometimes called "the stinking rose," is a member of the lily family and a cousin of onions, shallots, and chives. It comes to market as a bulb enwrapping many cloves in a papery membrane, and, is virtually odor-free. Scratch, crush, or even lightly brush those cloves, however, and you will instantly produce garlic's famous breath — a reek to some but a culinary stimulant to its many admirers. The more you slice and chop, the more odor will be released.

One of the first foods ever cultivated, garlic has a long, strong reputation in the history of food and preventive medicine. The first written reference to it showed up about 5,000 years ago, in Sanskrit. Chinese scholars had good things to say about garlic as early as 3000 B.C., and the ancient Egyptians would trade a healthy male slave for 15 pounds of it. According to the Old Testament, the Israelites wandering in the desert missed the flavorful foods they had known in Egypt, specifically "the leeks and the onions and the garlic" (Numbers 11:5).

From ancient times, impressive powers beyond nourishment, pungency, and flavor were ascribed to garlic — Aristophanes said it gave courage, Pliny said it cured consumption, and the prophet Mohammed said it eased pain. Crusader knights, returning from their campaigns in the Middle East, brought garlic home to Europe, where it was received as both food and medicine. Doctors in the 18th century said it was good against the plague, and as recently as 1963 the Russians sent out a call for garlic to help control a flu epidemic.

Modern medical research is investigating the curative claims made for garlic and has confirmed many of them. Garlic contains alliin, an amino acid. When a clove is crushed, the alliin reacts by enzyme action to form diallyl disulfide — the memorable breath — and diallyl thiosulfonate, the substance believed to be responsible for garlic's antibiotic and bactericidal effects. It certainly promotes cardiovascular activity and eases breathing.

A regular diet of garlic lowers blood cholesterol and hypertension, soothes asthma, and counteracts atherosclerosis. And in its spare time, garlic, raw and added to salads, or cooked and added to other foods, is the secret ingredient in many a tasty dish.

The Medical Record

Some of the uses of garlic and onion, since the days of the ancient cultures of Sumeria and Egypt:

Anticoagulants
Antiinflammatory agents
Antiseptics
Antitumor agents
Aphrodisiacs
Carminatives
Diuretics
Hair restorers
Poultices
Sedatives
Vermifuges

Among the ailments said to respond to garlic and onion:

Arthritis
Asthma
Atherosclerosis
Athlete's foot
Baldness
Bronchitis
Cancer
Catarrh
Chicken pox
Cholera
Common cold
Constipation
Dandruff
Diabetes
Dog bites

Dropsy
Dysentery
Dyspepsia
Epilepsy
Eye burns
Fits
Gangrene
Hypertension
Influenza
Intestinal gas
Jaundice
Laryngitis
Lead poisoning
Leprosy
Lip and mouth disorders
Malaria
Measles
Meningitis
Piles
Rheumatism
Ringworm
Scorpion stings
Scurvy
Septic poisoning
Smallpox
Splenic enlargement
Tobacco poisoning
Tuberculosis
Typhoid

Le Grand Aïoli

A little garlic can perform a lot of magic. In the south of France, in summer after the garlic harvest, many villages hold feasts they call Le Grand Aïoli. Tables are set up in the square and everybody comes. A traditional meal is served featuring salt cod (brandade de morue) with baby new potatoes, fresh vegetables, good wine, and huge bowls of aïoli — the aïoli is the true pièce de résistance of the occasion.

An aïoli is made by crushing garlic cloves in a bowl with a wooden spoon, beating in egg yolks and olive oil, and adding a soupçon of lemon juice or wine vinegar. And when you make aïoli you may not be in the south of France, but you'll feel like it, and the feeling will be grand.

Old Wives' Tale

According to an ancient Palestinian superstition, a clove of garlic worn in the buttonhole (or equivalent) of the bridegroom will ensure a successful wedding night.

ODD JOBS

A group of itinerant workers convenes every year during the garlic harvest at the Christopher Ranch near Gilroy, California, to braid specially grown garlic bulbs. Fast braiders can produce 130 braids a day composed of 19 to 21 bulbs each. Braids weigh three pounds and are two feet long.

Did You Know?

☞ Five California counties produce more than 250 million pounds of garlic every year. About 50 million pounds are sold fresh; most of the crop is dehydrated for use in ketchup, mustard, sausage, and pickles.

☞ The reason entree dishes are adorned with parsley sprigs is that fresh parsley, sometimes called nature's mouthwash, has long been been believed to smother garlic breath.

☞ The Native American people who lived on the shores of Lake Michigan called the wild garlic that grew there abundantly "chicagaoua" — and that is how the city of Chicago is said to have got its name.

☞ Legend has it that when Satan left the Garden of Eden in triumph after having put one over on Adam and Eve, onions sprang up in his right footprint, and garlic in his left.

☞ It is said that, in 1330, King Alfonso XI of Castile founded an order of knights based solely on a mutual hatred of garlic.

Books

Garlic
Janet Hazen; Chronicle Books, 1992; $9.95

Garlic Lovers' Greatest Hits
Gilroy Garlic Festival Association; Celestial Arts, 1993; $12.95

Glorious Garlic: A Cookbook
Charlene A. Braida; Garden Way/Storey Communications, 1986; $9.95

The Garlic Lover's Handbook
Lloyd J. Harris; Aris Books/Addison Wesley, 1988; $7.64

The Goodness of Garlic
John Midgley; Random House, 1992; $11.50

TIPS

Preparing

You need not peel garlic cloves before inserting them in a garlic press. Its pressure pushes the pulp through the holes, leaving the papery sheaths behind. Wash or soak the press in water immediately after using it; dried, the residue can be difficult to remove.

ALERT

Eating raw garlic regularly, for your health, can result in more than bad breath. Sometimes it can lead to anemia, stomach ulcers, and allergic reactions. Researchers suggest substituting cooked garlic and argue that garlic in its aged, deodorized forms seems to be as beneficial as fresh garlic, and without the side effects.

> *Garlick maketh a man wynke, drynke, and stynke.*
>
> — Thomas Nashe
> 16th-century poet

Good (Old) News

The not-exactly-late-breaking news that garlic is good for us increased sales of garlic supplements — tablets and oils — by 163 percent in 1992. Among the brands are Kwai, Nature Made, Private Label, Coles, Your Life, and Field of Nature. The USDA forbids mention of health benefits on the label because garlic is a food. But word of mouth (deodorized mouth, of course) has done the trick.

Gilroy Garlic

Garlic wasn't grown commercially in the United States until World War II, when a few California farmers responded to a government call for dehydrated garlic and onions to be included with other food supplies for troops overseas. In 1955, an adventurous farmer in Monterey County risked planting 10 acres of fresh garlic, though he saw little demand for it. Today, the same farm plants 2,000 acres of fresh garlic and packs about 25 million pounds annually; the nearby town of Gilroy proudly calls itself "The Garlic Capital of the World"; and the area's annual Garlic Festival regularly attracts more than 100,000 people.

Crazy for Garlic

In Miami, the new Garlic Grill is offering garlic soup, baked head of elephant garlic, garlic shrimp strudel, grilled garlic Romanian skirt steak, and garlic mousse. At a similar all-garlic restaurant in Stockholm, where garlic is even in the cheesecake, patrons may order extra garlic on all items if they wish, but never less.

GINSENG

> *I'm not sure ginseng is any better for you or me than a carrot, but just in case the Chinese are right, I grow it in my garden. I stick a root in a jug of gin and call it Old Duke's Gin and Ginseng.*
>
> — James Duke, USDA botanist,
> as quoted in *The Wall Street Journal*

WONDER ROOT

For thousands of years, ginseng root has been prized by the Chinese and Koreans as a regulator of basic body functions, a restorer of memory and sexual drive, and a general remedy for the ailments and incapacities of aging. In 1200 A.D., during the Song Dynasty, ginseng was recorded as one of ten medical herbs used to formulate Shi-Quan-Da-Bu-Tang (Ten Significant Tonic Decoction), a nostrum used in Chinese medicine to this day to strengthen health and immunity. The root of the herb takes the forked shape of a virile male, and because Chinese herbalists adhere to the principle that healing herbs are shaped like the body parts they can cure, ginseng has been closely identified in Asia, over many centuries, as an aid to sexual vigor.

Many Western researchers, however, believe that the extraordinary properties claimed for ginseng exist only in the imagination of the Chinese. One study, reported in the *Journal of the American Medical Association* in 1979, identified "ginseng abuse syndrome" — insomnia, nervousness, confusion, and depression resulting from the use of as little as 3 milligrams a day over a period of years. However, accounts of the effects were contradictory: There were indications of skin eruptions, nervousness, and morning diarrhea, but also of stimulation, well-being, and increased motor and cognitive function.

Though the American market for ginseng is negligible, the world market is immense. Some 8.5 million pounds of ginseng root are produced annually, and the worth of it is estimated to be in the neighborhood of $1 billion. Interestingly, the United States is a player: Marathon County, Wisconsin, is the third largest exporter of ginseng in the world. A few German-American farmers there began to grow the plant at the turn of the century, and their children and children's children have continued to cultivate it. Their ginseng is now one of the most lucrative crops in America, bringing $38 to $52 a pound. Established growers earn as much as $100,000 an acre. In 1991, the United States exported 1,289,000 pounds of cultivated ginseng, valued at $62 million, and 90 percent of it came from Marathon County.

North America exports well over 90 percent of all the ginseng it grows, while importing more than 90 percent of the ginseng it uses. The reason is laid to the West's prevailing fascination with the mystery of the East. More powerful by far the root that comes from far away across the sea, wrapped in exotic paper and indecipherable labels, than the scrubby old root we could grub from a nearby hillside or grow in our own backyard.

GOATS

You liberals think that goats are just sheep from broken homes.

— Line from a recent British play

Great Goat!

Goat meat is lower in calories, cholesterol, and fat than red meat, and more of the fat it contains is monounsaturated than saturated. Goat meat is also a good source of iron and vitamin B-12.

Goatspeak

To Americans, getting a person's goat simply means being irritating or annoying, with the object of "getting a rise out of" somebody. Its probable origin, though, is the French expression *prendre la chèvre*, meaning "to take the milch goat," which could well be a poor person's sole source of food or livelihood.

GOATS AGALLOP

It's fair to say that the New American Cuisine is based on soft goat cheese. We have eaten our way through mountains of it — warm with baby lettuce leaves, rolled in fruitwood ash, floating in sea-green olive oil, and in medallions decorated with a hail of nasturtium petals. How odd it is that we love this cheese and yet at the same time curl our lip at the notion of eating the meat of goat.

There is evidence of a rising enthusiasm for goat's milk yogurt, goat's milk ice cream, even goat's milk fudge. Why not the meat? I wonder if it has to do with billy-goats' beards. We have always been suspicious of beards, owing to their connection with intellectuals and other subversives.

Then I thought the problem might lie with goats' hooves, which are cloven. This has led to worrisome comparisons with the Devil, the goat god Pan, satyrs, and other symbols of bawdy behavior, which has fallen from favor in the present climate of modified Puritanism. And of course we all well remember the Bible's forecast of the Last Judgment, in which we will be separated into the sheep and the goats, and will receive our long-term assignments accordingly.

There are some 440 million goats in the world, but only in the Middle East are they brought to the table swaddled in myrtle leaves and roasted on a spit. Goats are eaten at Eastertime in some parts of Italy, and in the Caribbean at other times as well, and the Sofwa people of West Africa serve goat stew to celebrate a new baby's birth.

Clearly, if goats are to become part of *our* new culinary heritage, they must be repositioned. Congress recently instituted National Dairy Goat Awareness Week. This act was promptly followed by formation of a National Dairy Goat Association. Naturally, the association instantly published *The Dairy Goat Journal,* and before too many more days passed, there was a naming of the Queen of the Goats (a pretty blonde girl, not a female goat) as a program to educate the public was launched. What the association's awareness people want us to know is that goats absolutely never eat tin cans and that we should not concern ourselves with what goats do or do not eat. They are probably right. I am convinced that goat meat could provide us with another food fad, which we are so in need of. The young American superstar chefs are rapidly approaching middle age and have to come up with something fresh to recapture our attention. They could offer us roast goat wrapped in radicchio with black beans and pomegranate seeds, or maybe fricassee of blackened goat with sun-dried tomatoes and salsa on a bed of braised cabbage. The nutritionists, in league with the advertisers, could go wild with a new slogan: "Have an oat with your goat!"

As I was thinking about goats, I quite forgot that goats are also the source of mohair and cashmere, our softest, costliest wools. We could consider combining the MOhaiR with the CASHmere, and end up giving goats a new name: MOR-CASH. Then when this item appeared on the menu, we would call out with one voice, "What we want is MOR-CASH!"

Goat meat will be the fajita of the 1990s.
— Spokesperson for Texas A&I University

MORE INFORMATION

American Dairy Goat Association
P.O. Box 865
Spindale, NC 28160
704-286-3801

American Goat Society
R. R. I, Box 56
Esperance, NY 12066-9704
518-875-6708

GOOSE

> *Such a bustle ensued that you might have thought a goose the rarest of all birds . . . and in truth it was something very like it in that house.*
>
> — **Charles Dickens**
> *A Christmas Carol*

WHAT'S GOOD FOR THE GOOSE

The joyful sounds coming from the Cratchits' table in *A Christmas Carol* are seldom heard in America. Few families venture to cook a goose, and those who do have a hard time finding a fresh one, though only fresh are worth the time, trouble, and the space they take up in the oven.

Don't even think about buying a frozen goose. It will be a terrible, tough, and tasteless disappointment.

The goose is a willful bird that stubbornly refuses to bend its knee to modern farming techniques. It eats what it wants to eat, refusing poultry pellets, yet piles on layers of fat that it artfully conceals beneath its soft, downy white feathers. No amount of web-footed waddling will produce anything approaching an acceptable flesh-to-bone format. Indeed, some people think that the goose fat is the best part of the bird. In certain households, it is saved in an urn, like rejuvenating face cream, and measured in small spoonfuls to provide incomparable depths of flavor to cassoulet and other recklessly extravagant foreign fare.

If the decision is made to cook a goose, you simply must put it on a rack to allow the oven's hot air to circulate effectively. The bird should be trussed, drawing its legs close to the body. Count on cooking it at 350 degrees F. for 18 minutes per pound. By the end of this time the meat should register 185 degrees on a meat thermometer. Ten minutes before the cooking time is up, open the door of the oven and cautiously douse the breast of the goose with a cup of cold water. This will make a lovely, crisp brown skin and a terrible mess in the oven.

A 10-pound goose will serve six, though there will be few compliments on the hosts' generosity. The meat, all of which is rich and dark, is sparsely distributed around the bird's considerable carcass. To avoid keeping everyone waiting, it is wise to roast two birds and slice one of them in the kitchen, using an extremely sharp knife, meanwhile displaying its beautifully bronzed twin in the center of the table for all to admire as the plates are piled high with red cabbage, roast potatoes, and gooseberry sauce.

As for the stuffing: diced apples and potatoes, with breadcrumbs seasoned with sage and fortified with a snifter of brandy. The fruit helps cut the grease, as will a fine bottle of red Bordeaux.

GRAINS

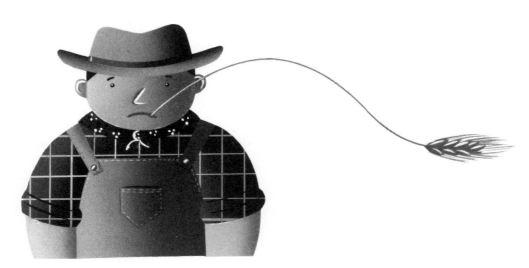

FOR AMBER WAVES

The word *grain* refers to any grasses that produce seeds we can use for human consumption or can feed to domestic animals. Today, more than half the arable land on earth is used to grow grain. The types most commonly cultivated are — in descending order of magnitude worldwide — wheat, rice, rye, oats, barley, corn, and sorghum. Wheat, rice, oats, and corn are discussed in detail in their own sections elsewhere in this book. The others, along with some other less common but potentially valuable grains, are included in the chart opposite, which describes some of their uses.

Man's discovery that wheat and barley could be planted, grown, cut and reaped, threshed, and winnowed — which occurred some 10,000 years ago in the Middle East — was a critical juncture in the development of civilization. In consequence of that realization, our hunter-gatherer ancestors no longer had to roam in search of food but could settle in one place, build homes, and domesticate animals. Thus, society as we know it began because of grain.

Thousands of different grains are grown and harvested throughout the world. In the West, machines began to replace manpower in the reaping of wheat with the invention of the McCormick reaper in 1834, followed by the later development of the combine harvester; in industrialized countries today, the work is entirely mechanized. In many underdeveloped countries, however, grains are still harvested and processed much as they were in ancient times. Even in 1994, it still takes a man 48 working hours to harvest an acre of grain if all he has to work with is a sickle. With a scythe, he can do the same job in 40 hours. If he has a scythe with a cradle, he can cut and gather the grain into bundles in one motion, thus cutting his working hours down to 37. Add an ox or a horse, of course, and the job moves exponentially toward modern times.

What's In A Grain

Various types of grain call for widely varying climatic and soil conditions; indeed, wheat alone grows in some 30,000 varieties around the globe, in many diverse natural circumstances. However, all grains are grasses, and all produce edible seeds, or kernels, with four basic features in common. The outer *husk*, or *hull*, is generally not edible and is usually removed. The *bran* is the layer that is richest in vitamins, minerals, and fiber. The *endosperm* is the starchy center, rich in carbohydrates. The *germ*, the embryo of the seed, contains enzymes, minerals, and vitamins.

RICE · WHEAT

In modern processing, different layers of the kernel are removed to create various kinds of foods, and the degree of refining determines the food value of the end product. Whole-grain breads, for example, make maximum use of the kernel. But when the grain is refined down to the starchy center, as it is for some white breads, many nutrients are lost.

It is ironic that in our zeal to refine grains as much as possible, we have steadily removed all the features that made the flours and cereals made from them our chief life support. Now we are trying to put all these nutrients back again, and adding to our diet new grains from ancient sources, which had never been refined in the first place.

OATS · BARLEY

New and Old Grains in Our Lives

Amaranth

The basic staple of the Aztecs, recently rediscovered, it is still chiefly found in health stores. A tiny grain with a nutty, spicy flavor, it is very high in protein; can be popped like corn or made into flours, pastas, and commercial breakfast cereals.

Barley

One of the earliest grains cultivated, it can grow in areas where wheat cannot. Extremely nutritious, but chiefly eaten pearled, or polished, with the hull removed, in soups; also available whole and unhulled, flaked, in grits, flour, or made into malt (sweet syrup).

Buckwheat

Not a true grain, but a grass, which means that people allergic to wheat can eat it. Brought to America by Dutch and German settlers, it is best known used in the form of flour to make pancakes; the rest is used agriculturally. Kasha is a classic Russian dish made with buckwheat groats.

Bulgur

Whole wheat that has been steamed, the hull removed, and cracked, shortening the cooking time. Because only the hull is gone, bulgur retains all its nutrients and is popular for use in salads such as *tabbouleh*, which mixes it with chopped mint, scallions, and tomatoes, flavored with cumin, and also in stuffings, soups, and entrees.

Millet

This ancient grain has been cultivated since Neolithic times. An important food source in the Far East, it is rich in iron and amino acids, and contains phosphorus and B vitamins; in the United States, however, it is still chiefly known as birdseed. Can be used as whole grain, without the inedible hull; also used like other cereals, ground into meal and flour and puffed.

Quinoa

Pronounced *keen-wah*, this was an Incan staple, along with corn and potatoes, and has only recently been reintroduced. Because it comes closer than any other food to supplying all the nutrients needed to sustain life, has been called "the supergrain," though it is in fact the fruit of an herb. Contains twice as much protein as barley or rice; available in whole-grain and flour forms, also made into pastas. As it is gluten-free, there are no allergic problems with quinoa.

Rye

Grown in Europe since medieval times, rye is hardy and thrives under poor conditions. It ferments easily for making whiskey, and has a strong, somewhat sour flavor in breads. High in protein, with low gluten content, it is available in whole grain, grits, groats, or meal forms, or ground into light, medium, dark, and pumpernickel flours.

Sorghum

Though in the United States it is used almost entirely as a feed grain for livestock, it is the third largest food grain for human consumption on the globe. It can be grown in areas where corn cannot be cultivated. Some U.S. mills sell it as flour; sorghum molasses — a thick syrup produced by boiling down the juice extracted from the stalks — is sold as a table syrup.

Triticale

A combination of rye and wheat that has a superior balance of amino acids and constitutes a nearly complete protein, it is a genetically unstable compound in nature. However, scientists have been able to breed it successfully in the laboratory, making it the first humanly engineered grain. It thrives in poor soil; the flavor is milder than rye, stronger than wheat. It is available as whole-grain berries or groats, or as flour.

Is It a Groat or a Grit or What?

Groats are the whole, unpolished kernels of grains. Grits, on the other hand, are kernels that have been ground down to three consistencies: coarse, medium, and fine. When rolled, kernels are steamed and flattened; when heated under pressure, they are puffed. Cracked, shredded, flaked — we do with kernels, or portions of kernels, what we will.

Books

Grain Power
Tamara Holt; Dell, 1993; $3.99

Great Grains
Linda Drachman and Peter Wynne; Simon & Schuster, 1991; $9.95

The Grains Cookbook
Bert Greene; Workman, 1988; $14.95

The Versatile Grain and the Elegant Bean
Sheryl and Mel London; Simon & Schuster, 1992; $27.50

GRAPES

HOW GRAPES ARE GROWN

More than most crops, the cultivation of grapes requires the skills of professionals, so it is not surprising that those who toil in the vineyards earn higher wages and enjoy better living conditions than other migrant workers. Their year begins in the early spring, when they are responsible for making an encircling cut at the base of each vine. This process, known as girdling, prevents nutrients from collecting in the vine's roots and trunk, diverting them instead into the grapes.

Pruning is the next stage; it requires considerable skill to ensure that enough light and air reaches the developing grapes. The fruit is picked at the peak of ripeness, when the sugar content of the grapes is fully developed. The bunches are carefully placed in boxes and arranged in a specific pattern to prevent jostling or bruising. Nor should single grapes fall from the bunch; few customers buy loose grapes.

The boxes are rushed from the field to the packing houses where they are immediately cooled to remove the "field heat" and sent off to market by rail or truck, still under refrigeration. Sophisticated instrumentation monitors the temperature minute by minute on the long journey, which can take up to five days from coast to coast.

The height of the grape season lasts from mid-May until well into September and once the grapes arrive at their destination, many markets display them outdoors in the hot summer sun. So it is important to buy them from a store that nurtures the fragile fruits with as much care and attention as do those who grow them.

BEAUTY IS SOMETIMES
SKIN DEEP

Calfornia supplies nearly half of all the nation's fruits and 97 percent of our table grapes, but few people are aware that grapes rank as high as *third* among all California's agricultural exports, surpassed only by cotton and almonds.

Each segment of this huge industry cultivates the fruit differently. The same kinds of grapes are not used for the table as for wine and for raisins, for canning, and for juice and jelly.

The table grape growers cultivate several varieties, matching them to the climate and the degree of sand in the soil. In their case, beauty *is* skin deep and the more attractive the grape, the more desirable it is to the buyer. Of course, the grape's sweetness and size are of great importance, too. Retailers and consumers often buy grapes solely on the basis of their color, and may be unaware of the many subtleties in taste between one and another. In larger American cities there may be as many as 20 grape varieties available in the course of the four-month season.

The warm climate in the area of Palm Springs ripens the Perlette Seedless grapes first. They are followed by the Thompson Seedless, Flame Seedless, and Exotic, which are also harvested from the arid soils of the Coachella Valley. Gradually, the grape harvesting moves to the southern tip of the San Joaquin Valley, then farther north along the 200 miles of the Central Valley. In the fall fresh grapes burgeon on the vines in vibrant shades of green, red, and deep blue-black, the rich colors of the Tokay, Red Globe, Queen, Emperor, Ruby and Flame Seedless, Ribier, and the beautiful Christmas Rose varieties.

The winemakers are less interested in the appearance of the grape than in how it may mature in taste on its own or combined with other varieties — what they call its "balance." Though Thompson Seedless grapes may sometimes be used for blending, the wineries grow the specific grape varieties that give Cabernet, Zinfandel, Pinot Noir, Merlot, Riesling, and many other wines their distinctive names — and unique flavors.

California Table Grapes

Perlette Earliest and hardiest, with almost frosty green round grapes, like "little pearls." May - July.

Thompson Seedless The most familiar variety, accounting for 40 percent of fresh production, with light green, oblong grapes. June - December.

Exotic A cross between red Tokay and blue-black Ribier grapes, with shiny blue-black grapes growing in long clusters. June - September.

Flame Seedless A flame-red cross between Thompson and other varieties that is starting to rival Thompson in popularity. May - November.

Ribier A 19th-century import from France via English hothouses, blue-black Ribier grapes are large and plump, with a fine flavor. August - January.

Superior Seedless An early-season bright-green elongated grape with a crunch. Mid-May - August.

Ruby Seedless Deep red, firm, and sweet, it freezes well. Mid-August - January.

Emperor A winter holiday favorite since the 1860s, with large, reddish-purple clusters. September - February.

Red Globe Recently developed from Emperor, with big, red, seeded grapes that grow in lush bunches. September - January.

Christmas Rose A cross introduced in 1980 as an early ripening variety with large, bright red grapes that have a tart-sweet flavor. August - December.

Calmeria A pale green, elongated grape with a mild, sweet, tangy taste. September - January.

Grape Bloom

That beautiful dusty film on grapes is produced by cells in or near the surface that form a natural waterproofing and prevent the skin from cracking. This film is no more harmful than the waxes that are applied to apples and cucumbers.

The nose knows ...

ODD JOBS

The inspectors who sample grape harvests sold to wineries first check to be sure that the grapes are properly labeled by type; then in examining the fruit they keep an eye peeled for material other than grapes, known in the trade as MOG (rhymes with fog). MOG could include leaves, rocks, and snakes. MOG in a shipment could result in fines to the grower.

MORE INFORMATION

California Association of Winegrape Growers
225 30th Street, Suite 306
Sacramento, CA 95816
916-448-2676

California Table Grape Commission
P.O. Box 5498
Fresno, CA 93755
209-224-4997

Concord Grape Association
5775 Peachtree-Dunwoody Road, Suite 500-G
Atlanta, GA 30342
404-252-3663

Napa Valley Grape Growers Association
4075 Solano Avenue
Napa, CA 94558
707-944-8311

PERIODICALS

For addresses, see Information Sources

Growers' Journal
Napa Valley Grape Growers Association
707-944-8311
Annually; $50

Grower Report
California Table Grape Commission
209-224-4997
Quarterly; free

GREEN MARKETS

GREEN MARKETS BLOOM

A handwritten sign tacked to a tree announces CORN, NEW-LAID EGGS, STRAWBERRIES, and the driver's foot eases off the pedal. The car slows as we scan the road ahead. And there it is — the roadside farm stand that is as much a part of the rural landscape as the white-steepled church standing calm and quiet in the fresh-cut lawn, and the blue-painted clapboard houses with the American flag moving softly in the summer morning breeze.

Around the rough wooden lean-to there are small family groups reaching for the just-picked fruits and vegetables. A wooden plank stretched between two sawhorses holds homemade jams and jellies and honey with their labels written in a spidery hand. There are mushrooms and berries: strawberries, blueberries, blackberries, and on two or three days a year, red currants and gooseberries and minuscule wild raspberries as sweet as sugar and as intense as stained glass. Fresh-baked breads and pies and cookies, gingerbread and muffins are proudly arranged in doily-lined baskets, and at the end of the table are bunches of basil, parsley,

thyme, and sage, and jugs of newly pressed cider.

On the ground are bushel baskets filled with apples and pears, plums and peaches, potatoes and onions, leeks and carrots, zucchini (always heaps of zucchini), burstingly ripe, juicy tomatoes, and big and small black eggplants. There are beets and lettuces, and shudderingly green greens, and brilliantly red radishes. On a side table are the eggs, brown and white, laid this very morning before the cock crowed.

The car is filled with more vegetables than we can eat in a month of dedicated consumption . . . but we will worry about that later. Nostalgia drives us to

buy too much. Temptation always overcomes reason.

The simple country farm stands are miniatures of the urban green markets that are springing up everywhere. These city markets are places where friends run into friends and pretty women wear straw hats and toddlers sleep in strollers while their parents amble from stand to stand. Here there is even more choice than in the country. There are dairy stalls displaying fresh goat and cheddar and cottage cheeses. There are a dozen kinds of wholesome breads, dark and raisin-studded or with a scattering of onion wisps baked into the crust. There are trays of good-for-you sprouts. The

chickens are free-range, the ducks plump, and the pheasants, quails, and little birds come from local farms. Smoked meats, bacon, and sausages sell fast, as do the blush wines from neighboring vineyards.

And in the fall there are a dozen kinds of apples, tiny squashes, and pumpkins big as a bathtub. Street musicians fill the air with the sound of fiddles, and children shyly step forward to drop a coin in the hopeful hat.

Shoppers buy from their favorite farmers, whom they know by name. Warm hands receive the money and pass the fresh foods they have themselves nurtured, hand-picked, and packed into trucks before first light.

These markets are our continuing link with our real or imagined past. Here we feel renewed and refreshed, for there are few things that give greater pleasure than shopping at the market, carrying everything home, and transforming it into a beautiful lunch for friends who will spend the rest of the afternoon with their elbows on the table, blissfully satisfied.

WEDNESDAY TREASURES

ALICE WATERS

I like to be around on Wednesdays because that's the one day the vegetables come in from the Chinos' family way down in Rancho Santa Fe. The Chino family has the most beautiful farm in the world. There are just rows and rows of every sort of vegetable. You never know exactly what the Chinos are going to send so opening the boxes is like opening a big surprise treasure chest. Sometimes there are striped tomatoes or yellow ones with orange veins or little tiny mini-red tomatoes that are littler than peas. Sometimes there are all these different color peppers that are every color of the rainbow. Sometimes there are even brown ones. In the summer there's big and little corn and all different color basils or beets or whatever else the Chinos have been growing.

Excerpted from Fanny at Chez Panisse

THE CADILLAC OF COD

Haddock is first cousin to cod, hake, whiting, and pollock. It's easy to recognize haddock by the dark gray of its back, fading to silvery gray along the sides. A distinctive black line above the pectoral fin (behind the gills) and a dark spot — called "St. Peter's mark" — are unique to the species. There is no real evidence to suggest that the disciple Peter fished for haddock, but the fish is usually sold with the skin on so that consumers can identify it properly. (With its skin off, it is sometimes sold as scrod.)

The haddock weighs between two and five pounds and is a smaller but "richer" relation of cod. It is found only in the North Atlantic, at depths to 450 feet, usually along the Continental Shelf.

Like fruits and vegetables, fish have a season. The haddock harvest comes in the summer; this is the time to eat them fresh. New Englanders used to love to do so, but the numbers found in New England waters are declining; most U.S. haddock now is imported from Canada, Iceland, Norway, and Scotland.

Like cod, haddock flesh is lean, white, and arranged in overlapping large, firm flakes. It is wonderfully tasty; when smoked, it takes the name of *finnan haddie*, after the Scottish village of Findon in the Shetland Isles.

Finnan Haddie Fish Cakes

Serves 4

1 pound smoked haddock
1 cup milk
1¹/₂ cups mashed potatoes
1 teaspoon prepared mustard
1 large egg, lightly beaten with
¹/₄ cup milk
Freshly ground black pepper
¹/₂ cup flour
3 tablespoons vegetable oil
2 tablespoons butter
Salsa, for serving

Preheat the oven to 350 degrees F.

Put the haddock in a small dish, just large enough to hold it. Add the milk. Cover with oiled foil and bake for 20 minutes until the fish flakes easily. Leave to cool, then discard the cooking liquid, the skin, and the bones.

Combine the fish with the mashed potatoes, mustard, and egg and milk mixture. Season with pepper. Form the mixture into cakes and dredge them in the flour.

Heat the oil and butter in a skillet and fry the cakes for 3 minutes on each side. Serve with salsa on the side.

HADDOCK

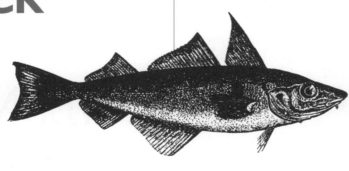

HALIBUT

HALIBUT HO!

ROGER FITZGERALD

Drifting in a heavy sea 50 miles off Alaska's Kodiak Island . . . waiting for the strike of 12: the hour of the halibut! Hundreds of boats circle the area like sharks, waiting to unleash thousands of hooks on millions of pounds of halibut. You can almost feel them under the keel: Pacific halibut, *Hippoglossus stenolepsis*, "hippos of the sea." In English, halibut means "holy fish" — a fish to be eaten on holy days (holidays). *"Five minutes!"*

Eighty "skates" of gear are baited and ready to go. With a skate equaling 1,800 feet, that's 25 miles of line — and 16,000 baited hooks — stretched across the bottom of the sea. Times

the other boats in the area, enough baited gear to wrap around the earth. *"Stand by with the flag!"*

The flag marks the start of the set. The captain, eyes on his watch, is waiting for the tick of noon. *"Let 'er rip!"*

Coils of baited gear sizzle over the stern, gulls wheeling and diving in a pandemonium after the flying morsels of bait; the greedier ones manage to get hooked, submarining to the bottom. Halibut love seagulls.

It takes only a few hours to set the gear, but a lot longer to pull it back — especially if there are 50,000 pounds of battling halibut on the line! . . .

In today's halibut fishery, instead of landing halibut six months out of the year, most of the annual allocation (some 60 million pounds) is harvested in a few 24-hour openings in May and June. Which explains why it's feast or famine (mostly famine) for fresh halibut.

"Flag!"

Now, the work begins. We are back to the first flag — the start of our set. Only 25 miles of line to pull in. . . .

The groundline is in the hydraulic hauler, and the hooks are coming up from the bottom. I'm leaning over the rail (a position I know too well), peering into the water. *"Halibut!"* It's a "chicken" — a halibut under 20 pounds. Most halibut fall into the 40- to 60-pound range, although 200-pounders are fairly common — with an occasional monster of 400 pounds. Only the females grow to any size, because they live longer — 50 years compared to 15 years for males (which seldom exceed 35 pounds).

The beauty of any hook-caught fish is that they come up one at a time, alive. Each fish is handled separately, reverently even, bled and cleaned and iced in a matter of minutes. Virtually all the halibut you buy are treated in this manner. Processors won't accept it otherwise. . . .

The deck was now flapping with fish.

"Whale!"

A whale is a halibut over 100 pounds. The roller man is yelling for assistance. A 200-pounder at least! Up over the rail — *groan!* — and into the fish-hold she goes. Holy halibut!

. . .All our gear is back aboard now, and the crew is in a state of collapse. We have about 35,000 pounds of halibut aboard (worth about $60,000), not a very successful trip —but enough for dinner.

Excerpted from Simply Seafood

Halibut Haul

There are two species of true halibut: Pacific and Atlantic. Of the 30,000 tons landed annually, about 90 percent is Pacific halibut, caught in the Gulf of Alaska. The Atlantic halibut catch, which once took fish around 800 pounds each, is dwindling fast from overfishing. A related species, the Greenland halibut, with softer-textured, fattier flesh, is sold as Greenland turbot.

Halibut Ceviche

Serves 6

Juice of 4 to 6 limes (³/₄ cup)
Juice of 2 oranges (¹/₂ cup)
1¹/₂ tablespoons chili paste with garlic
1 each small green and red bell peppers, stemmed, seeded, and diced
¹/₄ cup diced red onion
¹/₄ cup lightly packed fresh cilantro leaves, chopped
1¹/₂ pounds halibut fillet; boneless, skinless steaks; or cheeks
6 large red cabbage or lettuce leaves

In a large nonaluminum bowl, stir together the lime juice, orange juice, and chili paste until the paste dissolves. Add the peppers, onion, and cilantro.

Rinse the fish and pat dry. Cut it into ¹/₂- to ³/₄-inch-square pieces. Add to the bowl and gently stir the mixture until the fish is completely coated with the marinade. Cover and chill until the halibut turns solid white throughout (make cuts in several pieces to check this), about 8 hours or up to 24 hours.

Serve in individual portions in cabbage or lettuce leaves.

MORE INFORMATION

Halibut Association of North America
P.O Box 20717
Seattle, WA 98102
206-784-8317

International Pacific Halibut Commission
P.O. Box 95009
Seattle, WA 98145-2009
206-634-1838

HAM

FRESH AND CURED

Ham is among the few foods that are eaten for breakfast, lunch, or dinner, or between two slices of bread any time of day. Just about every country in the world produces ham and none calls this meat pigs' legs, though that is precisely what it is: the lean hind of the hog.

When it is uncured, it is known as fresh ham. This is the kind that is baked and carved from the bone and, with any luck, served with cornbread, sweet potatoes, dark greens, and a big pot of mustard. Cured hams go through a curing process that uses salt or brine, sometimes with sugar added, and is usually completed by smoking. Each ham has a "signature" taste, depending whether the pig was fed on corn, peanuts, apples, peaches, or acorns. But the truly unique characteristic of flavor is derived from the wood — apple, hickory, or oak — over which the ham is smoked, and the incarnation of the philosophy developed by generations of farmers in different parts of the world. In every country the curing process is undertaken as carefully as the making of fine wine.

Great Hams of the World

Bayonne Ham This boneless ham from the Pyrenees region of France is dry-cured and aged. Its flavor is similar to that of prosciutto.

Black Forest Ham A heavily smoked ham from Germany, smoked over pine wood and often dipped in beef blood to present a black surface.

Country Ham Traditional in the southeastern United States, these dry-cured hams vary according to locale and the processor. Many are smoked — though smoking is less common in country hams from the Appalachian region.

Parma Ham An Italian-style dry-cured ham that originates in the Parma region of Italy. Parma ham comes from hogs that are almost twice the size of American ones. Each ham is aged for more than a year.

Prosciutto An Italian-style dry-cured ham that is not smoked and is often produced boneless in the United States. Italian prosciutto tends to be larger than domestic varieties.

Smithfield Ham This best known of U.S. country hams must originate in Smithfield, Virginia. Smithfield hams are smoked and coated with black pepper.

Westphalian Ham A cured ham from Germany that derives its characteristic flavor from being smoked over juniper berries and beechwood.

TIPS

Shopping
Boneless or canned hams yield 4 to 5 servings per pound; bone-in hams, 2 to 3 servings.

Cooking
Most hams today come fully cooked. If a ham is not labeled "fully cooked," assume that it's a cook-before-eating ham.

Roasting: Place ham in an open roasting pan. Roast at 325 degrees F. to an internal temperature of 145 degrees F. for fully cooked hams and 160 to 165 degrees F. for cook-before-eating hams.

Cooking in liquid: This method is most commonly used for country-style hams. Cover the ham with liquid and simmer 4 to 5 hours to an internal temperature of 160 to 165 degrees F.

Broiling: Place the ham slice 3 to 5 inches from the heat source; broil until lightly browned. Turn and broil on the second side.

Pan broiling: Place ham slice in a heavy skillet. Do not cover. Brown slowly, turning occasionally.

Storing
If you have to freeze ham, use moisture-proof wrapping and do not leave in the freezer any longer than two months. Thaw in the refrigerator.

The Smithfield Statute

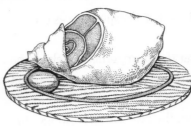

The reputation of hams from Smithfield, Virginia, predates by a century the naming of the town itself: as early as 1639 settlers in Virginia were exporting pork and bacon to New England. To safeguard this traditional industry from inferior imitations, Virginia's General Assembly passed a statute in 1926 defining a genuine Smithfield ham as "cut from the carcass of peanut-fed hogs, raised in the peanut-belt of the State of Virginia or the State of North Carolina, and . . . cured, treated, smoked, and processed in the town of Smithfield in the State of Virginia."

Q&A

Q Why do we eat ham at Easter?

A According to *Imponderables* author David Feldman, the ritual of eating ham around Eastertime predates Christianity. Ham was the main dish at spring feasts for a very practical reason: Fresh meats were not available at the beginning of spring, so pagans would bury fresh pork legs in the sand by the sea during the fall and winter. The pork was cured by the constant "marinating" of the salt water. Come spring, the preserved meat was cooked over wood fires.

James Villas' Country Ham
with Red-Eye Gravy

Serves 8

3 ¼-inch-thick center slices cured country ham
1 cup brewed coffee (or 1 cup water)

Score the fatty edges of the ham slices and place the slices in one or two cast-iron skillets. Heat to moderately low, slowly fry the slices till they are just slightly browned on each side, and transfer with a spatula to a heated platter just large enough to hold the slices.

Increase the heat, pour coffee or water into the skillet, scrape the bottom of the skillet with the spatula, and let boil till the liquid is reduced almost to a glaze. Pour the gravy over the ham slices and cut the slices widthwise into 2-inch serving pieces.

Reprinted from *Country Cooking*

☞ The pig is a symbol of good luck and prosperity.

☞ A three-ounce serving of ham has only about 150 calories; extra-lean ham averages around 100 calories. However, both are high in sodium.

☞ In France, a *fête du cochon* is a feast at which every dish, except dessert, contains a part of the hog.

☞ The expression "high on the hog" comes from the way meat was once portioned out in the British Army. The tender cuts "high on the hog" went to officers.

Carving a Country Ham

Turn the ham upside down and cut a thin slice from the top to allow the ham to rest firmly.

Set the ham right side up. Cut a triangular wedge from the shank end. With a long, sharp carving knife, cut very thin vertical slices straight down to the bone.

Holding the shank in one hand to steady the ham, slide the knife along the bone to release the thinly cut slices of meat.

Reprinted from *Food & Wine*

Ham with Orange-Honey Glaze

Serves 12

1 large (10 to 14 pounds) bone-in ham
1 cup honey, warmed
2 tablespoons orange juice
¼ teaspoon ground cinnamon
¼ teaspoon ground cloves

Preheat the oven to 325 degrees F.

Put the ham in a shallow roasting pan. In a small bowl, mix together the glaze ingredients. Glaze the ham with the mixture. Bake the ham in the oven until heated through, about 1 hour.

Baked Ham 300 – 325 degrees F. Oven Temperature

Source: CUTCO

Type of Ham	Approximate Weight in Pounds	Meat Thermometer Reading Degrees F.	Approximate Cooking Time (minutes per pound)
Ham (Cook before eating)			
Whole	10 - 14	160	18 - 20
Half	5 - 7	160	22 - 25
Shank or Butt portion	3 - 4	160	35 - 40
Picnic Shoulder	5 - 8	170	35
Ham (Fully cooked)			
Whole	10 - 14	130	10 - 15
Half	5 - 7	130	18 - 24
Loin	3 - 5	160	25 - 30

Books

A Ham for All Seasons
Bettie Clark; New England Press, 1985; $7.95

Hog Wild
K. C. McKeown; Warner Books, 1992; $9.99

The Ham Book: A Comprehensive Guide to Ham Cookery
Monette R. Harrell and Robert W. Harrell, Jr.; Donning Company, 1977; $14.00

Ham Everlasting

Asked for a definition of eternity, the writer Dorothy Parker suggested "two people and a ham."

Hamming It Up

For generations, American audiences have called certain showoff, showboating actors "big hams." What does ham have to do with bad acting? It's actually an almost completely forgotten abbreviation of "hamfatter," the name audiences used in the 19th century for just such actor showoffs. Hamfatter implied the second-rate; it referred to performers in minstrel shows who had to remove their makeup with ham fat because they couldn't afford cold cream.

HAMBURGERS

CARL SAGAN'S BILLIONS AND BILLIONS OF BURGERS

MENU

— STROMOSKI —

STAKING A CLAIM TO FAME

Every so often some well-intentioned person, usually one with a degree from a big-name university, decides to tinker with our national institution — the hamburger. Not so long ago the eat-no-fat crowd got McDonald's to replace the lovely, juicy fat in hamburgers with carrageenan, which is a plant extract that comes from seaweed. It was supposed to hold the moisture in the extra-lean meat, but the controversy it created pretty nearly tore it apart. It was bad enough that McD's had already been talked into substituting cholesterol-free vegetable oil for the beef tallow that had made their french fries into the stuff of dreams. Once they began altering the french fries, there was a terrible fear that next they would take away the bun. Everyone knows there is no such thing as a hamburger without a bun, just as there is no such thing as a hamburger without french fries.

Under no circumstances should hamburgers be treated lightly. One of the most truly dreadful ideas in the entire history of gastronomy is the special diet plate — a naked hamburger (without a bun), with cottage cheese and a pineapple slice. This is served to clutches of ladies who lunch in restaurants with green-trellised wallpaper, paper place mats, iced tea, and desperately young waiters whose trousers aren't long enough to reach their ankles.

This kind of fare is not for American families, who take hamburgers seriously. When they travel they always expect to find a burger place named after the local tourist attraction; Grand Canyon Burgers, for instance. They are not a bit afraid of riding an arthritic old horse down a treacherous mountain pass, but they think twice before taking a chance on lunch. A burger is what they all want. When they drive to the airport, they look for a place with a neon sign that says Airport Burgers. They no sooner arrive in Denver than they're looking around for a Mile-High Burger. In Miami there are dozens of places with sun in their name. Sam's Sunshine Burger is just one of them. Fred has Fred's Sunshine Beach Burger. Joe sells Big Surf Burgers. Most people like Big Burgers. And burgers with toppings; bacon, Cheez Whiz, and fried onions are popular.

Hamburgers are not like pizza, climbing weirdly upscale. Hamburgers are down home. Chili beans are the sort of thing most of us like on our beef burgers, not smoked salmon. It's nice when they call burgers beef burgers. We don't care much for burgers that are made out of fish or birds or plant life. And we don't trust places with women's names on the signs. Women's names are for beauty parlors operating out of the front room. Burgers need workingmen's names like Pete or Buddy or Charlie. Alfred and Bertie would never be able to make a go of it in the big business of beef.

What we expect to get when we study the menu is a nice burger that tastes just the same in Seattle as it did in Cincinnati — and crisp fries. We have enough surprises in our lives. Hamburgers are not things to mess with.

Hamburger As A Vision of Hell

by Henry Beissel

*O*ne day I dropped into one of these fast-food places for a coffee. Across from me at the next table sat a man in a business suit, decent, conservative, civilized. Suddenly he opened his mouth. Opened it and opened it 'til his chin touched his tie. Then he pushed a triple-decker hamburger into the opening and struggled to bring his teeth together. I thought he'd unhinge his jaw. I swear he bit off a chunk the size of your fist. He could hardly breathe. As he chewed and choked and mashed for dear life, a small trickle of ketchup ran down one side of his mouth as if he was bleeding. . . . Suddenly I had a vision of millions of mouths opening and closing. . . .

Excerpted from The Noose, A Melodrama

The Same Old Grind?

Beef that is ground in a meat-packing plant will carry the USDA-inspected shield, and beef delivered to the supermarket will also be graded, but the agency does not establish grades for beef that is ground in the store. The package may contain Prime, Choice, or Select grades, so consumers are advised to make their buying decisions based on the price and the fat content listed on the label.

Customarily, supermarkets label packages as ground chuck, ground sirloin, or ground round. Descriptive terms like "extra-lean" or "lean" may mean less fat, and this may be what you are looking for. It is well to remember that sometimes the less fat there is, the less flavor there will be. So you may want to add some ice-cube chips, a spoonful of V-8 or tomato juice, or even some breadcrumbs soaked in water or wine, to keep the beef patty moist as it cooks.

The Top Ten Hamburger Chains
Source:: *Restaurant Business*; Technomic Inc.

Rank	Chain	U.S. Sales ($000)	U.S. Units
1	McDonald's	$12,519,400	8,764
2	Burger King	(est.)5,330,000	5,557
3	Hardee's/Roy Rogers	(est.)3,580,000	3,954
4	Wendy's	2,940,000	3,414
5	Jack in the Box	977,984	1,094
6	Carl's Jr.	629,000	610
7	Sonic Drive-ins	518,765	1,112
8	Whataburger Restaurants	338,000	446
9	White Castle	302,549	257
10	Rally's	221,100	333

HAZELNUTS

HISTORY IN A NUTSHELL

Hazelnuts, also called filberts (after the French St. Philibert of Burgundy), have been known for close to 5,000 years and an ancient Chinese manuscript claims this nut as one of the five sacred foods bestowed by God upon mankind. Ninety-nine percent of U.S. commercial hazelnut trees — some 3.5 million — grow in Oregon's Willamette Valley. It was an English sailor who planted the first one. Two decades later, 50 more were planted along a fence row, and by the turn of the century planting began in earnest.

Unlike any other fruit- or nut-bearing tree, the hazelnut blooms and pollinates in the middle of winter. The pollen stays dormant until the early spring when the nut begins to form. The nuts reach maturity during the summer and are harvested in October. They are not plucked from the trees but allowed to fall when ripe, and are then swept into windrows to be picked up by a harvesting machine. This means there is virtually no hand labor in the cultivation or the harvesting.

The other good news for the growers — and for us because it keeps the costs down — is that orchards more than 50 years old are still producing abundant crops. A mature tree will yield nuts for hundreds of years or indeed until the saints come marching in. The 1992 crop was 26,000 tons.

Hazelnut Butter

Makes 1 cup

½ cup butter or margarine
2 teaspoons lemon juice
⅓ cup finely chopped hazelnuts
½ teaspoon salt
Dash celery salt
Dash cayenne pepper

Warm the butter or margarine to room temperature. Add the remaining ingredients, stirring until thoroughly combined. Serve on top of fish (especially salmon steaks), chicken, or vegetables, or as an alternative to peanut butter.

*Summer is come with love to towne...
The nut of hazel springeth.*

— *The Owl and the Nightingale, 1307*

Old Wives' Tale

Old wives put a lot of faith in the hazelnut. They say it cures chronic coughing if it is pounded with honey, and that when mixed with pepper it will get rid of the common cold. Better yet, if it is burned and mashed with suet and smeared on the head, it will cure baldness.

HEALTH FOOD

"Bran muffin?"

This stuff tastes awful; I could have made a fortune selling it in my health-food store.

— **Woody Allen**
Sleeper

Did You Know?

☞ Annual sales of health foods exceed $4 billion.

FORTY CARROTS, PLEASE — HOLD THE HORMONES

It all started in the psychedelic 1960s, with funky little stores on side streets in the wrong part of town. There would be bins and barrels full of mung beans and garbanzos, strings of dried chilies and garlic hanging from the rafters, and dazed shopgirls in long skirts who would invariably remark, upon hearing of any natural phenomenon, "Oh, wow, man!"

Nature was a trip then. And carrot cake and carob were king. And it all had to be talked about, there in those little stores with beat-up furniture, and a welcome always extended by their impoverished, patched proprietors. Health-food stores became the clubhouses of the freaked-out generation.

Times have changed. All the crazy foods we once thought were far out are now front and center in the supermarket aisles. Everyone drinks herb tea, claims to be vegetarian and organic, and simulates salivation over little squares of tofu floating in troughs of water. We are all carrying string bags, recycling, and saving the planet. Rice cakes and blue corn chips have found a home in homes that once scoffed at anything "natural." Tabbouleh, black beans, and dried banana chips occupy a place in our hearts as well as our cupboards. Tiger's milk never did quite make it into the mainstream, but there are more and more who agree with Madonna's decision and think it hip "to shun consuming flesh." Except once in a while.

When we speak of "health food," we are not talking refined. We are into whole, unprocessed food without additives and preservatives, though without them such foods quickly become rancid and provide a healthy diet for migrating colonies of bugs and weevils and small scurrying creatures.

Green is a hugely popular color among the politically correct. Brown is much in favor too, as in (like) brown sugar, brown rice, brown honey, brown pasta, and brown paper bags. Brown foods and brown bags share an aura of being natural, or better yet, "all-natural" and worthy. Which is probably why we can now buy brown, unbleached coffee filters — at a higher price, of course, than those that have been "purified." Way out.

"We believe in eating the whole food."

Health Food Goes Mainstream

Whole Foods Market Inc. is the largest health-food supermarket chain in the country, with 21 stores at last count. This expanding Austin, Texas-based group is riding atop a wave of new health-food stores that are large enough in size, and broad enough in selection, to fill a family's weekly grocery needs. In most operations, apart from aisles where New Morning Natural Otios replace Cheerios, fructose stands in for sugar, and there is an obvious preference for biodegradable detergents and other environmentally friendly products, the setup is that of a standard supermarket.

"There are a few differences, however," *Chicago Tribune* writer Janet Ginsburg observed following a visit to a local Whole Foods store. Among them were "an on-site massage therapist, presumably available to put customers in the right sort of New Age shopping mood, and a large herbal remedy department." There were no copies of the *National Enquirer* at the checkout counter, she noted, "but you can page through copies of *Yoga Journal, Animal's Agenda,* and *Bicycling* magazines."

Other chains in this genre include Wild Oats Markets, of Boulder, Colorado, which already has eight stores; Mrs. Gooch's Natural Food Markets, from Sherman Oaks, California, which operates seven; and the newest entry, Fresh Fields, based in Rockville, Maryland, which expects to have 14 stores in business soon.

General Nutrition Co. Inc. is in a different league, having evolved from a discount health-food store into a kind of Health 'R' Us mega chain with close to 1,400 stores selling merchandise along with brand-name vitamins.

What all these stores are banking on is that the organic foods market, currently growing at a rate of 20 percent a year, has nowhere to go but up. A recent comparison of 29 sample items featured in both conventional and health-food markets found that prices for similar items in health-food stores averaged about 40 percent higher.

HEART DIET

THE FRENCH PARADOX

What are we to make of the fact that the French eat, drink, and make merry at a rate far in excess of anything Americans deem prudent, yet are less than half as much at risk for heart disease as we are? The French eat a high-fat diet, they feast on cheeses and cream, and they smoke more and exercise less than we do. What makes the key difference? It seems to be the glass that cheers.

"No one needs to drink to lead a healthy, happy, rewarding life," writes Gene Ford in his recent book, *The French Paradox & Drinking for Health.* However, he says, "moderate drinking is *good for a person* in the same manner that aspirin or beef — in moderate amounts — add to the well-being of an individual. Ethyl alcohol provides calories and relieves stress. These physiological factors alone justify its moderate usage."

What's more, scientific studies have shown that the chances of suffering a cardiac death are dramatically reduced by drinking one or two glasses of wine a day, or equivalent amounts of other alcoholic beverages. According to a study in 1987 by Dr. Charles Hennekens and associates at Harvard University, "Analyses showed that compared with non-drinkers, people who drank 'moderate' amounts of alcohol every day — defined as two beers or wines or one mixed drink — had a 49 percent lower risk of a heart attack."

American scientists and medical researchers who are studying the paradox (which the French call their good luck) point to allied cultural influences on behavior. The French have an ancient gastronomical tradition. They learn in childhood to take a serious interest in the freshness and wholesomeness of food, and in its artful preparation. They eat three leisurely meals a day, never rushing food, rarely snacking. They eat more vegetables than we do and cook them less long. And they drink very little milk. But they do consume immense amounts of cheese and cream, for example, and in other countries the consumption of such high-fat foods is shown to have a strong relationship to mortality rate from chronic heart disease. In France, it shows little or none. What is the variable? The answer seems inescapable: a glass of wine a day keeps the doctor away.

A Dietary Prayer

I dare not taste one drop of oil
For if I do, my health I'll spoil.
I'd spread my bread with gobs of butter
But that would set my doc a-flutter.
Don't serve me poultry, pork, or beef
Or I will surely come to grief,
And that fine fish just from the sea
Would, fried, become the death of me.
At breakfast I must never poke
My fork at any golden yolk,
And salt, to which I was a slave,
Now lures me to an early grave.
Sugar, friend of childhood, sweet,
Is now a rare, forbidden treat.
A shot of gin, a glass of wine,
A vermouth cassis — sins times nine,
For Nathan Pritikin is my guide,
And by his Law I must abide.
Farewell to all the eats I love,
Farewell, so long, to all the above.
But as I chomp through fields of green
And shrink each day to sinewy lean,
Teach me, Lord, not to wish each course
Was rare roast beef with béarnaise sauce.

AHA's Dietary Guidelines

The Nutrition Committee of the American Heart Association offers these guidelines for a safe and prudent diet for healthy American adults and suggests that we translate them into eating patterns with the guidance of a physician and/or nutritionist.

1. Saturated fat intake should be less than 10 percent of calories.

2. Total fat intake should be less than 30 percent of calories.

3. Cholesterol intake should be less than 100 milligrams per 1,000 calories, not to exceed 300 milligrams per day.

4. Protein intake should be approximately 15 percent of calories.

5. Carbohydrate intake should constitute 50 to 55 percent or more of calories, with emphasis on increased complex carbohydrates.

6. Sodium intake should be reduced to approximately 1 gram per 1,000 calories, not to exceed 3 grams per day.

7. If alcoholic beverages are consumed, the caloric intake from this source should be limited to 15 percent of total calories but should not exceed 50 milliliters of ethanol per day.

8. Total calories should be sufficient to maintain the individual's best body weight.

9. A wide variety of foods should be consumed.

Books

Choices for a Healthy Heart
Joseph C. Piscatella; Workman, 1987; $15.95

Dean Ornish's Program for Reversing Heart Disease
Dean Ornish; Random House, 1990; $24.95

The American Heart Association Cookbook
Editors; Random House/Times Books, 1993; $14.00

In One Lifetime

The average human heart beats 2,500,000,000 times.

MORE INFORMATION

American Heart Association
7272 Greenville Avenue
Dallas, TX 75231-4599
214-373-6300

HERBS

Parsley, parsley everywhere —
Let me have my victuals bare.

— **Ogden Nash**
Plain-speaking poet

A GARDEN OF HERBS

No matter how many flowers, fruits, and vegetables they want to show off, gardeners always take you past their herb garden. These fragrant beds are often planted at the focal point of the garden around the sundial or behind the wooden bench so that you can breathe in their aroma as you sip your lemonade and admire your host's handiwork.

To be purely practical, though, it is best to plant herbs as close to the kitchen door as the sun will allow. It is easy, even on a rainy day, to dash out of the kitchen wielding a pair of scissors and snip off a few leaves, but if you have to go waltzing down the garden path you may just be lazy enough to use the dried ones that are handy, thinking no one will notice. They probably won't. But you will.

Not much space is needed for a small kitchen (as opposed to an ornamental) herb garden. A three-foot square will do nicely. Herbs don't need much watering, nor, except for parsley, do they require particularly good soil. About all they ask for is plenty of sunshine, and because this is often lacking, or the light is filtered, it's devilishly difficult to grow them on a window ledge, though the green of thumb claim to have success.

Fresh herbs can usually be found at farmers' markets or good produce stores. Herb catalogs exist, too, and, if you wish, Federal Express, like your personal gardener, will deliver freshly picked herbs overnight.

Old Wives' Tale

Drag a speckled toad by its hind leg around the herb garden and your herbs will grow abundantly. Plant an elder hedge around your garden; then if you stand still as a mouse beside it on Midsummer Eve, you will see the king of the elves and all his court go walking by.

Herbal Blends with Pizazz

When foods must be cooked without salt, herbs can come to the rescue. When using dried herbs, be sure that they are fresh; if possible, dry your own.

Saltless Surprise

2 teaspoons garlic powder
1 teaspoon each dried basil and oregano
1 teaspoon powdered lemon rind

Put the ingredients into a blender or food processor and give them a brief whirl. Store in a screw-topped glass jar; add a few grains of rice to prevent the herbs from clumping together.

Pungent Salt Substitute

3 teaspoons dried basil
2 teaspoons each dried summer savory, marjoram, and crushed sage
2 teaspoons celery seed

2 teaspoons ground cumin
1 teaspoon dried thyme

Combine all the ingredients in a blender or food processor or powder them with a mortar and pestle. Store in a screw-topped glass jar.

Spicy Saltless Seasoning

1 teaspoon ground cloves
1 teaspoon freshly ground black pepper
1 teaspoon crushed coriander seed
2 teaspoons paprika
1 tablespoon dried rosemary

Combine all the ingredients in a blender or food processor and whirl until thoroughly combined. Store in a screw-topped glass jar.

Drying Herbs

Air drying. Don't leave herbs out in the sun to dry or the oils will be lost along with the fragrance. Instead, tie small bunches of each herb together and put them, heads downward, in a brown paper bag. Leave undisturbed for a few weeks until completely dry.

Microwave drying. Put a single layer of the herbs between three or four thicknesses of paper towels and microwave on High for 2 minutes until they are dry. Add a few more seconds if necessary.

Stored in a cool, dark place, dried herbs have a shelf life of about six months. Stored near a hot oven, they have a life of six days. Herbs that are more than a year old have lost their savor; you might as well use a pinch of dust from the vacuum cleaner. Throw the rascals out and start over with a *fresh* fresh supply.

FDA Frowns on Self-Healing

Though herbal remedies may be quite safe when taken in small enough quantities, their legal status is murky. The FDA plans to institute stricter labeling requirements for many herbs that carry health claims. It is important to consult a physician rather than attempting self-medication, and always be extremely wary of promises of miracles.

What Goes with What

Soups
Bay, chervil, tarragon, marjoram, parsley, rosemary, savory

Poultry
Garlic, oregano, rosemary, sage, savory

Beef
Bay, chives, cloves, cumin, garlic, hot pepper, marjoram, rosemary, savory

Lamb
Garlic, marjoram, mint, oregano, rosemary, thyme

Pork
Coriander, cumin, garlic, ginger, hot pepper, sage, savory, thyme

Cheese
Basil, chervil, chives, curry, dill, fennel, garlic, marjoram, oregano, parsley, sage, thyme

Fish
Chervil, dill, fennel, garlic, parsley, tarragon, thyme

Fruit
Anise, cinnamon, coriander, cloves, ginger, lemon verbena, mint, rose geranium, sweet cicely

Bread
Caraway, marjoram, oregano, poppy seed, rosemary, thyme

Vegetables
Basil, burnet, chervil, chives, dill, marjoram, mint, parsley, pepper, tarragon, thyme

Salads
Basil, borage, burnet, chives, garlic, parsley, sorrel, tarragon

Planning a Herb Garden

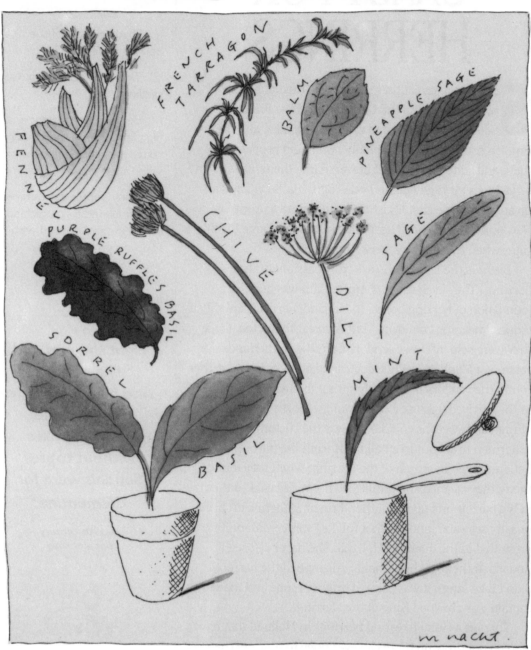

A herb garden may seem less appealing than a rose garden, but it gives every bit as much pleasure to the dedicated cook (and eater). There are hundreds of ways of arranging the plants, and this list of possible plants is just a beginning. A good gardener suggests a three-point plan:

1. Sit down with seed catalogs, books, garden layouts, and any other resources and read, read, read.

2. Outline your proposed garden first on paper or on the computer, starting with a blank layout. (Make lots of copies of the blank — it saves time when you change your mind.) Plant your garden on paper.

3. Carry out your plan.

Possible plantings:

Lamb Ears	Water Mint	Germander
Costmary	Wild Geranium	English Lavender
Chamomile	Southernwood	Peppermint
Bee Balm	Lady's Mantle	Wild Geranium
Lemon Balm	Betony	Creeping Thyme
Orange Mint	Lady's Bedstraw	Woolly Thyme
	Rose Geranium	Grey Santolina
	Green Santolina	Spearmint
		Dill
		Tarragon
		Rosemary
		Thyme
		Sage
		Marjoram
		Wormwood
		Winter Savory
		Chives
		Oregano
		Parsley
		Basil

The Right Spot

by Rosetta E. Clarkson

In every garden there is some spot just waiting for the right plant. . . . Some herbs fit into rock gardens; others make pleasing edgings for the vegetable plot, for bordering garden paths or roadways, for surrounding the sundial, or for tucking in among the flowers of beds or borders.

Begin with a few herbs and really get acquainted with them by growing them and by using them. You will find yourself wondering how you ever did without them and will be eager to become familiar with more and more of these ancient plants.

Excerpted from Herbs: Their Culture and Uses

There's fennel for you, and columbines; there's rue for you; and here's some for me; we may call it herb of grace o' Sundays.

— William Shakespeare
Hamlet

TIPS

Storing

Pick or buy any fresh herb in small quantities and tie the stalks together in a tight bunch. Wrap in wet paper towels and tuck the bunch into a plastic bag, leaving the end open to the air. Herbs will keep in the refrigerator for a few days. Or you can put the bunch of herbs in a small vase filled with water and keep them in the fresh air, but out of the sun.

Herbal Relations

Most herbs belong to either the carrot or the mint families. Included among the 3,000 species of carrots are anise, coriander, dill, fennel, and parsley. The mint family has 3,200 relatives and some of its cousins are basil, oregano, rosemary, sage, and thyme.

Books

Little Herb Gardens
Georgeanne Brennan and Mimi Luebbermann; Chronicle Books, 1993; $12.95

Recipes from an American Herb Garden
Maggie Oster; Macmillan, 1993; $30.00

Sage Cottage Herb Garden Cookbook
Dorry Baird Norris; Globe Pequot, 1991; $12.95

The Complete Medicinal Herbal
Penelope Ody; Dorling Kindersley, 1993; $29.95

The Herbal Tea Garden
Marietta Marshall Marcin; Garden Way, 1993; $12.95

Shepherd's Garden Seeds
6116 Highway 9
Felton, CA 95018
408-335-6910

Herb Society of America
9019 Kirtland Chardon Road
Mentor, OH 44060
216-256-0514

HERRING

Herring on the Run

There was a time not too long ago when herrings were the most abundant of all the world's fish, populating the oceans by the billions. Today their numbers have been decimated as a result of overfishing and loss of spawning habitat.

Like salmon, shad, and smelt, herrings are anadromous. They spend most of their life in the ocean and return to fresh water to spawn before swimming 300 miles or more back to the open, salty sea. But polluted water and high dams have effectively blocked their passage to the rivers where once they left their progeny in quantities so vast that the waters were thick with golden-green eggs, floating with the currents.

Conservationists, alarmed at the reduction in numbers of herring, have begun to realize the vital necessity of protecting all fish, not only specific species. Herrings, because of their sheer quantities, have constituted a particularly important link in the food chain: They feed on plankton and in turn provide food for larger species of fish. The decimation of the species threatens the balance of the entire ocean ecosystem.

Herrings are small, sleek fish, built for speed and agility — qualities that are called on to evade predators. But the most dangerous of these by far has been man, and no turn of speed can save a fish from the gigantic nets that can wipe out a whole school in one, long haul.

Fortunately, as many as a hundred herring runs in the New England area alone have recently been restored, thanks to the management of the Massachusetts Division of Fisheries. And more such action is needed. Today, the supply of fresh herring in the United States is so small that the fish is no longer considered commercially important. Most of the herring sold in our markets has come frozen from Iceland and Canada.

CRAZY FOR HERRINGS

Scandinavians eat them. So do the Russians, who pickle them, and the Germans, and the French. The Scots smoke them and call them *kippers,* and the English season them with plenty of salt and pepper, grill them and add a pat of sweet butter, name them *bloaters* and serve them for high tea. And years ago, coastal villages all up and down the East Coast of North America, from Newfoundland to the Chesapeake, hung out "Gone Fishing" signs when the herrings were running.

But it is the Dutch who are truly passionate about herrings. They even say that Amsterdam was built on a foundation of herring bones. In Holland, herrings are called *matjes,* meaning "maidens," but men eat them, too. Once they were sold by street vendors from the Netherlands version of Manhattan's hot-dog carts and folks would gather round the vendors in the early spring to greet the little fish as they arrived fresh and cold from the North Sea — young, plump, and sweet as could be. It was the custom then for fishermen to set out in small boats from the port of Scheveningen in search of the herring. When they found them, they cleaned and butterflied them and packed them in big barrels one upon another, brushing them with brine or salty seawater, and the first full keg was ceremoniously presented to the queen of Holland. She never refused it. And when the royal household had emptied the barrel (it didn't take long), it was painted bright orange and the sea captain was crowned King of the Herring.

There is a ritual to eating herrings in Holland that few who do not grow up there can ever hope to master. The raw fish, barely five inches long, is dipped in freshly chopped onions; then, with the eater's head tipped way, way back and the little fish held by its tail between the thumb and the first finger, the herring is swallowed in two or three heart-stopping bites of ecstasy with not the tiniest piece of onion falling from its silvery skin.

Herrings have suffered so grievously from overfishing that they are now almost as scarce in Holland as they are everywhere else. But for two or three weeks in May, herring fanciers can run to the Oyster Bar in New York's Grand Central Station, where KLM Royal Dutch Airlines flies in cargoes of herrings — enough to feed 15,000 people during the all-too-brief season.

Arthur Fiedler once instructed his orchestra to play the music "loud — but soft," and this is the way with herrings as well. They must be firm, but soft. In the Oyster Bar, which is the only restaurant we know of that offers the genuine Dutch herrings, the accompaniments are chopped hard-cooked eggs, chopped chives, and, of course, finely chopped onion. To set the scene properly, the drink of choice should be icy-cold Dutch gin — though the faint of heart may settle for beer.

*Light she was and like a fairy,
And her shoes were number nine;
Herring boxes without topses
Sandals were for Clementine.*

— *19th-century popular song*

Old Wives' Tale

A "red herring," to some people, may mean a diversion, but old wives believed that if a young girl ate a herring that had been preserved in salt for three months (which turned it red) and then went to sleep without taking anything to drink and without speaking a word to anybody, her future husband would appear to her in a dream. (And when she awoke she would have a powerful thirst!)

HOME COOKING

Granny's Kitchen

My grandmother wore one of those aprons with the big, scooped-out front and the crisscrossing at the back— a Hoover apron, I think it was called. And it bloused out over her very ample frame.

Everything was of scrubbed wood in her kitchen. The table, the floor, and even the sink was made of wood and lined with tin that was hammered in to form the lining. The water pipes were not attached securely to the wall. They came out under the sink, reached up the wall, and elbowed out over the sink.

When I was a little boy, I couldn't reach the faucet and I had to stand on something to turn the water on. And when it started coming, the pipe shook so much I had to hold onto it with one hand and hold the cup under it with the other.

I can still remember the taste of that water— it was so cold, so metallic, so crystal and pure. I have had more than my share of fine wines, but long for that brittle-hard, wonderful water in that bright kitchen.

— *Joe Baum*
President, The Rainbow Room, New York

My mother was a good recreational cook, but what she basically believed about cooking was that if you worked hard and prospered, someone else would do it for you.

— Norah Ephron
Sleepless author

THE KITCHEN CLOCK

In 1915, half of all American women had five or more children, and spent an average of five hours a day in the kitchen. Almost none were working mothers, and they had to shop around town for their food because supermarkets had not yet come into existence.

Today, a working mother with two children is the American norm. She shops quickly and efficiently in supermarkets, and the average amount of time she spends preparing the evening meal — which is often just a process of assembling and reheating components that have been prepared elsewhere, or "fixing" a salad — is 15 minutes. A recent study by *The Food Channel* newsletter asserted that only 3 percent of Americans admitted knowing how to cook. These amazing statistics are echoed by the questions asked when consumers call industry hotlines.

Yet people like to think of themselves as cooks if they can. Home bread-baking, for example, is very much on the rise, and people feel good when they can brag about producing their own loaves. But in fact this baking is usually done by a machine that requires no skill. Few if any of these "bakers" could understand basic instructions such as "bake blind," "stand under cold running water," "dredge," "flute," or "butterfly."

Typically, a contemporary working woman has little interest in home baking or other frills of the kitchen scene. Pressed for time on the job and short of time to spend on basic cooking, she elects to steal some time by buying prepared foods. Unhappily, her theft leaves her feeling guilty. However, if she can take fresh spaghetti made by someone else out of its refrigerated package and boil it up, and then stir in a jar of pasta sauce, she can tell herself that she has prepared a home-cooked meal.

In this way she buys some of the sense of worth that her great-grandmother took for granted in 1915.

The Top Ten

The foods most frequently found in American kitchens:

Ketchup
Mustard
Vegetable oil
Cinnamon
Margarine
Spaghetti
Seasoned salt
Chili powder
Potatoes
Soy sauce
(more people have soy sauce in their kitchen than have tea, coffee, milk, or salsa)

Reprinted from
The Food Channel

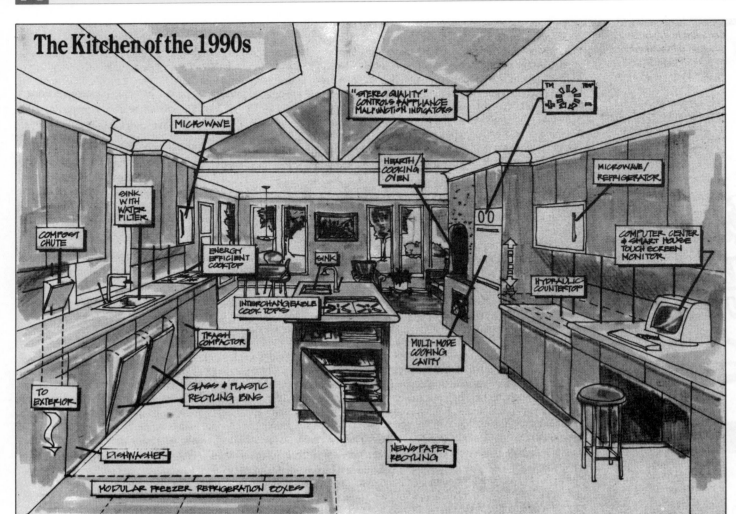

The Kitchen of the 1990s

(Labels: MICROWAVE; "STEREO QUALITY" CONTROLS + APPLIANCE MALFUNCTION INDICATORS; SINK WITH WATER FILTER; HEARTH/COOKING OVEN; MICROWAVE/REFRIGERATOR; COMPOST CHUTE; ENERGY EFFICIENT COOKTOP; SINK; COMPUTER CENTER + SMART HOUSE TOUCH SCREEN MONITOR; INTERCHANGEABLE COOK TOPS; HYDRAULIC COUNTERTOP; TRASH COMPACTOR; MULTI-MODE COOKING CAVITY; TO EXTERIOR; GLASS & PLASTIC RECYCLING BINS; NEWSPAPER RECYCLING; DISHWASHER; MODULAR FREEZER REFRIGERATION BOXES)

THE DISAPPEARING
"KITCHEN"

Periodically, the magazines declare that we are all going to return to the kitchen and gather round the family table. An unlikely story. Home cooking, despite what we may prefer to believe, is on the decline. Cooking is gradually becoming an optional recreation, like knitting.

Though it is likely that some will cook at the weekend, fewer people in succeeding generations will have the skills to prepare even the simplest dishes. Professional caterers will be brought in to provide the food for small dinners for four or six guests, and there will be more home delivery of hot food as the technology of cooking it en route is perfected.

Electronic shopping will eventually become the order of the day. Families will be ordering food from fine restaurants and fast-food places by fax, and franchised food facilities will have a nationwide 800 number, with operators who will direct a call to the nearest supplier.

Dinner won't be the only option after 6 p.m. Some of us may want to eat breakfast in the evening. As we gradually move to a global economy, there will be a huge growth in shift work. Those who now labor at night — medical, factory, and transportation workers, as well as police and other municipal workers — will be joined by office workers serving the new economy that must operate 24 hours a day. To service those who work at night, more retail operations, restaurants, and other businesses will remain open around the clock.

These radical changes will have an impact on what, when, and with whom we eat. The day is not too distant when we will be seeing four black "boxes" in our living room: the television, the computer, the microwave oven, and a small refrigerator-freezer. The utensils will be disposable or recycled and we will turn the kitchen into an exercise room.

But in the meantime there are still many food lovers who enjoy spending time in a well-designed kitchen — and sometimes actually *cooking* in it.

What Americans Do to Save Time

Eating Activity	Often	Sometimes
Eat at fast-food restaurants	22 percent	48 percent
Bring home take-out foods	14 percent	46 percent
Shop in convenience stores	13 percent	42 percent
Eat frozen prepared meals	10 percent	32 percent
Microwave main course	8 percent	23 percent

Source: Roper/Technomic, in *The Food Channel*

I never see any home cooking. All I get is fancy stuff.

— Prince Philip, Duke of Edinburgh
Crusty prince

American Family Arrangements

Married couple with children ....25.9 percent

Married couple without children ....29.4 percent

People living alone ....25.0 percent

Unrelated people living together ....4.7 percent

Other families without children ....6.5 percent

Other families with children ....8.5 percent

Source: U.S. Census Bureau

A PRIVATE EYE GETS A NICE HOME-COOKED MEAL

HOWARD ENGEL

In about 20 minutes, my mother called us to the table. The Friday-night candles had been lit, and there were two bowls of soup on the plastic cloth, one for me and the other for my father. It was canned vegetable.

"Where's your soup?" my father asked.

"I never eat soup," she answered. I was still in short pants when I first heard that exchange. "If anyone wants a salad, I can make one," she dared us. I said that a salad would be just the thing. She didn't budge. Pa went into the kitchen to retrieve the steaks from the broiler. "Manny, let Benny have the rare one." He placed the platter of steaming meat in the middle of the table, after I cleared a place. "You know how he likes it rare." He handed me my plate and I cut into the meat. It was liver gray all the way through. The vegetables were canned peas and carrots; lukewarm. Ma repeated her invitation to salad. Maybe there remained in the back of her mind the ghost of a servant lurking in the kitchen who could whip up these trifles at a moment's notice.

The meal concluded with the traditional passing of a tea bag from cup to cup, followed by the time-honored squirt from the plastic lemon. After his last sip of tea, Pa pushed himself away from the table observing, "Benny, it does you good to get a home-cooked meal for a change, after the *chazerai* you eat in restaurants."

Excerpted from
The Suicide Murders

A Man's Place

When it comes to cooking dinner, husbands always like to have a nice wife out in the kitchen, looking after things. It's true that times have changed, and working wives would like wives, too, but most married men still aren't helping with the family meal. There are some exceptions, particularly among the young and progressive-minded, but when we say that there's something about matrimony that works for the male, it's still more than likely to be the female.

HONEY

The only reason for being a bee that I know of is making honey . . . and the only reason for making honey is so I can eat it.

— **Winnie the Pooh**
in A. A. Milne's
The House at Pooh Corner

WHAT IS HONEY?

Honey is an invert sugar formed by an enzyme from natural floral nectar. The nectar is gathered by bees and manufactured into a stable, high-energy food. Its composition and flavor will vary depending on the floral source, but honey predominantly contains fructose and glucose, as well as maltose and sucrose. Most forms of honey contain about 17 percent moisture; approximately 98 percent of the remaining solid is carbohydrate. One teaspoon of honey contains about 21 calories.

Some say that babies should not be fed honey until they are at least a year old because it could contain harmful bacterial spores.

Honey Bear

Watch for the National Honey Board's bear logo on the label of the jar. It ensures that honey constitutes 51 percent or more of the total sweetener content of a product, or that honey is used in a higher proportion than any other sweetener. A panel of food scientists reviews each product to ensure that all the necessary criteria are met before awarding the bear designation.

MORE INFORMATION

American Beekeeping Federation
P.O. Box 1038
Jessup, GA 31545
912-427-8447

National Honey Board
421 21st Avenue, Suite 203
Longmont, CO 80501-1421
303-776-2337

MAIL ORDER SOURCES

✉

Champlain Valley Apiaries
P.O. Box 127
Middlebury, VT 05753
802-388-7724

Hanna's Honey
P.O. Box 17353
Salem, OR 97305
503-393-2945

HONEY VARIETIES

Honey is made throughout the world and in every state in North America. Color and taste vary greatly depending on the source of the nectar and the place where the honey is produced. Some honeys are almost colorless, while others are a deep, rich brown. Generally speaking, the lighter honeys have a delicate floral flavor while the darker varieties have a more mellow quality.

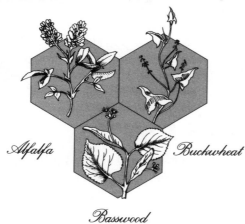

Alfalfa

Buckwheat

Basswood

Acacia honey is pale yellow with a delicate taste. China is the major supplier but it is also produced in California.

Alfalfa honey is produced throughout North America. It is light in color and has a delicate taste.

Basswood honey, characterized by its distinctive "biting" flavor, is the exception to the rule that color is an indication of the intensity of the taste. This honey is almost colorless but has a strong aroma and tang.

Buckwheat honey is dark and full-bodied. It is produced in Minnesota, Wisconsin, Ohio, Pennsylvania, New York, and eastern Canada, but has recently declined in popularity.

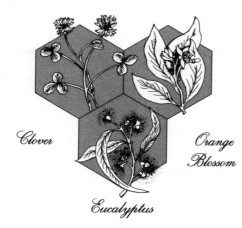

Clover

Orange Blossom

Eucalyptus

Clover honey has the mild, sweet taste we consider typical of honey. Clovers have contributed more to honey production in the United States than any other group of plants. White, yellow, and Alsike clovers are the most important for honey production. Depending on the clover's location and type, the honey may vary from almost clear to light amber in color.

Eucalyptus honey can come from any of many hundreds of species and hybrids, so the honey varies greatly in color and flavor; it almost always has a tang of eucalyptus. Australia is the major supplier.

Fireweed honey is light-colored; it comes from the showy

purple spikes of the perennial herb that grows wild in open woodlands and marshy spots.

Orange blossom honey often comes from a combination of citrus sources. It is usually light-colored, with a delicate flavor and a fresh scent reminiscent of the blossom. It is produced in Florida, and the southern counties of California and Texas.

Sage honey comes from any of several varieties of sage, but the chief source is the sagebrush of California. It is white, with a mild, delicate flavor.

Sourwood honey's source is a small to medium-sized tree that grows prolifically in the southern Appalachians, from southern Pennsylvania into northern Georgia. The honey is light-colored and has a fine, mild flavor.

Tulip poplar or tulip-tree honey has a less assertive flavor than one would expect from its dark amber color. It is produced from southern New England west to southern Michigan, and south to the Gulf states.

Tupelo honey is produced in the southeastern states; it is light-colored and has a mild but distinctive flavor.

Wildflower honey is a flavorful, versatile honey gathered from a variety of wildflowers and flowering trees and shrubs. It is usually quite dark, with a pleasingly bold flavor.

Sage

Tupelo

Tulip Poplar

While many of these types of honey are widely available in stores, most commercial honeys, especially those kinds produced in large quantities, are blended to create a unique and consistent taste and color, and are pasteurized by heating to 160 degrees F. This also prevents crystals from forming.

ODD JOBS

John Liska, the only commercial honey producer and packer in chilly Alaska, and his busy bees don't have much time in the year to do their work. Between mid-May and the first of September, when the state is free of snow and ice and flowers bloom, the hive hurriedly collects nectar from the blossoms of Alaskan fireweed and makes a honey that is as clear as corn syrup. Despite all the pressure, Liska and his natural associates manage to produce almost six tons of Raw Alaskan Fireweed Honey annually.

Books

A Book of Bees
Sue Hubbell; Ballantine, 1988; $8.95

Cooking with Honey: The Natural Way to Health & Better Eating
Marge Davenport; Paddlewheel, 1991; $13.55

Honey Cookbook: Recipes from the Home of the Honey Bee
Sharon L. Kraynek; A. I. Root, 1991; $12.99

Honey: From Hive to Honeypot
Sue Style; Chronicle Books, 1993; $14.95

Bee Scouts

When a hive needs food, a scout bee is sent to look for it. When she finds it, she returns and performs a complicated dance that is in fact an aerial map to the source. Follower bees in the hive read these instructions with their antennae. After millions of years, this honey-bee language is so refined that the follower bees can interpret the scout's message flawlessly, even if the conditions of their flight aren't exactly those of the reenacted flight.

For example, the scout bee conveys direction in terms of the position of the sun. As that changes, the follower bees adjust the directions. They do the same for distance, which the scout expresses in terms of energy (honey) needed to get to the source. Scientists have even discovered that if the follower bee is younger than the scout, she is able to know that she will need less fuel to reach the nectar.

Entomologists have unraveled the bee language by gluing a miniature bar-code device onto the back of the bee. The standard bar code can differentiate between as many as a million items, but postage-stamp size is far too big and heavy to suit a bee. Scientists turned to a scanner engineer, who developed a bee bar code just a tenth of an inch wide that can be attached to the bee's back. A scanner installed at the entrance to the hive monitors the bees' comings and goings, and reports on the vital role that bees play in pollinating crops.

HARVESTING THE HONEY

Traditional garb for a beekeeper is coveralls, hat with veil, leather gloves, and sturdy shoes. Many beekeepers, however, prefer to work with their bare hands, finding that gloves interfere with their dexterity.

To calm the bees during honey harvesting, the beekeeper "smokes" the hive, using a firepot with bellows. When smoke gets in their eyes, the bees' immediate reaction is to gorge themselves to save the honey. With their bellies full, the bees calm down.

The beekeeper "uncaps" the honeycomb, using a heated knife to remove the wax chamber covers, and places it in an extractor. The centrifugal force exerted as the extractor spins causes the honey to splash against its sides and run to the bottom of the container, where it passes through an opening and is collected below.

The honey needs no additional refining or processing, though a few other steps may be taken to prepare it for the supermarket shelf. For example, it can be strained through cheesecloth to remove particles of wax, or filtered to remove air bubbles, pollen, and other fine particles. But, basically, honey is ready to eat as soon as it has been gathered — as anyone who has ever enjoyed honey in the comb well knows.

TIPS

Buying
Buy mild-flavored honeys such as clover when you are looking for a delicate flavor, as for salad dressings. Choose darker-colored ones for long cooking procedures, including barbecue sauces and glazes for ducks.

Cooking
For best results choose recipes that specify honey. When substituting honey for granulated sugar, exchange honey for up to half the sugar. With experimentation, honey can be substituted for all the sugar in some recipes, but remember that because of its high fructose content, honey has a higher sweetening power than sugar.

Coat the cup or measuring spoon with vegetable oil or vegetable spray before adding the honey, and the honey will slide out easily.

One 12-ounce jar of honey is equal to a standard measuring cupful.

When using honey, reduce the amount of liquid in the recipe by ¼ cup for each cup of honey, because honey absorbs and retains moisture. (This is why breads, rolls, and muffins made with honey keep fresh longer.)

When baking, add ½ teaspoon baking soda for each cup of honey used; reduce the oven temperature by 25 degrees F. to prevent overbrowning.

Storing
Store honey at room temperature for up to one year. If it crystallizes, remove the lid and place the jar in warm water for a few minutes until the crystals dissolve. (They are not harmful.) Honey can be heated in the microwave for a minute or two, depending on the quantity. Stir it every 30 seconds and be careful not to let it burn.

Don't be tempted to taste it the second you take it from the microwave or you may scald your tongue. Honey heats more quickly than you may think.

Did You Know?

☞ The ancient Egyptians used to pay their taxes in honey.

☞ The honey bee has three pairs of legs, four wings, five eyes, a stinger, and a special stomach that holds nectar. It is the only insect that produces a food that we eat.

☞ The average worker bee flies 15 miles per hour and in its entire lifetime produces ¹/₁₂ of a teaspoon of honey.

☞ To produce 1 pound of honey, a bee colony will visit 2 million flowers and fly 55,000 miles.

☞ Utah is known as the beehive state.

HOTLINES

800-356-5941
National Honey Board

800-220-2110
Golden Blossom Honey

HOSPITAL FOOD

"I think Mr. Muskingham is on the mend. He sat bolt upright today and said, 'Bring on the hot hors d'oeuvres.'"

PRESCRIPTION FOR HOSPITAL FOOD

What is prompting the recent attention to hospital fare is, you guessed it, money. Money and health issues have recently become inextricably entwined. It caused a lot of pain to hospital administrators to see visitors streaming through the doors to return to the patients' bedsides carrying large square boxes that looked suspiciously as if they just might contain pizza. The solution: Install a pizza maker in the hospital kitchen and pocket the profits. The $11 billion hospital food industry is starting to look at food service as a profit center.

Mildly unwell patients — those with a broken bone or two, or post-birthing mothers — are more interested in meals than the seriously ill. For the restless confined to bed, the meal tray is an eagerly anticipated break in the day, providing a modicum of entertainment and something to do — if only to complain that the water for the tea is tepid, the macaroni and cheese on the dry side, and the Jell-O always red. And in cities where hospitals face stiff competition to keep beds filled, the food is picking up. The Children's Hospital in Los Angeles has an on-site McDonald's, whose food, to no one's surprise, the young patients prefer to the creamed chicken and pureed carrots of the hospital kitchen.

FAREWELL TO THOSE 5:00 A.M. BREAKFASTS

Food service is a difficult business in large hospitals, where kitchens have to cope with 20 or more menus and hundreds of orders every day, and meals must meet the guidelines of government mandates.

Ideally, of course, meals should be served at normal hours; hot food should arrive hot and cold food should be cold. But the distance between kitchen and destination often defeats those goals, particularly when food trolleys must compete for elevator space with other hospital traffic.

Promising solutions lie in developing food technologies, such as *sous-vide*, a new French method of preserving food so that it can be transported cold and reheated in hot water at the point of delivery. Also, with greater use of ready-to-eat meals and microwaves in patient locales, patients will be able to choose their own mealtimes as well as the kinds of foods they want to eat.

Discredited Diets

Borst Diet / *kidney failure*
Equal amounts of sugar and butter rolled into balls, melted, then served as "butter soup."

Caesar's Diet / *gout*
Milk and barley water.

Gerson-Hermannsdorfer Diet / *TB, cancer*
Fresh fruit, vegetables, and oatmeal, plus milk and vitamin supplements after six weeks.

Jarotsky Diet / *peptic ulcers*
A mixture of egg white and olive oil.

Salisbury Diet / *gout, psoriasis, dyspepsia*
Lean meat and hot water.

Sippy Diet / *peptic ulcers*
Hourly feedings of whole milk and cream.

Yolk Cure / *diabetes*
Ten to 40 egg yolks daily, plus leafy green vegetables.

Zomatherapy / *TB, anemia*
Raw meat juice.

Adapted from *Eating Well*

What people eat is at the very center of health.

— Carl Orringer, M.D.
Director of Preventive Cardiology,
University Hospitals of Cleveland

Dietary Outpatients

As in-hospital stays become shorter, the focus of food service in hospitals is changing. When a stay is limited to 48 hours, and when a period of fasting occupies a part of this time, many patients are more concerned about the quality of their medical care than of the cuisine. Nevertheless, diet may have been a contributory cause of a patient's illness and more hospitals are offering outpatient nutrition counseling.

HOT DOGS

The More Things Change. . .

by H. L. Mencken

I devoured hot-dogs in Baltimore 'way back in 1886, and they were then very far from new-fangled. . . . They contained precisely the same rubber, indigestible pseudo sausages that millions of Americans now eat, and they leaked the same flabby puerile mustard. Their single point of difference lay in the fact that their covers were honest German Wecke made of wheat-flour baked to crispiness, and not the soggy rolls prevailing today, of ground acorns, plaster-of-paris, flecks of bath-sponge, and atmospheric air all compact.

As quoted in A Food Lover's Companion

HOT DIGGETY DOG!

Frankfurters, a version of smoked, spiced, pork-and-beef German link sausages, were served and sold in America as early as 1860, from pushcarts in New York City. The bun came later, and regional debates still rage over who added it. No one, however, disputes who gave the hot dog its name. In 1901, Harry Mozley Stevens (founder of Harry M. Stevens Inc. of Cranbury, New Jersey, a contract management firm now run by third and fourth generations), then a concessionaire at the New York Polo Grounds, saw that cold foods weren't selling. So he sent his vendors to buy hot "dachshund sausages," and told them to hawk sausages by yelling, "Get your dachshund sausages while they're red hot!"

"Tad" Dorgan, a famous cartoonist of the time, was at the ball game. Next day, his cartoon featured barking dachshund sausages wrapped in warm buns. But because he had trouble spelling "dachshund," he substituted "Hot Dog" in the caption — and hot dog it has been ever since.

Adapted from *Restaurants & Institutions*

Did You Know?

☞ U.S. average annual hot dog consumption is close to 16 billion.

☞ Nathan Handwerker, the founder of Nathan's Famous Hot Dogs, hired young men wearing white coats and stethoscopes to gather round his cart and eat his "dogs," thus creating an impression of purity and cleanliness.

☞ Residents of Evanston, Illinois, can visit a hot-dog joint called Mustard's Last Stand.

☞ All beef, as in all-beef hot dogs, may not mean it is the kind of beef you might think of. But if by-products such as heart, spleen, and other innards are used, they must be listed on the label.

Let's Be Frank

The Center for Science in the Public Interest took an interest in hot dogs a couple of years back. To our surprise, though not to theirs, they discovered that turkey and chicken dogs scored among the fattiest. The winner among the best-tasting, lowest-fat dogs proved to be Hormel Light & Lean 97 percent Fat Free Franks, containing 45 calories, 1 gram of fat, and 350 milligrams of sodium. Healthy Choice also weighs in with a mere gram of fat and a bare 45 calories.

Manufacturers are still experimenting with meat mixtures that include carrageenan, the seaweed extract used to make low-fat ground beef. Low-fat hot dogs lack the taste and texture of the old-fashioned variety. But once they are nestled into a bun and blanketed with mustard, ketchup, relish, and sauerkraut, few notice the difference.

THE BEST OF
THE WURST

TIMOTHY WHITE

Throughout history, we've all been fed a lot of quasi-meaty hoodoo about the enduring Germanic grandeur of the frankfurter, the medieval invention named for the ancient city of Frankfurt. Frankly, hot dogs have always been Greek to me, and reached their apex, in my toothsome estimation, in the output of two family-owned chains that humbly sizzle and satisfy within 20 minutes of the George Washington Bridge. Of all the mobile meals created since antiquity (manna, pemmican, Mars bars), I don't think any rival the tongue-scalding superiority of a well-turned wiener in a toasted bun — that is, a bun whose sides are just high enough to contain a hearty slather of mustard and sauerkraut while you're trying to hold onto the wheel.

My late father was already renowned as a peerless one-armed hot dog chomper when he introduced me as a five-year-old to Teddy's in Paterson, New Jersey, and Papaya King in New York City. Guiding the family's wheezing, pea-green '53 Ford Custom wagon into the cramped parking lot of Teddy's or to the grimy curb at the Papaya King stand on 86th Street and Third Avenue, Dad was always boisterous in his ritual declaration that a good hot dog, rather than being ideal ball park fare, was actually best consumed in the comfort of the car — preferably with the motor running.

Excerpted from Roadside Food

Books

Hog Dog Cookbook
Jess M. Brallier; Globe Pequot, 1993; $9.95

I Love Hot Dogs
Pat Thompson; Olympic, 1981; $4.95

Make Mine Mayer

When Oscar Mayer's asked aerodynamic engineers to update their fleet of promotional Wienermobiles, they attacked the problem with relish and came up with motorized wieners capable of withstanding hurricane-force winds. Teenie-weenie teenagers are hired to drive the fiberglass "cars" wherever anyone wants to go. This includes getting wedding couples to the church on time and Oscar Mayer will not object if the Big Dog is draped with a banner that reads "Just Linked" or "For Better or Wurst."

HUNGER

We spend more money determining eligibility than on the service we are trying to provide.

— Attorney General Janet Reno

HUNGER IN THE
LAND OF PLENTY

A joint Task Force on Hunger and Malnutrition initiated by the American Institute of Nutrition and the American Society for Clinical Nutrition in 1988 defined hunger as "a recurrent, involuntary lack of access to food." The American Dietetic Association described hunger as "discomfort, weakness, or pain caused by lack of food."

But who needs a definition? Everyone has experienced temporary hunger and most of us can immediately do the obvious thing to alleviate it. When hunger is associated with the fear that there is no food to be had, we are looking at a far, far different thing from a momentary inconvenience.

The consequences of hunger are infinitely greater than the immediate problems of not having enough to eat. Being unable to find adequate amounts of food to support physical and mental health inevitably leads to the long-term hazards of the deprivation that comes from lack of income, lack of education, and lack of adequate housing.

There are 30 million hungry people in America — double the number of a decade ago. The United States, now the world's only superpower, would easily qualify for its own foreign aid.

A Call to Action

The old saying, "An ounce of prevention equals a pound of cure," makes good financial sense, a lesson that has hit home over and over again. For example, America has learned that improved highway design saved more lives than emergency medical services. Likewise, we learned that preventing smoking was cheaper than treating lung cancer, and reducing cholesterol was more cost-effective than bypass surgery, or caring for patients who had suffered a heart attack. Hungry children are literally a bad business because malnutrition can cause lifelong health problems. Feeding people now will save us a very hard lesson.

Hungry children and their parents do not have the strength to influence legislation. But corporate America does. And there are encouraging signs of increasing involvement from large and small companies. Their hunger-prevention activities include giving money and donating food surpluses to local food banks.

In addition, volunteerism is on the rise. Today there are more than 600 private emergency food provider agencies, many of them church-based, as compared with only 30 in 1981. Among the largest are Second Harvest, Share Our Strength (SOS), and Meals on Wheels.

God's Love We Deliver brings hot meals to homebound New Yorkers with AIDS. During the holiday season its volunteers deliver special gift baskets which also include nonfood items, a service meant to lift spirits in addition to filling stomachs. Even the needy cannot live on bread alone.

A SECOND HARVEST

DWIGHT GARNER

In the past, when a cereal company overshredded its wheat squares or a vegetable processor sliced its green beans the wrong length, the perfectly edible results went to the trash.

No longer. Thanks to an organization that transforms food-factory mistakes and distributes them to food banks, everyday production errors have become a weapon in the fight against hunger.

Armed with thousands of volunteers and food from nearly 250 corporate donors, Chicago-based Second Harvest National Food Bank Network has become the largest feeding program in the United States, second only to government food stamps. Last year, the nonprofit group distributed 400 million pounds of food across the country — everything from white bread to trout stuffed with crabmeat.

"Our standards for the goods we accept are very high," says Bud Jones, spokesperson for Second Harvest. "People don't just dump things on us. We've got teams of inspectors and we make sure we're providing food banks with quality goods."

Miriam Manyon, executive director of the Greater Pittsburgh Community Food Bank, which helps feed 23,000 households, says she remembers one opportunity when General Mills recalled thousands of boxes of Cheerios because a child choked on one of the toy balls enclosed as a premium. "Through Second Harvest, we got a lot of Cheerios," Manyon says. "All we had to do was fish all of those toy balls out."

While Jones is pleased with the support Second Harvest has received from large corporations, his goal is to have them give 1 percent of their food to the hungry regardless of production errors. The organization also invites individuals to donate groceries to their local food bank or contribute financially.

Excerpted from Eating Well

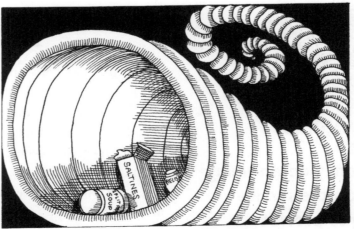

"HORN OF SOME"

Hungriest Populations

Mississippi	19.86%
New Mexico	18.77%
Louisiana	15.92%
Alabama	15.75%
Kentucky	15.75%
Washington, D.C.	15.58%
West Virginia	15.00%
Texas	14.66%
Arkansas	14.49%
Georgia	14.41%
Oklahoma	14.24%
South Carolina	13.74%
Indiana	13.15%
California	13.15%
Tennessee	12.99%
Montana	12.90%
Florida	12.90%
New York	12.82%
Missouri	12.40%
Arizona	12.40%

Source: Food Research and Action Center

MORE INFORMATION

Food Research and Action Center
1875 Connecticut Avenue NW, Suite 540
Washington, DC 20009
202-986-2200

National Charities Information Bureau
19 Union Square West, 6th floor
New York, NY 10003-3395
212-929-6300

Retired Senior Volunteer Program
1100 Vermont Avenue NW
Washington, DC 20525
202-606-4851

Second Harvest National Food Bank Network
116 South Michigan Avenue, Suite 4
Chicago, IL 60603
312-263-2303

Share Our Strength
1511 K Street NW, Suite 940
Washington, DC 20005
800-969-4767

It Costs More To Be Poor

One commonly believed cause of hunger — that children go hungry because poor people spend money wastefully or buy food that is not nutritious — is a myth. Poor people actually buy more nutritious food than the rest of the population. The average food stamp benefit per meal is 68 cents, which means the family must think about how to make wise choices in order to stretch each food dollar as far as possible. Yet the poorer the neighborhood, the higher the grocery-store prices and the lower the quality of foodstuffs and service. To feed a family of four over the course of a year, low-income shoppers pay at least $350 more than their middle-income counterparts.

Government Programs That Help

The Food Stamp Program, run by the USDA Food and Nutrition Service, is the largest of the federal food assistance programs, in terms of both amounts of money spent and numbers of people served. Between 1990 and 1991, federal expenditures for, and participation in, this program have increased. In 1993 it served 27.4 million people, close to half of them children. Food stamps, redeemable at retail stores, are available for eligible low-income households but many who could qualify fail to do so because they are unable to find their way through the bureaucracy or are too embarrassed to admit their need for "charity."

The Special Supplemental Food Program for Women, Infants, and Children (WIC) provides monthly vouchers for such foods as iron-fortified infant formula, eggs, fruit juices fortified with vitamin C, milk, cheese, and cereal. The program also offers nutrition education and referrals to health services. WIC's annual funding is less than $6 million and it serves slightly over half of those who are eligible.

The National School Lunch Program (NSLP) reaches about 30 million children, who receive meals at no cost or at a substantially reduced price. Its goal is to provide approximately one-third of the nation's children with the recommended dietary allowance for nutrients and calories. Participation is determined by household size and income.

The School Breakfast Program (SBP) is the most recent addition to programs designed specifically to help children. Recognizing that eating breakfast improves academic performance, Congress has mandated $5 million a year to help stimulate more schools to offer free breakfasts. But because of transportation problems and the belief that breakfast should be a family meal, many schools have been reluctant to adopt the program.

Aid for Families with Dependent Children (AFDC) is a primary lifeline for many children in poverty, but, unlike Social Security, benefits are not adjusted annually for inflation. In 1970, New York State considered $279 per month minimally essential for a family of three, and the benefit level was set accordingly. In 1989, AFDC paid $539. This is $325 short of what it would have been had the 1970 level been fully adjusted for inflation. That $325 shortfall can mean the difference between two meals a day and one or none for millions of children; for millions of babies, it is the difference between formula and water.

The Stealth Bomber Criterion

The director of Tufts University Center on Hunger, Poverty, and Nutritional Policy estimates that for $8 billion annually — the cost of producing ten F-117 Stealth bombers — we could totally eliminate hunger in the United States.

HYDROPONICS

WEATHERLESS WONDERS

Hydroponic farmers raise plants free of sand, herbicides, and pesticides. Plants are grown in a controlled greenhouse environment, in which the light, air, water, plant nutrients, and the spacing between plants are carefully monitored in order to achieve optimal growth in the least time and at the lowest cost. The work requires the skills of a scientist and the devotion of a mother.

The seeds are nursed from germination through maturity in an inert growing medium, usually gravel, through which is pumped water that contains a balanced mix of nutrients. As the plants grow, they travel in cradle-troughs along a moving conveyor belt. The cradles expand, allowing them more breathing room as they need it.

The overhead lamps emit three wavelengths of light: red, far red, and blue. Unlike sunlight, which varies according to weather, season, and the time of day, the constant, steady emission of artificial light stimulates photosynthesis and promotes efficiency. To take advantage of the lower cost of electricity during off-peak hours, the days and nights in a hydroponic facility are reversed. Plants innocently think they are awake all day when, in fact, they are up all night.

Potatoes and root vegetables are uneconomical; they take up too much space. However, 12 heads of lettuce can grow in a space where only three would grow in an open field. But the real jackpot is the tomato. Farmers can expect to pluck slightly more than a pound of tomatoes a week from a single plant. Many customers are willing to pay a premium for a pesticide-free, red, ripe, juicy tomato.

Hydroponic farming does carry a slight social handicap, however. Regular farmers tend to act superior, looking down from their 10-ton combine harvesters upon those who tiptoe among the troughs, using tiny scissors and tweezers to bestow the gift of fertility upon each tiny shoot.

But the hydroponic farmers don't mind. After all, the only heavy lifting they do is when they carry their cash receipts to the bank.

Marijuana Growers Take a Bath

It wasn't too arduous to grow marijuana hydroponically, and there were those who made pots of money at it until the law took the situation in hand. The Federal Drug Enforcement Administration used low-flying aircraft with heat-sensing devices to zero in on the emissions from the halogen lamps that nurtured the plants. The grass was green no more. From the moment of discovery, it was lights out all the way.

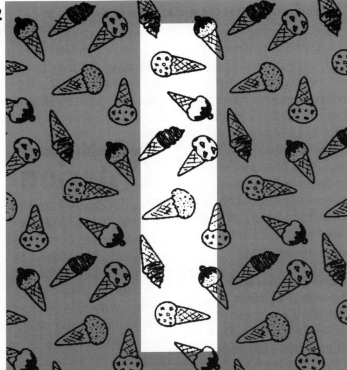

ICE CREAM ❖ INSECTS AS FOOD ❖ IRON ❖

IRRADIATION

ICE CREAM

*We dare not trust our wit for making
our house pleasant to our friend,
so we buy ice cream.*

— Ralph Waldo Emerson

A THOUSAND PINTS OF LITE

The original ices are thought to have been snow, flavored with fruit juices; certainly in the fourth century B.C. the Romans were eating ices of this type at their banquets. Flavored snow may not now seem a particularly exotic dessert, but the difficulty of keeping snow in its original form created plenty of challenge and excitement.

In the not very distant past, cold was a far greater luxury than heat. Anybody could get hot simply by lighting a fire and sitting close to it. Getting cold when the weather was hot was a much more complicated and expensive affair.

Wealthy men everywhere have in common a liking for creature comforts, and ice cream is way up there in this department. But Americans of all income levels are given a constitutional right to the pursuit of happiness — and this translates into creature comforts, which further translates into the right to have ice cream wherever and whenever we want it. We may not all be able to live like the Rockefellers, but we sure can eat the same kind of superpremium ice cream that they eat.

We eat it in restaurants, in ice cream parlors, in the street, in front of the television, and in bed. We eat it in summer and in winter. We eat it day after day and never tire of it. Ice cream seems to appeal to all ages, all income levels, all educational levels, all backgrounds, all religious groupings, and all political persuasions. Every year we each eat 26 pints of it — though perhaps some of us eat more than our share, just to make the figures work out correctly.

ODD JOBS

Ice cream runs in John Harrison's veins. His great-grandfather was an ice cream maker in 1880. His grandfather began the first dairy co-op in Tennessee. His father owned a dairy-ingredients business in Atlanta, and his uncle owned an ice cream factory in Memphis. So it's only natural that he would end up as one of the premier ice cream tasters in America — for Edy's on the East Coast, and Dreyer's on the West Coast.

Every morning a taster must confront 60 containers of ice cream, tasting every flavor at the beginning, middle, and end of its run. He tastes vanillas first, then chocolate chip cookie dough, mocha almond fudge, and mint chocolate chip. Harrison's discernment is highly valued. His taste buds are insured for $1 million.

Vanilla Is Tops

Baskin Robbins boasts 31 flavors, but when the chips are down, one out of four orders are not for cool jalapeño, or rose geranium, or mad mango, or purple passionfruit, or cotton candy, or quadruple brownie impasse — but for plain old vanilla.

A FEW DEFINITIONS

Superpremium ice cream contains up to or more than 16 percent butterfat.

Premium ice cream contains approximately 14 percent butterfat.

Regular ice cream contains about 12 percent butterfat.

Ice milk usually contains between 2 and 7 percent milk fat by weight. It often has more sugar than ice cream.

Frozen yogurt may or may not be low-fat or nonfat, depending on whether it is made from whole milk and cream or skim milk.

Fat-free frozen desserts usually have less than half a gram of fat per serving. Desserts made from skim or nonfat milk solids may actually contain more calcium than ice creams because the removal of the fat leaves more space for other nutrients to fill.

The Inside Scoop

You have to put it down to American ingenuity. Can you imagine any other nation taking a food that starts out higher in fat, calories, and cholesterol than any there ever was, and turning it into a good-for-you diet food?

Sales of frozen yogurt last year topped $474 million. Add the purchases of ice milk and you are looking at close to a cool billion. Maybe the big seduction is all those unpronounceable Scandinavian names that evoke butter and cream and snowy days and Nordic nights. But big business has known all along that the customer for the richest, most super of the superpremium ice creams on the market is the very same perverse person who also buys the fat-free diet desserts.

So a plethora of frozen desserts is being launched into the market in an effort to balance the scales of our desires. These products cannot legally be called ice cream but masquerade as something similar, made with less or no milk, but with carrageenan (a form of seaweed), guar and carob bean gums, egg whites and starch, coloring, flavoring, and sugar substitutes, plus a few other elements that hold everything together.

So far there have been few raves. It's hard to take a fancy to something that looks mighty like an ice, but doesn't melt in the hand, doesn't melt in the mouth — and, for heaven's sake, doesn't even melt in the dish. It just sits there.

I SING OF CHAMPAGNE AND RUM RAISIN

GAEL GREENE

Ice cream unleashes the uninhibited eight-year-old's sensual greed that lurks within the best of us. I do not celebrate the Spartan scoop of vanilla the incurably constricted grown-up suffers to cap a pedestrian dinner. I sing of great gobs of mellow mint chip slopping onto your wrist as your tongue flicks out to gather the sprinkles. I sing of champagne and rum raisin and two spoons in bed on New Year's Eve. I sing of the do-it-yourself sundae freak-out with a discriminating collector's hoard of *haute* toppings — wet walnuts, hot fudge, homemade peach conserve, Nesselrode, marrons, and brandied cherry — whisk-whipped ice cream, a rainbow of sprinkles and crystals and crisp toasted almonds, inspiring a madness that lifts masks, shatters false dignity, and bridges all generation gaps. . . . In these harsh and uncertain times, as the establishment cracks and institutions crumble, it is no wonder we reach out to ice cream. It is a link to innocence and security, healing, soothing, wholesome …

Excerpted from Bite, A New York Restaurant Strategy

Ben & Jerry Are Cool

Few companies have attracted as much customer affection as the almost grown-up ex-hippie founders of Vermont-made ice cream. With some $105 million in annual sales and a ranking of sixth among the giants in the business, they have played David to some pretty big Goliaths.

Ben & Jerry have succeeded partly because their exuberant approach to business has been unorthodox and full of fun and energy. It is hard to imagine corporate America giving the nod to a package with a photograph of rock star Wavy Gravy and his quotes, "The '90s are the '60s standing on your head" and "We are all the same person trying to shake hands with ourselves."

In many ways, Ben & Jerry *are* shaking hands with themselves and with their fans. It is no accident that they employ a Primal Ice Cream Therapist, whose task it is to dream up new flavors. This is no laughing matter. When the chocolate-chip cookie dough flavor was launched in 1991, it was a breakthrough in the ice cream business equivalent to that of Microsoft's Windows entry into the computer field. Currently, the cookie-dough ice cream sales amount to 17 percent of the Ben & Jerry empire. Cherry Garcia, too, is a flavor that makes us all eternally grateful to these pioneers. May it never rain on their forest.

Books

Ben & Jerry's Homemade Ice Cream & Dessert Book
Ben Cohen and Jerry Greenfield; Workman, 1987; $8.95

Ice Cream
Mable and Gar Hoffman; Fisher Books, 1993; $9.95

Ice Cream! The Whole Scoop
Gail Damerow; Glenbridge, 1991; $24.95

The Joy of Ice Cream
Matthew Klein; Barron's, 1985; $15.95/$10.95

A Lot of Cool Air

All commercial ice cream contains air. Whipping it in is a deliberate step in the processing; in the trade, it's called "overrun." Without air, ice cream would be solid as a rock and close to impossible to penetrate with a scoop. The air actually improves the texture, but there is no requirement to list air as an ingredient on the label, though, by law, ice milk and ice cream must weigh at least 64 grams (2¼ ounces) per half-cup serving.

TIPS

Preparing
If ice cream is too solidly frozen to eat, put it in the microwave on High, and count up to two, slowly.

MORE INFORMATION

National Dairy Council
O'Hare International Center
10255 West Higgins Road,
Suite 900
Rosemont, IL 60018
708-803-2000

**International
Ice Cream Association**
888 16th Street NW
Washington, DC 20006
202-296-4250

INSECTS AS FOOD

A LITTLE BIT CRACKLY, PERHAPS

Very rarely, if ever, does a group of hungry Americans sit down to a meal of cooked insects and say "Yum." Worms, beetles, and bugs are not as American as Mom's apple pie, and very probably never will be. But there was an occasion in 1992, at the Explorers Club in New York City, when the New York Entomological Society celebrated its hundredth anniversary with a banquet that began with snacks of roasted crickets and larvae and went on through mealworm ghanouj, waxworm fritters with plum sauce, cricket and vegetable tempura, and roasted Australian kurrajong grubs to roast beef and gravy. The dessert was

chocolate cricket torte, the centerpieces on the tables were live tarantulas (for decor, not for eating), and — in living proof of the rarity of the event — the room was jammed with journalists from many publications, including *The New York Times, Scientific American, Food Arts* magazine, and *The New Yorker.* Resulting stories were reliably sensational and revealed exactly how much Americans do not appreciate insects.

As it happens, insect bodies are quite nutritious. When dried, they have a protein content per pound that is higher than that of conventional meat. There are parts of Africa where 60 percent of dietary protein comes from caterpillars and other insects; what's more, people genuinely like the texture and taste. There are parts of Asia, too, where the three-inch Thai waterbug, sautéed, is all the rage, but not here. Most people regard its bloated resemblance to a giant cockroach as too off-putting.

These likenesses are indeed one source of Western resistance to eating bugs; we have *no* tradition of dining on them after stepping on them. Another is that we already get our protein more efficiently (and, we believe, more palatably) from our own larger traditional sources — the cow, the pig, and the sheep.

One passionate defender of insects as a potential food source in America is entomologist Dr. Gene DeFoliart, who addressed the New York anniversary dinner with an illustrated talk entitled: "Insects Are Food: Where Has the Western World Been?" Dr. DeFoliart is professor emeritus at the University of Wisconsin and publisher of a periodical, *The Food Insects Newsletter.*

Protein Content of Some Insects

Termites	20 - 45 percent
Grasshoppers	15 - 60 percent
Beetles	11 - 30 percent
Butterflies and moths	8 - 38 percent
Bees and ants	7 - 25 percent

PERIODICALS

The Food Insects Newsletter
Department of Entomology
University of Wisconsin,
Madison
237 Russell Laboratories
1630 Linden Drive
Madison, WI 53706
608-262-5958
Quarterly;
$1.50 per issue

IRON

HARDWORKING MINERAL

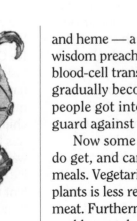

Iron-poor blood" is an advertising slogan that we know a lot more about than we know about iron itself. The concept of iron as being in chronic short supply in the adult body made generations of Americans afraid that they might not be getting enough iron. Many modern nutritionists, however, are saying just the opposite.

Unquestionably, iron is vital to us and has a big job to do for the body. It serves, in the composition of hemoglobin, as a kind of transportation conductor in the bloodstream. Hemoglobin, the chemical component of the red blood cells that carry oxygen from the lungs to the cells of the body, is made up of globin — a protein compound —

and heme — a pigment containing iron. The former wisdom preached that without super supplies of iron, blood-cell transportation would slow and we would gradually become headachy and lethargic and ill. Many people got into the habit of taking iron supplements to guard against this eventuality.

Now some nutritionists say that most people really do get, and can absorb, all the iron they need from their meals. Vegetarians are a possible exception; iron from plants is less readily absorbed by the body than iron from meat. Furthermore, it seems that taking iron supplements could cause damage to the liver, pancreas, and heart, and that people with high iron levels (which can be determined by a serum ferritin test) might consider giving blood a few times a year to reduce any excess of the mineral.

The recommended dietary allowance (RDA) of iron for men and for postmenopausal women is 10 milligrams a day. For women of childbearing years, the allowance is 15 milligrams. Anything over that amount is now being reevaluated.

Two Irons

Two types of iron — heme and nonheme — are found in food. Heme iron comes from meats, poultry, and seafood and is readily absorbed by the body; beef liver is the leading source. Nonheme iron, which is less easily absorbed, is found in dried beans (particularly kidney beans), vegetables, enriched breads and fortified cereals, eggs, blackstrap molasses, and dried fruits.

IRRADIATION

Irradiation is safe and can provide consumers with more food of higher quality.

— *Institute of Food Technologists*
Expert Panel on Food Safety and Nutrition

Q&A

Q What is irradiation?

A It is a relatively simple process that has been studied for 40 years. Food is sterilized by irradiation to make it safer and more resistant to spoilage. By destroying insects, fungi, and bacteria that cause human disease or cause food to spoil, irradiation makes it possible to keep food longer and in better condition.

Even its most outspoken critics do not contend that it will make the food or the person who eats the food radioactive, any more than a passenger will glow in the dark after retrieving luggage from the airport X-ray security system.

Q Does irradiation cause chemical changes in food, perhaps producing substances that aren't present in nonirradiated foods?

A The USDA's Food Safety and Inspection Service replies, "Any kind of processing causes changes in food. Heat produces chemicals that could be called *thermolytic products*, while irradiation produces similar chemicals known as *radiolytic products*. Radiolytic products are so minor that they are measured in parts per billion and can be detected only with sensitive laboratory equipment. Thermolytic products, on the other hand, can be smelled, tasted, and seen."

What's in a Name

The international logo for irradiation was first used in the Netherlands. It is a solid circle, representing an energy source, placed above two petals, which represent the growing food. The five breaks in the outer circle symbolize the rays coming from the energy source.

RADIATING CONFIDENCE

If we knew a way to remove the danger of salmonella and other forms of contamination from our food, and it was called irradiation, would we leap at it?

Not on your life.

Say that tomorrow somebody invented fire for the first time. Can you imagine how many forms would have to be filled out before the FDA would allow it to be used in the home? How righteously foes would rise up to condemn it for being hellishly dangerous? Well, fire *is* dangerous. So is irradiation. But both serve mankind when properly handled.

It's true that we already have the safest and least expensive food supply in the world. But this doesn't mean it is totally, absolutely, perfectly safe. It never will be, nor should this be a goal. If it were, we would never build up resistance and in a few hundred generations our immune systems would atrophy. But safety is, nevertheless, a train we should be traveling on. And irradiation is one more arrow in the arsenal of weapons against food-borne illness.

Say the word "irradiation" and it conjures up fearful visions of Chernobyl. But comparing food irradiation to nuclear devices makes about as much sense as saying that too many construction workers winking simultaneously at too many pretty girls leads to global warming. The simple fact is that we absorb more radiation taking a walk on a sunny day or lying on the beach than if our entire diet were made up of irradiated food.

MORE INFORMATION

Office of Public Affairs
Food and Drug
Administration
Room 1505, FDA
5600 Fishers Lane
Rockville, MD 20857
301-443-3285
The FDA publishes a pamphlet, *Food Irradiation: Toxic to Bacteria, Safe for Humans.*

Vindicator, Inc.
1801 Thonotosassa Road,
Suite 3
Plant City, FL 33566
813-752-3364

HOTLINES

800-535-4555
USDA Meat and Poultry
Hotline
202-720-3333
in Washington, D.C.

MOLECULAR ENERGY

Microwaves produce a form of energy that causes friction of the molecules within the food. As the molecules jump about and get very excited, they generate heat. It is this heat that "cooks" the food. In the irradiation process the energy level is too low to change the atoms of the food; the extent of molecular disruption depends on the power of the radioactive source and the length of time the food is exposed. This can be compared with cooking. Keep the heat low and you have a nice poached egg. Put an egg under the broiler for half an hour and you have a mess.

Of course, you wouldn't be dopey enough to put an egg under the broiler, and nor are all foods suitable candidates for irradiation. Only foods of very high quality are selected for the process. Fatty foods are out; irradiation oxidizes fats. Among fruits, only nine benefit from irradiation — among them bananas, mangoes, strawberries, papayas, and figs. Tests show that apples, pears, citrus fruits, and pineapples actually spoil more quickly after being irradiated. Wheat benefits (irradiation kills the bugs); beef, pork, and poultry profit, and probably seafood does as well, though fish has not yet been approved for irradiation processing.

Federal law requires irradiated food to be identified. Those who distrust the world's scientific establishment will no doubt consider such identification to be a warning. Those who have come to prefer pasteurized milk will recognize the international symbol as attesting that irradiated food is safe as well as good to eat.

— Editorial,
Miami Herald, January 2, 1992

"Apparently the chef's been experimenting with radiation. Wonder who ordered snails?"

MIRED IN CONTROVERSY

The controversy surrounding food irradiation is no small issue. As world trade expands, agricultural products may be accepted or excluded on the basis of how they have been handled. All but one of the food fumigants have now been banned, and irradiation is an alternative that could extend the life of some produce. Japan, an importer of huge quantities of Florida citrus fruits, permits irradiation. Thirty-four countries have issued unconditional or provisional clearances allowing irradiation of commercial foods; countries that operate irradiation plants include Israel, South Africa, China, France, and the Netherlands. Restrictions continue to exist in the United Kingdom, Australia, New Zealand, Denmark, and Sweden.

The U.S. General Accounting Office has said that the banning of food irradiation results from activist pressure, not scientific evidence. Secretary of Agriculture Mike Espy has urged the meat industry to study irradiation in the hope of preventing outbreaks of food-borne illness in the future. Strong leadership may sway public opinion, but many people prefer to let time be the ultimate judge.

Pro and Con

Food irradiation is supported by the scientific community and food safety experts including the following:

American Medical Association

United States Department of Agriculture

United States Food and Drug Administration

Institute of Food Technologists

Harvard Health Letter

Mayo Clinic Health Letter

Council for Agricultural Science and Technology

American Council on Science and Health

United Nations Food and Agriculture Organization

It is opposed by the following organizations:

Center for Science in the Public Interest

Food and Water

How Food Is Irradiated

The food irradiation plant in Mulberry, Fla., will be used to kill bacteria in fruit and vegetables. It can handle about 200,000 pounds of produce in an hour, passing it around a rack of cobalt 60.

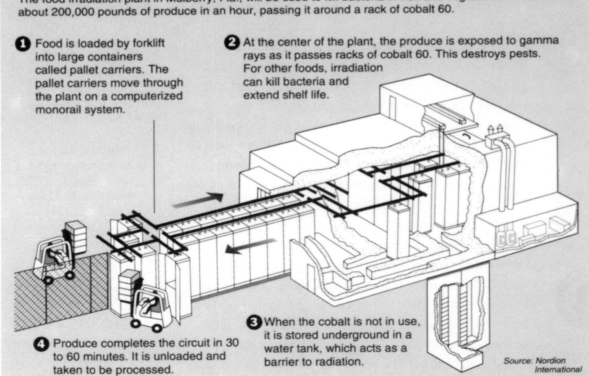

1 Food is loaded by forklift into large containers called pallet carriers. The pallet carriers move through the plant on a computerized monorail system.

2 At the center of the plant, the produce is exposed to gamma rays as it passes racks of cobalt 60. This destroys pests. For other foods, irradiation can kill bacteria and extend shelf life.

3 When the cobalt is not in use, it is stored underground in a water tank, which acts as a barrier to radiation.

4 Produce completes the circuit in 30 to 60 minutes. It is unloaded and taken to be processed.

Source: Nordion International

Reprinted from *The New York Times*

All We Have To Fear . . .

Wouldn't you think that industry would be happy about the possibility of irradiating products to extend their shelf life? Not all are. Some growers say they prefer their berries to have a shorter life, which means that we, the consumers, will buy more. Some poultry producers are giving the thumbs-up sign; others sit on their hands, afraid to antagonize their customers. As for big business, never before have so many hung back in the hope of winning the race by coming in second.

Supermarkets are of two minds about carrying irradiated food lest they get picketed by those who are passionately opposed. Florida, the only state with a food-processing irradiation plant, would prefer to keep it under cover in case fanatical public opinion boycotts all the state's agricultural products, to say nothing of its glorious beaches. Legislators, whose first task is to get reelected, cringe at the least whisper of controversy. The winner is Food and Water, an organization with about 3,500 dues-paying members dedicated to the eradication of irradiated food.

JUICES ❖ JUNK FOOD

JUICES

Throat-Tingling Hot Apple Juice

The following is a real (honest-to-Betsy) recipe. It is written, we assume, for a rank beginner. No heating instructions are included. Maybe the radishes are what make it hot?

3 medium red radishes (leaves and root removed: 2 ounces)
1 medium Golden Delicious apple (cored: 6 ounces)

Juice in the order of the listed ingredients. Makes about ⅔ cup.

Reprinted from *101 Ways to Juice It!*

SQUEEZING OUT THE TRUTH

Are you tired and listless? Are you concerned about those unsightly blemishes? Are you suffering from weight gain or hair loss? Are you seeking a new job, a new mate, a new car, a new life? Would you like to be six feet tall, slim, and gorgeous?

Do you truly believe that five glasses of juice will achieve all these goals?

For many people, the answer seems to be yes. Last year more than 3 million juice makers were sold to a nation thirsty for change. We bounce from one machine to another but exercise our credit cards more than our bodies. The latest toy for the health-obsessed is the juice machine.

Juice is where we think it's at. But now that we've found the fountain of youth, we're dismayed to discover it spouting kale juice, spinach juice, parsley, beets, rhubarb, celery, ginger, and wheat-grass droplets. Some are downing this stuff on three-day juice detox regimes. "Rids the body of impurities," they say, and there are plenty of people to accept the thesis. If a little juice is good, then surely jugs of juice will be better. It'll clear up that embarrassing little touch of impotence. Drink enough and you'll be able to dunk the dunk and walk the walk — and if not, you can get your money back. Maybe.

The Cons of Juicing

There is no evidence that you get more nutrients out of juice than you get out of whole food," says a spokesperson for the American Dietetic Association. Dr. James Duke, an economic botanist with the USDA, says that whole fruits average a little more vitamin C, about twice as much beta carotene, and nearly ten times as much vitamin E as juice. A pound of carrots yields just one cup of juice and you end up throwing away half a pound of fiber — a dietary disaster for fiber-deficient Americans. Fiber, as you know, lowers cholesterol levels and because some fat-soluble vitamins are often bound to the fiber, these too are lost, as they are not all transferred from the whole vegetable or fruit into the juice. The juicing regime

promoted by Jay Kordich, for example, will require you to buy and carry home 50 pounds of produce a week for a family of four. Juicing machines range in price from $50 to $300.

The process isn't inexpensive, and it is a remarkably labor-intensive hobby. It is faster to drink a kraut cocktail in a restaurant for only about $4 a glass. (Or you could eat a bowl of cabbage for a lot less and get a better health benefit.) Juice may be better than a package of french fries — but better than eating a whole carrot or a whole apple? Not.

But be aware, the safest, fastest, most economical, and surest path to good health is to exercise and eat a well-balanced diet. A glass of beer is nice, too — keeps the creative juices flowing.

Popular Drinks

The juices most frequently found in the home refrigerator are orange, apple, blended fruit, cranberry, grapefruit, grape, tomato, and blended vegetables.

Books

Juicing Book
Stephen Blauer; Avery Publishing, 1989; $8.95

The Juicer Book
Joanna White; Bristol, 1992; $7.95

The Juiceman's Power of Juicing
Jay Kordich; Morrow, 1992; $14.50

Total Juicing
Elaine LaLanne; Plume, 1992; $10.00

101 Ways to Juice It!
Carol Gelles; HarperCollins, 1993; $12.50

The Main Squeeze

Somewhere between the Psychic Friends Network, Cher's cascading hair, and Richard Simmons weeping with his newly thin disciples, you will find Jay — The Juiceman — Kordich. Revenues for Trillium Health Products of Seattle, the parent company of his infomercials, topped $100 million last year.

Kordich is a very golden goose. His book, *The Juiceman's Power of Juicing,* has sold close to a million copies. When he autographs it, crowds gather from near and far to touch the hem of his gown. Kordich advises his followers to drink six glasses of juice a day to obtain the maximum benefit. He says, "I believe that if you add juice to your life, you will contribute to your overall cardiovascular health, enhance your physical performance, help lower your blood pressure, sleep better at night . . . and have more energy and better health than you probably ever dreamed possible."

Reading the Fine Print

100 percent fruit juice is the real thing; nothing added and nothing taken away. Look for drinks labeled "100 percent pure juice," "100 percent fruit juice," or "100 percent fruit juice blends." A label read-ing "100 percent natural beverage" doesn't mean the drink is 100 percent juice. Water is a natural beverage, too.

100 percent fruit juice from concentrate may be 100 percent pure juice, but it could also contain sweeteners. Read the label carefully so you know what you are getting.

Fruit drinks, ades, punches, cocktails, and juice beverages may contain only 10 percent juice, yet cost more than 100 percent juice.

What's A Mother To Do?

Apple juice, a favorite with mothers of young children, is little more than flavored water that contains some natural fruit sugar. Unless it's fortified, in fact, a cup of apple juice provides almost no vitamin C, while a cup of orange juice has about double the daily recommended amount for a child. Note, also, that apple juice can cause diarrhea in some children.

Reprinted from Tufts Diet and Nutrition Letter

JUNK FOOD

LISA HANEY

THE JOYS OF EATING

JOYCE CAROL OATES

A compilation of the foods you once ate, and ate with zest, now banished from your life, denied, or, with the passage of time, simply lost: . . . Tootsie Rolls and Mallow Cups and Milky Ways and Mars Bars . . . Juicy Fruit and Dentyne . . . Hostess Cupcakes . . . pies that fit into the palm of your hand, to be eaten on the sidewalk outside the store . . . pop-, fudg-, and creamsicles of all lurid flavors . . . peanut butter sandwiches on soft white pulpy Wonder Bread . . . The Royale (hot fudge banana split with cherries, walnuts, whipped cream, decorated with a crown of sugar wafers — the specialty of the ice cream parlor) . . . glazed doughnuts, grease-saturated doughnuts, frosted dough-nuts, Freddie's Doughnuts (specialty of a Buffalo bakery: immense, sweet, doughy, covered in confectioner's sugar and filled to bursting with whipped cream) . . . the shame-lessly salty, greasy hamburgers, cheeseburgers, hot dogs, and french fries sold for human consumption in the Lockport, New York, area . . . the shamelessly salty, greasy, and stale popcorn sold in theater lobbies everywhere . . . pizza (of all varieties) . . . triple layer devil's food cake with fudge frosting . . . strawberry-banana cream pie with "Nabisco-wafer crust" . . . southern fried chicken, and sweet-glazed ham steaks baked with canned pineapple rings . . . homemade chicken soup brimming with globules of fat . . . all red meats, but especially fat-webbed roasts and 8-oz. sirloins . . . breaded things (fish, fowl, animal) . . . fish sticks dipped in catsup . . . Planter's Peanuts, so greasy and salty your fingers began to smart, eaten directly from the can . . . Royal Crown Root Beer, especially when insufficiently cold . . . cheese omelets the size of automobile hubcaps . . . canned pork and beans . . . canned applesauce . . . canned salmon . . . iceberg lettuce wilting beneath dollops of "Russian" dressing . . . the specialty (canned) fruit cup that is served only as a first course at formal, institutionally catered meals in your honor . . . the Parker House rolls that accompany the fruit cup . . . and the excruciatingly sweet, cloying, thick blueberry pancakes I prepared as a young wife, Sunday mornings in Detroit, in our single-bedroom uncarpeted apartment south of Palmer Park, festive concoctions out of a Pillsbury mix, presumably delicious, for, otherwise, how could we have eaten them?

Excerpted from "Food Mysteries," Antaeus: Not By Bread Alone

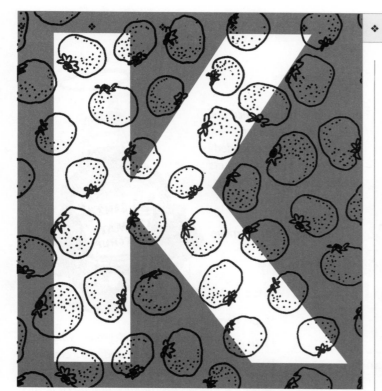

KALE ✦ KETCHUP ✦ KIWIFRUITS ✦ KOSHER FOOD

LOVELY — TO LOOK AT

If there were only two foods left in the world and one was ice cream and the other was kale, I know which one *I* would choose. Nevertheless, kale is a nutritious food, and there are those who regard it as very good eating, too.

Kale is a member of the cabbage family but it doesn't come to a head; instead, as it rises from the ground, it forms curly leaves. Like collard greens, turnip tops, and dandelion leaves, kale is a good source of vitamin A and is thought to help reduce the risk of cancer. It contains iron, but the human body has a hard time grabbing hold of it unless the leaves are eaten along with other vegetables that are high in vitamin C. Despite a virtuous nutrition profile, some people, especially those under the age of seven, find the taste of raw kale too assertive. Its tender young leaves have a bullying quality about them. Even when served hot, kale leaves many of us cold.

There are exceptions, of course. In Portugal, kale is the main component of an exquisite green broth. Small quantities of kale taste quite nice in mixed vegetable soups, such as minestrone. The Danes like it with roast pork, and the Germans are fond of it, too. The hardy Scots eat lots of it, but this is not much of a recommendation; the Scots also eat haggis, a dish someone once called a concoction brilliant in its conception but profoundly flawed in execution. I have heard the same description applied to the Southern way with kale — simmered in bacon grease. However, it was Northerners who were talking.

All things considered, I feel that this pretty, leafy plant is probably best used as a table decoration — unless, of course, there is no ice cream.

KALE

Kale makes a stunningly beautiful centerpiece.

KETCHUP

BLESSED RELIEF

The ploppy tomato ketchup we know is a far cry from what it once was. Originally, in China, it was *ke-tsiap*, a pickled fish sauce. The Malays adapted it for a mushroom base, called it *kechup*, and in the 17th century served it to some English sailors, whose taste buds were so enlivened that they rushed it home to perk up a languishing English cuisine. The Americans added the tomatoes — whereupon ketchup, more or less as we know it, was born.

The people of those first United States had no hamburgers or french fries to put it on, but they did have pork chops, so they put it on them. Ketchup was made at home for generations — a laborious process in which the tomatoes had to be parboiled and peeled and the puree continuously stirred. Then Henry Heinz introduced the commercial version in 1876, billing it as "Blessed relief for Mother and the other women in the household!" And so it was.

Many children grow up believing that ketchup has a mind of its own because it is often so reluctant to leave the bottle. In fact, ketchup belongs to a family of substances called plastic solids, which retain their shape until a certain level of stress is applied. The stress we all know well is a few firm thwacks with the heel of the hand on the base of the bottle. Technically, this mild violence is sufficient to make the ketchup flow. But there are those who have had such colorful experiences with recalcitrant ketchup that they will never believe it.

Tomato Ketchup
If you do not shake the bottle
None'll come and then a lot'll.
— Anonymous

Judgment Day

After too long an exile in the British Isles, the 18th-century philosopher Voltaire is said to have remarked that the British were a nation of 100 different religions, but only one sauce. He could as well have been describing present-day America, where there are at least as many forms of belief and a single sauce that is known and loved from sea to shining sea. Whether slipped in plastic packets into fast-food take-out bags or nestled in cruets on formica-topped tables, tomato ketchup is the ultimate road food; and a bottle or two have even been seen lurking in the shadows at smart restaurants, ready, if a diner *absolutely* insists upon it, to impart ketchup's homely red glow to a platter of upscale french fries.

Newlyweds

In nuptials announced by the H. J. Heinz Company in July of 1993, bachelor-about-town Tomato Ketchup was married to the sensationally popular, picante new Latin sauce, Salsa. After a private ceremony in which they promised to be both mild and medium, the couple left immediately on an extended wedding trip to supermarkets all over the country, traveling under their married name: Salsa Ketchup.

This was a fifth marriage

for the bridegroom, who was previously and unsuccessfully wed to steakhouse, chili pepper, hickory, and pizza flavors from 1969 to 1971 under the auspices of Hunt-Wesson.

How The Half-Billion-Dollar American Ketchup Market Divvies Up

Heinz	55 percent
Hunt-Wesson	19 percent
Generics and private brands	19 percent
Del Monte	9 percent
Gourmet and regional labels	2 percent

Source: Prudential-Bache in *The New York Times*

KIWIFRUITS

FAMILIARITY DOESN'T . . .

Thirty years ago, the American public was introduced to something called the kiwifruit. It was round and brown, like a small suede potato. Cut in half, it proved to have bright green flesh with a tart-sweet taste and crackly black seeds arranged in a neat circle. All of it was edible except for the skin, and, properly kept, it would stay fresh for weeks. Did we instantly adopt this new marvel? Not exactly. Was the kiwi's long journey worth the prize? Definitely.

Kiwifruits come originally from China, where they are called Yangtao. Their origins are in the Yang-tse river valley, where the vines have been cultivated for about 800 years on trellises. The fruit was imported to New Zealand early in this century and renamed the Chinese gooseberry. Grafting experiments there produced a larger and more flavorful variety of the original and the improved version reached the United States in 1962.

In Los Angeles, produce marketer and distributor Frieda Caplan took a fancy to the new fruit and decided to market it nationally under the name kiwi, after the small, brown, national bird of New Zealand. Caplan says that acceptance of the fruit took her 18 years. Retailers were reluctant to sell it and shoppers hesitated to buy it. But general public awareness perked up when fashionable young American chefs started using the kiwi in their designer dishes. For a meteoric moment the fruit was a nouvelle darling, then it plunged into the mass market, where it started showing up at highway truck stops, decorating plates of sausage and eggs.

At this point, however, the cute fruit has settled down to quiet general popularity, aided by the fact that kiwifruits are

HANEY

now grown in California as well as in New Zealand — making supplies available year round. California now provides the bulk of the crop, from November through May; then fruit ripened during the New Zealand summer (our winter) takes over from June to October.

In addition to its very agreeable flavor, the kiwi has a towering advantage over many of the unfamiliar fruits that have come on the American market; almost everyone can spell it.

TIPS

Storing

Kiwis that are not ripe (those that don't yield a little to the touch) can be held at room temperature until they start to soften slightly — a process that may take weeks unless hastened on its way by enclosing them in a brown paper bag. Once ripe, kiwis can be stored in the refrigerator for at least three weeks.

Frozen Chocolate-Dipped Kiwifruits

Serves 6

3 kiwifruits
6 ounces (1 cup) chocolate chips, melted

Peel and slice the kiwifruits into ¹⁄₄ -inch rounds; place on a baking sheet lined with wax paper. Freeze until firm. Dip half of each kiwi slice in the melted chocolate. Freeze until ready to eat.

KOSHER FOOD

KEEPING THE FAITH

There's a big difference between buying kosher and keeping kosher. The Jewish practice of keeping kosher, called *kashruth* or *kashrut,* meaning "fit" or "proper," stems from a complex set of biblical rules that govern all aspects of food preparation. These rules strictly prohibit the eating of certain foods and the mixing of certain others. For example, you can buy kosher hamburger and kosher cheese, but you can never make a kosher cheeseburger.

At the same time, many Americans who have no intention of bringing religion to the dinner table buy kosher products — especially kosher meats — because they worry about safety and quality. To be called kosher, meat has to be meticulously handled and independently certified; many people are willing to pay a higher price for such assurances.

Kosher meat contains no additives, preservatives, byproducts, or fillers. Kosher butchers, called *sochets,* have always been required to slaughter the animals quickly and painlessly, so kosher meat also appeals to those who are concerned about animal rights.

Kosher meat has been thoroughly cleaned and drained of blood, a process that reduces certain health risks, such as the presence of salmonella in chicken. However, the rules stem from religion rather than from science. The Union of Orthodox Synagogues puts a seal of approval on many kosher foods, but there is no uniform standard for what is or is not kosher except for what is written in the Bible, mostly in *Leviticus,* chapter 11, and *Deuteronomy,* chapter 14.

Many foods, not only pork and shellfish but a long list of other animals and fishes, can never be kosher. The mixing of milk and meat is forbidden and kosher foods with even the smallest traces of dairy products in them are specially marked to eliminate any confusion. People with lactose intolerances benefit from these special labels, which let them know what foods to avoid.

Milk and fish *can* mix, because the kinds of fish that qualify as kosher are *pareve,* neutral. Anything *pareve* can mix with either milk or meat. Vegetables, bread, and most staple foods — almost anything that is not meat or dairy — fall into this category. Some product labels add *pareve* next to their kosher seal if there's any chance of confusion.

The prohibition against mixing milk and meat extends to all eating utensils and implements used in cooking. Kosher households have designated sets of meat and dairy silverware, plates, pots, and pans, to avoid any possibility of contamination. Restaurants that cook meat and cheese on the same grill can never be certified kosher. This rule poses a problem for McDonald's in Jerusalem. This fast-food outlet uses only kosher meat, but the burgers and cheeseburgers are cooked on the same grill. Thus, religiously observant Israelis can't order any burgers on these premises. There's no such thing as "sort of" kosher.

Perplexed? Some Specifics

The Jewish physician Maimonides in his *Guide for the Perplexed* asserted that kosher foods are more healthful than non-kosher foods. Over the ages people have sought medical reasons for the complex dietary laws: in hot climates the prevalence of parasites or disease in pork may have made it a dangerous food (which could explain why Muslims also shun pork). But quasiscientific theorizing will not make *Kashruth* understandable to beginners.

The highly restrictive laws were codified well over a thousand years ago, when religious authorities constructed a "fence around the Torah," widening the scope of the law to safeguard against any possible transgressions. The Bible forbids boiling a calf in its mother's milk — so the rabbis established total separation of all meat products from all dairy, just to be safe. However arbitrary in its origin, this law does reduce a person's fat intake, creating a fence around the heart, as well as the Torah.

Some less explicable kosher laws:

• Only fish with fins and scales may be eaten; this excludes sharks, rays, and a long list of other species.

• The Bible lists 24 forbidden birds; any bird not listed is acceptable.

• Amphibians, insects, and "creeping things" cannot be eaten, with a few exceptions. Some species of locust are legally edible; others are not.

• Leviticus XI, 3 states: "Whatsoever parteth the hoof and is wholly cloven footed and cheweth the cud among the beasts, that you may eat." Cows meet these qualifications, but horses, obviously, do not. Animals with claws, such as dogs, cats, and rabbits, are off-limits. Certain mammals can be kosher, provided they are of high quality and properly prepared. Camels are not among them.

Glatt Kosher

Certain kosher foods are certified as *glatt* by ultra-Orthodox groups and are eaten by those who believe that this label denotes an even greater degree of purity. *Glatt*, a Yiddish word meaning "smooth," originally was applied to animals with smooth lungs, without adhesions or irregularities. Nowadays, *glatt* is a label that extends to many kinds of kosher foods.

KOSHER FOR PASSOVER

Seven or eight days out of every year, observant Jews alter their eating habits to commemorate the flight of their ancestors from slavery in Egypt more than three millennia ago. Tradition has it that the newly freed Jews had to mobilize their Exodus so quickly that the bread they baked for the trip never had time to rise, and Moses and his followers ate the unleavened bread to sustain them as they fled with the army of Ramses II at their heels.

At the **seder**, the traditional meal that is Passover's high point, foods are used to symbolize the ancestral ordeal.

Matzoh, flat unleavened bread, is the only bread that is kosher during this time.

A book called the *Haggadah* guides diners through the meal, which includes salt water, bitter herbs (usually horseradish), greens, wine, and **haroset**, a sweet and tasty fruit-and-nut paste, along with some of the best traditional Jewish cooking — gefilte fish, matzoh-ball soup — to be had on any occasion. Singing, ritual readings, and a hide-and-seek game involving a stolen piece of matzoh are integral to the meal, and the atmosphere is relaxed and merry.

More people celebrate Passover than any other event in the Jewish calendar. Other holidays center around prayer; perhaps people find the seder easier to swallow.

HOTLINES

212-563-4000
Union of Orthodox Jewish Congregations Kashruth

PERIODICALS

Kashrus Magazine
Yeshiva Birkas Reuven
P.O. Box 204, Parkville Station
Brooklyn, NY 11204
718-998-3201
5 times a year; $15 per year

Matzoh Fun

During the week following the Passover seder, matzoh becomes like turkey after Thanksgiving is over. Cravings arise for *hametz* dishes made with the leavened flour that is forbidden: cake, french toast, pasta…

So kosher cooks have concocted substitutes like multilayer matzoh cake, or matzoh *brei*, fried egg-soaked matzoh flavored with sugar and cinnamon, a traditional breakfast treat. And matzoh-ball soup, another Passover-inspired adaptation, became such a hit that millions never shed a tear for chicken noodle.

Books

Faye Levy's International Jewish Cookbook
Faye Levy; Warner Books, 1991; $29.45

Jewish Cooking in America
Joan Nathan; Knopf, 1994; $30.00

Our Food: The Kosher Kitchen Updated
Anita Hirsch; Doubleday, 1993; $25.00

The International Kosher Cookbook
92nd Street Y Kosher Cooking School; Fawcett, 1992; $22.50

The Passover Gourmet
Nira Rousso; Adams Publishers, 1987; $19.95

The Passover Table
Susan R. Friedland; HarperPerennial, 1994; $17.00

MORE INFORMATION

Union of Orthodox Jewish Congregations of America
333 Seventh Avenue, 19th floor
New York, NY 10001
212-563-4000

MAIL ORDER SOURCES

Hamakor Judaica, Inc.
"The Source for Everything Jewish"
6153 Mulford, Unit D
Niles, IL 60714-3427
800-426-2567

Kosher Cornucopia
Box 326, Beechwoods Road
Jeffersonville, NY 12748-0326
800-756-7437

Mrs. Maltz's Knishes
2686 Middlefield Road, Unit B
Redwood City, CA 94063
800-875-6474

Second Avenue Deli
156 Second Avenue
New York, NY 10003
800-692-3354

LABELING

3 grams fat/serving

The new food label is an unusual opportunity to help millions of Americans make more informed, healthier food choices.

— David A. Kessler, M.D.
Commissioner, Food and Drug Administration

A TOWER OF LABELS

"Man, the FDA is really cracking down on food labeling!"

The new political climate in the land of labeling demands honesty, integrity, and total disclosure — nothing hidden from public scrutiny and no more frivolous word games. No element on the new food labels is safe from legal toothcombing. No longer can we take litely such descriptions as *reduced, fewer, less, low, extra, ultra, fortified, improved, handmade, fresh-squeezed, country-fresh,* or *all-natural;* these are now loaded words, to be used only with discretion.

Those who process food must say what they mean and mean what they say. So if they intend us to buy beef and gravy, we must be sure they do not mean gravy and beef, or just beef gravy. The first contains 50 percent beef, the second 35 percent, and the third only 6 percent. Lasagna with meat sauce means that there is 12 percent meat in there somewhere; lasagna with meat *and* sauce requires only 6 percent meat. Chicken à la king positively *has* to contain at least 20 percent chicken, whereas chicken chop suey can accommodate as little as 2 percent chicken and still be within the law.

It's obvious we will have to do some homework to understand the new language of labels. Critics maintain that they are written for the guidance of those who can't read in a language they don't speak. They propose substituting symbols: an arrow pointing upward would mean loads of fat, pointing down hardly any. Then we could all see in a flash whether it would be wise to eat it — in moderation. (Was it Mark Twain who urged moderation in all things, including moderation?)

Nonetheless, the Nutrition Labeling and Education Act of 1990 is bringing about the most extensive food labeling change in the country's history. In place this year, for the first time ever, is a consistent, scientifically based system of identifying nearly all processed foods and some unprocessed ones as well. The intent is to provide accurate, easy-to-grasp information that will help us make informed choices about what we eat, with the end result that we eat a healthier diet, have fewer nutrition-based illnesses, and achieve huge savings in medical costs.

To this end, serving sizes are now defined realistically and consistently, reflecting the amount of a food that a normal person is likely to eat at any one time. A company can no longer make a slice of bread thinner and claim that it is "healthier" than a competitor's.

Of course, none of these changes have come about without some squabbles. The FDA wanted to base all the figures on a 2,000-calorie-a-day diet, having earlier proposed a 2,340-calorie ration. The USDA, which governs regulation of meat, poultry, and produce, insisted on a 2,500-calorie version and were summarily accused of cozying up to the agricultural community. In a compromise, both 2,000-calorie and 2,500-calorie diets appear on the labels. (A 2,500-calorie diet allows a person a higher number of grams of fat per day; there is a lot of fat in red meat.)

Then there was the question of which foods were to be labeled. The decision: Baked goods packaged in advance of the customer's arrival must bear a label; freshly baked goods need not. For similar reasons the deli counter is also exempt, as are take-out and restaurant foods — though fast-food restaurants have masses of nutritional information about their food available if you ask for it.

The law requires that informative posters be displayed at or near the fresh meat, poultry, and fish counters. Twenty-seven of the most popular meats and 20 of the most frequently purchased kinds of fish are listed.

When it comes to teeny-tiny items such as a single foil-wrapped chocolate, however, the government waives the requirement of an actual label (because it wouldn't fit) provided the item's nutrition profile is made available to customers requesting it. But how many people are really worried about the nutritional benefits, or lack of same, in something they regard as an indulgence? Some of us might be happier if we didn't read those newly accurate labels. The whole truth is not always easy to swallow.

The Process of the Process

Foods have to be tested in order to derive the specific information about their components required by the new descriptive labels. Most manufacturers use independent food-testing labs across the country, and Lancaster Laboratories, in Lancaster, Pennsylvania, has become a major player in the field.

Samples of foods to be tested arrive at the lab by overnight express or courier. The first step in testing is usually to grind them in a food processor. Gummi bears were an exception, staunchly refusing to disintegrate under the knife. The solution: freeze them, then spin.

Lancaster Labs puts its samples through close to 50 standard tests, most of them conducted under special yellow light in order to prevent the vitamins in the food from breaking down as they do when exposed to ordinary ultraviolet light. There are 12 ways of measuring fat in meat and snack foods, for example. Samples are weighed, ether is added, and the food placed in a fat extractor. The ether dissolves the fat, which drips into a container. The dissolved fat is weighed to establish the sample's fat content, then its cholesterol and saturated fat are measured by gas chromatography.

To measure fiber in a breakfast cereal, samples from a dozen containers are poured into a tray of warm water and gently rocked back and forth, imitating the process of natural digestion. When the allotted time has passed, the fiber that separates out is measured.

An analysis may take from 12 to 15 days.

Q&A

Q How much is a gram (g)? What does it mean if a food has 4 grams of fat in it?

A A gram is a metric unit of measurement. There are 454 grams in a pound. A single gram weighs about the same as a regular metal paper clip. Four grams of fat would be the equivalent of 1 teaspoon.

New Nutrient Content Claims

Free — The product contains only a tiny or insignificant amount of fat, cholesterol, sodium, sugar, and/or calories. For example, a "fat-free" product will contain less than 0.5 grams of fat per serving.

Low — A food described as "low" in fat, saturated fat, cholesterol, sodium, and/or calories could be eaten fairly often without exceeding dietary guidelines. "Low in fat" means no more than 3 grams of fat per serving.

Lean — "Lean" and "extra lean" mean the product has less than 5 grams of fat, 2 grams of saturated fat, and 95 milligrams of cholesterol per serving. Extra lean is leaner than lean, but not as lean as "low."

Reduced, Less, Fewer — Means that a diet product contains 25 percent less nutrient or calories than a comparable food. For example, hot dogs might be labeled "25 percent less fat than our regular hot dogs."

Light/Lite — Means a diet product with a third fewer calories or half the fat of the original. "Light in sodium" means a product with half the usual amount of sodium.

More — Means a food in which one serving has at least 10 percent more of the Daily Value of a vitamin, mineral, or fiber than usual.

Good Source of — Means that a single serving contains 10 to 19 percent of the Daily Value for a particular vitamin, mineral, or fiber.

Source: USDA's *Food News for Consumers*

Tuna Gets a Tail Bob

Labeling pressures as well as advertising concerns can force a packaging redesign. Chicken of the Sea tuna used to feature a seated blonde mermaid with her tail gracefully displayed, but the new label resulted in a shrunken image. The mermaid's tail was bobbed and she was pushed out to sea to make room for all the nutrients that had to be listed. Some icons must sacrifice a lot.

Did You Know?

☞ The cost of the new food labels is estimated at $2 billion.

☞ Labeling regulations apply to 139 different food categories, which translates to approximately 200,000 individual foods.

☞ Kraft alone had 16,500 products to repackage, and Quaker Oats Company formed a separate task force to oversee labeling changes on its own 1,700 different packages.

☞ If a food such as a pickle varies in size, the nutritional information is determined by measuring all the pickles in the jar, determining what constitutes a reasonable serving, and arriving at an average set of numbers.

☞ Once the new labels are on the market, the FDA will spot-check the foods to ensure no one is cheating or backsliding.

☞ Surveys claim that eight out of ten people read food labels.

Labels List Limited Health Claims

The only health claims that may be printed on packages are those that cite relationships between calcium and osteoporosis; sodium and hypertension; fat and cancer; fat-containing foods and heart disease; and foods such as fruits, vegetables, and whole grains that are high in antioxidant vitamins (including vitamin C) and cancer.

The rules also acknowledge that folic acid can benefit women of childbearing age.

How to Read a Label

New heading means label is new.

Consistent serving sizes, in both household and metric measures.

Nutrition Facts

Serving Size 1 cup (228g)
Servings Per Container 2

Amount Per Serving

Calories 260   Calories from Fat 120

	% Daily Value*
Total Fat 13g	**20%**
Saturated Fat 5g	**25%**
Cholesterol 30mg	**10%**
Sodium 660mg	**28%**
Total Carbohydrate 31g	**10%**
Dietary Fiber 0g	**0%**
Sugars 5g	
Protein 5g	

Vitamin A 4%	•	Vitamin C 2%	
Calcium 15%	•	Iron 4%	

* Percent Daily Values are based on a 2,000 calorie diet. Your daily values may be higher or lower depending on your calorie needs:

	Calories:	2,000	2,500
Total Fat	Less than	65g	80g
Sat Fat	Less than	20g	25g
Cholesterol	Less than	300mg	300mg
Sodium	Less than	2,400mg	2,400mg
Total Carbohydrate		300g	375g
Dietary Fiber		25g	30g

Calories per gram:
Fat 9 • Carbohydrate 4 • Protein 4

Nutrient panel lists percentages of nutrients most important to health of today's consumers, who are more concerned about getting too much of certain items such as fat than too few vitamins or minerals, as in the past.

Conversion guide shows caloric value of the nutrients that produce energy.

A new mandatory component, this helps consumers following diets that recommend fewer than 30 percent of calories be derived from fat.

Percent Daily Values of the components show how this food fits into the overall daily diet.

Reference values for 2,000-calorie and 2,500-calorie diets help consumers learn good diet basics; they can be adjusted according to individual calorie needs.

FDA, FSIS, and USDA Have A New Alphabet

DVs (Daily Values) — A new dietary reference term appearing on food labels, it is made up of two sets of references, DRVs and RDIs.

DRVs (Daily Reference Values) — A set of dietary references that applies to fat, saturated fat, cholesterol, carbohydrate, protein, fiber, sodium, and potassium.

RDIs (Reference Daily Intakes) — A set of dietary references based on the Recommended Dietary Allowances for essential vitamins and minerals and, in selected groups, protein. "RDI" replaces the term "U.S. RDA."

RDAs (Recommended Dietary Allowances) — A set of estimated nutrient allowances established by the National Academy of Sciences. It is updated periodically to reflect current scientific knowledge. The current recommendations are:

- Total fat: less than 65 grams
- Saturated fat: less than 20 grams
- Cholesterol: less than 300 milligrams
- Sodium: less than 2,400 milligrams

Vetting the Label

Twelve specialists at the Food Safety & Inspection Service (FSIS) in Washington, D.C., review and authorize 180,000 new product labels annually. Manufacturers submit products with formulations and label sketches; specialists check that the smallest letter is a third the size of the largest letter, that the weight is prominently displayed, and other minute details.

MORE INFORMATION

National Exchange for Food Labeling Education
Food and Drug Administration
Office of Public Affairs
5600 Fishers Lane, HFE-88
Rockville, MD 20857
301-443-3220

SPARE ME COOKED HAM AND WATER PRODUCT

BILL HALL

I have mixed emotions about accuracy in labeling the content of foods when I read an accurate label on a food package and it says "cooked ham and water product." Maybe there are some things we don't want to know. Wet ham is one of the things I don't want to know. . . .

Guess what goes into meat product. The parts left over after you have cut out and sold the chops, steaks, roasts, and ribs. . . .

We were once saved from specific knowledge of what meat product is. But the do-gooders are out to change that. Soon, you will no longer have to guess what is in meat product or hardly anything else. More and more the feds require product producers to list all the ingredients.

I have mixed feelings about that. On the one hand, I think I have the right to know. On the other hand, the information should be presented in ways I can avoid if I have a weak stomach. . . .

It should be like the movies. . . . There should be a rating system G (for godly), PG (for pretty-near godly), R (for rotten), etc. You have fair warning about [what] you will be buying if you go through that door.

Food labels require similar warnings in this candid new world, some indication on the label that you may not choose to read the label because the label now has the bad taste to be truthful.

There are days, looking at cooked ham and water product, when I long to be lied to again.

Excerpted from *Lewiston Morning Tribune*

"It's labeled 'high sodium, high cholesterol, low vitamins.' I think we should reward their honesty by buying it."

LAMB

Mary Had A Little Lamb and a Side Of Fries.

— STROMOSKI —

LAMB LOVERS, UNITE

No one would call sheep charismatic (in fact, some describe them as gentle, others as stupid), but any lack of character on their part is compensated for by their meat's sweet tenderness, complex flavors, and succulent juices.

Lamb has long been thought of as a special-occasion meat, but things have been changing in the lamb business. New breeding techniques have lowered prices and lamb is starting to show up in some unlikely places in unusual forms: filling fajitas, topping trendy pizzas, and even, ground up, transformed into lamburgers.

In Britain, where people eat five times as much lamb as Americans do, lamb still appears for Sunday lunch, invariably accompanied by a thin gravy, roast potatoes, green peas, and mint sauce. This thin sauce is made by pounding shredded fresh mint leaves with loads of sugar, then adding a few drops of boiling water and some salt and vinegar. It is quite mad, but every Briton expects it and swishes the gorgeous (though always well-done) meat about in it. Americans pander to this taste by offering mint jelly, which is sweeter and, if possible, still less appropriate.

The Greeks, Middle Eastern people, and North Africans also like mint with their lamb, but they make much more interesting dishes with it. Couscous is just one of them; yogurt often shows up with lamb, too. Then there are the go-with-lamb herbs and vegetables; in fact, I find it hard to think about lamb without imagining it roasted with rosemary and garlic and eggplant and white beans.

Lamb stews are eaten all over the world; curried lamb is fabulous with all its accompaniments: roasted chopped peanuts, toasted coconut, hot mango chutney, *raita* (very cold cucumber, diced and smothered with yogurt), crisp, peppery *pappadams* — and plenty of rice, of course. And the French casseroles of lamb with tiny carrots and onions are glorious with a bottle of red wine and their incomparable bread and sweet butter. . .

Oh my — so much to eat and barely 52 Sundays in a year. What a pity to waste even one on take-out pizza.

A Little (Leaner) Lamb

Lamb has always been an excellent source of protein, and contains several B vitamins, iron, and zinc as well. These days, it is leaner than ever, so certain cuts are part of any reduced-fat diet. A 3-ounce portion of roasted lamb from the shank half of the leg, for example, has just 153 calories, 6 grams of fat, and 74 milligrams of cholesterol.

TIPS

Cooking
Soak sprigs of fresh herbs such as basil, thyme, tarragon, sage, or oregano in water for about an hour, shake until partially dry, and lay them on the hot coals of your outdoor grill just before adding butterflied lamb.

Serving Sizes

Each of the following provides a serving of approximately 3 ounces of cooked, lean lamb:

1 loin chop
2 rib chops
1 sirloin steak
1 shoulder chop
4 spareribs or riblets
1 ground lamb pattie

With boneless lamb roasts, 1 pound of uncooked meat will yield 3 to 4 servings.

Lamb In A Pita Pocket

Serves 4

1 small cucumber, peeled, seeded, and diced
2 summer ripe tomatoes, sliced and cut into dice
1 jalapeño pepper, with seeds removed, finely chopped
2 tablespoons finely chopped fresh cilantro
8 ounces plain low-fat yogurt
Pinch of salt
4 pita bread pockets
Thin slices of leftover roast leg of lamb
4 leaves romaine lettuce, shredded

Stir together the cucumber, tomato, jalapeño, cilantro, yogurt, and salt.

Warm the pita pockets, then stuff with lamb slices and lettuce; spoon in the cucumber mixture.

Adapted from a recipe by Rick Rodgers and Stephanie Lyness

Q&A

Q Whatever happened to mutton?

A Nuttin' much. Federal regulations require meat from sheep over a year old to be sold as mutton. Although European sheep farmers swear that the best-tasting meat comes from two-year-olds, it is almost impossible to find mutton in the United States.

LEEKS

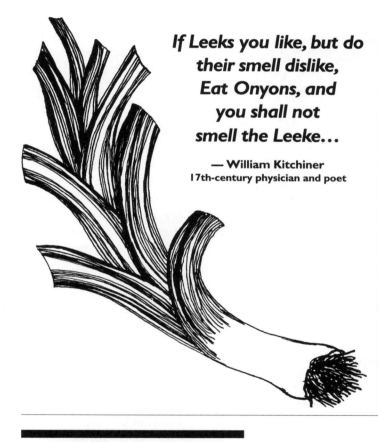

If Leeks you like, but do their smell dislike, Eat Onyons, and you shall not smell the Leeke…

— William Kitchiner
17th-century physician and poet

Legends of the Leek

Emperor Nero ate leeks regularly because he believed they were good for the vocal chords. Indeed, the Romans nicknamed him porrophagus, which means "leek mouth" — and the reference may not only have been to his singing.

Roman legions spread the leek as far as Wales, where it became the national emblem. It seems that either St. David or a Welsh prince named Cadwallader instructed his soldiers to wear leeks in their caps for identification during a big battle — and, of course, they were victorious. Ever since, loyal Welshmen bring out the leeks on March 1, St. David's Day.

Soup's Up!

The three great leek dishes are all soups. The Welsh are fond of a traditional broth made with leeks, called Cawl Cennin.

The Scots add a chicken and potatoes to the soup and call it Cockaleekie. But the most famous of all is a soup invented in a moment of desperate ingenuity by a chef at the Waldorf Astoria

in New York City, who added cream and flavorings to a cold version of French leek and potato soup and called it after his hometown of Vichy.

So Vichyssoise is in fact an American soup, available, in one spelling or another, all across the United States — but not in France.

LETTUCES

Lettuce is like conversation: It must be fresh and crisp, and so sparkling that you scarcely notice the bitter in it.

— C. D. Warner
19th-century garden lover

Many New Leaves To Turn

Arugula, watercress, and dandelion greens are peppery, mustard-flavored, and very perishable. They are particularly effective paired with mild lettuces such as Boston and Bibb.

Bibb lettuce has a small head of loosely grouped, delicate, light green leaves and an elusive flavor. It is excellent tossed with Boston, romaine, endive, watercress, radicchio, or watercress.

Boston lettuce, like Bibb, has a soft head. Like other loose-leaf lettuces it is useful for lining salad bowls and platters. Boston lettuce combines well with oak-leaf lettuce, endives, and young spinach leaves.

Chicory and **endive** are members of the same family, and the varieties are often confused with each other. True chicory has crisp, curly green leaves with quite a bitter taste; curly endive is often called chicory because it looks similar, but it has a whiter heart than chicory. Both should be eaten young, preferably with milder lettuces, such as Bibb and Boston; the bitterness increases as the leaves grow old.

Endive, or Belgian endive, has unmistakable white-and-yellow leaves, tightly wrapped into narrow cones a few inches long. Its crisp texture and slightly bittersweet taste are distinctive in mixed salads; it is also excellent braised. Endive is grown in darkness and turns green and bitter if exposed to light, so never buy any that is tinged with green.

Escarole is also an endive, with broad green leaves shading to white at the center. Its mild taste goes particularly well with an oil and lemon juice dressing.

Frisée is the least bitter of the chicory family. It has frilly light green leaves, firm white ribs, and a light yellow central core. It is excellent mixed with arugula, baby oak-leaf lettuce, and radicchio.

Lollo Rossa, a recent salad entry, originated in Italy. Its leaves are loosely bound at the root and form a lovely bouquet of red-tipped crinkly leaves.

Mâche is also known as **lamb's lettuce.** Its small, deep green leaves have a buttery flavor and soft texture. Serve it alone or with other lettuces and the best olive oil you can afford.

Marvel of Four Seasons, relatively new to the market, is a soft lettuce with a spectacularly good taste and marvelous coloration.

Mesclun is the darling of the salad set. It is not a single lettuce but an inventive mix of several baby lettuces, herbs, and colorful edible flowers. It costs as much as steak and vegetarians say it tastes better.

Oak-leaf lettuce has soft, dark green leaves that do indeed resemble oak leaves. The red oak variety is shaded from brown to crimson. Both kinds are very popular.

Radicchio's cupped leaves are deep crimson with white ribs running the length of them. A relative of the endive, it has a tightly bunched head that, pried open, releases an agreeably peppery flavor.

Romaine has long, flat, flavorful leaves that give crunch to salads, especially Caesar salads. The dark green outer leaves that are usually discarded are in fact the most nourishing, but most lettuce lovers prefer the sweetly crisp yellow heart. Red romaine's leaves are tipped with red; it has a milder taste than regular romaine but they mix together well.

Icebergs Do Not Sink

There may be as many as 30 different salad greens in a well-stocked grocery store, but until a few years ago iceberg was often the sole lettuce available in supermarket produce sections.

A lot of us grew up thinking that iceberg was the only kind of lettuce there was. Even today, it is second only to potatoes as the most popular fresh vegetable in the United States. It has all the virtues that appeal most to people who are not fond of vegetables. It is crispy, crunchy, low in calories, always in season, always in plentiful supply, inexpensive, and almost tasteless. (It is 90 percent water.) It keeps for a week or more in the refrigerator and, unlike all other lettuces and salad greens, will not become limp after it is doused with a dressing or laid upon a hamburger, chili, or tostadas.

The iceberg's only real drawback is its size. It is usually just too big to fit conveniently into the average refrigerator vegetable drawer, and there is too much of it to suit a single person who wants just a wedge or a few leaves. Recognizing this, the genetic engineers have engineered a tennis-ball-sized iceberg lettuce, small enough to fit in the palm of the hand. So far, iceberg remains green, but it will eventually become available in a rainbow of jolly colors. It's just a matter of time.

TIPS

Preparing
People who remain quiet on other matters don't hesitate to express firm opinions about lettuce. "Cut it," say some. "Tear it," others insist. In *our* not remotely humble opinion, the only lettuces that should be cut are iceberg, romaine, radicchio, watercress, and endives. All the rest should be torn before washing and whirled in a salad spinner.

Books

Fields of Greens
Annie Somerville; Bantam, 1993; $26.95

Salads
Leonard Schwartz; HarperCollins, 1992; $23.00

The Harrowsmith Salad Garden
Turid Forsyth and Merilyn Simond Mohr; Camden House, 1992; $19.95

MORE INFORMATION

California Iceberg Lettuce Commission
P.O. Box 3354
Monterey, CA 93942

Q&A

Q How many men does it take to make a salad dressing?

A Four. It takes a miser to measure the salt, a frugal man to measure the vinegar, a generous man to measure the oil, and a crazy person to mix them all together.

New Greens From Old Stock

In the process of collecting a worldwide gene pool of lettuces, the USDA has discovered red, yellow, and blue-green varieties. The last has a two-foot stem and is eaten like celery.

Researchers are working with lettuces from several countries, hoping to develop dozens of new nutritious varieties of salad greens. Recently, an experimental half-acre in California was planted with 400 varieties of lettuce, some of which were known in ancient Egypt and Persia 2,500 years ago. Many of the varieties now regarded as new were in fact well known in Europe in the Middle Ages, though only the wealthy could afford them then.

Times change. When the Illinois Central Railroad laid track from Chicago to New Orleans, thus offering the Windy City as a lucrative market for lettuce that could be transported at a popular price, common folk took to salad. Nor have we turned back. Today, air freight enables lettuce growers in California to fly their fragile crops to markets all over the world.

LOBSTER

A truly destitute man is not one without riches, but the poor wretch who has never partaken of a lobster.

— Anonymous

THE SEX LIFE OF THE LOBSTER

BRUCE BALLENGER

The female lobster's interest in sex is limited. She can mate only within two to four days of shedding her shell, which happens once a year or less, in the summer or fall. Though mating takes place rather quickly, often in less than a minute, it is not typically a one-night stand. A female lobster will often cohabit with her chosen male for a few days before mating, and may stick around with him in his burrow, usually under rocks or in a hole dug in the bottom mud, for up to a week after the act takes place. Both lobsters express their ambivalence about the arrangement with odd sexual displays, including a lot of aggressive "boxing" and friendlier "antenna feeling."

In the minute or so during which mating takes place, the male lobster gently turns the female over on her back, where she lies with front claws and tail fully extended. The male faces her, often resting his claws on hers, and with his walking legs grasps her body. Just aft of the male lobster's last pair of legs are modified swimmerets [small appendages rather like fins] which deliver the sperm to a receptacle on the female — a heart-shaped shield between her last two walking legs.

Remarkably, the female lobster can carry the live sperm for up to two years until she is ready to use them to fertilize her eggs. Usually, fertilization takes place in the next year, when the female lobster "extrudes" her eggs from little holes in the base of her second pair of legs. When she spawns, she flops over on her back and lifts herself up on her front claws, . . . the eggs stream out of the ducts on her legs and they end up cemented to the swimmerets on the underside of her tail, which is curled to form a pocket.

Because lobsters begin life with such a slim chance of surviving, females produce a lot of eggs — between 3,000 and 75,000 eggs every time they spawn. En route to the tail, the eggs are fertilized as they pass the seminal receptacle where the sperm are stored. The eggs hatch a year later, and the tiny lobsters begin their against-the-odds battle to make it to your dinner table.

Excerpted from *The Lobster Almanac*

Did You Know?

☞ Lobsters are crustaceans, often called "insects of the sea," because they belong to the same phylum, or division of living things, as insects and, like them, have exterior skeletons with a jointed body and limbs.

☞ Lobsters have been found at depths of 1,500 feet.

☞ The largest lobster on record weighed more than 40 pounds.

☞ It is illegal to trap lobsters without a license.

☞ In 1880, the wholesale price for lobster was 6 cents a pound.

☞ The annual advertising budget of the 1,500-unit Red Lobster restaurant chain is $60 million.

☞ Despite its rich taste, lobster is relatively low in fat and cholesterol.

A Lobster Roster

There are two kinds of cold-water lobsters, which are generally considered the most delicious: the **American** lobster (*Homarus americanus*), found off the eastern shore of Canada and New England, and the **European lobster** (*Homarus gammarus*), which is found from Norway to the Azores. These have slightly bluer shells and are smaller than the New England lobsters, but their meat is equally succulent and much prized by lobster lovers. Both species have hard, thick shells and typical lobster claws — a small, thin one for seizing hold of prey and a large, heavy one for crushing it.

There are also **spiny lobsters**, also known as **rock lobsters**, or **langoustes**, which are really seagoing crawfish and have no heavy claw; their bodies and legs are covered with thin spines. Some dwell in warm waters off Florida and the Caribbean islands; others in colder waters off South Africa, Australia, and New Zealand. The latter are usually imported to the United States in the form of frozen "lobster tails."

All lobsters are naturally a dark greeny-blue when alive; cooking turns their shells bright red.

Sex Discrimination

It is difficult to tell the male or "cock lobster" from the "hen" unless they are lying side by side on a chopping block. The male has slightly larger claws — and some claim their meat is firmer than the hen's. The female has a tail that is perhaps a shade broader — and some say its flesh is sweeter than the cock's.

A more reliable way of determining the lobster's sex is to turn it over and examine the rows of small appendages, called swimmerets, behind the four pairs of walking legs, on the underside of the tail. In the male they are hard and feel like small bones; in the female they are soft and feathery. And, of course, if there is any "coral" attached to them, there is no longer any question — other than whether the lobster should have been caught at all.

Repartee in Gay Paree

The writer Georges Feydeau, famous for his remarkable output of successful farces at the turn of the century, had ordered lobster at a Paris restaurant. Brought one that was missing a claw, Feydeau demanded the reason. The waiter murmured something about lobsters liking to fight each other in the restaurant's tank. "Then take this one away and bring me the victor," said Feydeau.

TIPS

Buying

Choose a busy fish store. A lobster that has languished too long in a tank moves sluggishly. Deprived of its natural habitat, it uses up its own resources and the quality of its meat diminishes. The livelier the lobster, the fresher it is, and the better it will taste.

Many connoisseurs think the small "chicken" lobsters weighing a little over a pound are the sweetest and most succulent. Others say a giant 5-pounder makes even better eating. (Just be sure you have a pot big enough to put it in.)

A 1¼-pound lobster for one person will yield about ⅓ cup (¼ pound) of meat.

A 2½-pound lobster will produce 2 cups or 1 pound of meat. This will be enough for four people.

"Culls" — lobsters that have lost a claw, or both — cost less than those that are intact, and can be used in cooked dishes or salads.

Storing

The best way to keep a lobster alive is to carry it home in a strong brown paper bag with some seaweed. Get it into the refrigerator as quickly as possible, still in the paper bag. Lobsters can survive out of the sea for a while because tides sometimes strand them ashore, but if you put one in a closed plastic bag, it will suffocate. And if, feeling kindly, you put it in a bath of cold tap water, it will drown.

It is always best to cook the lobster as soon as possible.

Serving

Should you have leftover lobster (an unlikely event), remove it from the shell and make a chowder with it, or prepare a lobster roll for a loved one. Don't try to freeze it; frozen lobster loses both flavor and texture.

ODD JOBS

To stop lobsters from pinching people and cannibalizing each other, their claws must be rendered useless. Out at sea in the lobster boat, the fisherman holds the lobster upright, which makes it stretch out its claws. He sets it, tail first, into one of the sections in a wooden crate like a soft-drink crate. Then, with the lobster's arms still open wide, he snaps a thick rubber band over each claw in turn. (Before rubber bands, wooden pegs were used.)

Books

A Lobster in Every Pot
Editors; Yankee Books, 1990; $10.95

The Complete Crab and Lobster Book
Christopher R. Reaske; Lyons & Burford, 1989; $16.95

The Lobster Almanac
Bruce Ballenger; Globe Pequot, 1988; $10.95

MORE INFORMATION

Maine Lobstermen's Association
P.O. Box 147
Damariscotta, ME 04543
207-563-5254

MAIL ORDER SOURCES

Boston & Maine Fish Company
6 Faneuil Hall Marketplace, 3rd floor
Boston, MA 02109
800-626-7866

Downeast Seafood Express
Box 138, Route 176
Brooksville, ME 04617
800-556-2326

Hunches and Honor

Lobsters live on the sea bottom, in fairly shallow water, feeding on the fallen organic materials they find there. Lobstermen note the lobsters' haunts, and drop down wooden traps weighted with stones and baited with stale fish. Each trap is attached to a buoy on the surface that carries the owner's individual mark. Lobstermen make it a point of honor never to steal from each others' traps.

Strict regulations govern the size of lobsters that may be caught. Each one must be measured; any with carapaces less than 3¼ inches long, from front of head to first tail joint, must be thrown back. Females with eggs must also be thrown back, after first being specially marked.

Approximately 90 percent of legally eligible lobsters are harvested annually. How, then, does the population renew itself? One theory holds that most breeding females dwell far offshore in very deep waters where — thank goodness — it is almost impossible to find them.

Hard Or Soft Shell?

By the time a lobster reaches the dinner table, it will probably have shed its shell more than 20 times. Before it loses the old shell, it is busy growing a new one underneath. The old shell begins to soften as the lobster borrows calcium salts and other minerals from it to make the new one, which is a slightly larger replica of the original.

The old shell cracks open along a line on its back and the lobster in its malleably soft new shell squeezes out as quickly as it can. The process usually takes from 5 to 20 minutes, and if any legs or claws have a hard time coming out, the lobster simply abandons them in the old shell and eventually grows back new ones.

The new shell takes several weeks to harden, so the lobster is now at its most vulnerable and an easy mark for underwater predators. Each time it sheds, the lobster expands, emerging some 14 percent longer and 40 percent heavier. To do this, it takes on a great deal of extra water, so a lobster that has just shed its shell will have very soft, watery flesh.

Summer is the shedding season for American lobsters of edible size, and diners cracking open summer lobster are likely to get a gush of water onto their plates, or their laps — which is why we have lobster bibs.

LOBSTERS DON'T CRY

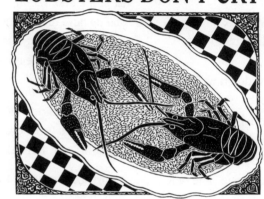

It has been said that the lobster is a primitive creature with such a rudimentary nervous system that it feels no pain when it is cooked. Just to be sure, the British Society for Prevention of Cruelty to Animals conducted a study to determine the least painful way for a lobster to meet its eater.

The researchers concluded that it would be best to lower the lobster into the pot head first — perhaps so that it can see where it's headed. Some say that it screams as it takes the big dive, while others hasten to assure us that this is merely the escape of air under high pressure.

The stout of heart prefer to introduce an element of surprise by plunging a knife into the lobster's spinal cord, thus severing all connection between head and body; however, lobsters treated in this manner thrash about rather alarmingly. If you fear that you will be upset by taking such drastic action, you can always buy a lobster that has been pre-cooked. Alas, it will be overcooked. That is one thing you *can* count on.

And like a lobster boil'd, the morn From black to red began to turn.

— Samuel Butler
17th-century satirist

LUNCH

"Just a sandwich, please — I'm working through lunch."

P.C. VEY

THE HEYDAY OF THE THREE-MARTINI LUNCH

Jerry Della Femina

We called them silver bullets — they were six-ounce martinis made up of six ounces of gin, a drop of vermouth and a thin strip of lemon peel floating on the top, surrounded by a handful of silvery slivers of ice. "Straight up" was the way most people drank in the 1960s; ordering "on the rocks" was seen as a sign of weakness, as was the substitution of vodka. Olives displaced too much gin, and the only people who drank Gibsons were the effete heads of publishing companies. The town's bartenders took pride in the picking up of their cocktail shakers the minute they heard the voices of their favorite customers booming "Hello, Dino." It was a simpler time — maitre d's names were limited to Dino or Gino in Italian restaurants and Pierre or Claude in French restaurants. By the time you made your way to the bar, your martini awaited you, drops of moisture icing the glass. You reached for it, took a first sip, and said out loud to no one in particular, "Ah, that feels like jumping into a cool freshwater pond on a hot day." Another business lunch of the '60s was under way.

The three-martini lunch with clients and colleagues was not an exaggeration of the IRS; it was real, and, one must admit, it was fun. In contrast to today's teetotaling investment-banker types ("Just bring me a diet soda and a knife to cut someone's heart out with, please"), we were a kinder, gentler group before politicians were telling us to be a kinder, gentler group.

The first martini at lunch always went down with talk about baseball or other sports: "I tell you, he can't carry Mantle's glove. Players today make too much money." Suddenly it was 1:00 p.m. and someone would catch the maitre d's eye, raise his empty glass, and nod his head. Soon, another tray of silver bullets would arrive. The talk would drift to business: "I tell you, it's getting ridiculous. That commercial cost $40,000 to produce. Someday, it'll cost $75,000 to make one."

Then someone would remember, "Hey, we forgot to order food. Waiter, can you bring us some menus and another round while we're waiting and, oh yes, bring us the wine list." Lunch for four would be consumed with two bottles of wine and, on rare occasions, three bottles. At 2:30, those of us who had a 3:00 meeting would go off to work sober and steady. Those who didn't would sit back and have a couple of Scotches on the rocks — for dessert.

Recently, I decided to reconstruct a lunch of the 1960s. After one silver bullet, I quit. I imagined my third martini arriving at the same time as the paramedics. The next day, I walked into my favorite restaurant and, when the captain asked if I would have "the usual," I said, "No, I'm in the mood for something different today. Let's try putting a lime in my club soda."

One martini is all right. Two are too many, and three are not enough.

— James Thurber
Luncher and laugher

Out Of It

When we say that somebody is out to lunch, we very often don't mean that he or she is at a restaurant. We mean that he or she is not functioning, intellectually absent, and, probably, wrong. This phrase can be applied to anyone, from corporate CEOs to office persons. And if it is applied often enough, and widely enough, it guarantees that the subject of our scorn is surely moving out of the loop and will shortly be put out to pasture.

What I Don't Do

• *I never stop for lunch at the same time every day. (I don't like routines, and I don't believe it was a real person who said that they free your mind to concentrate on more important things.)*

• *I rarely take even 20 minutes for lunch — it's much easier to sit at the desk with a sandwich and keep on working. (Though you do have to take care not to get grease spots on the paper, and someone always seems to call just as you're stuffing the egg salad back into the sandwich with your fingers.)*

• *It's silly to even think of going out for a stretch — I'm waiting for that phone call without which I can't complete the job that was due two hours ago, and I'll forget my train of thought if I break off now. Besides, it's raining and I haven't got my umbrella.*

• *Anyway, who was it said you shouldn't go for a swim after a heavy meal?*

Whoops!

How significantly a tiny typographical lapse can change one's understanding of an event.

The invitation read, in part:

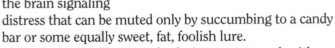

Lunch will be gin at noon.

Bag It

If we skip the noonday meal for some sensible reason — we needed to shop, go to the bank, or get other important business done — it throws the body for a loop. Instead of rewarding our sacrifice with weight loss, the body stubbornly sets us up for weight gain by sending repeated urgent and ultimately irresistible messages to the brain signaling distress that can be muted only by succumbing to a candy bar or some equally sweet, fat, foolish lure.

Having initially rejected calories, we get stuck with more of them in the end than if we had eaten our modest brown-bag lunch.

Free lunches are vastly overrated. What you gain in food stays with you, but what you lose in time and concentration is gone forever.

— Anonymous

Quick Snacks
for Lunch Skippers

Plain cheese pizza

Pop-top canned tuna, packed in water (3½ ounces)

Nonfat or low-fat plain, or fruit, yogurt

2 ounces low-fat cheese chunks and ⅓ cup dried fruits

Bagel with jelly or a smear of cream cheese

Low-fat cottage cheese (4-ounce container)

Low-fat breakfast bar

Books

Brown Bagging It — Lunches to Go
Jeanette L. Miller and Elisabeth Schafer; Pearl Publications, 1991; $12.95

The Creative Lunchbox
Ellen Klaven; Crown, 1991; $7.00

MAHI-MAHI

They are brilliantly colored fish with blue to turquoise backs, iridescent emerald-green bodies, and yellowish bellies. Most of their color fades, however, as they die: Their skin turns a silver gray the longer they are out of the water.

— **Shirley King**
Fish: The Basics

STRONG-STRONG

Up until about a decade ago, mahi-mahi was a fish dish you found on menus in Hawaii, and far out in the South Pacific. Almost everywhere else on the globe, the same fish went by the name of "dolphin" or "dolphinfish." It was an instant turnoff, of course. Most people, and especially Americans, were misled into thinking that a mammal was on the menu — Flipper, perhaps.

Recognizing the confusion, American fish purveyors united in promoting the Hawaiian name, and the result is that mahi-mahi has gone from strength to strength in the U.S. market. What's in a name? Everything. *Mahi-mahi,* in Hawaiian, means "strong-strong."

Mahi-mahis swim worldwide in tropical, subtropical, and temperate waters. In size they can reach 6 feet and 70 pounds; the average weight is 5 to 25 pounds. They feed on anything from flying fish to crabs, shrimp, squid, mackerel, and other small fish.

Japan catches from 50 to 60 percent of the world's mahi, with Taiwan trailing. In recent years, mahi is being fished vigorously off the Pacific coast of Latin America, from Costa Rica to Peru; most of the mahi we eat in U.S. restaurants comes from that catch.

Even in Hawaii, three-quarters of the mahi is imported; only about 500 tons of them are caught in local waters.

On the plate, mahi-mahi are sometimes compared to swordfish, though mahi flesh is sweeter and more moist, and has a large flake when cooked. Mahi tastes wonderful grilled, baked, pan-fried, deep-fried, broiled, braised, poached, smoked, dried — or raw (as sashimi or ceviche).

In fact, the fish may be strong-strong, but its taste is delightfully delicate-delicate, and that's of course the reason we like it so much-much. Even those people who once raised their fists in anger now beckon to the waiter so that they can order mahi-mahi in restaurants.

Did You Know?

☞ Female mahi-mahis are immensely fecund. They lay, on the average, some 50 million eggs per year.

☞ The flesh of the mahi-mahi contains less than 1 percent fat. Hollandaise sauce, which makes a lovely accompaniment to the mahi, is more or less solid fat — so things balance out quite nicely.

Baked Mahi-Mahi with Papaya Coulis

Serves 4

Papaya Coulis:
1 tablespoon corn oil
1 to 1½ pounds papaya, peeled, seeded, and diced
3 ounces finely chopped onion
Pinch of salt
6 ounces fish stock
Juice of 1 lime
8 tablespoons whipping cream
¼ teaspoon crushed red pepper

2 tablespoons lemon juice
2 tablespoons olive oil
4 6-ounce mahi-mahi fillets
Bouquet of fresh vegetables, for garnish

Preheat the oven to 400 degrees F.

Heat the corn oil in a medium saucepan over moderate heat. Add the papaya, onion, and salt to taste. Cook, stirring frequently, for 5 to 7 minutes, until onion is translucent. Pour in the fish stock and lime juice. Bring to a boil, reduce heat to low, and simmer, partially covered, for 10 minutes. Transfer the mixture to a blender and puree until smooth.

Meanwhile, pour the whipping cream into a skillet, add the crushed red pepper, and cook over medium-high heat until reduced by one-third. Add to the papaya puree and keep warm.

Brush the mahi fillets with the olive oil and lemon juice. Bake in the oven until done to medium temperature.

To serve, sauce each plate with Papaya Coulis, place a fillet on top, and garnish with fresh vegetables.

— Richard S. Viernes, chef at Tahitian Lanai, Honolulu

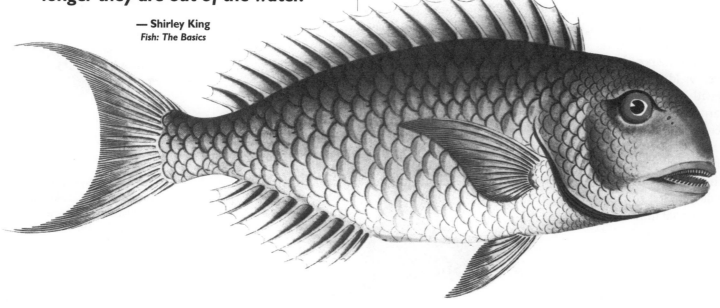

MAPLE SYRUP

HARVESTING LIQUID GOLD

The sticky brown stuff that sits in plastic bottles on supermarket shelves is very often an impostor passing itself off as maple syrup. These faux-maples blend sugars, corn syrups, flavorings, caramel coloring, and preservatives, sometimes adding from 2 to 15 percent *real* maple syrup for a more authentic taste. One hundred percent pure maple syrup contains only the cooked sap of North American maple trees.

The art of maple-tapping was practiced by Native American tribes of the Northeast such as the Algonquin, Iroquois, and Ojibway. Colonists learned their techniques and modified them, but the process has been largely the same all along.

Sugaring season runs from February into early April, from the time buds first appear on the maple trees to the moment the buds open. To harvest the rising sap, farmers drill from one to four ½-inch-wide holes in a tree, depending on its size, and insert a short, tapered tube called a spile through which the sap drips into a hanging bucket. Or they will run plastic tubing from many trees into a central collection drum. This method has become popular in recent years because it increases the trees' yield and cuts down on the labor required for collection without reducing the quality of the syrup. But many farmers still drive horse-drawn sleighs from tree to tree emptying buckets, just as they did a century ago.

Many gallons of sap have to be collected, because 97 percent of the sap is water, which has to be boiled off. The sap must be heated for an entire day, until it reaches exactly 219 degrees F., but there are a few crucial minutes that make the difference between good, slow-pouring maple syrup and a sticky, viscous blob. In this process of "sugaring," or "sugaring off," syrup makers will boil 30 to 70 gallons of sap down to 1 gallon of syrup — that's why it's like liquid gold at the supermarket. But no one doubts that

it's worth the labor-intensive long hours and every penny that pays for them.

Maple syrup producers hope for freezing nights and warm days, a combination that produces the maximum amount of sap; however, nature doesn't always deliver. The 1993 harvest yielded only about half of 1992 levels because of a short season. A surplus of Canadian syrup, held over from the previous winter, saved sweet-tooths around the world from having to go without.

Evening in a Sugar Orchard

From where I lingered in a lull in March
Outside the sugar-house one night for choice,
I called the fireman with a careful voice
And bade him leave the pan and stoke the arch:
"O fireman, give the fire another stoke,
And send more sparks up chimney with the smoke."
I thought a few might tangle, as they did,
Among bare maple boughs, and in the rare
Hill atmosphere not cease to glow
And so be added to the moon up there.
The moon, though slight, was moon enough
   to show
On every tree a bucket with a lid,
And on black ground a bear-skin rug of snow.
The sparks made no attempt to be the moon.
They were content to figure in the trees
As Leo, Orion, and the Pleiades.
And that was what the boughs were full of soon.

— **Robert Frost**

Odd Jobs

To make good maple syrup, you have to be patient as the sap boils down, and ready to recognize the moment when it finally reaches a state of ideal constitution. Bill Clark, of Clark Farms in Vermont, uses a metal scoop shaped like a dustpan for this job. During the last 15 minutes of cooking, he digs his scoop into the syrup. If an inch of syrup drips off the scoop when he withdraws it, the syrup is ready. Modern hydrometers could do this detective work, but Clark's test is 99 percent accurate.

Sweet-Toothed # Critters

Animals enjoy the maple's sweet sap at least as much as humans. Moose find young maple trees and help themselves to a few twigs every chance they get. Cows will lick sap oozing from the mature trees, and squirrels wait until it freezes into icicles for a frozen treat. Farmers who tap into their trees with plastic tubes have often found their hoses gnawed full of holes by woodland creatures.

Books

The Maple Syrup Baking and Dessert Cookbook
Ken Haedrich; American Impressions, 1985; $4.50

The Maple Syrup Cookbook
Ken Haedrich; Storey Communications, 1989; $7.95

Making the Grade

There are four different grades of syrup and not all are bound for the breakfast table.

Grade A light is almost transparent; its subtle flavor is best for foods containing fruit or nuts whose taste would be overpowered by a heavier syrup.

Grade A medium, with its golden color and mild flavor, is the most popular syrup.

Grade A dark, called Grade B before the state of Vermont changed the rating system a few years back, is stronger-tasting than the others — like a stout, say, compared to lager beer or espresso to regular coffee.

Grade B, formerly known as grade C, is used by commercial syrup companies because it is less expensive. They add other ingredients to achieve a taste somewhere between medium and dark Grade A syrups.

My Country, Sweet and Sticky

Canada has the maple leaf on its flag, but by no means a maple monopoly. Maple syrup is big business in Canada — more than three-fourths of the world's supply comes from there — but the syrup found in U.S. gourmet food stores usually comes from New York or Vermont. Massachusetts, New Hampshire, Wisconsin, and other northern states also produce moderate amounts, usually for local use.

There are 11 different varieties of maple, all of which have a sweet sap, but the sap of the sugar maple (which has the reddest leaves in fall) is about twice as sweet as any of the others. All maple syrup comes from North America, and the bulk of it is made from the sugar maples of the wintry northern states and provinces.

MORE INFORMATION

International Maple Syrup Institute
P.O. Box 715
Swanton, VT 05488
802-868-7244

North American Maple Sugar Council
W10010 Givens Road
Hortonville, WI 54944
414-779-6672

Vermont Maple Industry Council
R.D. 1, Box 1660
Ferrisburg, VT 05456
802-877-2250

MARGARINE

THE GREAT MARGARINE CONTROVERSY

Those of us old enough to remember World War II have indelible memories of the day when butter went to the war effort and margarine arrived in the family kitchen in the form of a large loaf of white stuff that looked like lard. A blister of yellow-colored powder came along to provide it with the look of butter, and children begged — at first — to be allowed to mix the color in. Later, of course, the glamour paled and it became a chore.

Margarine got easy after that. Even with improved taste and the color premixed it was cheap. And it gained a reputation for being good for us, with its unsaturated fat looking ever better when compared with the saturated fats in butter. In due course, margarine replaced butter altogether on many American family dinner tables. The ascendancy of margarine seemed secure — so secure, in fact, that many people felt free to spread it on as thickly as they had once, before they knew better, added butter.

Then came 1993, and a report of results from a massive research effort at the Harvard School of Public Health, which tracked the diets of more than 85,000 nurses over eight years and found that those who ate four or more teaspoons of margarine a day had a 50 percent greater risk of heart disease than those who ate margarine less than once a month.

While the margarine manufacturers insisted that

nothing could be proved by just one study, however long it had lasted, and reluctant margarine eaters swore that they had been betrayed, closer observers had already been noting some chinks in margarine's armor. A Dutch research group had established that hydrogenated oils raised cholesterol counts — though not to levels as high as those produced by saturated fats. Now it appeared that the true villains were the artificial trans fats created from the unsaturated fats in the course of the hydrogenation that makes margarine solid. These trans fats, absorbed by the body, acted like saturated fats and upset the body's balance of HDL and LDL cholesterols. The more the margarine was hydrogenated, the stiffer it became, and more trans fats were produced.

So the most recent consumer trend has been to margarines in soft cup forms, which have 50 to 80 percent less trans fats than stick margarine.

In the Harvard Nurses Study, butter consumption was not associated with any increased risk, and sales of butter have been up ever since those results were announced. However, this may be partly the result of pricing: butter and margarine are now more or less head to head in cost.

After all the controversy, it now seems that whether we choose to eat butter or margarine, the most important thing is to keep our consumption of fat of any kind as low as possible. Stinting is the best payoff. So if we *have* a piece of bread, we surely won't be slathering it with any yellow spread; it will be a lot more like applying a thin film of foundation makeup.

What a Promise!

Constituents of Promise Ultra Fat Free spread, in descending order: water, monoglycerides and diglycerides, gelatin, salt, rice starch, lactose, esters of mono- and diglycerides, potassium sorbate, lactic acid, artificial flavor, colors, and vitamin A. It contains 5 calories per tablespoon and tastes just like . . . margarine.

Alternative Formats

Butter and margarine combinations usually contain 40 percent butter to 60 percent margarine. Some people swear by them; others are reminded of the famous politician who, faced with two evils, invariably chose both.

Diet or reduced-calorie margarines derive all their calories from fat, about 45 percent by weight. The oils may be diluted with water until they have about half the fat and calorie contents of regular margarine. Diet margarines spread well, but if you cook with them, their water content makes them splatter all over the stove.

Liquid margarines, in squeeze bottles, have the lowest content of saturated fats. You can squirt them directly on corn on the cob, waffles, or toast, and use them for cooking.

Sprinkle-on powders are made from carbohydrates and are virtually free of fat and cholesterol. They will melt on hot, moist foods such as baked potatoes and vegetables, but can't be used for spreading on bread or for cooking.

Whipped margarine contains about 50 percent air, which is fine as long as you realize that you are paying for something that is not there.

MAKING MARGARINE

Most commercial margarines release the oils from their various vegetable sources — corn kernels, soybeans, peanuts, sunflower seeds, and so on — by a complex method of cleaning, then milling, steam-heating, and hot-pressing the seeds. Chemical solvents are used to increase the yield of oil. The extracted oil is then filtered, degummed, and neutral-ized, using sodium carbonate or bicarbonate; finally, it is washed, bleached, and deodorized.

So-called natural margarines are produced by a cold-pressing method that omits the use of solvents, and consequently does not need to clean up its act afterwards. This process does not create trans fats. Such margarines, said to taste bland but palatable, and definitely not greasy, have been made in Europe for some time and may soon be introduced in the United States.

Switch? Which?

Responding to public concern about the role of trans fatty acids in raising cholesterol and confusion about which spread to choose, the American Heart Association's Nutrition Committee issued an advisory in April 1994 suggesting that margarine is still a preferable substitute for butter and that soft margarines are better than hard ones. The AHA recommends shopping for a margarine with no more than 2 grams of saturated fat per tablespoon, choosing a soft rather than stick form, and limiting total daily intake of fats and oils to 5 to 8 teaspoons.

MORE INFORMATION

National Association of Margarine Manufacturers
1101 15th Street NW,
Suite 202
Washington, DC 20005
202-785-3232

MAYONNAISE

LISA HANEY

Over Aisy Now!

Mayonnaise, that delightful combination of egg yolks, oil, and vinegar, probably originated in Spain. It is said to have been brought to France by an 18th-century duc de Richelieu, who had been fighting the British at Mahon, a port on the Mediterranean island of Minorca. He named it Sauce of Mahon because that was where he first tasted it; later it was renamed mahonnaise, which means, roughly, "after the manner of Mahon," and this is how some people still pronounce it. Other egg-yolk-based sauces also have aise endings, including hollandaise, "after the manner of Holland," and béarnaise, "after the manner of Béarn."

Bringing Out The Best

Seventy-five years ago, a German immigrant named Richard Hellmann was operating a deli in New York City. The salads and sandwiches he sold were made with his wife Nina's homemade mayonnaise, and his customers raved about it.

Hmm, he thought. The secret of success here wasn't his doing; it was Nina's mayo.

In short order he filled two big containers with it, called it Blue Ribbon, and sold it for ten cents a dollop. That went so well that in no time at all he was distributing it to other stores. He bought first one truck, then a fleet of trucks. In 1912, he built a manufacturing plant, the forerunner of the many now spread over the continent, and started selling it in jars. He built an empire. And today we eat, every one of us, close to three pounds of mayonnaise a year.

Which all goes to prove that behind every successful man stands a good woman (especially if she makes good mayo).

Mayo Wisdom

"Hold the mayo" is not popular with mayonnaise makers, but health-conscious consumers know that the sauce is close to 100 percent fat. One tablespoon of commercial mayonnaise contains 100 calories and 80 milligrams of sodium, so an egg-salad sandwich with added salt isn't the wisest choice over a sardine and a prune.

Alternatives to regular mayonnaise: Mix half the amount with nonfat yogurt, or select a reduced-calorie or fat-free form. The good news: Even regular mayonnaises have only 8 milligrams of cholesterol per tablespoon.

Homemade Mayonnaise

Makes 2 ½ cups

Those who fear salmonella may ignore this recipe; those who are confident of the pristine quality of their eggs may want to try it — carefully. It's a winner, especially when enhanced with a handful of fresh herbs.

3 egg yolks
1 teaspoon mild Dijon mustard
½ teaspoon salt
Freshly ground black pepper
2 tablespoons fresh lemon juice
¾ cup light olive oil
¾ cup salad oil
¼ cup chopped fresh parsley, thyme, oregano, or other herb

Put the egg yolks in a food processor with the mustard, salt, pepper, and lemon juice. Turn on the power and whirl until thickened; then, very slowly, pour in the oils. When the sauce is completely emulsified, add the herbs.

MORE INFORMATION

Association for Dressings and Sauces
5775 Peachtree-Dunwoody Road, Suite 500G
Atlanta, GA 30342
404-252-3663

MEAT

Eliminating meat cuts out a major source of nutrients.

— **Mary Abbott Hess, R.D.**
Former president of the American Dietetic Association

LIVING CLOSE TO THE BONE

Reay Tannahill

In the very earliest days of human evolution, food helped to make man. It was roughly 4 million years ago — some authorities say 30 million — when the ape-into-man transmutation began, and it is generally accepted that the change was set in motion by a shortage of eggs, nestlings, and fruit which drove the ape down from his familiar habitat in the trees to forage in the grasslands.

He found lizards and porcupines, tortoises and ground squirrels, moles, plump insects and grubs, and took to them with such enthusiasm that, in time, he almost wiped out a number of the smaller species.

During the next 3 million years of development, he learned how to kill larger animals by hurling rocks at them, a hunting technique which required him to move on three or, ultimately, two legs instead of four. His wits became sharper as he competed with the lion, hyena, and saber-toothed cat who shared his hunting grounds. His teeth, no longer needed for fighting, changed shape — and human speech began to develop. His forefeet adapted themselves into hands, and these hands proved capable of making tools.

Excerpted from Food in History

Q&A

Q Is it better to eat chicken than meat?

A Maybe. Maybe not. Fried chicken may well contain more fat and calories than lean beef.

Slim As A Pig

In the never-ending search for leaner meat, genetic engineers have been able to introduce growth-regulating hormones into domesticated animals, primarily beef cattle; regulation of growth produces meat with less fat. The hormones are harmless to humans because they are destroyed when the meat is cooked. Even if they are eaten, they are broken down during the normal digestive process.

Applying genetics is not the only way we contrive to produce leaner meats. All or almost all visible fat is trimmed before most meats arrive in the store. When the fat is removed before meat is cooked, there is no chance of its migrating into the meat. In addition, broiling or roasting meat on a rack allows internal fat to drain from it.

In order to reduce the fat still further, however, it may be necessary to consider eating smaller quantities of meat. Our energy needs decrease by about 5 percent every ten years, so eating the same number of calories as we used to when we were teenagers will have an inevitable result: a depressingly steady weight gain.

Meaty Dimensions

Meat is described as "nutrient-dense," which means that it supplies a large amount of essential nutrients in relation to its calorie content. (By way of contrast, Cheez Doodles are not nutrient-dense.)

Health professionals recommend a diet that includes no more than 5 to 7 ounces of meat per day — about two 3-ounce servings. A 3-ounce serving is often compared with the dimensions of a deck of playing cards. This amount will provide plenty of protein, iron, zinc, phosphorus, thiamine, niacin, and vitamin B-12.

Making the Grade

Grades such as prime, select, choice, etc. are given for meat's quality and expected yield. The Federal Meat Inspection Act of 1906 made inspection mandatory for all meat that crossed state lines. The Wholesome Meat Act of 1967 required that meat sold within a state must meet requirements at least as stringent as those of the federal system. The United States requires imported meat to be of equal quality to domestic products. To ensure its safety, all imported meat is inspected by agents of the Food Safety and Inspection Service (FSIS), a division of the USDA.

A round stamp (made with purple ink) certifies that the meat has been inspected and the official establishment number assigned to each packing or processing plant is placed on each primal cut when it passes federal inspection. The stamp must also be on all prepackaged processed meat that has been federally inspected. If the meat is sold in a box, the inspection stamp is placed on the outside of the carton rather than on the meat itself.

Meat is subjected to more testing and inspection than any other food. The USDA devotes to meat and poultry inspection as much as eight times the resources that the Food and Drug Administration spends on monitoring the rest of the country's food supply.

In round numbers the federal government spends more than $1 million every day employing its 7,400 meat and poultry inspectors, who remain in every packing plant during every minute of operation. FDA-inspected food plants, in comparison, may receive a visit from an inspector less than once a year.

Federal inspection stamp used for fresh and cured meat.

Federal inspection stamp used for canned and packaged meat products.

State meat inspection stamp is often shaped like the state.

Books

Jack Ubaldi's Meat Book: A Butcher's Guide
Jack Ubaldi and Elizabeth Crossman; Macmillan, 1991; $12.95

Look and Cook: Meat Classics
Anne Willan; Dorling Kindersley, 1992; $19.95

Professional Charcuterie Series, Vol. 1
Marcel Cottenceau; Van Nostrand, 1991; $74.95

The Lobel Brothers' Complete Guide to Meat
Stanley and Leon Lobel; Running Press, 1990; $14.95

Everybody's a pacifist between wars. It's like being a vegetarian between meals.
— Colman McCarthy
Columnist, *The Washington Post*

MELONS

THE MARVELOUS MELON FAMILY

The melons are the sweet aristocrats of the very large gourd family; like the squash, the cucumber, and the pumpkin, they grow on vines, but to reach full splendor melons require warm weather, regular drinks, and watchful care as they pass through adolescence to the exact moment of fragrant maturity when they are ready to be picked and eaten.

There are two main kinds: muskmelons and watermelons. Muskmelons are round or oval and highly aromatic, hence their name. The two principal varieties are those with rough netted skins, such as cantaloupe and Persian melons, and the smooth-skinned winter melons, which include the casaba, Crenshaw, and honeydew. The soft flesh within spans a range of subtle flavors but the seeds are always grouped in the center. Watermelons are big, lozenge-shaped, and solid, with thick green skins, crisp, crunchy flesh, and seeds scattered all through their bodies.

Ripe muskmelons are fragrant, with a scar at the stem end that is slightly sunken. The more aromatic without, the sweeter the melon is within. Smooth-skinned winter melons have much less aroma, a more delicate taste, and juicier flesh. No melon ripens to full sweetness off the vine, but winter melons make a better stab at it than most.

Watermelons, which grow to superb sizes in the United States, are the most festive of outdoor summer party foods, easy to eat out of hand and with seeds that just beg for the spitting. A ripe watermelon full of juice responds with an echo when thumped, and its skin can be scratched with a fingernail.

Popular Melon Varieties

ROUGH-SKINNED MUSKMELONS

Cantaloupe — A variety of muskmelon brought into Italy, probably from Armenia, in the first century A.D. and grown in the town of Cantalupo — hence its name. Cantaloupes have a rough yellow "netting" on the outside and juicy golden-orange flesh on the inside. At their best in July and August, ripe cantaloupes are fragrant at their stem and blossom ends and their rinds yield slightly to gentle pressure.

Persian — This gray-green melon looks like a cantaloupe, but is larger, rounder, and more finely netted, with flesh that is firmer and deeper orange. A ripe Persian melon should weigh at least 5 pounds and have hints of bronze in the skin and a good aroma; either end should give slightly to gentle pressure. Persians are in high season in August and September.

SMOOTH-SKINNED MUSKMELONS

Casaba — A large, oval melon, the casaba has a pale yellow, slightly ridged skin and creamy white, moderately sweet flesh. At its best in September and October, a truly ripe casaba will have no green in the skin.

Crenshaw — Sometimes called a Cranshaw, this melon is often sold in halves because of its size (it can top ten pounds). A light yellow or golden yellow rind showing a minimum of green is the best indicator of ripeness. The golden to peachy-pink flesh has a spicy-sweet taste, at its peak in August and September.

Honeydew — The honeydew belongs to the winter melon family, but it is at its best from July through October. A honeydew should weigh around 5 pounds, with a smooth, almost cream-colored skin and pale green flesh; when ripe it will have a fragrant, somewhat softened blossom end and the outer surface of the rind will feel slightly soft. A hybrid known as the orange-fleshed honeydew melon resembles the cantaloupe in size and taste. Its rind looks like that of a regular honeydew but has a faintly pink cast.

WATERMELONS

A member of the cucumber family, the **watermelon** can vary widely in size and shape — from spheres the size of honeydew melons to submarine-shaped giants weighing well over 100 pounds that are sold in pieces. Their smooth thick rinds take on pale, dark, or mixed green hues that contrast strikingly with the firm, deep red flesh inside. Most watermelons are full of black seeds, but some farmers grow "seedless" varieties with small white seed pods that are undeveloped — and edible. Watermelons are at their be from June through August.

Tastes Good — Like a Cantaloupe Should

Half a 5-inch cantaloupe contains 100 percent of the recommended daily allowance of vitamins A and C; it is rich in beta carotene, has plenty of fiber, adds only 90 calories — and tastes great, too.

Melon Aplomb

Melons are one of the very few fruits that are never served cooked. They can also appear equally appropriately at either end of the meal.

A First for Japan

The Food Channel newsletter reports that a "biomelon," artificially rendered disease-resistant through recombinant DNA techniques, may prove to be Japan's first genetically engineered edible produce. The biomelon is an improved variety in which a gene from one species has been transferred to the cells of a different species, producing a new cultivar with no known ancestors. Seedlings of the melon were planted in May 1993 on a miniplot at Japan's National Institute of Agro-Environmental Studies where field studies are being carried out.

Cantaloupe Sorbet

Serves 4

Make the simple syrup first so that it has time to get cold. Try this recipe also with honeydew, orange flesh honeydew, and other ripe melons.

Simple Syrup:
2 cups granulated sugar
1 cup water

1 medium cantaloupe, fully ripe
2 tablespoons lemon juice

To make 2 cups of simple syrup, bring the sugar and water to a boil over medium heat, without stirring. Reduce heat to medium-low, cover the pan, and simmer for 5 minutes without stirring. Remove from the heat and let cool. Cover and refrigerate. Use 1 cup for the sorbet; the syrup will keep for several weeks.

Halve the cantaloupe and remove the seeds. Scoop out the flesh; there will be about 4 cups. Process in the food processor for 3 to 4 seconds, scraping down the sides until pureed Combine the puree, lemon juice, and 1 cup simple syrup until well blended. Pour into an ice cream machine and freeze according to manufacturer's instructions.

TIPS

Storing

How you store melons depends on the variety. Rough-skinned muskmelons, such as cantaloupes and Persian melons, if purchased when hard should be stored at room temperature until they soften and lose any green coloration. Then they can be kept for up to a week in the refrigerator, wrapped in plastic so that they do not absorb any odors.

As for the smooth-skinned muskmelons: Casabas that look greenish can be stored at room temperature until they turn yellow-white, and then refrigerated. A whole Crenshaw that is unripe will ripen at room temperature; halved ones will ripen no further and should be refrigerated as soon as they are bought. Honeydews should be chilled immediately. They do not become any sweeter if kept at room temperature; what you buy is what you eat.

Watermelons are often bought in sections because there is no way of determining how ripe an uncut melon may be; also, a whole watermelon can yield more fruit than a single family can handle. Keep whole watermelons at room temperature in a darkened, reasonably cool spot, but refrigerate any cut pieces.

Did You Know?

☞ Eat-it-all mini-melons with an edible rind have been developed by scientists at the USDA.

☞ Melons can be grown inside molds that form them into pyramids, squares, and other intriguing shapes.

☞ Watermelons are appropriately named, since water constitutes 88 percent of their (considerable) mass.

☞ The world record for watermelon seed spitting is held by Jack Dietz of Chicago, who launched a seed a distance of 66 feet 11 inches in March 1989.

MORE INFORMATION

California Melon Research Board
531-D North Alta Avenue
Dinuba, CA 93618
209-591-0434

National Watermelon Promotion Board
P.O. Box 140065
Orlando, FL 32814-0065
407-895-5100

MAIL ORDER SOURCES

Frieda's, Inc.
P.O. Box 58488
Los Angeles, CA 90058
213-627-2981

MICROWAVABLE FOOD

Microwaving has revolutionized the way we cook as no other technology ever has.

— Anonymous

FAKE AND BAKE — KIND OF

There is a story that sentries on alert close to a radar installation were stunned one day to see a flight of ducks collide with the mast and fall to the ground — cooked to a crisp.

The other popular tale is told of Percy L. Spencer, a Raytheon engineer, who stood close to a magnetron tube, a device that generates microwaves, and observed that the chocolate bar in his pocket had melted. A lesser man would have been appalled and petrified, but not this brave pioneer. Seizing the moment, he immediately launched the first research into microwaves as a means of cooking, while inadvertently spawning the horrid rumor that microwaves could creep stealthily into pants pockets and cause a meltdown into sterility. Thus important science advances into the mainstream.

Today, microwave ovens are an integral part of every kitchen, as indispensable as the sink and the refrigerator. They are also found in offices and company cafeterias, on trains and planes, in restaurants and submarines, in hospitals and in prisons, and soon will be installed in the glove compartments of cars so that driver and passengers will be able to fix a hot snack as they roll merrily along. Microwaves are where it's at, in terms of the food of the future.

Not everyone is pleased with this development. There is a minority that stoutly refuses to give house room to the microwave oven, while others use it to prepare all their meals. Stirring is for them a major culinary undertaking, and if the instructions require that the package be turned more than once, they won't buy it because they don't want all that trouble.

The microwave threatens to change the way we think about food in general and the family meal in particular. Fewer children will cherish loving memories of family meals. It is difficult indeed to know what kind of grace is appropriate for little children to offer when their frozen, microwavable evening meal is provided by a corporate conglomerate.

What Works, What Can't, And Why

Sooner or later we're going to stop calling microwaves "ovens" because they're *not* ovens. Ovens generate heat; microwaves generate microwaves.

Microwaves cook wherever they strike, and the heat is incidental. As the waves penetrate a potato, for example, they cook by causing the potato's molecules to vibrate. It is the agitation that creates heat — and when the waves converge at the center, as they do with spuds, you get a good result. A food's density and the amount of water it contains are also factors — soups, sauces, and stews will cook faster than a solid piece of meat.

Microwaves perform some tasks very well; vegetables, for example, can taste superb when cooked this way. Because they are prepared with little water they retain most of their nutrients and emerge bright in color, crisp in texture, and with a taste so brilliant that no butter or margarine is needed to make them moist.Fish, too, can be first class when timed carefully. At its best when used for steaming or braising, the appliance is also good for heating soups or warming moist foods that are immersed in sauces or covered with gravy.

Grilling, frying, roasting, and baking are the major methods of cooking with heat, while microwaving is an entirely different process. To be cross when a microwave fails to broil a steak is as irrational as trying to open a can with a wire whisk. The microwave can't do all things, and will never be tamed or reformed into producing an entire meal. One day we'll have to accept that it's not a magic box.

Microwaves can't compete with regular sources of heat. They can, however, perform a few incredible tricks of their own. In the moments it takes to create an ice cream sundae with hot chocolate sauce, for example, the ice cream stays hard and cold even while the sauce (which contains a high proportion of sugar) gets hot enough to scald your tongue.

The rules of microwaving are rigid, and few of us understand them. However, the microwave allows for only the slimmest margin of error. Leave some foods on for just a couple of seconds too long and they're inedible.

Some people value the microwave most for its efficiency at reheating coffee, but it is probably most reliable at boiling water, a job it accomplishes with admirable speed and divine predictability.

Coming Up Micro

The next generation of microwaves will make the current ones seem as old-fashioned as tail-fins on a pink Cadillac convertible. These new appliances will read the bar code on the package and figure out how long to cook the food. When it is ready, a light will go on or a heat-sensitive strip will change color. All food for very young children will take the same amount of time to cook, so little Mary Jane will know that if she presses her very own color-coded button, she will be able to provide herself with dinner while Mom and Dad are still at work faraway.

Eventually, all food may be grown in square or oval shapes, the better to be cooked in the microwave. Already, square eggs have been produced, which can accept microwave energy without exploding.

Books

Better by Microwave: Over 250 Recipes for the Foods Microwave Does Best
Lori Longbotham and Marie Simmons; NAL-Dutton, 1990; $19.95

Betty Crocker's Microwave Cookbook
Editors; Prentice Hall, 1990; $19.95

Good Housekeeping Illustrated Microwave Cookbook
Editors; Hearst Books, 1989; $24.95

Mastering Microwave Cookery
Marcia Cone and Thelma Snyder; Simon & Schuster, 1986; $24.95

Micro Ways
Jean Anderson; Doubleday, 1990; $29.95

The Microwave Gourmet
Barbara Kafka; Morrow, 1987; $25.00

The Microwave Gourmet Healthstyle Cookbook
Barbara Kafka; Morrow, 1989; $22.95

What Else Can I Do With My Microwave?
Ruth Spear; Dell, 1993; $7.99

PERIODICALS

Microwave Times
Recipes Unlimited, Inc.
P.O. Box 1271
Burnsville, MN 55337
612-890-6655
Bimonthly; $11.95 per year

Range Rovers

Microwaves come in four sizes — subcompact, compact, midsize, and full size — and in wattages ranging from 300 to more than 1,000. The absence of standardization leads to complications. Problems in timing are compounded by the fact that microwave energy is intense and constant and can be tempered only by a setting at half power, which delivers full power half the time.

Models producing 300 to 350 watts emit no more energy than the lowest setting of a gas flame, so when speed is the objective, they're not much help. Models that produce 650 watts or more are more useful. Most useful of all are the combination microwave/convection ovens that permit a range of cooking options.

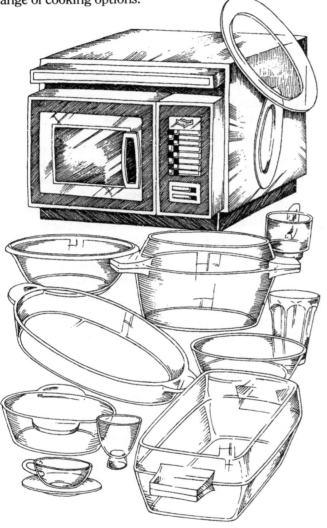

The microwave takes less than ten seconds to heat a moist towel for a quick refresher. But the washer/dryer takes more than an hour to wash and dry it ready for use again.

— Anonymous

Faster Feeding Speeds Up

Restaurants that rely on microwaves have solved the troublesome law of physics that states that if a single potato takes five minutes to bake, two potatoes require more than ten minutes, and three potatoes take more time than is practical. Some establishments use banks of microwaves, others invest in 3,000-watt models that cook the food in literally no time at all.

MACRO COMPANIES, MICRO WAVES

The food industry has spent an estimated $2 billion fruitlessly trying to formulate microwavable cakes, brownies, hamburgers, and pizza — a task as hard as trying to create a lawn mower that can vacuum rugs. The foods in question, with their light-as-air bubbles and delicious crispy brown bits, are produced by dry heat, and microwaves don't employ dry heat. Consumers might be willing to sacrifice a small degree of flavor in exchange for convenience, but when confronted with a microwavable cake mix that tastes like a wet sock, they balk. Sales for almost all microwavable foods have been declining steadily; even the market for diet meals is diminishing. New product introductions have been fewer in the last couple of years than before, and the bloom is off microwave cookbooks, too.

Meanwhile, after sampling several thousand microwaved foods, the industry has been able to identify specific chemicals in the process and the flavors they produce. The "good" chemicals (thiazoles, cafurans, and pyrazines) produce meaty, nutty, buttery, roasted, and caramel tastes. The "off" chemicals (thiophenes, pyrroles, and oxazoles) are associated with burned, rubbery, fishy, and haylike flavors. Unfortunately, the good chemicals are intermingled with the bad, and this situation has given rise to a growing business in the production of synthetic flavors. Expert tinkering with the chemicals results in the subtraction of certain tastes and their replacement with others more to our liking.

All Wrapped Up

Foods prepared for microwave reheating generate more than 4 billion pieces of packaging annually, a fact that concerns many environmentalists. The problem starts because we rarely cook whole food in the microwave; most people use food in packages, usually in single servings, and foods that used to come in all kinds of other forms now are packaged in plastic so that they can be put directly in the microwave.

One company has devised packaging for four strips of bacon that employs a quilted paper to absorb fat and repel water. The bacon cooks in about three minutes and produces more garbage than a full pound of bacon cooked in a skillet. An effort to make crisp french fries yielded some awesome packaging: a honeycomb container about the size of a cigarette packet, with each little fry in its own individual bed, on a mattress of strips of laminated aluminum. As the aluminum heats, the fry fries. An Einsteinian solution — but a costly one.

The FDA is worried about whether the sticky stuff that holds the packaging in place may find its way into the foods and has asked the microwave industry to prove that packaging is safe — which is a task akin to proving that something that isn't there *is* there, and that even if it weren't, it would still be OK if it were.

Microwaving Safety Tips

These apply especially to households with children, who are major users of microwaves.

• Make sure the microwave is in a convenient, easily reachable spot with a level surface.

• Never turn on an empty oven. It can damage or break the mechanism.

• Read the package directions and make sure the cooking time has been set correctly (it is easy to set the time for five minutes instead of five seconds).

• Use only microwave-safe cookware. Cold storage containers such as plastic margarine tubs, ice cream cartons, and styrofoam packages may collapse.

• Rotate the food in the microwave and stir halfway through the cooking time, if possible, to make sure no part of it is scalding hot.

• Always use pot holders to take the food out of the microwave — just in case the container is hotter than you expect it to be.

• If a plate or bowl is covered with plastic wrap, always turn up a corner to let the steam escape. Peel off the wrap or paper from that corner *toward* you, so that the steam is released at the far side of the dish, not up into your face where it could cause a painful burn.

• Break open jelly doughnuts and pastries carefully before eating them. The fillings can get fiercely hot because the sugar attracts the heat and holds it like a magnet.

• When preparing popcorn, be patient. The steam escaping from the packet (or the saucepan) can cause a nasty burn. Let the popcorn cool for a couple of minutes.

MILK

I don't believe you have to be a cow to know what milk is.
— Ann Landers
Wise woman

NATURE'S FIRST FOOD

Forty years ago, Elsie, the Borden cow, was America's national spokes-bovine for the virtues of milk. Dressed like an ideal American mother in a modest frock, frilly apron, and sometimes discreet jewelry, Elsie smiled at us from billboards and the pages of magazines, urging us kids to drink our milk and plenty of it.

In those days milk was a personal matter. It was delivered door to door by the milkman, in bottles; his jingly-jangly approach was anticipated by one and all, as was his cheerful chatter on the doorstep. Elsie and the milkman made milk a family institution. And if parents ever had to say, "Finish your milk now," they had Elsie and the milkman to back them up.

Today Elsie is out of the picture, the milkman has gone into some other line of work, and milk's national image is not what it was. The fact that milk is good for children has never been seriously challenged. Mother's milk can nourish infants safely for up to two years, and when cow's milk takes over, its pasteurization (partial sterilization to kill off any objectionable organisms) and homogenization (the blending of elements into a uniform mixture) makes it a healthy and palatable drink for most children. Furthermore, the milk industry is now investing in television ad campaigns aimed at showing that milk makes pretty girls even prettier.

However, milk's role as a beverage for adults has been under scientific review for many years. Milk is a terrific source of calcium for children and adults, but it has been argued that adults don't need the calcium that milk delivers. And there is some evidence that the cholesterol and saturated fat in milk contribute to the accumulation of plaque in the arteries approaching the heart. For adult milk lovers, the current alternative suggested by the experts is red wine.

One is left to wonder what Elsie would have to say about that.

Varieties of Milk

Whole milk contains not less than 3.25 percent milk fat and not less than 8.25 percent milk solids. Most milk, including whole, low-fat, and skim, is fortified with vitamin D.

Low-fat milk has a reduced milk-fat content. Because vitamin A is removed along with the milk fat, it is replaced in the same amount.

Skim milk, also called nonfat milk, has had as much fat removed as is technologically possible. The vitamin A lost in processing is replaced.

Chocolate milk is made by adding chocolate or cocoa and sweetener to whole or low-fat milk.

Evaporated milk is made by evaporating enough water from whole milk to reduce the volume by half. It is then homogenized, fortified with vitamin D, and heat-sterilized. **Evaporated skim milk** is concentrated and fortified with vitamins A and D.

Sweetened condensed milk is a canned milk concentrate of whole or skim milk with a sweetener added.

Buttermilk, originally, was the thick, butter-specked, slightly sour liquid left behind after whole milk had been churned into butter. **Cultured buttermilk** is made by adding a bacterial culture to milk to produce the acidity, body, flavor, and aroma.

Eggnog is a mixture of milk, eggs, sugar, and cream and may also contain flavorings such as rum extract, vanilla, and/or nutmeg.

Not Sour, Just Bad

When Louis Pasteur discovered how to wipe out bacteria by raising the temperature of the medium in which they were thriving, he invented a process that revolutionized public health and saved millions of lives. But he was no benefactor to anyone who, like Miss Muffet, liked to make good use of a bowl of naturally soured milk.

In the souring process, unrefrigerated raw milk separates into curds and whey, and home cooks used to enjoy straining off the whey from the curds through a layer of cheesecloth, then pressing the little packet of dry curds into a homemade cream cheese.

But pasteurized milk doesn't sour; it goes bad, and you will regret it if you eat over-the-hill cottage cheese, sour cream, and yogurt. Maybe there was a grain of truth in the anti-pasteurization protests of the early 20th century that the destruction of bacteria would hide spoilage.

HOLIER THAN COW?

Igor Kopelnitsky

Consumer groups have become vocal in their denunciation of milk produced using a genetically engineered hormone protein, bovine somatotropin (BST). They need not be alarmed. Solid scientific evidence has proved that the substance presents no health risk to consumers. Furthermore, increased milk production through the use of BST lessens the size of dairy herds, which in turn conserves valuable water resources and reduces the use of agrochemicals and the demand for acreage for grazing. Environmentally, it is benign; politically, it is a hot potato.

BST is a naturally occurring protein hormone made in the cow's pituitary gland. It is a growth hormone that is found in small amounts in all cows. Biotechnology has enabled it to be made inexpensively and in unlimited quantities. When injected into adult cows it results in an increased milk production of up to 25 percent.

Small dairy farmers are opposed to its use, not for health reasons but because it could lead to a glut of milk and a drop in wholesale prices. They point to the figure of more than 10 million cows on 220,000 farms, which annually produce close to 150 billion pounds of milk. No matter how much milk we drink, no matter how much cottage cheese and yogurt we eat every day, there is still a huge surplus. Farmers are paid less for their milk than they were ten years ago, and the government spends literally billions of dollars to buy and store surplus butter, milk, and cheese.

Despite all the good and valid reasons not to produce even more milk, farmers are facing a dilemma. If they warn consumers of the "dangers" of drinking milk that "contains hormones," they run the risk of lessening the overall demand. They managed to persuade legislators in the dairy states of Wisconsin and Minnesota to ban the use of BST temporarily, but the federal government formally approved it for use nationwide at the end of 1993.

The National Institutes of Health and the FDA are in agreement that the composition of milk is not altered when cows are treated with BST. It is already present in all milk and the amount in milk from BST-treated cows does not significantly differ from the amount in milk from nontreated cows. But in these emotion-packed situations facts count for less than perceptions. The public is more concerned about hormones in milk than hormones in meat. This could be because we have the option to refuse meat, but milk and milk products are essential to most people's daily diet.

Virtue does not entirely reside with advocates of BST. Opponents are worried about the stressed-out dairy cattle who are supplying all the extra milk. They already have hugely distended udders as a result of breeding to produce larger quantities of milk and are likely to develop mastitis, a painful udder inflammation, as a result of longer milking. Other detractors express concern that what may be an acceptable minimal residue in milk is more concentrated in cream, butter, and cheese. To ease this anxiety, scientists reiterate that BST has no biological effect on humans. Regardless of the form in which milk is ultimately consumed, it is broken down during the digestive process, just like any other protein.

Meddling with the Moo

Synthetic flavors — The Department of Agriculture has been working hand in glove with a company that concentrates on developing synthetic flavorings. Together they have cooked up a mixture of reconstituted dried nonfat milk, skim milk, fruit juice, and artificial flavorings. To this brew they add a sprightly fizz. Kids will love it. Parents will fuss about lowered nutrition, added sugar, and increased price compared with low-cost regular milk. But who do you think will win this battle of wills when the product comes our way?

Frozen milk — Efforts to produce frozen milk have been put on ice. Nevertheless, the USDA has patented a process that will keep milk fresh in the freezer for three months. The word "fresh" may be slightly misleading: Frozen milk is a low-fat emulsification of milk solids, water, and corn or soybean oil that, when combined with water in a 3:1 ratio, will yield a product similar to skim milk in taste, fat content, and calorie count. Sounds lovely.

Organizations Assuring Us
BST Is Safe

Groups that have confirmed the FDA's conclusion that BST-supplemented milk poses no safety risks:

American Dietetic Association
American Farm Bureau Federation
American Medical Association
Council of Agricultural Science and Technology
Grocery Manufacturers of America
International Dairy Foods Association
Joint FAO/WHO Expert Committee on Food Additives
National Institutes of Health
National Milk Producers Federation
(representing large farm cooperatives)
National Wholesale Grocers
— and regulatory agencies in at least 12 countries, including
Canada, France, Germany, and the United Kingdom

Those opposed:
Center for Science in the Public Interest
Community Nutrition Institute
National Farmers Union (representing small dairy farms)
National Resources Defense Council
Pure Food Campaign

*The cow is
of the bovine ilk;
One end is moo,
the other milk.*

— Ogden Nash
Wise man

MORE INFORMATION

**Milk Industry
Foundation**
888 16th Street NW,
2nd floor
Washington, DC 20006
202-296-4250

National Dairy Board
2111 Wilson Boulevard,
Arlington, VA 22201
703-528-4800

**National Milk
Producers Federation**
1840 Wilson Boulevard,
4th floor
Arlington, VA 22201
703-243-6111

**Wisconsin Milk
Marketing Board**
8418 Excelsior Drive
Madison, WI 57317
608-836-8820

MINERALS

Minerals: Facts and Myths

Mineral/Food Sources	What It Does	Myths
Macrominerals		
Calcium. Milk and milk products, sardines and salmon eaten with bones, dark green leafy vegetables, shellfish, hard water.	Builds bones and teeth, maintains bone density and strength; helps prevent osteoporosis; helps regulate heartbeat, blood clotting, muscle contraction, and nerve conduction.	Helps prevent insomnia and anxiety.
Chloride. Table salt, fish.	Maintains normal fluid shifts; balances blood pH; forms hydrochloric acid to aid digestion.	None.
Magnesium. Wheat bran, whole grains, raw leafy green vegetables, nuts (especially almonds and cashews), soybeans, bananas, apricots, spices.	Aids in bone growth; aids function of nerves and muscle, including regulation of normal heart rhythm.	Cures alcoholism, prostate problems, kidney stones, and heart disease.
Phosphorus. Meats, poultry, fish, cheese, egg yolks, dried peas and beans, milk and milk products, soft drinks, nuts; present in almost all foods.	Aids in bone growth and strengthening of teeth; important in energy metabolism.	Reduces stress; accelerates growth in children; helps reduce arthritis.
Potassium. Oranges and orange juice, bananas, dried fruits, peanut butter, dried peas and beans, potatoes, coffee, tea, cocoa, yogurt, molasses, meat.	Promotes regular heartbeat; active in muscle contraction; regulates transfer of nutrients to cells; controls water balance in body tissues and cells; helps regulate blood pressure.	Cures acne, alcoholism, allergies, burns, and heart disease.
Sodium. Table salt, salt added to prepared foods, baking soda.	Helps regulate water balance in body; plays a role in maintaining blood pressure.	Lowers fevers; prevents stroke.
Microminerals		
Chromium. Meat, cheese, whole grains, dried peas and beans, peanuts.	Important for glucose metabolism; may be a cofactor for insulin.	Cures diabetes and hypoglycemia.
Copper. Shellfish, nuts, beef and pork liver, cocoa powder, chocolate, kidneys, dried beans, raisins, corn oil margarine.	Formation of red blood cells; cofactor in absorbing iron into blood cells; helps produce several respiratory enzymes.	Stimulates hair growth in bald men; relieves anemia.
Fluorine (fluoride). Fluoridated water and foods grown or cooked in it; fish, tea, gelatin.	Contributes to solid bone and tooth formation; may help prevent osteoporosis.	Causes cancer.
Iodine. Iodized salt; also seafood, seaweed, dairy products, crops from iodine-rich areas.	Necessary for normal function of the thyroid gland and for normal cell function; keeps skin, hair, and nails healthy; prevents goiter.	Causes anemia.
Iron. Liver, kidneys, red meats, egg yolks, peas, beans, nuts, dried fruits, green leafy vegetables, enriched grain products.	Essential to formation of hemoglobin, the oxygen-carrying factor in the blood; part of several enzymes and proteins in the body.	Controls alcoholism and menstrual discomfort.
Manganese. Nuts, whole grains, vegetables, fruits, instant coffee, tea, cocoa powder, beets, egg yolks.	Required for normal bone growth and development, normal reproduction, and cell function.	Helps asthma, diabetes, sterility, and fatigue.
Molybdenum. Peas, beans, cereal grains, organ meats, some dark green vegetables.	Important for normal cell function.	None.
Selenium. Fish, shellfish, red meat, egg yolks, chicken, garlic, tuna, tomatoes.	Complements vitamin E to fight cell damage by oxygen-derived compounds.	Cures cancer and arthritis.
Zinc. Oysters, crabmeat, beef, liver, eggs, poultry, brewer's yeast, whole wheat bread.	Maintains taste and smell acuity; normal growth and sexual development; important for fetal growth and wound healing.	Relieves angina and cirrhosis.

Reprinted from *The Wellness Encyclopedia*

GOOD AS GOLD

Minerals are inorganic chemicals that play a vital role in the healthy maintenance of bodily functions. They are essential to the formation of bone mass and regulation of the heartbeat. They are also important in maintaining normal blood pressure and in regulating the digestive and other systems.

Minerals are divided into two groups. Macrominerals are needed by the body in relatively large amounts and include calcium, chloride, magnesium, phosphorus, potassium, sodium, and sulfur. Microminerals, or trace minerals, are also essential, but in smaller amounts, some so small that they are measured in micrograms, which are millionths of a gram. Together, minerals make up barely 4 percent of the body's total weight, but the presence of exactly the right amount of each one is critical to maintaining good health.

Because the balance of minerals in the body is so fragile, experts urge us not to play doctor and attempt to self-medicate ourselves. Mineral supplements should only be taken on professional advice. A sensible and varied diet will supply all our needs and there is little danger of overdosing on fruits and vegetables. On the other hand, too much calcium and too much phosphorus in the form of over-the-counter supplements may interfere with the body's absorption of iron, and too much iron, in pill form, may have a harmful effect on cardiovascular health.

The most-talked-about minerals — calcium, potassium, and iron — are discussed in more detail in their own sections; sodium is covered in the section on salt; and the chart on page 245 lists some of the true values of the main macro- and microminerals, and exposes some of the myths about their functions in our lives.

Did You Know?

☞ Minerals are sturdier than vitamins, but some of them are soluble, which means that they may be lost if water used in cooking is discarded.

☞ Minerals are present in the crust of the earth. They are carried into the soil and the water and absorbed by fruits and vegetables; we eat them and absorb the minerals they contain, in turn, in our food.

MONKFISH

Monkfish is called the poor man's lobster. As long as people never see what it looks like whole, they love it.

— Werner Auer
Executive chef, Hyatt Regency Hotel, Houston

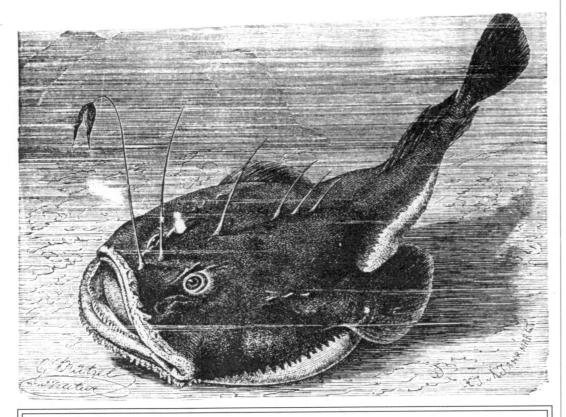

Not Nice Names

The monkfish has more names than those already mentioned, none complimentary: bellyfish, frogfish, goosefish, and sea devil.

NOT ANOTHER PRETTY FACE

Until very recently, New England fishermen didn't take the monkfish. It was too ugly, they thought, to consider. Not just rather ugly or somewhat ugly. We're talking hideous here — "a tadpole almost the size and shape of a baby grand piano," one observer wrote. It has too many teeth, wrinkly skin, knobby little fins like elbows, and a wiggly antenna on the top of its head.

This fish is not for your next soiree, you may exclaim. Ah, but it doesn't *want* to come to your party. It wants to blunder along the bottom of the sea as nature intended, looking morose and undesirable. Then, when a lesser fish comes swimming by, it wiggles its head antenna so that the prey will think it's a worm. Prey swims near, *gnash* go all those teeth, and that's the end of that. Not itself a pretty sight. But it is because of its natural skill as a fisherman that the monkfish is also called the angler fish.

This fish has always been popular in Europe, where it is known as lotte. European fishermen aren't at all concerned about its looks, and the restaurateurs know a good thing when they see it — a mild, sweet flesh, firm in texture, low in fat. Only the tail of this enormous fish is edible, but tail fillets weigh from 2 to 10 pounds.

So American fishermen finally got the point, and today, domestic monkfish is readily available in U.S. markets, sold fresh or flash-frozen to restaurants. The flesh is so sweet that sometimes chefs use it to extend lobster and scallops. Despite everything, it seems, the ugly monkfish has made it to the ball after all.

MONOSODIUM GLUTAMATE

FLAVOR LIKE NEVER BEFORE

Richard Atcheson

One evening at our apartment in New York City, my wife and I decided to order in some Chinese food for dinner. I put my hand on the shelf where I keep my thick sheaf of Chinese take-out menus, picked one at random, and we made our choices. I remember making the call: It was prawns for her and beef with garlic sauce for me. I had barely put the phone down before the doorman buzzed: Our dinner had arrived.

We agree that it was the *best* Chinese dinner we've ever had, and we speak as a pair who have been around, veterans of Chinese take-out in many parts of America, including Chicago, San Francisco, and Laguna Beach. This food was far, far better than any that had gone before. It was glorious, fabulous, exquisitely flavored. We waxed rhapsodic. We pressed tidbits upon each other. We raved. We were drunk with the sheer deliciousness of it all. And we ate everything in sight.

When the last scrap of food was gone my wife abruptly put her chopsticks down and departed urgently for the bathroom. In the same moment, I developed a piercing headache that was exactly like steel bands tightening around my cranium. I got up and paced the room. When my wife came back into the living room she said, "Well, I don't know what happened to me, but all of a sudden …" "I have the most terrific headache," I said, which is exactly what Franklin Delano Roosevelt said the moment before he had the stroke that killed him. And so to bed.

At *exactly* 3 a.m. — not 2:59, not 3:01 — I awoke from sleep and sat straight up in the bed, eyes wide, feeling that something was very odd. But what? Slowly I realized: I was breathing. Breathing fully, the air rushing in and out of me like winds at gale force. I've had sinus problems all my life. My nose is always dripping or stuffed up. So I had never ever had that precise sensation. "It's like a spiritual experience," I thought, then lay down again and went back to sleep.

Next morning we compared notes and agreed that something extraordinary had happened to us, and that it must have been an overload of MSG in the gravy. In fact, I thought it must have been a *jar* of MSG in the gravy to get me breathing like that. In one way or another — my wife digestively, I sinusitisistically — we had been opened up by monosodium glutamate, hollowed out like soda straws. Turned to pure spirit.

— stromoski —

My wife would never do it again, but I would. Breathing is a fabulous experience once you get over the shock. The only problem is that neither of us can remember the name of the restaurant we called that night.

The Chinese Food Syndrome

Monosodium glutamate, commonly known as MSG, is a flavor enhancer largely connected in the public mind with Chinese restaurants. It is a crystalline powder derived from glutamic acid, one of the 22 amino acids. MSG, which was discovered by Japanese scientists in the 1920s, is found in seaweed, vegetables, cereal gluten, and the residue of sugar beets. Now produced mainly through fermentation of molasses, glutamate in one natural form or another has been used in Asian cooking for 2,000 years without incident.

However, numbers of Americans have reported adverse reactions to MSG in recent years. Their complaints include nervousness, irritability, stomach problems, severe headaches, numbness of the limbs, tightness in the chest, heart palpitations, dizziness, asthma, flushing and burning sensations, and depression.

MSG is not merely a Chinese food ingredient; the substance is widespread in our food supply. It is added to canned and dry packaged soups and many snack foods such as chips, dips, and nuts. It can be found in deli meats, cured meats, canned fish, frozen dinners, salad dressings, croutons, sauces, and seasoning salts. It is also present in many fast foods, including fish and chicken items, sauces, and salad dressings.

If you look for MSG on the contents list of food packages, you won't always find it listed by that name. MSG is sometimes also known as Accent, natural flavorings, Aji-no-moto, Zest, gourmet powder, subu, Chinese seasoning, Glutavene, Glutacyl, and Kombo extract. Hydrolized vegetable protein, another alias, may contain 12 to 20 percent MSG.

Under Review

Some consumer groups have urged the FDA to put restrictions on the use of MSG, and in 1993 an advisory panel to the agency held hearings on the question. Scientists who testified said that the substance is harmless when used in typical small amounts. Some said they saw no reason to classify MSG as a health hazard.

The advisory panel could take up to a year to submit its findings. If it concludes that MSG is a health risk to some people, the FDA could rule that food labels be more explicit, or that MSG content in restaurant food be limited.

MORE INFORMATION

The Glutamate Association
5775 Peachtree-Dunwoody Road, Suite 500-G
Atlanta, GA 30342
404-252-3663

MUSHROOMS

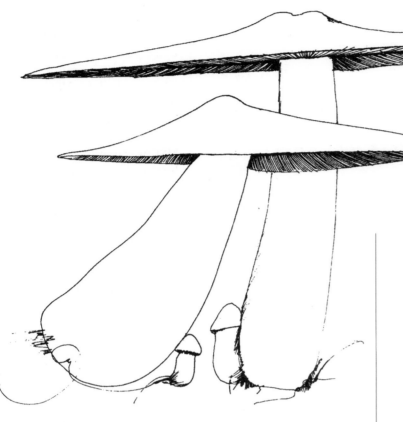

THE FASCINATION WITH FUNGI

When it comes to mushrooms, nothing should surprise us. They are full of mystery and intrigue, studied as much by toxicologists as by mycologists and those of us who like to eat them. They fascinate us like no other food.

It is astonishing to learn that there are 2,500 different kinds of mushrooms, and even more surprising that this is just the tip of the iceberg. Others, learned in these matters, claim knowledge of 5,000 fungi and the American Mushroom Institute states, quite matter-of-factly, that there are 38,000 varieties!

Mushrooms are not vegetables, though we find them in the vegetable section of the supermarket. They are fungi, and some can kill you. You are perfectly safe if you buy them in a reputable store, but if you pick and eat mushrooms in the field without knowing exactly what you are doing, it may be the last thing you ever do. There are no specific antidotes to some of their poisons.

If you disregard this advice, please leave one of your field-found mushrooms in the refrigerator. It will provide guidance for the coroner.

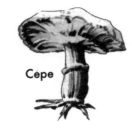

Cepe

Enoki

Oyster

Shiitake

Porcini

Varieties of Edible Mushrooms

Cèpe — A rich, meaty-tasting wild mushroom with a thick stalk and flat cap. It is highly regarded in European countries, notably France and Switzerland, and often used in quickly sautéed veal dishes with cream sauce.

Chanterelle — Found in Pacific Northwest forests by knowledgeable mushroomers, this wild variety with its frilly yellow trumpet-shaped head is another treasure of early fall.

Crimini — Closely related to the cultivated white mushroom, these are firm and brown. They are cultivated in Pennsylvania and have an attractively earthy flavor. They can be eaten raw or sautéed in butter and are particularly good made into a sandwich with bacon and chives (and a fried egg).

Enoki — The Japanese are great fans of these fragile, long-stemmed, pin-headed mushrooms. They are usually eaten raw, or sometimes floated in clear soups at the last minute. They don't have a lot of flavor and are chiefly admired for their graceful form.

Morel — The undisputed king of the mushroom family, this wild mushroom with its black spongy head and thick stem often appears following a forest fire. Morels are astonishingly delicious and make sublime marriages with veal and heavy cream sauces.

Oyster — This does have a silken texture reminiscent of a fresh oyster. Oyster mushrooms are eaten raw, but are better sautéed and added at the last moment of cooking to poached chicken breasts or a ragoût of vegetables.

Porcini — Native to Italy, and cousins to French cèpes, these mushrooms are usually sold dried. Their full flavor emerges when they are reconstituted in hot water and added to soups, sauces, and stews.

Shiitake — These Asian mushrooms are the current darlings among those who keep up with fashions in food. Now grown in the United States, they have become readily available in upscale markets. With their dark brown, meaty caps and a flavor reminiscent of the forest, shiitake can withstand long cooking in stews and soups.

Wood Ear — These wild mushrooms have been popping up frequently in what are known as your better-class grocery stores. Some people are crazy about their musty flavor.

Morel

Chanterelle

REFLECTIONS ON FORAGING

EDWARD BEHR

Part of the fascination of mushrooming is finding the order within disorder. In known patches in season, one gathers what one needs in a few minutes; similar results in new territory can require hours or days. A mushroomer is like a fisherman. Each devotes time to his or her pursuit. Each has an eye for natural detail, patience for efforts made in vain, and perhaps a liking for solitude. Successful mushroomers remember what fungus grew where and when and in company with which plants. Penetrating the untidy logic of nature is its own reward, but with mushrooms come qualities of flavor not found elsewhere in the animal or vegetable world.

Excerpted from *The Art of Eating* newsletter

Raw Mushroom and Endive Salad
with Lemon Dressing

Serves 6

This is a fast recipe from Albert Stockli, the first chef of The Four Seasons Restaurant in New York City.

12 large white mushrooms
Juice of 2 lemons
4 Belgian endives, cut into thin strips
1 teaspoon salt
Freshly ground black pepper
¼ teaspoon dried savory or oregano
1 tablespoon chopped chives
½ cup finely chopped celery
3 tablespoons olive oil

Wipe the mushrooms with a damp cloth, trim off the stems, and slice the mushrooms thinly into a bowl. Pour the lemon juice over them at once, coating them well. Toss in the endive strips, then add the salt, pepper, savory or oregano, chives, celery, and oil. Mix well and chill.

Reprinted from *Splendid Fare*

On The Button

Despite all the heady talk about rare, wild, and exotic mushrooms, the fact of the matter is that 99 percent of the close to $1 billion fresh mushroom crop is made up of the dependable, plain white button mushroom. It is the iceberg lettuce of the mushroom world. Maligned for its lack of flavor by haughty gourmets, it has an important role on the table and, unlike some of its wild relatives, most certainly won't cause anyone to become giddy or hallucinate. White mushrooms are bred in conditions more sterile than many a hospital operating room, and the process is among the most difficult in all of agriculture.

The mushroom seeds, called spores, are so incredibly tiny that they can barely be seen with the human eye. Technologists begin the growing process by inoculating them into cereal grain and incubating them until they become infinitesimal seeds. These seeds are planted in pure organic compost in air-conditioned windowless sheds. The identical "spawn" mature at different times. But barely 12 days later, the first mushrooms have fully matured and can be harvested. When the growing beds have yielded up all their crop, they are emptied and the entire mushroom house must be sterilized before the next batch can be started.

Pennsylvania produces close to half of all the mushrooms eaten in America. California is second and Florida third, but 23 other states are also raising mushrooms year round and supplying them to an eager and ever-growing market.

Too Late Now

After a robber snatched the cash in the register and ran, his victim, one of our best-known purveyors of exotica, noted wryly: "He should have taken the dried mushrooms; they're worth more than the money."

TIPS

Storing
Refrigerate mushrooms in the box or paper bag in which they were bought, covered with damp paper towels to keep them moist. Don't seal them in a plastic bag or they will quickly become slimy and horrible.

Preparing
It is not necessary to peel mushrooms. Most are free of dirt but sometimes sand or sooty particles are present. Wipe the mushrooms clean with wet paper towels. If you soak them they will drink up the water and their flavor will be lost.

Books

A Passion for Mushrooms
Antonio Carluccio; Trafalgar Square, 1991; $22.95

Gourmet's Guide to Mushrooms & Truffles
Jacki Hurst and Lyn Rutherford; Price Stern Sloan, 1991; $9.95

Mad About Mushrooms
Jacqueline Heriteau; Putnam, 1984; $4.95

The Edible Mushroom
Margaret Leibenstein; Globe Pequot, 1993; $8.95

The Mushroom Book: Recipes for Earthly Delights
Michael McLaughlin; Chronicle Books, 1994; $12.95

The Mushroom Feast
Jane Grigson; Lyons & Burford, 1992; $14.95

MUSSELS

NOT JUST FOR THE BIRDS

Consider that modest mollusk, the mussel, whose fabled "beard" is actually a tuft of long filaments known as byssus threads, by which it clings tenaciously to rocks and docks and to the ocean floor. You really should give mussels some attention, because it's conceivable that, like all too many Americans, you never have. Until very recent years, this succulent, thin-shelled bivalve wasn't even thought of as edible, and was literally spurned by all but the seagulls.

No more. In the most rapid turnaround in shellfish history, mussels in America have suddenly become the debutantes of the deep. Burgeoning demand created an industry, and has sparked tremendous growth in farming on both coasts, with the mussels grown on racks in flowing water, or on seeded and tended ocean beds.

Wherever they live, mussels are efficient eaters. Each mussel strains 10 to 15 gallons of water a day, consuming everything in it. This makes the mussel, as Waverley Root puts it in his encyclopedic book, *Food*, "the Typhoid Mary of the sea." As Root points out, mussels aren't poisonous in themselves, but "they can pick up toxins from their environment and pass them on to those who eat them."

Along the Pacific coastline, for example, mussels aren't edible from May through October, when they eat a variety of plankton that contains a poison called saxitoxin, which can build up to levels dangerous to humans. Native Americans living along the coast, for whom mussels were an important food, knew all the indicators. The proliferation of plankton causes the sea to glow with an eerie phosphorescence. When they saw that glow, they stopped eating mussels; when the glow had gone, they ate mussels again.

If you're at the shore and want to gather mussels on your own, it's best to be sure that you're in the right place and in the right season. Purveyors of these shellfish are, of course, scrupulously careful to procure mussels from safe waters.

Mussel Goo

The stickum mussels produce in order to glue themselves to underwater surfaces contains a protein that is highly resistant to corrosion and the marine industry hopes to replicate it for use in paint for the hulls of boats. Corrosion currently costs the industry some $25 billion annually.

All Sorts

Most commercial mussels in the United States are dark blue, with thin, shiny shells; they tend to be of fairly uniform size.

European mussels, all farmed (mostly in Spain and the Netherlands) are blue, too, and differ little from the American blue.

New Zealand greenshell mussels are also on the American market; they are rope-cultured (literally, they cluster and grow on ropes dangling in the ocean), and they are processed under FDA approval. Greenshells are larger than blues and resemble the razor clam.

Wild mussels have thick, ridged shells, usually with barnacles on them.

TIPS

Buying
Buy only live mussels with tightly closed shells.

Preparing
If you have wild mussels, you may have hell to pay to clean them. First, wash off the mud and silt, then scrub each one with a wire brush. Farmed mussels need only a couple of rinsings in cold water. Don't remove the beard until just prior to cooking: You can remove it by pulling it toward the smaller end, or by cutting with scissors.

Storing
Don't freeze live mussels. Keep them cold in a bowl in the refrigerator, and don't let them sit in melted ice or other standing water.

Cooking
To cook, steam with water or dry white wine for about 5 minutes, or until the mussels open.

Mussels in Broth

Serves 4

2 quarts fresh mussels
  or 2 (1 pound) cans mussels
1 cup dry white wine
1 cup water
¹/₂ teaspoon salt
4 scallions, finely chopped
¹/₂ teaspoon dried thyme
2 bay leaves
4 tablespoons finely chopped parsley
1 stalk celery, very finely chopped
1 tablespoon butter, softened
1 tablespoon flour

Scrub the mussels with a stiff brush and clean well. Remove beards. Place mussels in a large bowl and cover with water. Discard any open ones. Soak mussels for 15 minutes to allow sand to soak out. Rinse and place in a saucepan. Add wine and water. Add salt, scallions, thyme, bay leaves, parsley, and celery. Cover and simmer for 5 minutes.

Strain liquid from the pan into a small saucepan and return to simmer. Combine butter and flour into a paste and stir into simmering broth. Remove the top shell from each mussel. Place in individual soup bowls and cover with the sauce.

MUSTARD

WIDE SPREAD

Tangy mustard is called "the spice of nations" because it is cultivated all over the world, and has been since prehistory. In fact, "cultivation" of mustard is an overstatement; the plants — whose more mild-mannered cousins are broccoli, brussels sprouts, collards, kale, and kohlrabi — grow wild in most places, and where they don't, all you have to do is scatter some seeds. You'll have mustard greens soon enough.

Commercial processed mustard is made from the seeds, but the greens are edible, too, as the citizens of ancient Rome knew well. Today in the American South, a dish of peppery mustard greens, or a "mess of greens" with mustard greens prominent, is always a welcome accompaniment to a spring Sunday lunch.

For processed mustards, two species of seed, white and brown, are ground for their oils. White are the less pungent and are mostly used in American mustards. A blend of white and brown is employed for English and European mustards. Brown seeds are also used for pickling and as a seasoning.

Mustard seeds are sold whole, ground into powder, or prepared. To create the prepared version, powdered mustard is combined with seasoning and a liquid such as water, vinegar, wine, beer, and must (the pulp and skins of crushed grapes). A couple of decades ago, commercial American mustards, mild and yellow, dominated the market. Now, a multitude of domestic and imported mustards, and many special brands, jostle for notice on supermarket shelves, representing a range from very hot to sweet and mild.

Afterburn

The city of Dijon, in France, has been the home of fine mustards since the 13th century. According to a popular tale, the duke of Burgundy was gratified by Dijon's aid in a military campaign, and decided to confer a coat of arms upon the city. The motto was to read Moult Me Tarde, meaning "I Ardently Desire." However, the woodcarver accidentally omitted the middle word and the result was Moult Tarde, translated as "I Burn Much." Though this was a big mistake, it was also a nice reference to the city's main product. Everybody liked the error so well that they left it that way. Thus, the product acquired a name and the woodcarver kept his head.

Dijon continued to be the place of mustard, and in 1777, two fellows named Grey and Poupon went into partnership there to make a new mustard, stronger than anything then current: Poupon had the cash and Grey had a secret recipe. In time their mustard became the leader in the field. The factory where Grey and Poupon started out still stands in Dijon, and has become a shrine to mustard-lovers. However, Grey Poupon mustard is owned today by the Nabisco Company, and is made in Oxnard, California.

High Life — with Mustard

When newspaper magnate William Randolph Hearst entertained guests at San Simeon, his castle on the California coast, table settings in the magnificent Renaissance banqueting hall always included French's mustard, Hearst's favorite. Now visitors touring the castle marvel at the long oak table set just the way Hearst liked it — with silver salt and pepper shakers, and little pots of mustard, in their original labeled jars.

Lest We Forget

The Mount Horeb Mustard Museum and Fancy Food Emporium opened in Mount Horeb, Wisconsin, in 1989, with 365 mustards in one place. Since that time, curator and entrepreneur Barry Levenson has been ceaselessly adding to his collection, and now has 1,652 kinds, with all 50 states represented. He has also been publishing lots of improbable mustard talk in its newsletter, *The Proper Mustard*, which bears the motto: "Yellow Journalism At Its Best." A one-year subscription is available; so is a catalog of foods, and there is a hotline (800-GET-MUST) for mustard emergencies.

PERIODICALS

The Proper Mustard
Mount Horeb
Mustard Museum
109 East Main Street
Mount Horeb, WI 53572
608-437-3986
2 times a year; $5

NUTRITION ◆ NUTS

NUTRITION

If the doctors of today will not become the nutritionists of tomorrow, the nutritionists of today will become the doctors of tomorrow.

— *Thomas Edison*
Visionary inventor

AMERICA'S NEW NUTRITION AWARENESS

Pat Baird, R.D.

Hillary Rodham Clinton was the first major force in America to take a stand on nutrition services. As the director of President Bill Clinton's attempts to revise the nation's health care policies, Mrs. Clinton believes that nutrition must have a place in the new health care system.

In line with this thinking, Dr. Steven Woolf, a science adviser to the U.S. Preventive Services Task Force of the Public Health Service, has said that "the nutrition community should continue to send the message that dietary factors account for a large portion of diseases that people suffer in this country, and that prevention is a wise public policy and nutrition is important."

As exciting as this may seem, it is only the tip of the iceberg in terms of what is happening in the widely growing field of nutrition. In 1991, the National Cancer Institute launched the 5 A Day program encouraging Americans to eat at least five servings of fruits and vegetables each day. What the program *really* meant was that years of scientific research and data showing a relationship of diet to the prevention and reduction of certain cancers had convinced the institute to take up a formal position.

New food labeling laws, as mandated by the National Labeling Education Act of 1990, tried to address years of advances in nutrition. The first changes in more than 20 years clarified descriptions of products, sought to standardize portion sizes, and to clarify sound health claims while restricting ones that were frivolous or untrue.

Even nutritionists and dietitians are challenged to look at issues differently and to expand their horizons. The idea of using the chemical properties of foods and herbs in clinical and preventive medical situations has moved way beyond hocus-pocus into mainstream American life. Not only is food being used directly as a curative, but there is an active new interest in the actual growing and producing of "designer foods" containing key nutrients. This fresh awareness also involves the fields of food safety, the use of chemical pesticides, food additives, and preservatives, along with the role of nutrition in disease — and even more importantly, its role in *preventing* disease.

The major nutritional breakthroughs of the 20th century have opened American eyes to fresh possibilities at many levels. The 21st century will be a mighty exciting time for those who have always acknowledged the role of nutrition — and even for those who haven't.

Books

Eat for Life: The Food and Nutrition Board's Guide to Reducing Your Risk of Chronic Disease
Institute of Medicine, National Academy of Sciences, 1992; $18.95

The Corinne T. Netzer Encyclopedia of Food Values
Corinne T. Netzer; Dell, 1992; $25.00

The Mount Sinai School of Medicine Complete Book of Nutrition
St. Martin's Press, 1990; $35.00

The Pyramid Cookbook: Pleasures of The Food Guide Pyramid
Pat Baird, R.D.; Henry Holt, 1993; $24.00/$15.00

Food Guide Pyramid
A Guide to Daily Food Choices

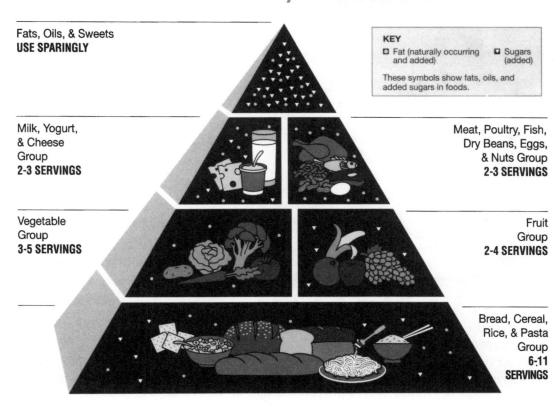

Fats, Oils, & Sweets
USE SPARINGLY

KEY
☐ Fat (naturally occurring and added)   ☐ Sugars (added)

These symbols show fats, oils, and added sugars in foods.

Milk, Yogurt, & Cheese Group
2-3 SERVINGS

Meat, Poultry, Fish, Dry Beans, Eggs, & Nuts Group
2-3 SERVINGS

Vegetable Group
3-5 SERVINGS

Fruit Group
2-4 SERVINGS

Bread, Cereal, Rice, & Pasta Group
6-11 SERVINGS

The Food Guide Pyramid Explained

Clamor, commotion, and confusion accompanied the U.S. Department of Agriculture's release of the Food Guide Pyramid in 1992. And once the idea of an Eating Right Pyramid was developed, another 11 months and close to a million dollars were expended on achieving final approval of the all-important graphic that would affect how nutrition is taught for decades to come.

Despite government denials that there had been industry pressure — from the meat and dairy commodity groups — to change the apparent ranking of foods, officials contended that a slightly modified Pyramid continued to be the best means of communicating the need to reduce consumption of fats, oils, and sugars, and to convey the appropriate amounts of food that should be selected from each of the five groups.

At a glance, the Pyramid shows which foods to eat the most of and which to eat the least: cereals and grains are the major focus, while fats, oils, and sugars are to be used "sparingly." According to the USDA's official Food Guide Pyramid booklet, "the Pyramid is an outline of what to eat each day . . . a general guide that lets you choose a healthful diet that's right for you." Technically, the Pyramid is the illustration of the research-based food guidance system developed by USDA to help consumers put its Dietary Guidelines into action. The messages of balance, variety, and proportionality (moderation) from older guides remain. The Pyramid's main focus is on the reduction of fat because most Americans' diets are too high in fat, and because fat is the single most important factor related to chronic disease.

The Pyramid also incorporates guidelines from other major health organizations, echoing the National Cancer Institute's advice to eat more fiber, the National Cholesterol Education Program's suggestion to lower saturated fat intake, and the National High Blood Pressure Education Program's reminder that it is important to cut down on salt.

The "basic four chart" that advised people to eat meats, breads, dairy products, and fruits and vegetables is amended to show choices from five groups with an emphasis on more whole grains, fruits, and vegetables, and on choosing low-fat meat and dairy products whenever possible. The number of servings is now clearly stated in a range intended to vary according to age and sex. The ultimate confusion, though, has been the definition of a serving; it is provided elsewhere in this section.

It's important to remember that there are no forbidden foods in the Pyramid, and that no one food group is more important than another. For good health you need them all.

Nutrition and Medicine

Yogurt fights certain types of infections. Fish oils are touted to help treat colitis. Broccoli and other vegetables contain sulforaphane, which means that these foods may help to prevent some forms of cancer. Food, nutraceuticals, and designer fruits and vegetables have created this growing and somewhat sensational area of nutrition. The ironic part is that the physicians themselves learn little or nothing of this important science in medical school. Few schools offer and still fewer require nutrition as part of their curriculum. In fact, in 1992, only about a third of the 125 or so U.S. medical schools required students to take courses in nutrition. Most of those courses are short — as brief as eight hours — and most of what is taught, unfortunately, concerns therapeutic rather than preventive uses of nutrition.

"Here's your problem. You've been reading the Food Pyramid upside down!"

Q&A

Q What can a nutritionist do for you?

A A nutritionist can evaluate your current eating patterns and suggest changes or modifications. If you're confused about the Food Guide Pyramid, or have a special clinical consideration such as diabetes, heart disease, or gall bladder or ulcer problems, a Registered Dietitian can offer guidance and advice about special diets. Nutritionists often help people taking medications know if there is any problem with malabsorption of nutrients. And vegetarians, who are especially prone to nutrition inadequacies, can benefit from a session or two.

Q How do you find a nutritionist?

A Choosing a qualified nutritionist is no easy task. Physicians, nurses, chiropractors, and Ph.Ds of all kinds like to hang out "Nutritionist" shingles. Slightly more than half the states have a legal definition, standards, or licensing procedures for nutritionists. The American Dietetic Association, the American Board of Nutrition, and the American Nutritionists Association are a few recognized professional organizations that can help you select a competent specialist.

But I Always Thought . . .

What we eat and what we know about food changes from decade to decade. After deaths from heart disease skyrocketed in the late 1950s and 1960s, scientists began to take a hard look at what we ate to see if it bore any relation to how long we lived. Lo and behold, it seemed that the substantial all-American meal of meat, potatoes, and gravy might have something to do with this predicament. It took another decade for us to realize that exercise — or the lack of it — might also contribute to the cholesterol-laden arteries that were advancing coronary heart disease. And while we once thought that three squares a day were the ideal way to feed a family, researchers now say that smaller, more frequent meals may keep our thinking clearer, improve digestion, and ward off excess pounds.

In relation to other sciences, nutrition is still in its infancy. It took World War II for the government to set any dietary allowances for its citizens. Several decades passed before the Surgeon General's Report in 1988 specified actual amounts of different nutrients. Now we get "breakthrough" reports on nutrition almost daily. Small pieces of information over the years have led to relatively speedy discoveries. It's usually wise to wait for the results of several studies before making up your mind, and important to know, and to trust, the source of the research. The comfort foods of America — mashed potatoes, rice pudding, oatmeal with butter and cream, apple pie, and ice cream — needn't be tossed out the window. With a little tailoring to trim the fat and reduce the cholesterol, Mom's meatloaf-and-mashed-potato dinner can still be placed on the table and end up as an empty platter.

"You figure it. Everything we eat is 100 percent natural, yet our life expectancy is only 31 years."

Burn, Burn

It takes 29 minutes of walking to burn up the calories from a half pint of milk; 59 minutes to burn off that lunchtime cheeseburger; 68 minutes to work off a quarter of a 14-inch pizza. There's more to this nutrition game than what we eat. Exercise burns calories, keeps up the metabolic rate long after work ends, and helps lower the risk of several diseases. The latest wrinkle: Those who are physically fit have a better self-image and a more positive attitude toward life. So burn it!

What's a Serving?

Perhaps the most confusing aspect of the Pyramid is the concept of a serving. Most people think that a serving is whatever they put on their plate, or what is placed in front of them in a restaurant. Far from it. A serving is a unit that has been designated by food and health professionals to represent an amount of foods within a group or category, and generally it's much less than most of us are accustomed to eating.

For instance, one serving of cooked rice is a half cup; if you eat about two cups of rice at a meal, that's actually four servings — more than half the number recommended for an average-weight woman.

Here's a list of some foods in each group and what counts as a serving

BREAD, CEREAL, RICE, AND PASTA GROUP

1 slice white, whole-wheat, unfrosted raisin, French, or Italian bread;
½ English muffin or hamburger bun; 1 6-inch flour tortilla;
2 4-inch-by-½-inch breadsticks;
4 Ry-Krisps or Saltines

1 ounce ready-to-eat breakfast cereal;
½ cup cooked cereal

½ cup cooked whole grains (quinoa, bulgur, or millet)

½ cup cooked rice

½ cup cooked pasta

FRUIT GROUP

¾ cup juice

½ cup cooked or canned fruit

¼ cup dried fruit

Fresh fruit:
1 medium-sized apple, banana, or orange

3 apricots

½ cup blackberries

½ cup blueberries

12 large cherries

2 2-inch figs

15 grapes

½ grapefruit

1 large kiwifruit

½ mango or papaya

½ cup melon cubes

½ cup raspberries

½ cup sliced strawberries

VEGETABLE GROUP

¾ cup vegetable juice

1 cup chopped raw leafy vegetables (spinach, kale, beet greens, etc.)

½ cup chopped raw nonleafy vegetables

½ cup cooked beans and peas (kidney, split, black-eyed) or lentils

½ cup cooked vegetables (corn, green peas, lima beans, sweet potato, winter squash)

1 6-inch corn on the cob

1 small (3-ounce) baked potato

MILK, YOGURT, AND CHEESE GROUP
(Select low-fat items whenever possible)

1 cup skim, low-fat (1 or 2 percent), whole, or chocolate (2 percent) milk

1 cup low-fat buttermilk

½ cup evaporated skim or evaporated whole milk

⅓ cup dry nonfat milk

1½ cups frozen ice milk

1 cup low-fat or nonfat yogurt, plain, flavored (lemon, vanilla, etc.), or with fruit

1 cup frozen yogurt

½ cup part-skim or nonfat ricotta cheese

2 cups cottage cheese

2 ounces process cheese

1½ ounces natural cheese (cheddar, mozzarella, etc.)

MEAT, POULTRY, FISH, DRY BEANS, EGGS, AND NUTS GROUP
(Select low-fat items whenever possible)

1 ounce cooked lean meat, poultry, or fish
(e.g., ½ medium-sized baked chicken breast = 3 ounces cooked meat; flesh of 1 drumstick = 1½ ounces cooked meat)

1 ounce cooked lean ground meat

1 ounce cooked lean game (rabbit, venison, buffalo, etc.)

1 ounce cooked lean sliced meat (ham, turkey, roast beef, roast lamb, etc.)

Protein Alternatives for 1 ounce of meat or fish:
½ cup cooked dry beans, peas, or lentils

4 ounces tofu

1 egg

¼ cup egg substitute

⅓ cup nuts

2 tablespoons peanut butter

FATS, OILS, AND SWEETS
(Use sparingly)

Butter, cream cheese, margarine, mayonnaise, salad dressing; sugar, honey, syrups, jam, and soft drinks; chocolate, sherbets, sorbets, and gelatin desserts are just a few of the higher fat- and sugar-laden foods we tend to eat a lot of. Keep fat to 30 percent of total daily calories and avoid over-indulgences of sugar.

The Freshest
Food

Fresh is best — or is it? Frozen foods often get a bad rap for being high in calories, fat, and sodium. Overall, they are perceived as less than adequate and devoid of nutritional value. And many Americans shudder at the very notion of eating canned fruits and vegetables. But, truth to tell, frozen and canned products may offer a variety of nutrition bonanzas.

During the actual freezing of vegetables, nutrient loss is usually less than 5 percent. One study showed that the vitamin C content of retail market produce had decreased almost 60 percent, while fresh frozen green beans lost only about 17 percent of their vitamin C. Likewise, canned fruits and vegetables are now packed with little or no added salt and can provide more nutrition than fresh equivalents that have been held too long in store or home refrigerators.

So when fresh items are not in season or are too expensive, don't cross fruits and vegetables off your shopping list. Use canned or frozen fruits in muffins and pancakes, or puree them for a sauce. Add frozen and canned veg-

"Breakfast ... usually a bran muffin or whole-wheat toast with grapefruit juice ... lunch is either a spinach or watercress salad with herb tea ... dinner is usually broiled fish with lemon, a vegetable quiche, or one of my favorite tofu dishes ..."

etables to soups, stews, and casseroles. Clearer food labels distinguish which varieties have added fat, salt, and sugar; modify your choices accordingly. With more than 50 varieties of whole, sliced, chopped, diced, and pureed fruits and vegetables now available you can meet your 5 A Day quota again — and again.

Special Needs for Special People

Fairness, equality, and impartiality may be the guiding principles for much of what goes on in this country, but there are special people with special nutrition needs and it's important to identify at least a few of them.

It is essential for pregnant women to maintain optimum nutrition. The critical time to set up good eating habits may start as early as two weeks after conception. Some experts say the time *before* getting pregnant is crucial: Loss of the fertilized egg or failure to implant can be a result of poor nutrition. Throughout an embryo's development the growth of cells, tissues, and organs depends upon its mother's healthy diet. Among the most important considerations: an additional 100 calories per day, extra protein, vitamins A, C, D, and several of the B vitamins, and minerals such as calcium, phosphorus, iron, and zinc. Alcohol, caffeine, and empty calories from sugar should be avoided.

All new mothers are encouraged to breast-feed, at least for a while, and an extra 500 calories and foods that contain calcium, protein, magnesium, and zinc will help to ensure a good flow of high-quality milk for the baby.

Infancy, childhood, and adolescence are filled with growth spurts and sudden changes of attitude toward foods. Serving healthy meals and snacks becomes more important than ever because children who don't eat properly are not resistant to diseases, their growth — both mental and physical — may be retarded, and behavioral problems can occur.

It's easy to get the notion that nutrition is not a vital concern in later years. People tend to slow down, retire, and think less about what they eat. In fact, good nutrition may actually retard aging; it certainly plays a role in reducing and preventing heart disease, diabetes, cancer, diverticulosis, bone disease, and other problems. There is also some evidence that people with diets low in vitamins C and B-12 are less able to think clearly, and those with diets low in riboflavin and folacin have poor memories.

Some research on arthritis indicates that low levels of vitamin E and zinc may contribute to it, although real cures are rare. Losing weight through sensible diet often helps, by lightening the burden on inflamed arthritic joints.

Immune response decreases and weakens with age. Dietary protein — lean meat, fish, and legumes; vitamin A, beta carotene, vitamins B-6 and B-12, folacin, vitamin E; iron, and zinc are some of the nutrients that maintain a healthy immune system. Certain viruses, cancer, and AIDS wreak particular havoc on the immune system. Anyone suffering from their inroads is at nutritional risk and needs the assistance of a physician and a Registered Dietitian.

In certain special situations supplements may be indicated, and there is evidence that, in some cases, they can even give the immune system a jump start. But don't give, or take, megadoses of nutritional supplements. They can often be toxic and are especially dangerous to those already at risk. For sound advice on your special need, always seek the services of a specialist.

"The milk is for your teeth and bones, the meat is for your muscles, the potatoes give you energy, and the lima beans are one of life's little inconveniences . . . eat them."

NUTS

TENDER IS THE NUT

There are so many kinds of nuts, with such different shapes, sizes, flavors, and characteristics that it hardly seems possible that they could all be classed as nuts. And, in fact, some of them are fruits while some of them are seeds, and peanuts, for instance, aren't even nuts at all but legumes that grow underground. It is fascinating to realize that pine nuts or pignolias, which are the tiny seeds nestling within the cones of the stone pine, which grows on arid mountain slopes, are related in a distant sort of way to coconuts, which are the fruits of a tropical palm tree.

The criterion linking them all is that human beings found out long ago that they taste good, store well, and can keep you going when other foods are scarce. Primitive peoples made use of whatever nuts they found in their region and were prepared to go to a lot of trouble to make bitter-tasting nuts such as acorns and beechnuts palatable. Now, we chiefly care about nuts that taste good from the start — almonds, Brazil nuts, cashews, chestnuts, coconuts, hazelnuts (also known as filberts), macadamias, pecans, pine nuts (pignolias), pistachios, and walnuts (black as well as English) — and are prepared to pay to import them from wherever they grow best.

One of the charms of nuts is that you can eat them in so many ways. They adapt equally well to being dredged in salt or hot pepper or coated with chocolate or honey. They may be roasted or toasted whole, halved, or in fragments. They are slivered, sliced, chopped, and ground. Some, like chestnuts, can be made into flour; others, including cashews, are formed into nut butters; and a few, such as walnuts and pistachios, are pressed into fragrant oils — which are another subject altogether.

Health Nuts Get Cracking

Though they are high in fat and calories, nuts reduce the risk of heart disease by lowering cholesterol — this by virtue of their high monounsaturated fat levels. To get the benefits without the drawbacks, we should eat them as part of a low-fat, low-cholesterol diet, adding them to vegetable, grain, and pasta dishes and to fruit salads.

ODD JOBS

Harvesting macadamia nuts requires someone strong enough to remain squatting from sunup to sundown, picking up the fallen nuts and bagging them. Workers can't kneel or their knees would be damaged. But mechanical harvesters can't match human ability: A hard worker can collect several hundred pounds in a day.

TIPS

Storing
Store nuts in the refrigerator to keep them fresh. They can also be frozen.

Cooking
Heating improves the taste of nuts. Spread them in a single layer on a cookie sheet and roast them in a preheated 350-degree F. oven for about 10 minutes, or fry them gently in a nonstick skillet over moderately low heat until they are lightly browned.

Books

Not Milk… Nutmilks!
Candia Lea Cole; Woodbridge Press, 1990; $7.95

Nuts: A Cookbook
Ford Rogers; Fireside, 1993; $18.00

The Goodness of Nuts and Seeds
John Midgley; Random House, 1993; $12.00

The Nut Lover's Cookbook
Shirl Carder; Celestial Arts, 1984; $6.95

MAIL ORDER SOURCES ✉

Carolyn's Pecans
P.O. Box 1221
Concord, MA 01742
508-369-8212

Evonuk Oregon Hazelnuts
P.O. Box 7121
Eugene, OR 97401
800-992-NUTS

Luke's Almond Acres
11281 South Lac Jac
Reedley, CA 93654
209-638-3483

Sunnyland Farms, Inc.
P.O. Box 8200
Albany, GA 31706
800-456-4299

Did You Know?

☞ Brazil nuts grow in the Amazon rain forest inside hard coconut-sized shells that weigh about 5 pounds each and enclose up to 18 nuts per shell.

☞ A handful of any shelled nuts contains about 170 calories. (A handful of unbuttered popcorn contains about 12 calories.)

☞ Nuts are so nutritious that the USDA guidelines permit them to be substituted for half the meat requirement in school lunches.

☞ Coconut milk is *not* the liquid in the middle of the coconut. It is made by combining boiling water with ground-up coconut, forming a thick liquid that is then squeezed through a strainer.

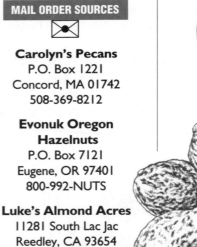

OATS

Once we sowed wild oats, now we cook them in the microwave.

— Anonymous

PORRIDGE EATERS
WEAR KILTS

O ats, not the inedible thistle, ought to be the national badge of Scotland. Oats do well in the Scottish climate, making them the cheapest grain available, admired for their filling, nutritious, and pleasantly chewy qualities.

Porridge, that gray, sticky, stodgy mass, fills the stomach and offers inner protection against the raw cold of winter mornings. Making it involves the skillful, slow drizzling of oatmeal into a pan of boiling water and much patient stirring of the gradually thickening contents before moving the covered pot to consolidate itself overnight at the back of the stove.

As day dawns the porridge is dumped into a bowl. As much salt as can be pinched between the thumb and first finger is scattered over the top. A spoonful of black treacle (molasses) or sweet golden syrup is puddled into the center and a circle of heavy cream is poured around the rim. Some Scots so admire porridge that they eat it standing up.

For tea, which all other countries call dinner, there is a plate of thin, flat oatcakes hot from the griddle, with a knifeful of butter that immediately melts and surges up your sleeve. If it's not oatcakes, then it's oats in the form of bannock buns or clootie dumplings or Athol brose, a drink of oatmeal, honey, cream, and whisky that makes the Highlands fling.

The Cholesterol
Connection

R eports that oat bran lowered cholesterol caused sales of the Quaker Oats Company's oat-bran hot cereal to skyrocket from 1 million pounds in 1987 to more than 20 million pounds within two years. Some 300 new oat-bran products were rushed to market; the miracle grain was turning up in everything from muffins to potato chips to cakes and cookies. Oats were "haute," the hottest health craze of the decade. Robert E. Kowalski's *8-Week Cholesterol Cure* (or How I saved my life by eating three oatbran muffins a day) generated sales of $40 million. We

were obsessed with cholesterol. Until . . .

Many contradictory studies later, it has been determined that oat bran does indeed reduce the level of LDL (bad) cholesterol in people with high blood cholesterol, but not by much. It does not change LDL levels that are within normal ranges nor elevate the level of HDL (good) cholesterol. On an average, when 1½ ounces of oat bran are incorporated into a low-fat, high-fiber diet, there is a 5 to 6 percent reduction in LDL cholesterol in six to ten weeks. It's the **soluble fiber** in the oat bran that does the trick.

Old Wives' Tale

Russians say that a poultice of equal parts of hot oatmeal and hot dry mustard will ward off pneumonia. In Switzerland, people smear a paste of oats pounded into cream onto painful chilblains. And in Germany, those who have drunk too deep swear that eating a bowl of oatmeal topped with fried onions *really* helps a hangover.

OCTOPUS

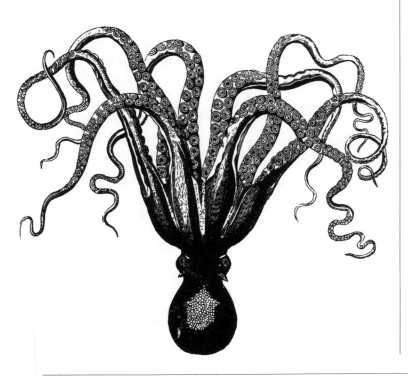

OCTO-PUSSIES DON'T PURR

Just because a particular species of octopus may grow into a 600-pound monster measuring 30 feet with tentacles outstretched, capable of enfolding an unwary prey and poisoning it with saliva prior to crushing it to death, does not mean that all octopuses are terrifying creatures.

Don't be intimidated. Most of those we find in the supermarket, already cleaned and often frozen, weighed barely a pound when alive and the largest tip the scale at a mere three pounds.

The Japanese are especially fond of octopus. They salt it and pickle it in a process that turns the skin a shocking purple that looks gorgeous when served on a hot-pink lacquered tray. Most other nations treat octopuses with less respect. The Greeks hurl them against rocks and the Portuguese beat them with bottles to tenderize them before they are cooked. We have to wonder why anyone goes to so much trouble. Octopus, raw or cooked, is pretty tasteless, with a texture that most closely resembles rubber bands.

OILS

SLICK AS A WHISTLE

Oil was one of the very first products manufactured by man, and the story of its proliferating uses and refinements traces the development of civilization from its birth. Recently, marine archaeologists found a round vessel of olives in the ruins of a prehistoric settlement off the Israeli coast; laboratory tests dated the olives back to the year 5000 B.C., and the researchers believe the vessel could have been an oil press.

So we know that even in prehistory, our ancestors had some oil to rub on roughened skin or soothe an upset stomach, to fuel their lamps or use for barter. More important, they had a sophisticated substance to cook with, a medium that lifted the preparation of food off the searing flames of campfires and into the realm of creativity. It was oil that greased the pan, hastened the cooking, and — most important of all — enhanced the food with delicious flavors and aromas, depending upon how artfully it was applied.

The good sense in pressing, grinding, or crushing a vegetable or nut or seed for its oily essence was recognized by early people in all cultures. In India, it was the groundnut and the mustard seed. In the South Seas, it was the coconut. In West Africa, it was the fruit of the oil palm. Everywhere, oil was the analgesic balm that made life better.

And it still is.

With olive oil, we are exactly where we were with wine in the 1960s.

— Darrell Corti
California olive oil producer

Oil Crazy

In 1982, the United States imported 32,000 tons of olive oil; in a decade, the figure has risen to well over 100,000 tons, mostly of cooking oils. California is now producing at least a dozen brands of fruity, extra-virgin varieties, for a total of some 200 tons of olive oil annually.

Oil
Names

In the language of olive oils, **extra-virgin** means the first oil from the first pressing, with perfect flavor, color, and aroma, and no more than 1 percent acidity; **fine virgin** oils are also from that pressing, but are less flavorful and slightly more acid; **olive oil**, formerly known as **pure olive oil**, is a blend of refined and virgin oils; **olive pomace** oil is extracted from the remains in the press with solvents (which then have to be removed); it lacks flavor but makes an inexpensive cooking oil. **Light** olive oil is a product created for the American market. The adjective refers to the milder taste; it has the same calorie count as any other oil, and is now being labeled as **extra mild**.

And don't bother to look for **cold-pressed**; all olive oils are cold pressed, by spinning a paste of ground-up olives in a centrifuge and filtering the oil that separates from the residue.

Q&A

Q What are tropical oils?

A There are no "tropical oils" as such. The term has been used to group certain oils grown in tropical regions of the world: palm oil, palm kernel oil, and coconut oil, but there are significant differences. Palm kernel oil and coconut oil have high levels of saturated fats; palm oil contains equal parts of saturated and unsaturated fats. The term "tropical oils" has appeared on some food labels, but it fails to meet any legal or technical definitions.

The World of Oils

Almond oil — Expensive, with a pronounced flavor; used in minute quantities to add to desserts and cookie recipes.

Canola oil — From a genetically engineered version of rapeseed, a wild mustard; has less saturated fat than any other oil — 6 percent — and 62 percent monounsaturated fat. Bland, good for both cooking and salads.

Corn oil — Made from the germ of the corn kernel, it has virtually no taste or smell, which can be useful when the properties of an oil are needed without the addition of another flavor. Good for frying because it heats to a high temperature without smoking; keeps well.

Cottonseed oil — Made from regular cotton seeds, usually used blended with other oils in vegetable-oil products such as margarines.

Olive oil — Most versatile of oils, highest in mono-unsaturated fat (77 percent); variety used will depend on the taste desired and budget available.

Peanut oil — Made by pressing steam-cooked peanuts; contains only 17 percent saturated fat. Valuable in home cooking because it doesn't absorb or transfer flavors and can be heated to 440 degrees F. without burning or smoking; can be clarified and reused.

Rice bran oil — An import made from rice polishings; high in monounsaturated fat and may contain a component that blocks the absorption of cholesterol.

Safflower oil — Made from a kind of thistle; has more polyunsaturated fat than any other oil but contains no vitamin E; popular in salad dressings because it doesn't become solid when chilled.

Sesame oil — The oldest flavoring of all, popular throughout the Far East. Untoasted seeds, pressed, produce a yellow oil good for frying; stronger-tasting brown oil from toasted seeds is used in minute quantities for flavoring foods.

Sunflower oil — Made from — you guessed it. Most of the world's production comes from Russia. Bland-tasting, good general-purpose oil, low in saturated fat (11 percent), high in polyunsaturates.

Vegetable oil — Accounts for 80 percent of the world market; usually made from **soybean oil**, which is high in polyunsaturated and monounsaturated fats, and low in saturated (15 percent). A good, inexpensive all-purpose oil.

New Nuts for Oils

Walnut oil, once used only to polish violins, is now lubricating lettuce leaves. Fragrant hazelnut oil is drizzled on warm salads. Pistachio oil is the ultimate choice for pale and delicate greens, and a mere drop of almond oil will send the mind reeling.

From the Fruit

Palm oil, second to olive oil in vegetable oil production worldwide, is pressed from the fruit of the oil palm tree. Cultivation of the palm began in West Africa 5,000 years ago; the industry now centers in Malaysia, where palm oil accounts for 10 percent of GNP.

Palm oil is used in making margarine and shortenings, and for frying. It consists in equal parts of saturated and unsaturated fats, and its vitamin E content acts as an antioxidant to lower cholesterol. Palm oil also remains semisolid at room temperature, which gives it a long shelf life without hydrogenation (which produces harmful trans fatty acids).

The Malaysian people use palm oil exclusively in their diet, and their good health is the oil's best advertisement.

Did You Know?

☞ Oil increases in volume when heated, which makes it a highly efficient cooking medium.

☞ All culinary oils contain 120 calories and 14 grams of fat per tablespoon.

☞ Peanuts supply one-sixth of the world's supply of vegetable oil.

☞ It takes 1,000 almonds to process just 1 pint of almond oil.

MORE INFORMATION

Institute of Shortening and Edible Oils
1750 New York Avenue NW
Washington, DC 20006
202-783-7960

OLIVES

The olive tree is surely the richest gift of Heaven.
I can scarcely expect bread.

— Thomas Jefferson

FULL CIRCLE

There was a time when olives were chiefly used as ballast and no one gave a fig about them until some entrepreneur decided to stuff them with pimientos. Adding value meant creating profit. Now olives are stuffed with miniature onions, hazelnuts, almond slivers, hot peppers, and anchovies — but what may look like pimiento has become a tasteless red paste extruded into the space left by the removal of the pit.

The science of stuffing olives is called condimentology, but its practitioners are an endangered species. A person can stuff only 18 olives a minute, or 8,640 olives a day — whereas a machine can stuff 1,800 a minute, once the pit has been removed.

Lindsay, the giant olive company in California's Central Valley, has machines that pit 14 million olives per day, and could stuff them as well, although, in fact, they only stuff some of the green ones. There is little point in stuffing black olives because they are all processed in cans, which means that no one could see the stuffing, if there were a stuffing. Besides, a stuffing would change the flavor, which admirers describe as "mild."

California olives lack flavor because, although they look ripe and black, they are in fact unripe green olives that are processed in a series of lye baths, while being oxidized with air, which turns them a browny-black. Then they are pitted, sorted, and ultimately, to protect them from bacterial contamination, cooked under pressure at 260 degrees F. for 14 minutes. Glass would fracture at this temperature, which is why black olives are canned.

Green olives, which have a higher acid content, do not require extensive processing. They are not "cooked" but cured with lye. And it is worth the trouble of stuffing them because customers will pay more if they like the way the olives look in their gleaming glass jars.

Olive Drab

by Nick Richards

At Christmas in 1958, during my Army days, I found myself seated at a holiday party next to a young trooper named Hanby. Spying a dish of black olives on the table by his elbow, I said to him, "Hanby, please pass the olives."

He looked at me with scorn. "Richards," he said, "them ain't olives. Olives is green. Them's plums."

"They are not," I said. "If you think they're plums, try one."

He did, then spat it out. "Worst plums I ever et," he declared.

Tapenade

Makes ¾ cup

Serve as an appetizer, spread on freshly made toast.

1 cup Greek kalamata or other flavorful olives
2 2-ounce cans anchovy fillets, with their oil
3½-ounce can tuna, packed in oil, drained
½ cup capers
1 teaspoon mustard
1 cup light olive oil
Juice of ½ lemon
2 tablespoons brandy (optional)

Put the olives, anchovies, tuna, capers, and mustard into a food processor or blender and process to form a puree. With the motor running, add the oil slowly through the top, then add the lemon juice and brandy, if using. Spoon the tapenade into a container. Cover and chill for at least 4 hours. It will be quite thin when first made but becomes thick when chilled.

Olives Grow on Branches

The Bible refers to the olive as "the king of trees," and most food historians agree that olive trees originated around the shores of the Mediterranean at least 5,000 years ago, and were first brought to America in the 15th century. Today, the United States's annual production, chiefly from the San Joaquin Valley of California, is close to 150,000 tons — less than 5 percent of the world crop from roughly 50 million olive trees. Only a tiny fraction of their fruit, about 3 percent, ends up as table olives; almost all the rest are pressed into oil.

Olives Pack a Punch

Olives get close to 85 percent of their calories from fat. Though this is predominantly the desirable mono-unsaturated variety, olives also contain a colossal amount of sodium — close to 350 milligrams in just three large green ones.

Books

The Feast of the Olive
Maggie B. Klein; Aris Books, 1983; $16.95/$10.95

Travels of an Olive Eater from Pit to Pit Plus How to Cure an Olive
Virginia P. Ryder; Amigo Press, 1991; $12.95

Olives & Olive Oil for the Gourmet: 100 Recipes of Foods Made with Olives & Olive Oil
George F. Steffanides; Steffanides, 1980; $2.50

MAKING THE GRADE

Olives are too bitter to be eaten fresh, whether they are picked green and unripe, or have been allowed to ripen on the tree. They need first to be cured by immersing them in a solution of lye or in a bath of brine or in dry salt; extra flavorings are added later. The method of curing makes a huge difference in the olives' flavor.

The majority of European olives are brine-cured, with a vast range of flavors and sizes; some black olives are oil-cured, such as French Nyons, or dry-cured, such as Moroccan. But you can't rely on the name to know what you are getting. Niçoise olives, for instance, are grown in several countries and each region's soil, climate — even the quality of the air — will produce quite different-tasting olives.

Nor is size an indication of flavor. Small are not necessarily sweeter than large. In Europe olives vary in size from as tiny as a chick-pea to as large as a fresh date. In the United States small olives are almost impossible to find; most are graded extra-large, jumbo, colossal, and super-colossal (although a 1½-inch, 16-gram super-colossal olive is far from gigantic).

Black olives . . . A taste older than meat, older than wine. A taste as old as cold water.

— Lawrence Durrell
Prospero's Cell

MORE INFORMATION

California Olive Association
660 J Street, Suite 290
Sacramento, CA 95814
916-444-9260

Green Olive Trade Association
325 14th Street
Carlstadt, NJ 07072
201-935-0233

International Olive Oil Council
800-232-OLIV

MAIL ORDER SOURCES

Fusano Valley Specialty Olive Company
P.O. Box 11576
Piedmont, CA 94611
510-530-3516

Santa Barbara Olive Company
P.O. Box 1570
Santa Ynez, CA 93460
805-688-9917

The Olive Company
11746 Route 108
Clarksville, MD 21029
800-515-5330

OMEGA-3

WHO KNEW?

Omega-3 fatty acids weren't a subject of conversation ten years ago. The old rule, "fat is bad," prevailed. Then researchers figured out that there are "good fats" in the world, ones that actually help to keep arteries clear, and they are fats that contain high levels of these acids.

Where are they found? Seal blubber is one good source, first identified when scientists observed that seal blubber is the main element in the diet of polar bears, and that they thrive on it. The human denizens of the frozen north, the Eskimos and Inuits, also hunt seals, eat the blubber, and remain very healthy. Scientists finally concluded that it's not the blubber but the seal's diet that's operative here:

Seals eat enormous quantities of fish, and those fish are the dietary source of omega-3 fatty acids.

Exactly how these acids work is still not fully understood, but people who eat fish regularly have lower cholesterol levels and a lower incidence of cardiovascular disease, by 40 percent or more. It's also believed that these acids are effective against psoriasis, arthritis, diabetes, migraines, and cancer. It appears that the acids reduce LDL levels and raise HDLs.

Some people eager to increase their omega-3 intake have started taking fish oil capsules, but these capsules are not recommended. Many hazards are associated with taking such supplements; too much may induce a stroke, and some contain cholesterol and raise blood cholesterol levels. Also, fish oils are notorious for accumulating toxins. The bottom line is that no facts have yet been established about fish oil, except that some fish — such as salmon, fresh tuna, swordfish, and halibut — are the best sources of omega-3 fatty acids.

The Healthy Bird Sings

Canary owners may be feeding their songbirds the best known dietary source of omega-3 fatty acids: hempseed, also known as marijuana seed. Pet store owners recommend hempseed to make canaries sing, and hemp is a key ingredient in birdseed mixes. Sterilized hempseed is exempt from the laws that ban the importation of leaves, buds, and other parts of the plant that people often smoke.

Although hempseed does not contain as much omega-3 fatty acid as flax seed, it contains a balance of omega-3 and omega-6 polyunsaturates that is preferable for a healthy human diet. It also tastes better. Recently, people have been importing hempseed, milling it into a nutty-tasting flour and baking with it, or using hempseed oil for frying food. They're eating hempseed for its nutritional value and the novelty of eating legal pot, but they don't do it to become intoxicated. The seed contains none of the psychoactive ingredients found in the hemp leaves and flowering buds. So the caged canary may sing well but it never gets high.

MAIL ORDER SOURCES

Ohio Hempery
14 North Court Street, Suite 307
Athens, OH 45701
800-BUY-HEMP

ONIONS

NO ORDINARY ONIONS

Onions are extraordinarily versatile. They can be eaten raw, baked, stuffed, sautéed, creamed, boiled, and, best of all, made into deep-fried onion rings in the hands of a master cook who has a good supply of fine, fresh oil.

The Milds
Chives, shallots, and scallions make docile yet attractive additions for delicate-tasting dishes. Debonair leeks are braised or made into leek and potato soup. Small white pearl onions have an appealing flavor that makes them suitable for boiling, creaming, and pickling. The even tinier crisp white onions pack a surprising and fantastically good wallop and are indispensable in an icy-cold Gibson martini, which is likewise sometimes indispensable.

The Strong
Rustic white and yellow onions are part of the aromatic vegetable group that includes carrots and celery. Together with garlic, they are essential components of literally thousands of dishes; without them, soups and stews have no life.

The Sweeties
The market for sweet onions has been growing rapidly and there are now several varieties to choose from. Raw, they are added to salads and hamburgers; cooked, they become integral parts of chutneys, marmalades, and jams.

Texas Sweets or 1015s — so named because they should be planted on October 15 — are prized for their sweet dispositions. California's Italian Reds and Sweet Imperials, New Mexico's Carzalias, and Hawaii's Maui Sweets are becoming more plentiful but are rarely found outside the regions where they are grown. Vidalias now have nationwide distribution and have recently become available for most months of the year as a result of advances in storage facilities. They flourish in the sandy soil around Vidalia, Georgia, and along with Washington State's Walla Wallas join the familiar Bermudas in the family of mild, easily digestible onions.

Serving
Slice red and white onions paper-thin, toss with anchovies, capers, and vinaigrette dressing for a good-tasting onion salad.

• Alternate slices of tomatoes, sweet onion, and mozzarella cheese. Drizzle with olive oil and top with fresh chopped basil for a classic Italian appetizer.

• Garnish salads with thinly sliced onion rings.

• Make onion canapés by topping buttered, trimmed, sandwich bread with thinly sliced onions and watercress. Cut the bread into decorative shapes.

• Bake small onions stuffed with wild rice and top with grated cheese, or fill onion shells with mustard and mayonnaise-coated crabmeat for an unusual appetizer.

• Top halved baguettes, rolls, or bagels with flavored cream cheese, paper-thin onion slices, and fresh herbs.

• Create a Mediterranean-style pizza with caramelized onions, olives, and goat cheese on a whole-wheat crust.

• For a savory side dish, season whole, peeled onions with butter, soy sauce, or other marinade and bake until tender.

• Roast whole onions dotted with butter and garnish with chopped parsley and fresh herbs.

• Stuff onion shells with creamed spinach, broccoli and cheese, or other vegetables for simple vegetarian dishes.

Did You Know?

☞ Rubbing with lemon juice or salt removes the smell of onions from your hands, knife, or chopping board.

☞ In ancient times, people believed onions were a symbol of eternity because of the concentric circles that make up their unique internal structure.

☞ For the same reason, onion-shaped towers were popular decorations in Russia and Eastern Europe; they guaranteed the building would stand more or less forever.

☞ During the Civil War, General Ulysses S. Grant sent an urgent message to the War Department: "I will not move my army without onions." The very next day, three trainloads were on their way to the front.

Old Wives' Tale

In the Middle Ages, doctors prescribed onions to alleviate headaches, provide protection against snakebites, and prevent hair loss. They were eaten raw, too, to soothe a sore throat, ease the pain of burns and bee stings, cure athlete's foot, and remove warts. Bela Karolyi, now-retired coach of Olympic gymnasts, swears by the old Transylvanian remedy of applying a cooked onion to an inflamed joint.

Books

The Elegant Onion: The Art of Allium Cookery
Betty Cavage; Storey Communications, 1987; $6.95

The Onion Cookbook
Jean Bothwell;
Dover, 1976; $4.50

Onions can make even heirs and widows weep.

— Benjamin Franklin

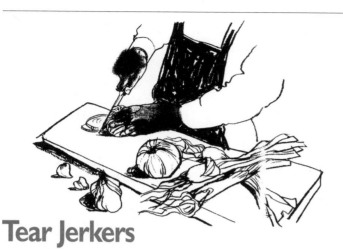

Tear Jerkers

It is the sulfuric compounds in onions that irritate the eyes and make cooks cry when they chop onions. To stem the tears, cut the top from the onion and peel the skin downwards. Wait as long as possible to trim off the root because the sulfuric cells cluster at the base of the onion.

Another solution is to chill the onions before chopping them. This will help a little with fairly docile onions but the lusty yellow ones will get you every time.

Braised Onions with Herbs

Serves 4

Braised onions make an excellent side dish. As they cook, the onions become sweet and mild and make an ideal accompaniment to roasts. Use small fresh onions or already peeled, frozen onions.

3 tablespoons butter or margarine
12 small onions (about 1½ pounds) blanched and peeled
¼ cup beef broth
2 teaspoons finely chopped garlic
2 teaspoons dried rosemary
1 bay leaf
Salt and freshly ground pepper

Preheat the oven to 350 degrees F.

Put the butter in a shallow flameproof dish, about 8 inches in diameter, over medium heat. When the butter starts to brown, add the onions and cook for 3 or 4 minutes, stirring frequently, until the butter is nut-brown and the onions start to darken.

Stir in remaining ingredients and cover the dish. Bake in the oven for 30 minutes, until the onions resist only slightly when pierced with a skewer or knife. Remove the bay leaf before serving.

ORGANIC FOOD

ORGO 101

The word *organic* has several meanings. To a chemistry teacher, it's a word that describes compounds containing carbon, which is found in all plant and animal life. To a grocer who sells organic vegetables, fruits, and meats, the term means that no synthetic chemicals have been used in the production or storage of foodstuffs. To the farmer, organic means a great deal of work.

Keeping food chemical-free is easier said than done in a civilization as reliant on chemicals as ours is. Organic farmers have to imitate nature as closely as possible. Instead of spraying crops with pesticides, the organic farmer sends in squadrons of ladybugs, praying mantises, and other insect-eaters to guard the fields and gardens. Organic farmers must use fertilizer that meets the chemically correct meaning of organic — carbon-based substances, usually plant and animal waste, instead of the synthetic fertilizers conventional farmers use to maximize their yield. By recycling waste matter into fertilizer, organic farmers hew to another definition of the term: a whole, cyclical, sustainable system.

An organic farmer has to pull up weeds or smother them one at a time, while other farmers often use chemical weed-killers. Producers of organic meat and poultry can't use growth-promoting hormones or antibiotic feeds. These competitive disadvantages, plus all of the extra care required, will usually increase the cost of organic foods by 20 to 50 percent over nonorganics.

What's more, crops have to be grown for at least three years without pesticides and two years without certain fertilizers in order to meet the certification standards of industry

The first time I ate organic whole-grain bread I swear it tasted like roofing material.

— **Robin Williams**
Comedian

Health nuts are going to feel stupid someday, lying in hospitals dying of nothing.

— **Redd Foxx**
Comedian

watchdog groups. But even with all of these requirements and more, purity can be difficult to achieve. Organic farmers can do very little to protect against contaminated groundwater and wind-borne toxins. In addition, some suppliers have been known to cut corners, prompting consumers and other farmers to call for nationwide certification standards.

Perfectly Natural

Organic foods were once to be found only in health-food stores. However, during the alar apple scare in the 1980s, the public grew suspicious of regular supermarket produce, and managements scrambled to stock organically grown fruits, vegetables, and other organic products.

Initially they were a hit, and sales have been growing at about 15 percent a year, a rate higher than that of the food market overall. Some chains have cut back on organic foods because of their higher price and shorter shelf life, but shoppers can still find at least some organically grown produce in mainstream stores in most parts of the country.

Growth has also been hampered by the reluctance of major American food companies to develop and market organic brands of their own, possibly out of fear that the public would then question the quality of regular brands.

The 1990s are seeing a boom in prepackaged organics, which are more supermarket-friendly than perishable fruits and vegetables. Blue corn tortilla chips were first. Then Scotland's Caledonian Brewing Company introduced Golden Promise, an ale brewed from organic ingredients. Now new organic olive oils, pizzas, peanut butters, pastas, and cookies are hitting the shelves almost daily,

directed (and priced) to appeal to upscale buyers.

Organic foods have come a long way since they were the staple of the hippies, but that's not surprising, considering that yesterday's hippies and today's customers are one and the same.

Tea Thyme

Leftover tea makes a good organic fertilizer. Just pour it on the plants or mix it into foliar spray solution. For kitchen-window herb gardens, nothing could be more convenient.

Organic? Yes!

Percentage of Americans who would buy organic food if it were available	84.2
Percentage who would pay more for organic food	49
Percentage of U.S. agriculture that is organic	1

OSTRICHES

Everything But the Beak

Ostriches not only provide meat; their distinctively patterned skins furnish leather for all kinds of luxury items from wallets to cowboy boots. Their fabulous feathers turn up in fans, outfits for the Folies Bergère chorus line, and dusters for polishing BMWs and Mercedes-Benzes; even their exceptionally long eyelashes are made into artists' paintbrushes. As yet, no one has found a use for the beak.

Scans Replace Brands

As a precaution against theft, valuable ostriches are being fitted with numbered implants. To check on a bird's identity, a scanner can be passed over the bird's neck and its owner's ID number appears on the screen.

RISING LIKE A PHOENIX

I n our never-ending search for the exotic we are prepared to settle for the strange. Ostriches have entered the realm of the rare and remarkable, entitling them to a place on the menus of some of our most exalted restaurants. Despite their disagreeable dispositions, ostriches are sought after because their meat is reputed to taste — no, not like chicken, but very similar to lean beef, but with ultralow cholesterol, fat, and calorie counts. (Emus, their slightly smaller Australian cousins, are said to taste great on the barbie.)

In anticipation of a big rush of orders, would-be ranchers are setting up operations whenever they can scrape together the $5,000 required to buy a pair of three-month-old chicks. (Mature mating pairs can cost up to $60,000.) There are already more than 2,000 ostrich breeders bopping about from Connecticut to Texas; the big swivel-necked adult birds procreate readily and constantly, but it takes from five to eight years before the young grow large enough to be worth killing for their meat.

The center of ostrich ranching is still Oudtshoorn, in South Africa, where the birds are esteemed so highly that there is a brisk business in smuggling fertilized ostrich eggs out through Bophuthatswana to anonymous customers in parts unknown.

MORE INFORMATION

American Ostrich Association
3840 Hulen Street, Suite 210
Fort Worth, TX 76106
817-731-8597

OYSTERS

He was a bold man that first ate an oyster.

— Jonathan Swift
18th-century satirist

DISCOURSE ON OYSTERS

ALEXANDRE DUMAS

T he oyster is one of the most deprived mollusks in the kingdom of nature. Being acephalic, that is to say having no head, it has neither an organ of sight, nor an organ of hearing, nor an organ of smell. Its blood is colorless. Its body adheres to the two valves of its shell by a powerful muscle, with the aid of which it opens and closes the shell.

It also lacks an organ of locomotion. Its only exercise is sleep and its only pleasure is to eat. Since the oyster cannot go and look for its food, its food comes to find it or is carried to it by the movement of the waters.

The eggs of the oyster are almost invisible; a million of them would be needed to constitute the volume of a child's marble. The tiny oysters, when they come out of their mother's shell, are capable of movement. Nature provides this faculty for the larvae of all stationary animals, and thus allows them to affix themselves where they wish. Only they must choose their abode with care; for once fixed in it, they are stuck with it for the rest of their lives.

What is the length of an oyster's life? This is still a mystery. To begin with, few oysters die of old age. And those who do, perish unknown.

Excerpted from Dumas On Food, translated by Alan Davidson

The Prince Of Tides

Thomas H. Greene won his world title in an open challenge oyster-eating contest in Annapolis by downing 288 oysters in 1 minute, 33.34 seconds. His winning technique: swallowing preshucked oysters out of one-pint Mason jars. Asked why he enters oyster-eating contests, the boat repairman seemed surprised by the question. "I like them," he said.

TIPS

Buying

It's a lot better to be safe than sorry. Buy raw oysters only from approved, licensed stores. If you're at all worried about freshness, ask the sales clerk to show you the certified shipper's tag that must accompany all "shell on" containers, giving the license number of the shipper. Knowing this enables you to rebuke the shipper should you later succumb to sudden illness of a fishy nature.

Such an unfortunate eventuality ought not to happen. The American waters where shellfish are harvested are regularly tested by authorities in the coastal states, in cooperation with the FDA, to meet standards set by the National Shellfish Sanitation Program.

Storing

Don't put oysters in closed plastic bags; they will suffocate. If you are refrigerating them, keep them in containers loosely covered with clean, damp cloths. And don't keep them in the refrigerator for longer than 12 hours. Most refrigerators maintain a temperature of about 40 degrees F., and oysters (and other shellfish, too) soon deteriorate if kept at a temperature higher than 32 degrees. A solution is to fill the vegetable drawer of your refrigerator with ice and stash the shellfish among the cubes. Alternatively, you can bury them in an ice-filled casserole or roasting pan.

• Shells of live oysters may gape naturally, but will close tightly when tapped, indicating that they are alive. Discard any that don't close at once.

• Wash all towels, cloths, and sponges that have been used in handling oysters before using them again. And wash knives and cutting boards with hot, soapy water.

• Don't keep raw oysters out of the refrigerator for longer than a couple of hours, even if they are displayed on a bed of ice.

A HARVEST OF OYSTERS

In the Chesapeake Bay, oysters have been harvested in the same way for more than 100 years — requiring a combination of long hours, great patience, and enormous physical strength to gather them from the floor of the bay. The most interesting method, and certainly the most picturesque one, is oyster-dredging by skipjack. There are still about 25 of these small, V-shaped boats on the Chesapeake, and they make up the last big commercial sailing fleet in the United States.

By far the more common method of oystering is "tonging," or "hand-tonging." The waterman lowers a pair of scissorlike tongs over his low-sided boat, opening and closing them to rake together a few oysters at a time. The arms of the tongs are anywhere from 8 to 20 feet long — long enough for a standing man to reach the floor of the bay.

The design of the tongs and the skipjacks has remained virtually unchanged since the peak of the popularity of oysters in the late 1800s; it is thought that Chesapeake Bay oysters have been gathered for 6,000 years or more.

Things are changing rapidly in the oyster business, because of declining harvests. The catch in 1990 was 3.7 million pounds, which seems a lot until you compare that figure with those of a decade earlier. In 1980, Chesapeake oyster production exceeded 22 million pounds, and in the late 19th century, the oystermen were dredging up an astonishing 111.3 million pounds annually.

In recent years the oysters have been ravaged with shellfish diseases. While these are natural occurrences and not due in any way to pollution, the stock has been severely depleted. Happily, however, indicators are pointing to good times ahead, as large numbers of healthy "spat" (baby oysters) have been sighted. They will reach maturity within the next couple of years. Another encouraging sign for oyster lovers is that aquaculture is growing rapidly around the Chesapeake and in Virginia, where there are already ten companies producing oysters with the same flavor characteristics as those that are harvested wild.

Oysters Rockefeller

This famous dish made its first appearance at Antoine's restaurant in New Orleans in the late 1800s, and was given the name Rockefeller because it is so gloriously rich. The oysters, on the half shell, are nestled in indentations on a platter of rock salt, covered with a blanket of breadcrumbs, dotted with butter, seasoned with salt and pepper, then grilled briefly and served hot, in their shells, on a bed of chopped spinach.

Books

Consider the Oyster
M. F. K. Fisher; North Point Press, 1988; $7.95

Oysters
Karen Warner and Lonnie Williams; Ten Speed Press, 1990; $14.95

The Celebrated Oyster House Cookbook
Frederick Parks; Seven Hills, 1985; $8.95

R Doesn't Count Anymore

Said Dr. William Butler, in his *Dyet's Dry Dinner,* published in 1599: "It is unseasonable and unwholesome in all months that have not an R in their name to eat an oyster."

Truth to tell, part of Dr. Butler's theory lost credence a hundred years ago, with the arrival of refrigeration. But his theory about the seasonal high point in the life of an oyster remains valid today.

Some oyster beds are closed during the summer months — May, June, July, and August — because this is the breeding season. At this delicate time in their life cycle, oysters tend to be thin, watery, and tasteless — ghosts of their otherwise firm, plump, and succulent selves.

MORE INFORMATION

Pacific Coast Oyster Growers Association
120 State Avenue NE
Olympia, WA 98501
206-459-2828

MAIL ORDER SOURCES

Bivalve Packing Company
P.O. Box 336
Port Norris, NJ 08349
800-524-2833

Taylor United, Inc.
SE 130 Lynch Road
Shelton, WA 98584
206-426-6178

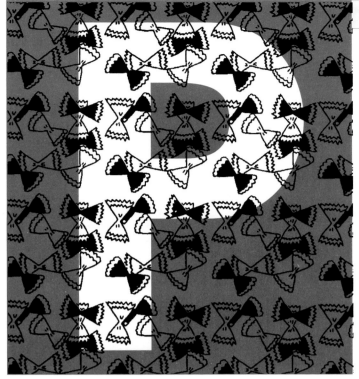

PACKAGING

> **In this uncertain world, the food is disposable. It is the wrappings that are permanent.**
>
> **— Anonymous**

THE PACKAGE IS THE PRODUCT

For the industry, the goal is to create a package that has the greatest shelf appeal at the lowest cost. The average customer perceives little difference between one brand and the next, so it is often the attractiveness of the container that results in the purchase, if the price is right.

The manufacturer of food products must wrestle with several other factors as well. The packaging must slow the rate of spoilage — currently less than 3 percent — which is one of the important factors in keeping prices low. Wrappings must not allow any leakage — of meat juices, for instance — and the food must not stick to the carton. The container has to be unbreakable, uncrushable, and lightweight to minimize its transportation costs, and it must stack equally well on shipping pallets or supermarket shelves. And its label must list every ingredient in order of importance yet also make the contents look so luscious and mouth-watering that consumers will grab it up instantly.

In addition to conforming to all safety and regulatory legislation, food packagers must arrive at the right answers to several other riddles: Exactly how many M&M's will be perceived as an extra-large pack; whether to package the same number of hot dog buns in a bag as there are wieners in the most frequently bought package of dogs; what is the ideal (most profitable) quantity of cereal for an individual serving; or whether, if all the blue cheese is formed into pyramids, "they" will buy more of it. And there's no way to find out except by creating the package — and learning yet again that the majority of customers buy on impulse.

Recyclable Doesn't Always Mean Better

Almost everyone thinks that the less packaging foods receive, the better. Many who believe this also think that biodegradable materials are better than plastic and that recyclable packages are best of all. But this ain't necessarily so. Plastic actually occupies less space in landfills than paper, and its production eats up fewer resources. And if a consumer buys a product that is theoretically biodegradable or recyclable, but there are no facilities nearby to do this work, the product gets tossed into the garbage and ends up in landfills anyway.

We should be cautious about confusing environmental issues with garbage disposal problems. Biodegrading and recycling are garbage issues; environmental concerns are with improper or extravagant use of scarce resources such as water, trees, and energy, for instance, in the transportation of heavy containers.

This is no semantic distinction but a matter of vital importance if, as seems likely, legislation currently pending attempts to solve short-term garbage disposal problems at the expense of long-term environmental concerns.

☞ Packaging is a $70-billion-a-year business.

☞ If the 50 percent of vegetables that are sold frozen or canned were instead sold fresh, the hulls, husks, pods, and stems that now wind up as animal feed would add 3 million tons of solid waste to landfills each year.

☞ One in every four Americans lives alone, yet single-person households take in (and throw out) relatively more packaging than the others. Why? Because larger families buy food in larger containers.

The buzzwords of the 1990s are recycle, bicycle, and life cycle.

— Hilary Philips
Ardent cyclist

Milk Keeps Fruit Fresh

By using enzymes to make the proteins in milk whey stick together, USDA researchers are using "linked" milk to coat sliced fruits and vegetables and keep them fresh for up to three days. The milky barrier looks like cellophane and is completely safe to eat. It seals the food almost completely, permitting carbon dioxide gas to escape but refusing passage to either water molecules or oxygen, which could spoil the contents.

Soon, maybe, we will be able to buy sliced fresh foods coated in protein film that will be superior to the frozen foods of today — with the bonus of needing less energy for preservation.

BIG IS GETTING BIGGER

For a while everything was getting smaller and smaller. Vegetables shrank so drastically that it began to look as if they might eventually just be painted onto the plate. Portions grew smaller. Square meals were reduced to a mere 300 calories and served from square boxes. Cookies and candies were miniaturized and bread was sliced so thinly that you could read the morning newspaper through it.

Then suddenly everything changed direction and started getting big again. Muffins grew so large that it took two hands to lift them. Cookies grew, too, and so did bagels, croissants, and biscuits. Thomas's sandwich-sized English muffins saw a 2,500 percent increase in sales in just one year, while sales of two-foot-wide Big Foot Pizzas neared $1 billion. Purchases of Hungryman Dinners soared. Bigger hot dogs were advertised by big man and former boxer George Foreman. Immense drinks, gigantic buckets of popcorn, and sandwiches generous enough to feed a family of four in a third-world country are routinely ordered and partially eaten. Restaurants are serving enormous meals on huge plates (orders for 12-inch plates rather than the traditional 10-inch ones have skyrocketed).

So what is happening? Some interpret the trend toward massive meals as a revolt against being told what to eat by nagging nutritionists. Others, predictably, note that pendulums that swing too far in one direction compensate by swinging out of control in the other. Whatever the reason, the packaging industry has often taken advantage of our inborn craving for the largest slice of the pie.

But what of the customer who purchases that nice *big* package only to discover that the contents of the box have been reduced while the cost remains the same? That customer gets mad, because it is really just a sneaky way of raising the price while we weren't looking.

WHAT TERMS MEAN

The Federal Trade Commission has established the following advertising and labeling voluntary guidelines.

Degradable, biodegradable, photodegradable — The product will break down and return to nature within a reasonably short time after it is disposed of in the customary way.

Compostable — All materials in the product or package will break down into, or otherwise become part of, usable compost (e.g., soil-conditioning materials, mulch) in a safe and timely manner if processed correctly.

Recyclable — The product can be collected, separated, or otherwise recovered for use as raw materials in the manufacture or assembly of a new product or new package.

Recycled content — The product has been made from materials that were recovered from the solid-waste stream (either pre- or post-consumer).

Catching Up With Ketchup

For years, Heinz's ketchup competitors watched enviously as that glass bottle was up-ended and its thick crimson contents inched toward the plate, capturing the largest market share of ketchup buyers on its stately way. The message was, of course, that the slower it poured, the better it tasted. Thickness was the secret, it seemed, and at last the rivals figured out how to get their ketchup thick enough to pour equally slowly.

At that very moment, everything changed. Heinz introduced its new plastic squeeze bottle that got the ketchup out onto the fries in double-quick time, and ever since then, squeezable bottles have replaced glass ones in the affections of the nation.

Why are we so enraptured with the idea of squeezing cheez, or squirting jelly, synthetic whipped cream, and other toppings onto our food? Maybe the old-fashioned ways have simply become . . . old-fashioned. We want action, even in our packaging.

Brand-New Breakthrough for Bags

Dow Brands recently introduced two sizes of plastic bags that will keep unwashed produce fresh for up to 14 days in the refrigerator, thus cutting down on waste and saving time and money, too. Supermarkets should be happy about this new packaging concept because customers are more likely to buy produce in larger quantities if they are not worried about fast spoilage.

Once saving the planet meant fighting communism. Now it means buying biodegradable packaging.

— Anonymous

Ready When You Are

The Japanese are combining packaging and chemistry to develop self-heating and self-chilling cans. According to a report in *Science of Food and Agriculture,* the first self-heating (exothermic) can, containing sake rice wine, was introduced in 1985; coffee in self-heating containers arrived in 1987, followed by a line of self-heating lunches including roast chicken, rice, and vegetables.

Self-chilling containers are in the development stages.

The invention of the microwave popcorn bag has meant more to mankind than the discovery of a galaxy of new stars.

— Anonymous

Control At All Costs

Controlled-atmosphere packaging, developed during the Gulf War, vacuum-seals food within a series of layers that keep out moisture, bugs, and sand and keep in freshness and flavor. The process radically cuts down exposure to oxygen, thus slowing the food's spoilage rate, reducing the need for preservatives, and lengthening its shelf life. Other advantages: The lightweight wrapping avoids losses from breakage and lowers transportation costs significantly.

Packages Repackaged

Designers are developing packaging concepts that will result in less waste. Each container will be protected by a tamper-evident seal.

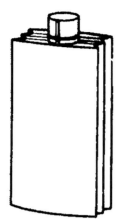 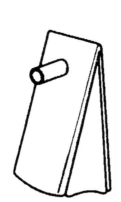 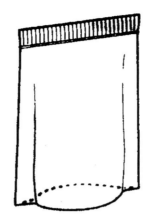

Containers with folding walls take up less space when thrown away.

Another folding-wall container designed for liquids. The fold can also act as a hand pump.

Instead of being packaged in a cardboard box and plastic bag, cereal can be sold in just a bag with a rigid base and resealable top.

Source: Gerstman & Meyers Inc.; *The New York Times*

THE BEST PACKAGE: NO PACKAGE

Like all big business, packaging is constantly seeking new solutions to new circumstances. The biggest changes to come will be in microwave packaging: The food will get brown and crisp in a package that becomes a mini-oven to finish the cooking process. Sensors will change color to indicate when the food is ready.

Regular containers will be returned for recycling or refilling. Imagine supermarkets set up with vats and casks of foods from which you help yourself. This is really just a step from self-service salad bars and selecting our own breads, coffee beans, and candies from open bins. A parallel trend in packaging concerns itself with tamper-proofing. The two concepts coexist remarkably well.

Eating Beats Recycling

Styrofoam packaging pellets are being replaced by vegetable starch bubbles that dissolve almost instantly in water and can be added to the compost or flushed down the drain. Still better for the environment: packages cushioned with marshmallows, popcorn, or peanuts. No waste, just more waist.

Glass Milk Bottles Stage a Comeback

The recent return to glass milk bottles prompts the question why they disappeared in the first place. It wasn't chance. As small dairy farms were consolidated into larger cooperatives they no longer served local communities, so it became impractical for milk to be delivered door to door. And it was prohibitively costly to haul bottles back and forth over long distances for cleaning and sterilizing. Today, a few local dairies have reappeared and some customers are willing to pay a premium for these services because those shiny glass bottles reflect an image of their users as subscribing to the best and the purest. Little thought is given to the amounts of water required to wash the bottles or the energy required to heat the water.

Buying milk in clear, attractively shaped bottles is a big-city thing to do. In Wyoming, where the empties would have to be picked up by plane, they would think it a daft idea.

The Price of Packaging

Product	Packaging	Cost	Price Difference
Tomatoes	wrapped	$2.22 per pound	24 percent
	naked	$1.79 per pound	
Corn chips	snack size	$4.10 per pound	47 percent
	family bag	$2.79 per pound	
Coffee	prefilled filters	$6.74 per pound	70 percent
	can (plus 50 filters)	$3.95 per pound	
Apple juice	minibrick pack	$9.36 per gallon	180 percent
	½-gallon bottle	$3.34 per gallon	
Sugar	paper packet	$2.18 per pound	459 percent
	bulk	$0.39 per pound	
Rice	microwavable	$5.71 per pound	1,531 percent
	bulk	$0.35 per pound	

Source: Paul Ligon, Tellus Institute; *Garbage*

MORE INFORMATION

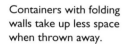

Committee for Environmentally Effective Packaging
601 13th Street NW,
Suite 5105
Washington, DC 20005
202-783-5588

Council on Packaging in the Environment
1001 Connecticut Avenue
NW, Suite 401
Washington, DC 20036
202-331-0099

Flexible Packaging Association
1090 Vermont Avenue NW,
Suite 500
Washington, DC 20005
202-842-3880

Foodservice and Packaging Institute
1901 North Moore Street,
No. 1111
Arlington, VA 22209
703-527-7505

Paperboard Packaging Council
1101 Vermont Avenue NW,
Washington, DC 20005
202-289-4100

Polystyrene Packaging Council
1025 Connecticut Avenue
NW, Suite 515
Washington, DC 20036
202-822-6424

Research and Development Associates for Military Food and Packaging Systems
16607 Blanco Road, No. 501
San Antonio, TX 78232
210-493-8024

PERIODICALS

Packaging Briefs
Packaging Education Forum
481 Carlisle Drive
Herndon, VA 22070-4823
703-318-8975
3 to 4 times a year; free

PASTA

Everything you see I owe to spaghetti.

— **Sophia Loren**
Donna bellissima

PASTA PRIMO

Spaghetti's popularity in the United States dates back barely 50 years. It arrived here originally with the wave of immigration from southern Italy, which began in the 1920s. Like other new arrivals, the Italians soon opened restaurants to serve their own communities and before long pasta was on its way, greatly assisted, as it turned out, by Prohibition. The only places where a glass of wine could be drunk more or less legally were the Italian speakeasies, and they all served spaghetti, partly because it was the dish every true Italian thought of first, and partly because it was cheap, quick, and easy for even the most inexperienced cook to prepare.

Its next wave of success came from the voluntary and involuntary travelers to Italy who returned from vacations and wars alike with shared nostalgia for pasta. Spaghetti has a lot going for it: noodles are inexpensive, bland, easy to eat, and seem to appeal to all nationalities and all ages, all creeds and all income levels.

And the pasta boom shows no sign of diminishing. The National Pasta Association estimates that the average American now eats almost 20 pounds of pasta every year.

Why Macaroni Has Elbows

In the pasta factory, the dough passes through machines that extrude it through dies — metal disks pierced with holes. The configuration of the disks determines the final shape of the pasta. Round or oval holes produce solid rods, such as spaghetti and linguine. For macaroni, a steel pin is placed in the center of the hole in the die, which forces the dough to flow around it and form hollow rods. For elbow macaroni, the pin has a notch on one side of it, which allows the dough to pass through more quickly, creating a

curve. A revolving knife attached to the die cuts the bent pasta into the desired lengths.

And Then There Was Chocolate Pasta

There are two types of pasta: dry, which is made with only flour, salt, and water, and no eggs, and the fresh version that is made with eggs. There are literally hundreds of different shapes of macaroni, from spaghetti to elbow macaroni. If you tire of these, there are stars and shells, bow ties, and pearls to choose from. Though they are all made in roughly the same way from the same ingredients, their shapes create the illusion of being quite different. Sauces snuggling inside a curled shell or a hollow tube can be carried to the mouth in greater quantity than the tiny amounts that fall from a star or a string of spaghetti.

Dry pasta is made from water and hard durum wheat, the same wheat that has been used since ancient Roman times. Huge quantities of this grain are now grown in Canada and in North Dakota, as well as in Minnesota, South Dakota, Montana, Northern California, and Arizona; some of it is even exported to Italy.

Fresh pasta is made with semolina flour and formed into noodles, tortellini, ravioli, cannelloni, and many other forms of pasta specifically designed to be filled with other ingredients.

Colored pastas are made with the addition of a range of natural colorants, from black squid ink to spinach, beet juice, tomato paste, truffles, herbs, carrots, and even chocolate.

Clever chefs like to make "pretend" pasta dishes: Jimmy Schmidt, owner of the Rattlesnake Club in Detroit, enchanted his guests by making a *trompe l'oeil* dessert that looks like ravioli but turns out to be white chocolate filled with dark chocolate. Martin Johner of the Culinary Center of New York was the first chef to create chocolate fettuccine that was not fettuccine at all but strips of chocolate crêpes, served with dark chocolate sauce and whipped cream.

Books

Joy of Pasta
Joe Famularo and Louise Imperiale; Barron's, 1989; $9.95

Look and Cook: Perfect Pasta
Anne Willan; Dorling Kindersley, 1992; $19.95

Pasta
Lorenza de Medici; Time-Life Books, 1992; $14.95

Pasta Dishes: La Pastasciutta
Anna Del Conte; Simon & Schuster, 1994; $14.00

The Classic Pasta Cookbook
Giuliano Hazan; Dorling Kindersley, 1993; $24.95

We Called It Macaroni
Nancy V. Barr; Knopf, 1990; $23.00

MARCO POLO'S REPUTATION'S GONE?

PAUL LEVY

The Oxford Symposium on Food and Cookery, an annual gathering for academics and food writers, has lately become a fertile source of high-minded scandal. . . . Some eminent Sinologists think that Marco Polo never went to China at all.

The whisper was that the great 13th-century Venetian traveler only got as far as Persia, where he constructed his vivid account of life at the court of Kublai Khan and in other parts of China from Persian merchants, who knew China well because of their extensive trade with the khan's empire.

I was told that it is now known that the text Marco Polo is supposed to have dictated to Rusticiano of Pisa, when they were both prisoners at Genoa after his capture in 1298, was not in Latin or the Venetian dialect, but in Provençal. The clincher is that the transliterations of Chinese terms used are always Persian.

The news is devastating for several foodie scholars, particularly for one symposiast who is working on a learned history of ice cream. Marco Polo is, of course, the source for the tale that the Chinese invented ice cream. He is also cited to prove that the Chinese discovered pasta before the Italians. But the macaroni researchers are not upset. They say they have known for years that Marco Polo did not bring pasta back from China.

Excerpted from the London Observer

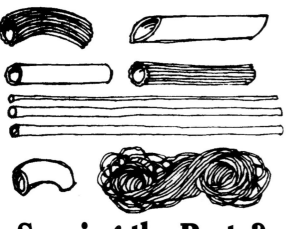

Saucing the Pasta?

When choosing a sauce for pasta, visualize its shape in the palate of your mind. Thin spaghetti looks lovely coated with a simple dressing of warm olive oil and a generous handful of freshly grated Parmesan cheese. Smooth sauces are generally served with thin strands of pasta. Chunkier pastas go better with chunkier sauces containing seafood, meat, or vegetables.

Hookers' Pasta

Serves 4 or 6

This is Carlo Middione's recipe from Vivande Porta Via in San Francisco. Asked why this pasta should be named after the ladies in the world's oldest profession, he suggests, "Perhaps the fact that it can be eaten cold may mean they could cook, do some business, and have a tasty cold meal ready."

2 or 3 tablespoons olive oil
2 garlic cloves, minced
2 ounces or more kalamata olives, pitted and coarsely chopped
1 teaspoon coarsely chopped capers
1 large fresh tomato, peeled and coarsely chopped
4 or 5 anchovy fillets, coarsely chopped
1 pound spaghetti
1/3 cup finely chopped parsley
Salt and freshly ground pepper, to taste

Place the olive oil in a frying pan and add the minced garlic. When it is golden, add the olives, capers, tomatoes, and anchovy fillets. Stir well and heat through for about 6 minutes.

Cook the pasta al dente and drain it. Place it in a warm bowl and add half of the sauce. Toss well. Add the remaining sauce and sprinkle on the parsley. Season with salt and pepper to taste.

TIPS

Buying
As a rough guide, figure 1 pound of spaghetti to serve 6 as an appetizer or 4 as a main course. If served with a substantial sauce, you will need less.

Cooking
Cook pasta uncovered at a fast boil, using at least a quart of salted water for every 4 ounces of dry pasta. A rapid boil helps circulate the pasta for uniform results.

Stir frequently, preferably with a wooden fork.

• If pasta is to be used as part of a dish requiring further cooking, undercook it slightly.

• Drain pasta to stop further cooking. Do not rinse unless the recipe says to do so.

• Follow package directions for the degree of tenderness desired. Cooking time varies from 5 to 20 minutes.

MORE INFORMATION

National Pasta Association
2101 Wilson Boulevard, Suite 920
Arlington, VA 22201
703-841-0818

MAIL ORDER SOURCES

Al Dente, Inc.
9815 Main Street
Whitmore Lake, MI 48189
313-449-8522

Bel Canto Fancy Foods
555 Second Avenue
New York, NY 10016
212-689-4433

Buckeye Beans & Herbs
Box 28201
Spokane, WA 99228
509-926-9963

Gaston Dupre
7904 Hopi Place
Tampa, FL 33634
813-885-9445

Rossi Pasta Factory
P.O. Box 759
Marietta, OH 45750
800-227-6774

PERIODICALS

For address, see Information Sources

Pasta Journal
National Pasta Association
703-841-0818
Bimonthly; $18 per year
for members; $28 for
nonmembers

Positively Pasta
National Pasta Association
3 times a year; $4 per year

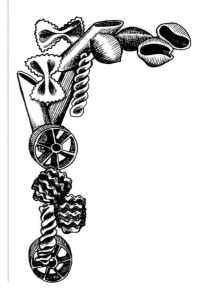

PEACHES

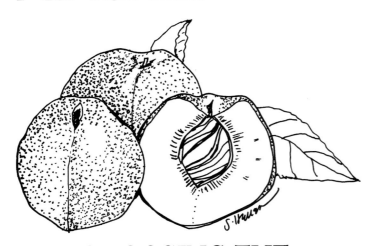

CHOOSING THE PERFECT PEACH

MOLLY O'NEILL

Tender them," an old-time grower at a farmers' market in North Carolina admonished me several summers ago. I was prodding and squeezing his crop, oblivious to its nuance, not really thinking about how hard it is to be a ripening peach in this vacu-sealed world.

"Sniff, don't pinch," he said. "The blush don't matter," he said. "The rosiness, that's just Maybelline." He sounded like a father offering marriage advice to a son.

"The shape don't count, it's just a feeling you get when you look and take a whiff of the perfume, and make your mind up to take a chance."

Excerpted from *The New York Times Magazine*

ODD JOBS

To assess the ripeness of peaches that are still on the tree, pickers use a set of color chips on a key chain, rather like color samples from a paint store, and match the fruit to a chip in a range of approved colors from orange to yellow to green-yellow.

MORE INFORMATION

California Cling Peach Advisory Board
P.O. Box 7111
San Francisco, CA 94120
415-541-0100

Georgia Peach Commission
328 Agricultural Building,
Capitol Square
Atlanta, GA 30334
404-656-3678

MAIL ORDER SOURCES

✉

Harry and David
P.O. Box 1712
Medford, OR 97501
800-547-3033

Walnut Acres Organic Farms
Penns Creek, PA 17862
800-433-3998

HANEY

Books

Peaches 'n Cream
Brenda McKnight; Eakin Press,
1988; $12.95

PEANUT BUTTER

ONE WAY

Peanut butter is a sticky business. Europeans don't understand it at all — it's virtually unknown abroad — and even many Americans never get the hang of it. Kids of six and seven who are unloosed on their family kitchens for the first time always try combinations they believe are original but that are generations older than they — peanut butter and jelly sandwiches, peanut butter and banana sandwiches, peanut butter and bacon sandwiches — and smart manufacturers now market some of these combos premixed, sparing children the necessity of invention.

However, for true aficionados, all these devisings are ridiculous. Luscious, beguiling peanut butter, they say, should always stand on its own, never sullied by jelly, bacon, or other distracting bad companions. We applied to one such expert for a description of the *right* peanut butter experience, and she obliged. We offer it here as a public service.

1. Always use Wonder Bread, or some comparable airy American bread product; butter both slices with *real* butter.

2. Choose a moderately moist chunky peanut butter — that means one with nuts — and spread it generously on one buttered slice of bread; top with the other slice.

3. Accompany with a large glass of cold whole milk.

4. Take a bite of the sandwich and follow with a sip of milk, then repeat, meditating on the tastes, until the sandwich is entirely consumed.

Our expert promises that if her method is strictly followed, the result will be a smooth, focused experience of "pure heaven."

My favorite sandwich is peanut butter, baloney, cheddar cheese, lettuce, and mayonnaise on toasted bread with catsup on the side.

— Hubert H. Humphrey
Former Senator from Minnesota

How Peanut Butter Is Made

Peanut butter comes chiefly from runner-type peanuts grown in Georgia, Alabama, and Florida, which are inexpensive, uniformly sized, and have good flavor. Peanut butter must contain at least 90 percent peanuts, so each of the various manufacturers uses an almost identical production process.

Once the peanuts have been harvested, inspected, and shelled, they are processed by roasting and blanching to remove the papery skin that surrounds the kernels, then ground until the texture is smooth. A stabilizer (hydrogenated vegetable oil), salt, or natural sweeteners (corn syrup or dextrose) may be added during the grinding (and must be listed on the label); these extend a jar of peanut butter's shelf life to nearly one year after being opened.

The grinding process usually heats the peanut butter to about 170 degrees F. De-aerators remove any air bubbles from the butter before it is pumped into jars, sealed, and cooled, then labeled and packed into cases. It takes the equivalent of 548 peanuts in the shell to produce a 12-ounce jar of creamy peanut butter.

Crunchy peanut butter is made in the same way, but tiny peanut chunks (from 10 to 25 percent of volume) are added to the peanut butter after it is ground.

So-called old-fashioned peanut butter, sold as "natural" in health-food stores, contains no stabilizers, so the oil soon separates from the ground peanuts and can oxidize and become rancid if the peanut butter is not refrigerated. Most such butters don't have salt or sweeteners either, though regular peanut butter brands may contain as much as 1.5 percent salt and 7 percent sweeteners. (No-salt varieties are available, however.)

Manufacturers are prohibited from adding any artificial flavoring or sweeteners, chemical preservatives, color additives, or additional vitamins to their product, and its fat content must not exceed 55 percent by weight.

Better As Butter

The ancient inhabitants of South America liked to eat a kind of paste made from peanuts. But modern peanut butter came into being about 1890 as the bright idea of a St. Louis physician, who thought it would be a good health food for elderly people. It was not linked with jelly until the 1920s.

PEANUT BUTTER IS GOOD FOR YOU

Peanut butter, though admittedly fattening, is a nutritional powerhouse: a two-tablespoon serving supplies about 15 percent of an adult's daily protein needs (ounce-for-ounce more than hamburger, cheese, or bologna); has as much fiber as two slices of whole-wheat bread; and is a source of niacin and zinc. It contains no cholesterol and its calories are derived primarily from monounsaturated fats.

Two tablespoons of peanut butter contain 190 calories. Two tablespoons of peanut butter plus a couple slices of crispy bacon plus a cold beer eaten in pajamas with bare feet in the middle of the night contain more calories than a glass of cold water.

Fans in the Wind

Yes, there really is an Adult Peanut Butter Lovers Fan Club, and it has 60,000 members. Other than consuming peanut butter in all its forms, their chief activity seems to be sending contributions to the club's official newsletter Spread the News, noting showbiz and other personalities who openly declare their fondness for peanut butter or who have been spied sneaking Reese's Pieces while on a diet . . . whereupon the famous names are made honorary members. Some might call this buttering up; others, just nutty.

Books

The Big Little Peanut Butter Cookbook
Norman Kolpas; Contemporary Books, 1990; $6.95

The Great American Peanut Butter Book
Honey Zisman and Larry Zisman; St. Martin's, 1985; $4.95

Did You Know?

☞ It takes 3,650 peanuts to fill a 5-pound container of peanut butter.

☞ Half of all edible peanuts consumed in the United States are used to make peanut butter.

☞ Skippy creamy peanut butter was first sold in 1933. Now we buy over 93 million jars of it annually.

☞ East Coast people prefer creamy peanut butter; West Coast folk like theirs chunky.

☞ Americans eat enough peanut butter in a year to make over 10 billion peanut butter and jelly sandwiches (estimating 2 tablespoons per sandwich). At graduation, the average high school student will have consumed 1,500 peanut butter and jelly sandwiches.

☞ Peanut butter is one of the most frequently purchased items in the supermarket, with sales of about $1 billion a year.

MORE INFORMATION

Peanut Butter and Nut Processors Association
9005 Congressional Court
Potomac, MD 20854
301-365-4080

PERIODICALS

For addresses, see also
Information Sources

Peanut Butter and Nut Processors Association Bulletin
Peanut Butter and Nut Processors Association
301-365-4080
2 to 3 per month; free with membership

Spread the News
Adult Peanut Butter Lovers Fan Club
P.O. Box 7528
Tifton, GA 31793
Occasional; free with $3 membership

PEANUTS

*I hate television.
I hate it as much as peanuts.
But I can't stop eating peanuts.*

— Orson Welles
Massive moviemaker

Peanut Speak

Peanut gallery, as a term for the seats farthest from the entertainment, dates from the time when such seats were occupied by poor families who brought peanuts to the show as cheap snacks for the children.

Working for peanuts, as an expression meaning "working for nothing," originated because the value of this commodity was, at one time, virtually nil.

Q&A

Q If four monkeys can eat four sacks of peanuts in three minutes, how many monkeys will eat 100 sacks of peanuts in one hour?

A Five.

THE FATHER OF PEANUTS WAS NOT THE PLANTER

The Spaniards first stumbled across peanuts in South America, where the Incas stashed them in jars at burial sites to nourish departed spirits. Later, slaves from West Africa planted peanuts in the southern colonies of North America as a food crop for themselves. They called the nut *nguba*, which was the origin of the word "goober." During the Civil War, soldiers on both sides ate a crushed peanut porridge to provide themselves with protein.

At the turn of the century, botanist George Washington Carver arrived at the Tuskeegee Institute in Alabama and made peanuts his field of expertise. Newly invented equipment had made it possible to cultivate peanuts mechanically, without stoop labor, and Carver urged Southern farmers to plant peanuts in rotation with cotton, thus laying the foundation for an annual harvest that today is worth more than $3 billion. Carver also developed more than 300 ways to use peanuts in human food and as pig fodder that produced superior hams. Ever since, the peanut industry has honored Carver as its pioneer.

Human consumption of peanuts got a rousing boost at about the same period, when Amedeo Obici and Mario Peruzzi, two young Italian immigrants, founded the Planters Nut and Chocolate Company in a two-story loft that they rented for $25 a month in Wilkes-Barre, Pennsylvania. Obici already had developed a method of roasting and salting peanuts and adding them to candy, and the company was an instant success. In 1916, the Planters partners offered a prize for a company trademark. A schoolboy won the competition with a drawing of an animated peanut — and soon afterward, Mr. Peanut was on his way. He has never lost it since.

Peanuts Don't Grow On Trees

Peanuts are not nuts but legumes, members of the pea family. The yellow flowers appear above ground, pollinate themselves, then lose their petals as the fertilized ovary at each flower's center enlarges. It grows down, away from the plant, forming a "peg" that extends to the soil, with the peanut embryo in its tip. So the peanut actually develops *below* the soil, hence its other name, groundnut.

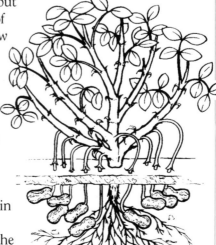

PEARS

> *There are only ten minutes in the life of a pear when it is perfect to eat.*
>
> — **Ralph Waldo Emerson**

A PICK OF THE PEARS

Pears are usually picked when not fully ripe and kept in controlled-atmosphere storage, which ripens them very slowly. Ripened at home in a lightly closed paper bag, a pear is ready to eat when it has softened slightly near the stem.

SUMMER PEARS

Bartlett pears, also known as **William pears**, are bell-shaped and the most familiar of the summer varieties. The new crop becomes available in August and continues into early winter. Bartletts change color from green to yellow as they ripen; ripe **Red Bartletts** have spectacularly crimson-colored skins; both have white, juicy flesh and superb flavor.

WINTER PEARS

Anjou and Red Anjou pears are almost egg-shaped with a slight "shoulder" and a short stem. They are wonderfully juicy when ripe and have a mild, spicy taste. Anjous are the most abundant of the varieties, excellent for salads and for juicing; available from October to June.

Bosc pears are symmetrical with a long tapering neck and slightly rough, golden-brown skin, which does not change color when ripe. Their creamy taste and attractive shape makes them ideal for poaching, baking, or preserving; good for eating fresh, too. Available from August through May.

Comice pears are greenish yellow with sometimes a rosy blush. They have a short neck and stem and are superbly sweet. Harvest starts in October, so these are the pears frequently seen in holiday gift boxes, prized for their abundant juice.

Nelis pears are small with brown russeting over a light green skin. They are sweet, flavorful, and firm enough for cooking and canning; available from October onward.

Forelle pears are small and bell-shaped with sweet, juicy flesh and crimson "freckles" that develop as the fruit ripens. The season lasts from February to September.

Seckel pears, the smallest variety, have a dark red blush, particularly sweet taste, and are delicious eaten fresh. Available from August to January.

PEAS

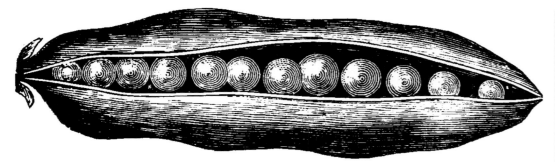

> *As their savory odor drifts upward, a dreamy look will overspread your countenance, and as you taste their rare succulence, their yielding tenderness, their glorious just-off-the-vine flavor, a feeling of blissful satisfaction will literally permeate you.*
>
> — **Advertisement for frozen peas in *The New Yorker*, January 1936**

ENOUGH AND ALL READY

JEAN ATCHESON

In the old days, the only people who fully understood the pleasures of eating fresh peas were those who grew their own. What a pleasure it was then to sit on the porch with the basket of peas, running your thumb down each pod in turn to reveal its moist, shiny innards for the first time ever, then scooping down the line of tiny peas and hearing them rattle into the colander in your lap. You could steal one or two to eat raw: sweet, crunchy, delicious. And there would be just enough to boil with a leaf or two of fresh mint; or maybe they would need to be extended in the French style with onions, chopped lettuce leaves, and butter (plenty of butter); certainly there would soon be peapod soup, turning all the discarded pods' goodness into a dark green bisque with a distinctive tang. And there would be that unmistakable dirty green under your fingernails to be scrubbed away.

Nowadays, the freshest peas you can buy are those that are frozen straight from the field and turn up in plastic bags of ever-increasing sizes in the supermarket. And as they rattle into the saucepan, there are plenty for everyone. You could steal a whole spoonful — but what would be the point?

Beans in Disguise

Black-eyed peas and chick-peas are actually beans. Because black-eyed peas have a black "eye" in a small beige-colored bean, they were once called cowpeas and fed to animals. Chick-peas, also known as garbanzos or ceci, are also buff-colored, but larger, with a marvelously adaptable texture and flavor.

The Popular Peas

All the varieties of peas contain vitamins A and C, as well as niacin and iron, but they are chiefly popular because they are sweet and easily digested.

English, green, or garden pea — Eaten shelled and cooked, occasionally raw. The peas are green and sugary sweet when just picked, but the sugar speedily converts to starch.

Petits pois are young, tiny green peas; now available frozen as well as canned.

Field pea — Smaller than the garden pea, grown to be used dried. Yellow or green, the peas tend to split along a natural seam, so they are also known as "split peas."

Snow pea — Thin, crisp, bright green with tiny peas within, these are eaten whole, barely cooked through, in stir-fries, or uncooked in salads.

Sugar snap pea —Also known as *mange-tout*, because you really do "eat it all," this cross between garden and snow peas has a crunchy pod filled with sweet, small peas and is usually served raw or very briefly cooked.

PECANS

NATIVE NUT

The pecan gets its name from paccan, an Algonquian word meaning "nut with a hard shell to crack."

The pecan is the most American of nuts. Before recorded history, pecan trees grew wild along the river banks of Texas and Mexico, spreading gradually east and north, and accounts by early Spanish and French explorers show that the Native Americans planned their migrations around the harvesting of these nuts. Cabeza de Vaca, held captive by one tribe from 1529 until his escape in 1535, wrote that the pecan "is the subsistence of the people for two months of the year without any other thing."

Nutritionally speaking, the indigenous peoples were in luck. Pecans provide protein and fiber and also contain some iron, calcium, phosphorus, potassium, and B vitamins. And they taste great. However, like all nuts, they are high in fat — not that these early Americans would have known or cared.

Colonial gentlemen farmers planted pecan trees, and it's said that George Washington always carried a few pecans in his pocket, but commercial production didn't begin until early in the 19th century, and then only in a small way. As late as the 1870s, when Gustav Duerler decided to start a pecan candy business in San Antonio, he had to go to the Native Americans for his supplies of pecans, and they delivered them to him wrapped in deerskins.

In Duerler's first shelling operation, he cracked the nuts with a railroad spike and picked out the meats with a sack needle.

Today, Duerler wouldn't have to take the trouble. Professional growers — many of them in Texas, where the pecan tree is the state tree — produce millions of pecans annually, shelled and unshelled. What happened to Duerler's candy isn't recorded, but pecans show up today in many salads and desserts. And for two of America's greatest, richest treats they are absolutely essential: fruitcake and pecan pie.

States That Major in Pecans

States	Annual Pecan Crop (in pounds)
Alabama	27 million
Arkansas	2 million
California	3.5 million
Florida	6 million
Georgia	130 million
Kansas	1.8 million
Louisiana	24 million
Mississippi	8 million
New Mexico	36 million
Oklahoma	4 million
South Carolina	70 million

Source: USDA crop forecast, December 1993

Books

Pecans: From Soup to Nuts
Keith Courrege; Cane River, 1984; $5.95

Pecan Lover's Cookbook
Mark Blazek; Golden West Publishers, 1986; $5.00

The Great American Cookbook: Featuring Pecans, America's Favorite Nut
Rebecca Johnson and Sharon Rousseau, editors; National Pecan, 1984; $3.95

PENGUINS

ALL DRESSED UP

We don't normally regard penguins as a source of food. These Chaplinesque Antarctic birds capture our fancy largely because when we see pictures of them at home on their pebble beaches and ice floes, they have the look of so many swells in tuxedos, waddling en masse to some big party. And we like them not only because their style strikes us as comic. They win our admiration, too, for being so well able to survive in the most punishing climate on earth. The down side, however, if you look at it from their point of view, is that they're not very bright, and have no fear of human beings. Thus, if you were an Antarctic explorer and short on supplies, the first thing you'd go look for would be a fearless penguin.

It's happened on many expeditions that an emergency ration of pemmican — dried penguin meat, pounded fine, and mixed with melted fat — has made all the difference between the loss or survival of groups of explorers. Reportedly, pemmican is no taste sensation — the staple of a penguin's diet is the shrimplike krill, a tiny, planktonic larva that they dive for in their daily foraging. Scientists have said that krill has the flavor of "fishy cellophane," and the same taste is passed on to the penguins. We are, after all, what we eat, and that's why penguin drumsticks are unlikely ever to show up in the supermarket. But no explorer who's owed his life to a penguin has ever been heard to complain.

Did You Know?

☞ Penguins are marvelous swimmers, able to travel at 25 miles an hour underwater by moving their flipperlike wings, using their stubby feet as a rudder. On land, they waddle very awkwardly and often find it easier to toboggan on their bellies.

☞ The big Emperor penguins lay one egg each year in the depth of the Antarctic winter, incubating it for two months in the warmth of a fold of skin between their feet. They eat nothing until the chick hatches, and a four-foot-tall bird may lose up to 75 pounds.

PEPPER

MASTER SPICE

Owing more to legends than to facts, we know that pepper came out of India some 4,000 years ago, moving westward in the caravans of early traders. It was called the master of spices because people everywhere found it irresistible, among them the ancient Greeks and Romans, at a time when the distance between the Mediterranean and the pepper ports of Tellicherry, Alleppey, and Pandjang was scarcely an easy skip and a jump.

Like ourselves, classical cooks liked both black and white peppercorns. Both derive from the same tropical vine — the difference is that the berries picked for black pepper are plucked before they're ripe and are left intact, while the ones to be sold as white are allowed to ripen completely before the dark outer husk is removed. In America we much prefer the black to the white; in Europe it's the reverse.

Today the world's pepper supply comes from India, southeast Sumatra, Sarawak, Sri Lanka, and equatorial Brazil. Though Brazilian pepper is relatively new on the scene, it is the pepper now most commonly marketed in the United States.

A Sampler of Peppers

Pepper fanciers are as particular as wine fanciers. Typically, they look for special peppers in specialty stores, not supermarkets, and so should you. Grind is a consideration. The number of openings per linear inch in the screen used to sift pepper determines the nature of the grind, from the finest (30/60 mesh) to the largest cracked (6/10 mesh), which is about the size of half a peppercorn.

BLACK PEPPER

Tellicherry — in aroma sweet-spicy and fruity, with hints of ginger and pine, this is considered the most balanced and elegant of peppers.

Malabar — this widely produced Indian black pepper has a resinous aroma; it's very hot.

Lompong — produced in Indonesia; it's not as perfumed as Indian peppers but has a nice balance of heat and pungency.

Sarawak — this area of Malaysia was once a British colony, and this pepper is its primary export; well-balanced, similar to Lompong.

Brazilian — tends to be hot and sharp; not notable for aroma.

WHITE PEPPER

Muntok — the only white pepper to bear a name of origin; Muntok lies off the southwest coast of Sumatra, and its white is considered the finest in the world. Earthy, with less heat and pungency than the blacks.

GREEN PEPPERCORNS

These are pepper berries that have been picked while green and still unripe, then dehydrated and freeze-dried or liquid-packed. (Pink peppercorns are not peppers at all; they are the dried, pungent berries of a tropical rose.)

Pepper Voyager

The first American millionaire was Elias Haskett Derby, who made a fortune importing black pepper into the United States. The East Indies pepper trade flourished between the 1780s and the 1870s, richly rewarding financiers like Derby, but yielding little to the tough sailors who managed to survive 24,000-mile voyages that kept them at sea for two to three years of hardship, deprivation, and danger.

In the end, Elias Derby used his considerable profits to endow Yale University, which is no place to sneeze at.

As Good As Gold

In 408, the Visigoths were besieging Rome and demanded 3,000 pounds of pepper as part of the city's ransom. (They sacked Rome anyway, in the end.)

Books

Great Shakes: Salt and Pepper for All Tastes
Gideon Bosker; Abbeville Press, 1985; $19.95

TIPS

Storing

If you store whole peppercorns in airtight containers, away from light and dampness, they'll last indefinitely. However, pepper will deteriorate after being ground. The finest grinds will last at most only for a few months; cracked peppercorns will last up to a year. Store powdered white pepper in glass containers; it can penetrate plastic.

PEPPERS

Peppers are a rainbow of good nutrition. These sweet and crunchy vegetables lend their pizzaz to soups and salads as well as entrees.

— Lou Seibert Pappas (not peppers)

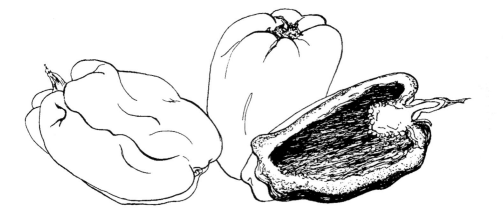

FROM ICY COOL TO RED HOT

C hristopher Columbus discovered peppers in the Caribbean in 1492 and took them back to Europe, where they were a culinary hit. Eventually, they worked their way back to America, where the mild varieties soon made it onto the family table. The hot and spicy kind, however, were banned from respectable tables for generations and barely tolerated in Mexican restaurants until, relatively recently, they became the darlings of the smart set, which is always restlessly seeking new sensations.

All peppers are members of the nightshade family of tomatoes, potatoes, eggplants, and tobacco, and all belong to the genus *Capsicum*. But because of the immensely wide range of their hundreds of types, from very sweet and mild to fierce enough to blow your head off, and in the strict division traditionally kept between them in American culture, their family relationship is sometimes overlooked.

In the world of food purveyors, peppers are grouped into two practical and applicable categories: sweet-mild (the bright green and red and yellow and orange and purple and black bell peppers belong here) and the hot-spicy varieties that head upward from jalapeños, which are covered as Chilies elsewhere in this book.

Sweet bell peppers are abundant in the markets, although the recently introduced colored ones, Le Rouge and Le Jaune Royale, cost more than the green peppers we've

eaten all our lives, stuffed with spiced meat or sliced into salads. Peppers are low in calories — about 35 per large bell — and deliver a lot of nutrition. The greens have twice as much vitamin C as citrus oranges, and the reds and yellows nearly four times as much. Claims for the new hybrids include, for 5.3 ounces of a new red pepper, more potassium than a banana and as much fiber as a bowl of bran flakes. A single pepper is also claimed to be a good source of folic acid and vitamin B-6. Unlike their red-hot cousins, they can be freely handled without incident — thank goodness.

PESTICIDES

Purity Preferred?

Up to 80 percent of the pesticides used on oranges and 60 percent of those used on tomatoes are there for cosmetic purposes. A recent poll found that 80 percent of Americans would be willing to trade more surface blemishes for the assurance that the produce was grown with reduced pesticide levels.

WHO PAYS THE HIGH PRICE OF PESTS?

Lisa Rathke

I f half the chemical pesticides used in this country were replaced by alternative pest controls, food prices would rise by less than 1 percent, according to a recent Cornell University report. Although that would cost consumers up to $1 billion a year, the expense would be more than offset by environmental and public health benefits.

Each year, 1 billion pounds of pesticides are used in this country, including 700 million pounds applied to farmland at a cost of $4.1 billion. The amount of pesticides used on cropland has increased 33-fold since the 1940s, yet crop losses due to insects, fungi, and weeds have actually increased during that time, from 31 percent to 37 percent.

The cost to farmers represents only part of the pesticide bill. The Cornell report estimates that indirect costs range from $2 billion to $4 billion a year. Among those costs are:

- Pesticide poisonings and related illnesses: $150 million a year.
- Damage to agricultural ecosystems: $525 million.
- Testing drinking water for pesticide contamination: $1.3 billion.
- Destruction of fish and wildlife: $15 million.

- Livestock poisonings combined with contamination of meat and milk: $15 million.
- Pesticide regulation and monitoring: $150 million.

The researchers examined the feasibility of using alternatives to pesticides on 40 major crops. According to David Pimentel, a Cornell professor of entomology and agricultural sciences and leader of the study, some alternatives would be more expensive because of increased labor costs and less effective results. But in other instances, replacing pesticides would actually increase yields and save money.

Reprinted from "Counting the Costs of Chemical Agriculture," *Harrowsmith Country Life*

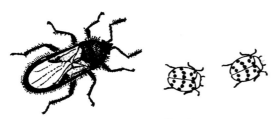

Catching Up With The Facts

Of the 400 or so chemical pesticides currently used in American farming, more than 70 have been found to cause cancer in laboratory animals. Some environmentalists want these pesticides banned. However, a recent study by the Food and Drug Administration, titled *Residues in Foods*, reported that 99 percent of domestically grown foods showed either no pesticide residues, or safe levels when tested.

So far, the Environmental Protection Agency has been unable to act on the latest scientific findings. The reason: The Food, Drug and Cosmetic Act, which governs food safety, has a provision called the Delaney Clause that bans any additive in food that has been shown to cause cancer in animals. The law was enacted in 1958, before researchers had established that only 1 to 3 percent of all cancers are caused by environmental exposure to toxic substances, and had cited smoking, alcohol consumption, and fatty diets as the primary causes of cancer.

Meanwhile, the Insecticide, Fungicide and Rodenticide Act, which governs the use of pesticides on farms, provides that chemical compounds found to cause cancer in animals are permissible as long as their residues in food don't pose "an unreasonable risk" to humans. Thus the agency is set upon the horns of a legal dilemma — unable to approve the use of new, less toxic chemicals if manufacturers' tests show that massive doses of them, far larger than the fractions that humans might receive in food residues, produced tumors in the rats or mice studied.

Last year the EPA's administrator, Carol M. Browner, named 35 pesticides that fall into this category and are commonly found in trace amounts in processed food; she suggested that Congress consider changes in the law that would prevent their being banned under the Delaney Clause. "There are scientific anachronisms that get created any time you have a 30-plus-year-old environmental regulation," she said.

In the resulting outcry, Browner retracted her remarks, but this spring returned to the fray with a proposal that would allow pesticide residues in food if "a reasonable certainty of no harm" could be shown. However, both industry and environmental groups were opposed.

TIPS

Buying
Buy locally, and in season.

Preparing
Wash produce under clean, running tap water. Add a drop or two of mild, unscented soap.

Peel away and discard outer leaves, skin, or rinds, or scrub those portions thoroughly with a brush.

To remove the edible waxes often applied to cucumbers, peppers, and apples, scrub with a brush and a little vinegar or mild detergent diluted in water.

Trim away fat from meat, because if residues are present, they are more likely to be stored in fatty tissues. (They are also most likely to be present in organ meats.)

It is not possible to add a pesticide to water anywhere without threatening the purity of water everywhere.

— Rachel Carson
Silent Spring

Toxins Everywhere

Forget about pesticide spraying for the moment. Did you know that there are natural toxins in almost everything we eat? This was the conclusion of two University of California scientists, who set out to show that laboratory animal studies inflated actual risk levels, and ended by estimating that 99.9 percent of the chemicals in America's food supply are present naturally.

For example: Organic apple juice can contain up to 137 volatile chemicals, at least two of which have been found to be carcinogenic in lab animals. One cup of coffee contains 17 substances that cause cancer in the hapless lab rat, the researchers wrote, "about equivalent in weight to the potentially carcinogenic synthetic pesticide residues one eats in a year."

Thinking of hiding at Grandma's for respite? Think again. The American Council on Science and Health has analyzed a typical Thanksgiving dinner from a toxicologist's viewpoint and found that turkey, cranberry sauce, and pumpkin pie each contain two, different, suspected carcinogens, and the pumpkin adds myristicin, a human hallucinogen. Don't even ask about the whipped cream.

IPM Pays Off

The progressive farming policy of Integrated Pest Management, or IPM, has spread widely in recent years. Whenever possible, IPM growers raise disease-resistant plants that can fend off predators naturally. Other IPM practices include crop rotation (so that single-crop eaters don't settle in), close observation and control of pest populations, and reliance on the built-in defense mechanisms both of plants and predators to create a natural balance. Some farmers even encourage weeds among the plant rows because they provide homes for pest-eating bugs, add beneficial nitrogen to the soil, and act as bait for predators who would otherwise feed on the crop itself. Pesticides are used only as a last resort.

In California, 60 percent of tomato growers and 70 percent of strawberry growers practice IPM. Gerber, the baby-foods giant, has been a leader in IPM farming methods since 1991. And Indonesia, which inaugurated IPM techniques in the 1980s, has halved its use of pesticides and raised rice yields by 12 percent.

Genetic Rx
For Plagued Plants

Biotechnologists are perfecting an antipest vaccine for plants that may reduce the need for chemicals. Bacteria called endophytes, genetically altered to carry a protein that kills insects, are injected into the plant's seeds. As the plant grows, endophytes protect it from root to bloom.

In related developments, a San Diego-based company called Mycogen won a government go-ahead in 1993 to genetically engineer a bacterial insecticide called MPV, and Crop Genetics, of Hanover, New Hampshire, found that its biopesticide product had reduced crop damage from corn borers by 60 to 80 percent in field tests.

And there's always nature's own way. When California farmers were besieged by the Mediterranean fruit fly in 1991, Mexican roundworms, which attack the flies' larvae, were employed in conjunction with sterile Medflies in the state's population control program. Farmers have also called in frogs, snakes, lizards, toads, ladybugs, and guinea fowl to go after cutworms, caterpillars, and beetles. Geese make good weeders, but require supervision to ensure they don't gobble up the crop as well.

Kids And Chemicals

For decades, the determination of safe levels of chemicals in the food supply has been based on average consumption by an adult male weighing 160 pounds. But recently the National Academy of Sciences noted that children might be at greater risk of consuming toxic residues than adults are — children weigh less, and eat larger quantities of fresh fruits and vegetables than adults do. The Academy urged more stringent testing of pesticide levels in children.

However, "we are not saying that parents should rush out and radically change their children's diets to avoid certain foods," the Academy emphasized. And some nutritionists question whether children are in fact eating *enough* fruits and vegetables. Same old story — what's a parent to do?

MR. NUTRICLEAN

When environmental concerns peaked in the 1980s, a California chemist named Stanley Rhodes saw a way of providing a service that would alleviate fears. He founded NutriClean Inc. to test pesticide levels in produce, using a system based on FDA trials. Supermarkets signing up with the service deliver random samples of their produce to NutriClean before they offer it for sale. The company tests for up to 200 pesticides and notifies the store manager if any are found; the manager can return shipments with levels in excess of federal limits. NutriClean also issues a weekly report to suppliers, listing whose produce passed muster and whose didn't.

To win NutriClean's Silver Seal, a fruit or vegetable must not exceed one-tenth of allowable pesticide residue levels, and must contain at least 75 percent of the levels of key nutrients established by the USDA. Gold Seal requirements: no detectable chemical residues either on the produce or in the soil and water used to grow it, and 100 percent of USDA nutrients.

The world is experiencing a resurgence of deadly diseases spread by insects because pesticides like DDT have been prematurely outlawed.

— Ronald Reagan

Cautious of Cauliflower?

When you reach the supermarket's produce counters, you don't have to be locked in fear's cold grip. Whatever concerns may have been published about trace elements of pesticides in food, our produce is perfectly safe to eat. The toxic chemicals that occur naturally in plants far exceed any traces of chemical pollutants in food; even so, they are not concentrated enough to be dangerous.

In this respect, there is little difference between domestic and imported produce. The FDA inspects both; further, producers who grow for the U.S. market are aware of our more stringent regulations. If they want to sell here, they must abide by our rules.

MORE INFORMATION

National Coalition Against the Misuse of Pesticides
701 E Street SE, Suite 200
Washington, DC 20003
202-543-5450

National Pesticide Telecommunication Network
Texas Tech University
Department of Preventive Medicine
Thompson Hall, Room S-129
Lubbock, TX 79430
800-858-7378

Pesticide Action Network North America Regional Center
116 New Montgomery Street, Suite 810
San Francisco, CA 94105
415-541-9140

PERIODICALS

For addresses, see Information Sources

Global Pesticide Campaigner
Pesticide Action Network North America Regional Center
415-541-9140
Quarterly; $25 per year

Pesticides and You
National Coalition Against the Misuse of Pesticides
202-543-5450
Quarterly; free with membership; $25 per year for nonmembers

Banned But Not Broken Down

Although use of the pesticide DDT has been banned since 1972, it is one of the slowest chemicals to break down in the environment and DDT residues are still commonly found in many foods grown in this country.

PET FOOD

A Savvy Dog Story

A *clever dog owner trained her pet to take a written order for his favorite treat — beef sausages — to the neighborhood butcher, who became accustomed to preparing the order as soon as the emissary arrived with the paper between his teeth. But when the dog's weekly visits became daily ones, the butcher grew suspicious. Coaxing the piece of paper from the clenched jaws, he discovered that the "order" was blank.*

Whenever the dog had a hankering for sausage, it seems, he would simply grab whatever paper he could find and make for the charcuterie.

"The table scraps look good . . ."

BEST FRIENDS DESERVE THE VERY BEST

Americans spend an average of $5,845,205 a day on cat food and $8,550,685 on dog food, making pet food a $8-billion-a-year industry. It may be worth noting, too, that in 1991, introductions of new baby-food products went *down* by 41 percent, while offerings of new pet foods went *up* 27 percent. The more expensive and anthropomorphic they are (strips that look like bacon, tiny little pork chops, salmon mousse that lacks only a copper mold), the better they seem to sell.

But do bells, whistles, and premium price points really make a difference to Fido and Fluffy? Experts suggest that the best way to shop for pet food is not to scan price tags or serving suggestions but to read the nutritional label. Often, good nutrition doesn't cost more.

First, check the guaranteed analysis statement on the label, which states the food's percentages of protein, fat, fiber, moisture, and minerals. Remember: Dogs generally need far less protein than cats, and too much can result in severe urinary problems. For adult dogs, protein contents should remain below 20 percent; cats should have foods that contain 30 to 32 percent protein. Try to mix animal and plant proteins, and don't forget that an egg (cooked) or a piece of cheese makes a tasty booster.

Both cats and dogs need fat in their diets. Cats should get about 60 percent of their calories from fat, dogs around 10 percent.

Pets need dietary fiber in smaller amounts than humans do — it usually makes up about 5 percent of pet foods.

Canned, dry, and semimoist foods are equal in nutritional value; most vets recommend serving a balanced variety.

Are premium brands worth the 30 to 40 percent more usually charged for them? Maybe. They tend to offer higher quality protein, less sugar, and few artificial dyes or additives. Pets fed high-end kibble tend to eat less of it (either because it's so good for them or because it *tastes* as if it's good for them), and require less medical attention.

TIPS

Feeding Cats
Saucers of milk aren't a good treat because lactose can be difficult for cats to digest. For a special tidbit from the dairy counter, try yogurt or cottage cheese — both low in lactose — instead.

• For an alternative cat munchie, offer crudités. Felines have been known to crave string beans, peas, cantaloupe — even potato peelings.

Feeding Dogs

Feeding the pet from the table isn't just bad manners — table scraps aren't even good for dogs. People-food contains higher levels of protein and fat than animals can digest properly.

• It's even a matter of contention whether bones are good for dogs — they can splinter, either in the dog's stomach or on their way down. Rawhide "chewy" bones are better.

• Death by chocolate? Maybe not, but too much can be toxic for dogs. (Cats don't have a "sweet" taste bud, so they will probably turn up their noses at a chocolate kiss anyway.)

Meowing the Lawn

Keep a decorative planter full of flat-bladed grass handy for your cat to munch on between groomings. The greenery helps it to digest hairballs and maintain healthy levels of folic acid. But beware of some other houseplants — English ivy, dieffenbachia, and caladium — which are toxic.

Old Wives' Tale

If your pet has fleas, sprinkle some brewer's yeast on top of its food. The powder is said to make fleas flee — and add valuable vitamins.

MORE INFORMATION

Pet Food Institute
1101 Connecticut Avenue NW, Suite 700
Washington, DC 20036
202-857-1120

— stromoski —

" That's right . . . a large meat loaf and anchovy pizza lightly sprinkled with suet."

Books

Bone Appetit: Gourmet Cooking for Your Dog
Suzan Anson; New Chapter Press, 1989; $9.95

Cat Nips!
Rick and Martha Reynolds; Berkley, 1992; $8.95

Dog Bites!
Rick and Martha Reynolds; Berkley, 1992; $8.95

Feed the Birds
Helen and Dick Witty; Workman, 1991; $8.95

PICKLES

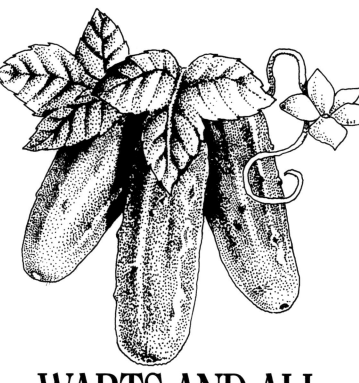

WARTS AND ALL

In the last analysis, a pickle is nothing more than a cucumber with experience. But not all cucumbers are suited for a pickle's journey from the long bath in brine to a place on the plate as the garnish for a deli sandwich. Too many cukes are thick-skinned. It takes a specially bred, thinner-skinned cucumber to absorb the brine and thus preserve itself.

According to an association of commercial picklers called Pickle Packers International (of One Pickle and Pepper Plaza, St. Charles, Illinois), there are 36 basic varieties of pickle, and 26 billion of them are packed annually in the United States. Every person in the country, they say, eats nine pounds of pickles every year — a rise of 50 percent over a quarter century ago.

When fresh cucumbers hit the factory, they go through one of three processes to control their natural fermentation. In the first, called "curing," the cucumbers are stored for as long as three years in tanks filled with salt brine. Then they're rinsed, put in a vat of fresh water, and heated to remove excess salt. Whether cut, sliced, or left whole, they are packed in a finishing "liquor" and end up dark green in color, flavorful, and crisp. Relishes and food-service pickles are often handled this way.

The "fresh pack" process eliminates the holding tanks and rushes the cucumbers immediately into flavored brine or syrup, after which comes pasteurization. The resulting pickles are less salty than the cured kind, and light green in color, though they may darken and soften as they age in the jar.

In the third method, the entire process takes place under refrigeration. Candidates for this category, known as "deli dills," are cleaned, graded, and go straight into flavored brine without any intermediate steps. Because they're never cooked or pasteurized, they remain very cucumberlike in texture, but also very flavorful. They must be kept refrigerated at all times.

All three methods produce three basic flavors: dill, sour, and sweet. With dills, known as "genuine," the dill weed may be added at any stage, from initial immersion in salt brine onwards. Kosher dills are made in the same way, except that fresh garlic is added to the brine. Pickles that go through a rapid, refrigerated cure in brine with a high vinegar content (taking only two or three days) are called "overnight dills."

Sour pickles are finished in a solution of vinegar and spices, "half-sours" in a spiced brine. Sweet pickles are sour pickles that have been drained of brine and placed in baths of mixed vinegars, sugar, and spices. The most popular sweet-pickle products are gherkins, bread-and-butter chip, and relish.

Pickles made under refrigeration will keep up to about 90 days. The other sort, if stored out of direct sunlight, will keep up to 18 months.

Did You Know?

☞ Amerigo Vespucci, after whom America was named, was a pickle merchant before he went into the exploration business. As a ship's chandler, he outfitted ships with pickled vegetables for long voyages.

☞ Pickling is one of the oldest forms of preserving food. It has been traced to Mesopotamia at the dawn of civilization, more than 4,500 years ago.

☞ Europeans want their pickles to have smooth skins. Americans prefer theirs with warts.

☞ The first pickles in America were made by Dutch farmers in the vicinity of what is now New York City.

☞ An average-sized dill pickle contains about 15 calories . . . and about 800 milligrams of sodium.

15 calories

Far-Fetched

According to the people at Pickle Packers International, if all the pickles Americans eat in a year were placed end to end they would:

❶ **make a ribbon of pickles 1,829,422 miles long, which could**

❷ **wrap 73.17 times around the earth at the circumference; or could**

❸ **reach to the moon and back 8.25 times.**

A Pickle Limerick

There was a young man named Perkins

Who was specially fond of small gherkins.

One fine day at tea he ate forty-three,

Which pickled his internal workin's.

Books

Blue Ribbon Pickles and Preserves
Maria P. Robbins; St. Martin's Press, 1987; $11.95

Pickles and Relishes
Andrea Chesman; Storey Communications, 1990; 12.95

Saving the Plenty: Pickling & Preserving
Richard Humphrey; Teaparty Books, 1987; $11.95

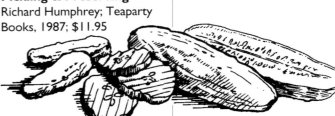

MORE INFORMATION

Pickle Packers International
P.O. Box 606
St. Charles, IL 60174-0606
708-584-8950

PICNICS

PICNICS ARE SO MUCH FUN — SOMETIMES

Eating outdoors is not everyone's idea of a picnic, but there are plenty of people who think that nothing is finer than to eat sandwiches in the sand, bake a clam on the beach, barbecue in the backyard, or carry a boxed lunch to the bleachers. Churches still hold a lot of outdoor suppers and campfires burn as brightly as ever they did. Uncounted millions picnic in the park, backpack along country trails, and toy with tidbits at the intermission of charming concerts in museum courtyards. Then there are the fortunate who feast alfresco at rock music festivals, families who bring food on board boats, and yet more who spend their summers eating while comfortably seated around swimming pools or perched on patios. Dining out is the *in* thing to do.

Americans have overcome a lot of the unpleasantness that people in other countries have to deal with: ants, for instance, and the mosquitoes that are almost certainly there although invisible in those pastoral paintings of picnics that Manet did so well. *We* spray the hell out of the area where we plan to eat — and a generous radius around the picnic site, as well. Then, just to be sure, we hang up those blue electric devices that zap any flying object that gets too close.

In Europe, picnickers go in for fancy picnic hampers that have leather loops for holding a service of fine tableware for eight, but give no thought to napkins. No one outside the United States bothers with napkins. *We* bring paper napkins to every occasion. Even if the picnic is just a buttered roll and some coffee there are always far more napkins than we could possibly use. Paper plates and plastic forks are the American way to go when we commune with nature.

TIPS

Preparing
Make a list of everything you could possibly need before packing the coolers. Nothing puts a damper on a cookout faster than forgetting to bring matches. Keep them dry in a covered jar, just in case of spills.

• Take along garbage bags and paper towels for cleanup — and damp washcloths in resealable plastic bags.

• Tape the lids down on all plastic containers; cover lidded plastic bowls with plastic plates and tape them in place. This may seem obvious (when it's too late), but pack the most fragile stuff on top of the heavier food.

• Pack hot foods and cold foods in separate containers. In the event of a disaster, better that the hot pea soup taken to a football game spills over the chicken than into the apple pie.

• Don't fill a cooler too full or the air will not circulate adequately to keep the food cold.

• Pack raw vegetables such

as tomatoes and cucumber separately, then slice and add to sandwiches at the last minute so that the bread does not get soggy. (In fact, all sandwiches made at the picnic site will look and taste fresher — but not all sites suit sandwich preparation.)

• Pack cookies in containers between sheets of paper towels to keep them crisp and cushion any blows.

• Consider taking an upside-down cake. It will spare you the surprise if that's how you find it.

Exploding Myths

Some away-from-home truths, courtesy of the USDA:

• Mayonnaise-based dishes such as potato, chicken, or tuna salad are *not* likely to cause food-borne illness, provided they are properly chilled. Commercial mayonnaise is pasteurized, so it is as safe as any other food. Keep all foods chilled in thermal containers or packed with ice or frozen gel pouches.

• Hard-cooked eggs *are* safe to take on a picnic, but must also be kept cold. Although long cooking destroys salmonella organisms, other bacteria could creep in later if there are cracks in the shell.

• Take-out cooked food must be kept chilled, too, to ensure its safety — or, more precisely, your safety. Bacteria thrive on warm food.

• Don't think you are saving time by partially precooking chicken or burgers that you plan to grill; you are courting disaster. Better by far, if you must prepare ahead, to cook everything completely, bring the food chilled to the picnic, then reheat it on the grill.

• Cook all hot foods to at least 160 degrees F., keep chilled foods in the refrigerator at 40 degrees until ready to leave, and remember that the picnic danger zone lies between 140 and 45 degrees. Preheat or prechill insulated, thermos-type containers by filling them with boiling or iced water and leaving to stand for 15 minutes. And carry the cooler in the car, not in the trunk where it will warm up more quickly.

When the Living Was ... Easier

by Kenneth Grahame

The Rat brought the boat alongside the bank, made her fast, helped the still awkward Mole safely ashore, and swung out the luncheon-basket. The Mole begged as a favor to be allowed to unpack it all by himself; and the Rat was very pleased to indulge him, and to sprawl at full length on the grass and rest, while his excited friend shook out the tablecloth and spread it, took out all the mysterious packets one by one and arranged their contents in due order, still gasping, "O my! O my!" at each fresh revelation.

Excerpted from The Wind in the Willows

PINEAPPLE

A PROMISE OF PLENTY

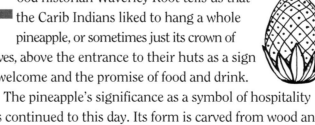

Food historian Waverley Root tells us that the Carib Indians liked to hang a whole pineapple, or sometimes just its crown of leaves, above the entrance to their huts as a sign of welcome and the promise of food and drink.

The pineapple's significance as a symbol of hospitality has continued to this day. Its form is carved from wood and molded from precious metals, often inlaid with jewels. Pineapples are stenciled on floors, painted onto china, printed on wallpaper, and no festive table would be complete without a splendid pineapple at the center of a cornucopia of fresh fruits. Its prickly exterior hides the promise of the luscious sweetness that lies within — so maybe it should also symbolize the old-fashioned virtue of perseverance.

Double Pineapple Breakfast Shake

Makes 2 12-ounce drinks

3 cups cubed fresh or canned pineapple
12 ounces lemon yogurt
1 ripe banana, sliced
¼ teaspoon powdered cinnamon

Process in a blender or food processor until smooth.

How to Prepare a
Pineapple

1. Lay the pineapple on its side on a shallow dish that will catch all the juices. Holding the fruit steady, cut off its leafy crown.

2. Slice through the pineapple crossways at 1/2-inch intervals. Cut away all the tough rind.

3. Stand each slice on its side in turn. Holding it steady, flick out the small, woody "eyes" with the tip of the knife.

4. Lay each slice flat again and cut out the hard core with a small pastry cutter, an apple corer, or a small, sharp knife.

5. To serve in wedges, quarter the whole fruit lengthways and remove the core. Separate the fruit from the rind and cut into wedges.

Did You Know?

☞ Pineapple has a soothing effect on a sore throat, possibly because its juice contains the antiinflammatory enzyme bromelain.

☞ Hawaii is now the world's leading producer of pineapples.

☞ Pineapples need 18 months until they are ready for their first harvest, and another 12 months before the second harvest. Three years and they're out.

☞ If the base of a pineapple smells sweet and you can pull a leaf easily from its crown, it is ripe.

☞ A pineapple's cut crown can propagate a fresh plant.

☞ Pineapple contains an enzyme that breaks down the fibers of meat, so the juice can be used as a meat tenderizer.

PISTACHIOS

AN ANTIQUE NUT GOES WEST

Pistachios' original home was the Middle East, where they still are a centuries-old trading commodity, valued for their delicate taste and attractive green color.

The nuts were first brought to the United States in the 1880s, but it would be many decades before pistachio growing got beyond the experimental stages. In 1929, American plant scientist William E. Whitehouse spent six months in Iran, seeking the plumpest pistachios with the most complex flavors. He came back with a 20-pound sack filled with seed and established his first plantings in the San Joaquin Valley, which has a desert climate similar to their original environment.

Years of experimentation produced the Kerman, named for the city where its seed had originally been collected, which was grafted onto strong rootstocks. More farmers started planting pistachio groves, and, finally, in 1976, the first commercial crop of pistachios was harvested — 1.5 million pounds, grown on fewer than 1,500 acres. California's newest agricultural industry was born.

The severing of relations between Iran and the United States in the 1980s resulted in the loss of the American market for Iranian pistachios, and subsequently there was a huge surge in U.S. domestic production. The most recent harvest was more than 129 million pounds, produced by 525 growers on close to 62,000 acres. California is now the world's second largest pistachio producer.

Health Nuts

Pistachios are a nutrient-dense food, a source of protein, complex carbohydrates, and fiber, as well as the B vitamins, vitamin E, and minerals including potassium, iron, and calcium. They are also fairly high in monounsaturated fats, believed to lower blood cholesterol. An ounce of shelled nuts (about 20 nuts) contains around 160 calories. A cup of unshelled pistachios produces about 1/2 cup of nutmeats.

Did You Know?

☞ The pistachio is a distant relative of the turpentine tree.

☞ Pistachios are naturally green with pale beige shells, but Middle Eastern merchants dyed them red to hide blemishes caused by primitive harvesting methods and travel hazards.

☞ Pistachio groves are planted with one male to every ten female trees. The wind does all the pollinating.

☞ Pistachio shells split as they ripen, so unopened ones almost always contain immature nuts.

PIZZA

PIE IN THE SKY

In the beginning, pizza was a simple affair, a 14-inch round of hand-twirled dough topped with sausage, pepperoni, cheese, anchovies, and tomato sauce. Today's pizza can be anything from 3 inches to 3 big feet.

Once it took 40 minutes to melt the cheese to strings-falling-down-your chin perfection. Now it takes 4 minutes and the industry talks of laser-operated ovens, which will reduce the cooking time to seconds.

Pizza may appear with an ultrathin crispy, crunchy crust or a thick doughy base. It may be deep dish or square dish or no dish at all. And it isn't just for lunch or dinner anymore. Now we can have breakfast pizza with bacon, sausage, eggs, and hash browns and ice cream sundae pizzas topped with split bananas, raspberry sauce, whipped cream, grated chocolate, chopped nuts, and, of course, a cheery maraschino cherry on the top.

Some of the finds we have stumbled across lately:

Southwestern burrito pizza with lime-marinated chicken breast, black beans, mild chilies, grated aged cheddar cheese, green tomato salsa, and sour cream.

Pizza topped with smoked salmon, crème fraîche and red, black and golden caviar.

Pizza topped with prosciutto, caramelized onions, artichoke hearts, fresh figs, and grated Parmesan.

Pizza topped with duck sausage, sliced duck breast with rosemary, grilled eggplant, and goat cheese.

Tortilla pizza with blackened ostrich meat, papaya, and sun-dried cherry vinaigrette.

Now really!

Godfather Is Mum

Pizza is big and getting bigger by the minute. Together, the Big Eight pizza chains have annual sales approaching $11 billion — a huge number by any measure. Little Caesar's sales are mighty close to $2.3 billion, and Domino's have fallen only a hair's breadth behind at $2.2 billion. It's not all pleasure and profit, though. Domino's achieves sales of this magnitude after spending an estimated $50 million a year on advertising. And massive advertising has helped Pizza Hut build the biggest mansion of all, with sales of almost $5 billion.

Even the pizzas are increasing in size. Pizza Hut offers a pie so massive it can be cut into 24 slices; its Big Foot pizza has put its stamp on the industry. Godfather's Jumbo Combo has achieved success with its 18-inch pie and the company has even larger plans for the future.

Meanwhile, the big players are constantly seeking new areas of expansion. Pizza Hut has opened 1,573 parlors overseas, in addition to close to 9,000 units at home. Pizza is hot everywhere and even the frozen varieties rack up huge numbers. The leader, Tombstone, heads the field with annual sales in the $200 million range (big, but just a fraction of the overall frozen pizza segment, which is estimated to be worth $3 billion a year).

If you aren't close to a pizza restaurant or don't feel like making it or waiting for home delivery, there are plenty of other options. The giants have rolled out new pizza eating opportunities at airports, hospitals, industry cafeterias, school lunchrooms, sports stadiums, and in kiosks at 1,200 K-mart stores and there is tight-lipped talk about expanding to in-flight service and delivery to cars stuck in traffic jams.

Pizza makers fear competition from within their own ever-vigilant industry, but their biggest worry is that McDonald's will get into the McPizza business — which could add another 9,000 outlets to the already existing 50,000 pizza restaurants and result in higher prices for flour, sauce, and cheese.

White House Snoop

According to *The Wall Street Journal*, pizza orders from the Clintons and their hardworking staff are up 31 percent compared with the best year for the Bush administration. When Hillary is out of town, the figures increase even more.

Hot Tips From All Over

Pizza delivery people have made these discoveries:

• Women tip better than men.

• The longer the driveway, the lower the tip.

• The best tippers own Corvettes, Camaros, and Novas.

• A new car in the driveway usually means a lower tip.

• During TV newscasts, most pizza is ordered while the weather report is on.

• TV shows most frequently being watched during pizza delivery: "The Simpsons," "60 Minutes," and "Saturday Night Live." All-time highest demand so far was during programs on Amy Fisher and the Buttafuoccos.

• Most people answer the door shoeless.

Books

Chez Panisse Pasta, Pizza, and Calzone
Alice Waters et al.; Random House, 1984; $22.00

Pizza
Lorenza de Medici; Time-Life Books, 1993; $14.95

Vegetarian Pizza
James McNair; Chronicle Books, 1993; $11.95

Pizza Yankee

*T*he story goes that a pizza parlor waitress asked Yogi Berra whether he wanted his pizza cut into six or eight slices. "Six, please," he said. "No way am I hungry enough to eat eight."

Free and Fast Future

A toll-free 800 number will access a pizza chain from anywhere in the country. The telephone operator "reads" the address, locates the nearest pizza parlor within 7 to 11 seconds, and speeds your order to your door. The pizza is cooked en route to your couch.

PLUMS

VERY DESIRABLE

*T*he plum is such a luscious and sought-after fruit that in the English language a secondary meaning of its name is "something superior or very desirable" — as in sugarplums, for example, and plum pudding.

Our forefathers on Plymouth Rock turned up their noses at native American wild plums, including the beach plum that still grows in some profusion along the Atlantic coast. They had brought their own plum-tree seeds from Europe, seeds with a sophisticated lineage, having been cultivated, after all, for some 2,000 years — and these they planted. Subsequent proliferation, however, got the better of control. By the mid-19th century there were at least 150 varieties of plum in America, and today there are unknown multiples of that number.

Fresh plums have more than a delicious taste to recommend them. They are free of fat and cholesterol, low in sodium, and each one contains only about 33 calories.

Did You Know?

☞ The plum tree grows on every continent of the globe except Antarctica.

This is just to say I have eaten the plums that were in the icebox and which you were probably saving for breakfast; forgive me, they were delicious, so sweet, and so cold.

— William Carlos Williams
American poet

The Queen's Behind

*T*he prized plum known in England as the greengage is in France called the reine-claude, *named after the famously fat Queen Claude, François I's first wife, who was very fond of this fruit. However, according to legend the naming was not so much in her honor as she might have thought. It's said that because the plum in question is deeply cleft from stem to stern, its shape reminded her courtiers of nothing so much as her royal backside.*

A Guide to Plums

Plum	Skin Color	Flesh Color
Sweet Clingstones		
Santa Rosa	Red	Yellow
Friar	Black/red	Yellow
Nubiana	Black/red	Yellow
Laroda	Deep red	Red
Eldorado	Deep red	Red
Black Amber	Black	Golden
Elephant Heart	Black/red	Red
Kelsey	Green/golden	Yellow
Sweet Freestones		
Italian Prune	Purple	Green/amber
Emily	Purple	Green/amber
President	Purple	Green/amber
Tart Plums for Cooking		
Damson	Purple	Purple
Mirabelle	Golden	Golden

POLLOCK

THE MEGA-CATCH

*Y*ou may have eaten a lot of pollock in your time, but it's unlikely that you ever asked for it by name in a fish restaurant. This plentiful whitefish, which averages 12 to 20 inches in length and a half pound to 2 pounds in weight, swims in schools so deep and vast that, on radar, they show up as the equivalent of a 19-story New York skyscraper. They are tracked and netted by fleets of factory trawlers from many nations, and processed into a variety of packaged, frozen food products right on board.

If you met a pollock recently, it was probably under an assumed identity — as fish sticks, perhaps, or as surimi, the imitation crab or lobster meat now found in supermarkets. Because of the factory finish provided by suppliers, fast-food chains are big customers for pollock. The fish is precut into skinless, boneless fillets and frozen into blocks for storage and shipment.

Alaskan pollock is the most abundant seafood in American waters, and more than 3 billion pounds (1.4 million metric tons) of it is caught each year in the Bering Sea and Gulf of Alaska. The Russian share of the pollock harvest from these waters is believed to be about double our own.

POPCORN

Incredible Origins

According to legend, popcorn was introduced to the Pilgrims by the Wampanoag tribe on the first Thanksgiving Day. It seems that the Wampanoag chief's brother presented the settlers with a deerskin bag full of popped corn. The enterprising colonial cooks served it the next morning with sugar and cream, thus inventing the first puffed cereal.

Did You Know?

☞ The oldest ears of popping corn so far discovered were found by archaeologists in a bat cave in west-central New Mexico. According to radiocarbon tests, they are about 5,600 years old.

☞ Movie popcorn is popped in super-fatty coconut oil. A large box of plain popcorn packs the saturated fat wallop of six Big Macs. With butter, make it eight.

Betty Bopper

*This is Little Betty Bopper.
She has popcorn in the
    popper.
Seven pounds of it! Please
    stop her.
That's more popcorn than is
    proper
In a popper. Someone drop
    her
Just a hint! Mommer!
    Popper!
Betty's going to come a
    cropper!
Look, it's starting! Get a
    chopper.
Chop the door down!
        . . . Well, too late.*

— John Ciardi
Mummy Took Cooking Lessons

A LOTTA HOT AIR

Popcorn has long been a showbiz treat. As caramel corn it made its theater debut in boxes of Cracker Jack, sold in the aisles at the vaudeville show. Plain popped, it was a home treat during the Depression, cheap and easy. But when it showed up fresh, hot, and buttery at the concession stand in the first ornate lobby of the first movie palace, a national passion was born. For one thing, the popcorn poppers at the movies produced far fewer unpopped kernels (UPKs, as they're known in the trade, or "old maids") than turned up in a bowl of popcorn at home. For another, popcorn is so addictive when the lights are out that most Americans found they just couldn't sit through a movie without a bag or box of it in their laps.

The movie monopoly on popcorn consumption continued until the late 1950s. Then came TV, drawing us and our snacks to the home screen. Since 1966 we've eaten about 70 percent of our popcorn at home. Overall, we consume — every single one of us — 56 quarts of popcorn a year, according to the Popcorn Institute. Consumption has increased by more than 50 percent in the past decade, says the Snack Food Association, with sales now exceeding $2 billion a year.

A major factor fueling popcorn's popularity now is its association with the lite-and-healthy school of nutritional thinking. Popcorn can be a wholesome, high-fiber, whole-grain food, and air-popped (no oil, no butter, no salt) it contains a mere 92 calories in a 4-cup serving. Microwave popcorns (starting with the Orville Redenbacher brand in 1976) have now introduced light versions that come plain or with butter flavor and no cholesterol. Flavored popcorns (with real cheddar cheese, for example) are also now on the market in dozens of varieties and colors.

Popcorn may have been born in a trunk like all the other stars of stage and screen, but in America's search for the magic snack — great taste, no weight gain — this exploding kernel of hot air has dramatically transcended the stage.

Popcorn Nutrition

4-cup serving	Calories	Grams of Fat
Regular, air-popped, plain	92	1
Regular, air-popped with 1½ tablespoons butter	254	19
Regular, oil-popped, plain	120	8
Orville Redenbacher's Butter Microwave, popped	133	8
Orville Redenbacher's Light Butter Microwave, popped	93	4
Smartfood White Cheddar, popped	320	20

Source: *Eating Well*

Pop Goes the Corn

Many Indians popped their corn by placing the kernels on hot sand. The old American at-home method is not very different. Warm a heavy pan and add about ¼ cup oil. Heat the oil and drop a few kernels into the pan. If they pop, proceed.

The kernels for good popping corn contain about 14 percent moisture. When this moisture is heated, it turns to steam, creating a pressure inside the kernel of about 135 pounds per square inch. Then the kernel explodes, leaving behind a puff of starch and protein. The puffs form in two different basic shapes: snowflake — popped big and shaped like an unruly cloud — or mushroom — popped into a ball.

Books

For Popcorn Lovers Only
Diane Pfeifer; Strawberry Patch, 1987; $9.95

MORE INFORMATION

Popcorn Institute
401 North Michigan Avenue
Chicago, IL 60611-4267
312-644-6610

PORK

JURASSIC PORK GETS A MAKEOVER

Americans are consuming almost 40 percent more pork than they did just a decade ago. We can credit the current popularity of "the other white meat" to the pork industry's vigorous advertising and promotion campaigns and recognize today's pig as a very different animal from its ancestors, which were bred as much for the value of their lard as for meat. Before the commercialization of vegetable oils, lard was the primary fat used for cooking.

Beginning in the 1950s, the pork industry embarked on an aggressive effort to reduce the fat in its animals by more than 50 percent in order to lower calories and enhance the health profile of most cuts. In 1955, the average hog yielded 127 pounds of meat and nearly 40 pounds of lard. Today, its descendants produce 167 pounds of meat apiece and only a "trace" of lard — a mere 10 pounds. This reduction passes its benefits onto the plate. A 3-ounce serving of pork contains 24 grams of protein and only 6 grams of fat (compared with 16 grams of fat in 2 tablespoons of peanut butter), and pork is also a source of iron, zinc, and B vitamins.

Contemporary pork tenderloin has become so slim, in fact, that it compares favorably with chicken breast stripped of its skin. But not all cuts of pork win high points in the health department. Much depends on preparation: Batter-fried chicken contains far more fat than a dish of stir-fried pork, just as a carton of Chinese take-out sweet and sour pork will contain more fat and calories than a turkey sandwich without mayo. However, pork always has the advantage of contributing more flavor. It is as delicious at a barbecue as in the dining room in the form of an elegant crown roast — truly a meat for all seasons.

TIPS

Buying
Boneless cuts of fresh pork provide three to four servings per pound, so they are a better value than ribs, which are fun to eat but long on bones and short on meat.

Cooking
You don't have to overcook fresh pork to ensure its safety. Trichinosis is now so rare that you can pretty much forget about it. Experts recommend cooking pork to an internal temperature of 160 degrees F. If you overcook it, the flavor and juiciness are lost.

Books

Hog Wild
K. C. McKeown; Warner Books, 1992; $9.95

Hot Links & Country Flavors: Sausages in American Regional Cooking
Bruce Aidells and Denis Kelley; Knopf, 1990; $19.95

The Useful Pig
Roberta Wolfe Smoler; HarperCollins, 1990; $22.95

Oink!

In the 17th century in New York City, farmers built a wall to keep pigs from roaming. The street bordering the wall was called Wall Street. This is why there are no greedy pigs in that part of town, even to the present day.

Did You Know?

☞ It is because pigs have no sweat glands that they wallow in water or mud to keep cool.

☞ Until the end of World War II, pork fat was an essential ingredient in the manufacture of explosives.

☞ Pigs aren't being kicked around anymore — not for sport, anyway. Footballs, or "pigskins," are now being made from cowhide.

Noel Coward Considers The Pig

Any part of piggy
Is quite all right with me.
Ham from Westphalia, ham
from Parma,
Ham as lean as the Dalai Lama,
Ham from Virginia, ham from
York,
Trotters, sausages, hot roast
pork,
Crackling crisp for my teeth to
grind on,

Bacon with or without the
rind on.
Though humanitarian,
I'm not vegetarian.
I'm neither crank nor prude
nor prig
And though it may sound
infra dig
Any part of darling pig
Is perfectly fine with me.

"Why, just look at what this place can do with a baked apple . . ."

POTASSIUM

MAJOR MINERAL

Potassium is a major mineral in the human body, along with calcium, chloride, magnesium, phosphorus, sodium, and sulfur. It is called major, or macro, because in a healthy body it is present, like its counterparts, in quantities larger than 5 grams, and because it has profoundly important work to do in the smooth operation of the human system. There are 22 minerals that are essential to health and a total of 60 minerals present in the body in trace amounts.

Potassium promotes regular heartbeat, assists in muscle contraction, regulates the transfer of nutrients to cells, controls water balance in body tissues and cells, and helps to regulate blood pressure. It is the major positive ion inside the cell.

In recent years many tests have been run seeking to determine whether potassium plays a role in preventing and controlling high blood pressure, but the results have been inconclusive. Current thinking: Any role potassium may have in prevention is less than that associated with weight control or reduced sodium intake.

Potassium is so plentiful in the normal diet that deficiencies are unknown. Recent USDA surveys found that American men and women from 19 to 50 customarily have potassium levels above the minimum requirement estimated by the Food and Nutrition Board of the National Academy of Sciences. A diet that contains plenty of grains, fruits, and vegetables supplies an abundance of potassium.

Foods High In Potassium

500+ milligrams
½ cup dried apricots (unsweetened)
½ cup cooked lima beans
Baked or boiled potato
½ cup cooked winter squash
8 ounces low-fat yogurt

350 - 499 milligrams
1 ounce 100 percent bran cereal
1 medium-sized banana
¾ cup orange juice (unsweetened)
½ cup cooked prunes (unsweetened)
1 medium-sized baked sweet potato
¾ cup canned tomato juice
1 lean broiled pork cutlet
1 lean pan-broiled veal cutlet
3 ounces broiled flounder
1½ cup cooked kidney beans
½ cup cooked lentils
1 cup buttermilk
8 ounces whole-milk yogurt

Source: USDA Handbook 8

POTATOES

A Potato Prayer

**Pray for peace and grace and spiritual food,
For wisdom and guidance,
For all these things are good.
But don't forget the potatoes.**

— Anonymous

Potato Talk

Couch potato — one who is watching television and is too lazy to get up and go to the gym, the cleaners, the supermarket, or the video store.

Hot potato — something too hot to handle; could be a project with doubtful or sensational implications.

Meat-and-potatoes man — one who likes simple fare, a person of uncomplicated tastes and strongly held opinions.

Mashed potato — a disco dance of the 1960s.

Potato slot — a mouth.

Potato head — a stupid person.

Small potatoes — something insignificant.

Spud — a potato; possibly an acronym for The Society for the Prevention of an Unwholesome Diet, which was founded to keep the potato out of England; more likely, the word for a digging fork used in cultivating potatoes.

"Tu me dices papas" — a Spanish expression, literally "you are telling me potatoes," meaning "you are telling me lies."

One Potato, Two Potato...

Though regarded in the first half of this century as starchy and fattening, the potato has now been recognized as an ideal food. It contains only a trace of fat and little sodium. A medium-sized potato delivers about 220 calories, and it's an excellent source of vitamins C and B-6 and of niacin, and a good source of fiber and potassium. It is, in fact, the second highest source of vitamin C in the American diet.

The USDA reports that per capita we eat 124 pounds of potatoes a year; put another way, potatoes are included in one of every three meals Americans eat.

A GOOD
POTATO DAY

TRUMAN CAPOTE

I live in Sagaponack by the sea. The house, which I love, sits smack in the middle of potato fields. In Fall, when harvesting is done and the tractors are gone from the fields, I amble out through the empty rows collecting small, sweet, leftover potatoes for my larder.

Imagine a cold October morning. I fill my basket with found potatoes in the field and race to the kitchen to create my one and only most delicious ever potato lunch. The Russian vodka — it must be 80 proof — goes into the icebox to chill. The potatoes into the oven to bake. My breathless friend arrives to share the feast. Out comes the icy vodka. Out comes a bowl of sour cream. Likewise the potatoes, piping hot.

We sit down to sip our drinks. We split open steaming potatoes and put on some sour cream. *Now*, I whisk out the big tin of caviar, which I have forgotten to tell you is the only way *I* can bear to eat a potato. Then caviar — the freshest, the grayest, the biggest Beluga — is heaped in mounds on the potato. My friend and I set to. This simple tribute to the fruit of Eastern Long Island farming makes an exhilarating country lunch, fuels the heart and soul and empties the pocketbook.

Some of the potato fields, so beautiful, flat and still, may not be here next year. And fewer the year after that. New houses are steadily popping up to mar the long line where the land ends and the sky begins.

The Hampton Day School is on a farm among these fields. It is as open in spirit as its surroundings and for that we can be thankful.

Excerpted from the Foreword to
Myrna Davis's *The Potato Book*

Best Uses For Specific Varieties

Variety	Uses
Round white group	Frying, scalloped, gnocchi, pancakes
Idaho (Russet Burbank)	Baking, frying, mashing, soups
Red round group	Roasting, boiling, salads
Long white group	Roasting, boiling, salads

Potatoes are to food what sensible shoes are to fashion.

— Linda Wells
Food writer

I now dismiss the Potato with the hope that I shall never again have to write the word, or see the thing.

— William Cobbett
19th-century English political writer

My idea of heaven is a great big baked potato and someone to share it with.

— Oprah Winfrey
Former eater of bountiful food

Lydie Marshall's Mashed Potatoes Anna

Serves 4

2 pounds russet or Yukon Gold potatoes, peeled and cut into 2-inch cubes (5 cups)
1 cup milk
4 tablespoons (½ stick) unsalted butter
⅓ cup heavy cream
1½ teaspoons salt
Freshly ground pepper

In a large saucepan, cover the potatoes with cold salted water. Bring to a boil, partially cover and cook for 20 minutes, or until the potatoes are tender.

Scald the milk. Drain the potatoes and mash them in the cooking pot with a potato masher, a ricer, or through a strainer back into the pot. Turn on the heat and gradually whisk in the hot milk, butter and cream. Season with salt and freshly ground pepper and serve immediately.

Reprinted from *A Passion for Potatoes*

A BRIEF HISTORY OF FRENCH FRIES

Good ideas in food travel fast, but they have to occur to somebody first. French fries, the deep-fried sliced potatoes that the French call *pommes frites,* were a popular feature of the French table for many years. But it wasn't until the middle of the 19th century that some Parisian pushcart vendor got the idea of offering them on the street as a deep-fried snack in a twist of paper. By the 1880s, street vendors of fried potatoes were all over town, and a canny Englishman, noting the popularity of the treat, decided to export the same to London. There, introduced as *pommes de terre à la mode française* (and called "alamodes" for short), these new-fangled potatoes caught on like a house afire, particularly with the working classes. Since the 17th century, fried fish had been for sale in London streets. A wedding of the fish with the *frites,* wrapped up together in a page of yesterday's paper, salted and liberally doused with vinegar, soon proved to be a soggy match made in heaven and known ever since as fish and chips.

How the chips eluded the fish and escaped to America is not a matter of record, but we can be pretty sure that some canny American was in Paris or London or both in the 1880s, knew a good thing when he saw it, and brought it straight over with the good honest name of French fries. In this country, French fries returned to the better restaurants and the tables of respectable homes, and never reverted to the streets. However, they became a sizzling feature of fast-food operations all over the world. And in far-flung outposts of McDonald's and Burger King, in cities like Moscow and Beijing, they are known today as "American fries."

WE'VE GOT 'EM UNDER OUR SKIN

It was the Spanish conquistadors, searching for gold in Peru in the 16th century, who discovered the potato (which they originally thought was a truffle) and brought it home, using it first as a cheap food for sailors on the Spanish Main, then cultivating it at Seville. Some Spaniards called it *papa,* which is the Peruvian word for tuber, some called it *turma de tierra,* Spanish for "testicle of the earth." When potatoes washed up on the Irish coast after the defeat of the Spanish Armada, the Irish didn't know *what* to call them. But the English name we now use derives from *batata,* the West Indian name for the sweet potato — no kin at all to the *Solanum tuberosum* that we're talking about, but in those days, who knew?

The potato was not an overnight sensation in Europe. It had a louche reputation for a long time, suspected of being poisonous, or aphrodisiacal, or both. And fundamentalist reformers did it no good, denouncing it because it isn't mentioned in the Bible. But in the end this abundant food — benign, essentially unerotic, and humble — made its way onto all the tables of the West, saving whole generations of Europeans from starvation from time to time en route to becoming indispensable in our diet in the present day.

Best Companions

Potatoes in the ground don't thrive in just any old society; they do poorly in the vicinity of apples, pumpkins, squash, and tomatoes. They perk up, however, in the company of beans, cabbage, corn, lettuce, radishes — and petunias. Helpful neighbors, because they deter the potato beetle, are catnip, coriander, horseradish, and onions.

Types and Tips

There are hundreds of varieties of potatoes, but 80 percent of the national crop is derived from only six varieties. Among the best known are the russet baking potato, the Superior and Kennebec (or Katahdin) all-purpose potatoes, and the red boiling potato (sometimes called Red Bliss, though the Red Bliss variety isn't planted anymore).

In Europe, potato wholesalers identify potatoes by their varieties. American wholesalers designate the location where the potatoes were grown — as in Idaho, Long Island, and Maine — but that doesn't really tell us much about taste and characteristics, because one or more varieties can be grown in the same place.

Confusing — but there are a few useful guidelines. Maine and Long Island potatoes should be used primarily for mashing and frying. Use Idaho potatoes for baking, and small new California and so-called Red Bliss potatoes for potato salad. Peel old potatoes and cook them in boiling salted water. Cook new potatoes unpeeled and start them in cold salted water.

MORE INFORMATION

Idaho Potato Commission
P.O. Box 1068
Boise, ID 83701-1068
208-334-2350

Maine Potato Board
744 Main Street, Room 1
Presque Isle, ME 04769
207-769-5061

The Potato Board/ National Potato Promotion Board
7555 East Hampden Avenue, Suite 412
Denver, CO 80231
303-369-7783

MAIL ORDER SOURCES

New Penny Farm
P.O Box 448
Presque Isle, ME 04769
800-827-7551

Seeds Blum
Idaho City Stage
Boise, ID 83706
208-342-0858

POTATO CHIPS

Bob's Texas-Style Potato Chips
Route 1, Box 66-A
Brookshire, TX 77423
800-833-0205

Vermont Old-Fashioned Potato Chip Company
266 Pine Street
Burlington, VT 05401
802-863-3203

Books

A Passion for Potatoes
Lydie Marshall;
HarperPerennial, 1992; $13.00

Potatoes: A Country Garden Cookbook
Maggie Waldron; Collins Publishers, 1993; $19.95

The Perfect Potato
Diane Simone Vezza; Villard Books, 1993; $16.00

The Potato Garden
Maggie Oster; Crown, 1993; $17.00

POTATO CHIPS BREAK THE SOUND BARRIER

It has been said that the yearning for potato chips is one of mankind's deepest emotions. It is odd that this craving should have lain dormant in the human breast from the beginning of recorded time until 1925, when the invention of the potato slicer changed everything.

The thickness of an ordinary potato chip is 55/1,000 of an inch. Your everyday potato chip will be that thick. Ridged chips may be four times as thick — up to 210/1,000 of an inch. In the unending search for a potato chip that might taste more like a potato, the potato chip engineers boldly broke the thickness threshold.

In doing so, they had to respect the potato's natural fracture pattern and discover where its structural weakness lies, so that when the chip is edged into the mouth, it will not shatter like glass. The miracle of ridged potato chips is achieved by running the ridges parallel on both sides of the chip, but slightly out of sync, so that they resound with a crisp crackle and crunch.

Furthermore, when it is well into the mouth, a chip mustn't mash down into a mushy consistency but melt away at a precise (very precise) moment, otherwise we may eat them too slowly and delay reaching into the bag for more and yet more. It must also be possible to reproduce an identical chip with precisely the same characteristics in manufacturing plants throughout the country, day and night, summer and winter.

A diet that consists predominantly of rice leads to the use of opium, just as a diet that consists predominantly of potatoes leads to the use of liquor.

— Friedrich Nietzsche
19th-century philosopher

Maybe Silicone Chips Are Slimmer

The potato chip industry racks up $3.9 billion a year making a total of 1.5 billion pounds of chips. The Snack Food Association assures us that every day Americans spend a total of $10,410,959 on potato chips, which is equivalent to an average consumption of 6 pounds of potato chips per year for every man, woman, and child in this country.

Now, 18 regular Ruffles contain 150 calories and 9 grams of fat, and when you multiply these numbers by 6 pounds (having first figured out how many chips there are in a 4-ounce bag), you will understand why your belt is getting tighter.

POULTRY

POULTRY
IS FLYING HIGH

What's got into us lately, a lot, is poultry. We are eating more of it in more ways than ever — around 70 pounds a year. And the numbers are on the rise. Poultry is showing up in pretend bacon and sausages, burgers and "meat" balls, cold cuts and hot dogs. Hardly any companies advertise all-beef franks anymore, which is a real pity.

Everywhere we turn we are being urged to eat more poultry and less red meat, but the fat, cholesterol, and calorie content of the substitute may not, in fact, be anything like as healthful as we imagine. It all depends on how it is prepared and how much we eat of it. Chicken nuggets and other microwavable magic bullets aren't going to win any awards for promoting longevity.

Many experts say it is short-sighted to ignore other meats that contain important nutrients. Everyone knows, of course, that white meat without its skin is "better" for you than dark, but this doesn't mean it tastes better. It could be successfully argued that a stolen piece of juicy leg, right out of the oven, eaten while nobody is looking, is more deeply satisfying than the sliver of breast that lies later on the plate, thin and white and wan.

You can carry things a heap too far in the quest for a diet of denial. In some circles it is considered bad manners to discuss what food doesn't have in it while one is in the act of consuming it. This is not to cast a pall over poultry consumption; far from it. Everyone knows that there are few things in life more fabulous than a nice roast chicken or Thanksgiving turkey dinner, especially if there are plenty of mashed potatoes to go along with it.

Books

Poultry Cook Book
Sunset Editors; Sunset
Publishing, 1991; $7.95

The Complete Guide to Poultry
Lonnie and Falon Gandara;
Price Stern Sloan, 1990; $14.95

Swan Songs

Since the old Romans first spied a swan skimming serenely over the water, cooks have tried, unsuccessfully, to seduce us into thinking that these pretty birds are good to eat.

They aren't.

Despite appearances, they are tough old birds. However, during the Middle Ages they were served to kings, accompanied by a flourish of trumpets, and to this day they appear on the menu at the annual banquet of the Guild of Vintners in London, which is lorded over by the River Thames Master of the Swans.

Brimming glasses are raised and five cheers given (instead of the customary three) in honor of the kings of England, Scotland, France, Denmark, and Cyprus who once ruled the waves. Then everybody sits down to an inedible portion of roast swan.

Q&A

Q When you ask the butcher for a chicken breast and you get two chicken breasts, what should you do?

A Ask for half a breast, then seize the moment to explain what you *really* mean.

TIPS

Preparing
You do not usually need to wash fresh poultry under cold running water.

Cooking
Cook whole birds until the internal temperature reaches 180 degrees F.

• Cook poultry breasts to a temperature of 170 degrees.

• Reheat leftover poultry to 165 degrees, preferably covered with a sauce or gravy; this will prevent it from becoming dry.

PRISON FOOD

FORGET THE FOIE GRAS

Going to prison is never any picnic, of course, but if you get sent up the river these days into the keep of state or federal penal systems, you can expect to be fed adequately, if never lavishly, for the duration of your stay. A diet of bread and water is definitely off the menu, three square meals are mandated, and as many as 12 different food programs — from Muslim to kosher to diabetic to low sodium — are available for special needs in most institutions. In fact, one of your first intake interviews is liable to be with a nutritionist.

American prison administrators don't treat felons with kid gloves, and they're not trying to show them a good time. But incarceration breeds resentment, prisons are powder kegs, and jailers want to ensure the least amount of trouble from large prison populations. Like children at school, inmates are creatures of routine. Say that spinach is always on the menu on Thursdays. Well, if it's Thursday and the spinach isn't there, or the kitchen runs out of it during a meal shift, the shock waves can lead to strikes and violence. Same goes for size of portions, which are kept adequate without being heaping, and must be uniform. Meal time is the only event in prison life that everyone looks forward to; if one inmate were to receive a larger portion than another, a fight could break out. You better believe it.

In prisons, security is a matter of crucial importance. For example, inmates are never served meat with the bones in, and all scrap bones in the kitchen must be accounted for. All food preparation is done by inmates, and a stolen bone can be made into a lethal weapon. For the same reason, food is served on paper plates and inmates must turn in their plastic spoons and forks at the end of every meal.

Can food be used in this environment to punish or restrain? Well, yes. The states of Oregon, Washington, Arizona, and Michigan have experimented with something called a "food loaf" as a means of discouraging prisoners who throw food and disrupt routines. If the day's dinner menu calls for pork chops, rice, and broccoli, all three elements are pureed in a blender, then poured into pans, baked, and served, more or less predigested, to the perpetrators. In Arizona, a convicted murderer who had been fed this way sued prison officials for violating his rights under the Constitution, and won his right to better food.

A version of the diet loaf appears in this section. When test cooks made it for a Seattle newspaper, one reporter pronounced it unspeakable; another said he wouldn't mind a second helping. But, of course, there are no second helpings, or second chances, in prison.

The food is bad and there isn't enough of it
—Fed-up prisoner

Nutra-Loaf

Makes approximately 20
10-ounce servings

As served in Clark County Jail, Washington State.

10 pounds ground beef or ground chicken
1 cup sliced celery
1 cup sliced carrots
1 cup beans (white, red, chili, or baked)
1 cup cooked rice (white or brown)
1 cup cored and chopped apples
1 cup tomato product such as diced tomatoes or salsa
2 cups chopped cabbage
2 cups miscellaneous vegetables (corn, peas, green beans)
8 cups oatmeal (or bread chunks or crackers)

1 dozen eggs
¼ cup seasoning salt
2 cups potatoes (mashed, dehydrated, scalloped, or fresh, diced)

Preheat the oven to 325 degrees F.

Run everything through a grater or chopper. Shape into 2 meatloaf-shaped loaves on cookie sheets or other large flat pans. Cover with foil. Bake for 2 hours, or until done.

Reprinted from
The Seattle Times

Rotten Deal

A convicted criminal receives three meals a day. Many poor people and the frail elderly cannot count on receiving food regularly.

Conversation
with a Former Inmate

Recently we learned that a California friend of ours did brief time at the Santa Clara County Detention Farm after a minor conviction. Going to first things first, we asked him to describe the dining experience there.

"Meals aren't social hours in jail," he told us. "There's no time for chatting. The farm is overcrowded and prisoners have to eat quickly to make room for the ones who are still waiting in line behind them. So I was surprised at my first meal when a guy struck up a friendly conversation with me as we walked from the chow line — where they put our food on steel trays — to the tables. Then, when we sat down, he suddenly asked if he could have my string beans.

"The beans were a very faded shade of green, and I didn't mind parting with them. What was left? Some off-white corn, a breaded hamburger patty, and a nondescript roll. It wasn't terrible, but none of it would pass muster with anybody's mother . . . even a neglectful mother.

"There was never enough food on the tray and there were never any seconds. The administrators used hunger to keep the inmates motivated. They had an angle: If we signed up for work details during the week, which they wanted us to, we could earn a few cents an hour, and on weekends we could spend our earnings at the prison commissary on tobacco and Cup O'Noodles.

"Believe me, in the long hours between the evening meal and lights out, a serving of Cup O'Noodles is a tasty prospect.

"In a place like that, food is very important. You see, it's against the rules for inmates to take any food out of the mess hall. So if you're found later with an apple in your pocket, they punish you by adding three days to your sentence.

"So it was no wonder that my 'friend' in the chow line on my first day wanted my string beans."

PROTEIN

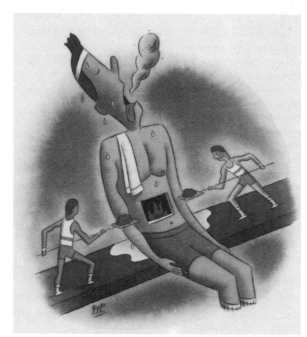

Nobody wants protein. The best-educated, most affluent people in America want to pay top dollar to eat a third-world diet.

— Clark Wolf
Restaurant consultant

PRIMARY STUFF

The word *protein* is taken from the Greek for "primary" because it is the protein in our food that is essential in sustaining our lives. We get it in a complete form from animal sources such as meat, poultry, fish, cheese, milk, and eggs, and incompletely from plant sources, such as grains, cereals, and legumes.

Eaten in combination — rice and beans, for example, or peanut butter and whole-wheat bread — incomplete proteins are enhanced or completed. From prehistoric times, particularly when animal sources of protein were scant or nonexistent, many cultures obtained essential nutrients by growing staple crops in such combinations: in Asia, rice and soybeans, for example; in the Americas, corn and black beans.

In the process of eating, we digest dietary protein into separate amino acids and synthesize our own proteins from them. All the chemicals that keep us growing and functioning are proteins: the enzymes that build up and break down molecules; the antibodies that fight off disease; the hemoglobin that carries oxygen through the system; even certain hormones. In the composition of the body, protein is second only to water: Organs, muscle and skin tissue, nails, hair, teeth and bone — all are protein.

A century ago, no amount of dietary protein was deemed enough, particularly from meat. A Dr. Salisbury, popularizing his chopped-meat diet (and thereby lending his name to Salisbury steak forever), recommended no less than three pounds of meat a day when two pounds (about 120 grams of protein) was the standard. Today, the World Health Organization sets 40 grams a day as adequate, and nutritionists argue that no more than 10 to 12 percent of our daily caloric intake needs to come from protein. Nevertheless, Americans remain protein-prone: individually, we consume about 90 grams of protein a day.

Protein Overload

Diamond Jim Brady, a 19th-century hero of conspicuous consumption, would drop in at Delmonico's to snack on six or eight beefsteaks at a sitting. Of course, he took on a ton of lard with all that marbled meat, and his body could use only a fraction of the protein he consumed, so it stored that as *more* fat.

Diamond Jim ended up as big around as the Ritz.

PRUNES

BUT CAN YOU PUT IT ON POPCORN?

In yet another valiant attempt to get us to eat our prunes, the California Prune Board has come up with a sure winner: prunes as a fat substitute. A recent study conducted by the board found that replacing butter, margarine, or oil with prune puree in tested baked goods reduced their fat content by 75 to 90 percent, decreased calorie content by 20 to 30 percent, and dropped cholesterol to zero. The puree is made by whipping together 4 ounces of pitted prunes and 5 tablespoons of water. Among the suggested uses for it: a Low-Fat Devil's Chocolate Fudge Cake, which one food writer reported as having a texture almost that of a good Sachertorte, but a bit chewier, and a flavor "both chocolaty and prunous, as you might expect."

Many Are Called, Few Are Chosen

Although all prunes were once plums, not every plum can be a prune. Only the sweetest, most flavorful varieties have what it takes to stay sweet, plump, and flexible when sun-dried — or, as is more common nowadays, dehydrated by machine.

MORE INFORMATION

California Prune Board
P.O. Box 10157
Pleasanton, CA 94588
510-734-0150

Books

The Prune Gourmet
Donna Rodnitzky, Jogail Wenzel, and Ellie Densen; Chronicle Books, 1990; $9.95

Did You Know?

☞ A mature plum tree produces between 150 and 300 pounds of prune-plums every year; it takes 3 to 4 pounds of fresh plums to produce each pound of prunes.

☞ The state of California produces more than 70 percent of the world's prunes. Almost all the rest come from France.

☞ Some researchers believe prunes are such an efficient laxative because they contain a substance — similar to an ingredient in most over-the-counter laxatives — that induces intestinal contractions.

PUMPKINS

NO FAIRY GODMOTHERS NEEDED HERE

Howard Dill is the grand master of the pumpkin, regularly beating out competitors at growing the world's largest pumpkin. He's even patented his giant pumpkin seeds, called Atlantic Giant hybrid, and penned his autobiography, *The Pumpkin King*. For his contributions to the sport of giant pumpkin growing, Dill, who lives in Windsor, Nova Scotia, has won a spot in the World Pumpkin Confederation's hall of fame.

The first champion grower was William Warnock, of Ontario, Canada, who entered a 400-pound pumpkin at the Paris World's Fair in 1900. Since then, pumpkins have hit the 800-pound mark, some bruisers putting on 10 to 15 pounds a day. (When Howard Dill sent a 616-pound pumpkin to the United States for a competition, customs officials, skeptical that such a large crate could contain one pumpkin, called the drug squad.)

For Dill, winning competitions brings more substantial rewards as well. For his world championship pumpkin in 1992 he received $11,500 from a California restaurant that wanted to display the squash, and $3,000 from the World Pumpkin Confederation. The confederation, located in Collins, New York, boasts 3,000 members in some 30 countries, including Japan, Australia, and Zimbabwe. Quite simply, editorialized the pumpkin growers' journal, *Esprit de Corps,* "Howard is part and parcel of our *raison d'être.*"

Keep the Seeds!

Remove any fibers from the fresh seeds and spread them on a baking sheet to dry overnight. Toss with 1 tablespoon of olive oil and bake at 350 degrees F., stirring occasionally, until they are golden brown, between 15 and 20 minutes. Pat with paper towels, sprinkle with salt, or with curry, chili powder, or grated Parmesan cheese — and munch away.

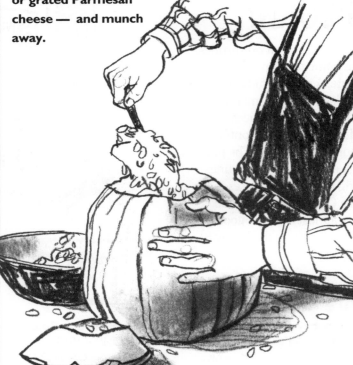

Pumpkin-Walnut
Muffins
Makes 12 muffins

**2 cups flour
³/₄ cup light brown sugar
2 teaspoons baking powder
¹/₂ teaspoon salt
¹/₄ teaspoon baking soda
1¹/₂ teaspoons pumpkin-pie spice, or mixed cinnamon, ginger, nutmeg, and cloves
1 cup unsweetened pumpkin puree
4 tablespoons butter, melted and cooled
2 eggs
¹/₄ cup buttermilk
2 teaspoons vanilla extract
¹/₂ cup plus 2 tablespoons coarsely chopped walnuts or green pumpkin seeds**

Preheat the oven to 350 degrees F. Butter 12 muffin cups.

Sift the flour, brown sugar, baking powder, salt, baking soda, and spice into a large bowl. In another bowl, whisk the pumpkin puree, melted butter, eggs, buttermilk, and vanilla.

Make a well in the center of the dry ingredients and stir in the pumpkin mixture until just combined. Stir in the ½ cup nuts or seeds. Spoon the batter into the prepared cups, filling them three-quarters full. Sprinkle with the remaining 2 tablespoons nuts.

Bake for 18 to 20 minutes, or until the muffins spring back when pressed with a finger.

Did You Know?

☞ The word "pumpkin" is probably derived from the Greek *pepon,* meaning "cooked by the sun."

☞ Pumpkins are actually fruits — melons — one of the largest in the gourd family.

☞ Of all canned fruits and vegetables, pumpkin is the best source of vitamin A: a half cup has more than three times the daily U.S. recommended daily requirement.

☞ If you run out of pumpkin, other winter squashes such as acorn, butternut, or Hubbard, can pinch-hit.

Books

Pumpkin Cookbook
Richard L. Gilberg; Gilmar Press, 1983; $6.95

Pumpkin, Pumpkin! Lore, History, Outlandish Facts & Good Eating
Anne MacCallum; Heather, 1986; $8.95

The Best of the Pumpkin Recipes
Helen O. Dandar and Emil P. Dandar; Sterling Specialty, 1989; $7.95

The Great Pumpkin Cookbook
Norma S. Upson; Maverick, 1984; $6.95

MORE INFORMATION

International Pumpkin Association
2155 Union Street
San Francisco, CA 94123
415-346-4446

World Pumpkin Confederation
14050 Route 62
Collins, NY 14034
716-532-5995

RASPBERRIES ❖ RESTAURANTS ❖ RICE ❖ ROBOTS ❖

ROOT VEGETABLES

RASPBERRIES

The juice of the Raspberry is exceedingly luscious, and possesses a peculiarly rich aroma, for which reason it is much used by cooks, confectioners, and the manufacturers of liqueurs.

— *The Encyclopaedia of Practical Cookery, 1890s*

A PASSION FOR RASPBERRIES

There are more than 200 species of raspberries in the world, and they are popular wherever they grow because of their intense flavor, which no other berry can match. Pliny praised them 2,000 years ago, and Martin Van Buren, campaigning for the presidency in 1840, was said by his opponents to "wallow in raspberries," which they regarded as a shocking extravagance. In our own day, raspberries are turning up everywhere, as salad ingredients as well as in vinegars used to dress them, and on just about every dessert menu, usually in company with chocolate — although the very best way of eating truly fresh raspberries is quite plain, with cream, and perhaps a hint of sugar.

Thanks to the marvels of air travel and controlled-climate packaging, raspberries' availability is no longer limited to their two brief domestic seasons at the beginning and end of summer; berries are imported from as far away as Chile and New Zealand, countries whose summer is the U.S. winter.

The major U.S. berry-growing area is the Pacific Northwest, notably the Willamette Valley of Oregon, but varieties of raspberry are raised in fruit farms nationwide, as well as in countless backyards. Raspberries grow wild in the woods, too, wherever there are sunny patches to bring forth the soft, ruby-red treasures sheltering beneath the canes' green leaves.

From Snow White to Rose Red

If legend is to be believed, in the days when the gods were young, all raspberries were white. Then one day when Zeus was a baby, "making the mountains echo with the sound of his cries," the nymph Ida went searching for berries to soothe him. She scratched herself on the thorns of the raspberry bush, and since that time raspberries have been tinged with her blood.

And that is why the botanical name for raspberry is Rubus idaeus; rubus *means "red" and* idaeus, *"belonging to Ida."*

Pros and Cons

Raspberry virtues: Great taste, a good source of vitamin C, and only 30 calories in ¹/₂ cup of berries.

Raspberry failings: Seeds get between the teeth, berries are soft and spoil easily.

TIPS

Buying
Fresh raspberries deteriorate rapidly, despite careful packing and climate control. Be sure the berries are plump, dark red, and well mounded in the package; check its bottom, too, and if there are any stains, don't buy it!

Storing
If you can't use raspberries right away, freeze them in a single layer on a cookie sheet, then pour the frozen berries into a plastic bag, and store in the freezer to brighten future recipes. Or make jam with the berries (and strain out the seeds before bottling).

Books

Berries: A Country Garden Cookbook
Sharon Kramis; Collins Publishers, 1994; $19.95

Remarkable Red Raspberry Recipes
Sibyl Kile; BCG Ltd., 1985; $7.95

Very Special Raspberry Cookbook
Very Special Raspberry Cookbook Committee; Jumbo Jack's Cookbooks, 1993; $15.00

MORE INFORMATION

Oregon Caneberry Commission
247 Commercial Street NE
Salem, OR 97301
503-399-8456

MAIL ORDER SOURCES

Maury Island Farm
Route 3, Box 238
Vashon, WA 98070
800-356-5880

Trader Joe's
P.O. Box 3270
South Pasadena, CA 91030
818-568-9254

RESTAURANTS

WHITE TABLECLOTHS IN THE '90S

In the dark days before decaffeinated espresso, when chefs were cooks and waiters were called "waiter," dinner out was an important occasion. Today, meals eaten away from home are more commonplace, although dinner in a fine (expensive) restaurant is still a treat. We expect a high degree of value and service — though these words mean different things to different people.

For some, perfection means an elegant room with an ambiance of sophistication and luxe. The tables are far apart and at just the right height for your elbows. The flowers are extravagant. The linens are crisp, the crystal sparkles, and the gleaming silver is heavy in your hand. The lighting is warm, soft, and flattering. The movement in the room flows evenly, as if an unseen hand were conducting the orchestra. There is a feeling of being in the right place, what someone has called "a hushed perception of rich people quietly eating meat." The waiters know instinctively when and how to wait. The food is consistent and the only surprises are enchanting, and infinitely pleasurable.

These restaurants are temples to traditional elegance, and their admirers adore them.

Others are made uneasy.

These others prefer a place where the noise level is equal to that of an indoor swimming pool. Waiters are pals. Plates are as big as bicycle wheels. Ribs drip sweet brown sauce, the baked potatoes are huge, oozing butter *and* sour cream. Enormous burgers come with the works — toasted bun, thick slice of tomato, crisp bacon, melting cheese, fries, sliver of pickle, lettuce, ketchup, mustard, ridged potato chips. There's a monster red lobster on a white oval dish with lemon wedges, a bib, and a big, wet beer. An immense piece of broiled fish wears brown fins, and there are as many shrimp as you can eat. There's crisp Southern-fried chicken in a basket, with plastic portions of honey and pats of margarine tucked into the fries. There's plump roast chicken with mounds of mashed potatoes, and breads and cornbreads and corn sticks and muffins, and salads with a choice of dressing. You select from the salad bar and won't even have finished your salad before the food arrives, and you have to lean across the table because in the din you can't hear the waiter's "Who gets the steak?"

All the food is crowded together and the table is wobbling until someone puts a matchbook under one leg. There is one second's pause, one all-enveloping happy smile around the table, and then . . . all set for the good-time crowd on Saturday night. Yo!

Everything OK, folks?

Relishing one kind of restaurant doesn't for a minute mean you can't enjoy the other. Good eating is what it's all about.

> *Restaurants want to be judged on their intentions — not the results.*
>
> — Mimi Sheraton
> Restaurant critic

Q&A

Q Why do chefs wear those pouffy hats?

A When kings went around in deathly fear of being poisoned by their cooks, it was of vital importance that the food be prepared by a trusted member of the royal household. When the chef had proved his worth, a *toque blanche* was placed on his head. Its pleats represent the vertical bars of the monarch's golden crown. Legend says the tall hat was originally designed to keep the head cool, but modern cooks say this explanation is just a lot of hot air.

Dial A Dinner

Good evening.

If you wish to receive a fax of the menu, press 1, followed by your seven-digit fax number preceded by the area code.

If you wish to place your order in advance, press 2, followed by the number of guests and the telephone numbers of two references.

If you wish to receive a nutrition analysis of your order, press 3, followed by the date of your birth and your most recent blood pressure and cholesterol reading.

If you wish to receive a video of the kitchen or the dining room, press 4.

If you wish to be seated next to the window, press 5.

If you wish to be seated before or after 8 p.m., press 6.

If you wish to make a reservation, press 7, followed by your credit card number and the date of expiration.

Sorry, the restaurant is full this evening. If you would like to make a reservation for another evening, press 8.

Good evening. If you wish to receive a fax …

RESTAURANT HIERARCHY

The maitre d' (pronounced "mater dee" — an abbreviation for *maître d'hôtel*, which freely translates into master of the universe) decides the seating arrangements, sometimes dotting the room with decorative guests, sometimes finding a table where previously none was to be had, occasionally warning a newly arriving guest of the presence of an ex-spouse. A salaried member of the staff, he expects to be tipped only if he has performed extraordinary service.

The captain is the supervisor of the staff. There may be several captains in a large dining room and to them falls the minute-by-minute decision-making and the writing of the food order. The captain may expect, though usually in vain, to receive 5 percent of the before-tax check.

The sommelier is becoming one of an endangered species. His role is to recommend a wine or wines appropriate to the food that has been selected by the guests. Usually the sommelier will be knowledgeable, helpful, and not apt to choose the most expensive wine on the list. His tip is traditionally 10 percent of the cost of the wine. (But if it is

an $18 bottle, we wouldn't suggest counting out $1.80 and slipping it to him in cupped hand behind your back.) If you bring your own bottle to a restaurant that has a wine list, you can anticipate paying a corkage fee of up to $10.

The busboy sets and clears the table. He will not be able to answer your question concerning the toughness of the meat nor provide you with a satisfactory explanation of why your fish is overcooked. Neither is he authorized to make adjustments to the check. So don't ask. To spare embarrassment, complaints should be taken up with the captain or maitre d' away from the table. A well-modulated voice should be employed and hands kept in a nonthreatening position.

The chef is not part of the hierarchy; rather, he or she is the star of the show, and these days often its owner as well. Even the most distinguished chef, however, should be willing to prepare a simple dish for a guest who is feeling under the weather, or has a dietary need. Good chefs are measured by their ability to prepare a stunning array of steamed vegetables without salt or butter, and to readily accommodate guests' whims and needs. Celebrities ask for such odd things: Andy Warhol studied the menu at one of the nation's finest restaurants, then ordered a cookie; another famous person routinely arrived at his favorite restaurant bringing his own tunafish sandwich.

Based on reporting by Bryan Miller
for *The New York Times*

Given the choice, most people would prefer to dine with an inspired companion than to dine on inspired food.

— Anonymous

The Role of the Waiter

A lot of people think of waiters as temporary, transient folk, working in a restaurant until they get a more desirable job (except at the top restaurants, where the professional staff may have been working for decades). But as restaurants (and schools for waiters) proliferate, the social status of waiters may change, just as the role of the chef has.

Basically, waiting is not compatible with the American view of democracy.

Service, it has been said, is given and accepted more comfortably at a gas station than in a restaurant, where the role of the guest in relation to the waiter is uncertain and the prestige of waitresses is even more

ambiguous. Recently, a cocktail waitress struck a blow for equality when she filed a sexual discrimination suit against a restaurant that allowed a waiter to wear comfortable loafers while she was required to lower her neckline, raise her hemline, and totter about all evening on five-inch heels.

Part of the problem lies with the job description. Waiters and waitresses are both pressing to make their occupation unisex; everyone would be called waiters just as dancers are called dancers and writers are writers and mailmen are known as letter carriers. (One wit suggested we should acknowledge that anyone who brings food and takes it away again is really called a Mommy!)

Every now and again there is anguished talk about elevating the public's perception of waiters by putting them on salary, giving them benefits, and entitling them to paid vacations, just like everybody else. Sensible as this proposal seems on the surface, it continues to face implacable opposition. Management says that if the extra costs were added to the check at the end of the meal, the public would be shocked at the total. Besides, giving tips makes patrons feel in charge and gives them the option of bestowing or withholding a gratuity based on the perceived quality of the service rendered. So ingrained is this master-slave view of things that no big changes can be expected anytime soon.

Many waiters don't want to upset the apple cart either. Though the base pay

". . . and now I'd like to sing you a song about our specials for the evening."

hourly may be around $2.60 — half the standard minimum wage — a skilled waiter can earn astonishingly large tips in a successful restaurant (up to $80,000 a year in top New York restaurants). He can increase his take-home pay, too, by suggesting that the host may want to order mineral water "for the table" (if he refuses, he looks cheap). He can artfully and archly persuade at least three of the four guests to have the "unbelievable" dessert he was lucky enough to have sampled in the kitchen only moments ago, or propose another cappuccino all round — and perhaps an after-dinner drink? "Right away, Mr. Jones." (Chortle, chortle.)

There is nothing wrong with this, mind you. A good waiter deserves every penny he can hustle, for he can make or break the evening. Far more people return or fail to return to a restaurant on the basis of the service than of the quality of the food.

A waiter who understands the rules of service doesn't remove one person's plate while others are still eating, or intrude when guests are deep in conversation. He remembers to give a gracious goodbye instead of a cold shoulder after the account has been settled, knowing that a good (high-tipping) guest will ask for him to serve his table on his next visit. Though in many restaurants tips are pooled and shared, a well-satisfied customer may reward outstanding service with a crisp bank note indicating "This is just for you."

The Role of the Critic

Restaurant critics must learn to live in an atmosphere that mixes groveling, cringing fear with hostile loathing. Being liked is not part of the job. Honesty is. Lately, though, there have been fewer poisonous reviews and markedly less inclination to go out of the way to decimate a restaurant with a hail of contemptuous comments. More reviewers are concentrating on seeking out the best restaurants and ignoring those they don't like. It is rare to see a critic frankly deploring the lamentable.

When critics do go out on a limb, though, the First Amendment guarantees their right to express an opinion, and there is not much an aggrieved restaurant owner can do about it. Given a choice, however, he would probably prefer a hatchet to a lawsuit.

Restaurant critics are powerful people and *The New York Times* reportedly pays its influential critic $120,000 a year, plus an expense account that may come close to this figure. So it is not surprising that the restaurant world watches the appointment of new critics with a certain trepidation, wondering how they will use or abuse their power.

The Role of the
Guest

Just as guests expect, indeed demand, a level of professionalism on the part of a restaurant, they, too, have clear responsibilities. The most basic one is to honor a reservation. A reservation is a contract that, if broken, results in loss of income not only for the restaurant but for the staff who are cheated out of their earnings.

The no-show problem is a mounting one, with a startling number of callers who fail to notify the reservations desk of a change of plans. Newly arriving guests are often angered at being turned away when they can clearly see empty tables. The idea of charging the anticipated average check and tip to the credit card of a patron who has failed to appear has often been discussed, but few restaurants are willing to offend even a rude customer.

The worst kind of guests are those who change their minds after the drinks order has gone to the bar, or the order for food to the kitchen. The indecisive holdout's order has to be handled separately, meaning that the waiter has to get on line a second time.

Annoying as this is on a frantically busy evening, a bigger problem is the guest who returns his dinner. Not that he shouldn't if there is a problem, but when it is for a frivolous reason, it disturbs the rhythm of the meal entirely and creates an awkward situation for everyone. Others at the table don't know whether to allow their food to cool until everyone is served, or to start — and probably finish their food while the complainer chomps glumly on. Conversation becomes focused on the food in all the wrong ways and no matter how well the meal started out, it will leave a bad taste. A dissatisfied customer will tell 20 others about his lousy experience, and the ripples will spread, causing unfavorable and often unwarranted bad publicity. If there is genuine cause to complain, however, it will probably get an immediate response if the unhappy diner writes a letter to the owner, calmly stating the facts.

Finally, there is the thoughtless behavior of guests who either argue at the table or, worse, fall in love on the banquette. Hand clasped on hand, they linger on into the night gazing longingly at each other, oblivious of the waiting staff who yearn only to go home.

Actual Selections From Menus and Specials Boards Found in Manhattan

Cream cheese and ox

Breast sandwich

Tuna Nickwash

Sauteed couch

Angel-hair pasta with wild mushrooms, sun-dried tomatoes and basil. After five years, as great as ever...

Fish curry: Fish marinated in intricately blended spices in the Stone Age

Grilled fresh tuna served with soap

Olive leaf on roll

Fluffy balls of milksolids in syrup

Sodas by Coke and Pepsi

Ask waiter for availability

Compiled by Henry Alford for *The New York Times Magazine*

The Role of the Proprietor

A well-known restaurateur has asked that the following words be written on his tombstone: "This is the only stone I left unturned."

A typical restaurant owner does everything possible to ensure that his guests have a lovely time. He is at his post every night. From the moment he arrives, often early in the morning, until the moment he leaves, often early the next morning, he will know what is going on in the kitchen, in the dining room, in the refrigerator, and on the stove. He opens the door and knows immediately whether the temperature of the room is within a degree or two of the comfort zone. He knows if the soup needs more salt. He knows who is expected and whose name to star to ensure they get the best table, which does not always mean the one with the best view but the one that is served by the most skilled wait staff. He smiles on his favorite guests and most frequent visitors and extends a cordial welcome to new ones. He dispenses favors like a bee hovering in a field of flowers, distributing pollen to the most exotic blooms and saving the sting for the youngest waiter.

Over the years it has become customary for the owner or chef/*patron* to leave his kitchen or his counting house and chat with the guests. Bryan Miller, the now-retired *New York Times* restaurant critic, compared the passage of one owner on such a mission with that of "a prowling long-tailed cat in a roomful of rocking chairs." No matter what the style, the guests seem, for the most part, to welcome a nod from such a grand personage. Some diners feel quite slighted if the restaurateur/chef whom they saw on the TV just the other night doesn't come and lean his hand on the back of their chair for even a fleeting moment.

This urge to roam around the room is unique to restaurants. You certainly don't expect the manager of your local bank to wander about among his depositors asking if they are enjoying all the nice new bills his tellers have dispensed, nor will he offer to reveal how they were made. The restaurateur shoulders the responsibility for all aspects of the operation and if something has gone the teensiest little bit wrong, all but the most shortsighted will turn cartwheels to soothe even the most demanding (and inebriated) guests. A long wait for a table will often be mollified by complimentary drinks or appetizers, and an inconvenience caused by the restaurant or its staff may be recompensed with a deluge of desserts.

Joe Baum

It is impossible to talk about restaurants without mentioning Joe Baum. Craig Claiborne called him the restaurateur of the century and the praise is well deserved because everyone who dines out in America feels the influence of his ideas. He was the first to bring art and architecture into restaurants, working with such luminaries as I. M. Pei and Philip Johnson. He was the first to bring distinctive signature plates and menus to the table, employing a distinguished graphic designer to produce them. Baum restaurant tableware designs are now on permanent exhibit at the Museum of Modern Art. He employed a theatrical costume designer to create staff "uniforms" that suited their various occupations (and he also introduced the idea of "name" waiters). He was unique in creating theme restaurants: La Fonda del Sol, The Tower Suite, The Forum of the Twelve Caesars, Zum Zum. . . . And he was the first restaurateur to formally institute seasonal foods, contracting with farmers to grow specific crops for his restaurants. When he created The Four Seasons, he brought to America its first "world class" restaurant, which became the inspiration for our own distinctive American cuisine. His legendary attention to detail resulted not only in changing the menu and the foliage with the season, but even the colors of the ribbons in the typewriters. His restaurants, particularly Windows on the World and The Big Kitchen in the World Trade Center, boosted the economy in the parts of the city where they were located.

All his skills were assembled when he undertook the historical renovation of the legendary Rainbow Room, faithfully reproducing in exquisite detail the splendor of one of the best loved and longest operating restaurants in the country.

Many have called Joe Baum a genius.

"I'm not a genius," he responds.

This is one of the few things he is wrong about.

"The porridge looks good."

Let Me Count The Ways

Money magazine ranked the country's 15 finest eating-out cities of 1993 as follows:

1.
New York

2.
San Francisco

3.
Los Angeles

4.
Chicago

5.
Washington, D.C.

6.
New Orleans

7.
Miami

8.
Seattle

9.
Boston

10.
Houston

11.
Philadelphia

12.
Phoenix

13.
Atlanta

14.
Santa Fe

15.
Dallas

MORE INFORMATION

National Restaurant Association
1200 17th Street NW
Washington, DC 20036
202-331-5900

The Art and Craft of the Menu

Before the menu is replaced by a computer printout, let us trace its origins. The first menu we know of was written on a Sumerian clay tablet that dates to about 3000 B.C. It listed in cuneiform a proper meal for the gods. A scholarly writer tells us: "Tradition has it that the modern menu was devised by the Duke of Brunswick in 1541 to give his friends a choice among the dishes his chef could prepare but another, earlier version of the menu served an entirely different purpose. It was not a menu in the sense of a bill of fare at all, but a set of instructions for the kitchen staff of a royal or princely household and also a rendering of accounts to the chamberlain. The menu, or *escrieau*, as it was known in old French, told the staff the order in which various courses were to be served. The cost of buying foodstuffs was also indicated on the menu for the convenience of the chamberlain."

The menu as used today serves two purposes. It indicates what food is available and notes the price.

Psychologist Diane Kochilas says, "If restaurants had windows into their souls they would likely be in the form of a menu." She also says that if you think you are making up your own mind about what it is you want to eat, think again. You may be manipulated into making a decision to spend more money than you intended.

It can cost anywhere from $2,000 to $25,000 to produce a menu that will be read for less than three minutes, so you can be sure the restaurant owner gives a lot of thought to the way the menu looks and the placement and description of the foods on the page.

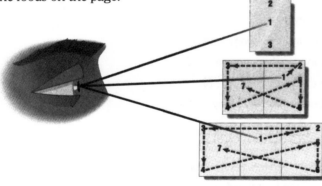

One of the ways to steer diners toward the dishes that produce the highest profits is a subtle technique known as motion. In theory, every menu has a "sweet spot" — the place where the eye falls first. An astute artist (or menu engineer) can lead the eye wherever desired.

On the classic magazine-style or two-fold menu, the dominant space is on the upper right-hand side. On one-page and three-page menus, the sweet spot is in the center. Conversely, if the owner wants to hide a popular but less profitable dish, the lower left is the place to put it. Other attention-getting techniques include boxing the item, underlining, circling or shading it, lengthening the description, and enlarging the type size — which can be done so subtly that it is only observed subliminally.

The best number for a dinner party is two — myself and a damn good head waiter.

— Nubar Gulbenkian
A not-so-easy-to-please guest

WHY EATING OUT IN NEW YORK COSTS $60 A PERSON EXCEPT WHEN IT COSTS EVEN MORE

JEFFREY STEINGARTEN

A celebrated chef explained it to me this way: Take an entree of Skate with Brown Butter. Fourteen ounces of skate costs $1.31 wholesale. The ingredients for the quart of nage in which it is poached cost $1.92. The sauce requires four ounces of butter ($.44), an ounce of capers ($.26), two ounces of fish stock ($.22), salt and pepper ($.04), and a half-ounce of vinegar ($.01). Total cost of these ingredients is $4.20, plus a 5 percent allowance for waste and spoilage, or $4.41.

The restaurant lists every dish at five times the cost of its ingredients to cover rent, labor, and interest on bank loans and yield a profit. *This is the key*. This is why what sells for $25 in a New York restaurant sells for $8 in the suburban Midwest, if you can find it. The customer is renting an extravagantly decorated 20 feet in Manhattan for two or three hours.

So the Skate with Brown Butter will be priced at $22. The cost of an appetizer, dessert, and coffee approximately equals that of the entree, say another $18. Half a modest $25 bottle of wine is $12.50; half a bottle of sparkling water is $2.

The total so far is $55.50. Tax adds $4.50, a 15 percent tip another $8.85. Grand total: $67.85.

And it all started with $1.31 worth of skate.

Excerpted from *Vogue*

"Here comes the first course ..."

Books

America Eats Out
John Mariani; Morrow, 1991; $25.00

The Restaurant Companion: A Guide to Healthier Eating Out
Hope S. Warshaw, R.D.; Surrey Books, 1990; $11.95

Zagat Restaurant Surveys (for major U.S. cities)
Zagat Surveys, annually; $9.95 (New York, $10.95)

PERIODICALS

For addresses, see also Information Sources

Food Arts
P.O. Box 7808
Riverton, NJ 08077
800-848-7113
10 times a year;
$30 per year

Restaurants & Institutions
Cahners Publishing
44 Cook Street
Denver, CO 80206
303-388-4511
Biweekly; $104.95 per year

Restaurant Business
355 Park Avenue South
New York, NY 10010
212-592-6262
18 times a year;
$79 per year;
free to trade

Restaurant Hospitality Magazine
Penton Publishing
Subscription Lock Box
P.O. Box 96732
Chicago, IL 60693
216-696-7000
Monthly; $60 per year

Restaurants USA
National Restaurant Association
800-424-5156
11 times a year;
$125 per year

RICE

THE REMARKABLE GRAIN

R ice is the staple food for more than half the world's population, and consumption is booming in the United States. We now eat close to 21 pounds of rice a year, more than double what we ate just a few years ago. There has also been a huge increase in multicultural immigration in the same period, so the figures may be deceptive. It could be that some of us are eating far more and others considerably less than the calculated average. Our bowls are relatively empty, though, in comparison with those of Asians, who eat as much as 300 pounds of rice per person per year. But as we are coaxed, prodded, and nagged to eat healthier diets, the prognosticators are predicting a rise in rice consumption that will parallel our passion for pasta.

Rice is just about as healthy as any single food can be. It is rich in complex carbohydrates, low in fat, and packed with vitamins, minerals, amino acids, and fiber — and it's inexpensive, too.

Whenever I am homesick for Japan, I have to have rice. If I don't have rice for a whole week, I have a terrible desire for it, even just plain rice on its own.

— Takani Yao
Expatriate in New York City

A Roster of Rices

Long grain rice is four to five times as long as it is wide. When cooked, the grains tend to stay separate and are light and fluffy. It is a good all-purpose rice and recommended for use in curries, pilafs, and paella.

Medium grain rice is plump but not round. When cooked, the grains are moister and more tender than long grain.

Short grain rice is almost round in shape. The grains are softer than the medium or long grain and tend to stick together when cooked; for this reason this variety is good for sushi and rice pudding.

Arborio rice from Italy's Po Valley is a superior variety used for making risotto. It is a short, shiny, pearly-smooth grain that gradually absorbs hot broth when patiently stirred for 45 minutes.

Basmati rice is one of the fragrant, aromatic rices from India and Pakistan. It is now grown in Texas and is gaining converts every day. Its long, tender grains and distinctively nutty taste make it the rice of choice for curries and pilafs.

Spanish rice, a medium grain rice grown in Valencia, is the one to select for paella.

Brown rice is the unpolished grain and retains its valuable bran. A storehouse of good nutrition, it contains both soluble and insoluble fiber and vitamin E, which is believed to strengthen the immune system. Brown rice takes longer to cook than white, but its dense, nutty flavor is worth the wait. Some quick-cooking forms are now available.

Converted (parboiled) rice has been steamed and dried prior to removal of the hull and bran. The result is a fluffy rice, with grains that do not stick together, but during the conversion and washing nutrients are lost and must be replaced.

Instant rice is precooked and dried. The grains are cracked to allow the water to enter so that they cook almost instantly, which is why the taste is disappointing. However, it is predictable, which in times of uncertainty is certainly something.

Wild rice is not rice at all; it is a marsh grass.

Breakfast Competition

W hen the Quaker Oats Company made their rice cakes taste like buttered popcorn, sales soared to more than $100 million a year. With a thin spread of whipped cream cheese and a touch of preserves, a rice cake (or two) makes a great-tasting nutritious breakfast. Move over, oatmeal!

Did You Know?

☞ Fifty percent of all the world's rice is eaten within eight miles of where it is grown.

☞ Rice should *never* be rinsed before cooking. When the starch is released too quickly, the grains will not thicken.

☞ White rice has such a low fiber content that it takes only an hour to digest. (Most foods require two to four hours.)

☞ Archaeologists have traced the cultivation of rice back at least 5,000 years. Rice, millet, and sorghum are thought to be the first crops ever cultivated.

☞ A common Chinese greeting translates as "Have you eaten rice yet?"

☞ More than 1 billion people throughout the world are actively involved in growing rice.

☞ Seventy-one percent of the U.S. rice crop is long grain, 27 percent is medium grain, and only 2.5 percent is short grain.

Books

Quick and Natural Rice Dishes
Editors; Natural Health Books, 1992; $8.95

Rice: A Food For All Seasons
H. D. Akins and Ellen F. Lew; H. D. Akins, 1989; $10.00

Rice: The Amazing Grain
Marie Simmons; Henry Holt, 1991; $24.95

Risotto
Judith Barrett and Norma Wasserman; Macmillan, 1989; $12.95

The Carolina Rice Kitchen: The African Connection
Karen Hess; University of South Carolina Press, 1992; $24.95

What We Miss

Rice bran is the outer layer of the grain that lies directly beneath the hull. It is removed during milling. Rich in protein, fiber, minerals, and B vitamins, the bran is used to manufacture vitamin concentrates and rice oil, a high-grade cooking oil. Rice oil contains orysanol, a fatty acid-free lipid that is thought to block the production of LDL cholesterol. Claims have been made that it is twice as effective as other vegetable oils in lowering cholesterol.

MORE INFORMATION

U.S.A. Rice Council
P.O. Box 740123
Houston, TX 77274
713-270-6699

HOTLINES

800-421-2444
Rice-A-Roni
(for rice recipes)

ROBOTS

MECHANICAL SLAVES

For hundreds of years, visionaries anticipated a technological zenith when robots would work tirelessly on all the dreariest chores, and human beings would go into virtual retirement from physical tasks. Computers have shortened and lightened our tasks in ways both obvious and indirect. R2D2s, though not yet physically present in American homes and businesses, are not far off. But the idea of robotics threatens us as much as it excites us — fear of being eliminated, perhaps. Here's a very short list of the state of the art, as it now exists out there on the edge of tomorrow, or nearer.

The Pizzabot
A new robot powered by a Macintosh computer can make pizzas by voice command. It sits behind a semicircular workstation within reach of bins of food ingredients and does everything but retrieve the pizza from the oven.

Robo-Vision
"Washdown" robots can identify types of products via a "vision system," transfer a product to bulk shipping boxes or individual shipping trays, and are capable of moving 60 to 90 products a minute. They currently handle preformed hamburger patties, lunch meats, and "uniform" meats processed by slicing machines.

Soda Jerk
PepsiCo, which owns KFC, Pizza Hut, and Taco Bell, has developed a prototype for a new automated beverage dispenser that will drop a cup, fill it with ice and soda, and put a lid on it. A conveyor belt moves the drink to the customer. Time elapsed: 15 seconds.

The Vittleveyor
Arby's has been experimenting with a conveyor-belt system that serves multiple drive-through lanes. The customer places an order at a drive-through microphone, then pulls into a stall, puts money in a capsule, and shoots the capsule into the restaurant via conveyor belt. A clerk sends the food and change back the same way.

Robotic Bun Filler
A Burger King test unit has designed a robot to perform jobs currently done by high-school kids. This prototype can put burgers on buns at the rate of three a minute.

Automated Cake Decorator
Dressel's Bakeries Inc., in Chicago, is trying this device, which is guided by software smart enough to make it write "Happy Birthday" in frosting. Unlike human cake decorators, the robot doesn't get carpal tunnel syndrome.

Robo-Moo
A Dutch machinery company has developed a cow-milking robot. The robotic system "knows" the cow and adjusts the milking device to her teats; when it senses milk has ceased to flow it detaches the device for automatic cleaning.

Laser Peeler
H. J. Heinz has developed a potato peeler that employs three 25-watt lasers to zap off potato skins at a rate of one per second. Price of the lasers: $1 million each.

MORE INFORMATION

Robotic Industries Association
P.O. Box 3724
900 Victors Way
Ann Arbor, MI 48106
313-994-6088

Robotics International of the Society of Manufacturing Engineers
P.O. Box 930
1 SME Drive
Dearborn, MI 48121
313-271-1500

PERIODICALS

Advanced Manufacturing
Center for Robotics and Manufacturing Systems (CRMS)
College of Engineering
University of Kentucky
Lexington, KY 40506-0108
606-257-6262
Bimonthly; free

The moment [this business] tilts too far toward automation, the human spirit that sparks food service would be severely and sadly damaged.

—Charles Bernstein
Consulting editor, *Restaurants & Institutions*

ROOT VEGETABLES

When we talk about returning to our roots, we don't necessarily mean turnips.
— **Anonymous**

UNDERGROUND DELIGHTS

Jean Atcheson

In Paris, years ago, looking for lunch after a morning's sightseeing, I turned into a small restaurant in the Latin Quarter. When the menu was offered, I decided on a pork dish.

When it came, I was surprised to see, perched around the edge of the plate, a series of brilliantly colored cones — orange, yellow, green, white, red — each finished with a dexterous twirl at the top. Each was a pureed root vegetable — carrot, parsnip, potato with spinach for color, turnip, beet — seasoned simply yet subtly to reveal its own, uniquely different taste.

That meal with the jolly little hats, made with the humblest vegetables from underground, was one of life's great moments.

Back to the **Roots**

Root vegetables, traditionally associated with winter, are now in the spotlight year-round. Beets, carrots, celeriac, and potatoes have entries elsewhere; also popular are:

Jerusalem artichokes (sunchokes) — These are not artichokes but tubers of a kind of sunflower which the Italians call **girasole**, hence the name "Jerusalem." A good source of iron, they can be eaten raw, boiled, steamed, or made into soup or gluten-free flour.

Parsnips — Medieval folk believed parsnips to be an aphrodisiac, but in fact they contain mostly soluble fiber, potassium, and other micronutrients, and only about 100 calories per cup.

Radishes — Admired by the Pharaohs and a popular snack food in ancient Rome, radishes today are used more for their color and crispness than for any nutritive value.

Turnips — A common food in classical Greece and Rome, and revived in 16th-century French stews, the turnip's keeping qualities soon established it throughout northern Europe. The tops, a popular soul food, are a good source of vitamins A and C.

Books

Essential Root Vegetable Cookbook
Sally and Martin Stone; Clarkson Potter, 1991; $22.50

Roots: The Underground Cookbook
Barbara Grunes and Anne Elise Hunt; Chicago Review Press, 1993; $9.95

Suzanne Taylor's
Parsnip & Potato Casserole

Serves 4 to 6

4 medium-sized potatoes
4 medium-sized young parsnips
3 tablespoons milk
2 tablespoons sherry or Madeira
3 tablespoons unsalted butter
2 eggs, separated
¹/₂ teaspoon freshly grated nutmeg
Salt and pepper to taste
Dry breadcrumbs for topping
Chopped parsley or watercress sprigs for garnish

Preheat the oven to 375 degrees F. Lightly butter a baking dish.

Scrub, but do not peel the potatoes. Boil them in salted water until soft. Boil the parsnips until soft but not mushy. Peel the potatoes and parsnips and force them through a ricer or a food mill into a bowl. Add the milk, sherry or Madeira, 2 tablespoons of butter, the egg yolks, nutmeg, salt, and pepper, and stir all together to blend well. Adjust the seasoning to taste.

Whip the egg whites until they hold peaks, and fold them gently into the mixture. Turn the mixture into the prepared dish, cover with breadcrumbs, and dot with the remaining butter. Bake in the preheated oven for 35 to 40 minutes, or until the breadcrumbs become golden. Garnish with chopped parsley or sprigs of watercress.

Reprinted from Cooking from a Country Kitchen

SALAD BARS

SALAD DAZE

Standing in front of a salad bar the length of a bowling alley, faced with a bewildering choice of items, leaves me utterly cold. I know that the bright green peas (newly defrosted), the yellow corn (recently uncanned), the green beans (hard and undercooked), the stiff, tasteless broccoli, the mayonnaise-drenched fake crab, and pallid potato salad will all taste the same.

Every now and again I check out a newly opened salad bar and find it is every bit as dreary as the last. Why is this so? Lack of salt is one reason. The long, chilly exposure to air trapped beneath the clear plastic sneeze-protective cover is another. The flavor has fled. The food is lifeless and boring.

I have a dreadful suspicion that an army of gnomes wearing rubber gloves has filled up all those trays and catapulted them to their destinations along an underground network of steel troughs.

Salad bars aren't cheap. They aren't particularly healthy. They certainly aren't satisfying. So why are they sprouting up everywhere? It's because they're fast, clean, safe, and convenient — as is indoor plumbing.

The Sprouting of Salad Bars

Serve-yourself salad bars probably started in the early 1970s (in Californian restaurants, of course), and their appeal was instantaneous. College campuses took them up at once — they cut down on service costs and hungry students could load up their own plates as high as they liked (with a couple of extra rolls or pieces of fruit for the pocket). In restaurants, they provided welcome distractions for children and conversational breaks for adults; for everyone, a chance to be greedy on the sly.

Then the health craze swept across the country, reinforcing the trend toward salad meals and adding an ever-increasing number of foods that happened to be in vogue, in season, or inexpensive. Now there are salad bars from coast to coast, in fast-food restaurants, supermarkets, malls, specialty stores, Korean groceries, and corner cafes. Their offerings are the 1990s version of the American melting pot — temperature a strict 30 degrees F., nutrition counts posted above the low-fat salads, no sulfites allowed, everything super hygienic, Japanese sushi right next to the Mexican taco salad, Chinese stir-fried vegetables and tortellini in pesto flanking the sliced kiwifruit. But if you spoon up a generous mouthful of what looked like guacamole beside the California rolls and it turns out to be *wasabe,* that exquisitely green Japanese horseradish, you may lose your cool.

Q&A

Q How can we be sure the foods displayed in salad bars are fresh?

A All salad bars, like delicatessens, restaurants, and shops offering take-out foods, must comply with sanitation standards imposed by the specific local health authority for the city or county concerned; they are inspected regularly.

Pacific Overtures

Say good-bye to Thousand Island and Roquefort. The salad dressings of tomorrow will borrow from other cultures — especially Asian — in their ingredients. But remember that although these may offer some new and different tastes, such as cilantro, fish sauce, ginger, lemon grass, and tamari, they tend to use oils, peanuts, and macadamia nuts with abandon. So hedge your bets when making dressings, marinades, or pasta sauces and concentrate on achieving flavor with as little fat as possible.

Trimming the Dressings

Mix Dijon mustard into balsamic vinegar for a fat-free topping. Or try rice vinegar with tamari sauce, honey, and chopped fresh ginger. Some salad lovers swear by the easiest one of all: spicy salsa as a salad dressing.

SALMON

SALMONBURGERS SIZZLE INTO THE MAINSTREAM

It is Monday morning along the Alaskan coast and a few hundred high rollers are setting out on one of the highest-risk jobs in the country. They are going fishing — commercial fishing. This endeavor is an entirely different kettle of fish from game fishing, which involves spiffy boats, jaunty caps, a lizard embroidered on the left breast, and a slightly more than adequate supply of beer. Commercial fishermen don't have much fun. They don't even wear matching socks, let alone color-coordinated slacks and shirts. They go to sea in terrible weather and battle moving ice packs, freezing water — and time. An average of 25 fishing boats capsize and sink every year. The death rate for commercial fishermen is seven times greater than in heavy industry.

So what are they doing out there? They're looking for canned salmon, in a manner of speaking. Their purpose is to catch as many pink salmon as possible in the shortest possible time.

Along the coast of Alaska and way up into the Bering Sea is where the salmon thrive. It is from this icy water, too, that the regal king salmon are troll-fished one by one, and, as soon as they are brought aboard, cleaned and glazed in a thin overcoat of ice. Lifted aboard hovering helicopters, they are transferred to jumbo jets and arrive within 48 hours on the tables of the finest restaurants in Los Angeles, New York, London, Paris, and Tokyo.

The demand for fresh, high-quality fish is expanding every day, and this leaves the fishermen who depended on the canneries for their income out in the cold. There were once 50 salmon canneries dotting the Columbia River. They are all gone now.

To counteract the anti-canning trend, the salmon-canning industry is trying to tout us onto new ways to use their product. Lately, their public relations people were proposing that we give up hamburgers and switch to salmonburgers served on sesame-seed buns.

Perhaps there is hope for canned salmon yet.

It's in the Can

Pink salmon, the kind that ends up in a can, is a good source of omega-3 fatty acids, and its soft bones are rich in calcium. Remove any large, hard bones, then use a fork to mash the remaining ones with the salmon for use in salads and casseroles, or turn into a food processor to puree for soups or sauces.

Did You Know?

☞ Radiocarbon dating of skeletons proves that cavemen were eating salmon 100 million years ago.

☞ Native American tribes in the Pacific Northwest made their staple food, pemmican, out of dried, ground-up salmon.

☞ The "juice" in canned salmon comes from the fish itself, whereas tuna has oil or water added in the canning process.

☞ Salmon will travel 3,000 miles to spawn. Some theorize that it is their sense of smell that brings them back to the precise spot where they hatched.

☞ Norway and Chile are the leading suppliers of farmed salmon.

Salmon Are Vanishing from the Pacific ...

The Wilderness Society has declared that nine out of ten species of Pacific salmon are in danger of extinction. Once, some 16 million salmon a year would enter the Columbia River from the Pacific Ocean, and swim quickly up to their spawning grounds far inland to reproduce and die, leaving their young to grow for a year or more in the fresh water before making their way downstream back to the sea. Eventually, they, too, would return to the river of their birth to repeat the process.

These days, barely a million fish make the perilous journey. Their habitat has fallen victim to the ravages of several forces. Extensive logging has devastated the hillsides; without trees to hold the soil along the river banks in place, the sediment has clogged the once pristine waters, depriving the fish of oxygen. Urbanization has resulted in contamination from sewage and has raised the temperature of the water. Industry has contributed to the pollution.

Most damaging of all has been the building of dams that harness the river's precious energy, slowing its current and along with it the progress of the young fish returning to the ocean. The most serious problem is created by the electricity-producing turbines. It is said that as many as 95 percent of all young salmon are trapped and killed in the churning machinery.

To preserve salmon stocks in the Columbia River Basin, the Pacific Fisheries Management Council in April 1994 banned all commercial and sport fishing for salmon from the coast west of Portland, Oregon, north to the Canadian border, save for a limited catch for Indian tribes in northwest Washington. No coho salmon may be caught commercially anywhere.

. . . And the Atlantic

Atlantic salmon were once so plentiful that they were used as fertilizer. Now they are almost fished out, and few commercial fishermen are able to reach even half their quota. In an effort to preserve wild salmon, Norway and Iceland bought out the Faroe Islands' salmon-fishing rights, compensating the fishermen for *not* fishing; this quickly increased the number and size of the fish in the North

Atlantic. Now other countries are joining forces to buy out Greenland's salmon-fishing quotas. They believe that the investment will eventually pay off. Meantime, the cost is considerably lower than that of stocking the area with hatchery-raised salmon.

Currently, almost 96 percent of the salmon sold in supermarkets is farm-raised.

MORE INFORMATION

Alaska Seafood Marketing Institute
1111 West Eighth Street, Suite 100
Juneau, AK 99801
907-586-2902

Atlantic Salmon Federation
P.O. Box 807
Calais, ME 04619-0807
506-529-4581

Pacific Salmon Commission
1155 Robson Street, Suite 600
Vancouver, BC V6E 1B5
Canada
604-684-8081

Books

James McNair's Salmon
James McNair; Chronicle Books, 1987; $11.95

Salmon Recipes
Cecilia Nibeck; AK Enterprises, 1987; $10.95

Simply Salmon
Linda Martinson; Lance Publications, 1988; $14.95

The Salmon Cookbook
Jerry Dennon; Globe Pequot, 1987; $8.95

The Salmon Cookbook
Tessa Hayward; Trafalgar Square, 1992; $29.95

SALMONELLA

WHAT IS SALMONELLA?

Food-borne intestinal illnesses range in severity all the way from a mild tummy upset to death. But they are unlikely to be terminal unless a person's health is already precarious. The several kinds of bacteria that cause food poisoning are detailed in the section on Food Safety, but we tend to be most concerned about *Salmonella enteritidis* bacteria, which produce salmonellosis, the most common infection. The Centers for Disease Control estimate that there are about 2 million cases of salmonellosis each year, with 1,000 to 2,000 illnesses proving fatal; 96 percent of the outbreaks are caused by contaminated food. Those at greatest risk are infants, the frail elderly, and people with impaired immune systems.

Trouble may appear any time from 12 to 36 hours after eating contaminated food with the onset of symptoms that include high fever, stomach cramps, vomiting, diarrhea, and dehydration. The problem rarely lasts long — two to four days — but it can be memorably unpleasant. A severe infection usually responds quickly to treatment with antibiotics.

Better Safe Than Sorry

Improper food handling accounts for 85 percent of salmonellosis outbreaks, so clearly the first line of defense is a hygiene attack — at home as well as in restaurants and institutional cafeterias. The danger of developing disease can be avoided almost totally by safe handling, careful cooking, and proper storage of all foods.

Keep your hands, working areas, and all utensils spotlessly clean. Use a separate cutting board for meats and poultry to avoid any danger of transferring bacteria from one food to another. Always wash all knives and boards with hot soapy water.

Use a thermometer to cook foods thoroughly and to the proper internal temperature. Keep hot foods hot (above 140 degrees F.) and cold foods cold (below 40 degrees F.). Serve foods containing milk, eggs, or meat at once; cover all foods properly and refrigerate leftovers.

ALERT

One bacterium kept in a moist environment at a temperature of 80 degrees F. will increase to 16 million in 8 hours. Flavor and odor give no indication of contamination, so never taste a suspect food. If in doubt, throw it out!

Salmonella Suspects

The Centers for Disease Control and Prevention tracked known sources of salmonellosis from 1973 to 1991. The breakdown:

Poultry	17.2 percent
Beef	9.5 percent
Pork	2.8 percent
Other meats	3.2 percent
Eggs	3.2 percent
Dairy foods	3 percent
Fruits and vegetables	2.4 percent
Seafood	0.9 percent
Other sources (Including food combinations)	57.8 percent

Altered Egos

Genetic engineers have conceived an oral vaccine developed from Salmonella *bacteria that holds promise as an easy and inexpensive method of birth control. Still in early research stages, such a vaccine could be used by men and women, and a single dose would last for several months.*

It works by altering part of the bacterium's genetic code so that instead of causing diarrhea, as it customarily does, it forms proteins that are almost identical to those of human sperm. The body mistakes these for dangerous invaders and creates a reservoir of antibodies, which coat the cells and block their activity. The antibodies go to work on the lookalike real sperm cells, trapping sperm inside and preventing them from fertilizing the egg.

The researchers hope this new technology may become a useful tool for limiting human and animal populations.

SALSA

Feel that happy, mouthfilling wow? Taste that gimme-some-more-of-that, boy-that's-great-flavor? That's salsa! That's musica for your mouth!

— Reed Hearon
Author of Salsa

Doctor Pepper
Prepares A Hot Pot

Chilies are the ingredient common to all salsas. Among those frequently used, in ascending order of fire, are ancho, poblano, Anaheim, serrano, jalapeño, and habañero.

Anything goes when it comes to salsa (the Spanish word for sauce). Uncooked salsa fresca mixes onions, garlic, tomatoes, chilies, cilantro, oil, and lime juice. It is designed for cold foods. Other salsas, made with onions, garlic, blistered and roasted peppers, and cooked tomatoes, turn up on everything from potatoes to eggs — even meat loaf. Another family of salsas is made with fruits: pineapples, mangoes, peaches, melons. There is even rumor of a tomatillo and white chocolate salsa waiting to surface; more traditional is salsa *mole*, a long-simmered sauce made with ground peanuts.

Each condiment in a salsa is a piquant counterpoint that adds a dash of brilliance to the main act on the plate. Well choreographed, a salsa can be as elegantly balanced as a C-major chord, with no one flavor dominant. Tastes range from tame and timid to incendiary, to fairly flamboyant, to powerful enough to strip paint.

Salsas are the Caribbean, Mexican, and South American counterpart of Indian chutneys and chowchows, Eastern European pickles, North American relishes, and Far Eastern ginger-mustard-soy sauce combinations. And we had best get used to them. Prognosticators say that Mexican foods — tacos and salsa — are about to overtake the popularity of pasta and pesto.

HOTHEADS TURN ON

Bland white Anglo-Saxon food has bitten the dust. Hot is what is haute now. With unaccustomed ardor we are embracing burning sauces that leave us with face flushing, eyes gushing, nose streaming, knees buckling, and breath coming in short pants.

In our youth we became accustomed to dips and chips as the traditional way to start the evening, but lately, serving blazing salsas at sunset seems to be the right way to go (with Margarita as a companion).

The tide turned when the demographics took a detour and mainstream snacks found themselves in the outfield. Waves of immigrants brought their fiery foods to the attention of a nation eager to find instant satisfaction without (undue) guilt.

Unscrew a jar lid and tear open a bag of tortilla chips. Who could ask for anything more?

Some Salsa Sobriquets

Cactus Salsa

Chipotle Cha Cha Cha

Coyote Cocina Fire-Roasted Salsa

Crazy Gringo

Desert Pepper Trading

Desert Rose Salsa

Green Mountain Gringo
(made in Chester, Vermont)

Hotlicks

Miguel's Stowe Away Salsa
(made in Stowe, Vermont)

Newman's Own Bandito Salsa

Shotgun Willie's Picante

Snakebite Salsa

ODD JOBS

Once a week, El Paso neighborhood women crush chipotle chilies for the El Paso Chile Company's Chipotle Cha Cha Cha salsa. They boil 100-pound batches of mesquite-smoked dried red Mexican jalapeños with water in big vats; then they cool, puree, and finally strain the contents through a giant strainer. On a hot day they can literally taste the fire in the air.

Skinny Dipping

Pace Thick & Chunky salsa contains only four calories, provided that you dunk only four corn chips. Even a realistic snack of four ounces of salsa has only about 50 calories (not counting the chips and beer, of course).

Books

The El Paso Chile Company's Burning Desires
W. Park Kerr; Morrow, 1994; $15.00

Salsa
P. J. Birosik; Collier Books, 1993; $13.00

Salsa
Reed Hearon; Chronicle Books, 1993; $12.95

Salsas, Sambals, Chutneys and Chowchows
Chris Schlesinger and John Willoughby; Morrow, 1993; $20.00

Salsas!
Andrea Chesman; Crossing Press, 1985; $8.95

MAIL ORDER SOURCES

D. L. Jardine's
P.O. Box 1530
Buda, TX 78610
800-544-1880

El Paso Chile Company
909 Texas Avenue,
Downtown
El Paso, TX 79901
800-27-IS-HOT

SalsaExpress
P.O. Box 3985
Albuquerque, NM 87190
800-43-SALSA

SALT

Salt is what makes things taste bad when it isn't in them.

— Anonymous

A FAIR SHAKE?

JEFFREY STEINGARTEN

The Yanomami Indians of northern Brazil have the most famous blood pressure in the world because it is the lowest. You can hardly read an article about blood pressure these days that doesn't drag in the Yanomamo Indians. I am amazed that the Yanomami can stay so calm surrounded by giant bugs, snakes, and investigators forever taking their blood pressure, which at last report averaged an amazingly low 95 over 61. . . . A fifth of all Americans are hypertensive, but none of the Yanomami are.

The Yanomami eat incredibly tiny amounts of salt, and we eat lots of it, which has led some doctors to imagine that eating salt causes hypertension. The Yanomami consume about 87 milligrams of salt a day, which occurs naturally in their food and equals two shakes from a standard saltshaker. Americans eat 12,000 milligrams of salt, about 266 shakes, a day. (The weight of an average shake has, to my knowledge, never before been published. To compute it, I loaded my saltshaker with 15 grams of salt, counted 330 shakes before it was empty, did it again for accuracy's sake and reached the same result, divided 330 shakes into 15 grams and arrived at 45 milligrams per shake.)

Does eating salt cause high blood pressure? Every human society with easy access to salt eats 40 times the minimum, and the reason is simple. Salt gives us pleasure by making food taste better. Then, after dinner, our bodies eliminate the salt we don't need. That is why God gave us kidneys. If salt caused high blood pressure, the average American would be hypertensive, which is not the case. I eat all the salt I want, and my blood pressure is slightly below normal. My wife's is even lower, and she eats what I do because I do all the cooking.

Excerpted from *Vogue*

Types of Salt

Table salt, which has small crystals, is used to enhance flavor in cooking and as a condiment. It usually contains additives to ensure that when it rains, it pours.

Iodized salt, which has had sodium iodide added, is particularly valuable in areas that lack natural iodine because it prevents hypothyroidism (goiter).

Kosher salt has larger crystals and gives food a brighter taste than table salt.

Sea salt is evaporated from seawater and formed into fine or large crystals, which retain more trace minerals than other salts that are mined and refined, and give foods a fillip.

Rock salt looks grayish because it is less refined than other salts. It is used in ice cream makers.

Q&A

Q What is the difference between salt and sodium?

A Sodium is a basic chemical element that occurs in nature in a large number of combinations, one of which is the crystalline form of sodium chloride (40 percent sodium, 60 percent chlorine) or *common salt* we cook with. Other sodium compounds are present naturally in foods and beverages or are added to them to alter consistency, enhance flavor, or aid in preservation. People on low-salt diets automatically reduce salt intake, but it is just as important to avoid eating processed or natural foods that are high in sodium.

Feeling Shaky?

The salt controversy rages on, though indications that sodium is a main culprit are diminishing. Researchers now think there is a link between hypertension and an imbalance of calcium.

We throw up our hands when we read seemingly conflicting information. An epidemiology study can point to high-risk factors for an entire population. But Asians, for example, eat large quantities of soy sauce, every tablespoon of which contains around 1,000 milligrams of sodium, without developing a marked degree of hypertension.

Many findings may prove irrelevant for healthy individuals. Nevertheless, when the American Heart Association recommends that sodium intake should not exceed 2,400 milligrams a day, it would seem wise to heed the warning.

Did You Know?

☞ All the salt we use comes originally from the sea, either from salt mines that excavate deposits laid down by long-dried-up seas in earlier eras, or from evaporating seawater.

☞ Salt is central to human life because it helps regulate the balance of bodily fluids and plays a role in muscle contractions — especially heart muscle — and the transmission of electrical nerve impulses.

☞ One tablespoon of table salt contains almost 2,000 milligrams of sodium.

Are Salt Cravings Calcium-Related?

The craving for salt has been discovered to indicate a calcium deficiency. In one study, rats that were fed a no-calcium diet increased their salt intake by 500 percent; in another, rats fed a low-calcium diet drank significant amounts of a salty solution when offered the choice along with sweet, sour, and bitter alternatives. The reason? Scientists think it may have something to do with the receptors in the liver that indicate salt satiation, which shut down when calcium levels drop; this might apply to similar receptors in the mouth. Although no official recommendations have emerged from the studies, says researcher Michael Tordoff, "The implication is that if people are like rats, consuming more calcium should reduce their desire for salt."

MORE INFORMATION

Salt Institute
Fairfax Plaza, Suite 600
700 North Fairfax
Alexandria, VA 22314-2040
703-549-4648

SANDWICHES

A CUT ABOVE THE REST

At a fund-raising luncheon in Omaha, former President George Bush finally articulated the vision thing:

"We need to keep America what a child once called 'the nearest thing to heaven.' And lots of sunshine, places to swim, and peanut butter sandwiches."

Right.

The trouble is that everyone has their own personal view of heaven and of what constitutes a good sandwich. For one person it is peanut butter with bacon, for another, peanut butter with a sliced banana is the best thing on earth. One fella says the greatest sandwich in the world is leftover turkey with dressing in the middle of the night; another yearns for Italian sausage, fried onions, and peppers on a hard roll.

The mile-high sandwiches Dagwood Bumstead heaped up, made with every blessed thing he could find in the refrigerator, are designed for good eats enjoyed in your undies at the kitchen table.

Neatly stacked turkey club sandwiches on toast or delicately sliced cucumbers on barely buttered, crustless white bread evoke visions of the ladies in hats and white gloves who used to meet for lunch at Schrafft's ("separate checks, please").

A two-fisted deli pound of corned beef on rye with a Dr. Brown's cream soda is another kind of experience, amplified by the bulbous sour pickles in a steel bowl beside the cash register.

And, of course, there are soggy sandwiches on the Amtrak train, dreary sandwiches on the plane, bacon and egg and ketchup sandwiches in the corner coffee shop — with a paper cup of coffee to go that always spills, soaking first the napkin, then the bag.

There are regional sandwiches, too: Philadelphia cheese steak sandwiches that you have to be a native to fully understand, North Carolina shredded mystery pork barbecue on a hot dog roll in a crinkled paper boat, Maine lobster rolls, Howard Johnson's fried clams on a bun, and New Orleans Po' Boys — the stuff of dreams — with crisp batter-fried oysters pressed between the halves of a gigantic roll with a side of slaw.

Then there are "occasion" sandwiches, such as lox and bagels on Sunday morning, a baguette with country pâté and French mustard for a picnic, a club sandwich and a glass of white wine in the hotel room after a long journey.

And there are the sandwiches you stand in line for at the counter, unable to decide what to have, though you have ordered there a hundred times. You look up at the big board and ponder — liverwurst, egg salad, chicken salad, tuna, grilled cheese . . .

"Ham and Swiss," you say.

"What kind of ham? What kind of bread? You want it toasted? You want mayo? Mustard? Lettuce and tomato?"

So many questions. So many choices.

I think I'll change my mind. Instead of a BLT, I'll have prosciutto, arugula, and sun-dried tomatoes on toasted brioche . . . or maybe a seafood club with smoked salmon, sliced scallops, baby shrimp, and belon oysters, with jalapeño mayonnaise on lightly toasted focaccia . . . or perhaps a submarine or a torpedo or a grinder or a hero or a hoagie . . . or a muffuletta stuffed with ham and salami, mortadella and provolone . . .

Hold it!

I'll have my absolute most favorite sandwich. Make mine a hamburger . . . and french fries!

Sandwich Ideas from The Silver Palate

Put thinly sliced roast veal, spread with anchovy mayonnaise, on black bread. Sprinkle with capers.

Try smoked filet of beef, equal parts of Roquefort and cream cheese, and sprigs of watercress on pumpernickel rolls.

Spread black bread with anchovy butter, then pile high with thinly sliced radishes and watercress.

Stack steak tartare and thinly sliced red onions on a black bread roll. Grind on lots of black pepper.

Mix lump crabmeat, diced green pepper, and cream cheese to a spreadable consistency and spread on a bagel.

It has been well said that a hungry man is more interested in four sandwiches than four freedoms.
— Henry Cabot Lodge, Jr.
American statesman-diplomat

Do not make a stingy sandwich; Pile the cold cuts high. Customers should see salami Coming through the rye.
— Alan Sherman
Sandwiches

Too few people understand a really good sandwich.
— James Beard

Books

Gourmet Sandwiches
Norman Kolpas; HP Books, 1993; $8.95

Grills and Greens
Linda Zimmerman and Gerri Gilliland; Clarkson Potter, 1993; $25.00

The Art of the Sandwich
Jay Halow; Chronicle Books, 1990; $14.95

SARDINES

A FLASH OF SILVER

The true sardine is the young of the pilchard and is found with diminishing frequency in the Mediterranean and off the coasts of Portugal and Spain. Farther north, the Norwegians catch small fish known as sprats, which they pack in oil under the name of brisling sardines. The fish caught and canned as sardines on the Atlantic coast of Canada and Maine are usually small Atlantic herring. The Pacific catch of true sardines has been almost totally depleted, and there are now too few left for commercial fisheries to bother with.

In fact, all these species (and anchovies, alewives, and shad) are members of the very large and widely distributed herring family. In canned form, they vary in taste and quality according to size, species, the type of oil used to preserve them, and the amount of time they are matured.

Silvery fresh sardines are quite fabulous when grilled over fragrant wood embers and eaten hot with a touch of lemon juice. When cold and soused (in vinegar), they should properly wear tiny tutus of onion rings, and be arranged like a corps de ballet on a bed of grape leaves. French bread and flinty, well-chilled white wine are suitable companions, along with a salad of brilliantly ripe tomatoes, orange segments, and black olives in a bright blue bowl. Make a dressing for the salad that includes fresh thyme.

Did You Know?

☞ Sardines are caught in large quantities off the coast of Sardinia — hence (no surprise here) their name.

MORE INFORMATION

Maine Sardine Council
P.O. Box 337
Brewer, ME 04412-0337
207-989-2180

Make Mine Sardine

Canned sardines contain more cholesterol than canned tuna or canned salmon, but 100 grams (about eight fish) of the kind that are packed bones and all provide 40 percent of the recommended daily allowance of calcium and 100 percent of the vitamin D that is essential for its absorption. Sardines are now packed in tomato sauce and water as well as oil; any which way, devotees adore them in salads, and a sardine sandwich on toasted brown bread with a soft lettuce leaf makes a nice lunch, especially if you have run out of tuna. In times of trouble the tasty little fish give solace.

SCALLOPS

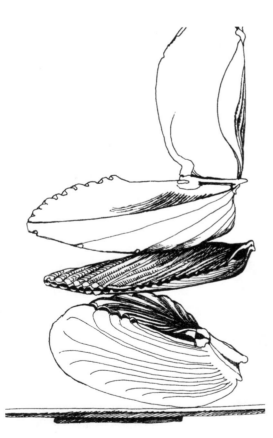

Making Do with the Best

At Le Bernardin, a renowned fish restaurant in Manhattan, sea scallops are served with foie gras, chopped black truffles, and julienned artichoke hearts, enrobed in an intensely flavored sauce of lobster broth, truffle, and veal juices. It is a memorable dish.

BEGUILING BIVALVES

The scallop shell is so geometrically pleasing that it has been reproduced by artists, architects, and gas stations everywhere. Fishermen don't give a fig about the shells and just toss them overboard at sea. But even a half shell has its uses. Half a shell was all Botticelli needed to bring about the Birth of Venus.

We never see the scallop's lovely coral-colored roe either. That, too, is wantonly chucked overboard. Nobody wants it, "they" say, though "they" don't give us much of a chance to have *our* say in the matter. Europeans say the coral is the best part; the Japanese eat every bit of the scallop, with passion.

Americans get two kinds of scallops; the sea variety, which can span up to six inches, and tiny sweet ones, the bay scallops, which are delicious when marinated in fruit juices or steamed for a moment or two and added to salads.

A Saintly Shell

The scallop shell is the emblem of St. James, and medieval pilgrims who made the dangerous journey to his shrine at Compostela in Spain always wore a scallop shell in their hats. Scallops were abundant off the coast nearby, so the first *coquilles St. Jacques,* which means "scallops of St. James," may well have been served to thankful pilgrims.

Seviche

Serves 4 as an appetizer

1 *pound ultra-fresh bay scallops*
½ *cup fresh lemon juice*
¼ *cup fresh lime juice*
¼ *cup fresh orange juice*
4 *scallions, thinly sliced*
⅛ *teaspoon red pepper flakes*
Boston lettuce leaves
2 *tablespoons finely chopped coriander or parsley*

Put the scallops in a china bowl and add the juices, scallions, and red pepper. Marinate in the refrigerator for 6 hours. Drain and serve on lettuce leaves, garnished with parsley.

Books

Clams, Mussels, Oysters, Scallops & Snails: A Cookbook & A Memoir
Howard Mitcham; Parnassus Imprints, 1990; $12.50

Stalking the Blue-Eyed Scallop
Euell Gibbons; A. C. Hood, 1988; $14.95

A Mighty Muscle

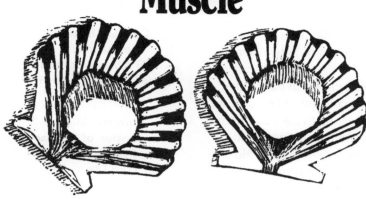

Like its fellow bivalves, oysters, clams, and mussels, the scallop has two shells. But unlike them, it swims in the water or moves along the surface of the sand. Its twin shells are rounded and fluted, with wavy "scalloped" edges. The large adductor muscle that controls the scallop's movement is the only part of the creature that we eat. Sometimes this muscle is called the eye, perhaps because it opens and closes the shells to see what's for dinner.

When scallops try to escape from danger, the adductor muscle proves its worth, clapping the shells together smartly while simultaneously squirting out, with great force, a stream of water that propels the scallop upward off the ocean floor. It travels in a zigzag for about a yard before dropping back down again. Scallops can travel about in spurts like this for quite a while.

Did You Know?

☞ Every year Americans eat 36,000 metric tons of scallops of one kind or another, and the catch worldwide is nearly 1 million tons.

☞ Sea scallops are found far out at sea at depths of up to 900 feet. Bay scallops live in shallow coastal water and are harvested by hand.

SCHOOLS, COOKING

GOING TO THE RIGHT SCHOOL

Once, fine cooking was considered an entirely European domain; no fine restaurant was complete without a chef trained in France or a Swiss-schooled *patissier*. These days, American chefs are training at U.S. schools and displaying their credentials with pride. And they are achieving a level of performance in cooking innovative, healthy, delicious dishes that is matched by growing public interest in learning how they do it. At the White House, Hillary Rodham Clinton has asked such culinary pioneers as Alice Waters and Larry Forgione to help institute a more American style of eating, and the French chef was recently replaced with an American. The line-up of Saturday-afternoon television cooking shows grows ever longer, and some avocational cooks are seeking more than holiday classes in order to increase their skills.

The Shaw Guide to Cooking Schools opens the door to the kitchen. This invaluable directory accurately describes itself as the only comprehensive source of information about cooking courses, apprenticeships, tours, and culinary arts schools worldwide, containing information about 664 programs in 39 states and 22 countries. Whether you cook for pleasure or profit, the *Guide* will help you find the programs that best fit your interests, schedule, and budget.

Schools range from facilities in cookware shops, restaurants, resorts, and individuals who offer classes primarily for the nonprofessional cook, to private institutions, community colleges, trade schools, and earn-as-you-learn apprenticeships for those pursuing a culinary career or seeking to improve their professional skills. More than 150 of the schools that offer career training report a job placement rate for their graduates that varies from 90 to 100 percent.

How to Be a Chef

Some chefs have served apprenticeships with master chefs in renowned restaurants; many are culinary-school graduates; and some switched from other professions because they were fascinated by food and what could be done with it. But no one gets to the top without hard work in the kitchen.

PROFESSIONALISM IN THE KITCHEN

The not-for-profit International Association of Culinary Professionals was founded in 1978 as the International Association of Cooking Schools, in order to link culinary educators in a worldwide network. It now has more than 2,500 members from 20 countries, predominantly from North America, and includes many of the most famous names in the field. Widely known as the IACP, it provides continuing education and professional development through regional and international conferences. Its major conference is held once a year, culminating in the presentation of the Julia Child Cookbook Awards honoring the best books published during the previous year. The organization offers a certification program for cooking school teachers and other culinary professionals, and also funds a series of scholarships for outstanding students in various culinary specialties.

There are five categories of membership: Professional Members are individuals who derive their income from food-related activities; Cooking School Members are vocational or avocational schools that focus on culinary education; Business Members are small, entrepreneurial food-related service businesses; Corporate Members are companies and organizations that produce or promote food and cooking-related products.

Teachers within the group offer classes in basics (including microwave and vegetarian cooking and specialized courses in everything from barbecueing to cake decorating) and beyond, to include the international cuisines of England, France, Greece, India, Ireland, Italy, Mexico, Morocco, Sicily, and Spain. Travel and vacation cooking schools operating year-round offer students the opportunity to learn on location from masters in each specialty.

The Other CIA

The Culinary Institute of America has been described by *Time* magazine as "the nation's most influential training school for professional cooks." Founded in 1946, the CIA has 1,900 full-time students, 20 percent of them women, and more than 23,000 alumni who are among today's leaders in the restaurant, food service, and hospitality fields. The 21-month course costs $21,705. (Happily, this fee includes two square meals a day.) The school also offers courses for nonprofessionals at its campus in Hyde Park, New York.

A Matter of Degree

Johnson and Wales College and Boston University now offer, in addition to practical training, academic courses in culinary history, anthropology, sociology, and the role of food in world culture.

MORE INFORMATION

Culinary Institute of America
433 Albany Post Road
Hyde Park, NY 12538-1499
914-452-9430

International Association of Culinary Professionals
304 West Liberty Street,
Suite 201
Louisville, KY 40202
502-581-9786

Johnson and Wales College, Culinary Arts Division
1 Washington Avenue
Providence, RI 02905
401-456-1130

Books

The Shaw Guide to Cooking Schools, 1995
Editors; Shaw Guides, 1994;
$19.95

SEAFOOD

FISH POPULATIONS ARE FADING FAST

For years there have been dire warnings of global warming, global cooling, and predictions of the near extinction of several forms of marine life. We are still unable to forecast the weather accurately, but scientists and industry analysts *can* prove that their worst fears are being realized as they document alarming declines in several species of fish.

The United Nations Food and Agriculture Organization monitors close to 1,000 fish species around the world and attributes the losses to several causes, chief among them being the unintentional capture of what are considered trash fish that are caught up and die in the vast trawling nets. One of these nets is big enough to accommodate 12 Boeing 747 jets side by side; others still in the design stages are 30 percent larger. The trawl nets scour the oceans like insatiable vacuum cleaners, scooping up all the living creatures in their path and wantonly destroying the fragile ecological balance of the oceans' life forces.

Industrial and agricultural pollution have caused changes in water temperature and altered salinity levels, and the draining and development of coastal marshlands and damming of rivers that used to play significant roles in fish breeding and feeding cycles have further diminished the populations of several species, but overfishing by commercial fisheries is the chief culprit in what may well become an irreversible loss of wild fish. In the future, we may come to be totally dependent on farmed fish for supplies of certain species, and know them in their wild form only in aquariums.

Fish Safety

Some 60,000 people became ill last year after eating contaminated fish — a distressingly large number that will surely be reduced once stringent new government rules are enforced. However, the FDA estimates the chances of succumbing to food-borne illness from seafood other than raw shellfish as one in 5 million.

Believing that the public will be more inclined to buy fish that carries a safety guarantee, domestic seafood suppliers have welcomed the new regulations. New laws will also mandate close scrutiny of imported fish and shellfish to be sure that they originated in waters free from pollution or pesticide contamination.

There has been concern about other potential dangers from toxic chemicals and heavy metals such as mercury and lead, or from man-made compounds such as PCBs. There have been no known human deaths from seafood tainted with PCBs, which are now strictly regulated. But their residual presence in inland waters remains a problem and although PCBs tend to concentrate in the fish's skin and liver and are eliminated in cooking, many sport fishermen do not eat their catches.

Our descendants are going to be mightily peeved to learn that they're going to have to wait 10 million years — or five times the full length of the entire history of the human species since its evolutionary origin — to see biodiversity recover from what we're doing in less than 100 years.

— Edward O. Wilson
Biologist

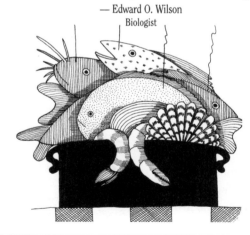

A Hole in the Sea

To give the stock time to rebound, the nations that fish in the Bering Sea have agreed to steer their nets clear of an area known as "the donut hole" in the center of the ocean between the territorial fisheries of the United States and Russia. Because Alaska's island chains extend across the North Pacific, the off-limits international zone is surrounded by still-active American and Russian fisheries, hence the name "donut hole." In 1995, international authorities will decide whether or not to extend the fishing moratorium for another two years.

"I'm in the mood for fish but I don't want anything that tastes like fish."

Fresh Fish to Fry

Futurists think we will soon be seeing brand-named fish in our markets in much the same way as we now buy fruit and vegetables marked with company logos. Brand-naming will provide assurance that the fish has come from clean water and was processed under the strictest safety standards.

Technological breakthroughs will rid fish of skin and bones, although this will rob it of flavor. But on the whole, we seem willing to sacrifice taste for convenience.

New varieties of fish will start showing up in the stores. Look for Nile perch, spearhead, arrowtooth flounder, and a welter of seafood sausages, fish "dogs" on a stick to eat while driving, and catfish burgers served with "frickles" (fried pickles).

Q&A

Q Do saltwater fish taste saltier than freshwater fish?

A No. Fish have a special physiological mechanism that prevents them from becoming as salty as the water in which they live. They are actually quite low in sodium — a 3½-ounce portion of raw fish contains only 100 milligrams, barely 5 percent of the daily amount suggested for someone on a low-sodium diet.

MORE INFORMATION

National Fisheries Institute
1525 Wilson Boulevard
Arlington, VA 22209
703-524-8880

National Seafood Educators
P.O. Box 60006
Richmond Beach, WA 98160
206-546-6410

PERIODICALS

Seafood Current
Sea Grant College Program
North Carolina State University
P.O. Box 8605
Raleigh, NC 27695
919-515-2454
Quarterly; free

Simply Seafood
Waterfront Press
115 NW 46th Street
Seattle, WA 98107
Quarterly; $8.95

Books

A Seafood Celebration
Sheryl and Mel London; Simon & Schuster, 1993; $30.00

Fish: The Basics
Shirley King; Simon & Schuster, 1990; $24.95

Great American Seafood Cookbook
Susan Herrmann Loomis; Workman, 1988; $12.95

Seafood: A Connoisseur's Guide and Cookbook
Alan Davidson; Fireside Books, 1989; $29.95

The Legal Seafoods Cookbook
George Berkowitz and Jane Doerfer; Doubleday, 1988; $12.95

SEAWEED

A Serenade to
Kelp

Giant Pacific kelp, popular in Japanese dishes under the name of *kombu*, grows up to a foot a day and can extend more than 400 feet — taller, in marine terms, than a giant sequoia. And if you cut a kelp "tube" to an appropriate size and fit it with a mouthpiece, you can play it like a French horn.

Featherweight Floater

What is edible, made of seaweed, 10 percent lighter than air, and biodegradable? It's SEAgel, a remarkable material that can support thousands of times its own weight. Its inventor, Robert L. Morrison, a physical chemist at the Lawrence Livermore National Laboratory in California, foresees its usefulness as an insulation material for both sound and heat. He suggests that it could also be used as a time-release packaging for medicines, insecticides, and fertilizers. SEAgel's source is the kelp that washes up on the Pacific coast by the crateload after a storm, so the product should be easy and inexpensive to make. Add some soy sauce and it could even become a genuinely light and healthy snack.

A NEW WAVE

If you think the idea of eating slimy seaweed is something you would as soon forget about, forget the thought. We are already deeply into seaweed. Colloids derived from marine algae are used to make ice cream, puddings, and salad dressings smooth as silk, to beef up "leanburgers," to bulk pie fillings, and to induce chocolate milk to mound in the mouth. Carrageenan, better known as Irish moss, is responsible for putting a nice frothy head on many a pint of beer. Dulse, or Neptune's Girdle, a tasty dried red seaweed, beats out potato chips in healthy circles. Nori sheets are familiar everywhere Japanese food is offered, toasted as sushi wrappers and holders for hand rolls. Varieties of seaweed such as bright green *wakame* or jet-black *hijiki* show up as a garnishes for soups and components in salads. And seaweeds are also good for you — most contain significant amounts of vitamins A and C as well as some of the B vitamins, iodine, and potassium.

Now that seaweeds are riding high, they're slipping into drugs and cosmetics as well as food and drink. Guess what makes toothpaste stay in the tube without getting stuck? What else but seaweed.

Weeds Are the Harvest

Seaweeds are really sea vegetables and deciding which to raise is like choosing to plant radishes rather than lettuces. *Undaria* and *Laminaria*, for instance, are both species of brown kelp, but their taste and texture are quite different from each other. Others popular for eating are the red seaweed *Porphyra* (which the Welsh call laver and the Japanese know as nori) and the crinkly green sea lettuce.

The seaweed farmer "seeds" thin threads with seaweed spores and cultures them in laboratory tanks until the young plants are visible. The threads and their plants are then inserted between rope strands for transfer to the open sea. Some varieties are suspended from individual ropes slung horizontally between buoys and weights, others are woven into 6-by-60-foot nets, which hang a few yards below the surface. The growing seaweeds' chief need is pollution-free water with the right combination of light, nutrients, currents, and wave action. The farmers select appropriate spots; if they've chosen well, nature goes to work and a few months later they can come back with clippers and harvest the bounty. At last count, it amounted to more than 4 million tons worldwide and there's plenty of room for more.

*Where the salt weed sways in the stream;
Where the sea beasts rang'd all round
Feed in the ooze of their pasture-ground.*

— Matthew Arnold
The Forsaken Merman

MORE INFORMATION

Maine Seaweed Company
Box 57
Steuben, ME 04680
207-546-2875

New Beginnings Seafood Company
16 Cornish Road
Carmel, NY 10512
914-220-6186

Books

Cooking with Sea Vegetables
Peter Bradford and Montse Bradford; Inner Traditions, 1985; $8.95

Sea Vegetables: Harvesting Guide and Cookbook
Evelyn McConnaughey; Naturegraph, 1985; $15.95/ $8.95

Spuds! Dulse! Fidddleheads!
Judith Comfort; Nimbus, 1986; $9.95

Vegetables from the Sea
Seibin Arasaki and Terulo Arasaki; Japan Publications, 1983; $13.95

SEEDS

PRECIOUS HEIRLOOMS

In 1975, Ken Whealy of Decorah, Iowa, founded the Seed Savers Exchange after he and his wife received a traditional wedding gift of heirloom seeds from her grandfather. Since then, the exchange has passed along almost half a million open-pollinated seed varieties, which are fertilized the old-fashioned way — by breeze or bee. Each season, growers select seeds of the best plants, and hardy, tasty strains are replanted. Seed savers let plants go to seed on purpose, tending them until they blossom, then extracting the seeds and sending them back to the exchange. (No nibbling allowed.)

These grass-roots heroes are shoring up the gene pool, which has been rapidly depleted since the 1940s. As conglomerates buy up seed companies, they crowd out heirlooms with more profitable high-tech varieties, whose produce looks perfect, travels well, and ripens almost simultaneously. Each new variety has to yield consistent, true-to-type produce that represents an improvement, they point out, otherwise farmers wouldn't buy it. Breeding to achieve this is costly and takes years — and meanwhile the seed catalogs drop more and more of their older, open-pollinated varieties.

Seed savers are also helping to stem the destruction of the 50,000 plant varieties that are predicted to vanish in the next 30 years or so. Seventy-five percent of native food plants have disappeared from the Americas since the time of Columbus, according to Kenny Ausubel, director of Seeds of Change, an organization working to preserve those that are left.

Far more important than the environment or history, of course, is the taste of what grows from these special seeds. A panel of *COOK's Magazine* tasters unanimously pronounced the heirloom Early Blood Turnip Beet sweeter and with "more beet flavor" than its supermarket competitors, while an heirloom Ruby Crescent potato beat the more common Red Bliss and California White potatoes hands down, with "a full, buttery, almost tropical flavor and firm, yellow flesh that had tasters raving."

Evocative Seed Names

Batavia Rouge Grenobloise lettuce

Bill Jump's Soup peas

Blacktail Mountain watermelon

Comtesse de Chambord beans

Cow Horn potatoes

Deer Tongue lettuce

Earliglo sweet corn

Lazy Wife beans

Mandan Blue corn

Mirabelle plums

Moon and Stars watermelons

Papa Amarilla potatoes

Saladmaster lettuce

Seek-No-Further apples

Six Week beans

Talley's Sulphur beans

Did You Know?

☞ The world's first seed bank was founded in 1921, by a Russian biologist named Nikolai I. Vavilov, who had tramped five continents in search of wild and domestic seeds, and on his return, set up the Vavilov Plant Industry Institute to house his collection. Today, it holds more than 380,000 gene types representing 2,500 plant species.

☞ Kansas artist Stan Herd has created many-acre-sized reproductions of paintings by artists such as Cézanne and Van Gogh, designed to be seen from the air, by selecting seeds that yield plants with the exact colors he needed.

MORE INFORMATION

American Seed Trade Association
601 13th Street NW, Suite 570 South
Washington, DC 20005
202-638-3128

Native Seeds/SEARCH
2509 North Campbell Avenue, No. 325
Tucson, AZ 85719
602-327-9123

Seeds Savers Exchange
3076 North Winn Road
Decorah, IA 52101
319-382-5990

Shepherd's Garden Seeds
6116 Highway 9
Felton, CA 95018
408-335-6910

MAIL ORDER SOURCES

Johnny's Selected Seeds
Foss Hill Road
Albion, ME 03910-9731
207-437-4301

Seeds of Change
621 Old Santa Fe Trail, Suite 10
Santa Fe, NM 87501
505-983-8956

Shepherd's Garden Seeds
30 Irene Street
Torrington, CT 06790
203-482-3638

SHARK

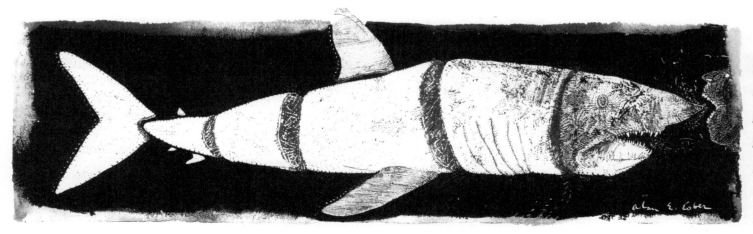

For every person attacked by a shark, 1,000,000 sharks are killed by people.

MAC THE SHARK

The shark's teeth are indeed pearly white . . . and if he should lose one, another promptly pops up in its place. Which is only one of the phenomenal characteristics, along with a ruthless appetite for just about anything dead or alive, that have made the shark the lord of the seas since dinosaurs ruled the earth.

Sharks are called the "apex" or top predators in the ecology of the sea; they face no competition whatsoever from animals lower in the food web, but what happens to them for good or ill has critical resonance down the line.

Right now their population is shrinking, thanks to their only predators: us. According to the National Marine Fisheries Service, large coastal sharks are being killed annually in numbers that exceed their reproduction rate. The peak year was 1989, when the total came close to half a million.

Americans were a long time joining Europeans and Asians in appreciating the delicious qualities of shark meat — dense, flavorful, nutritious, and totally free of bone because the shark's skeleton is made of cartilage to give it lightness. It seems incredible that many fishermen so hated sharks that they threw away their flesh as trash.

But the growing market for shark meat in the United States is not the major cause of the depredations. Part of the problem is that many sharks get caught and killed in the nets of fishermen who are after tuna, or other more conventional catches. Then there's the Asian market for shark fins, which soared in the 1980s. The demand drove the price for the most desired fins and tails, those of the great white shark, up to $100 a pound.

Sharks take years to mature and they reproduce infrequently; most give birth to live babies, one at a time, in small litters. Scientists and conservationists have warned that it takes decades for a shark population to recover from decimation, but they know little about the exact ecological effects, or even how to measure the degree of fishing that constitutes overfishing. Still, Florida, where the commercial and recreational shark fishery is the state's fourth largest finfishery, has passed a law protecting 39 of the most threatened species.

Shark Species

Spiny dogfish, destined for export, make up half the American shark harvest. Fished commercially for U.S. consumption are blacktip and mako from Florida, mako and thresher from the West Coast, and two species of angel shark — one from Texas, one from California. The angel shark resembles skate in shape and taste. None of these species is related to either the pool shark or the loan shark.

Did You Know?

☞ Pacific Islanders, who are totally at home in the ocean, have great respect for sharks but don't fear them. They swim with them, feed them, and often eat them.

☞ The shark has been called a "swimming computer" because it has more sensory inputs than any other animal, and a large brain for integrating information. It can detect an ounce of blood in a million ounces of seawater, and sense underwater vibrations so acutely that its ability has been called "touch at a distance."

☞ Sharks' teeth and vertebrae have been found in prehistoric trash heaps, indicating that our distant ancestors ate sharks. How did they catch them? Possibly by trapping them in tidal creeks, with nets.

☞ Bull sharks can live for long periods in fresh water. They have been found in the upper Amazon, and in landlocked bodies of water such as Lake Nicaragua.

ALERT

Very fresh shark meat is bright and firm, with distinctive, marbled swirls; it should smell fresh or slightly metallic. Because sharks carry urea in their tissues and blood, ammonia can build up if they are not properly handled and chilled. If shark meat has darkened or smells of ammonia, discard it.

SHELF-STABLE FOOD

Q&A

Q What is a shelf-stable food?

A According to the FDA, the term covers any food that has been processed to limit or control the growth of microbes within it, enabling it to maintain its qualities over a specified period. That period will vary, depending on the product and on whether outside conditions have altered. Shelf-stable foods include dehydrated products, canned goods, and staples such as sugar and cheese, when properly wrapped, as well as vacuum-packed and aseptically packaged foods.

The Future Is Aseptic?

Those brightly colored "drink boxes" so popular with children no longer contain only juices and beverages; latest foods to be found in aseptic packaging are whipping cream, tomatoes, scrambled egg mix, tofu, and pancake syrup. The process sterilizes the food without altering its taste, then seals it in a multilayered laminated package. An added benefit: Because the printing inks are applied only to the outer lamination, the inner layers are easily recycled into white, high-quality pulp.

Did You Know?

☞ Shelf-stable milk, or ultra-high temperature (UHT) milk has been heated to 284 degrees F. for 3 seconds to kill all bacteria, then quickly cooled and sealed in aseptic containers. It is guaranteed to keep fresh for at least six months without refrigeration.

☞ In 1989 Stanford University buried 40,000 dehydrated meals in 12 locked holds at secret locations to feed its 8,500 students for two days in the event of another earthquake.

☞ Shelf-stable food should be stored where temperatures will remain between 32 and 85 degrees F.

The Humanitarian
Ration

The armed forces are the major commissioners and consumers of shelf-stable foods. With existing stockpiles of MREs (Meals Ready To Eat) running low, the Defense Department has designed new rations that are suitable also for feeding to hungry, possibly vegetarian refugees. This typical meal package has a shelf life of 18 to 24 months; it contains about 1,900 calories and costs $3.95.

Tangy beans
Navy beans with tomato sauce

Lentil stew
Stew with lentils, navy beans, and assorted vegetables
Crackers
Bread

Jelly
Apple or grape

Fruit snack
Confection of various fruits and sugar

Granola
With raisins
Spoon

Future Foods May Last for Years

Among 1990s food trends, shelf-stable foods — packaged products that can sit safely in a cupboard for months before being opened and eaten — seemed the hottest. Because convenience and health are the two major consumer concerns, a product that is portable, takes only minutes to prepare, and is free of additives and preservatives looked like a sure thing. Many food companies dropped the canning of some products and switched to microwavable tubs and vacuum-packaging that needed no refrigeration.

Consumers have been slow to respond, and the momentum has faltered temporarily. However, high-pressure processing and aseptic packaging are on their way, and will transform the way we eat before another decade has passed.

When the foods of the future remain "fresh" for 18 months to five years, we'll shop a couple of times a year, browsing the supermarket like a bookstore, and stacking our selections at home in pantries that resemble libraries. And all these marvels will meet their maker at the kitchen's new center, the microwave; stoves will have become antiques. An electronic

chip, activated by pulling a strip on the package, will chill any food that needs it. And the refrigerator, shrunken in size (and energy demands) to meet the negligible need for cold storage, will lurk on the sidelines — or even in the laundry room.

But where will we post all the messages?

SHRIMP

SMALL, BUT MUCH APPRECIATED

Shrimp is called "the seafood for people who don't like seafood," and the reasons for that are obvious enough — the flesh is firm and meaty, the flavor is mild and likeable, and (for those afraid of fish, this is important) *there are no bones*. Indeed, shrimp is so popular in the United States that it ranks second only to canned tuna. On a per-capita basis, each American eats about two and a half pounds of shrimp a year; in actual fact, some people up north must not be getting their quota, because there are good ole boys living along the Gulf Coast who think nothing of eating that much shrimp in a *day*.

There are several thousand species of shrimps in the world's waters, ranging in size from behemoths that weigh three or four pounds apiece to Lilliputians so tiny that the normal human eye can barely see them. Of the thousands of kinds of shrimps in existence, only about 300 species are harvested. Like crabs and lobsters, shrimps have ten legs and external skeletons.

Commercially, shrimps are divided into two types: cold-water or northern shrimps, and tropical shrimps. Tropical shrimps are further categorized commercially according to shell color — white, brown, pink, red, and striped (or tiger). The term "green shrimp" means that the shrimps are raw, not literally green. A subgroup of shrimps are those caught in fresh water; internationally, these are called prawns — a term also used arbitrarily on the West Coast to describe big shrimps from the ocean.

The United States imports about 80 percent of the shrimp we eat from the some hundred countries that export their catches. World shrimp production is about 5 billion pounds a year; U.S. shrimp production is only around 300 to 400 million pounds a year, but it is of consistently higher quality than most imports.

About a fifth of the world's shrimp supply currently comes from aquaculture. Shrimps take well to farming, and it has been predicted that by the first decade of the 21st century more than a third of the shrimps eaten around the world will be farm raised.

At The Supermarket

Shrimp species you are most likely to encounter at your local supermarket include:

Gulf White — May be wild or farm-raised. Usually gray-white in color. Good flavor, firm texture, and expensive.

Ecuadorean or Mexican White — Likely to be wild. The United States imports more shrimp from Ecuador than from any other country.

Black Tiger — Farmed in Asia. May be dark gray with black stripes and red feelers, or blue with yellow feelers. Flavorful and firm; pink when cooked.

Gulf Pink — May be wild or farm-raised. The shell may be red or light brown. Excellent quality.

Gulf Brown — Easily confused with Whites and Pinks. A wild shrimp, most likely to taste of iodine.

Chinese White — Farm-raised in Asia. Gray-white, usually inexpensive.

The World's Top Ten Shrimp Producers

1. China
2. Indonesia
3. Thailand
4. Ecuador
5. India
6. Philippines
7. Vietnam
8. Taiwan
9. Bangladesh
10. Colombia

PERIODICALS

Shrimp Tales
Texas Shrimp Association
2101 South IH35, No. 107
Austin, TX 78741
512-448-3828
Bimonthly; free with membership

Counting Shrimp

If you start with two pounds of raw, headless, unpeeled warm-water shrimp, cook them, peel them, and devein them, you'll end up with about one pound of edible meat.

Books

The Art of Catching and Cooking Shrimp
Lynette Walthers; Sussex Prints, 1986; $5.95

Shrimp
Jay Harlow and Victor Budnick; Chronicle Books, 1989; $16.95

Simply Shrimp
Glenn Day; Crossing Press, 1990; $14.95

Did You Know?

☞ Like most seafoods, shrimps are about 78 percent water by weight; they contain about 18 percent protein and less than 1 percent fat.

☞ Cooked, peeled shrimps look quite alike (and nicely pink), no matter what the color of their shells or the waters of their origin.

☞ Shrimps are sold in numbered or sized counts per pound; ideally, all shrimps in a count are identical in size.

☞ Large brown shrimps often taste of iodine, which is present in the plankton they feed on. But if little shrimps sold in the fish market smell of iodine, have nothing to do with them.

☞ Our word *shrimp* comes from the German *schrumpfen*, which means "to shrivel." And this is what our opponent or enemy is supposed to do when we call him a "little shrimp."

SMELL

MEMORIES ARE MADE OF THIS

Strolling down the street, thinking of something entirely other, you are aware of the fragrant smell of fresh-baked bread. Breathe it again. Inhale it. Wham!
In a flash you are transported to a long-forgotten landscape that you first glimpsed 20, 30, 40 or more years ago. You are seven years old . . . on your way to school with a bag of books on your back. You are back on the street where you lived. For a fleeting moment the long-ago past becomes the immediate, vivid present. It is as though our brain were a computer and a file we thought was lost is suddenly restored.

We have all experienced this extraordinary jolt from a sudden encounter with a smell in the course of daily life. In the course of an operation, however, a neurosurgeon can touch part of the brain with the tip of a fine probe and elicit an instantaneous response from the conscious patient, as though he could smell that nonexistent bread being baked right there in the operating room.

It may seem like a minor miracle but the explanation is relatively simple. Inhaled air passes through the back of the nose and the mouth where the two passageways join to form a chimney. The moistened odor molecules converge on the area called the hippocampus in the brain's limbic system, which is the part of the brain that interprets smell. It is also the center for memory and for emotion. Memories of smells are deposited there when we are very young. The more times a child is exposed to a certain aroma, the stronger will be the imprinting. When a good or bad odor is smelled again, it can bring with it a linkage with a definite experience.

A scent can carry not only the perfume of flowers or spices, but the memory of mother, a lover, a time, a place, a sadness or a pleasure — or, if your name was Marcel Proust, a madeleine and the remembrance of things past.

Detective Nose at Work

The eye can recognize a few from among a cast of thousands of faces owned by friends, family, film stars, and TV personalities. The ear identifies a "Hello" on the telephone from the voices of hundreds of acquaintances. The tongue detects a myriad shades far beyond the broad boundaries of sweet, salt, sour, and bitter. But when it comes to detection, the nose is in a class by itself.

Some connoisseurs possess noses that can detect the differences among 200 to 300 wines without peeking at the label, fragrance makers are able to differentiate 500 chemicals that go into the construction of a perfume, and a few country people will sniff the air, tell you that a thunderstorm is on its way — and be proved right.

The human nose is a mighty powerful possession. Sticking straight out from the center of our face, it detects and identifies an odor that measures less than a billionth of an ounce as it floats in the air.

Every living thing has a nose . . . sort of. Even brainless invertebrates like jellyfish "smell" their dinner and wiggle their way toward it. Bees and snails and ants and other insects have the equivalent of noses in their antennae which they wave in the air to sense the whereabouts of a potential food source.

Humans have their smellers *inside* their noses as do mice, pigs, and dogs. But human noses can't compare with those of animals, which must live or die by their ability to smell (and avoid) predators and to sniff out their own prey. Animals are far more choosy about what they avoid than what they eat. A cat will eat not only the same food, but the same commercial brand of Nine Lives Tuna and Chicken Dinner (33 cents a can), for an entire lifetime. But human beings depend for good health on a varied diet, and a nose that found only one food acceptable would be maladaptive to the species.

Did You Know?

☞ A house sells faster if it is perceived by potential buyers as a home; this effect is achieved by putting some bread in the oven or simmering cider with cinnamon sticks.

☞ Some restaurants ask their patrons not to wear heavy perfumes because they overwhelm the wondrous smells of the food. (Some perfumes can overwhelm a dinner companion, too.)

☞ Aromatherapists hope to harness the power of smell to alleviate stress. A whiff of vanilla helps to relax patients who are feeling tense while undergoing magnetic resonance imaging (MRI). The fragrance of jasmine acts as a pick-me-up; that of lavender induces sleep.

☞ Newly minted money has a nice smell — very seductive.

Nosing It Out

It is the smell of certain foods that attracts or repels people, so when children refuse "even to taste a little bit," it is because in a very real sense they have already tasted it by smelling it. They don't want to put it in their mouth if they have already put it in their nose — and rejected it!

MORE INFORMATION

Olfactory Research Fund
145 East 32nd Street,
14th floor
New York, NY 10016
212-725-2755

Smell is a potent wizard that transports us across thousands of miles and all the years we have lived.

— Helen Keller

SMOKED FOOD

American food is going up in smoke — fragrant coils of smoke rising from hickory logs, fruity clouds ascending from pecan wood, apple, and cherry. In an effort to increase flavor while reducing fats, more and more chefs are turning to smoked foods and smoke cookery.

— Steven Raichlen
Food writer

SMOKING COMES
BETWEEN OAK AND ASH

Because bacteria cannot survive in a dry environment, people have been smoking food as a means of preserving it for thousands of years.

In theory, any food can be smoked, but those that are most successful have a naturally high oil content. Among the most familiar smoked foods are ham, bacon and sausages, chicken and duck breasts, and quail and other small game birds. Several traditional cheeses that used to be made in farmhouses are smoked over fragrant wood chips, and with the new popularity of smoking more and more cheeses are being offered in smoked form.

But for most of us, it is smoked fish we yearn for. It could be herring and kippers, oysters and mussels, Sunday-morning sable, whitefish, chubs, or sturgeon, or, most luxurious of all, lox and its classy relative, smoked salmon from Scotland, Ireland, Canada, Norway, and Chile.

It is the choice of wood that gives the food its characteristic flavor. Fruit and nut woods — peach, cherry, pecan, even grape prunings — are soaked in water so that they will smoke slowly and impart their fragrance to the food before eventually burning to ashes. Apple, with its sweet, mild smoke, is among the favorites for chicken and turkey, and oak chips, juniper, and beech are used wherever these woods are plentiful. Birch, which gives a slightly resinous smoke, is used in the Midwest and Northeast, and corncobs are a favorite fuel in New England. In Texas, the abundant wild mesquite bushes were considered a perfect pest until tangy mesquite smoke became an admired addition to millions of backyard barbecue grills and fired a mesquite boom in the Lone Star State. The fresh, pungent smoke of alder wood is preferred for smoking salmon in Alaska and the Pacific Northwest.

These are all considered to be specialty woods, but the wood used in more than 95 percent of commercial houses for smoking meats is hickory, which imparts a splendid depth of mellow flavor and turns ham a deep russet color.

Firing Up at Home

Home smoking has become popular lately and reliable stovetop and electrical and outdoor equipment can be found in cookware catalogs and specialty stores. Home-smoked food should always be eaten within a day or two, which is rarely any problem.

Smoking Hot and Cold

In the two chief methods of smoking food — hot smoking and cold smoking — the portions of fish, meat, or poultry are hung in the smokehouse for a specific period at consistent temperatures until they have the desired flavor and consistency. For hot smoking, the temperature ranges between 120 and 180 degrees F. and the food is smoked for up to 12 hours, depending on its size. For cold smoking, temperatures are much lower, from 70 to 80 degrees F. and the food may be smoked for days or even a week or two, again depending on size and the flavor desired.

Before being smoked, fish especially is immersed in a salt-water bath. The salt acts as an initial preservative that adds flavor and firms the flesh; it also helps to draw out water during the smoking process. Some producers add herbs and other seasonings to the brine.

SNACKS

A Cheeto by another name is still a Cheeto.

— Janet Siroto
Food writer

ANIMAL BEHAVIOR

WAYNE JEBIAN

Sitting or standing, busy or not, a sudden hunger can creep over us: snack attack! In animal response we search for food. It doesn't much matter what it is — prepackaged, salty, sweet, crunchy, fat-filled, fresh from the cupboard, fridge, nearby store, or vending machine — we eat it.

The objects of edible desire can be basics like chips, candy, cookies, nuts, and raw vegetables; also, sometimes, dry cereal from the box, fluffy extruded pseudo-dairy crunch products, and preprepared logs of chocolate-chip cookie dough. Classics like ice cream and popcorn have an irresistible pull under the right conditions. And some snacks are specifically de rigueur for movie dates, sporting events, and late-night TV.

We amass tomatoes, sour cream, dip, herbs, ketchup, peanut butter, and chocolate bits, or cheeses from Cheddar to Brie, cottage to string, goat cheese to cheese-free cheese, and put them on crackers, wafers, apples, celery, matzoh, a spoon, or fingers. We make mini-pizzas, hand-held salads, soft-boiled eggs, spread-on-bread or potato-anything, and stuff them greedily into our mouths.

We snack when we're bored or tense or angry or on the go. Is there any time when we're *not* inclined to snack? Since the olden days when an apple a day would do, it's been as much a tradition as apple pie, which, come to think of it, sounds pretty good right now.

Munch Trends

• Mini-munchables, such as Bagel Bites, Snickers Miniatures, and Oreos, barely a quarter the size of the originals. Popular because they leave fewer crumbs and give the impression, frequently false, that the snacker is eating less.

• Unsalted pretzels, significantly lower in salt and fat than potato chips; a big comeback.

• White corn and blue corn tortilla chips, sweet potato chips, vegetable chips, bean chips, taro chips, and a myriad other thin crunchables; a rainbow of tastes for chip fans.

• Exotic mixes, prompted by a dramatic rise in sales of snack mixes such as trail mix and Chex; look for new inventions. Imagine, for example, a combo of oriental rice crackers, Cajun hot sticks, honey-roasted peanuts, and the ever-popular cheddar Goldfish.

Health in Grazing

As the ever-quickening pace of life undermines the traditional idea of three square meals a day, the country is turning to other ways of eating: grazing on mini-meals and frequent mouthfuls. Will this snack-centric life-style undermine our good intentions to cut back on saturated fats, sodium, and excessive calories? After all, people tend to regard snacks as tasty treats, not building blocks to better nutrition.

According to the Department of Health and Human Services, there is a way to graze healthfully. We should vary the kind of snacks we eat, rather than downing the same fat nuggets all day. Children's and teenagers' metabolisms burn snack calories rapidly, but adults should consider putting themselves on a "fat calorie salary" and not exceed it. We can make this task easier by stocking wholesome munchables within easy reach. Most recommended: cucumbers, celery sticks, cherry tomatoes, graham crackers, melon slices, air-popped popcorn, pretzels, baked tortilla chips, whole-wheat muffins, and nonfat plain yogurt mixed with fresh fruit.

Snack companies, realizing that the right products could become dietary staples, have been lowering the fat content of their chips, the sodium content of their crackers, and the cholesterol count in their cupcakes. Real fruit juices are increasingly edging out artificially flavored drinks. Even teenagers, the backbone of the snack industry, are turning away from "junk" food and leading America into a brave new world of natural, organic, light, and vegetarian noshing.

Some evidence suggests that frequent mouthfuls can be easier on the body than large meals. Researchers at the University of Toronto fed two groups of men the same number of calories per day for two weeks, one group eating three meals and the other eating a little bit once per hour. The snackers, it turned out, showed lower levels of insulin and cholesterol in their blood. In addition, the switch from three big meals to frequent small meals can boost the metabolism and burn more calories.

Woe Are We

According to a survey by the Hostess cupcake folks, more than a third of Americans made New Year's resolutions in 1994 to cut down on between-meal snacks. A minority — 11 percent — feel more guilty about snacking than they do about cheating on taxes. Women are more than twice as likely (40 percent) as men (19 percent) to suffer guilt over their munching habits.

MORE INFORMATION

Snack Food Association
1711 King Street, Suite 1
Alexandria, VA 22314
703-836-4500

SNAILS

*A snail's pace is
anything short
of eight miles
per hour.*

— *Sporting Magazine, 1826*

GESTURE OF FAITH

It is very hard to believe that you would ever voluntarily eat a snail. Until you do. Well, usually, it isn't something you actually *choose* to do. More often it just happens. Usually in the presence of one whom you hope may become a significant other. While gazing fondly into the eyes of the beloved, amid the heady fumes of garlic butter, the little morsel slips succulently down almost unnoticed, followed fast by another.

And . . . suddenly, the deed is done. You discover you love snails with a fondness that will long outlive the companion of the moment.

SNAPPER

NEW OPENINGS FOR RED SNAPPERS

In the last decade our consumption of all fish has increased nearly 25 percent to some 16 pounds per person per year, and snapper is one of the most popular, in restaurants as well as at home. Its fine white flesh has a fresh, sweet taste and lends itself well to all methods of preparation. There are about 200 species within the snapper family — 34 of which are fished in American waters. The American red snapper is regarded as best of the best, and, perhaps because lesser fish such as porgies and rockfish are sometimes passed off under its name, the true red snapper is always sold and often served with its rosy skin attached. (In fact, only its skin and the iris of its eye are red; like all snappers, it is white-fleshed.)

Snappers are found in tropical and subtropical waters worldwide; domestic species come from the coast of North Carolina to Florida, and in the Gulf of Mexico, and are most abundant in late summer. Most of the snapper eaten in the United States is imported, however; Mexico and Brazil harvest large quantities of red snapper, but by far the largest catch of all kinds of snappers comes from Indonesia and Southeast Asia. Because most snapper species are deepwater fish that tend to live close to reefs where large trawlers dare not venture, they are largely caught at night by fishermen in small boats using hook and line.

Snappers can weigh as much as 40 pounds, but we mostly see fish from 5 to 10 pounds that are sold filleted. Smaller red snappers weighing less than 2 pounds are available whole and are good for stuffing and grilling or baking.

Did You Know?

☞ Some of the red snapper pretenders' real names: blood, blubberlip, Colorado, crimson, dog, graytail, humpback, Malabar, midnight, mutton, ruby, rufous, silk, spotted rose, yellowtail.

☞ Snappers are probably so called because they have large mouths and sharp teeth with which they snap up smaller fish. Their family name, Lutjanidae, is a bit of a mouthful, too.

SOUP

**Between soup and love,
the first is better.**

— Old Spanish saying

The Campbell's Tomato Soup label has changed since 1897 — left to right, the original label, 1905 label, and current design — but the red and white colors haven't. They are based on those of Cornell University's football team.

Q&A

Q What is the difference between bouillon, broth, stock, and consommé?

A Bouillon, broth, and stock all refer to the liquid that is left after cooking vegetables, meat, or fish in water, then removing the solids; the strained liquids are used as soup bases. Bouillon (from *bouillir,* "to boil," in French) is most familiar in concentrated, dehydrated cubes or granules, to which water is added. A consommé is an absolutely clear soup made from a combination of meats or fish that has been strained, clarified to remove any vestige of fat, and usually reduced to intensify its flavor. It can be served hot or cold, sometimes jellied.

A SUPER SOUP

A friend of mine loved to tell of the time when he was an apprentice at a formidable French restaurant, where the proprietors used only ingredients at the very peak of perfection. All the vegetables and herbs were grown on their own property and the fish was brought in daily from rivers and lakes in the vicinity.

The fish chef was an irascible fellow who worked alone, snarling at anybody who came near his section of the kitchen. Early every morning, he would don his white chef's hat, stride into the kitchen garden, and gather bouquets of herbs, which he laid out in neat bunches along the length of his chopping block.

Next, he arranged one of each type of fish in military formation, heads forward, tails to the rear. Stooping, he confronted each fish, eyeball to gleaming eyeball. Hands bent on chubby knees, he smelled every fish and herb in turn. Very slowly, he would select one herb from this bunch and one from that and chop them into dozens of combinations, putting a little tarragon into this group, a touch of sorrel in another, a few curls of parsley here and there. The gentle, constant chopping continued until each herb was minced to the size of a pinhead and every fish on parade was flanked by green mounds of fragrance.

The inspection then began again. The chef picked up the first fish in line, rubbed a generous pinch of herbs onto its shiny skin, sniffed it delicately, and smiled. He then wiped his hands on his clean white apron, and proceeded to the next fish. By the time he had reached the end of the line, he was supremely content. His apron was green from the sweet-smelling herbs and *very* fishy.

One night, the apprentice stole the master's apron, which had become a historical record of the day's activities, and dropped it into a pot of boiling water. Ten minutes later, he had a glorious fish soup!

That is the way soup is made. You take a little of this and a little of that, and if it pleases you, you put it all together.

(The apprentice eventually became the executive chef of The Four Seasons restaurant in New York. His name was Albert Stockli.)

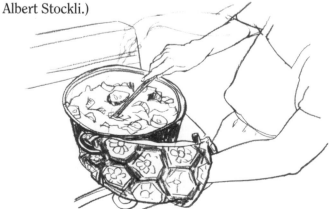

Books

Dairy Hollow House Soup and Bread
Crescent Dragonwagon; Workman, 1992; $12.95

Sensational Soups
Judy Knipe; Ballantine, 1994; $20

Soup, Beautiful Soup
Felipe Rojas-Lombardi; Henry Holt, 1992; $14.95

Soup Suppers
Arthur Schwartz; HarperPerennial, 1994; $15.00

Splendid Soups
James Peterson; Bantam, 1993; $29.95

Albert Stockli's
Cream of Broccoli Soup

Serves 4 to 6

1 tablespoon butter
½ medium-sized onion, coarsely chopped
1 small leek, coarsely chopped
1 stalk celery, coarsely chopped
1 tablespoon flour
4 cups chicken broth
1 bunch fresh broccoli, trimmed
Salt and pepper
Dash nutmeg
1 cup light cream
1 tablespoon parsley or chives, finely chopped

Melt the butter in a large saucepan and gently fry the chopped onion, leek, and celery for 5 minutes. Sprinkle the flour over the vegetables and combine. Stir in the broth, bring to a boil, then lower the heat, and simmer uncovered for 15 minutes.

Trim the head of the broccoli from the coarse stalk just where the florets begin. Break or cut the head into small florets and add to the soup, then cover, and simmer for another 15 minutes. Pour the mixture into the blender and puree until smooth. (You will have two blender loads.) Strain through a fine sieve into a clean saucepan. Season with salt and pepper, add a dash of nutmeg, and stir in the cream. Reheat the soup, but do not allow it to boil. Garnish with chopped parsley or chives.

SPACE FOOD

REMEMBRANCE OF THINGS FUTURE

ANN HORNADAY

When NASA's space station — equipped to hold a crew of up to eight for three months at a time — becomes permanently manned in 2001, it will house the kitchen of the future: state-of-the-art, but *cozy*.

Dr. Charles T. Bourland, the food system manager, says he wants the kitchen to feel like home, to give the astronauts relief from the stressful workouts of the usual spaceship day. Aside from some typical household debates like where the oven should go and how much storage space the craft can afford, Dr. Bourland's plans seem to be swimming along nicely. Unlike other spacecraft that use purified water left over from their fuel cells to rehydrate dehydrated food, the space station will be run on solar panels, which don't need or create water. So the meals taken on board will be more similar to normal earth food, which has psychological advantages, according to Dr. Bourland. Being cooped up in a space station for months, the astronauts will surely crave some reminders of home.

Although the team will be able to choose their personalized 28-day flight menus 120 days ahead of the launch (fresh supplies will be delivered by shuttle), there are some off-limits choices. Things that crumble easily — like cookies — present problems. In a gravity-free cabin the crumbs fly about like so much airborne dust. Eggs can't be cracked in space for the same reason, so the station's eggs are likely to be precooked and frozen.

Dr. Bourland has been figuring out how to get fresh fruits into space (he's developing a special container to keep apples and pears fresh for several months), and he would like to provide the crew with fresh-baked bread. He has played around with the idea of taking dough on board in frozen form, giving it time to rise, then baking it during the trip. Frozen dough would take up little space, he points out, and the smell of baking bread would be good for the astronauts' psyches. There's only one catch: astronauts tend to suffer from nasal congestion in weightless conditions, and there are no convection currents in the air to transmit odors.

Food in Space: A Timeline

1962 — John Glenn becomes the first American astronaut to eat in space, sucking applesauce from a tube connected to the food port of his helmet. Later Mercury missions feature bacon squares, brownies, coconut blocks, and squares of cinnamon toast.

1965 — NASA discovers that meat, bread, fruit, and desserts, which crumble and disperse in the gravityless capsule, can be compressed into cubes and coated with gelatin to hold together.

1968 — NASA graduates its boys to eating with a spoon.

1969 — NASA's generosity extends to providing precooked hot dogs and freeze-dried scrambled eggs.

1972 — Irradiated ham steaks are introduced to the menu.

1973 - 74 — Skylab features the first heated food on a space mission, thanks to a specially designed warming tray, as well as a freezer on board. Each astronaut plans his own menu: prime ribs, lobster Newburg, and filet mignon were all requested.

1985 — French astronaut Patrick Baudry joins Discovery with a basket of delicacies such as jugged hare *à l'Alsacienne* and crab mousse; on his return to France he forms a company to supply gourmet space meals.

1993 — Breakfast, lunch, and dinner menus on space flights may include peaches, fruit yogurt, beef pattie, scrambled eggs, bran flakes, cocoa, and orange drink; frankfurters, turkey tetrazzini, bread or tortilla, bananas, and lemonade; and shrimp cocktail, beefsteak, rice pilaf, broccoli au gratin, fruit cocktail, vanilla, chocolate, or butterscotch pudding, and grape drink. Unrefrigerated fresh fruits and vegetables are available for the first couple of days; after that, it's on to trail mix and other nonperishable snacks.

1994 — A shelf-stable tortilla is developed that will stay fresh for up to six months. Applesauce is still on the menu.

Loss in Space

Whatever they eat, astronauts return to earth with less than they went up with. One of the side effects of space travel is the loss of bone and muscle tissue, both of which atrophy regardless of dietary calcium and protein supplements, and even though the astronauts exercise vigorously. Scientists attribute the loss to the fact that there is no resistance to movement in zero gravity, so that flight-time activity doesn't "count."

Did You Know?

☞ Each astronaut's food for the day must not weigh more than 3.8 pounds, including 1 pound of packaging.

☞ Shrimp cocktail is still the most requested food item.

☞ There has been one vegetarian astronaut, who was able to select a balanced diet from NASA's basic food list.

☞ There's no dishwashing in space. Containers go into the trash; eating utensils and food trays are cleaned with premoistened towelettes at the hygiene station.

SPICES

THE ORIGINS OF SPICES

AVANELLE DAY AND LILLIE STUCKEY

Like rivers of fragrance, all the spices of the East — pepper, poppyseed, ginger, cloves, and sesame; nutmeg, mace, turmeric, cinnamon, and basil — have poured forth to bring their bounty. For thousands of years these insignificant curls of bark and shriveled seeds, these dried leaves and gnarled roots have flowed along the curving trade routes of antiquity into man's legend and history. From the perfumed ritual of the bath and the aromatic goodness of the hearth to the sacred worship of the gods, spices have added their magic. This was so, in whole or in part, when man was prehistoric; it was thus with the ancient Babylonians and Assyrians and Hebrews. Today the routes are buried by time, but time's tradition remains.

Excerpted from *The Spice Cookbook*

Q&A

Q What's the difference between a spice and an herb?

A Spices are seasonings made from the bark, roots, stems, buds, fruits, or seeds of tropical plants and trees, and are mostly used dried. Herbs are the fragrant leaves and young stems of plants from temperate areas; they may be dried but are better when fresh.

Spice Sources

Cardamom and ginger are related tropical plants, but we use aromatic cardamom seeds and pods dried, but only the leathery-looking root of fragrant, hot ginger, in fresh, dried, pickled, and crystallized forms. Cloves are the dried, unopened flower buds of a tropical member of the myrtle family. Cinnamon is the aromatic bark of a tree from the laurel family. Nutmeg and mace are the seed and its surrounding membrane from the peachlike fruit of an evergreen tree that is kin to almonds and peaches.

Anti-Arthritis
Tisane

¾ ounce of cinnamon sticks or twigs
1 ounce of fresh ginger root
Hot water

Combine the cinnamon and ginger in enough water just to cover them. Boil over moderate heat until the liquid is reduced by half. Drink a cupful three times a day to relieve the pangs of arthritis.

Pepping Life Up

Increasingly, physicians are looking to the curative powers of spices to treat common diseases. Cinnamon, cloves, turmeric, and bay leaves all may be able to lower blood-sugar levels because they affect the production of insulin, the hormone that controls the absorption of blood sugar. As we age, insulin works less efficiently, and blood-sugar levels can rise high enough to be toxic; untreated, this situation can turn into diabetes.

When USDA researchers applied 22 spice extracts to rats' cells and measured insulin production, they found that cinnamon, nutmeg, turmeric, and bay-leaf solutions tripled the hormone's usual activity level. Some diabetics have reported that about ¼ teaspoon of cinnamon a day is good for keeping glucose levels normal. And Dr. Richard Anderson, who conducted the study, recommends that *everyone* put a little spice in their life, to prevent adult onset of the disease.

Old Wives' Tale

Cumin is said to inspire faithfulness in men. In Europe, when young men went off to war, their sweethearts would bake a loaf of bread sprinkled with cumin seed, to send with them — and bring them home again.

Chinese herbalists say that cinnamon twigs are like the streets of a city, branching out and carrying their beneficial effects to every part of the body. And that is why cinnamon is good for arthritic fingers, which are our most remote extremities.

The Best Root en Route

If you suffer from motion sickness, next time pack some ginger root for the road. Tests have shown that ginger, either fresh or preserved, is more effective than Dramamine and lacks the drug's dizzying effects. Ginger is also a supposed cure for vomiting, fever, diarrhea, lumbago, coughing, and stomach pain. In New Guinea it's a contraceptive, in Africa an aphrodisiac. Truly, a root for all reasons.

Did You Know?

☞ U.S. annual spice consumption a decade ago was 486 million pounds; it currently averages about 730 million pounds. Do we like spices better or are our tongues simply becoming sensitized?

☞ Saffron is the most expensive spice. It is made from the bright orange stigma at the center of each purple flower of the autumn crocus, and 14,000 stigmas must be hand-picked to make 1 ounce of saffron.

☞ When Columbus discovered the New World, he was actually looking for spices, and he didn't come home empty-handed: Both allspice and chili pepper were discovered on his journey.

☞ Poppy seeds contain morphine in trace amounts — not enough to produce an effect but just enough to show up as an opiate in routine urine tests.

Books

Skinny Spices
Erica Klein; Surrey Books, 1993; $12.95

The Complete Book of Spices
Jill Norman; Viking, 1991; $21.95

SPINACH

Spinach is susceptible of receiving all imprints: It is the virgin wax of the kitchen.

— Grimod de la Reynière
Gastronomic historian

Green Queen

Catherine de' Medici, daughter of Lorenzo, duke of Urbino, left Florence in 1533 to become queen of France and mother of three kings. But she was also the mother of French haute cuisine, which had not existed until she arrived with her skilled Italian chefs and a passion for fine food. She was so fond of spinach that she had to have it at every meal, and the royal cooks learned to adapt it to all kinds of dishes. To this day, any dish employing spinach is called Such-and-such "Florentine" after Catherine.

GREAT GREENS

There is not a lot more to say about spinach than has already been demonstrated by Popeye, The Sailor Man, the vegetable's greatest champion and propagandist, in cartoons that date back over many decades. Squinting, muscular Popeye has shown many generations of young Americans that if we eat our spinach, we will grow up to be big and strong. And if we go on eating it as adults, as he does, we will always have boundless energy in a pinch.

Of course, in those early days, the health-giving properties of spinach, though well known to mothers trying to get their children to eat it, had only the authority of folklore: Its virtues had been observed, but not studied. Today, scientists are able to tell us, with confidence, that spinach is a real fighter against a variety of diseases, including cancer and cataracts. Rich in beta carotene, spinach has high concentrations in its stems and leaves of cancer-inhibiting carotenoid compounds, plus other anticancer compounds such as folic acid. Studies show that spinach is a regular feature in the diets of groups of people who have a low incidence of both heart disease and cancer.

Spinach has been cultivated for thousands of years, but the varieties of plants grown today, developed through the efforts of American breeders, are far more luxuriant than their predecessors, and their leaves are far more tasty than those that were plucked in the southwestern part of Asia in the dawn of cultivation. That Popeye never seemed to be particularly interested in the *taste* of spinach — he always ate it directly from the can, and in one gulp — is the one aspect of spinach promotion in which he failed us. Spinach is not only one of the most healthful vegetables we can have in our diet, it's wonderfully delicious, too.

Did You Know?

☞ Winter spinach has a stronger flavor than the young leaves of summer. To mute it, toss with butter and a pinch of salt.

MORE INFORMATION

Leafy Greens Council
33 Pheasant Lane
St. Paul, MN 55175
612-484-3321

Spinach to Die From

The eminent French gastronome Anthelme Brillat-Savarin considered that the best dish of spinach he had ever eaten was at Sunday dinner in the home of his friend the Abbé Chévrier, and he wanted the recipe. But the abbé was reluctant to confide it, and only after much prying and pressing did Brillat-Savarin discover the following facts:

1. For a Sunday dinner, cook the spinach for the first time on Wednesday, using a quarter pound of butter for each pound of spinach. Cook over very low heat for 30 minutes, then allow to cool in the pan.

2. On Thursday, cook the spinach again for 10 to 15 minutes in 2 more tablespoons of butter for each original pound, then allow to cool.

3. Repeat the process every day until Sunday.

4. On Sunday, cook the spinach again with 2 more tablespoons of butter, and serve.

By this time, the spinach will have absorbed three-quarters of its own weight in butter.

SQUASHES

FOR GOURDNESS' SAKE

Squashes sustained the starving Pilgrims during their first perilous winters because their hard skins (the squashes') allowed them to keep for a long time without spoiling. Though few ingenious ways were devised for cooking squash, the hungry colonists found them satisfying enough when there wasn't much else to eat.

In bygone times we had the quaint idea of eating fruits and vegetables in their appointed seasons. Today there are no seasons; both summer and winter squashes are available year-round, produced in some part of the United States or imported from other countries.

All squashes are members of the gourd family and are native to the Americas. Nature has created dozens of fanciful shapes, colors, and sizes for them. Some are bite-sized, others large enough to feed an army. Last year, incredulous reporters spread the news of an 800-pound pumpkin that was grown in a (very large) patch. Let's hope the prize was an immense pie plate.

Winter Varieties

The squashes that once heralded the fall are golden within their hard-shelled exteriors.

Butternut, one of the most popular varieties, is pear-shaped, with a light brown skin, yellow flesh, and inedible seeds clustered in its bulbous base. Butternuts weigh from 2 to 5 pounds each.

Delicata is shaped like a grooved watermelon with creamy-yellow mottling and dark-green stripes. Some claim it tastes like sweet corn, others liken it to sweet potatoes.

Turban really does look like a turban. It comes in all sizes, some large enough to hollow out and use as a soup tureen. (A voice of experience suggests that you make sure you haven't inadvertently poked a hole in the skin before you pour hot soup into its depths.) Smaller varieties can be used as table decorations. **Buttercup** is a variety of turban squash, although it does not look like one.

Acorn is one of the most familiar squashes. A favorite way of cooking it is to halve it horizontally, and fill the emptied seed cavity with apple sauce and maple syrup. Like all winter squashes, it is best served with spices, such as cinnamon, nutmeg, and allspice.

Golden nugget is shaped like a small pumpkin and has a pronounced pumpkin taste.

Hubbard squashes weigh up to 12 pounds; with their knobbly green skins, they look as though they might have been kissed by a frog. Inside, the flesh is a brilliant orange. Its taste, when cooked, is mild and pleasant, proving again the old adage about not judging a squash by its warts.

Sweet dumpling is a diminutive pumpkin-shaped ball with dark-green striations interspersed with mottled white skin. Most weigh only about half a pound and can be stuffed.

Spaghetti squash really can substitute for spaghetti because, when cooked, the yellowish flesh separates into long, thin, translucent strings that resemble pasta, but with many fewer calories. Even so, children may ask for more.

TIPS

Cooking

Cooking a winter squash can be speeded up by enclosing it, either whole or halved, in a plastic bag and microwaving it, cut side down, for 15 minutes or more. Make holes in the bag to allow the steam to escape.

Squash Nutrition

All squashes contain vitamins A and C (though deep-colored ones have the most beta carotene), along with some of the B vitamins, and are good sources of fiber. One cup of cooked squash contains about 100 calories.

Summer Varieties

All the summer squashes are delicately flavored and do not keep for more than three or four days in the refrigerator. They cook quickly and benefit from the company of onions, tomatoes, and eggplants. One of the best-tasting is the **chayote**, which is about the size of an avocado and is beloved in Mexico, South America, and the Caribbean, where it is also known as vegetable pear.

The little green **pattypan squash** and its relatives, the golden **sunburst** and dark green **scallopini squash,** are all identified by their scalloped edges and may be used interchangeably in recipes.

Marrow is an enormous squash that grows as long as your arm and as thick as your waist. It has what some call a mild (others vacuously bland) flavor. Savvy farmers in Maryland grow it for those who know how marvelous it can be with a savory stuffing or reposing in pristine splendor beneath a blanket of well-made white sauce laced with freshly chopped parsley.

But what most people think of as summer squash are the yellow **straightneck** and **crookneck squashes** and shiny green **zucchini**. Both are plentiful, inexpensive, and cook very quickly. Buy small ones, because when a squash grows too big, its seeds suck up all the flavor. Summer squashes are at their best steamed or grated into a salad.

For a while cute chefs made much merriment with fanciful presentations of **squash blossoms**, fried, stuffed, and strategically inserted among other nouvelle cuisine extravagances. They were almost always zucchini blossoms, because there are always *too many* zucchini in anybody's garden (which is why there is no separate category for zucchini in this book).

Spaghetti Squash with Garlic

Serves 6

1 large spaghetti squash
4 tablespoons butter or margarine
3 to 6 cloves garlic, finely chopped
2 tablespoons chopped parsley
Salt and freshly ground pepper

Fill the bottom of a vegetable steamer with enough water to come to within 1 inch of the steamer insert. Cover the pan and bring the water to a simmer over medium heat.

Cut the squash in half lengthwise and scoop out the seeds. Put the squash on the steamer insert, cut side down. Cover the pan and steam the squash for 40 minutes.

Heat the butter in a large frying pan over low heat. Add the chopped garlic and cook, stirring, for 2 minutes. Scoop the squash out of its skin, pulling it into strands. Add it to the garlic butter and toss. Add the chopped parsley and season with salt and pepper to taste. Toss again and serve.

Books

Harriet's Zucchini Lover's Cookbook
William Root; Harriet's Kitchen, 1986; $7.95

The Best of the Zucchini Recipes
Helen O. Dandar and Emil B. Dandar; Sterling Specialty, 1988; $7.95

The New Zucchini Cookbook
Nancy C. Ralston and Jordan Marynor; Storey Communications, 1990; $9.95

MORE INFORMATION

Frieda's Inc.
P.O. Box 58488
Los Angeles, CA 90058
800-241-1771

Melissa's World Variety Produce, Inc.
P.O. Box 21127
Los Angeles, CA 90021
800-468-7111

SQUID

Squid Are Swift

Using a siphon in their mantle, squid travel by squirting themselves through the water — and sometimes skim the waves as well. Able to aim, they can dart forward, backward, or sideways at will.

The favorite prey of most larger sea creatures, squid confuse their attackers by squirting black ink into the water. They are fierce predators themselves, consuming 14 percent of their body weight daily in crustaceans, small fish, and other squid.

LITTLE MONSTERS

Americans never really took to squid. In fact, until a very few years ago, we wouldn't even touch them except for bait. It was a matter of aesthetics: We had a hard time even *considering* trying to like a mollusk so ugly and oogy. As for those ten wriggly tentacles — ick.

However, the squid's time has come in the American market basket. Acceptance has soared so steeply in recent years — particularly when it's presented as *calamari*, as the Italians know and love it — that squid is now referred to as the "Cinderella seafood."

Getting past the creature's appearance — imagine a pale white two-eyed torpedo with a bad hairdresser — there are lots of good reasons why it promises to be the really big aqua-food of the future. For one thing, it's plentiful and cheap, weighing in at less than half the cost of all its competition, including its ritzier cousins, the clam, the mussel, and the oyster. And you get more for your money: The squid has no fuselage; more than 80 percent of what you buy is edible.

Nutritionists praise it because it's high in protein but low in fat and calories. Cooks like it because it's quick and easy to prepare — about two minutes is all it takes; keep it on the fire longer than that and it toughens up. But there's an escape clause that's called the 2/20 rule. If you cook it past two minutes, keep right on cooking for 20 minutes more, and it will get tender again.

The main thing, of course, is that squid has a firm texture and a sweet and nutty flavor. It's just delicious, as the people of the Mediterranean basin have known, to their great advantage, for at least a thousand years.

Did You Know?

☞ Squid can be eaten raw, baked, fried, or sautéed. It is user-friendly in salads, ceviches, empanadas, burritos, pastas, and pizzas.

☞ The largest squid ever caught was taken in Thimble Tickle Bay, Newfoundland, on November 2, 1978. It was 55 feet long and weighed two tons.

☞ The Japanese love squid; they call it *ita*. The Vietnamese also love it, and call it *muc*. The Basques love it so much that it's the central ingredient in their national dish, *calamare en su tinta,* or squid in its own ink.

Books

Calamari Cookbook
Joseph Schultz and Beth Regardz; Ten Speed Press, 1987; $9.95

The International Squid Cookbook
Isaac Cronin; Addison Wesley, 1981; $8.61

STRAWBERRIES

Doubtless God could have made a better berry, but doubtless God never did.

— Dr. William Butler
17th-century English writer

BEST OF BERRIES

Plump, red, and juicy, the strawberry has no rival in the hearts of Americans. Ninety percent of us eat them, according to the California Strawberry Advisory Board. Or, to put it in per-capita terms, each of us consumes 3.4 pounds of fresh strawberries every year, plus another 1.8 pounds frozen. California produces the lion's share, some 75 percent of all strawberries grown in the United States. The crop is available from January through November, with peak quality and supply from March to May. Florida ranks second to California in production; its berries are available from December to May, at a peak in March and April. Imports join the market from November to May.

The strawberry, a member of the rose family, grew wild

in Europe (where it was first cultivated in the 13th century) and in North and South America. Greatly prized in Europe for their sweetness are the tiny, fragile, wild Alpine strawberries called *fraises des bois*, "strawberries of the woods," because they grow in open glades in the conifer forests.

The basic strawberry we know today in America is a much bigger and hardier variety, the result of several centuries of cross-breeding of the native Virginia wild strawberry and a Chilean variety.

Why are strawberries called strawberries? It may have to do with the fact that in earlier times farmers brought berries to market threaded on straws. Straw has a role in strawberry farming to this day: Growers still put down a layer of straw to cover and protect strawberry beds.

Strawberry Marks

1. Good flavor

2. Size and shape — large, conically shaped berries are most popular

3. Texture — berries should have structural integrity, neither mushy nor crunchy

4. A fine strawberry scent

Books

Berries: A Country Garden Cookbook
Sharon Kramis; Collins Publishers,1994; $19.95

From the Strawberry Patch
Sharon K. Alexander; ABC Enterprises, 1982; $12.95

One Hundred One Strawberry Recipes
Carole Eberly; Eberly Press, 1987; $2.95

Simply Strawberries
Sara Pitzer; Storey Communications, 1985; $6.95

Strawberries
Carol Shirkey; New Win Publishing, 1992; $19.95

Strawberries: Recipes for America's Favorite Fruit
Nan Whalen; American Cooking, 1983; $2.95

Strawberry Cookery with Flavour, Fact, Folklore
Beatrice Ross Buszek; Nimbus, 1984; $9.95

Did You Know?

☞ Madame Tallien, a prominent figure at the court of the Emperor Napoleon, was famous for supplementing her bath water with the juice of strawberries — 22 pounds of them per *bain*.

☞ Driscoll Associates is the largest producer of fresh strawberries in the United States and the first to add its brand name and special packaging to the top-quality fruit it sells.

☞ Researchers have recognized that strawberries have a tranquilizing effect; the fragrance of strawberries is now being impregnated into the masks used for children's anesthesia.

☞ Eight medium-sized fresh strawberries contain

MORE INFORMATION

California Strawberry Commission
P.O. Box 269
Watsonville, CA 95077
408-724-1301

Florida Strawberry Growers Association
P.O. Box 2631
Plant City, FL 33564
813-752-6822

50 calories, 140 percent of the recommended daily allowance of vitamin C (more than is present in an orange), 3 grams of dietary fiber, and 240 milligrams of potassium.

STREET FOOD

When people wore hats and gloves, nobody would dream of eating on the street. Then white gloves went out of style and, suddenly, eating just about anything in the street became OK.

— Jane Addison
20th-century spectator

DINING A LA CART

FLORENCE FABRICANT

New York, of course, has it all. Or nearly all. It does not yet boast a fleet of boats in the harbor dispensing noodle dishes and stir-fries like the ones in Hong Kong, or the Navajo fry bread of Shiprock, New Mexico.

But if anything epitomizes the melting pot in this city, it is the street vendors. Hungry for Italian sausage sandwiches, calzones, and pizzas? No problem. Chinese noodles, dumplings, and egg rolls? Step right up. Jewish knishes and pickles, Mexican tacos and burritos, German bratwurst, Indian samosas, Philadelphia cheese steaks, Japanese yakitori and tempura, Caribbean roti and patties, Argentine empanadas, and good, dense New York cheesecake are also on the sidewalk menu.

Wagons throughout the city purvey chestnuts in season, soft pretzels, ice cream, and drinks. In the morning on Canal Street near Bayard, a cart serves steaming crab rolls in rice-flour wrappers, while on West 14th Street you can sometimes snack on Philippine lumpia. Uptown, on the corner of 86th Street and Central Park West, fresh muffins and hot coffee are often available to subway commuters in the morning rush.

The roasted sweet potatoes, oysters, and charlotte russes of yore have disappeared. Good Humor has been all but eclipsed by a dozen fancy competitors. But there are now french fries, giant cookies, fresh-squeezed orange juice, and cappuccino. And it seems as though more food vendors than ever ply the streets.

— Excerpted from *The New York Times*

SUGAR

SUGAR TAKES ITS LUMPS

In 1979, when Dan White was on trial for killing San Francisco Mayor George Moscone and City Supervisor Harvey Milk, sugar was declared the real villain. White's defense was that he had been of unsound mind as a consequence of bingeing on Twinkies. The argument that "sugar made me do it" was accepted by a sympathetic jury.

Sugar has taken a lot of bum raps. "They" say it makes holes in your teeth. Wrong. Rats in a San Bernardino lab were force-fed fruit or refined sugar 17 times a day for 30 days and the cavity culprits turned out to be, in descending order, bananas, oranges, and apples. Close to innocent was sugar. In fact, it is no more guilty of causing dental caries than are raisins and dates.

Sugar has been blamed for disagreeable behavior, inattention, and hyperactivity in children. This case has also been dismissed for lack of evidence. The fact is that sugar has a calming effect. Give a crying baby a bottle of sugar water and you will get a happy smile.

Sugar is also accused of causing obesity. There *is* something to this, but those who claim to have a "sweet" tooth are more likely to have a "fat" tooth. Many desserts that we think of as sweets are really fats. And don't be beguiled by labels claiming "sugar-free" foods. They may contain other high-calorie sweeteners such as honey, corn syrup, molasses, or concentrated fruit juice.

Finally, to clear up another myth, the FDA confirms that sugar does not cause diabetes, although it can exacerbate the symptoms. (In primitive cultures, diabetes is diagnosed by urinating against a tree. If the ants come running, the proof is positive.)

Sugar
Substitutes

Saccharin, a petroleum derivative 300 times sweeter than sugar, was discovered, accidentally, in 1879. For nearly a century it was the only synthetic sugar substitute — a teaspoon has only $1/8$ calorie — but its somewhat bitter aftertaste, noticeable when heated, and possible carcinogenic effects have made it less popular, though it is widely used as Sweet n' Low sweetener.

Aspartame, a synthesis of two amino acids, was licensed in 1981 after years of safety review by the FDA, and is sold under the brand name NutraSweet, and as Equal sweetener. Low in calories and 200 times sweeter than sugar, aspartame now dominates the packaged food and soft drink market in more than 90 countries. It loses its sweetness when heated because its components break down, but it can be added successfully to a product at the end of processing.

Acesulfame-K (Sunette) contains no calories and is about 200 times sweeter than sugar. FDA approval is still pending for its use in sodas and commercial baked foods.

ODD JOBS

The bag checker at C & H Sugar sits within a maze of eight conveyor belts, looking for leaks as the sugar bags speed by on their way to the warehouse. Even a small hole can rain sugar, which upsets consumers and messes up the machinery. The bag checker's position has been integral to C & H's operation since the firm opened in 1906, and has survived the plant's full automation.

Sweetness and Light

Sugar (sucrose) is a carbohydrate found in many fruits and some vegetables. It is the result of photosynthesis, a process in which plants transform the sun's energy into food. It is most concentrated in sugarcane (a giant grass that stores sugar in its stalk) and in the sugar beet (which stores sugar underground in its big white root). There is no difference in the sugar produced from these sources.

Sweet Deals

The trading of sugar is subject to incredibly complex sets of import and export quotas and tariffs. Exports from developing countries, amounting annually to $16 billion, have a direct effect on the global economy. Sugar is among the most highly political of all commodities. The 1993 passage of NAFTA legislation hinged on Mexico's agreement not to dump surplus sugar in the United States and depress prices.

MORE INFORMATION

American Sugar Alliance
1225 Eye Street NW,
Suite 505
Washington, DC 20005
202-457-1437

The Sugar Association, Inc.
1101 15th Street NW,
Suite 600
Washington, DC 20005
202-785-1122

SUPERMARKETS

THE CHANGING SCENE

Want a car loan? Go to the supermarket. Want a croissant, a lawn mower, a vacuum cleaner? Want a video, a potted plant, postage stamps, a toaster, a toy, a tire? Go to the supermarket.

While you're at it, have a sit-down lunch from the salad bar, or pick up a pizza or a plate of sushi, or choose among the fast and ethnic food franchises that are taking up residence there. In some markets you can sip a cappuccino, in others you can order, and have delivered, a complete Thanksgiving dinner for 12. (All you need do is heat it and eat it.)

Stimulated by vigorous competition, supermarkets continue to trade in new services — bakeries, pharmacies, florists, and film processing centers. They have long been selling magazines, books, school supplies, and hardware. Now they're adding dry cleaners, cooking and English language schools, and varied financial services and banking facilities.

You can't as yet get married in a supermarket, although some do feature dating nights for singles. (And others have always been the best pickup places around — just pop your honeydew melon into the right wrong shopping cart for starters.) The latest wrinkle to attract more customers is a service that enables shoppers to buy tickets for movies, concerts, and sporting events. Will we be running to the supermarket to pick up a plane ticket, get a haircut, or have our palms read? Already there are rumors that we may soon be able to find a doctor in the house — as emergency walk-in clinics are established where most people are, most of the time, anyway.

Features of the markets of tomorrow:

• Because fewer people will be cooking from scratch, we'll be buying more ready-to-eat and microwavable foods, in amounts for one or two.

• Prepared foods will constitute more than 90 percent of food sales and supermarket aisles will be arranged not by product but by time taken in preparation — 15 minutes, 10 minutes, and so on.

• A supermarket chef will be on hand to cook customer meals to specifications.

• Packaged prewashed salad greens and precut brand-name fruits such as melon and pineapple will be labeled with place of origin and degree of ripeness.

• When customers open refrigerated cabinets, jingles advertising particular brands of soda will play.

• Supermarket chains will offer credit cards rewarding high spenders with bonus coupons. Chain "clubs" will give member discounts on large orders of staple products.

Putting the Cart First

The promised revolution in "smart" shopping carts has been slow to pick up steam. Some customers refuse to have anything to do with them; others stand in line to use them.

Some carts are smarter than others. A few have liquid crystal screens that display signals as they roll down the aisle, alerting customers to sale-priced items. Some can remind a customer buying hot dogs, say, to pick up buns, mustard, relish, paper plates, and as many add-ons as possible. Some carts talk back to you when you ask for guidance on locating up to 2,000 items in the store, or for specific nutrition information. Ask what healthy snacks are in stock, and the cart displays a list of choices. Ask for a seasonal or economical menu — and you get suggestions, plus a free recipe.

Some carts even dispense electronic coupons, which show up on the screen as the customer passes an item (not necessarily of the same product — stores find these a useful way of cross-merchandising). Pushing a button tells the cart's computer which coupon is being used, the message is passed to the cash register, and when the customer checks out, the reduced price is charged automatically.

Carts with pushbar calculators aren't popular, it seems. Fewer than half the shoppers questioned in a recent survey knew the cost of any item they were buying, and those who care about cost bring personal calculators along.

How $100 Is Spent

The most recent annual report on the grocery industry identified where the money goes by category in the average supermarket:

Perishables	**$50.08**
Bakery foods, packaged	$3.36
Dairy products	$7.79
Deli	$2.95
Florals	$0.29
Frozen foods	$5.82
Ice cream	$0.89
In-store bakery	$1.70
Meat and seafood	$17.44
Produce	$9.84
Nonedible Grocery	**$11.90**
Beverages	**$9.62**
Miscellaneous Grocery	**$8.24**
Snack Foods	**$5.27**
Main Courses and Entrees	$4.31
General Merchandise	**$4.07**
Health and Beauty Care	$3.93
Unclassified	**$2.58**

Many Tiny Returns

The average supermarket earns as little as half a cent on the dollar for staples such as bread, milk, flour, and coffee, but higher markups on nonessentials such as potato chips, deli sandwiches, and luxury foods. The giants in the field, who can pressure suppliers for the best deals, and count on high volume and a wide range of merchandise to achieve profits, drop prices the lowest.

ALL BASED ON BAR CODES

Efficient Consumer Response, familiarly known as ECR, is just one of the ways that advanced technology has sprinted into the supermarket. The new system is expected to save the industry up to $30 billion by streamlining its operations. It tracks the supermarket's inventory (an average of some 18,000 items) by using information from the bar codes, and automatically delivers new supplies on a "just in time" schedule, thereby reducing labor costs and losses from wasted perishable foods.

The bar code contains information about manufacturing, shipping, inventory control, and pricing. It speeds checkout time by providing more accurate tallies than the human hand that frequently falters. Newer codes are printed in ink invisible to the human eye, so that they can be bigger and contain more information, enabling the scanner to identify each object from any angle.

A Dutch company with more than 6,000 stores is testing a hand-held scanner, which the customer passes over the bar code of each item selected. When the shopping is done, the scanner issues a statement and the customer pays the bill at the express checkout counter.

And a naughty customer who has attempted to steal a chicken by hiding it under her hat will be summarily arrested at the door, betrayed by a loud wail from a bar code on the wrapper that has not been properly deactivated by the scanner.

Why Can't I Find What I Want?

Have you noticed some gaps in the supermarket shelves lately? Even old trusties like Ry-Krisp or Pecan Sandies disappear for a while, then return once more, but in a fresh position. There are more and more offerings from giants with familiar names, but there are fewer and fewer varieties to choose from — especially alternatives that bear small companies' names.

It's the slotting, you see, that determines the stocking. For some years now, supermarkets have been charging manufacturers so-called slotting fees for the use of the prime shelves in the store (those at eye level in the most frequented aisles), and to cover the risk of stocking new and unproven products. Fees depend on individual practices, but can run upwards of $20,000 per product per chain. A new business entering the market must budget millions to pay the up-front price.

Sometimes, supermarkets will reduce or waive slotting allowances in order to be able to stock new products that look like winners — especially in the now-booming health foods field, which is still largely a province of small, independent manufacturers. But achieving a slot does not necessarily mean a product will keep its place if it doesn't turn sales quickly enough. Supermarkets work on such a narrow markup that they must make money from every square inch of space, and they are ruthless in their discards.

What you are being offered, in fact, are those brands that your supermarket chain's distributor stocks, which may vary by region as well as by amounts paid in slotting fees. A brand made on the West Coast, for instance, may no longer be stocked in East Coast supermarkets because alternatives closer at hand can be brought in more cheaply. They may not have the flavor of the one you were looking for, but you'll get used to it.

The Inner City Supermarket

Some profound changes are afoot in the nation's cities. Community Development Corporations (CDCs) are encouraging the large chains to build new stores in some of the poorest neighborhoods, aided by generous funding and tax concessions from state and federal governments. These markets can serve as stabilizing anchors and encourage investment by other merchants. But the participating chains don't view this as a purely philanthropic investment: Inner-city supermarkets have almost double the sales potential of suburban ones because the population density is so much greater.

The small inner-city supermarkets and corner stores are often accused of price gouging because they sell at prices 10 to 25 percent higher than those charged for comparable products in suburban stores. Managements justify this on the grounds of having higher security costs, but their chief customers are the captive population who can't go elsewhere to shop. Those who can, do. A recent Consumer Reports survey found that in Oakland, California, for every $100 that low-income shoppers spent on food, only $34 was spent in neighborhood stores, whereas middle-income consumers spent $83.25 on food purchases *within* their own communities.

As the big chains move back into America's cities, however, they can offer fairer prices because of their ability to buy in quantity and spread the costs more widely. They also regularly maintain security forces and in-store surveillance systems because "crime is in all areas," as one executive put it. His company already has 20 inner-city stores and rates them among its most successful.

Did You Know?

☞ Fifteen percent of husbands whose wives earn more than $30,000 do all the grocery shopping, but only 7 percent of the husbands whose wives earn less than $20,000 shop regularly.

☞ When grocery shopping with children, women spend nearly 30 percent more than if they had shopped alone; men spend 66 percent more.

☞ More than two-thirds of buying decisions are made when the customer is in the store.

☞ Men prefer paper grocery bags, women prefer plastic.

☞ Six percent of the items stocked in the average supermarket account for 40 percent of the store's total sales volume.

☞ The Kroger Company is the largest publicly owned supermarket chain.

☞ Americans spend more than $286 billion at the supermarket every year. Seven percent of disposable income is spent on food to eat at home.

☞ A record 7.7 billion manufacturers' coupons were redeemed last year, saving consumers close to $4.5 billion. Most popular: breakfast cereal, candy, pet food, cookies, cheeses, and condiments.

Coupons have become America's other currency.

— John Naisbitt
Thinker

Money-Saving Tips

• Shop where you are familiar with the layout of the store so you are less likely to make impulse purchases as you roam the aisles.

• Using coupons for such staples as coffee, prepared foods, cereals, flour and flour mixes, and pet foods can save 10 percent on your grocery bill. But when you're clipping coupons, only clip those for foods you normally use.

• Buy store or regional brands. Research shows that doing this will cut your overall grocery bills by 10 percent.

• If a pound of breaded flounder fillets costs $4.99, while a pound of unbreaded fillets costs $6.39, this adds up to nearly 9 cents per ounce extra for the unbreaded fish.

But wait a minute. Breaded coatings on fish can account for 40 percent of the total weight. By buying the unbreaded, you pay $1.93 less per pound of real fish.

• Pancakes made from a complete mix are a quarter of the cost of frozen pancakes and a third of the price of ready-to-pour batter.

• It makes good sense to buy store brand products such as sugar, bleach, flour, and vinegar. Sugar is sugar. There is no difference in quality between a high-priced bag and one with a lower price. A 5-pound bag of store-brand sugar costs $1.99 compared with a brand name at $2.29.

• A 10-pound bag of baking potatoes is $1.99, while individual potatoes in the bin cost 50 cents a pound. (An equivalent amount of instant potatoes from a box costs about 45 cents.)

• The price per pound for shredded Swiss cheese is close to twice the amount for a wedge.

• You get more meat per pound when you buy a turkey weighing 12 pounds or more. For example, a 15-pound turkey will feed 18 to 20 people while a 10-pounder will feed only 6 to 8. At $1.39 a pound, you save up to 92 cents a serving. A smaller turkey has a larger ratio of bone to meat than the bigger bird.

• A 12-inch deli pizza costs $6.50, a frozen one $4.50, and a refrigerated "make your own" pack with rolled-out crust, pizza sauce, and mozzarella cheese $5.99.

If you were really to make your own — by buying a frozen 2-crust package ($1.69) or a pound of frozen pizza dough ($1.38), a 16-ounce jar of pizza sauce ($1.86) and 8 ounces of shredded mozzarella ($2.50) — you would spend about the same amount, but get two pizzas for the money!

• Sugared cereals cost more than plain. Add 1 teaspoon of sugar and plain corn flakes are still 4 cents per bowl less than sugared.

• Buying a frozen beef entree costs you about one and a half times what it would to cook the same meal yourself. Being your own cook can save you about 80 cents per serving.

• There's not much difference in the cost of frozen or canned vegetables, but the cost of vegetables frozen in butter sauce is nearly twice as much.

For example, store-brand frozen peas cost 85 cents per 10-ounce bag while a 10-ounce package of brand-name buttered peas costs $1.69. Even when you add a tablespoon of butter (which hardly anyone does these days), you save a dollar by buying plain peas.

Based on "Save Over $1,000 a Year on Your Weekly Shopping List," *Woman's Day*

Comparing Prices, Competing Brands

Shelf-mounted unit price labels show both the actual price being charged for each item and its price per unit — dry products such as flour and coffee are measured by the pound, liquids by the quart, and paper products by the per-100 count.

Unit price labeling aids the store, because it removes the necessity of labeling each item individually (and relabeling every time there is a price change). The side-by-side comparisons also enable the customer to compare competing brands and make informed choices. For instance, if a specific brand of coffee is $1 a pound and another is $1.50 a pound and you want to buy a 2-pound can that is on sale, you can check the unit prices against each other to determine which is the better buy (which may not be the sale item).

Though smart shoppers may think there is no difference between a brand-name and a private-label bag of sugar or salt, they will frequently buy the more expensive product. In a 1993 Yankelovich survey, 72 percent of consumers said they selected a brand-name food rather than a less costly private-label alternative. To encourage this way of thinking, some brands reward loyal customers with a points system entitling them to discounts or gifts.

"It's a male thing, Martha. Just humor me."

SURIMI

NAKED LUNCH

Surimi is the people-fodder of the future, a seafood with a thousand false identities but none of its own. It's a tasteless, odorless paste manufactured — usually on factory trawlers — from the minced, rinsed, mild white flesh of Alaska pollock. The rinsing dissolves water-soluble elements, leaving behind a residue of tightly bonding proteins with such extraordinary "gel strength" that this raw material can be molded into any shape desired, and will keep that shape subsequently. Natural flavors can be blended in, and color and texture imposed.

Surimi is the basic stuff for many faux seafood products, which are called analogs. It made its debut in the American market a decade ago, mixed with mayonnaise and celery and posing in delicatessens as "seafood salad" or "Neptune salad." Public acceptance was so rapid and avid that the market ventured further with specific imitations — of crab, lobster, shrimp, and scallops, looking just like the real thing — and U.S. consumption now is at an estimated 100 million pounds annually. With these imitations we are still often able to astonish our friends — "You mean this *isn't* lobster?" they say.

But surimi has many more surprises in store. It's already being used as the phony baloney in low-cal hot dogs, it poses as potato chips and ice cream, and it can be made into a "chicken breast" so authentic that most people who tasted the prototype couldn't tell it from poultry.

Japan is the largest surimi producer in the world; in that country, more than 300 food products made from it are already available on the market. The United States is the second largest world producer, and lags well behind the Japanese in numbers of surimi food products already in the stores. But the lag probably won't last long. Says Roy Martin, vice president of science and technology at the National Fisheries Institute: "As with soy proteins, the only limit to the use of surimi is the imagination and the market."

SUSHI

SWOONING AT THE SUSHI BAR

RUTH REICHL

The first time I ate sushi I fell in love. I could hardly believe that I had spent 20 years on this planet before my introduction to this incredibly delicious food.

I was later to learn that there are people — lots of them — for whom the very idea of eating raw fish is disgusting. It never entered my mind. I was lost in the joy of discovery. I loved the clean, clear flavors of the fish and the soft velvety textures. I loved the subtle flavor differences between one fish and another: the richness of yellowtail; the robust, almost meaty taste of tuna; the subtlety of halibut. As one piece of sushi after another slipped down my throat, I thought how lucky I was to have made this discovery. I was greedy for the buttery softness of red snapper, the smoothness of squid, and the resiliently crunchy character of giant clams. I had only one thought: How soon can I come back?

Since then I have eaten sushi hundreds of times, but the essential experience has never changed. Every time I walk up to a sushi bar I go into a trance of anticipation. I bow to the sushi chef. I inspect the fish in the case. I rub the hot towel across my hands. I say that I will start with sashimi. (This, I have discovered, brands you as a serious sushi eater.) And then I tell the chef that I am in his hands….

Now the chef spoke. "Sushi?" he asked. Of course. A new board appeared in front of me….

First came *tai*, the sweet lean fish that is a relative of sea bream. The flesh was so soft it seemed to melt into the rice on which it was served. The chef picked up a large clam that was still moving and sliced it. The flavor was clear and piercing and clean…. Then a variety of fish roe served in little seaweed bundles: large bright pearls of salmon roe that popped lazily between the teeth and the tiny, brighter smelt roe that popped with a staccato rhythm….

"More?" the chef wanted to know.

"Just one more flavor," I replied.

Excerpted from The New York Times

Record-Setting Robot

A Japanese company has introduced a sushi robot that can produce up to 1,200 pieces of sushi in an hour. This performance beats the record of Japan's finest human sushi chefs, who even under the most optimal conditions can produce no more than about 200 pieces an hour by hand. The sushi robot costs $65,000.

A Matter of the Greatest Delicacy

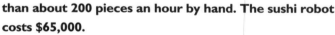

Sushi is the national dish of Japan. The word itself refers to the one constant and basic ingredient of the dish — vinegar-seasoned rice, carefully fanned dry, to which vegetables, condiments, and fish are added.

There are three kinds of sushi: *nori-maki*, in which the sushi are rolled in sheets of nori seaweed; *chirashi-sushi*, rice balls with other ingredients scattered in; and *nigiri-sushi*, ovals of rice with other ingredients layered over the top.

The raw fish that is served before (or in some cases, with) a meal of sushi is called sashimi. To ensure the most subtle and delicate of flavors, only the freshest fish is used, artfully carved and exquisitely presented.

Sashimi is eaten with chopsticks. Sushi is taken in the hand.

Books

Sushi Made Easy
Nobuko Tsuda; Weatherhill, 1982; $9.95

SWORDFISH

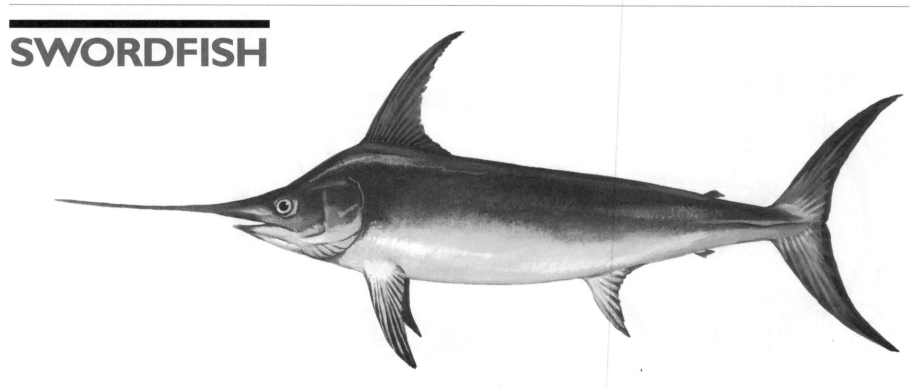

BROADBILL

The most hunted of fish in the sea is the broadbill swordfish. A solitary, unique species, it wanders, a long-range traveler, through all the tropical and temperate oceans of the world. Its food is smaller fish such as mackerel, which it kills by rising suddenly beneath a school near the surface and slashing or impaling fish with blows from its remarkable bill. Appropriately, its species name is *Xiphias gladius* — from the short sword of the Roman soldier.

Swordfish can be 15 feet long and weigh as much as 1,000 pounds, and in some parts of the world they still do. But not in the coastal waters of New England, where they have been fished almost out of existence. In 1958, the average size of a swordfish landed there was 130 pounds. Today, it's more like 50.

More than 20 nations send fishing fleets worldwide after swordfish. The most productive area — the western Pacific, from Japan to the Philippines — yields 20 percent of the world catch. Swordfish are also taken in the eastern Pacific from California to Chile. In the Atlantic they are pursued from Newfoundland to Uruguay to the coast of Africa, and they are sought in the Mediterranean as well. The United States is the world's leading consumer of swordfish, but is only a minor producer. Japan leads in production, but Spain, Italy, South Korea, Taiwan, Chile, the Philippines, Portugal, and Canada are also significant producers. Swordfish are often referred to by the nationality that took them — Portuguese sword, Chilean sword, domestic sword — because the manner of handling, which differs from country to country, greatly affects quality.

The newest source of swordfish is in the waters of Hawaii. This fishery has risen from virtually nothing at all to very significant landings in just a few years. In the swordfish business, Hawaii is now "hot."

Swordfish with Tomato Sauce

Serves 4

3 tablespoons olive oil
1 ½ to 2 pounds swordfish steaks, ½- to ¾-inch thick
Salt and freshly ground pepper
¾ pound Italian plum tomatoes, seeded and cut into ½-inch pieces
1 large scallion, chopped
1 tablespoon balsamic vinegar
1 tablespoon chopped fresh basil

Heat 1 tablespoon of the oil in a large frying pan over medium-high heat. Sprinkle the fish lightly with salt and pepper and cook for 4 to 5 minutes on each side until the steaks are opaque at the center. Remove the fish from the pan and keep warm on a serving platter.

Add the remaining 2 tablespoons of oil to the pan along with the tomatoes and scallions. Cook over medium-high heat for 3 to 4 minutes until the tomatoes are softened. Add the vinegar and cook for 1 minute. Stir in the basil and season to taste with salt and pepper.

Spoon the tomato sauce over the fish and serve.

A Mercury Fix?

The U.S. swordfish industry, which was flourishing in the early 1970s, met a crisis when it was found that swordfish were exceeding U.S. allowable mercury levels of 0.5 parts per million. Catches, especially of the larger fish, had to be dumped. However, in 1978 the FDA solved the problem in a curiously Alice-in-Wonderland fashion by raising the permissible mercury level to 1 part per million, where it has remained ever since.

The Power of the Sword

The swordfish isn't fond of man — why should it be? — and in the days of wooden sailing vessels, sailors feared its wrath. According to one 19th-century account, a swordfish stabbed a whaling ship right through to the heart, penetrating a layer of copper sheathing and the wooden hull, a 3-inch hardwood plank, a 12-inch timber of white oak, and 2½ inches of hard oak ceiling, finally imbedding the point of its sword in a cask of oil.

TIPS

Buying
Domestic swordfish is usually sold fresh; almost all frozen swordfish is imported and somewhat less costly. The color may vary depending on how the fish was caught, but white flesh should never be gray, darker flesh never brown, and the bloodline always reddish. Rely on your nose as well; buy fish that smells fresh and sweet.

Cooking
Grilling is the most popular way to cook swordfish, but you can also bake, broil, or pan-fry it. Even the best cuts easily dry out, so be generous with the oil or butter and cook only until the flesh just becomes opaque.

SYNTHETIC FOOD

SEE YA IN THE FUNNY PAPERS

RICHARD ATCHESON

I've been expecting synthetic food to show up for decades, ever since I first read about it in a Mickey Mouse comic book back in the 1940s. In a story that utterly captured my childish imagination, Mickey and Minnie journey in space to the world of the future, where they wander city streets that are remarkably like the city streets of . . . well, of the 1940s. But when they go into a restaurant that's like the Automat and put coins in a slot, out comes a plate with nothing on it but a tiny pill.

Mickey and Minnie react with comic astonishment, gawping and pointing as exclamation points of surprise ring their heads. But then they are told to water the pill (little watering cans are on every table), and when they do, the pill blossoms into two huge pork chops, a big dollop of mashed potatoes with a pool of gravy, and a pile of peas — all piping hot.

Faux fats and seaweed posing as ice cream are all very well, but they are food from food. Food from *no* food — preferably pork chops — is what I'm waiting for.

Microbes and Men

If you grow your own tomatoes, you'll have heard of *Fusarium graminearum*, a pesky fungus that can destroy tomato plants. But as with so many microbes, one variety of this fungus has its good side: Biotechnologists can use it to make high-quality protein by mixing it with carbohydrate in the form of glucose, adding oxygen, nitrogen, and minerals, and fermenting the mixture in a bioreactor. The combination grows rapidly and can be harvested within a few days, pro-

ducing, once the liquid has been drained off, a fibrous substance, rather like meat, with fibers formed from fungal threads.

Sounds horrible? That's why it took eight years for a British food company to develop an effective marketing strategy for its mycoprotein product (*myco* actually means "fungus"), called Quorn. Its debut in 1990 featured TV ads showing a group of happy animals rejoicing because they had been saved from slaughter by "a tiny relative of the

mushroom" ("mushroom" sounds more friendly than "fermented filamentous fungus").

Mycoprotein has great possibilities as a cheaper, tenderer, healthier alternative to meat. It seems that the fungus makes protein four times more efficiently than the best animal. The problem is, simply, acceptability. Most of us would rather eat a factory-farmed chicken than a synthetic microbial protein fermented in a bioreactor. Though what is a chicken grown to be eaten, if not a bioreactor on two legs?

If we are what we eat, then what the hell are we?
— A 20th-century wit

MAN MADE

So you say you had a nice breakfast this morning — orange juice, bacon and eggs, buttered toast, and coffee with cream. Dreamy.

But . . .

if the orange juice was reconstituted from a powder . . .
and the bacon was made from a soybean analog . . .
and the scrambled eggs were poured from a carton . . .
and the butter was shaken from a container of flakes . . .
and the coffee was decaffeinated and came from a jar . . .
and the non-dairy creamer had never seen a cow . . .
and the sugar and salt were substitutes in little paper packets . . .

Could you really claim to have had breakfast this morning? Or were you living without noticing it in somebody else's technological dream?

Because in the colder light of day, what you *really* had this morning was an ingenious variety of fake foods made into fake shapes, and cooked in the microwave with — this is the dreamiest thing of all — fake heat.

A Mystery on Every Plate

At the turn of the century, government, science, industry, and technology changed not only what we ate but also how we thought about it. Food was reduced to those physical properties that could be analyzed and synthesized chemically.

— Betty Fussell
Food writer

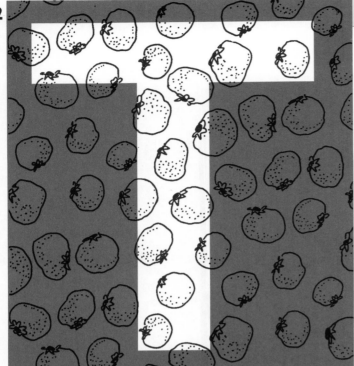

TABLE MANNERS

How Time Flies

*A*ccording to Michael Bateman, writing in London's The Independent on Sunday, *there are several ways to let dinner guests know it's time to leave. "A Frenchman may ask if you'd like something, a fruit juice perhaps? The Elizabethans played nasty practical jokes on guests who outstayed their welcome. . . . If you still haven't left the house after several days, the Ainu of Japan give a feast for you entitled The Feast of Having Been Sent Back, the Mouth Having Been Cooked For. If the guests still fail to take the hint, the host and hostess move out and go to stay with relatives. That usually does the trick."*

WAITER, BRING ME ANOTHER SEA SHELL

HENRY PETROSKI

Of the common eating implements, the fork was the last to develop. Spoons can be traced back to prehistoric times, when shells were an improvement over cupped hands for holding water and other liquids. Fingers had long served to convey solid food to the mouth. The first knifelike objects were fashioned 8,000 years ago from sharp pieces of chipped flint and obsidian, and were used as weapons and butchering tools. By the Middle Ages they had achieved a recognizably modern form, with pointy-ended blades and handles of wood, bone, brass, or horn. They were the only eating utensils for solid food....

Early in the 17th century, a desire to eat foods that didn't cut easily under a single knife caused a second pointed knife to appear at well-set tables, or to be brought to the table by the sophisticated traveler. One knife held the food steady while the other cut it, and then the cutoff piece of food could be speared and carried to the mouth. Since the cutting knife demanded the greater dexterity, a right-handed diner would naturally use the knife in his left hand to steady the meat while the knife in his right hand did the cutting.... The use of two knives remained the custom of well-mannered diners until a new implement became available.

The earliest European table forks appeared in Italy a thousand years ago but fell out of use until the 14th century. They moved westward to France in 1533 and to England nearly a hundred years later. At first, they were used only sparingly, by royalty and in the most fashionable homes, to replace the knife that held the food. During this time, forks had two straight (rather than curved) tines, and were grasped in the left hand. They were a great convenience for eating meat, because the separate tines held the meat much more securely than a single knife point could.

In the American colonies, however, forks were not readily available.... The customary way of eating was the old way, with a pair of pointed knives. When the new blunt-ended knives began arriving from across the ocean — unaccompanied by forks — colonists, who had never used a knife blade to scoop up food, had to adopt the spoon as the utensil that conveyed food from plate to mouth.... The knife was laid down after being used for cutting and the spoon in [the colonist's] left hand was passed to his right.... By the time forks finally became widely available in the 19th century, the manner of using the knife and spoon had become so customary that the fork merely replaced the spoon in the left hand and was used as the spoon had been.

Excerpted from *Wigwag*

What To Eat With Your Hands

Maryland steamed crabs

Lobster

Fried chicken

Hamburger

Pizza

Corn on the cob

Artichokes

Overstuffed sandwiches, including Po' Boys

Ribs

Watermelon

What Not to Eat With Your Hands

Spaghetti

Jell-O

Keeping the Fur From Flying

Leonardo da Vinci was known to keep detailed notebooks about many things that interested him. Recently, Shelagh and Jonathan Routh published a fascinating translation of Kitchen Note Books, attributed to Leonardo, in which the great painter complains about the table manners of his patron, Lodovico Sforza, duke of Milan, whom he served as Master of the Revels and Feasting:

"My Lord Lodovico's habit of tethering beribboned rabbits to the chairs of his table guests, that they may wipe their grease-ridden hands upon the beasts' backs, I find unseemly for the day and age we live in. Also, when the beasts are collected after the meal and taken to the laundry-room, their stink pervades the other linens with which they are washed.

"Neither do I care for My Lord's habit of wiping his knife upon his neighbor's skirts. Whyfor can he not, like the other members of his Court, wipe it upon the tablecloth which is so provided?"

Number of chairs you will need for a six-person dinner party. Plus a table, of course.

Books

Elements of Etiquette
Craig Claiborne; Morrow, 1992; $15.00

Much Depends on Dinner: The Extraordinary History and Mythology, Allure and Obsessions, Perils and Taboos, of an Ordinary Meal
Margaret Visser; Grove, 1986; $19.95

The Rituals of Dinner: The Origins, Evolution, Eccentricities, and Meaning of Table Manners
Margaret Visser; Viking, 1992; $14.00

TAKE-OUT FOOD

GETTING CARRIED AWAY

We have come a long way since we thought it thrifty to steal a march on tomorrow's dinner by bringing home a doggie bag of leftover meat loaf. Today we are willing to spend extravagantly for a grilled chicken breast with jalapeño mayo between two slices of toasted focaccia, a slice of duck pâté with sun-dried cherries on a baguette, or a single portion of triple chocolate cake and a paper cup of frothy cappuccino — to go.

Take-out stores are thriving because they fill a real or perceived need for busy people to provide themselves with something pretty and pretty good to eat at almost any time of day. What could be more convenient than to zip into our favorite take-out trattoria and emerge with breakfast, lunch, or dinner clutched in our hand. At home or at work, we can eat without lifting a finger — just a plastic fork. There's no one to tip, no dishes to wash, and, if we live alone and buy two pieces of pie, no one to scowl.

Take-out food is what keeps us going when we're too weary to even *think* about what's for dinner, let alone shop for it. And it's for hotel guests who don't want to wait for room service, airline passengers who prefer to bring their own picnic, late-night workers who refuse to eat Chinese food two nights in a row. (Only the Chinese are prepared to do this.)

A lot of people readily acknowledge that there are not enough hours in the day. Diving into an à la carte carton of dinner enables them to count those that are left with considerable comfort. They may transfer the food onto china plates, but often lack the energy to bother. Instead, they settle for a skimpy paper napkin hardly large enough to wipe a tooth, let alone a whole mouth. This is the time of day when we let the devil deal with decorum.

Take-out food has a lot going for it. It is freshly made and mostly healthy. It contains no additives, preservatives, stabilizers, emulsifiers, or gums. And we can buy as much or as little as we want (or can afford). Having a take-out store nearby is the closest thing to having a live-in cook — and no worries about Social Security.

Take-out stores appeal particularly to HWW (harried working women,) TS (tired singles), and FICs (financially independent couples). All have kitchens but few use them on a regular basis.

— Anonymous

Take-Out Tips

• The simpler and more robust the food, the better it travels.

• Choose cold or room-temperature food over hot dishes — especially those with heavy sauces, which tend to congeal.

• Fried foods quickly become soggy; order them freshly made from a take-out source close to home.

• Pasta, great served cold in salads, is less satisfactory when ordered hot because it continues to cook in the container and the strands stick together. A better buy: Choose an unusual sauce and fresh pasta from the take-out store and cook and combine them in minutes at home.

• Order in quantity only from stores whose foods you know you like. Take out small amounts to sample the offerings of an unfamiliar store; take-out dishes don't always live up to their looks, and none are inexpensive.

• If you are confident about its source, sushi is a good food to order.

Take-Out Stores Are Here To Give

The best of the take-out stores are architect-designed boutiques with bouquets of flowers, backlit breads, vibrant displays of vegetables, and perfect pasta salads. They are the modern counterpart of the old-fashioned neighborhood store, run by people who, for the most part, understand food and care about their customers. They operate in the best tradition of Mom and Pop, setting their own prices and hours and making their own decisions. They don't have to abide by the rules of corporate franchises but can instead pay attention to the needs of their clientele; some are even willing to prepare a stew in the customer's own casserole dish, or deliver a complete dinner and stay on the phone in case of a crisis.

The Tiffany of the trade is New York-based Dean &

DeLuca, which sets the standard for others throughout the country. Its imaginative food and packaging has become a model for countless small businesses to try to emulate. The cooking is done off the premises, so there is plenty of space for their skilled cooks to produce a fabulous variety of seasonal dishes. In the SoHo store itself, the staff constantly replenish the platters so that they are at the peak of appeal, and loyal customers are always offered new and exciting choices. For food lovers, a visit to Dean & DeLuca is a profoundly gratifying experience.

A Take-Out Sampler

Here are some dishes that will overcome guacamole gridlock any day:

Swiss cheese soup

Asparagus vichyssoise

Green gazpacho

Chicken chili with white beans

Mediterranean vegetable tart

Napoleon of vegetables

Saffron risotto with wild mushrooms

Fettuccine with crawfish and roasted red peppers

Ravioli with goat cheese and thyme

Pheasant pot pie

Soft-shelled crabs with citrus sauce

Macaroni with baby shrimp, peas, and shallots

Roast duck with couscous

Salmon, shrimp, and black bean salad

Coulibiac of salmon

Striped bass wrapped in phyllo leaves

Shredded pork with pecans and wild rice

Pasta with fresh clam sauce

Chicken breast in champagne sauce

Roasted sliced leg of lamb with artichoke hearts

Fresh tuna-fish salad

Caramelized apple tart

Mango mousse with melba sauce

Poached white peaches

Cold hazelnut soufflé

Cheesecake

Strawberry and rhubarb brown betty

TEA

Love and scandal are the best sweeteners of tea.

— Henry Fielding
18th-century novelist

ODD JOBS

Peter Goggi, who slurpingly sips 200 to 300 cups of tea a day for the Lipton Tea Company, can tell by taste the country a tea comes from, the plantation on which the tea was grown, and even the hillside on which the leaves were harvested. It is Goggi who creates the blend that issues forth from Lipton in 40 million tea bags every day.

THE PLEASING DRINK

Tea-drinking is a daily ritual for more than four-fifths of the people in the world, and whether it's early-morning tea in England or an afternoon work break in Japan, a certain ceremony attaches to the brewing and drinking of it. For all those who make tea a regular part of their lives, it is more than a quick and convenient pick-me-up; it's also an occasion, a deliberate pause for pleasure and relaxation.

Few Americans have any such ritual attachments to tea, but we drink a lot of it, and we've made some significant contributions to its lore. There was the Boston Tea Party, of course, when colonials dressed up like Indians and threw boxes of tea into Boston Harbor to protest the English tax on tea; no American schoolchild ever forgets that tale. Then there's the fact that in the great American search for something faster, we invented the tea bag. And it was Americans, too, who first drank tea on ice — on a blistering hot day at the St. Louis World's Fair, in 1904.

Now we're picking up the pace again, this time with ready-made iced tea. In a market sensation, iced tea is now sold as a soft drink, in bottles, cans, and boxes. Snapple Beverage was first in the field and cleaned up. Lipton's (teamed with PepsiCo) and Nestea (from Nestlé in partnership with Coke) jumped in with rival drinks, spending millions in advertising to catch up with and surpass the leader. Ads emphasize tea's healthy associations in the public mind, and ready-made iced tea is flying off the shelves. Industry observers now look deeply into the tea leaves and see a billion in sales of ready-made iced teas before the end of 1994.

In the middle of the afternoon when your batteries are run down, it's very nice to have tea.

— Michael Twomey
Manager of the Palm Court, Ritz Hotel, London

The Early Murk

The first written reference to tea appears in a Chinese dictionary of the fourth century A.D.; the word we use comes from the Chinese "t'e," pronounced "tay." And while nobody knows for sure who first brewed tea, or where or when, most sources point to China.

According to an ancient Chinese legend, it was the Emperor Shen-Nung, known as "The Divine Healer," who stumbled on the possibilities of tea in 2737 B.C., when some tea leaves blew into an open pot of boiling water. Shen-Nung tasted the brew, felt wonderfully refreshed, and declared that the drink was heaven-sent. After that, the word went out all over Asia, and the future of tea was guaranteed.

Types of Tea

All tea leaves come from the same species of an evergreen shrub related to the magnolia, but each tea has individual characteristics imparted by growing conditions and the processing of the leaves.

The leaves of **black teas**, such as Darjeeling, English Breakfast, and Lapsang Souchong, are fermented, then heated and dried; they produce a dark red-brown brew.

Green teas, such as Gunpowder, are unfermented; their greenish, slightly bitter taste is preferred in Asian countries.

Oolong teas, such as Formosa Oolong, undergo partial fermentation and produce a brew with milder characteristics of both black and green teas.

MAIL ORDER SOURCES

**Alaska Herb and
Tea Company**
P.O. Box 201871
Anchorage, AK 99520
907-522-3499

MacKinlay Teas
5025 Venture Drive
Ann Arbor, MI 48108
800-TEA-FOR-U

**Ridley's Country
Chandlers Teas**
c/o MacKnight, Inc.
1836-6 Stout Drive
Ivyland, PA 18974
215-230-8650

Did You Know?

☞ The "orange" in Orange Pekoe doesn't refer to color. It's an ancient Chinese way of identifying a certain size of leaf that once was scented with orange blossoms.

☞ American Health Foundation studies indicate that tea has the potential to lower cholesterol levels and reduce the risk of heart disease. Tea also protects against forms of skin, lung, and esophageal cancer.

☞ Tea contains 60 milligrams of caffeine per cup, coffee 100 milligrams.

MORE INFORMATION

Tea Council of the USA
230 Park Avenue
New York, NY 10169
212-986-6998

TILAPIA

MULTITUDES FOR THE MULTITUDES

Though relatively new in the American market, tilapia have been a very abundant fish in Africa since before the dawn of time. In Egyptian bas-reliefs that are more than 4,500 years old, lively schools of tilapia, a small fish similar to perch, show up in depictions of fish farming.

And some biblical scholars have named them as the fish that Peter caught and Jesus multiplied — thus the name that tilapia bears in many other parts of the world: St. Peter's Fish.

The modern technology for farming tilapia was developed in Israel, where this fish is hugely popular, valued for its mild taste — similar to sole and flounder — and pinky-white flesh. Because of their great hardiness, tilapia are now farmed far afield of their Nile origins. Asia produces in excess of 300,000 metric tons a year, Africa is next with more than 200,000 metric tons, and South and Central America are burgeoning new sites of production. There are also several tilapia farms in the northeastern United States and Canada, whose joint annual production amounts to just under 100,000 metric tons.

Tilapia are superb for aquaculture. On average, they can grow to 2 pounds in about 230 days. When they are fed a high-protein grain diet on farms where the water is kept free of algae, their flavor is delicate and sweet. But when they feed on algae, the taste will be "off," so it's important to find a reliable supplier for this excellent fish.

Did You Know?

☞ Tilapia live only in waters above 60 degrees F. and below 73 degrees F.

☞ When a male tilapia fertilizes a female's eggs, she carries them in her mouth for 10 to 14 days, until they hatch.

☞ In Israeli tilapia farming, fish are raised at densities as high as 25 fish per cubic meter.

TOFU

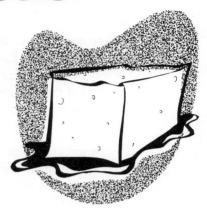

Vegetarians Paradise

NATURE'S PERFECT PROCESSED FOOD

Some Americans still don't like tofu. Could it be because of the mushy dessertlike texture of even the firmest varieties? Or are people just hooked on the old-fashioned notion that food should have flavor? But then again, what's not to like? Lower in calories and saturated fat than most other protein sources, tofu contains no cholesterol. And because it's a vegetable product, it's lactose-free. You might say that it's "lite meat," healthful filler stuff, just the thing almost all of us could use in our diets. A flurry of research suggests that eating soybean protein can lower cholesterol levels and even reduce rates of certain types of cancer.

What is tofu? Everyone says "bean curd," but that doesn't paint a clear picture. Soybeans are soaked, ground up, and then cooked. The soy milk is separated in an extractor, then poured into a pan, where a coagulant is added — and bean curds form. The longer they are allowed to drain, the firmer the tofu. Firm and extra-firm varieties hold their shape and often find their way into dishes where meat might otherwise be found: in soups, stews, and stir-fries. Soft tofu has a somewhat custardy texture and is good for making thick shakes, dips, sauces, and salad dressings.

The jury is still out on the question of flavor; that is, whether or not tofu has any of its own. Connoisseurs insist that it has a subtle, nutty taste that blends remarkably well with just about anything. Perhaps the taste is just too subtle for the uninitiated palate, but the debate is moot anyway because tofu has the ability to assume the flavor of whatever herbs, spices, or other ingredients share the same pan.

Picking up on this advantage, health-conscious Westerners have been slyly substituting soft tofu for sour cream and cream cheese, mixing it with chives, onions, garlic, or lox for supposedly guilt-free snack spreads. But despite all of tofu's splendidly healthy characteristics, it is also quite high in fat — about 55 percent of firm tofu's calories are derived from fat, in fact — although most people probably have just the opposite notion.

The Chinese, who have used tofu for over a thousand years to convert vegetable dishes into well-balanced meals, have found tofu fertile ground for spicy, sweet, or tangy sauces. In consequence, some Americans think of tofu as an exotic substance that they will only eat in Asian restaurants. Others consider it a fad food, a pet ingredient of vegetarians and health food fanatics. In reality, tofu is none of the above. It can fill manicotti or blintzes. It can accompany pasta in lieu of meat or cheese. It can stuff enchiladas, casseroles, pies, and cheesecakes; the possibilities are as endless as the chef's imagination.

Slabs of broiled tofu on a plate with fries and a parsley sprig will never replace you-know-what in American hearts. But tofu's hour has come, and it's here to stay.

Meat, Move Over

The Chinese call tofu "meat without bones," but it costs far less than meat, often selling for $1.00 per pound in health-food stores and Asian delis.

Books

The Book of Tofu
William Shurtleff and Akiko Aoyagi; Ten Speed Press, 1987; $11.95

The Taming of Tofu
Kerri B. Williamson; Pacific Press Publishing, 1991; $9.95

The Tofu Book
Jon Paino and Lisa Messinger; Avery, 1991; $12.95

Health In High Places

Reporting on the President's diet, Hillary Rodham Clinton is reported to have said, "We've made a lot of progress on pasta and things like that — but tofu has been hard for us."

MAIL ORDER SOURCES

✉

Frieda's Inc.
P.O. Box 58488
Los Angeles, CA 90058
800-241-1771

TOMATOES

It's not hard to breed a tomato that looks great and tastes like hell.

— Charles M. Rick
Preeminent U.S. tomato breeder

Fried Green Tomatoes

Serves 4

4 large green or firm pink tomatoes
¼ cup all-purpose flour
1 tablespoon sugar
1½ teaspoons salt
⅛ teaspoon freshly ground black pepper
2 tablespoons bacon drippings

Cut the tomatoes into ½-inch-thick slices. In a small bowl, combine the flour, sugar, salt, and pepper. Lightly coat the tomato slices on both sides with the seasoned mixture.

Heat the drippings in a large skillet. Arrange the tomatoes in a single layer and fry until brown on both sides. Remove to a hot platter and repeat with the remaining tomatoes. Add additional drippings if needed.

TEMPT ME NOT WITH TOMATOES

RAYMOND SOKOLOV

In a world riven by hate, greed, and envy, everyone loves tomatoes. I have never met anyone who didn't eat tomatoes with enthusiasm. Like ice cream, the whole, perfect, vine-ripened tomato is a universal favorite. The old-fashioned kind of tomato, not the hard-walled hybrids picked green, engineered to survive long truck rides, and ripened with gas on the way to market.

Real (as I will call vine-ripened, soft-walled, acid-flavored, summer-grown) tomatoes are an article of faith, a rallying point for the morally serious, a grail. And the real tomato's acolytes are not some ragged little band of malcontents. They are us, brothers and sisters in tomatomania, converts to the first Western religion since the Stone Age to worship a plant.

Excerpted from Natural History

Who Gets the Cents

Picker:
1.5 cents per pound
Packer:
10 cents per pound
Repacker:
4 cents per pound
Trucker:
5 cents per pound
Wholesale distributor:
1 cent per pound
Retailer:
17.5 to 37.5 cents per pound

Source: *Eating Well*

Tomato Nutrition

For just 35 calories one medium-sized tomato supplies almost half the recommended daily allowance for vitamin C, and about 20 percent of the RDAs for vitamin A and fiber. Tomatoes also contain lycopene, flavonoids, and other phytochemicals that play a role in fighting cancer and some forms of heart disease.

Antisense Gene
Functions Logically

The idea of eating out-of-season tasteless tomatoes is a peculiarly American custom, though we keep being baffled and bewildered when we discover that each new one is just as awful as the last. The nation is devoted to terrible-tasting junk food, but when it comes to tomatoes we get despondent and dejected when we buy red and get what tastes dreadfully green.

The problem is that growers must harvest tomatoes while they are still unripe and resort to ripening them with blasts of ethylene gas. If they were completely ripe, it would be impossible to pick, sort, pack, and transport them to supermarkets before they spoiled.

All this may change following Calgene, Inc.'s much publicized development of a flavorful tomato named Flavr Savr. Calgene has managed to alter this tomato by splicing an extra instruction called an "antisense" gene into its genetic code. The gene switches off production of a fruit-softening enzyme made by unmodified tomatoes. In other words, it makes sense for the tomato to ripen and rot. It makes sense for mankind to slow the process. The antisense gene says, in effect, "Hey, tomato, wait a few days. Stay ripe and good-tasting long enough for us to enjoy you."

The antisense gene allows growers to leave the tomatoes on the vine longer to ripen, yet they will still resist softening during handling and transportation.

Calgene has spent ten years and $25 million to develop a better-tasting tomato, but when it is offered to the public, fists are raised in protest. "Don't fool with Mother Nature," we bellow. No, we don't want your new, improved, better-tasting red ripe tomato. Give us hard, green, tasteless tomatoes — though that way of thinking doesn't make any sense at all.

☞ Refrigerating a tomato ruins its flavor.

☞ The average American buys 18 pounds of tomatoes a year — more than any other vegetable except potatoes and lettuce.

☞ According to the National Gardening Association, 85 percent of the 32 million U.S. households with gardens grow tomatoes in them.

Books

Fried Green Tomatoes at the Whistle Stop Cafe
Fannie Flagg; McGraw-Hill, 1987; $5.95

Lee Bailey's Tomatoes
Lee Bailey; Clarkson Potter, 1992; $14.00

Tomatoes
Jesse Ziff Cool; Collins Publishers, 1994; $19.95

Tomatoes! 365 Healthy Recipes for Year-Round Enjoyment
Garden Way Editors; Storey Communications, 1991; $12.95

TROUT

HOOK AND LINE SINK SOME OF US

The first time I went trout fishing I got the hook caught in my hair. The second time I went trout fishing I got the hook caught in my thumb and had to rush to hospital to get it surgically removed. The second was the last time I went trout fishing. However, my fondness for the fish is undiminished, as is my awe of those skilled fishermen who are devoted to the sport.

Trout are quite oblivious of how we feel about them, our romantic association of them with cold, crisp winter days, snow-capped mountains, and the clearest of crystal waters where the tastiest of them reach maturity. Rainbows, named for the colorful stripe that runs the length of their backs, are preferred by some; others hold out for bolder-tasting steelheads, which are more on a par in size with salmon and can weigh as much as 40 pounds.

Farm-raised trout, which we are almost certain to find on our plate unless we have caught the fish ourselves, weigh less than a pound. Those who haven't tasted the wild fish don't realize that the domesticated ones have barely a shadow of the fine, full flavor of those that have struggled their way upstream and down. Like salmon, wild trout have a pinkish cast to their flesh and are firm to the tooth and moist in the mouth.

Trout is a serious, sophisticated fish dish that has few bones to wrestle with — just the thing to serve to those who are reluctant to make any effort at the table and fretfully treat bones as foreign objects. Fortunately, trout is at its best when prepared simply and quickly.

Broiled Trout

Serves 4

4 small (¾ pound each) whole
   trout, cleaned
1 tablespoon vegetable oil
4 tablespoons butter, melted
2 tablespoons freshly squeezed
   lemon juice
2 tablespoons finely chopped
   fresh herbs

Preheat broiler for 10 minutes.

Wash and dry the trout thoroughly. Brush the broiler rack with oil to prevent the fish from sticking. Combine the butter, lemon juice, and herbs. Brush the cavity and surface of the trout with the flavored butter.

Broil the fish 4 inches from the broiler, allowing 6 minutes on each side. Baste each trout with the remaining flavored butter as it cooks.

Serve with baby potatoes steamed over white wine and the sweetest, freshest young asparagus you can lay your hands on. A little hollandaise sauce on the side will do no harm, particularly if the dinner is accompanied with a well-chilled, crisp white wine and strawberries are served for dessert.

Books

The Trout Cook: 100 Ways with Trout
Patricia A. Hays; Trafalgar Square, 1991; $22.95

MORE INFORMATION

Brown Trout Club
134 Skillings Street
South Portland, ME 04106
207-773-8561

Trout Unlimited
1500 Wilson Boulevard
Arlington, VA 22209
703-522-0200

Greater Ecosystem Alliance
P.O. Box 2813
Bellingham, WA 98227
206-671-9950

MAIL ORDER SOURCES

New Beginnings Seafood Company
16 Cornish Road
Carmel, NY 10512
914-228-6186

Red-Wing Meadow Trout Hatchery
528 Federal Street
Montague, MA 01351
413-367-9494

TRUFFLES

Truffles make the women more tender and the men more passionate.

— Anthelme Brillat-Savarin
A connoisseur in all things

"Class — you'll never get anywhere keeping your nose clean."

BLACK TRUFFLES ARE VERY DEAR

JOSEPH WECHSBERG

On a large desk was a basket filled with what looked like black oranges. I noticed that the room was filled with a strong, piquant scent.

"*Voilà*," M. Barbier said, presenting the basket as a guide at the Louvre would present Leonardo da Vinci's Mona Lisa. "Truffles. Great mystery of the vegetable kingdom. Highly appreciated by epicures for their flavor and taste long before the days of the Roman emperors. . . . They grow under the ground, and are found only on the poorest soil, where nothing else will grow, and they have resisted all attempts at cultivation. Thank God," he added as an afterthought. "Otherwise they would be as commonplace and cheap as potatoes, and we would be out of business."

The truffles, M. Barbier went on explaining, come in 140 variations and in all sizes, from that of a pea to that of an orange. The best-flavored specimens have the size of an English walnut. There are white truffles in Italy and chocolate-colored ones in other parts of France but the finest of all are black, outside and inside. (They are always black on the outside, but white or gray inside until they have fully matured and gained their strong flavor.) They should be firm but not hard, and they should have a marble grain.

M. Barbier broke one of the truffles in half. "See what I mean? Finely marbled; flesh of a jet-black color. Innocent-looking fruits, but, like the roulette tables of Monte Carlo, they've ruined quite a few people. Truffles are almost as much of a gamble. No one knows exactly how they come into being. . . . The peasants say that they are a product of soil fermentation, somewhat like mushrooms. Truffles, however, grow only in light soil, in the vicinity of trees. There are some truffles near maples, beech trees, junipers, elms, poplars, and willows, but most of them appear around a species of oak, called truffle oak. Our peasants say: 'If you want truffles, you must sow acorns.' Unfortunately, it takes 20 years for the oaks to reach sufficient size, and even then there remains the question whether you'll find any truffles."

Excerpted from Blue Trout and Black Truffles

Did You Know?

☞ In 1990, Luciano Pavarotti was awarded a 1½-pound white truffle by the mayor of the northern Italian town of Alba. The truffle of the year is given annually to the person who has best promoted Italy's image.

☞ The best black truffles in the world come from the Perigord region of France.

☞ Geneticists have discovered that insects, attracted by the truffle's aroma, carry its spores to the leaves of surrounding trees. There the spores develop and when the leaves fall to the ground, they start the formation of new growth.

☞ Truffles cost between $800 and $1,500 a pound.

Books

Gourmet's Guide to Mushrooms and Truffles
Jacki Hurst and Lyn Rutherford; Price Stern Sloan, 1991; $9.95

MORE INFORMATION

North American Truffling Society
P.O. Box 269
Corvallis, OR 97339
503-752-2243

MAIL ORDER SOURCES

Maison Glass
111 East 58th Street
New York, NY 10022-1211
212-755-3316

Truffles are sniffed out by specially trained female pigs which apparently detect a chemical also found in a male pig's saliva. This substance, which prompts mating behavior in the sow, is also found in human males' underarm sweat.

— Harold McGee
On Food and Cooking

TUNA

IN DEFENSE OF CANNED TUNA

BARBARA KAFKA

A short word for canned tuna fish, one of America's great contributions to the world of food, and no, I am not jesting. I am not about to make an attempt to bring back tuna-noodle casserole, occasionally topped with cornflakes, but I will stake my gastronomic laurels on the fact that tuna salad makes one of the all-time great sandwiches. In the effort to defend canned tuna, I sometimes give my own recipe for tuna salad. This requires that we note that not all canned tuna is created equal. I am not, however, talking about fancy French tuna, in cans like those for sardines, packed flat in olive oil; although this is also a great delicacy and hard to obtain. Nor do I mean the very good Italian tuna packed in olive oil in conventional round tins — expensive and strong in taste. What I do mean is fancy, white albacore tuna solidly packed in either water or a neutral oil, both of which are discarded in any case. Beware canned tuna in chunks, which tastes like dry, shredded, limp cardboard.

Too often, I have been assaulted in restaurants that think themselves very *à la page* with salade Niçoise containing fresh tuna. Usually, it is very badly cooked. Even when it is well cooked, fresh tuna does not have the rich, slightly mysterious flavor so necessary for the enrichment of this dish. Canned tuna is also essential for various Italian dishes. These are the recipes in which to use Italian tuna. Cannellini beans with tuna and red onions, pasta with tomato, olive, and tuna sauce, and tuna in antipasto are all unthinkable with fresh tuna.

It is all very well for all of us to learn about relatively new ingredients. The many varieties of fresh tuna are well worth enjoying. That does not mean that we have to insult and demean staples that we enjoyed in a more innocent time. Especially when, as in the case of neat cans of tuna, we can have them waiting on our shelves when need arises. Long live canned tuna.

Reprinted from *The Opinionated Palate*

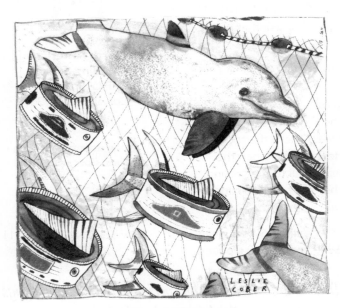

KID POWER

Millions of dolphins had died in tuna nets when, a few years back, the nation's schoolchildren rallied to save the dolphins by spearheading a national revolt against tuna-fish sandwiches. Children no higher than the kitchen counter demanded that tuna be taken off the school lunch menu; bigger kids orchestrated letter-writing campaigns using words like slaughter and boycott. Restaurants stopped serving tuna; characters in comic strips refused to eat it; sales were sinking fast. Then the producers of Starkist, Chicken of the Sea, and Bumble Bee announced a new dolphin-safe policy — just in time to save our (almost) national dish. The capitulation was not due to loss of money, it's said, but to the sheer embarrassment of having brand-name products publicly derided. Pride, we see, really does have a fall.

Tuna Types

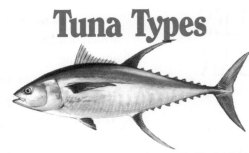

Tuna is the largest member of the mackerel family. There are 13 species, but only five are commercially harvested in the United States.

Albacore is the only sort that is labeled "white meat tuna" in cans. It's caught off the West Coast and around the Hawaiian Islands at a weight of 10 to 30 pounds. In Hawaii it's known as *tombo*.

Yellowfin, found off the coasts of California, Hawaii, and Florida, is so called for its yellow dorsal and anal fins and the yellow stripe on its sides. Hawaiians know it as *ahi*. Yellowfin can grow to 400 pounds, but is usually taken in the 20- to 100-pound range.

Bluefin, the largest tuna, can grow to 1,500 pounds. It is steely blue in color, and migrates up the Atlantic coast from South America. In Japan, the biggest market for bluefin, choice cuts cost upward of $25 a pound.

Bigeye, which can grow to over 400 pounds, is prized by the Japanese for sashimi.

Skipjack is taken at 6 to 8 pounds and has dark longitudinal stripes on its belly. In Hawaii it's known as *aku*; in Canada it is marketed as oceanic or arctic bonito. (**Bonito** is a small tuna found in the Pacific and the Atlantic that is not sold as tuna because it is not thought to be of good enough quality; it's chiefly used as bait.)

MORE INFORMATION

United States Tuna Foundation
1101 17th Street NW
Washington, DC 20036
202-857-0610

Books

Cooking with Tuna
Cheryl Bennett and Geri Pollock; Authors Note, 1986; $7.95

MAIL ORDER SOURCES

Port Chatham
632 Northwest 46th Street
Seattle, WA 98107
800-872-5666

Simply Shrimp
7794 Northwest 44th Street
Fort Lauderdale, FL 33351
800-833-0888

TURKEY

THANKS BE TO . . . WHOM?

When those early Pilgrims celebrated their first Thanksgiving dinner, the wild turkey was cooked on an open fire and fresh cider was the accompanying beverage. Whatever their ethnic heritage, almost all Americans eat turkey on this national holiday, but our domestic bird has become a very different creature. Because we prefer white meat, turkeys have been bred until their breasts are so huge that they can't get close enough to mate and have to be artificially inseminated. After the pre-Thanksgiving massacre, all the plucking and drawing is done for us and some birds are even injected with a yellow fluid to impart "buttery" flavor with no bother. The open fire has transmogrified into a microwave oven, and the pop-up thermometer has spared us the guesswork of knowing when the bird is ready to eat. The drink of preference is likely to be a diet cola. When it comes to turkeys, the more things change, the more things change.

WHAT *REALLY* HAPPENED TO TURKEY LURKEY

BRYAN LYNAS

One day, Henny Penny was out pecking and scratching in the yard when — WHACK! — something hit her on the head. Remember the old tale? Henny Penny goes off to tell the king "the sky's a-falling" and collects a menagerie of other animals on the way. One of these is Turkey Lurkey … which is what we called our first — and last — turkey. And that naming was our first mistake. My wife, Val, suggested we call it Chris (short for Christmas Dinner) but somehow that never stuck. I selected Turkey Lurkey from her bedraggled companions in the local market, which was how she came to live with us for a brief but happy life.

Now I didn't want to be special friends with her because she was destined for our Christmas dinner table. In fact, I didn't want to be friends at all. "Animals are my friends and I don't eat my friends," said George Bernard Shaw, but he was a vegetarian.

Turkey Lurkey had other ideas. She set out immediately to become a Person. Our second mistake was to notice this. She was a quick learner. She learned how no one could resist her gentle, whispering greeting, which she delivered each time she saw any of the family. She'd sidle up, oink-oinking, her ludicrous red wattles flapping like tiny flags. My, she was ugly. If she could, she'd stand right on my feet and talk: oink-whistle. She'd gaze up into my eyes with love and — it hurts to write this — total trust, as if she were saying, "I adore you. You're so kind to me. I just want to be near you."

She wasn't perfect, though; she had a darker side to her character — she learned to sulk. If at feeding time she didn't get fed first, she'd throw a tantrum, flop down on the ground, and refuse to eat … unless I took her special bowl of food to some select place and begged her forgiveness. In short, she had Presence. This resulted in our third mistake, which was to become fond of her.

And so things went along and went along, like Henny Penny and her troop who searched for the king, until one day, two days before Christmas to be precise, Turkey Lurkey's sky fell forever. But not without much wailing and gnashing of teeth, mostly from me. For had I not declared that I would partake no more of meat unless I had raised the animal myself, thus ensuring it a happy life? And had I not committed myself to the final killing to ensure a quick death, avoiding the miserable journey to the slaughterhouse that supermarket meat must endure?

To be sure, I'd dispatched many of my own animals for the family table, mostly dull, insipid rabbits. But now Turkey Lurkey was for the chop and I was distraught. Arguments for and against execution flashed through my head. I couldn't do it. I must do it. But she loves and trusts you! What about your principles now?

Val clinched it by stating that if I couldn't do it, she'd go right out and buy a turkey, frozen solid in a plastic bag, from the local supermarket. What, she asked, was the point of buying a bird at no small expense, feeding and caring for it, and then not eating it? Where were my principles now?

So I did it. I caught the poor, terrified creature. And you can be sure she knew I meant to kill her — me, the man she'd loved and trusted — the moment she saw me, sneaking guiltily about, searching for her. In the story, Foxy Moxy kills Turkey Lurkey, having inveigled Henny Penny and friends into his cave by telling them, trusting souls all, that he would show them a shortcut to the king. Like Foxy Moxy, I broke her neck. It was one of the hardest things I ever did. I killed my friend.

Then I sat and wept real tears over the body as I plucked out her feathers, hiding shamefaced under the old carob tree in my vegetable patch. And I decided there and then that once I had eaten her flesh (very tasty, I have to admit) I would never again kill an animal to eat. As I had already forsworn buying animals that other people had killed, that meant only one thing: I had to turn vegetarian.

That was three years ago. I haven't eaten flesh since and neither has Val. Neither of us has regretted our decision because we feel good being vegetarians. So Turkey Lurkey's death was not in vain.

Books

The Turkey Cookbook
Rick Rodgers; HarperCollins, 1991; $10.95

Turkey, the Magic Ingredient
Coleen Simmons and Robert Simmons; Bristol Publishing, 1990; $6.95

Turkey: The Perfect Food for Every Occasion
Kristie Alm and Pat Sayre; Berkley, 1993; $3.99

MORE INFORMATION

National Turkey Federation
11319 Sunset Hills Road
Reston, VA 22090
703-435-7206

Blow in its ear.

— Johnny Carson,
asked how best to
thaw a frozen turkey

*I just yell at the bird
and hope the meat
will fall off.*

— Jeff Smith,
TV's Frugal Gourmet,
asked about his carving skills

Turkey Truths

U.S. per-capita consumption of turkey has risen 64 percent in the last decade, to about 18 pounds annually. Turkey is Americans' fourth largest source of meat protein (after chicken, beef, and pork), and, save for the dark meat, which is higher in fat, it is slightly lower in calories, total fat, and cholesterol than our other favorites.

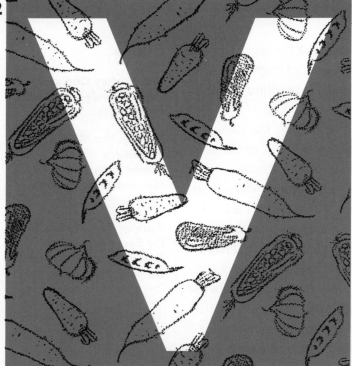

VEAL ❖ VEGETABLES ❖ VEGETARIAN DIET ❖

VENDING MACHINE FOOD ❖ VINEGAR ❖ VITAMINS

VEAL

A VERY DELICATE
MATTER

Veal is a very tender subject in the United States. Many people boycott the meat altogether because of stories they've read in the press and images on television of pitiful calves raised under appalling conditions — snatched from their mothers at birth and imprisoned in pens so small that they can neither walk nor turn around.

However, this is not by any means the way *all* calves are treated in veal production. At Summerfield Farm, for example, in the foothills of the Blue Ridge Mountains, Jamie and Rachel Nicoll take a free-range approach to the raising of their calves, who grow up in large open spaces and are fed on whole milk direct from the cow.

Unfortunately, the Nicoll method remains an exception to the rule. A veal tasting at *Eating Well* magazine gave top marks to Summerfield, noting, however, that "those who love traditional veal scallopini may have to go without if they find conventional veal husbandry unacceptable. The difference between free-range veal and traditional veal seems more pronounced than, for example, the difference between foie gras from force-fed French ducks and that from more humanely raised American birds."

Meat lovers who shy away from veal for fear that it came inhumanely to the table rarely exhibit similar reservations about eating lamb or young poultry. In a curious way, most of us distance ourselves from the troubling thought of connecting *any* meat to its origins.

Osso Buco

Serves 6

¾ **cup all-purpose flour**
2 teaspoons salt
**1 teaspoon freshly ground
  black pepper**
6 2-inch slices veal shank
4 tablespoons vegetable oil
1 large onion, thinly sliced
1 large carrot, finely chopped
1 stalk celery, finely chopped
1 bay leaf
**15-ounce can whole tomatoes,
  coarsely chopped, juice
  reserved**
2 tablespoons tomato paste
1 cup dry white wine
½ **cup finely chopped parsley**
Grated rind of 1 lemon

Combine the flour with 1 teaspoon salt and ½ teaspoon pepper in a paper bag. Pat the veal pieces dry with paper towels, put them in the bag, and shake until they are coated with the seasoned flour. Shake off any excess.

Heat the oil in a large casserole over high heat, add the veal, and cook, turning until browned on all sides. Remove the meat from the pan. Add the onion, carrot, celery, and bay leaf to the pan and cook over moderate heat until the onions are softened and translucent. Add the tomatoes with their juice, the tomato paste, and the wine and bring the mixture to a boil. Reduce the heat to low and return the meat to the pan. Put a circle of wax paper directly onto the surface of the stew. Cover the casserole and cook for 2 hours or until the meat is very tender.

Combine the parsley and the lemon rind in a small bowl. When the veal is cooked, stir the parsley-lemon mixture into the stew and simmer for 1 minute. Using a slotted spoon, transfer the veal to a heated serving platter. Spoon the sauce over the meat and serve at once.

Did You Know?

☞ Veal is a naturally lean meat — an average three-ounce portion of cooked, trimmed veal contains only 166 calories, less than a third of them derived from fat.

☞ Bull calves are raised for slaughter as veal until they are 16 to 18 weeks old and weigh about 450 pounds.

☞ Milk-fed veal is white in color. The meat is pink if the feed includes grain or the animal has grazed on pasture.

Of Veal and Milk

The veal industry is closely linked with dairy farming, which is the reason veal calves are raised primarily in milk-producing states.

In order for dairy cows to continue to be milked, they must give birth once a year. Female calves are usually kept by farmers to replace older cows in the herd. Male calves, on the other hand, are of little value to dairy farmers; Hereford bull calves are raised for veal until they are 16 to 18 weeks old.

A surfeit of milk once allowed the farmers to use it to feed the calves, but most are now fed on soy milk fortified with vitamins and minerals.

MORE INFORMATION

**National Live Stock
& Meat Board**
444 North Michigan Avenue
Chicago, IL 60611
312-467-5520

MAIL ORDER SOURCES

Summerfield Farm
10044 James Monroe Highway
Culpeper, VA 22701
703-547-9600

VEGETABLES

IT'S STILL SPINACH

RICHARD ATCHESON

Vegetables aren't really about nutrition. They're about power in the American home. Parents have it. Kids want it, and the struggle is usually engaged at the dinner table.

My own first encounter with this issue happened in the classic way when I was five. Seated on a telephone book for Sunday lunch, I remarked that I wouldn't have any black-eyed peas.

"Don't want any black-eyed peas?" my father asked. "Don't want some part of this good dinner that your mother has worked her fingers to the bone to put on this table?"

"No, thank you," I replied.

To my surprise, my father dumped the whole dish onto my plate. "Now, young man," he said. "You'll sit here until you eat every one of those peas."

I sat there until nine o'clock that night, but I never touched a single black-eyed pea — not from that dark day to this. And everybody I've ever known turns out to have made a childhood vow like mine, never again to touch some hated bean or legume that was once shoved down their throat.

Only in very recent times, feeling portly, have I taken up with *any* vegetables. And vegetables have been good to me. Cleaving *only* unto them, I have lost a total of 18 pounds in the past two months. It's been amazing: The lard melted off me like candle wax.

I love my vegetables now and take them on by the barrel load. But never while I live will a single black-eyed pea ever pass my lips. When it's a question of power, my inner child is still sitting up high and proud on that 1940 Houston telephone book.

The Meaning of Shelf Life

Vegetables, like fruits, continue to breathe after being harvested. They exhale ethylene, which speeds their ripening but also hastens deterioration. The riper the vegetable, the faster its respiration rate and the quicker the result: Just one baddie can turn the whole crate to trash.

Producers have enlisted a new pair of bad-breath fighters: CAP (controlled atmosphere packaging) and MAP (modified atmosphere packaging). CAP is a means of enclosing produce in a thin plastic "breathable" film that regulates the exchange of gases and can extend shelf life up to three weeks; MAP is a technique in which the produce is cleaned, cooled, flushed with a mixture of oxygen and nitrogen, and sealed within the package. Inside, the vegetables inhale the gases and emit carbon dioxide, which escapes harmlessly through the package's film.

MAP has also helped to create a new and ever-growing line of "value-added" produce. Items such as salad mixes, broccoli florets, and mini-carrots are prewashed and trimmed, so that they need virtually no preparation before cooking. In 1993, sales of these items surged 93 percent, to more than $323 million.

Vegetables are interesting but lack a sense of purpose when unaccompanied by a good cut of meat.

— Fran Lebowitz
Culture critic

Vegetable Respiration Rates

The rate is measured in milligrams of carbon dioxide given off per kilogram per hour when each vegetable is held at optimum temperature. The faster the rate (the higher the number of milligrams), the faster the produce ages and the more quickly it must be used.

Vegetable	Respiration Rate
Asparagus	82
Avocado	67
Broccoli	97
Lettuce	23
Mushroom	71
Tomato	22

Source: *Fresh Produce Academy;* Hercules Inc. Research Center

---

Did You Know?

☞ The most popular vegetables, in order, according to the FDA: potatoes, iceberg lettuce, tomatoes, onions, carrots, celery, corn, broccoli, green cabbage, and cucumbers. (You will note the absence of okra.)

☞ Frozen vegetables ought to rattle when the box is shaken. If they have thawed and frozen again, they become soft and unable to rattle.

☞ The USDA puts our annual vegetable consumption at 102 pounds per capita, compared with 81 pounds a decade ago. Yet, according to one National Cancer Institute survey, only 9 percent of us eat the recommended five or more servings of fruit and vegetables daily. Some 10 percent of U.S. adults don't eat *any* fruits or vegetables in a given day.

☞ Leafy greens lose up to a full day of shelf life for every half hour they spend unrefrigerated.

Books

Greene on Greens
Bert Greene; Workman, 1984; $15.95

Look and Cook: Main Dish Vegetables
Anne Willan; Dorling Kindersley, 1992; $19.95

The Victory Garden Cookbook
Marian Morash; Knopf, 1982; $35.00/$24.95

Too Many Tomatoes, Squash, Beans and Other Good Things
Lois M. Landau and Laura G. Myers; HarperCollins, 1991; $14.00

Vegetables: Artichokes to Zucchini
Joe Famularo and Louise Imperiale; Barron's, 1993; $12.95

VEGETARIAN DIET

I won't eat anything that has intelligent life, but I'd gladly eat a network executive or a politician.

— Marty Feldman
Actor

CULINARY CORRECTNESS

Every day, it seems, there is mounting evidence that eating more vegetables and less meat can take pounds off midsections and add to the life spans of those accustomed to meat-heavy diets. In a 1992 survey, 12.7 million Americans (7 percent of the population) termed themselves vegetarians and the numbers have surely increased since then. And in the latest version of the Food Guide Pyramid, the USDA has pictured the status of meat in smaller amounts than most of us are accustomed to.

Eager to assist the nutritional news in converting Americans to veggiecentrism, spokespeople from various creeds are crusading to get us to break our beef habits, adopt a cruelty-free diet, or not eat anything with a face, depending on the approach. Vegetarians, especially the most outspoken ones, are far from a monolithic group. Only a fraction of all self-described vegetarians are vegans, those who eliminate all animal products — meat, milk, eggs, and in some cases, honey — from their diets. Others are ovo-lacto vegetarians, meaning that they don't eat meat but consider milk, cheese, and eggs acceptable. Many people choose not to eat red meat, which makes them fish-and-fowl vegetarians, and some will eat just about anything but still call themselves vegetarians because they have de-emphasized meat in their diets. A few will make exceptions for particularly cherished categories, such as one "Texas vegetarian" whose only exception is barbecue.

While vegetarianism is moving into the mainstream, militant vegetarians still figure in stand-up comedy jokes. "My girlfriend's a vegetarian and she's trying to get me to become a vegetarian because . . . that's what vegetarians do," was a recent San Francisco one-liner.

Some new vegetarians have converted in response to bad news about overgrazed prairies, declining world food production, and the chopping down of the rain forests to make pastures for cattle. Others believe that because production of vegetable foods is some ten times as resource-efficient as meat production, drastically reducing the consumption of meat is the only way to feed the world's burgeoning population. But there are many who feel the most compelling argument for vegetarianism is the idea that animals should coexist with humankind peacefully and not be exploited for food, clothing, or scientific research.

Whatever the rationale, anyone switching to a vegetarian diet should take advice from more experienced practitioners or a nutritionist to ensure that vital nutrients find their way into meals. Whether you end up saving the planet or simply becoming more accepted at gatherings of the culinarily correct, your body will thank you for it.

The Good News

A considerable body of scientific data links vegetarian diets to lowered risks of obesity, coronary artery disease, hypertension, diabetes mellitus, and colon cancer. According to the American Dietetic Association, properly planned vegetarian diets are healthful and adequate to meet all nutritional needs.

Single Most Important Reason for Becoming a Vegetarian

Health Reasons
48 percent

Animal Welfare
15 percent

Influence of Family and Friends
12 percent

Environment
4 percent

Ethical Reasons
5 percent

Not Sure/Other
18 percent

Source: *Vegetarian Times*

"Look, Sylvia, it's just not working out. I like the mountains, you like the plains, I like red meat, you're a strict vegetarian, I'm an Aquarius, you're a rhinoceros..."

Keeping the Baby in the Bath

New vegetarians worry about discarding beneficial aspects of their diets along with all those saturated fats and cholesterol; indeed, intakes of protein, iron, zinc, vitamin B-12, and, to a lesser extent, vitamin D may decline with the elimination of red meat. Fortunately, there are ways to make up the losses.

Although meat is the most complete source of dietary protein, elimination of animal protein need not give cause for alarm. There are many common nonmeat protein sources, especially legumes: peas and beans such as lentils, navy beans, black-eyed peas, garbanzo beans (chick-peas), peanuts, and soybeans (including tofu). When eaten with grains, these foods will yield all of the amino acids necessary to build protein. Eggs and milk products are eaten by all ovo-lacto vegetarians, but anyone planning to bring up an infant on a vegan diet — without any animal products at all — should use fortified soy milk. According to nutrition experts, vegetarians who eat a variety of foods almost never suffer protein deficiencies. Nor need they worry about combining or complementing plant proteins at the same meal. The body will utilize what it needs from different foods throughout the day. And Americans have been so imprinted with the importance of eating protein that we're unlikely ever to eat too little.

Iron intake is a more legitimate concern, especially for women. Spinach and broccoli contain iron, but not nearly enough; you would have to eat at least three pounds of spinach, or eight and a half pounds of broccoli, to meet the daily requirement. Peas and beans are better sources, and potatoes (with skins on) and tomatoes are efficient suppliers because they contain a lot of vitamin C, which aids the absorption of nonheme (nonmeat) iron. Red meat and liver are the undisputed best sources of iron, and some people might want to consider making exceptions to vegetarian rules for the sake of maintaining their iron levels. Iron supplements and fortified breakfast cereals are also options, but supplements should always be taken under the guidance of a doctor.

Vitamin D and vitamin B-12 are not found in vegetable products, but intake of dairy foods, especially vitamin-D-fortified milk, should provide enough of these nutrients. The human body needs very little B-12, and sunlight can provide some vitamin D; nevertheless, vegans may need to consider supplements.

The key to eliminating potential deficiencies is to choose a variety of foods. With meat and other animal products gone or greatly de-emphasized, it is vital to take advantage of the remaining options: grains, seeds, greens, nuts, legumes, seaweed, and so on. Such a strategy not only makes dietary sense but greatly assists in making a vegetarian life-style palatable for the whole family.

Books

Fields of Greens
Annie Somerville; Bantam, 1993; $26.95

Madhur Jaffrey's World-of-the-East Vegetarian Cooking
Madhur Jaffrey; Knopf, 1981; $16.95

Recipes from an Ecological Kitchen
Lorna J. Sass; Morrow, 1992; $23.00

The Savory Way
Deborah Madison; Bantam, 1990; $24.50

VENDING MACHINE FOOD

CHINKA-CHUNKA-CLINK

Americans now buy a prodigious $26 billion in goods every year from vending machines. This includes more than 12 billion cans of soft drinks and more than 8 billion packs of candy, cookies, crackers, snacks, nuts, gums, and mints. But just because we use these machines a lot doesn't mean we're not suspicious of them. Though they have become a significant point of sale in national food distribution, we still have a love-hate relationship with them: We're glad to see them when we're needy and they come across with what we want. But when they silently swallow our coins and give us nothing back, or worse, disgorge stale products in return for our good money, we want to take an axe to them. Our main frustration is that we can't argue with them.

Still, they're here to stay, and there's every sign that they'll soon improve in performance. If we ever get a one-dollar coin into broad circulation, it will be because traffic in vending machines demands such a coin to simplify the coin-slot, change-making process. Meanwhile, debit cards are already in place in some corporations: Employees buy cards for a given amount, then the card is debited each time they insert it to purchase items.

The National Automatic Merchandising Association estimates that there are some 25 million full-time workers for whom vending machines are the sole source of food on the job, and those numbers are rising as more and more corporations replace company cafeterias with vending sites. Sophisticated machines are filling the need, among them a french-fry machine that uses hot air instead of oil, several kinds of pizza makers, frozen-food machines dispensing microwavable meals — even coffee-dispensing machines that can grind fresh beans and make a cup of coffee in 20 seconds from the push of the button and top a cappuccino with milky foam.

With all the creativity being expended by the vending industry to invent the nearest technological equivalent to a live foodservice person, the vending machine is becoming more responsive — and we'll want to use it more. But it will still be a machine, and you can't argue with that.

Did You Know?

☞ Cost of a new vending machine: about $5,000.

☞ Tutti-Frutti gum machines, installed more than 100 years ago on subway platforms in New York City, were the first vending machines in America.

MORE INFORMATION

National Automatic Merchandising Association
20 North Wacker Drive
Chicago, IL 60606-3102
312-346-0370

A Nickel in the Slot

The first Horn & Hardart Automat opened in Philadelphia in 1902, and the last one closed in New York in 1978 — slain by the technology of fast food. For decades Americans had enjoyed peering through little glass windows at foods in individual compartments, putting coins in slots, turning knobs to open the doors, and reaching in for the goodies. But the system demanded a big staff behind the scenes to keep those compartments supplied. So the Automat can be seen today only in the Smithsonian.

VINEGAR

PUCKER UP

The Vinegar Institute tells us that vinegar is one of the oldest fermented foods known to man — predated only by wine and possibly by certain fermented foods made from milk. The word *vinegar* is derived from the French *vin,* "wine," and *aigre,* meaning "sour," indicating that it first occurred naturally from the spoilage of wine, and as early as 5000 B.C. the Babylonians were making vinegar as an end product of a wine from the date palm. It was the strongest acid known to the ancient world, and has been used since then as a condiment, a food preservative, a primitive antibiotic, and even as a household cleansing agent.

Its infamous place in history was secured when the Roman soldiers offered a vinegar-soaked sponge to Jesus as he was dying on the cross. History has reported this action

Vinegar Varieties

White distilled vinegar has the sharpest, strongest taste of all vinegars. It is fermented naturally from ethyl alcohol and used primarily for pickling.

Cider vinegar has the sharp taste of the apples it is made from; it is used in cooking and for pickling.

Wine vinegars have a wide spectrum of flavors derived from the grapes that form their base. Red and white wine vinegars are used in salad dressing and for marinating meats and poultry.

Sherry vinegar at its best is imported from Spain. It is aged in wood like a fine wine and has a lovely full-bodied flavor. A touch of vinegar added to a soup or stew focuses the flavor and heightens the taste of the dish.

Balsamic vinegar is a gift from Modena in Italy. It is deep brown in color and has a complex, smooth, mellow taste with barely a hint of sharpness. It is made from the Trebbiano grape and is aged in a series of casks made from different woods. It is used in small quantities as a flavoring vinegar, and can be sprinkled, sparingly, over fried and grilled foods, or made into a vinaigrette dressing.

Malt vinegar is a full-bodied British favorite and is used most frequently on fish and chips. It can also rescue french fries to which you have added too much salt.

Herb- and fruit-flavored vinegars are much admired by some and regarded as something of an affectation by others. They are effective in salad dressings, in vegetable purees, and in some sauces.

as a cruel mockery of Christ's plea for water, but physiologists think it may have been a well-intentioned gesture. Vinegar causes the taste buds to atrophy, and by squeezing out the last drops of moisture in the mouth, it gives a temporary illusion of quenching thirst.

Did You Know?

☞ Vinegar is an essential ingredient in the production of cheeses and of animal feed.

☞ Lord Byron, the romantic poet, was said to drink lots of vinegar in the unpoetic belief that it would regulate his weight.

☞ Heinz is the leading maker of vinegars. When its spokesperson, Heloise, produced a pamphlet on vinegar's many household uses, there were 400,000 requests for copies.

ODD JOBS

Heinz employs a vinegar taster to examine the company's vinegars for clarity, color, and aroma. He dips a sugar cube into each sample and sucks up the vinegar. To keep his taste buds up to snuff, he nibbles unsalted crackers and drinks plain water. Faced with Heinz's new super vinegar, 50 percent stronger than any of its predecessors, the taster turned up his toes and declared himself in heaven.

Vinegar Lasts a Lifetime

Throughout its long history, vinegar has always been fermented naturally, and this is still the case. It undergoes a procedure in which alcohol made from any crop that contains sugar — grapes, apples, and grains such as rice, corn, and wheat — is converted into acetic acid. The resulting vinegar is then pasteurized and filtered.

As many as 50 different trace elements occur during the processing. It is these components that give each type of vinegar its distinctive taste.

All vinegars are shelf-stable and last almost indefinitely. Over time, though, a vinegar may take on a rusty color and become cloudy, which doesn't look good, but won't be harmful. Passing it through a coffee filter will improve the vinegar's appearance.

MORE INFORMATION

The Vinegar Institute
5775 Peachtree-Dunwoody
Road, Suite 500
Atlanta, GA 30342
404-252-3663

VITAMINS

"A little vitamin C ought to clear that up in no time."

A PERSONAL VIEW

On these pages you will find a variety of views on the use of vitamins and vitamin supplements. To all of these I add my own, which is that I have infinitely greater respect for the body than those who suppose they can improve on it by advocating radical changes in diet. Swallowing quantities of vitamins may not be harmful, because we simply excrete the excess. But we take supplements at our own risk. In the beginning, research on the properties of vitamins was conducted by witholding one vitamin at a time and studying the results. We can't hope to isolate one element or another in our diet and tinker with it, and suppose that we can do a better job on our bodies than thousands of years of human evolution have already neatly done.

The Great Vitamin C Debate

Adherents of vitamin C swear on Bibles, or whatever they hold dear, that large doses of vitamin C help to prevent colds; their experience has persuaded them that this is so. However, medical experts say there's no scientific proof of it. While some small studies have tended to show that vitamin C may act as a shield against cold viruses, these tests haven't been comprehensive enough to produce results the experts consider reliable.

Meanwhile, a "Vitamin and Mineral Guide" in a recent issue of *Health* magazine flatly stated that "moderate doses [of Vitamin C] can lessen cold symptoms," and went on to note that the vitamin is currently under study to determine whether it also has an ability to slow the onset of heart disease and cancer, and lower the risk of cataracts.

The Food and Nutrition Board of the National Academy of Sciences has recommended that the amount of vitamin C *derived from food* should be 60 milligrams daily. A diet that includes plenty of fruits and vegetables every day — particularly citrus fruits, broccoli, leafy greens, cabbage, and red and green peppers — should provide at least that amount.

The Little Facilitators

Vitamins keep our skin healthy, our bones strong, and assist in the upkeep and repair of body tissues. But do we need mega-doses? Dietary-supplement sales have soared in the past decade, creating a business worth more than $33 billion a year; today, 45 percent of American men and 55 percent of American women are regular users. As the Center for Science in the Public Interest attests,

people seeking high doses of vitamins E, C, and beta carotene would have a tough time getting them from regular diets.

The supplement tsunami suffered a setback in April of 1994, when *The New England Journal of Medicine* reported that a study of lifelong smokers in Finland showed that supplements of vitamin E or beta carotene or both offered no protection from lung cancer or cardiovascular disease and suggested that smokers might possibly be harmed by taking daily supplements of beta carotene. The *Journal* said that the results "do not disprove the potential benefits of antioxidant vitamins, but they do provide timely support for skepticism and for a moratorium on unsubstantiated health claims."

That position suited the FDA, which is campaigning to prevent the vitamin industry from making health claims for its products. Vitamin deficiency diseases are rarely seen in America.

A Quick Sketch of the 13 Major Vitamins

Vitamins are soluble either in oil or in water. The fat-soluble vitamins A, D, E, and K can be stored in the body and need not be consumed daily.
Water-soluble vitamins (those in the B complex and vitamin C) are stored in smaller amounts, so we need to eat them more often.

Vitamin A (retinol) is fat-soluble and is stored in the liver. We need it for new cell growth and healthy tissues. It helps maintain gums, glands, bones, and teeth, wards off infection, and is essential for night vision, but can be toxic in large doses. Vitamin A is found in the carotene pigment in green, orange, and yellow vegetables and yellow fruit, and in animal sources including fish oils, liver, eggs, and fortified milk. (Carotene is nontoxic but may cause skin discoloration when consumed in large amounts.)

Vitamin B-1 (thiamine) is water-soluble, as are all the B-complex vitamins. We need it for normal digestion, growth, the functioning of nerve tissue, and carbohydrate metabolism. Vitamin B-1 deficiency causes beriberi, a dysfunction of the nervous system. Pork is an excellent source of thiamine; seafood, fortified grains, and cereals also contain this nutrient.

Vitamin B-2 (riboflavin) helps the body get energy from carbohydrates and protein. Deficiency causes lip sores and impaired vision. Riboflavin is found in leafy vegetables, enriched and whole-grain breads, liver, dark meat of poultry, beef, lamb, milk, and eggs.

Niacin (nicotinic acid), also called vitamin B-3, promotes proper nerve function, normal appetite, and digestion, and is needed in many enzymes that convert food to energy. A niacin deficiency causes diarrhea and, in extreme cases, pellagra. Its most abundant sources are peas, beans, enriched and whole-grain cereals, poultry, and fish.

Pantothenic acid (sometimes called vitamin B-5) is needed for adrenal hormones and chemicals that regulate nerve function and the metabolism of food. Deficiency is unknown in humans. Found in almost all plant and animal foods; also manufactured by human intestinal bacteria.

Vitamin B-6 (pyridoxine) has three forms, all of which are used by the body in the same way. This vitamin is essential to the utilization of protein, the formation of red blood cells, and proper nerve function. Deficiency may cause mouth soreness, weight loss, and sometimes nervous disturbances. It is found in meat, poultry, fish, whole-grain cereals, sweet and white potatoes, green vegetables, bananas, and prunes.

Vitamin B-12 (cobalamin) is necessary for the normal development of red blood cells and the functioning of all cells, particularly in the bone marrow, nervous system, and intestines. A deficiency causes pernicious anemia. Sources include organ meats, lean meats, fish, milk, eggs, and shellfish. (Because this vitamin is not present in plants, strict vegetarians need to take it as a supplement, as do, in some cases, the elderly, and people with malabsorption problems.)

Biotin, once called vitamin H but reclassified as a member of the B complex, is important in the metabolism of glucose and certain fatty acids. Deficiencies are rare except in infants, probably because bacteria in the intestinal tract also produce it. Food sources include eggs, milk, meats, vegetables, legumes, and nuts.

Folic acid (also known as folate or folacin), another B-complex vitamin, helps in the making of red blood cells and is essential in normal protein metabolism. A deficiency may result in anemia, bleeding gums, and diarrhea, and in neural-tube defects in infants. Abundant sources include poultry and liver, navy beans, dark-green leafy vegetables, nuts, fresh oranges, and fortified cereals and whole-wheat products.

Vitamin C (ascorbic acid) promotes healthy gums, growth, and tissue repair, including the healing of wounds. When added to food, ascorbic acid acts as a preservative. Extreme lack of this vitamin causes bleeding gums and tooth loss, unmistakable signs of scurvy, one of the oldest human diseases. Other deficiency symptoms include dry, rough skin, easy bruising, and slow healing. Sources include leafy greens, bell peppers, broccoli, citrus fruits, strawberries, and tomatoes.

Vitamin D exists in several forms, including D-2 (from plants) and D-3 (from animals). Converted in the liver and kidneys to a hormonelike substance, Vitamin D aids in the absorption of calcium and phosphorus and helps to build and maintain bones. Deficiency causes rickets in children and osteoporosis and osteomalacia (bone softening) in adults. Excess can cause nausea, weight loss, hypertension, and calcium deposits in soft tissues. Abundant sources are fish, egg yolk, and vitamin-D-fortified foods such as milk and margarine. Vitamin D is also formed when the skin is exposed to the ultraviolet rays in sunlight.

Vitamin E acts as an antioxidant that helps to prevent oxygen from destroying cells. No illnesses are associated with low intake; deficiency is unknown in humans. Abundant sources include vegetable oils, beans, eggs, the germ of whole grains, poultry, seafood, and vegetables.

Vitamin K is partially manufactured in the human intestinal tract. It is essential to blood clotting, and also has a role in bone metabolism. Deficiency causes hemorrhage and liver injury, though this is rare. (Occasionally, newborns may be deficient because they lack the intestinal bacteria to manufacture it.) Vitamin K is found in a wide variety of foods, including green leafy vegetables, liver, and egg yolk.

Did You Know?

☞ There's no difference between natural and man-made vitamins. Their chemical formulas and usability by the body are identical.

☞ On an average day, Americans spend $3,673,973 on vitamins.

☞ Sylvester Stallone takes 50 to 75 vitamin supplements every day.

Books

The Essential Guide to Vitamins and Minerals
Elizabeth Somer;
HarperCollins, 1992; $15.00

Recommended Dietary Allowances (10th edition)
National Academy Press, 1989; $19.95

WALNUTS ■ WATER ◆ WEDDING FOOD

WALNUTS

STRANGE FRUIT

The walnut tree, which flourishes wherever the climate is temperate, is one of the oldest sources of food known to man. The Romans had such a high opinion of these nuts that they called them *Juglans regia* ("nuts of Jove, the king") to honor their chief god, Jove, or Jupiter.

When the trees were introduced to Britain in the 16th century, the English called them *walnuts* because, in the language of the time, the term *wal* meant "foreign." But walnuts were soon very much at home there, and today the two most popular varieties of walnuts in the world are the English walnut and the black walnut.

The vast majority of walnuts marketed in the United States are the English variety. They vary greatly in size and in thickness of shell, but will usually yield kernels (nutmeats) that are plump, meaty, and crisp. The nuts of America's native black walnut, *Juglans nigra*, are less popular because they are hard to remove from the shell and have a somewhat oily texture. White walnut or butternut hulls yield good dyes (they were used to dye Confederate uniforms), but the soft, sweet nutmeats are not available commercially.

Walnuts in the shell will keep for up to three months, stored in a cool, dry place. Shelled and tightly sealed, the nutmeats can be refrigerated for six months, or frozen for up to a year.

ODD JOBS

Dwayne Lindsay, who works in research and development at Diamond Walnut Growers, has the final say in the crunch department. During the nut harvest, Lindsay chews walnuts all day every day to determine their crispness. On the basis of his judgment, certain batches of walnuts may go right to the top, and end up, say, in Post's Banana Nut Crunch cereal.

Did You Know?

☞ Walnut trees start bearing nuts six to eight years after being planted, and will continue to bear for about a century.

☞ The walnut's slightly bitter flavor is caused by tannic acid in the skin. It can be removed by blanching the nutmeats in boiling water.

☞ Walnuts grown in California account for two-thirds of the world's walnut trade. More than 200,000 tons of nuts are harvested annually, between late August and early November.

☞ One pound of in-shell walnuts yields 2 cups of shelled nutmeats; one pound of shelled nuts yields 4 cups.

MORE INFORMATION

Diamond Walnut Growers
P.O. Box 1721
Stockton, CA 95201
209-467-6000

WATER

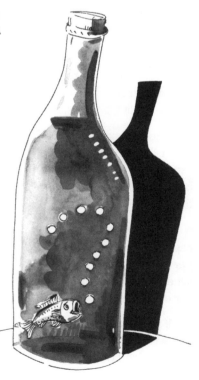

Water is the only drink for a wise man.

— Henry David Thoreau
19th-century ecologist

THE PRECIOUS RESOURCE

SANDRA DIBBLE

Do you know where your water was last night? Last month? Last year? Or where it's headed as it swishes across the slick surface of the sink and vanishes through a pipe? And what you've done to it while washing clothes, watering the garden, taking a bath? As more people reach for the tap, these become pressing questions. A growing population requires more food, more houses, more shopping centers, more roads, more cars — all of which increase demands for clean, fresh water.

The 20th century has seen great changes in the way Americans use water. As the century opened, the United States government launched a massive dam-building program aimed at bringing irrigation — and people — to the West. In the decades that followed, dams were raised across rivers around the country, providing not just water for agriculture, recreation, and navigation but also protection against floods and electricity to power the industrial development of entire regions.

Large-scale exploitation of groundwater resources began in the 1930s, when new pumps and cheap power allowed a growing number of farmers to economically lift water from as deep as 1,000 feet below the surface. From the Great Plains to California's Central Valley, vast regions with little rainfall assumed new prominence as agricultural land. In recent decades Americans have begun to feel the limits of their water supply. Pollution of lakes and streams and overpumping and contamination of groundwater sources have, in some areas, sharply reduced the available amount of fresh water. People are being forced into choices: Should we water fields or supply cities? Generate electricity or support fish habitat? Build an airport or preserve a wetland?

Reprinted courtesy The National Geographic Society

A Sparkling Success

Of the 700 or more bottled waters on the market, producing annual sales of nearly $3 billion, San Pellegrino — the leading Italian producer — is among the most popular. This sparkling mineral water is naturally carbonated — meaning that it contains enough carbon dioxide gas to bubble on its own. Its pleasant taste and light effervescence make it an excellent accompaniment to food and a fitting companion for fine wine.

San Pellegrino first bubbled into recorded history in the 13th century, when it was discovered 2,000 feet underground in the Italian Alps. Its healthy properties are derived from 14 important minerals and trace elements. Leonardo da Vinci drank it, and its contemporary devotees include Madonna, Tom Cruise, and Sylvester Stallone.

Drinking Waters

Sparkling water may be naturally carbonated with carbon dioxide (CO_2) gas or have carbonation (fizz) added.

Seltzer water is artificially carbonated filtered still water. It is often unsalted and no minerals are added.

Club soda is also artificially carbonated filtered still water, but contains added mineral salts.

Mineral water may be naturally rich in minerals or have minerals added. The minerals in the underground source of the water give each kind its distinctive taste. Most waters are named for their place of origin.

Spring water is bottled from underground springs that rise to the surface naturally. It can be labeled "natural" only if it is bottled just as it comes from the ground and receives no further processing.

WATER BABIES

Water is as integral to our lives as the air we breathe. Of the six nutrients — protein, carbohydrate, fat, vitamins, minerals, and water — water is the most essential. We can lose almost all our body fat and about half our protein and stay alive, but take away 40 percent of the water in our bodies and we are gone. The most dehydration we can survive is 25 percent of normal body weight.

To replenish this life force we must drink at least 8 cups of fluid a day for optimal health, and take on more liquid as we eat. We moisten foods by cooking them in water. We can eat only substances that have water in them — even foods such as bread or cereals contain at least 8 percent water.

As the creatures of planet Earth we owe our existence to the water in the oceans, in the air, in the ground, and in our bodies. As embryos we are 95 percent water; as newborns, about three-fourths water. In old age, the body's water content has dwindled by about half, depending on individual age and body fat.

Did You Know?

☞ Even naturally carbonated waters may be reinjected with carbon dioxide in the bottling process.

☞ The International Bottled Water Association estimates that 25 percent of bottled water is in fact just tap water, in a bottle.

☞ U.S. average daily residential water demand per person is 100 gallons. One thousand gallons of tap water cost less than $2.50.

☞ If you add ice cubes to imported bottled water you have a mixed drink.

MORE INFORMATION

International Bottled Water Association
113 North Henry Street
Alexandria, VA 22314
703-683-5213

HOTLINES

800-426-4791
EPA's Safe Drinking Water Hotline

WEDDING FOOD

OF LOVE AND LUNCH

Richard Atcheson

Weddings are very sexy occasions — not only for the bride and groom, whose passion is on display for all to see, but also for those who come to witness the joining of two into one: It gives us all a lot of great ideas. However, lest the wedding feast turn into a riot, these ideas must be channeled toward more discreet appetites, which in our culture are traditionally the lures of food and drink.

Wedding food has been a subject on my own mind since childhood, when my grandfather would take me on his knee and sing "Froggie went a-courtin' and he did ride, uh-huh." I loved the verse after Froggie wins Missy Mousie's heart: "What shall the wedding supper be, ah-hah?" In my grandfather's version, it was "parsnip soup and catnip tea, oh-ho, um-hum." That menu always cracked me up, because even at the age of three I knew that catnip tea wasn't going to cut it with *my* family at a wedding. Uh-uh.

Also, I worried that Froggie and Missy Mousie had no *cake*. The wedding cakes of my childhood were big, smushy angel-food confections with colored icing, the kind a boy likes. On the other hand, when my wife and I got married we had a very different kind, a classic English wedding cake direct from Fortnum & Mason in London. It traveled on a steamship to get to us in time, and when we took it out of its box we found three perfect white tiers without a dent.

Not surprising: When we tried to cut the bottom tier at the reception, the "royal" icing proved to be as thick as commercial drywall paneling, and the cake inside had the density of plum pudding. It did, however, have the advantage of keeping almost indefinitely. (We served the top tier at our first child's christening, a year later.)

When I was a young man, other people's weddings weren't really about the food; they were about drinking a lot of champagne and making passes at the bridesmaids. This activity continues to be the done thing at wedding receptions — youths drinking, dancing, flirting, even going off in pairs into the bushes with bottles of Perrier-Jouët boosted from the host's supply — and this is as it should be.

It is left to the rest of us — the middle-aged and our seniors — to turn our attention to the tables. And that we do, along with Aunt Maud and Uncle Harold and all, getting there on sticks if necessary. I have seen wedding feasts in Westchester County so opulent that the food seemed to be literally oozing out of the walls in cascades of fresh shrimp, oysters, and clams, while waiters circulated with trays of canapés and hungry guests shouldered each other out of the way to get at chafing dishes sizzling with mushroom caps wrapped in bacon. Under many a glowing tent — erected by a host I sometimes scarcely knew, whose blushing bridal daughter or son I knew not at all — I have sat like a pasha at a table for 12, placecard in spidery script before me in the shade of a giant, candlelit epergne, while four and more courses were set down for my delectation. After that I'd waddle to the dance floor to gracefully perform the cha-cha-cha. I'm sure the Romans never had it so good.

In contrast, I've stood on California hillsides, perfectly barefoot, while bearded boys and girls with flowers in their hair plighted their troth in the evasive language the young always try to find when the idea of commitment comes up. Once, I remember, the hillside wedding feast was restricted to a loaf of sourdough bread and a jug of good old California Mountain Red — and that was fine, because the "thou" was so poetically evident in the occasion. As it turned out, everybody got drunk sooner than at your usual reception because there were two more jugs of wine, and the one loaf of bread was all there was to eat.

In my view, it doesn't matter what the food is at a wedding if the zing of sex and the light of love are there. But if there are any more of those mushroom caps wrapped in bacon, I won't say no. Uh-uh.

The greatest of all arts is the art of living together.

— William Lyon Phelps
Optimist

Queen Victoria's Wedding Cake

*V*ictoria and Albert were married in February 1840, and the 1840 Annual Register described the "elegant emblem of the felicities of marriage," a 300-pound cake, 3 yards around and 14 inches high, which was served at the wedding breakfast.

"It is covered with sugar of the purest white. On the top is seen the figure of Britannia in the act of blessing the illustrious bride and bridegroom, who are dressed somewhat incongruously in the costume of ancient Rome. These figures are not quite a foot in height; at the feet of his serene highness is the effigy of a dog, said to denote fidelity; and at the feet of the queen is a pair of turtle doves, denoting the felicities of the marriage state. A cupid is writing in a volume expanded on his knees the date of the day of the marriage, and various other cupids are sporting and enjoying themselves as such interesting little individuals generally do."

YOGURT

YOGURT

THEY WANT YOGURT HILDA, YOGURT! NOT YOGA!

Right On — Dannon

The first commercial yogurt dairy was founded in Barcelona by Isaac Carasso; he named it Danone after his son, Daniel. When the company moved to New York after World War II, Danone was Americanized to Dannon, and it really got around after that.

WHITE VELVET

It's nature's way. If you leave milk at 110 degrees F. for a day you'll get yogurt, a velvety curd created in cow's milk (and most other milks) when friendly bacteria invade and cause fermentation and coagulation. Balkan nomads noted and adapted the process thousands of years ago, probably by means of the "Oops, I left the milk out" method, and it traveled eventually to the Middle East and Asia, where it's been a diet centerpiece for centuries.

Yogurt caught on relatively late in the United States. Back in 1960, American consumers satisfied their dairy needs (and got most of their calcium) from whole milk. That year they bought only about 44 million pounds of yogurt, on average only about a quarter of a pound per person. But things changed rapidly when we woke up to the goodness and good taste of this natural food. Today, we consume more than a billion pounds of yogurt a year.

In the modern production of yogurt, makers leave nothing to chance. The essential live bacteria — "active cultures" of *Lactobacillus bulgaricus* and *Streptococcus thermophilus* — are deliberately added to the milk during the manufacturing process. For people who want the calcium (higher in yogurts than in milk) but can't digest lactose, this is a particular advantage: The bacteria digest the lactose for them, in advance.

Anyone who's ever browsed supermarket shelves knows that whole sections are devoted to yogurt these days. Categories include original, custard, fruit, fruit-on-the-bottom, fresh flavors, Swiss-style, low-fat, nonfat, plain whole milk, plain low-fat, and plain nonfat, not to mention yogurt drinks and many other hugely popular products.

Did You Know?

☞ Bulgarians, renowned for longevity, consume so much yogurt that researchers sought a connection. Diet proved irrelevant, though; the elders were lying about their age.

☞ Dr. Khem Shahani, a food scientist at the University of Nebraska, is persuaded by lab work and field studies in yogurt-eating nations that yogurt fights diarrhea and food poisoning.

☞ When volunteers ate six ounces of yogurt daily for a year, those who ate live cultures had 25 percent fewer colds and 10 times fewer symptoms of hay fever and allergies than those who ate yogurt with killed cultures.

COLD Cultures

Frozen yogurt is one of the boomingest food products in America, with sales up 2,900 percent since 1951 and tripling annually. Its success is founded on the fact that it delivers great taste with healthy implications: The milk in it is usually more than 90 percent fat-free, and the yogurt cultures contribute that creamy experience.

But lest buyers get too carried away, they need to keep in mind that the word "nonfat" on the label refers strictly to the yogurt, not to interesting elements that makers sometimes add to the mix — cookie crumbs, for example, or cheesecake. Nor should they let a product's advertising tempt them into spooning up too much of a good thing. It's true that frozen yogurts have much less fat per serving than ice creams, even the ones with the highest fat content. But if you eat too much frozen yogurt you can get just as portly as you would on a normal-sized scoop of Häagen-Dazs.

One last caveat: While frozen yogurt is a healthful treat, it lacks the believed advantage of ordinary yogurt — that of keeping the intestinal system populated with good bacteria — because most bacteria are destroyed in the freezing process.

ZZZ – BEDTIME FOOD

ZZZ–
BEDTIME FOOD

I Vaunt To Be Alone

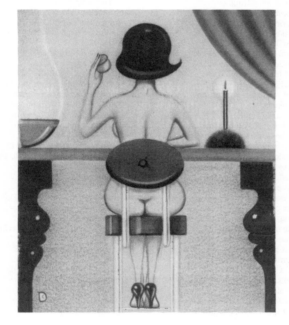

Sharing a meal with a loving mate may be the very best thing in life, but eating alone is the next best. You come home after a trying day with a chicken under one arm and a bottle of good red wine under the other. You put the bird in the oven, uncork the wine, change into something comfortable — and ah! Dinner is served when you serve it, and enjoyed in perfect peace.

IN MY OWN
SMALL CORNER

Eating in bed is one of the greatest pleasures I know, but I find that it takes a certain amount of planning to do it right. You *can*, of course, just leave everything to chance and knee-jerk reactions — throwing off the covers and rushing to the kitchen when you see, for example, a luscious burger commercial on TV — but this is a perilous policy: You'll be lucky to find anything out there more exciting than leftover Chinese food. Even drearier options abound: gingersnaps, a bowl of cereal, a sandwich. These boring solutions aren't what you want in bed.

I believe that the first step to a successful eating-in-bed experience begins by filling the refrigerator with far more food than you can possibly eat, even if you plan to stay in bed over a four-day weekend. This provides the luxury of choice and the opportunity to relax, free of all anxiety of running out of this or that. And you can eat at any time of day or night when craving commences.

There are good and better weathers for spending the day in bed. A heat wave is excellent, if you have an air-conditioner. A cold, rainy day is better, and a severe snowstorm is best of all. When blizzards approach, the TV weatherman tells you to stay indoors, and though he doesn't say "in bed," we know that's what he means.

If eating in bed is your cup of tea, you probably have rituals similar to mine. A comfortable backrest is important to me, as is a generous bed tray and a television set. A large bedside table is essential to hold the radio, the CD player, and the movie videos I plan to watch. On the bed are strewn the 30 or so magazines that I bought when I went out to get the movies, and two books: a worthy one, and a mystery novel in case the worthy book is too heavy. Naturally, I want something very nice to drink as I review all these opportunities.

After a decent interval, I get hungry. This is my signal to get up and look for something to eat. This is the best part. I rummage in the refrigerator and choose, choose, choose.

There's a risotto, saffron yellow, brilliantly colored with red onion, garlic, and red and yellow peppers, and topped with fresh tomatoes that I chopped and tossed in olive oil. There's a big-breasted roasted chicken near a dish of thinly sliced grilled eggplant with rosemary. Behind the chicken is a homemade quiche and some soft, buttery Bibb lettuce. The smoked salmon, wrapped as it came from the store, sits by a tub of fresh-from-the-dairy cream cheese and a skinny baguette. The prosciutto, also still in its wrappings, is nearby: What a fantastic flavor it carries in the thinnest slice, and wouldn't it be lovely with a slice of that ripe Persian melon! There's some cold butterflied lamb, too: That would be fabulous with the marinated artichoke hearts. Or how about the poached salmon with the cucumbers and fresh peas? Do I feel like shelling peas? Maybe.

But first I'll have just a little herring in sour cream . . . and some icy-cold vodka from the freezer. Then I'll decide between the linguine with fresh clam sauce and the chicken pot pie. I'll save the chili for later, to have with a piece of cake. Chili and cake is a nice combination to have with Jay Leno. Or David Letterman. Or will I be ready by then for the mango ice cream and fresh raspberries?

I wonder. This is something I obviously have to think about. And so to bed. Cheers!

Authors Quoted

Illustrations

Zimmerman; Dan Kirk **157** Merle Nacht **158** Merle Nacht — photo Ray Kroc courtesy McDonald Corporation; photo David Thomas courtesy Wendy's **159** Roger Roth — Victoria Roberts **160** David Calver; Marc Rosenthal **161** Rick Stromoski **162** Philippe Petit-Roulet **163** Courtesy National Fisheries Institute — Courtesy White Lily Flour **164** Steven Guarnaccia **165** Nurit Karlin — Rosmarijn van Limburg Stirum **167** Michael Witte **168** Henry Zamchick, courtesy Maturity Magazines Group **169** Joe Troise and Phil Frank **170** Nurit Karlin; Isadore Seltzer **171** Horacio Cardo **172** Matthew Martin **173** Virginia Halstead — Robert Zimmerman **174** Susan Blubaugh **175** (left) Courtesy New York Public Library Picture Collection **176** Steven Guarnaccia **177** Jose Cruz — Paul Hoffman **179** Dana Burns — Courtesy New York Public Library Picture Collection **180** Courtesy *The Observer* **181** Joanna Roy (top) **182** P. C. Vey — Robert Zimmerman **183** Julia Gorton — Joanna Roy **185** Bob Penny — Courtesy Christopher Ranch of Gilroy — Alina Wilczynski **188** Julia Gorton — Joanna Roy **189** Courtesy California Table Grape Commission **190** Courtesy California Table Grape Commission — Michael Witte — Lisa Haney **191** Paul Hoffman — Robert Zimmerman **193** Michael Witte **194** Margaret Scott; Bob Penny — Kassie Schwan; Michael David Biegel **195** (bottom) Rick Stromoski **196** Dan Kirk — Abe Gurvin **197** Courtesy Oregon Hazelnuts — Tom Cheney **198** P. C. Vey — Robert Zimmerman **199** Lisa Haney — Alina Wilczynski — P. C. Vey **200** Paul Hoffman — Courtesy Shepherd's Garden Seeds **201** Merle Nacht; Bob Penny **203** Robert Zimmerman — Steven Guarnaccia **204** Courtesy *COOK's Magazine* **205** Michael Witte — Julia Gorton **206** Courtesy National Honey Board; Margaret Scott **207** Merle Nacht — Drawing by H. Martin, © 1982 The New Yorker Magazine, Inc. **208** (bottom) Dan Kirk **209** (top left) Lisa Haney — Paul Hoffman **210** Carol Fabricatore — Margaret Scott **211** Alina Wilczynski **212** (top) Nurit Karlin — (bottom right) Julia Gorton **213** Margaret Scott — Rich del Rosso **214** Michael Witte; Robert Zimmerman — Courtney Graner; Robert Zimmerman **215** Merle Nacht **216** Tony Saltzman — *The New York Times* **217** Michael Witte — (left) Paul Hoffman **218** Lisa Haney **219** Alina Wilczynski — Lisa Haney **220** Greg Clarke; Michael Witte — Courtesy New Zealand Kiwifruit Company — Lisa Haney **221** (bottom) Debra Solomon **222** Seymore Chwast **223** Walt Handelsman, The Times-Picayune, Tribune Media Services — Hedy Klein **224** Leslie Cober **225** Label courtesy FDA — Ed Fisher, courtesy Modern Maturity Magazine **226** Rick Stromoski — Bob Penny **227** Rosemarijn van Limburg Stirum — (bottom) Nurit Karlin **228** Courtesy California Iceberg Lettuce Commission **229** (middle) Michael Witte **230** Shawn Banner; Shelley Heller — Merle Nacht; Bob Penny **231** Joanna Roy — P. C. Vey **232** Robert Zimmerman (middle right) — Alina Wilczynski (bottom 3) **233** Courtesy New York Public Library Picture Collection **234** Dave Calver — Courtesy Borden, Inc. **235** Nurit Karlin **236** Lisa Haney **237** Bob Penny — Joanna Roy **240** Robert Zimmerman **241** Tom Bloom **243** (left) Julia Gorton **244** Igor Kopelnitsky **245** Rolla Herman **247** Rick Stromoski **248** Rene Rickabaugh; Courtesy *Vegetarian Times* **249** Beata Szpura **250** Susan Grey; Courtesy National Fisheries Institute — Rosmarijn van Limburg Stirum **251** Bob Penny — Courtesy Mount Horeb Mustard Museum — Denis Vanderpuf **252** Robert Zimmerman **253** Courtesy USDA; A. A. McCourt **254** Michael Witte — John Jonik **255** Tom Cheney (both) **256** P. C. Vey — Alan Witschonke **257** Robert Zimmerman — (left) Jonathan Royce **258** (bottom) Beata Szpura **259** Sean Banner **260** Heather Calder **261** Alina Wilczynski **262** Paul Hoffman; Robert Zimmerman **263** Carol Fabricatore; Tom Bloom — Courtney Graner **264** Chris Van Dusen; Tom Bloom — Alan E. Cober **265** Michael Witte — Bob Penny **267** Dave Calver **268** Julia Gorton **269** (left) *The New York Times* **270** Peter de Seve; Merle Nacht **271** Donald Hendricks — Donald Hendricks; Alden Wallace; Judy Francis **272** Shelley Heller; Lisa Haney — Courtesy Peanut Advisory Board **273** Dan Kirk **274** Michael Witte; Tom Bloom — Courtesy Peanut Advisory Board **275** Margaret Scott; (right) Rene Rickabaugh **276** Bob Penny; Joanna Roy — Courtesy National Pecan Marketing Council **277** Abe Gurvin **278** Dale Glasser — Madeline Sorel **279** Lisa Haney —

(bottom) Nikki Middendorf **280** Tom Bloom (both) **281** (bottom) Steven Guarnaccia **282** Michael Witte; Michael Witte — Robert Zimmerman — Rick Stromoski **283** Bob Penny; Rick Stromoski — Courtesy Pickle Packers International and DHM Group **284** (left) Michael Witte — (bottom) Margaret Scott **285** Nurit Karlin; Paul Hoffman; Shelley Heller **286** Shelley Heller — Courtesy California Pistachio Commission **287** Michael Witte; Nurit Karlin; Michael Witte — Dan Kirk **288** Julia Gorton — (middle) Courtesy New York Public Library Picture Collection **289** Julia Gorton **290** Tom Bloom — Lisa Blackshear; Bob Penny **291** Michael Witte — (bottom) Bob Penny **292** Michael Witte; Abe Gurvin — Lisa Haney **293** Bob Penny — Dan Kirk **294** Dan Kirk — Merle Nacht **295** Courtesy New York Public Library Picture Collection; Nurit Karlin — Rick Stromoski **296** Tom Bloom; Tim Gabor — Alina Wilczynski **297** Greg Clarke — Bob Penny **298** Shawn Banner — Carol Fabricatore **300** Tom Cheney **301** Nicolae Asciu; P. C. Vey **302** (both) Michael Witte **303** Peter de Seve; Michael Witte — (bottom middle) Rick Stromoski **304** Tom Bloom; Nurit Karlin — Steve Stankiewicz; Rick Stromoski **305** USA Rice Council; Madeline Sorel **306** USA Rice Council — Rolla Herman **307** (top) Rene Rickabaugh **308** (bottom) Joanna Roy **309** Courtesy New York Public Library Picture Collection — (left) Chris Van Dusen **310** Chris Van Dusen — Sean Banner **311** Abe Gurvin — Courtesy El Paso Chile Company **312** Alina Wilczynski — Roger Roth **313** Julia Gorton — Robert Zimmerman **314** (both) Rene Rickabaugh **315** Joanna Roy — Michael Witte **316** Robert Zimmerman — (bottom) Paul Hoffman **317** Lisa Haney; Rick Stromoski — (far right) Lisa Blackshear — Margaret Scott; Lisa Blackshear **318** Mark Steele **319** Robin Jareaux — Alan E. Cober **320** Courtesy Aseptic Packaging Council **321** Margaret Scott **322** Courtesy National Fisheries Institute — Arnold Roth **323** John Kleber — Lisa Haney **324** Courtesy FDA **325** Lisa Haney — Rene Rickabaugh; Keith Graves **326** Nikki Middendorf — Duane Raver **327** Roger Roth — Courtesy Campbell Soup Company — Carol Fabricatore **328** Rich del Rosso **329** Joanna Roy — (bottom right) Madeline Sorel **330** Chris Van Dusen — Robert Zimmerman **331** Rich del Rosso — Jennifer Skopp **332** Lisa Blackshear — Joanna Roy **333** (left) Joanna Roy — Robert Zimmerman **334** (top) Billy Paul, courtesy Sugar Association **335** Tom Bloom — Lisa Haney; Tom Bloom **336** Michael Witte — Abe Gurvin **337** Tom Bloom — Rich del Rosso **338** Elwood Smith **339** S. Neil Fujita — Duane Raver **340** (bottom) Lisa Blackshear **341** Robert Zimmerman **342** Tom Bloom **343** Rust Hills — Tom Bloom **344** Michael Witte — Tom Bloom **345** Courtesy Tea Council; Tom Bloom; Courtesy Rainforest Aquaculture Products, Inc. **346** Lisa Blackshear — Michael Witte — Nurit Karlin **347** (top right) Tina Vey — Joanna Roy **348** Duane Raver — Rich del Rosso **349** Joanna Roy **350** Leslie Cober; Duane Raver — Roger Roth **351** Rick Meyerowitz — Tom Bloom **352** Dan Rosandich **353** Tom Bloom; Nikki Middendorf **354** Julia Gorton — Rick Stromoski **355** Robert Zimmerman **356** Tom Bloom — Courtesy Shepherd's Garden Seeds **357** V. Gene Meyers; Chris Van Dusen — Tom Bloom **358** Rolla Herman — Robert Zimmerman **359** (bottom) Yvonne Buchanan **360** P. C. Vey — Alina Wilczynski — Courtesy San Pellegrino **361** Nikki Middendorf **362** Julia Gorton — P. C. Vey; Merle Nacht **363** Merle Nacht — Dave Calver

Credits

13 "Those Dumb Birds," adapted from "Animals Bring Charm To Ads But Create Grief For Agencies," by Ronald Alsop in *The Wall Street Journal*, October 16, 1986. Reprinted by permission of *The Wall Street Journal*, © 1986 Dow Jones & Co., Inc. All rights reserved worldwide. **14** "A Few Minutes With Andy Rooney." Copyright © CBS Inc. Excerpted from 60 Minutes — A Few Minutes With Andy Rooney, "Ad Words." Reprinted with permission of the writer. **19** "Gator Nip," by Ernest Matthew Mickler. Reprinted from *White Trash Cooking*. "Scallopini of Alligator," from *American Game Cooking*, by John Ash and Sid Goldstein, Aris Books, 1991. By permission of the authors. **22** "The Barbarity Of Meat," by Nick Fiddes from the *UTNE Reader*, March/April 1992. Originally from *Meat: A Natural Symbol*, copyright © 1991, Routledge. **23** "Food Fright," by William Geist, from *New York* Magazine, August 7, 1989. Reprinted by special permission of the author. **27** "How The Taste Bud Translates From Tongue To Brain," by Jane E. Brody, in *The New York Times*, August 4, 1992. Copyright © 1992 by The New York Times Co. Reprinted by permission. **28** "The Joys Of Eating." Reprinted with the permission of Charles Scribner's

Sons, an imprint of Macmillan Publishing Co., from *Of Time And The River*, by Thomas Wolfe. Copyright © 1935 by Charles Scribner's Sons, renewed © 1963 by Paul Gitlin, Administrator CTA. **30** "Eating Humble Pie," from *Cooking in a Country Kitchen*, © 1983 by Suzanne Taylor, Irena Chalmers Cookbooks, Inc. **42** "Warfare At The Supermarket," from "Life In The 30's," by Anna Quindlen in *The New York Times*, April 8, 1987. Copyright © 1987 by The New York Times Co. Reprinted by permission. **43** "Breast Is Best," from *The Nursing Mother's Companion*, by Kathleen Huggins, R.N., M.S., Harvard Common Press, 1990. Used with permission. **44** "Infant Feeding In A Glance," from *The Baby Book*. Copyright © 1993 by William Sears, M.D., and Martha Sears, R.N. By permission of Little, Brown & Co. **45** "Begetting The Bagel," from *Craig Claiborne's New York Times Food Encyclopedia*. Copyright © 1985 by The New York Times Co. Reprinted by permission of Random House, Inc. **48** "Manly Chores," from "The Cookout; Barbecuing: A Manly Art," by William Geist, in *The New York Times*, May 17, 1987. Copyright © 1987 by The New York Times Co. Reprinted by permission. **50** "Bats Have A Role In The Food Chain, Too," from a transcript of The Charlie Rose Show, WNET-TV (13), 11:00 p.m., January 13, 1993, with guest Merlin Tuttle. Reprinted by special permission of Charlie Rose. **51** "Leaning Toward Lentils," by Jon Carroll, from the *San Francisco Chronicle*, April 22, 1991. Copyright © San Francisco Chronicle. Reprinted by permission. **53** "10 Beans And Their Flatulence Levels," compiled by Corby Kummer, *The Atlantic Monthly*, April 1992. Used with permission. **60** "Alice In Biotechland," from "Last Word," by Charles Memminger, Jr., in *OMNI* Magazine, August 1986. Reprinted by permission of *OMNI*. © 1986, Omni Publications International, Ltd. "A Dinner of Transgenic Treats," reprinted from *National Culinary Review*, November 1992. Courtesy *Restaurant Hospitality* Magazine. **62** and **234** "Blueberries" and "Evening In A Sugar Orchard," from *The Poetry of Robert Frost*, edited by Edward Connery Lathem. Copyright 1951, © 1958 by Robert Frost. Copyright © 1967 by Leslie Frost Ballantine. Copyright 1923, 1930, 1939, © 1969 by Henry Holt and Co., Inc. Reprinted by permission of Henry Holt and Co., Inc. **63** "Down With Catch-All Loaves," from *Beard On Bread*. Copyright © 1973 by James A. Beard. Reprinted by permission of Alfred A. Knopf, Inc. **64** "Primal Kneads," from *Ken Haedrich's Country Baking*. Copyright © 1990 by Ken Haedrich. Used by permission of Bantam Books, a division of Bantam Doubleday Dell Publishing Group, Inc. **65** "Nutritional Content Of Breads" from *The Wellness Encyclopedia*. Copyright © 1991 by Health Letter Associates. Reprinted by permission of Houghton Mifflin Co. All rights reserved. **66** "A Typical English Breakfast," from *George Lang's Compendium*, Clarkson Potter, 1980. Reprinted by permission of George Lang. **70** "The Virtuous Cabbage," from "With All Its Virtues, The Poor Cabbage Remains A Pariah," by Judith Valente in *The Wall Street Journal*, June 18, 1991. Reprinted by permission of *The Wall Street Journal*. Copyright © 1991 Dow Jones & Co., Inc. All rights reserved worldwide. **71** "Messing About in the Ultimate Company Cafeteria," from *The New Yorker*, March 15, 1993, "Messing About." Reprinted by permission. © The New Yorker Magazine, Inc. **73** "Not All Calories Are Alike," from *Eating Smart — The ABC's of The New Food Literacy*. Copyright © 1992 by Jeanne Jones. Macmillan Publishing Co., New York. Reprinted by special permission of the author. **74** "Fruits and Vegetables Prevent Cancer," from *Food: Your Miracle Medicine*. Copyright © 1993 by Jean Carper. Reprinted by permission of HarperCollins Publishers, Inc. **83** "Fiber in the Belly," from *Men's Health*, March/April 1993. Reprinted by permission of Colin McEnroe. Copyright © 1993. **84** "Dr. Kellogg's Dream" as quoted in *A Food Lover's Companion*, by Evan Jones, Harper & Row, 1979; original source unknown. "Making Sense of the Cereal Aisle," from "Eating Well," by Marian Burros in *The New York Times*, January 3, 1990. Copyright © 1990 by The New York Times Co. Reprinted by permission. **93** "Why It Works in Scientific Terms..." from the abstract "Chicken Soup Inhibits Neutrophil Chemotaxis," by B.O. Rennard et al., Pulmonary and Critical Care Medicine, University of Nebraska Medical Center and VA Hospital, Omaha, NE. By permission of the authors. **95** "Andrew's Turkey," from *L'Enfance de la Cuisine*, Pentagram Designs, New York. Reprinted by permission. **98** "Marcel Desaulniers' Bittersweet Chocolate Sauce," from *Death By Chocolate: The Last Word On A Consuming Passion*. Copyright © 1992 by Marcel Desaulniers. Rizzoli, Publisher. Reprinted by permission of the author. **100** "It's In The Blood," from "The New Bloodline," by Scott Mowbray in *Eating Well*, July/August 1992. Reprinted with permission, *Eating Well* Magazine, Ferry Road, Charlotte, VT 05445. **104** "Cod-Liver Oil: Tastes Terrible, Works Wonders," from "In Cod We Trust," by Penny Ward Moser, *Health* Magazine, March/April 1993. Reprinted by permission. **105** "The Classical Coffeehouse Revival," from "Ballad of the Glad Cafe," by Joseph Mazo, in *Food Arts*, June 1990. Reprinted by permission. **112** "So You Want To Write A Cookbook." Reprinted by permission from *Restaurants & Institutions* Magazine, October 14, 1988. **117** "The Lore of Corn," from "Growing Up," by Anne Raver in *The New York Times*, May 21, 1992. Copyright © by the New York Times Co. Reprinted by permission. **120** "Inside A Chesapeake Crab House," from *Beautiful Swimmers*. Copyright © 1976 by William Warner. By permission of Little, Brown & Co. **122** "A Crawfish Legend," from *Bernard Clayton's Cooking Across America*. Copyright © 1993 by Bernard Clayton, Jr. Reprinted

by permission of Simon & Schuster, Inc. **123** "How To Eat Crawfish," from *Emeril's New New Orleans Cooking*, by Emeril Lagasse and Jessie Tirsch, Morrow, 1993. Reprinted by special permission of the author. **123** "Jude Theriot's Crawfish Skillet," from *La Cuisine Cajun*, copyright © 1986, 1990 by Jude W. Theriot. Pelican Publishing Co., Inc., 1101 Monroe Street, Gretna, LA 70053. By permission of the author. **127** "To Live and Diet," from *Bachelor Girls*. Copyright © 1990 by Wendy Wasserstein. Reprinted by permission of Alfred A. Knopf, Inc. **128** "The Right Shape," from "Use of the Danish Adoption Register for the Study of Obesity and Thinness," by A. Stukard, T. Sorensen, and F. Schulsinger, in *The Genetics of Neurological and Psychiatric Disorders*, edited by S. Kety, 1980, p. 119. Copyright 1983 by Raven Press. Used by permission. Caption adapted from "How Do You See Yourself," by Joel Gurin in *American Health*, October 1986. Copyright © 1986 by Joel Gurin. Used with permission of *American Health*. **132** "Lunch Wagons with a Curfew," from "Lunch Wagons with a Curfew" and "Diner Speak," by Sylvia Carter in *New York Newsday*, September 19, 1990. Reprinted by permission of the Los Angeles Times Syndicate International and Sylvia Carter. **139** "Mother Hen," from *Much Depends On Dinner*. Copyright © 1986 by Margaret Visser. Used with the permission of Grove/Atlantic, Inc. **144** "The African Legacy," from *Southern Food*, by John Egerton. Copyright © 1989, Alfred A. Knopf. Reprinted by permission of the author. **147** "The Endangered Kitchen Table," by Rob Kasper from *New York Newsday*, November 13, 1991. Copyright 1991 by the Los Angeles Times Food Styles Syndicate. Reprinted by special permission of the author. **148** "The Challenge of the 21st Century," from "Meeting the Food Needs of the Coming Decade," by Orville Freeman in *The Futurist*, November/December 1990. Reproduced with permission from *The Futurist*, published by the World Future Society, Bethesda, MD. **154** "The Farm Of The Future," from "The Great Energy Harvest," by Helena LiChum et al., in *The Futurist*, May/June 1993. Reproduced with permission from *The Futurist*, published by the World Future Society, Bethesda, MD. **155** "Tractors Run On Software," from "Farming From Space." Copyright © 1992 *Harrowsmith Country Life*, published bimonthly in Charlotte, VT. 800-344-3350. "There's No Place Like a Farm," from *Food From An American Farm*, by Janeen A. Sarlin. Copyright 1991, Simon & Schuster. Reprinted by special permission of the author. **156** "A Burger King Fry Work Station," from *Making Fast Food: From the Frying Pan into the Fryer*, by Ester Reiter. Copyright 1991 by McGill-Queen's University Press, Quebec. Reprinted by permission. **163** "Flour Power," from *Food Lover's Companion: Comprehensive Definitions of over 3,000 Food, Wine and Culinary Terms*, by Sharon Tyler Herbst. Copyright © 1990, Barron's Educational Series, Inc. Reprinted by special permission of the author. **166** "The Fat of Our Fathers," from *Foie Gras, Magret And Other Good Food From Gascony*. Copyright © 1990 by Andre Daguin and Anne de Ravel. Reprinted by permission of Random House, Inc. **172** "A Food Pharmacy," reprinted with permission from *Eating Well* Magazine, Ferry Road, P.O. Box 1001, Charlotte, VT 05445. **176** "Jumping Off The Bandwagon," from "Frogs' Legs, Hunt to Table," by Elizabeth Schneider, in *The New York Times*, September 7, 1988. Copyright © 1988 by The New York Times Co. Reprinted by permission. **179** "Fruitcake Is Forever," from "Sunday Observer; Fruitcake Is Forever," by Russell Baker in *The New York Times*, December 25, 1983. Copyright © 1983 by The New York Times Co. Reprinted by permission. **182** "Janie Hibler's Big Game Hash," from *Fair Game*. Copyright © 1983 by Janie Hibler, Irena Chalmers Cookbooks, Inc. **191** "Wednesday Treasures," selected excerpt from *Fanny At Chez Panisse*, by Alice Waters. Copyright © 1992 by Tango Rose, Inc. Reprinted by permission of HarperCollins Publishers, Inc. **192** "Halibut Ho!" by Roger Fitzgerald, in *Simply Seafood* Magazine, summer 1991. Reprinted by permission of the author. **194** "James Villas' Country Ham With Red Eye Gravy," from *James Villas's Country Cooking*. Copyright © 1988 by James Villas. By permission of Little, Brown & Co. "Carving A Country Ham," reprinted by permission of Michael David Biegel and *Food & Wine* Magazine, April 1993. **196** "Hamburger As A Vision From Hell," from "The Noose," a play by Henry Beissel, published in *The Noose & Improvisations For Mr. X*, Dunvegan, Canada: Cormorant Books, 1989. Reprinted by permission. **201** "The Right Spot," from *Herbs, Their Culture and Uses*, by Rosetta E. Clarkson, Macmillan © 1961. Reprinted by permission of the publisher. **205** "Granny's Kitchen," by Joe Baum. Reprinted by permission of the author. **205** "A Private Eye Gets A Nice Home-Cooked Meal," from *The Suicide Murders*, by Howard Engel, as it appeared in *Canlit*, by Margaret Atwood. **208** "Discredited Diets," adapted from "Crazy Old Hospital Diets," by Irene Wielawski in *Eating Well* Magazine, May/June 1993. By permission of the author. "The More Things Change..." by H. L. Mencken, as quoted in *A Food Lover's Companion*. "Hot Diggety Dog," adapted from reporting by *Restaurants & Institutions* Magazine. **209** "Best of The Wurst," by Timothy White, from "Hot Dogs (Our Counterman's Special)," in *Roadside Food: Good Homestyle Cooking Across America*. Copyright © 1986 Stewart, Tabori & Chang. Reprinted by permission of the publisher. **210** "A Second Harvest," by Dwight Garner, from *Eating Well* Magazine, November/December 1991. Reprinted by permission of the author. **213** "I Sing Of Champagne and Rum Raisin," from *BITE: A New York Restaurant

Strategy*, by Gael Greene, with permission of W.W. Norton & Co., Inc. Copyright © 1971 by Gael Greene. **216** "How Food Is Irradiated," from *The New York Times*, January 21, 1992. Copyright © 1992 by The New York Times Co. Reprinted by permission. **218** "The Joys of Eating," from "Food Mysteries," by Joyce Carol Oates © 1993 by the Ecco Press. From *Not For Bread Alone*, edited by Daniel Halpern, published by the Ecco Press. Reprinted by permission. **225** "Spare Me Cooked Ham and Water Product," by Bill Hall from *Lewiston Morning Tribune*, November 29, 1991. Reprinted by permission of the author. **229** "The Sex Life of the Lobster," reprinted with permission from *The Lobster Almanac*, by Bruce Ballenger, Globe Pequot Press. **231** "The Heyday of the Three-Martini Lunch," by Jerry Della Femina. Reprinted by special permission of the author. **234** See p.62 **237-238** "Living Close To The Bone," by Reay Tannahill, from *Food In History*, Crown Publishing, copyright © 1973 (original edition), by permission of the author. **245** "Minerals: Facts and Myths," from *The Wellness Encyclopedia*. Copyright © 1991 by Health Letter Associates. All rights reserved. Reprinted by permission of Houghton Mifflin Co. All rights reserved. **249** "Reflections on Foraging," from the newsletter *The Art of Eating*. Copyright 1992 by Edward Behr. Reprinted by permission of the author. **265** "Discourse on Oysters," from *Dumas on Food*, translated by Alan and Jane Davidson, Oxford University Press. Copyright © Alan and Jane Davidson 1978. **269** "Packages Repackaged." Copyright © 1992 by the New York Times Co. Reprinted by permission. **270** "Marco Polo's Reputation's Gone?" from "Why Did The Chinese Pasta Cross the Sea?" in *The Observer*, London, September 15, 1991. Copyright © Paul Levy. Reprinted by permission of the author. **272** "Choosing The Perfect Peach," from "On the Peach," by Molly O'Neill in *The New York Times*, August 30, 1992. Copyright © 1992 by the New York Times Co. Reprinted by permission. **279** "Who Pays the High Price of Pests?" Excerpted by permission from *Harrowsmith Country Life*, May/June 1992. **285** "When The Living Was...Easier," reprinted with the permission of Charles Scribner's Sons, an imprint of Macmillan Publishing Co., from *The Wind In The Willows*, by Kenneth Grahame. Copyright 1908, 1933, 1953, Charles Scribner's Sons; copyrights renewed © 1961, 1981. **289** "Betty Bopper," from *Little Betty Bopper* in *Mummy Took Cooking Lessons*, by John Ciardi. Copyright © 1990 by Judith C. Ciardi. Reprinted by permission of Houghton Mifflin Co. All rights reserved. **291** "Noel Coward Considers The Pig," from *Any Part of Piggy*, copyright © 1967 by Noel Coward. By permission of Michael Imison, Playwrights Ltd., 28 Almeida Street, London N1 1TD. **292** "A Good Potato Day," by Truman Capote, from the foreword to *The Potato Book*, by Myrna Davis © 1972. Benefit of the Hampton Day School, Bridgehampton, New York. **293** "Lydie Marshall's Mashed Potatoes Anna," from *A Passion For Potatoes*, copyright © 1992 by Lydie Pinoy Marshall. Reprinted by permission of HarperCollins Publishers, Inc. **296** "Nutra-Loaf," from "Is Nutra-Loaf Cruel, Unusual?" by Jack Brown in the Seattle *Times*, April 17, 1993. Reprinted with permission of the Seattle *Times*. **302** "Actual Selections From Menus And Specials Boards Found In Manhattan," from "Endpaper; You Could Look It Up," by Henry Alford in *The New York Times* Magazine, April 3, 1994. Copyright 1994 by the New York Times Co. Reprinted by permission. **304** "Why Eating Out In New York Costs $60 A Person Except When It Costs Even More," by Jeffrey Steingarten. Reprinted from *Vogue* Magazine, September 1990, by permission of the author. **307** "Suzanne Taylor's Parsnip and Potato Casserole," from *Cooking in a Country Kitchen*, copyright © 1983 by Suzanne Taylor, Irena Chalmers Cookbooks, Inc. **312** "A Fair Shake," from "Salt," by Jeffrey Steingarten. Reprinted from *Vogue* Magazine, August 1990, by permission of the author. **327** "Albert Stockli's Cream of Broccoli Soup," from *Splendid Fare*, copyright © 1970 by Albert Stockli, Inc. Reprinted by permission of Alfred A. Knopf, Inc. **333** "Dining A La Cart," from "De Gustibus," by Florence Fabricant in *The New York Times*, April 17, 1991. Copyright © 1991 by The New York Times Co. Reprinted by permission. **337** "Money-Saving Tips," from "Save Over $1,000 A Year On Your Weekly Shopping List" in *Woman's Day* Magazine. Copyright 1991 Franny Van Nevel. **339** "Swooning At The Sushi Bar," from "Restaurants," by Ruth Reichl in *The New York Times*, January 28, 1994. Copyright © 1994 by The New York Times Co. Reprinted by permission. **342** "Waiter, Bring Me Another Sea Shell," from "Henry Petroski On Why Americans Eat With Their Hands," *Wigwag* Magazine, December 1990. Reprinted by permission of the author. **347** "Tempt Me Not With Tomatoes," from "Square Gassed Tomatoes And Other Modern Myths," by Raymond Sokolov in *Natural History* Magazine, July 1989. Reprinted by permission of the author. **349** "Black Truffles Are Very Dear," from *Blue Trout And Black Truffles*, copyright © 1953 by Joseph Wechsberg. Reprinted by permission of John Hawkins & Associates, Inc. "In Defense Of Canned Tuna," from *The Opinionated Palate*, by Barbara Kafka. Copyright © 1993, by permission of William Morrow & Co. **360** "The Precious Resource," by Sandra Dibble, from the map, "Water: The Precious Resource," November 1993. Produced by the Cartographic Division of the National Geographic Society. Reprinted by permission.